19

Environmental Psychology
People and Their Physical Settings

HOLT, RINEHART AND WINSTON New York Chicago San Francisco
Atlanta Dallas Montreal
Toronto London Sydney

Second Edition

Environmental Psychology

People and Their
Physical Settings

Edited by

HAROLD M. PROSHANSKY
Environmental Psychology Program, The City University of New York

WILLIAM H. ITTELSON
University of Arizona

LEANNE G. RIVLIN
Environmental Psychology Program, The City University of New York

Library of Congress Cataloging in Publication Data

Proshansky, Harold M   1920–   comp.
    Environmental psychology.

    Bibliography: p. 574
    Includes indexes.
    1. Environmental psychology—Addresses, essays,
lectures   I. Ittelson, William H., joint comp.
II. Rivlin, Leanne G., joint comp.   III. Title.
    DNLM: 1. Architecture.   2. Behavior.   3. Environ-
ment.   4. Psychology.   BF353 E613
BF353.P7   1976   155.9   76-2336

ISBN 0-03-089679-7

Printed in the United States of America
0   1   2   038   9 8 7 6 5 4

Preface
to the Second Edition

In a short time environmental psychology has come a long way. A number of relevant volumes have been published, some journals have been created, and above all, many more theoretical and empirical studies of environmental issues can be found in the older and established journals. What this has done for the authors has been to both complicate and simplify our search for works to make up this revision of our original volume. Clearly one of our greatest difficulties arose from the increasingly cross-disciplinary nature of the work, which required that we search a wide variety of sources to review and understand specific issues. The growth of the field, of course, had also a very clear positive side from our point of view. There has been a growing acceptance of the value of studying people and their physical settings. In the years since publication of the first edition of this readings book, not only have environmental journals been established but environmental professional groups both formal and informal have come on the scene. Environmental psychologists no longer need to defend their work or the value to be derived from it. Although the field is still in its very formative stages, it has been able to provide new insights to and ways of analyzing, if not resolving, environmental problems. The terms "environmental studies," "environmental psychology," "environmental sociology," "person–environmental relations," and others like them have become part of the language of the behavioral sciences.

The development of adequate theory and the isolation of significant environmental constructs is a continuing task. While the first edition of this readings book was primarily devoted to the definition of the substantive and conceptual boundaries of the field of environmental psychology, the revision seeks to do more. It reiterates the interdisciplinary nature of the field but also seeks to flesh out its form. The outline of the field is there, but what is needed now is the articulation of its structure and detail in terms of critical problems, essential concepts, and tentative generalizations.

The single greatest problem for this edition was to select from a wide variety of published and unpublished papers, monographs, and books that extended over a number of disciplines. What we often found was work of considerable significance but which was so extensively reported and presented that it had to be omitted. It was not possible in effect to do justice to many of these works. Since our revised volume provides references and bibliographies, we expect that it will assist the interested readers to locate these valuable resources. We had a choice to make: a revision of the same size as the original volume whose cost would make it less accessible to students or a smaller volume which, although not as representative as we would like, would be more accessible for students to purchase. We choose the latter. Thus the present book is smaller and the choices we had to make far more difficult than we had expected.

On the other hand we chose in a way so that each paper represents a larger literature. The increasingly empirical study of physical settings has been a significant development of the years since the first edition. Thus, the papers we have selected often reflect similar research and related findings and provide the reader with the references to be pursued in other scholarly works.

Of course, our choices reflected our own interests and biases and this means that more than a few significant environmental issues and analyses of physical settings are omitted from the present volume. We arrived at these choices on the basis of the decision to attempt to tailor the revision of the first edition of our readings book to a text we recently published with Gary Winkel entitled *An Introduction to Environmental Psychology*. It was our intention that the readings we selected and the organization in this volume would enable it to be used in conjunction with the textbook. Having made our choices of major topics, the rest of our selections were based on our experience in using the first edition of the readings book as well as the reactions we received from those who used the book in the past and were good enough to provide feedback.

Although the readings can be used as a companion volume to our textbook, they have been organized and introduced in a way that makes them entirely independent. They can be coordinated with other texts, in other areas, and the sections used in any order. In fact, readers can impose their own conceptual framework, whether developmental, in terms of a specific built form, or related to specific issues.

The preparation of a readings book is always a cooperative effort. A major expression of appreciation must be extended to two institutions whose assistance and encouragement directly led to both this and our earlier volume. For a number of years the National Institute of Mental Health has supported our research on the relationship between physical settings and behavior, leading to the specialty that we have identified as environmental psychology. Some of our empirical work is reported in papers included here but all the assistance is reflected in the thinking that has led to this volume.

To the Graduate School and University Center of the City University of New York goes another expression of appreciation. Through its support and that of our colleagues in the doctoral program in psychology, the Environmental Psychology Program was established at the Graduate Center. Our teaching and research, and the efforts of other members of our program, especially Gary Winkel, Maxine Wolfe, and Susan Saegert, have helped to stimulate the growth of our special interest area. Our students too have contributed in a very concrete way to our work, and ultimately to the definition of the field.

Specific editorial assistance in the preparation of material for this volume has come from Emilie O'Mara, Ellen Proshansky, and Timothy O'Hanlon with Beth Merritt, Wendy Gaynor, Elizabeth Gay, Linda Guthrie, Ben and Marc Rivlin providing a variety of specialized skills. We are grateful to all who have aided this group effort, including Deborah Doty, Psychology Editor, and Brian Heald, Senior Project Editor. A final but very special appreciation must be directed to the contributing authors, who come from a variety of disciplines, but who have permitted us to use their work as part of this volume. They and other colleagues in environmental psychology have stimulated our thinking, and in a very real sense, have helped in the formulation of this book and the growth and development of the field.

H. M. P.
W. H. I.
L. G. R.

Contents

Environmental Psychology
People and Their Physical Settings

Introduction

In the introduction to the first edition of this book two general goals were set forth: to provide a working definition of what was then the newly emerging field of environmental psychology and to bring it to the attention of specialists in a wide variety of related areas of study. Neither of these aims is as urgent to this second edition. In the very brief intervening time, environmental psychology has become a recognized and identifiable subject within the whole of psychology, and one that has attracted considerable interest among professionals representing a wide range of study from architecture to zoology.

This second edition is therefore addressed to issues more relevant to developing a mature field than to nurturing a new one. With this in mind we hope, first, to provide a representative selection of detailed up-to-date readings with which the student can supplement his broader, but perhaps shallower, coverage of the field offered by any of the now available introductory books and articles. While the organization of the readings is keyed to *An Introduction to Environmental Psychology* by the editors together with Gary Winkel, it is believed to be appropriate to almost any organization that may be chosen to introduce the student to the subject matter of environmental psychology. The number of readings has been reduced from that of the first edition. The breadth of coverage previously required is no longer necessary, as the field centers its work and thinking on more sharply specified subject areas. In addition, much of the material is new to this edition, mainly from the past year or two. In this way, we hope that this second edition will fill a need which was not previously appropriate—that of supplementing an introduction based on other available texts.

The second goal of this edition is related more directly to one of the stated aims of the earlier edition, which perhaps needs even further emphasis today. As the study of environmental psychology takes on an identity of its own, it becomes more and more necessary for it to develop a theoretical framework that is appropriate to its own particular problems. Many of the selections have been chosen to illustrate the various directions from which such a theory is being approached. But the task still remains unfinished, and much of what was said in introducing the first edition is equally valid and relevant today. People as builders, conquerors of their environment, form such a central place in the human self-image that we sometimes forget that when we seek to modify our environment we are actually doing something that is a biological commonplace. All living organisms engage in a complex interchange with their environments in the course of which they modify, and are modified by, what they encounter. Some such interchange is essential for the maintenance of life, and usually is involved in definitions of the concept of life itself. Living necessarily involves changes wrought on the environment by the organism —changes that may subsequently alter the organism itself, chemically, biologically, or behaviorally. In plants and primitive organisms, the interchange is of a most elementary form. The activity of the organism may change, for example, the chemical nature of the medium, and this change in turn may alter the range of possible activities of the organism. A dynamic equilibrium of some kind must be reached, or the

1

organism perishes. More complex organisms engage in more complex interchanges —hunting, fishing, building, destroying, transporting, reproducing—and respond to environmental changes in more complex and varied ways.

It is quite clear that life on this planet depends on a delicate ecological balance among many forms of life at all levels of complexity. Each organism contributes to and takes from its surroundings in such a way that an overall equilibrium is maintained. Upset this equilibrium at any point, and monumental consequences ensue. Each organism, and each group of diverse organisms, must somehow achieve an environment that all find at least reasonably congenial if they are to survive. Only today, and slowly, are we coming to recognize that this great imperative of nature applies as much to us as to the creatures from whose study we have gained this knowledge. We can no longer blindly change the world about us, ignoring the consequences of change, without threatening our own survival as a species.

The malleability of the environment in the face of the cumulative onslaught of groups of organisms has long been recognized as an important biological fact. The archaic view of a fixed environment that organisms must adapt to or perish has been replaced by a view that emphasizes the organism's creative role in shaping its own environment. Although the extent to which we shape our environment is unique, in a sense the relative impact on our immediate environment is perhaps less than that of some other organisms on theirs. Certain insects, for example, may live their entire life span in a totally artificial, insect-made environment without once coming upon undefiled nature—a fact that, happily, is still reserved for relatively few humans. The absolute magnitude of man's effect on the environment needs no documentation, however. Through our efforts, the entire face of the globe is being transformed at a rapidly increasing rate.

Closely related to its magnitude is the complexity of our relationship with the environment. It is both physically and biologically complex. Vast and permanent changes in the composition of the earth's crust and atmosphere, widespread changes in the ecological equilibrium of huge numbers and many forms of life, will have a complex and unpredictable influence on all forms of human activity. From the viewpoint of the social sciences, the social and psychological environment is largely a product of our own creation, and we in turn are fundamentally influenced by this product. Indeed, the social effect of the environment we ourselves have created may prove to be the most important aspect of this relationship. For, in the long run of history the product becomes the master. We have produced modifications in the environment that have set irreversible evolutionary trends in motion.

The magnitude and complexity of the effect of human activity on the environment would be little more than an interesting biological curiosity were it not for the uniquely human capacity to predict the consequences of our own behavior. This characteristic makes it possible for us to do more than blindly operate on the environment; it permits planned manipulation of the environment.

The builder is thus also the planner. But for the most part planning with respect to the environment has been limited to the physical effects of alterations. Understanding and predicting the effects of these manipulations upon ourselves, although operationally inseparable from the fact of manipulation, have tended to be separated conceptually and, until quite recently, largely ignored.

The capacity to predict the consequences of behavior, in addition to making planning possible, has another and perhaps further-reaching significance. It places on us a responsibility for our behavior which is biologically unique. Whether we accept it as a moral imperative or simply as a necessary condition for survival, it is evident that the scope of our manipulations of the environment makes essential an understanding of the consequences of these manipulations for human life itself.

The broad topic of societal goals cannot be avoided in a complete discussion of the environmental sciences, since knowledge of the consequences of environmental manipulation implies choice among those consequences. In this sense environmental studies are involved in the determination of both short- and long-term societal goals. Such studies recognize that every action shapes its own consequences. The choice of means and the choice of ends are inseparable, both in theory and in practice. In planning for the totality of human needs, hard and irreversible choices must be made as to where we are going, as well as how we will get there. Environmental sciences have not discovered the environment, nor are they pioneers in dealing with problems of man's environment. Science has always been interested in the environment; indeed it is impossible to imagine a science that is not a science of the environment. In this sense all science is environmental, and there is nothing new or distinctive in the body of studies labeled "environmental."

From another point of view, however, the study of the environment is not synonymous with environmental science. All science studies the environment. Environmental sciences, as we use the term, are characterized by certain distinctive features that set them off as embracing a definite subject matter.

First and most obvious, the environment that is of primary concern to the environmental sciences is a limited and particular one. Every science may study the environment, but the environmental sciences undertake investigations specifically of the environment as it is ordered and defined by human activity. Instead of asking, "What has nature wrought?" the environmental sciences ask, "What have we done to our natural heritage?" The modifications that we have imposed on our physical environment in the past, those we are undertaking now, and those we plan for the future represent the unifying reference of the environmental sciences.

Certainly these sciences do not suffer from a shortage of raw material to study. It is probably true that today no place on earth is untouched by human hands. And it is almost certain that in the future every place on earth will be significantly altered by human activity. One is tempted to write, "altered for better or worse." That almost compelling addendum points to a second characteristic common to the environmental sciences: their scientific problems grow out of pressing social problems. Take away the social issue and the scientific problem ceases to exist; at least, it ceases to excite the interest and the energies of the environmental scientist. The recognition that we can alter our environment favorably or unfavorably is a crucial identifying feature of the environmental sciences, which bear a unique value orientation. Indeed, they owe their very existence to a value judgment. We have already emphasized the close relationship between the environmental sciences and the goals of society. Here we suggest that this relationship is one of the identifying features of environmental science.

One cannot fully understand the environmental sciences without taking into consideration their particular and universally held value orientation. Similarly, although the environmental sciences have grown out of pressing social problems, it is a mistake to think of them strictly as applied science. Their value orientation undoubtedly commits them to a greater interest in future technologies than some of the more traditional sciences would claim. But it has become abundantly clear that the solution of environmental problems requires a vast addition to our store of basic scientific knowledge, and the environmental sciences are actively addressing themselves to this end.

Perhaps the relative lack of knowledge about environmental problems stems in part from a characteristic they seem to share. Not one of them fits neatly into an established scientific discipline. Each demands a multidisciplinary approach. Unfortunately, it is clear that after years of interest in interdisciplinary problems, we are still far from any effective understanding of how to deal with them. We do not yet know how to handle problems whose solutions require knowledge that can only be gleaned from the empty interstices between disciplines. The multidisciplinary nature of the environmental sciences represents both one of their chief identifying features and one of their major challenges.

A final common feature of the environmental sciences is that in them the person, above all else, is the measure. Perhaps this follows as a necessary corollary of what has already been said, but it merits separate attention. No matter how remote from human concerns some of the aspects of an environmental problem may appear, the study of people is a crucial part of the study. This importance is self-evident in such pressing problems as air pollution and urban design. We suggest that the study of people as part of the field of inquiry is one of the necessary defining features of all the environmental sciences.

In summary, the environmental sciences, as we understand them, have four identifying and defining characteristics: they deal with the environment ordered and defined through human actions; they grow out of pressing social problems; they are multidisciplinary in nature; and they include the study of people as integral parts of every problem. In short, the environmental sciences are concerned with human problems in relation to an environment of which people are both victims and conquerors.

Each of these characteristics raises important theoretical issues, but probably none more difficult than those concerned with the multidisciplinary aspects of environmental psychology. Nevertheless, while it must be firmly rooted in psychology, environmental psychology must at the same time be more than psychological in its total scope. We have suggested that environmental psychology is concerned with establishing empirical and theoretical relationships between behavior and experience and the physical environment. The far-reaching implication of this definition cannot be ignored. It means, on the one hand, that we need to be concerned not only with the individual's experience in and of the environment but also with all aspects of his individual and social behavior in relation to that environment; and, on the other hand, we cannot avoid looking at the environment as well and including within the reach of environmental psychology aspects of those fields concerned with planning and designing the human environment. Today's social problems express the complexity of existence in a complex and changing environment. They have no simple solutions because what determines them is not simple. Problems in the nature of air pollution, the urban ghetto, and the loss of individual privacy are multicausal in character. They are rooted in a pattern of interrelated determinants that express the human condition at complex levels of social organization. And herein lies the critical requirement that environmental psychology be multidisciplinary in its approach, a requirement that creates many of its difficulties in establishing a viable structure and, therefore, in undertaking meaningful research.

In considering the relationship between physical setting and human behavior, the environmental psychologist is confronted with the special problem of deciding which of the various levels of human or social organization he should undertake to conceptualize and study. This relationship can be defined and analyzed, for example, at the level of the individual who experiences as well as behaves in the physical environment. At this level, inner experience in the form of perceptions, feelings, values, and underlying motivations assumes considerable significance both in determining the meaning of the environment for the individual and in evoking responses to it. This, of course, is the more strictly psychological aspect of the study. But it must not be assumed that the psychological or individual level of analysis is the primary, if not the sole theoretical orientation of the field. This is not true. What binds the various presentations in this volume together is concern with the behavior as it is expressed at all levels of social organization.

The fact is that the individual can never really develop and live in social isolation. Experience is defined by membership in a variety of face-to-face groups and still larger social units. At this level of analysis one can ask, reflecting the approach of the sociologist and the social psychologist, how normative patterns of behavior and the group structure in which they are embedded influence and are influenced by the physical environment in which social groups exist. Here the unit of analysis is not the experiencing individual, but rather the characteristic pattern—of behavior, values, or standards—that comprises the organized nature of group life.

There remains a still more encompassing kind of social organization. Groups are organized into even larger social systems that may take the form of a community or even a nation. Here the approach of the sociologist, anthropologist, and political scientist assumes a theoretical role of major importance. How an urban community "lives its life" in terms of intergroup relations, economic productivity, political process, and other institutional activities can be studied in relation to the physical setting of the community and, more particularly, the design of its neighborhoods, parks, recreational areas, and so on.

If human behavior in relation to the physical setting can only be understood by analyzing it at all levels of social organization, then from a theoretical point of view there is no physical environment apart from human experience and social organization. The physical environment that we construct is as much a social phenomenon as it is a physical one. The constructed world, whether it is a school, hospital, apartment, community, or highway, is simply a particular expression of the social system that generally influences our activities and relationships with others. Furthermore, the individual's response to the physical world is never determined solely by the properties of the structures and events that define it. Spaces, their properties, the people in them, and the activities that involve these people represent significant systems for the individual participant and thereby influence his responses to the physical setting. "Crowding," for example, either for the member or the observer of the crowd, is not simply a matter of the density of persons in a given space. For the crowded person, at least, the experience of "being crowded" depends also to some degree on the people doing the crowding, the activity going on, and previous experience involving numbers of people in similar situations.

Two things are suggested by this discussion. First, environmental psychology is a discipline that must evolve an interdisciplinary superstructure of theoretical constructs and principles rooted in the basic formulations and empirical findings of many separate disciplines. Second, this superstructure can emerge only from the cooperative theoretical and empirical endeavors of the researchers representing these various disciplines.

Interdisciplinary cooperation, however, entails its own set of problems that must be overcome before the needed theoretical superstructure can even begin to take shape. Many of the social science disciplines upon which environmental psychology must rest have not themselves established a coherent theoretical structure supported by a firm foundation of empirical findings. It is true that the many methodological and theoretical developments in the fields of psychology, anthropology, sociology, economics, and political science have contributed to a vast "explosion of knowledge" in these areas. But as yet there is little evidence that this knowledge is cumulative or capable of being integrated to reveal solutions to social problems in cause-and-effect terms.

To ask why the various behavioral science disciplines have not cooperated more touches upon a host of issues that concern the structure of science as a social institution and the professional and organizational consequences of this structure. Apart from these issues, however—and they need not concern us here—it can be said that in terms of the simple requirement for theoretical communication between disciplines, such cooperation is not easily achieved. More is involved than a mere lack of familiarity with conceptual tools and methodological orientations of each discipline with the others. Difference in levels of analysis, styles of formulating concepts and problems, and empirical procedures tend to limit fruitful cooperation between two fields.

For environmental psychology this difficulty is compounded by the fact that its disciplinary focus extends beyond the boundaries of the social sciences. For some of its problems it must also rely on concepts and data from the natural sciences, and for others it must embrace the thinking and orientation of the architect, designer, geographer, urban planner, conservationist, and ecologist. However, these problems have been inherent in the field ever since its inception. The difficulties must not be allowed to obscure the fact that important steps have been taken which serve to bind together into a coherent field of study what was just a few short years ago a rather formless group of individual and relatively unrelated endeavors. Most of these developments have occurred since the completion of the first edition of this book, and taken together they serve as an indication of the progress in the fields to date.

Perhaps the most immediately obvious and dramatic change in the past few years is the growing number of professionals who choose to identify themselves as environmental psychologists. Most, as would be expected, come from the various other areas of psychology. Social psychologists, experimentalists, personality psychologists, psychometricians, and industrial psychologists are all represented among those who have seen their personal research and theoretical interests moving away from the more traditional concerns of their separate areas of specialization, and who have found that environmental psychology offers a consensus and a focus within which they can feel comfortable. Others have been drawn into the field simply because of the pressure for teachers and researchers in the many academic institutions that now offer everything from a single course to a full-fledged program in environmental psychology. However, the list of those identifying themselves as environmental psychologists is not exclusively drawn from these groups which would be expected to provide the nucleus of the field. In addition, some individuals professionally identified with other behavioral sciences as well as with some of the design and planning fields have chosen to describe their work as environmental psychology, although usually without abandoning their professional identity with their other field of specialization. This development is of particular interest because if the numbers grow to any sizable extent it may have significant implications for the disciplinary structure of all the various fields that impinge upon the problem areas relevant to environmental psychology.

The past few years have also witnessed a less dramatic but perhaps more important consolidation of the field of environmental psychology, as the particular areas of research recognized as part of the field of environmental psychology have become more sharply defined, not through any formal procedures, but rather through the concentration of efforts by workers in the field. It is still not possible, and perhaps never will be, to offer an exhaustive list of research topics in environmental psychology, but one can note the growing concentration of efforts on particular problem areas. The built environment and its effects on behavior, together with implications for the design of built environments, continues to draw considerable interest. The general questions related to environmental quality and environmental hazard form another set of issues around which much investigation is taking place. The study of privacy in relation to space, both personal and territorial, attracts much attention, as does the related issue of crowding. Not sharply delineated from the others, but nevertheless drawing attention as a specific area, is the whole question of environmentally induced stress. As a final example, environmental perception and cognition has been set out as a special area deserving of its own study. These illustrations do not exhaust the research interests of environmental psychology, but they probably encompass the greatest part of the current effort, and they are all well represented in the readings offered in this book.

Perhaps the most important indicator of the maturity of a scientific field is the level of its theoretical formulation. In this regard it must be said that environmental psychology is still very much in its infancy, although the infant has indeed grown considerably in the past few years. Most theory in environmental psychology remains at the level of rather limited empirical generalizations. These have important and demonstrated practical and heuristic values but do not as yet offer a theoretical integration of the field. For the closest approximation to theory on that general level one must turn, as would be expected, to the set of concepts that have the oldest history and firmest foundation. We refer to the interrelated set of concepts variously labeled as territoriality and personal space, shading off into questions of crowding, and probably most fruitfully conceptualized within the general topic of privacy. The most advanced theorizing is proceeding in these areas, and if a generally accepted and unifying theory has not yet emerged, one is nevertheless quite clearly in its developmental stages.

The preceding discussion of the current state of environmental psychology is reflected in, or perhaps more correctly stated, forms the rationale for the organization of the eight sections in this second edition, which differs in format somewhat from the first edition. The continuing need for theory development has dictated a first and enlarged section (Part I) on theory containing almost entirely material new to this edition. Similarly, the growth of the field of environmental perception and cognition has suggested a section (Part II) specifically devoted to that topic and again containing almost entirely material that did not appear in the first edition. In contrast Part III, on social processes in the environment, represents, as we have suggested earlier, the most maturely developed aspects of the field and as such is both a large section and one in which we have chosen to retain a fairly large number of the more classical and seminal pieces from the earlier edition. Part IV, on individual development and the environment, is both an entirely new addition to this edition and an attempt to represent and encourage a newly emerging area of interest. Part V, on search for relevant and productive research methods in environmental psychology, continues to be an important issue, and we have chosen to recognize that fact by retaining a section on that topic in this second edition. Parts VI, VII, and VIII—the natural environment, the built environment, and the city and urban design—represent what have come to be a generally accepted way of categorizing research in those types of environments. Work in all these areas has been proceeding rapidly and the selections in these three sections are more or less evenly divided between work that appeared in the previous volume and work new to this edition.

The preceding rationale for the structure of the book and of the separate sections follows rather directly from our general understanding of the current status of environmental psychology. It does not, of course, provide guidelines for the choice of any particular selection. In most cases the decision was difficult. Including one article almost always meant excluding two or three others of equal merit. We have tried to be guided by the principle of representing the field of environmental psychology rather than the individuals in it. In areas where many more people are working than could possibly be included, this has demanded the omission of many important and significant contributors. We hope that those who have been omitted will view that fact as a tribute to their having chosen to work in such an important and rapidly expanding field.

Part I

Theoretical Conceptions and Approaches

The development of concepts and theory in the behavioral sciences has not been and undoubtedly will not be an easy or simple endeavor. Over some fifty or more years the accumulation of research findings in these fields of inquiry has accelerated at an extraordinary rate, while the formulation of viable concepts and theories has lagged far behind. The problems involved in developing these concepts and theories extend from epistemological considerations on the one hand, to a variety of connotative and denotative issues in the definition and elaboration of concepts and conceptual schemes on the other. Of course without viable concepts and theories to guide ongoing research, the increased research findings for any number of specific problems reveal little indication of becoming a cumulative, verifiable body of knowledge. Furthermore, in some problem areas theoretical formulations and systematic investigations continue to take place, not just at differential rates of growth, but as more or less isolated and unrelated enterprises.

Against this backdrop and in the light of the relative youth of environmental psychology as a scientific endeavor, it should be evident that theoretical conceptions and approaches in this new field can best be described as in the "prenatal" stage. Indeed it can be said that its birth depends to some extent on advances made in the various behavioral sciences, particularly in sociology, psychology, anthropology, and ecology. However, notwithstanding such advances, there are particular issues and problems that beset the development of concept and theory in environmental psychology that transcend its relationships to the other behavioral sciences. We consider three of the more significant of these problems and issues in the discussion below in the belief that the reader will then be better able to order and give meaning to the diversity of theoretical conceptions and approaches presented in this section of our volume.

From the Introduction presented earlier it is clear that environmental psychology is a problem-focused scientific endeavor. Its concern is with the actual problems that emerge from the individual's use of and adaptation to the physical environment, and in particular that environment we identify as the urban setting. The environmental psychologist seeks to solve these problems using a critical underlying assumption as to the best way this can be done. It is assumed that out of the analysis and systematic study of these problems as they develop and unfold in the context of everyday life, there will emerge the empirical generalizations necessary to solve them. The approach then stands in rather sharp contrast to the other behavioral sciences where there is attempt to develop a set of general principles by means of basic research, with the intention to apply these principles—but only after they have been established—to the range of complex individual and social problems that are inherent in the continuous process of human adaptation to changing built and social environments.

It is because of its almost exclusive focus on the solution of ongoing problems, that environmental psychology necessarily emerges as interdisciplinary in its approach, another characteristic of the field noted in the Introduction. The problems involved require definition and investigation at not one but a number of levels of analysis; they are rooted in and express psychological, sociological, anthropological, political, economic, and historical processes. However, if, as we have already noted, theoretical developments in each of the various behavioral sciences are still relatively primitive, problem areas requiring an interdisciplinary approach derived from these disciplines present some formidable obstacles, to say the least. Although attempts have been made, the very great difficulty of bridging the theoretical gaps between two or more of the analytic approaches of these fields by means of appropriate "conceptual linkages" has yet to be overcome.

For the environmental psychologist this problem is compounded by still another interdisciplinary issue. The interdisciplinary conceptual schemes must be at least responsive to, if not actually inclusive of, the thinking, concepts, and principles involved in the orientation of architects, planners, designers, and other practitioners responsible for the design, implementation, and use of space. The assumptive structures that determine the products of these professionals include not just criteria and standards for making physical settings work as physical settings, but also include interpretations about people in general and various groups of people in particular, for example, types of users, builders, owners, and so forth. Any theory or conceptual framework for defining and understanding the relationships between the behavior and experience of individuals and given physical settings will have to take account of these groups as they relate to each other through the structured influence of the design process itself and those who determine this process.

The conceptual and theoretical integration of environmental psychology that includes at some level the thinking and activities of the architect, planner, and interior designer will be quite long in the coming. In part this is because environmental psychologists must confront and indeed solve a still more fundamental problem in their attempts to establish an interdisciplinary structure of concepts and principles. Both the environmental psychologist on the one hand, and the architect, designer, and planner on the other, have a critical interest in human environments generally and the physical characteristics of these environments in particular. But at this point, environmental psychologists are limited in their responses to the designer's questions concerning the general conceptualizations or ways of analyzing these physical settings that have been established by their colleagues in the other behavioral sciences.

Not unlike human beings, space in terms of its organization and content can be defined in a variety of ways. Yet the development of conceptual schemes for defining physical settings based upon systematic research has almost no history in the traditional behavioral sciences. In their concern with human problems—whether at the individual, a group, or societal level—"behavior and experience" rather than "space and place" had dominated the theoretical formulations and conceptual schemes that have developed in these fields. The problem of the physical environment is frequently formulated either in highly mechanistic or abstract conceptions, for example, stimulus patterns, or in elaborate programmatic statements of the importance of physical settings with little substantive relevance for the formulation of concepts and hypotheses. It is no exaggeration to say that the task of conceptualizing human physical settings—settings that both determine and emerge as a result of human behavior and experience—is one of the major tasks now facing the environmental psychologist.

The third and last problem in formulating concepts and theories in environmental psychology may well overshadow in significance the other two problems we have raised above. *Historical considerations* and the *dimension of time* play a relatively small role in the theories and analytic frameworks that have emerged in the traditional behavioral sciences, although this is somewhat less true for some theorists and some areas of specialization. On the other hand, these considerations force themselves on the environmental psychologist. The concern with given physical settings means a concern with correlative human activities, and these settings and their human activities are embedded in a rapidly changing sociocultural system that alters the nature, meaning, and relevance of both the people and places involved. Thus the analysis of person/environment relations must deal not just with the events involved but with the specific meaning of these events in relation to time as well as place. It may well be that insofar as general principles are concerned, theory and concept in environmental psychology may have to play a problem-oriented role. The broader generalizations may have to be relegated to future work by many disciplines seeking to establish the general fundamental processes that underlie human behavior and experience at all levels of personal and social organization.

It should be compellingly evident by now that the environmental psychologist is confronted with a host of problems in the search for viable theory and concepts.

The search itself is proceeding and will continue to proceed at a snail's pace, particularly if one keeps in mind that problems in concept and theory have consequences for the quality of research that goes on and the critical task of developing a cumulative body of knowledge. Whether the snail's pace will eventually give way to a more rapid progress in establishing concepts and theory in environmental psychology depends on many factors, including the extent to which the behavioral sciences can establish independently and in relationship to each other valid theoretical structures.

1. On the Nature of the Environment
ROGER G. BARKER

Two themes stand out strongly in my memory of Kurt Lewin from the time I was a post-doctoral fellow with his group at the University of Iowa in 1935 and 1936.

One theme was Lewin's vigorous presentation of psychology as a conceptually autonomous science. In his view, psychology is independent of biology, physics, and sociology; its constructs and theories are not reducible to those of any other science. Heider (1959) has reminded us that this was a guiding conviction of Lewin from his earliest days, and that it is expressed in his theory of the life space. Kurt Lewin brought this view to Iowa, and under the impact of his brilliance and enthusiasm all who worked with him there operated within its framework. But his conception of the place of psychology among the sciences did not go unchallenged; in fact, it was an explicit and a lively issue. The philosophy of science had recently come to the University of Iowa directly from Vienna. Under these circumstances, Lewin, who would certainly have chosen to let history settle the argument, had to enter into discussions of what, for him, were the familiar issues of positivism, reductionism, and the unity of science. These discussions were landmarks of the Iowa landscape of those days and surely everyone who participated in

them, even from the periphery, will always remember them.

The essence of science for Lewin was a system of explicitly stated concepts by means of which exceptionless derivations could be made. Since, in this view, the concepts of physics, biology, and sociology are incommensurable with those of psychology, he concluded that only probabilistic, empirical relations could be discovered between variables of psychology and those of other sciences. It was impossible, as he saw it, to make derivations to behavior from the nonpsychological environment, to use his own term, or the preperceptual or ecological environment to use Brunswik's terms.[1] It was this that made it essential for Lewin to limit psychology to an encapsulated system of purely psychological constructs.

My experience at Iowa convinced me that psychology was faced with a three-way dilemma and that it had to choose between achieving a truly Galilean psychology of precise derivations, but with

[1] *Nonpsychological environment, preperceptual environment, ecological environment* and *environment* are used interchangeably in this essay to mean the environment as described by the physical and biological sciences, and by those social sciences that are not adumbrations of individual psychology. *Psychological environment* and *life space* are used interchangeably as Lewin used them.

From *The Journal of Social Issues*, Vol. 19, No. 4 (1963), pp. 17–38. Reprinted by permission of the author and the publisher.

the ecological environment omitted, accepting a probabilistic functionalism of the kind advocated by Brunswik, with the ecological environment included, or retreating to a fractionated psychology of specialties and microtheories without conceptual unity. I am now beginning to see the issues differently. But before turning to this, I must report another theme that is prominent in my memory of Kurt Lewin and which helps to define the issue I want to discuss.

This theme is the overriding influence of the ecological environment in Lewin's own life. How well I remember a summer day I spent with him in the Sierra Nevada mountains of California. It was a beautiful day. Then the news came over the automobile radio that Hitler's German armies had invaded Poland. This was an event in the objective geo-political-social world; this was an occurrence in the ecological environment. It was hard, indeed, to follow Lewin's scientific tenets here. It was difficult to think that this occurrence had no certain consequences for him, or for me, or for multitudes of others from whom it had as yet no life-space representation whatever. Lewin was among those men who have had to contend in their own lives with the most striking evidence of the coercive power of the political-social environment. Indeed, two ecological realities, Jews and Nazis, were in some way causally implicated in the strange fact that Lewin was carrying on his work in an Iowa town. He recognized this, of course. He often emphasized the profound importance for people of nonpsychological events; but despite their saliency for him personally, he could not incorporate them into a science of psychology, as he understood science.

So Lewin led an uneasy life with this dilemma. He saw very clearly that an adequate applied behavioral science requires conceptual bridges between psychology and ecology, and even though his conception of science told him that this is impossible, much of his effort from the Iowa period

onward was preoccupied with it. Sometimes he approached the psychological-ecological breach directly and explicitly, as in his gatekeeper theory of the link between food habits and food technology and economics (1943, 1951); sometimes he approached it obliquely and implicitly, as in his attempt to treat the social field as a psychological construct (1951). He seemed unable to avoid the interface between ecology and psychology and to work within his own system, as he had done in the earlier studies of tension systems, psychological satiation, and level of aspiration. I think the reason is clear: Lewin's total life experience and his conception of psychology as a science were in irreconcilable conflict. He could not ignore his life experiences, and he could not give up his conception of psychology. It was a painful conflict.

It seems to me that, as psychologists, we are all confronted with the same dilemma today. And for those with the concerns represented by the Society for the Psychological Study of Social Issues the conflict is especially crucial. The environment which man is creating for himself is surely even more threatening (and, also, more promising, if we are able to call the turns) than it was twenty-five years ago. Who can doubt that changes in our environment ranging from new levels of radiation, to increased numbers of people, to new kinds of medicines, and new kinds of social organizations, schools, and governments are inexorably changing our behavior, and that our new behavior is, in turn, altering our environment. Can this total eco-behavioral system be incorporated within an explanatory science? Can we understand and control the total array and flow of what is happening to us, or must the couplings between the environment and behavior always be dealt with fragmentally, probabilistically, empirically, and *post hoc?* It is to this problem that I should like to direct your attention today.

I shall, first, define the dilemma, or rather the dilemmas, more precisely.

Problems Along the Environment to Environment Circuit

We can trace the round of events in which behavior is involved from distal objects in the ecological environment (say a fly ball in a baseball game) to proximal events at receptor surfaces (the image of the approaching ball on the retinas); to afferent, central, and efferent processes within the silent intrapersonal sector of the circuit (e.g., perceiving the approaching ball); to molecular acts (e.g., raising the hands) and finally to molar actions which alter the ecological environment (catching the ball). This is the environment to environment circuit, the E-E arc, which Brunswik (1955) and others (Murray, 1959; Miller, Galanter, & Pribram, 1960; Zener & Gaffron, 1962) have considered the fundamental psychological datum.

I have mentioned one dilemma of the E-E arc, namely, that it involves such alien phenomena in its various parts that a conceptually univocal treatment has seemed impossible. But there are other dilemmas.

Most psychologists, including Lewin and Brunswik, have found the ecological environment on the afferent side of the person to be unstable, and to exhibit at best only statistical regularities (1955). This disordered input has confronted students of the total E-E arc with the difficult problem of accounting for its transformation within the circuit into an ordered output. In consequence, the selective and organizing powers of the intrapersonal segment of the E-E arc, which to quote Leeper, "yield relatively stable effects out of the kaleidoscopically changing stimulation they receive" (1963, pp. 387–388), has undoubtedly claimed the greatest efforts of psychologists; here fall the problems of perception and learning. This is the second dilemma of the E-E arc.

Furthermore, it is generally agreed by students of perception and learning that the ecological environment does not demand behavior, but that it is, rather, permissive, supportive, or resistive. It is true that a language is often used that implies at least a triggering function for the ecological environment: events in the environment are said to stimulate, to evoke, to instigate behavior. And the fact that experiments are by design usually conducted within environments that are, indeed, stimulating gives support to the language used. However, the fine print of psychological theory always, so far as I have been able to determine, makes the intrapersonal sector of the arc the arbiter of what will be received as stimuli, and how it will be coded and programmed in the intrapersonal sector before it emerges as output (Lawrence, 1963; Ratliff, 1962; Schoenfeld & Cumming, 1963). The simple fact is that to function as a stimulus, an environmental variable must be received by the organism. In fact, the S-R formula would be more in line with basic psychological theory if it were recast as an R-S formula: R for *reception* by the organism followed by S for *submission* of the coded information back to the environment. It is safe to say that in most psychological thinking, ecological occurrences at the afferent end of the E-E arc are assumed (a) to be indifferent to their ends via the arc, and (b) to be endowed with directedness and purpose only within the intrapersonal sector. This is the problem of motivation, and it is a third dilemma of the E-E arc.

These three dilemmas rest upon certain conceptions of the ecological environment, namely, that it is disordered, that it is without direction with respect to behavior, and that it is conceptually incommensurate with the intrapersonal sector of the E-E arc.

Since psychologists usually consider the environment only insofar as it is propaedeutic to their main concern with behavior, it would appear desirable to examine, again, the ecological segment of the E-E arc as it exists before being received, coded, and programmed within the silent intrapersonal sector of the circuit. Egon Brunswik wrote, in this connection:

> . . . both organism and environment will have to be seen as systems, each with properties of its own, yet both hewn from basically the same block. Each has surface and depth, or overt and covert regions . . . the interrelationship between the two systems has the essential characteristic of a "coming-to-terms." And this coming-to-terms is not merely a matter of the mutual boundary or surface areas. It concerns equally as much, or perhaps even more, the rapport between the central, covert layers of the two systems. It follows that, much as psychology must be concerned with the texture of the organism or of its nervous processes and must investigate them in depth, it also must be concerned with the texture of the environment as it extends in depth away from the common boundary (1957, p. 5).

I raise the question then: What *is* the texture of the ecological environment?

Attributes of the Ecological Environment

The physical and biological sciences have amassed almost limitless information about the environment, and some of it bears directly and univocally upon the issues before us. The three environmental attributes I shall mention have been independently affirmed and reaffirmed by many observing techniques and instruments. They are far removed from the human observer; most of them are properties of the environment as revealed directly by photographic plates and recording instruments. They are elementary facts.

1. Order in the Preperceptual Environment. The environment as described by chemists, physicists, botanists, and astronomers is not a chaotic jumble of independent odds and ends, and it has more than statistical regularity. It consists of bounded and internally patterned units that are frequently arranged in precisely ordered arrays and sequences. The problem of identifying and classifying the parts of the environment, i.e., the toxonomic problem, is very great, but the problem is not, primarily, to bring order out of disorder. On the contrary its first task is to describe and explain the surprising structures and orders that appear in nature: within carbon atoms, within DNA molecules, within developing embryos, within oak trees, within baseball games, within hotels (if you will), within nations, within solar systems; and to account for the occasional absence of order and organizations, in atomic explosions, in cancerous growths, and in social disorder.

It must be noted, however, that order and lawfulness are by no means spread uniformly across the nonpsychological world; not every entity is lawfully related to every other entity. The preperceptual world is not one system but many, and their boundaries and interconnections have to be discovered.

A frequent arrangement of ecological units is in nesting assemblies. Examples are everywhere: in a chick embryo, for example, with its organs, the cells of one of the organs, the nucleus of one of the cells, the molecular aggregates of the nucleus, the molecules of an aggregate, the atoms of one of the molecules, and the subatomic particles of an atom. A unit in the middle ranges of a nesting structure such as this, is simultaneously both circumjacent and interjacent, both whole and part, both entity and environment. An organ, the liver, for example, is whole in relation to its own component pattern of cells, and is a part in relation to the circumjacent organism that it, with other organs, composes; it forms the environment of its cells, and is, itself, environed by the organism.

2. Direction and Purpose in the Pre-perceptual Environment. Most units of the ecological environment are not direction-less in relation to their parts. They are, rather, self-regulated entities (or the prod-ucts of such entities) with control circuits that guide their components to characteris-tic states and that maintain these states within limited ranges of values in the face of disturbances. Some of the strongest forces in nature and some of the most ubiquitous patterns of events are found within ecological units: in atomic forces and in developmental sequences, for ex-ample. The new understanding of cyber-netic processes makes it no longer necessary to be skeptical of the reality of target-di-rected systems within the ecological en-vironment.

There are mutual causal relations up and down the nesting series in which many environmental entities occur; the pre-perceptual environment is made up of sys-tems within systems. An entity in such a series both constrains and is constrained by the outside unit that surrounds it and by the inside units it surrounds. This means that entities in nesting structures are parts of their own contexts; they influence them-selves through the circumjacent entities which they, in part, compose. A beam de-termines its own strength by its contribu-tion to the structure into which it is built; a word defines itself by its contribution to the meaning of the sentence of which it is a part.

3. Incommensurability in the Preper-ceptual Environment. The conceptual in-commensurability of phenomena which is such an obstacle to the unification of the sciences does not appear to trouble na-ture's units. The topologically larger units of nesting structures have, in general, greater variety among their included parts than smaller units: an organism encom-passes a greater variety of structures and processes than a cell; a river is internally more varied than a brook. Within the larger units, things and events from conceptually

more and more alien sciences are incor-porated and regulated. In an established pond, a great variety of physical and bio-logical entities and processes are integrated into a stable, self-regulated unit; the com-ponent, interrelated entities range from oxygen molecules to predacious-diving beetles. This suggests that within certain levels of nesting structures conceptual in-commensurability of phenomena does not prevent integration and regulation. In fact, self-regulated units with widely varied component entities are, in general, more stable than units with lesser variety (Ashby, 1956).

In summary, the sciences which deal with the entities and events of the non-psychological environment directly, and not propaedeutically as in psychology, do not find them to be chaotic or only probabilistic in their occurrence. It is within the physical and biological sciences that the greatest order and lawfulness have been discovered, an order and lawfulness much admired by psychologists. These sciences do not find environmental entities to be without di-rection with respect to their component parts, and conceptual incommensurability does not prevent the integration and lawful regulation of ecological entities. One can-not avoid the question, therefore: Why has psychology found the ecological environ-ment to be so different ?

Let us take seriously the discoveries of the bio-physical sciences with respect to the preperceptual environment, and identify and examine the environment of behavior as they identify and examine the environ-ments of physical or biological entities: of animals, of cells, of satellites. This is neither more nor less difficult than it is to identify and examine the habitat of an animal, the organ in which a lesion occurs, or the planetary system within which a satellite orbits. The investigator first identifies the animals, the lesion, the planet, or, in this case, the behavior unit with which he is concerned, and he then explores the surrounding area until he identifies and then examines the circumjacent environmental unit.

But first we must have a unit of behavior. One cannot study the environment of behavior in general.

The Environment of Behavior Episodes

Psychology has been so busy selecting from, imposing upon, and rearranging the behavior of its subjects that it has until very recently neglected to note behavior's clear structure when it is not molested by tests, experiments, questionnaires and interviews. Following the basic work on behavior structure by Herbert F. Wright, (Barker & Wright, 1955), Dickman (1963) has shown that people commonly see the behavior continuum in terms of the units (or their multiples) which Wright identified, namely, behavior episodes. Here, for example, are descriptive titles of consecutively occurring episodes from the behavior stream of six-year-old Belinda Bevan during a 10-minute period beginning at 2:22 p.m., on July 18, 1957 (Barker, Wright, Barker, & Schoggen, 1961):

Watching bigger girls form a pyramid
  (gymnastic)
Taking off her shoes
Going closer to the big girls
Putting on her shoes
Admiring bracelet on Alice
Poking Alice
Looking at Winifred's ladybug
Following Alice
Watching boys
Looking into porch of schoolroom
Closing door of schoolroom
Watching girls play hopscotch
Giving Harry his shoe
Getting bracelet from Alice
Interfering in Delia's and Winifred's
  fight
Admiring bracelet on Alice
Behavior episodes, such as these, are not

arbitrarily imposed divisions of the behavior continuum in the way that microtome slices of tissue and mile-square sections of the earth's surface are imposed divisions. They are, rather, natural units of molar behavior (Barker, 1963) with the attributes of constancy of direction, equal potency throughout their parts, and limited size-range. Like crystals and cells which also have distinguishing general attributes and limited size-ranges, behavior episodes have as clear a position in the hierarchy of behavior units as the former have in the physical and organic hierarchies. It makes sense, therefore, to ask what units of the ecological environment encompass behavior episodes.

Consider, for example, Belinda's behavior episode, Looking at Winifred's Ladybug, from the series just given.

The record of this episode of Belinda's behavior stream reads as follows:

Belinda ran toward Winifred from Miss
  Groves' room.
Winifred had found a ladybug and was
  walking around with this ladybug saying, "Ladybug, ladybug, fly away
  home."
Belinda went up to Winifred.
She pulled Winifred's arm down so she
  could see the ladybug better.
She smiled as she watched the beetle.
She watched the ladybug for 10 or
  15 seconds.

This episode constitutes an E-E arc originating in the ecological event, "Winifred . . . was walking around with this ladybug" and ending in the ecological events, Belinda, "pulled Winifred's arm down . . . she watched the ladybug. . . ."

The environing unit in which this episode occurred was easily identified. It extended in depth away from the junction points between Belinda and Winifred-with-the-ladybug with a characteristic pattern of people, behavior, and objects which abruptly changed at a surrounding physical wall, and at temporal beginning and end points.[2] The environmental unit was After-noon Break, Yoredale County School Play-ground, North Yorkshire, England, 2:22–2:31 p.m., July 18, 1957.

We have studied many behavior epi-sodes, and we have always found them within ecological units like the one sur-rounding the episode Looking at Winifred's Ladybug. We have called these ecological units *behavior settings*. Our work in Mid-west, Kansas, and Yoredale, Yorkshire, has demonstrated that behavior settings can be identified and described reliably without an explicit theory and by means of a variety of survey techniques. This is of some im-portance, we think, as an indication that behavior settings are tough, highly visible features of the ecological environment.

There is only a beginning of a scientific literature on behavior settings. Except in their applied phases, the biological and physical sciences have eschewed ecological units with human behavior as component elements. They have stopped with man-free ponds, glaciers, and lightning flashes; they have left farms, ski-jumps, and pas-senger trains to others. And psychology and sociology, have, for the most part, shied in the other direction; they have avoided whole, unfractionated ecological units with physical objects as well as people and be-havior as component parts. So be-havior-setting-type units have almost com-pletely fallen between the bio-physical and the behavioral sciences, and this has been a source of serious trouble for the eco-behavioral problem: there have been no solid empirical ecological units. Un-

[2] In other cases the boundaries may not be so definite, they may in fact be boundary zones; and there are sometimes alternative bounds to an environmental unit. In these cases detailed judgments have to be made re-garding the location of the boundary, but the principle does not change (Barker & Wright, 1955).

bounded, demi-theoretical, demi-empirical units do not provide the firm base an em-pirical science must have. Floyd Allport (1961) has persuasively pointed to one difficulty of such demi-entities: they dis-appear when the attempt is made to touch them, as is essential if they are to be studied; in their place one encounters in-dividuals. And there is another difficulty: a universal attribute of the environment of a person, whatever its other characteristics may be, is a univocal position in time and space. The units of an eco-behavioral science must have time-space loci. Behavior settings fulfill both of these requirements: they can be encountered, qua environmental units, and re-encountered; and they can be exactly located in time and space.

It is not often that a lecturer can pre-sent to his audience an example of his phenomena, whole and functioning *in situ* —not merely with a demonstration, a description, a preserved specimen, a pic-ture, or a diagram of it. I am in the for-tunate position of being able to give you, so to speak, a real behavior setting.

If you will change your attention from me to the next most inclusive, bounded unit, to the assembly of people, behavior episodes, and objects before you, you will see a behavior setting. It has the following structural attributes which you can observe directly:

1. It has a space-time locus: 3:00–3:50 p.m., September 2, 1963, Clover Room, Bellevue-Stratford Hotel, Phila-delphia, Pennsylvania.
2. It is composed of a variety of interior entities and events: of people, objects (chairs, walls, a microphone, paper), behavior, (lecturing, listening, sitting), and other processes (air circulation, sound amplification).
3. Its widely different components form a bounded pattern that is easily dis-criminated from the pattern on the outside of the boundary.

4. Its component parts are obviously not a random arrangement of independent classes of entities; if they were, how surprising, that all the chairs are in the same position with respect to the podium, that all members of the audience happen to come to rest upon chairs, and that the lights are not helter-skelter from floor to ceiling, for example.

5. The entity before you is a part of a nesting structure; its components (e.g., the chairs and people) have parts; and the setting, itself, is contained within a more comprehensive unit, the Bellevue-Stratford Hotel.

6. This unit is objective in the sense that it exists independently of anyone's perception of it, qua unit.

You will note that in these structural respects, behavior settings are identical with bio-physical units.

This, then, is a behavior setting; within it is displayed, for you to see, the finer-grained texture of the environment as it extends around and away from the behavior occurring here. What is this texture and how does it affect behavior? This leads us to the more dynamic characteristics of behavior settings.

Every stable, patterned, and bounded assembly of phenomena (whether this be in the particles of milker's nodule virus, in the lines of a spectrograph, or in the position of chromosomes in meiosis) indicates that *some* regulator is operating. And where in nature is stable patterning clearer than in a baseball game, a church service, a law court, or a highway, i.e., in behavior settings? The question in all of these cases is: What is the source of the order?

It does not require systematic research to discover that the patterns of behavior settings do not inhere in the people or the objects within them. It is common observation that the *same* people and objects are transformed into different patterns as they pass from one variety of setting to another. This is exemplified by numerous pairs of behavior settings in Midwest and Yoredale with essentially the same people and objects as component parts but with quite different patterns. For example:

Church Service—Church Wedding
High School Senior Class Play—Senior Graduation
School Playground: Recess—May Fete on School Playground

It is common observation, too, that *different* sets of people and objects exhibit the same pattern within the same variety of behavior setting. This is exemplified by the almost complete turnover of persons each year in academic behavior settings, with the patterns of the settings remaining remarkably stable. One of the striking features of communities is how, year after year, they incorporate new people, despite the idiosyncratic behavior and personality traits of these people, into the characteristic patterns of their stable behavior settings: of Rotary Club meetings, of doctors' offices, of garages, of bridge clubs. Obviously, whatever it is that impresses the characteristic array and flow of behavior settings upon their interior entities and events is largely independent of the persons who participate in them.

However, these general observations do not tell us the degree of change in the behavior of *individuals* as they move from setting to setting. It is possible for the *patterns* of behavior settings to differ greatly without a similar difference in the behavior of the individuals involved. The standing behavior patterns made by the inhabitants of a track meet and by the same people as inhabitants of a ball game are quite different, yet the behavior of most of the individuals within these settings appears to be quite similar: by and large, the runners and throwers run and throw in both, and the cheerers cheer in both settings.

A considerable number of investigators have made quantitative studies of the differences in the behavior of the same persons in different behavior settings (Goffman 1963; Gump, Schoggen & Redl, 1963; Gump, Schoggen, & Redl, 1957; Gump & Sutton-Smith, 1955; Jordan, 1963; Raush, Dittmann, & Taylor, 1959a, 1959b, 1960; Soskin, 1963). I shall not survey this rather extensive body of research; the findings are in general agreement on the issue of importance to us here, and they are represented by the research of Raush, Dittmann and Taylor. Working within a therapeutic milieu with disturbed boys, these investigators found that on the behavior dimensions hostility-friendliness and dominance-passivity there was as much variation between behavior settings, with boys constant, as between boys with settings constant.

Altogether, then, there is abundant evidence that behavior settings, like many bio-physical entities, are strongly self-regulated systems which regulate the behavior episodes within them as molecules regulate atoms, as organs regulate cells, and as structures regulate the beams of which they are constructed. (Barker & Wright, 1955; Barker & Barker, 1961). To the extent that this is true, it means that the ecological environment of behavior is not passive, is not directionless, is not chaotic or probabilistic.

The Regulation of Behavior Settings

But how do behavior settings regulate themselves, including the behavior episodes within them? How does "the texture of the environment as it extends in depth away from the common boundary" influence individual behavior?

One can ask, of course, why one should bother with the distal texture of behavior settings. Whatever this texture may be, it ultimately has to be translated into input at the junction points with particular persons. Why not, therefore, get down to brass tacks at these junction points, i.e., at the sensory surfaces?

There are a number of reasons why this cannot be done. For one thing, behavior settings have so many richly interconnected elements that their tremendous complexity at the sensory surfaces of all inhabitants concurrently cannot, at the present time, be dealt with conceptually or practically. Behavior settings are often very large systems, and simplification is necessary. But what may appear to be the most obvious simplification, namely, dealing with the input to single inhabitants, or to a sample of inhabitants, does not reveal behavior settings. It is not only in perception that the attributes of parts differ from those of the whole. In any system with interdependent parts the order obtaining at a point of the system varies with the portion of the total system within which the part is considered. It is easy to overlook how greatly attributes vary with context. Take, for example, a visual target, a spot on the tire of an automobile moving forward at a road speed of 50 miles per hour. The spot will display simultaneously the following motions: (1) a random vertical vibratory motion within the field of a stroboscope focused on the spot at a single point in the wheel's revolution; (2) a uniform circular motion of about 1000 RPM within the context of the wheel; and (3) a cyclical forward motion varying from zero to 100 miles per hour within the context of the auto-highway traction system. The same state of affairs occurs in a behavior setting. Suppose one were to study input and output of a second baseman in a ball game. By careful observation, all incoming and outgoing balls could be tallied, timed, and their speeds and directions recorded. The input itself would be without a sensible order, and there would be no relation between baseball inputs and outputs. But within the behavior setting, baseball game, the record would be sensible, orderly and lawful. It is important to note that it is not the player who converts this into order, it is the game, the behavior setting. The player acts as the game's agent and is able to receive and throw the ball in an orderly way because the rules (the program) of the game, and all information about the momentary state of the game available to him through a variety of inputs, guide his actions. However, all the inputs and outputs of a single player, of a sample of the players, or of all the players if considered outside the context of "the game" would be without sensible order. It is important to note, too, that a much greater quantity of information would be required to discover "the game" from the inputs and outputs at the junction point with the individual players than is contained in the program of "the game" itself (Maruyama, 1963).

A special difficulty with the ecological input at the junction points with individuals arises from the difference in the temporal dimensions of the inputs at these points, i.e., of the stimuli, and the behavior output with which we are concerned, i.e., behavior episodes. Stimuli are very short units occurring in unpredictable sequences during the period of any episode, while episodes are much longer units with direction and interdependence from their points of origin. However, episodes are not determined by their internal states alone; they are guided in their details by the ecological environment. To predict a behavior episode it is necessary to know the prevailing conditions throughout its entire course, but the ecological input of stimuli during an episode can only be known at the completion of the episode. What is needed as an ecological anchor for behavior episodes is a stable unit with at least as long duration as episodes. Behavior settings, whole and undismantled, fulfill this minimal requirement; they are episode-sized ecological units. And behavior episodes are setting-sized behavior units.

Behavior settings do have unitary textured properties which can be dealt with as bridge builders deal with the span of a bridge rather than with its atoms. One such property is number of inhabitants. In the reminder of this paper, I shall present some evidence that this ecological variable influences individual behavior and some ideas as to how it does so.

Behavior Setting Size and Individual Behavior

There is evidence, some of which I have presented to you, for each of the following statements, but I shall consider them, here, as hypotheses that were investigated by the research to be reported. Behavior settings are bounded, self-regulated entities involving forces which form and maintain the component inhabitants and objects of settings in functioning patterns with stable attributes. One of the stable attributes of a setting is its functional level, and another is the optimal number of inhabitants for maintenance of this level. The optimal number of inhabitants may be precisely specified by the setting (a bridge game requires four inhabitants), or may fall within a range (a First Grade reading class in Midwest functions well with 15 to 25 pupils). When the number of inhabitants of a behavior setting is below the optimal number (within limits), the homeostatic controls of the setting maintain the total complement and pattern of the setting's forces essentially intact, and this produces differences, in comparison with an optimally populated setting, that ramify to the level of individual behavior. The differences reach the level of individual inhabitants by two main routes, one a rather direct route involving behavior setting structure and dynamics, the other more indirect via control mechanisms. I shall consider the more direct route first.

Behavior settings with fewer than optimal inhabitants are less differentiated, and their networks of forces are interconnected through fewer junction points than otherwise equivalent settings with optimal numbers of inhabitants. It follows from this that on the level of individual dynamics, the inhabitants (i.e., the junction points) of the former, or "underpopulated," settings are points of application of more behavior setting forces with wider ranges of direction than are inhabitants of the latter, or optimally populated, settings. Behavior setting forces cause participation in behavior settings, and persons and objects which receive more forces in more varied directions will participate with greater forcefulness in more varied ways. On the level of particular activities, far-reaching differences will result, all characterized by stronger motivation, greater variety, and deeper involvement in the settings with less than the optimal number of inhabitants.

When people are more than optimally abundant in behavior settings, the differences noted will be reversed.

At some point in the linkage between behavior setting population (an ecological fact) and forces upon individual inhabitants (psychological facts) a transformation from nonpsychological to psychological phenomena occurs. But in the present analysis we are not concerned with where or how this takes place, but only with the fact that as between behavior settings with the same number and pattern of forces (however the forces may operate), the settings with fewer than optimal number of inhabitants will bring more forces to bear per inhabitant in more directions than settings with an optimal or greater number of inhabitants. I have elsewhere indicated that while a person's perception is obviously involved in his degree of participation in a behavior setting, he need not be aware of the population of the setting as such (Barker, 1960). Prediction can be made from ecological facts to individual behavior via behavior settings without any knowledge of the channels or transformations involved and without previous observation of the phenomena.

The derivations from behavior setting size to individual behavior were investigated recently at the Midwest Psychological Field Station in the behavior settings of high schools. The settings were equivalent in all respects except number of inhabitants, which ranged from below to above optimal. Prototypes of the settings that were studied are the Junior Class Play of a small high school where each of the 22 members of the class participated in presenting the play to an audience of about 350 persons and the Junior Class Play of a large high school where about 100 (14 per cent) of the 700 members of the class had some part in presenting the play to an audience of about 2000 persons. Only behavior settings where attendance was voluntary were included in the studies.

The data showed that the students of the small high schools, in comparison with those of the large school:

entered the same number of behavior settings (although there were fewer available),

held important, responsible, and central positions in a greater number of the settings,

experienced more attractions and more pressures toward participation in the settings,

entered a wider variety of behavior settings, and

held important, responsible, and central positions in a wider variety of the settings.

These differences were not slight. Over the 17-week period of the study, the students of the small high schools participated in central, responsible positions (as members of play casts, as officers of organizations, as members of athletic teams, as soloists, etc.) in over three-and-a-half behavior settings per student, on the average (3.7), while students of the large high school participated in these important roles in 16 per cent as many settings, i.e., in just over one-half setting per student (0.6). The students of the small schools held central, responsible, and important positions in twice as many *varieties* of behavior settings as the students of the large school. (Gump & Friesen, 1964a). In short, these data showed, as the theory predicted, that the students of the small high schools (with fewer than optimal inhabitants per setting) were more strongly motivated, engaged in more varied activities, and were more responsibly involved than the students of the large school (with more than optimal inhabitants per setting). These are direct symptoms of the predicted differences in the strength and range of direction of forces. There is much additional evidence from research in industry that supports the predictions (Willems, in press), and the investigations and theories of Calhoun (1956) on population density and behavior velocity in animals are in general accord with the predictions.

There are less direct consequences of behavior setting population differences. When the participants in behavior settings fall below the optimal number and become points of application of more forces, they have increased functional importance within settings, and the situation may be reached where everyone is a key person for the stability, and even for the survival of settings. These are ecological facts. To the degree that the inhabitants are aware of their own behavior in behavior settings their experiences will pertain to their own efforts, achievements, and contributions to the functioning of settings. In fact, Gump and Friesen (1964b) found that the students of the small schools exceeded those of the large schools in satisfying experiences related to the development of competence, to being challenged, to engaging in important activities, and to being involved in group activities. When the number of inhabitants of behavior settings are greater than optimal, where there is a surplus of people, and people are the points of appli-

cation of fewer forces, the functional importance of all inhabitants is reduced on the average, and the situation will be reached where almost no one will be crucially missed as a contributor to the functioning of settings. Under these circumstances, it is to be expected that the inhabitants' experiences will pertain to behavior settings as detached, independent phenomena, to the performances of others, and to their own standings in comparison with others. In fact, the students of the large school exceeded those of the small schools in number of satisfying experiences related to the vicarious enjoyment of others' activities, to being affiliated with a large institution, to learning about the school's people and affairs, and to gaining "points via participation." These data may be summarized in terms of Dembo's distinction between *asset* values and *comparative* values (Dembo, Leviton, & Wright, 1956). The small schools more frequently generated in their students self-valuations based upon how adequately the students saw themselves contributing to behavior settings, i.e., being assets to settings. The large schools more frequently generated in their students self-evaluations based upon the students perception of their standing in comparison with others. There are fundamental differences: in terms of asset values, everyone in a behavior setting can be important and successful; in terms of comparative values, only a few can be important and successful.

I shall turn next to the connection between behavior setting population and individual behavior via the regulatory systems.

The inhabitants of a behavior setting always have the potentiality, and usually the active tendency, to exhibit a greater variety of behavior than the setting requires or can tolerate. The behavior setting control mechanism reduces this variety to the amount appropriate to the setting, and maintains it within an acceptable range of values. One type of control mechanism found in connection with behavior settings is a direct, deviation-countering servo-mechanism that counteracts any deviation beyond the acceptable values; a restaurant hostess who supplies coatless patrons with "appropriate" jackets functions as a deviation-countering homeostat and exemplifies this type of control. Another frequent behavior setting control is a vetoing-type mechanism that provides just two states with respect to the variables it governs: *in* and *out* of the setting (member-nonmember, pass-fail, alive-dead, permitted-not permitted, free-trapped) (Ashby, 1956). A restaurant hostess who refuses admission to coatless, aspiring patrons exemplifies this control mechanism. In general, deviation-countering controls are more efficient, but they are more difficult to devise and more expensive to operate than vetoing regulators. The latter are abundant in nature, e.g., vetoing the "unfit."

The regulation of behavior settings is usually a complex process, involving alternative mechanisms, and the continual selection of the most effective regulators for the conditions obtaining. In other words, regulation operates directly on behavior setting patterns and indirectly via the regulators themselves. In general, behavior settings with fewer than the optimal number of inhabitants must use deviation-countering control mechanisms, or they will perish; inhabitants are functionally too important to be vetoed out. I have seen a four-man baseball game of nine-year-olds tolerate and nurse along with carefully applied deviation-countering controls a four-year-old participant, or even a mother. In this case one outfielder, even an inefficient and inapt one, is likely to produce a better-functioning game than a game with no outfielder. On the other hand, if there are 30 candidates for players in the game, a better game will result with less fuss and bother if all four-year-olds, mothers, and other inapt players are vetoed out. And nine-year-olds have ways of doing this, and they regularly do it. Those vetoed out

become substitutes, bat-boys, and spectators. In behavior settings with more than the optimal numbers of inhabitants, efficiency usually moves behavior settings toward veto-type control mechanism.

Both deviation-countering and vetoing controls, insofar as they are effective in stabilizing the functioning of behavior settings, apply their differing influences more frequently to marginal inhabitants, likely to engage in deviant behavior than to focal, conformable inhabitants, unlikely to engage in deviant behavior.

In the case of the high school study we expected that deviation-countering control measures would be more frequent in the small than in the large schools, and this excess frequently would be greater among the academically unpromising than among the academically promising students. Willems' data bear upon these issues. He called the deviation-countering influences *pressures;* they included all the forces toward participation which the subjects reported as originating outside themselves, e.g., "My friend asked me to go"; "Band players were expected to come," etc. Over all, students of the small schools received two times as many deviation-countering influences as the students of the large school, and academically marginal students of the small schools (i.e., students without academically favorable abilities and motivation) received almost five times as many deviation-countering measures as marginal students of the large school.

Both deviation-countering and vetoing control mechanisms produce uniformity of behavior, but with very different consequences for people. In settings where people are at a premium, uniformity is necessarily achieved as we have seen, by the regulating *behavior*, without limiting the interests, abilities, and motives of inhabitants. In settings where people are surplus, uniformity is achieved to a considerable degree by vetoing, not behavior, but inhabitants who exhibit deviant behavior; and this amounts, in effect, to selecting inhabitants for conformity and uniformity with respect to personality characteristics (interests, abilities, motives). There are secondary resultants of these control processes which cannot be considered here; but it is immediately clear that the settings with fewer than optimal inhabitants, within which behavioral uniformity is engrafted upon personality diversity, are desegregated, egalitarian, functionally tolerant settings, while settings that veto the unfit and retain the fit are segregated, uniform, specialized settings.

Data were not secured upon details of the vetoing control processes in the schools. But the consequences were apparent: students who did not participate on a responsible level in any voluntary school activity, i.e., that were vetoed out of all but spectator participation, constituted 2 per cent of the students of the small schools, and 29 per cent of the students in the large school. It is from the nonparticipating students that great numbers of school "drop-outs" come (Williams, in press).

An essential feature of the regulation of behavior settings is that there be two-way communication between a setting and its parts. In particular, it is essential that both a participant and the setting be informed of the adequacy of the participant's functioning. In general, behavior settings are lavish with alternate and emergency circuits to carry these messages. This may be illustrated on a simple, but fundamental level. It is important in a ball game that fly balls be caught, and if not caught, otherwise dealt with; so the ball catcher must know if he did actually catch the ball. Going through the motions is not enough. Consider the player at the moment when his task as a participant in the setting is precisely defined, namely, to catch a fly ball: there is the ball in the sky; the ball's image is on his retinas; his perception of the ball is veridical; the ball approaches, the player's arms raise, his catching hand encounters the ball, but feedback #1, via

proprioceptive channels, reports to the player that the ball is not caught; feedback #2, via visual channels, reports that the ball is not caught, but is rolling along the ground; feedback #3, via auditory channels from the umpire, reports that the ball is not caught (and the batter safe); feedback #4, via auditory channels from the other players and spectators, reports that the ball is not caught (the batter safe and the game in jeopardy). If these channels fail to deliver the message of what happened along this E-E arc, there is delayed feedback. Feedback #5, via the manager's memory storage, his verbal mechanism, and the player's auditory channels, reports 10 minutes later that the ball was not caught (the batter safe, and the game lost); finally feedback #6, via the sportswriter's story in the paper and the player's visual channels, reports five hours later that the ball was not caught (the batter safe, the game lost). The ball game takes no chances in delivering to the player the report of his behavior deviancy. Those who know the plans of the setting Baseball Game know that if the message of the non-caught ball is not received by the player immediately via feedback channels #1, #2, or #3, and if he gives no return message to the game that he has noted his behavior deviancy, the message will be greatly amplified in channels #4, #5, and #6, and radically altered from a factual message to a strong deviation-countering influence.

Behavior settings and their inhabitants are mutually, causally related. Settings have plans for their inhabitants' behavior, and inputs are activated within the limits of the settings' control systems to produce the planned behavior.[3] If one channel to this behavior is closed, the setting "searches" within the life-space arrangements of the subjects for another open cir-

[3] The term *plans* is used here as Miller, Galanter, and Pribram (1960) have defined it with reference to individuals.

cuit. This is the meaning of Willems' findings that the deviation-countering influences of behavior settings were neither uniform for all inhabitants nor randomly distributed among them, but varied systematically with the personal characteristics of the inhabitants.

From this merest beginning of an eco-behavioral science, one is tempted in many directions and challenged by many problems. But the E-E circuits of the present behavior setting inform me that it has completed this phase of its plans, and that deviation-countering homeostats are warming up. So let me close by returning briefly to Kurt Lewin's dilemma, and to our dilemma.

The conceptual breach between psychological and ecological phenomena is, of course, not closed by behavior settings, it is as great as ever. But within the behavior setting context, the problem is restated so that breach can be by-passed on certain levels: the approach is re-directed from the sublime but millenial goal of developing a single conceptual system, and also from the discouraging prospect of mere empiricism, probablism, and fractioned micro-sciences, to the more modest and hopeful goal of discovering general principles of eco-behavioral organization and control without regard for the conceptual or substantive content of the phenomena regulated.

The recasting of the eco-behavioral problem does not abandon a first approximation to Kurt Lewin's conception of science: it does not abandon derivations; and the life space remains intact. Within a behavior setting a person contributes to the setting by which he, himself, is constrained. The life space is the means by which the setting secures the behavior appropriate to it. And in this connection, it is important to note that in any self-regulated system variety within the system is necessary if varied disturbances outside the system are to be countered. This is true of behavior settings, too, diversity of life space among the inhabitants of a setting makes possible behavior setting *unity* and *stability*. One problem of an eco-behavioral science, is to investigate how diversity and uniformity on the level of persons contributes to the unity and stability of behavior settings. In the past, important resources of psychology have been committed to the development of vetoing regulators which reduce diversity within settings. There is great need now to understand how the powerful deviation-countering control mechanism of behavior settings can produce unity and stability in conjunction with variety among its inhabitants.

Behavior settings have their roots in Kurt Lewin's conceptions of quasi-stable equilibria, in his treatment of parts and wholes, in his concern for the total situation, in his teaching that theory always must defer to data, and in his preoccupation with the eco-behavioral problem. How greatly the plant that has grown from these roots would have benefitted from his cultivation and pruning! Whether or not behavior settings prove to be a fruitful approach to the eco-directional problem, they serve at least to continue Lewin's multi-directional approach to it, and to emphasize the crucial importance of the eco-behavioral problem for the science of psychology.[4]

---

[4] The following volume which deals with a number of aspects of the environment of behavior became available after this essay was completed: Sells, S. B. (Ed.) *The Stimulus Determinants of Behavior*. New York: Ronald Press, 1963.

2. Some Perspectives on the Study of Man-Environment Phenomena[1]
IRWIN ALTMAN

Introduction

From the perspective of one who has been both a witness and participant, the field of man-environment studies has been growing continuously and is presently characterized by theoretical, methodological and substantive diversity, confusion and controversy. Considerable energy is being directed toward man-environment phenomena by practitioners and academic researchers, conferences are frequent and well-attended (even poor papers are received with attentiveness and rapture), organizations and newsletters are endlessly spawned, and the various disciplines try frantically to communicate with one another. In many instances, the alienated from several disciplines have come together, disenchanted by the provincialism of their parent professions. These include practitioners who want to build environments in terms of man's capabilities and needs and who criticize their own disciplinary "establishments" on the grounds that they are largely interested in creating personal monuments to designers. And, there are behavioral scientists who feel that their disciplines have neglected man's unity with his physical environment. Some talk of a coming unity of the scientist and the practitioner. Others foresee a Tower of Babel which will ultimately lead all back to their provincial disciplinary languages, values and approaches.

This paper examines the historical and sociological status of the man-environment

From *Representative Research in Social Psychology*, Vol. 4, No. 1 (1973), pp 109–126. Reprinted by permission of the author and the publisher.

[1] A lengthier version of this paper appeared in *Representative Research in Social Psychology*, 4, 1973, revised with permission of the editor, D. Stokols.

field, with an eye toward providing some perspective about its roots, progress to date, philosophical underpinnings and potential future. The first section contrasts styles of problem-solving by practitioners and behavioral scientists (primarily psychologists). The second section discusses the history of relations between behavioral scientists and practitioners. The last part of the paper outlines some philosophical "models of man" implicit in present-day work in the man-environment field, which may be considered as alternative strategies. The discussion is designed to provide an historical and philosophical perspective, to facilitate decisions by researchers and practitioners about how to expend their energies, and to assist them in consciously moving the field in directions which they consider worthwhile.

The Differing "Psyche" of Practitioners and Behavioral Scientists

A major barrier to progress in man-environment research is lack of productive communication between practitioners and behavioral scientists. It is our thesis that there are, in fact, basic differences in strategies among practitioners and behavioral scientists. But, their different approaches should not necessarily be compromised. Rather, each side should learn the other's strategy, gain skill in translating from one approach to the other, and should begin to develop some "role-playing" skills so as to be able, temporarily, to get into the "psyche" of one another. Thus, understanding and solution of man-environment problems may well come from preservation of the divergent approaches of practitioners and scientists, not from a search for consensus or the elimination of differences.

But how do their strategies differ? Figure 2–1 differentiates practitioner and

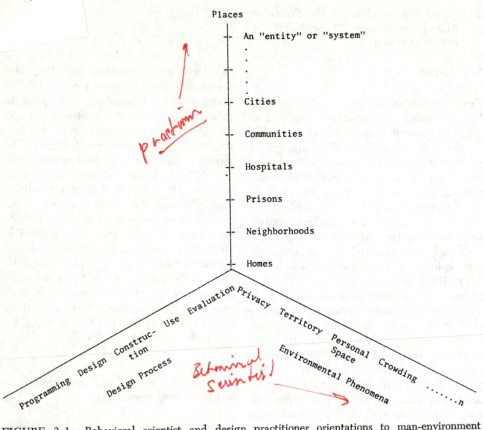

Places

An "entity" or "system"
.
.
.
Cities
Communities
Hospitals
Prisons
Neighborhoods
Homes

practitioner

Programming Design Construction Use Evaluation

Design Process

Privacy Territory Personal Space Crowding .... n

Environmental Phenomena

Behavioral Scientist

FIGURE 2–1. Behavioral scientist and design practitioner orientations to man-environment issues.

researcher approaches in terms of units of study, environmental phenomena and stages of the environmental design process.

The first dimension, *unit of study*, refers to *places*, from molecular units such as individual family homes to complex units such as cities and urban areas. The second dimension refers to *environmental phenomena* or social processes, e.g., privacy, territoriality. The typical practitioner, whether he be an architect or urban planner, usually focuses on a particular *unit* or *place*—a home, neighborhood, or city. His interest is in specifiable environmental units having spatial boundaries. In designing a place he necessarily deals with a variety of processes, whether they be the ones listed on the second dimension (pri-

vacy, territoriality) or other issues such as economic, political, and technological matters. In short, he fixes at a particular level on the place dimension and scans across phenomena or processes.

On the other hand, the behavioral scientist is usually *process* oriented. He studies such issues as privacy, territoriality or crowding, often in *any* setting which facilitates answers to his questions. For example, Galle, Gove and McPherson (1972) examined the impact of various types of crowding in terms of people per room in apartments (home unit), number of apartment units per house (apartment house unit), number of apartment houses per residential neighborhood (neighborhood unit) and number of residents per census tract (community unit). Thus, they scanned across places in studying the phenomenon of crowding. As another example, studies of proximity and friendship are often not concerned with family, neighborhoods and communities *per se*, but compare such places to the extent that they provide information about the phenomenon of friendship. In short, the behavioral scientist focuses his microscope on processes and scans across places, whereas the practitioner examines places and scans across phenomena. Obviously, not all behavioral scientists rigidly adopt this strategy; a number emphasize a particular cell in the two-dimensional space, e.g., privacy in the home. And, others emphasize more than single processes, e.g., the sociology of the family may involve study of privacy in the home and the role of the family in the community. Thus, some deal with a block of space, not just a vertical or horizontal slice. In general, however, the typical practitioner and the typical behavioral scientist seem to have different approaches in their respective emphasis on units and places vs. processes and phenomena.

The third dimension refers to the *design process* or the steps necessary to create a building, home, or city (Zeisel, 1972). Briefly, *programming* involves identification of design criteria or the goals of the unit; *design* is a specific plan to achieve programming goals. *Construction* includes building the place; *use* refers to user activities and adaptations to completed units. *Evaluation* includes assessment of whether the completed unit satisfied original programming goals. Historically, researchers have not been involved in the design process. And, when they have participated, it has largely been in the evaluation stage, i.e., Is the place doing what it was supposed to do; does it have "validity"? For example, Bechtel (1972) identified problems associated with a low-cost housing development. Unique to his approach was the feeding of evaluative limitations into a rehabilitative design process.

While practitioners have occasionally recruited behavioral scientists to participate in the design process, their success has been limited. Researchers are not prone to deal easily with such questions as: "How can the cultural background of group X be translated into the design of a home?" or "What design features should be built into this specific community for poor people?" Researchers do not typically pose questions in such specific place/locale form. The average scientist often replies that he can research the problem, but that his answers will be tentative and restricted in generality, and that the problem will require many studies, long-term funding and development of a body of theory. The practitioner, caught in the bind of a place to be built immediately, and operating with limited dollars, often throws up his hands in dismay, pleading that the design process must go on, and that decisions must be made in spite of incomplete knowledge. He goes on to say that he will accept educated guesses, but that the behavioral scientist must assume some responsibility, in spite of his uncertainty. The behavioral scientist often then steps aside, unwilling to assume such responsibility, to be driven by schedules and dollar limitations, and to act in the absence of thorough and scholarly documentation. Furthermore, he is often not interested in an applied product focused on a particular place or entity.

Implicit in this three-dimensional framework and in the paraphrased dialogue of miscommunication are several other differences in approach.

1. Criterion-oriented vs. process-oriented approaches.

So-called "applied" researchers who work on weapon, transportation, education, and health care "systems" share much in common with environmental designers and are divergent from "basic" researchers. The practitioner and applied researcher are typically criterion- or problem-oriented in that they *begin* with a statement of goals or endpoints to be achieved. They have a known criterion with known properties, e.g., a building or community to house X people and to provide X services, a transportation system which is to achieve a given flow of traffic in a specified period of time, etc. The job is to solve a specific problem and to produce a workable product. The practitioner or applied researcher then proceeds *backwards* from the criterion, gathering information and conducting research directed specifically towards problem solutions. While there may be by-products which go beyond immediate concerns, their perspective is directed primarily toward solving a particular problem. Thus, the practitioner and applied researcher are *dependent* variable oriented and work backwards only to those independent variables which may affect goal achievement. The basic researcher generally proceeds in the opposite direction. While interested in behavioral outcomes, his style is to pose first the question "What are the major classes of factors which affect behavior X?" His specification of behavior X is initially in fairly global terms. The next step, particularly if the researcher is experimentally oriented, is to design a multifactor study, with considerable attention devoted to properties of the laboratory setting and to careful specification and manipulation of *independent* or antecedent variables. In a sense, detailed description of behavioral or dependent variables comes *last* and is often contingent on what *can* be measured in the situation. And, the researcher is usually not concerned with a particular level of behavioral proficiency, but wishes to demonstrate how independent variables produce reliable differences in behavioral outcomes. In summary, he tends to be independent variable oriented, at least in terms of starting point.

Is it any wonder that practitioners and researchers encounter communication difficulties, when the practitioner poses a criterion or dependent variable question, e.g., "How can we satisfy people's needs for privacy in the design of this home?" and the researcher translates this into an inde-

pendent variable framework, "What factors can I study as independent variables which will yield demonstrable effects of privacy?" The practitioner will not obtain the answer to his specific problem from the researcher's strategy, and the researcher is not accustomed to posing his research in the form requested by the practitioner. The result is an impasse.

2. Analysis vs. synthesis

Embedded in the preceding discussion is an issue which has been of philosophical and scientific interest for centuries. The practitioner often describes his job as "putting everything together" to solve problems. Not only must he worry about an array of technological questions—architectural design, plumbing, electricity, materials, transportation, building codes—but he must also deal with sociological and psychological matters. His job is to *synthesize* these different areas in order to create a viable entity.

Implicit in many behavioral science approaches is an *analytic* strategy, i.e., the unraveling of the contribution of individual and clusters of variables to behavioral outcomes. Thus, scientists usually focus on specific behaviors, specific settings, and specific independent variables. While the ultimate goal is broad generalization, immediate goals usually involve dimensionalizing phenomena, partialling out of variance, and detailed *analysis* of the impact of specific variables on specific behaviors. Or, to put it somewhat facetiously, the behavioral scientist is primarily interested in *behavior*, and only secondarily in putting information together to describe *whole people* or *whole groups*. So, when the practitioner poses the question "What does this particular cultural group need by way of privacy, availability to transportation, cultural centers, etc.?" the behavioral scientist not only translates this into the independent variable strategy described above, but he also may reply, "I am a specialist in religious institutions of rural members of that group and, therefore, can only speculate about the many other parts of your question." The result is another mutual frustration.

3. Doing and implementation vs. knowing and understanding

The environmental practitioner is action-oriented; he is a "doer" whose energies are directed toward a specific end product. The typical behavioral scientist is less compelled to achieve an immediate "real world" product. His goal is usually a published study or a theory, with unknown or limited immediate application. Again, these differences in orientation can lead to an impasse. The practitioner, geared toward rebuilding a city or designing a low-cost housing project, must take *immediate action*. The behavioral scientist devotes his energies to understanding rather than to direct action, and in controlled settings where he can tease out relevant sources of variance. He is generally less driven to directly and immediately apply his knowledge.

While these distinctions are not categorical, they collectively point to differences in approach of behavioral scientists and practitioners. And, as noted earlier, the ideal relationship is not necessarily one of consensus or homogeneity of style. Divergencies in approach are probably healthy, for they will bring to bear a variety of knowledge and strategies to the same problems. Furthermore, it will be particularly unhealthy if divergencies are seen by either party as *inadequacies* on the part of the other, or if there is a refusal to undertake translation between approaches. Such translation can take any of several forms. Practitioners and researchers can shift roles, i.e., the scientist can attempt occasionally to translate his work into the practitioner's framework, and vice versa. Or, we can try to develop a new breed of scientist-practitioner, who has a commitment to both types of professions, who works at the boundary of disciplines, and who becomes skilled at

the translation process on an everyday basis. In any case, the theme proposed here is that differences in style exist, and need to be understood and bridged, not obliterated.

Evolutionary Stages of Researcher-Practitioner Contacts

The momentum for researchers and practitioners to join forces began in the late 1950's, when long smoldering discontents began to surface in the design professions and in behavioral science fields. Many practitioners rebelled against what they termed an egocentric approach to the design process, where the main product was accused of being for the benefit of the designer's aesthetic and personal aspirations, and not for the benefit of the human user. The needs of the environmental consumer became primary in the eyes of the malcontents, even at the expense of beauty in design. This led to a reaching out toward disciplines who presumably knew something about man's limitations, motivations and needs—sociology, psychology, political science, anthropology.

In the social and behavioral sciences (speaking primarily of psychology), a complementary discontent mounted about the same time. Some began to question the use of laboratory experimentation as the *sole* approach to understanding behavior and called for the study of behavior in "real world" settings. The hold of the laboratory was quite firm at the time, and it was not popular to conduct field research. However, there had been several notable field studies (Barker & Wright, 1955; Barker, 1963; 1968; Sommer, 1969) which demonstrated that meaningful information could be obtained using field experimental or observational techniques. Nevertheless, those who advocated field studies were often alienated from the mainstream of research. Second, a realization grew that psychology traditionally had been examining behavior almost independent of the physical environment. When it was considered, the environment had been treated primary as an independent variable and physical determinant of responses, e.g., lighting, noise, color. It was not really conceived of as a social milieu or as a modifier of social structures and interaction patterns. Furthermore, the environment had rarely been studied in a dependent variable sense, as a manifestation and extension of behavior, e.g., privacy mechanisms, personal space, territorial behaviors.

Sommer (1969) and Barker (1963; 1968; Barker & Wright, 1955) demonstrated how environments serve as a social milieu, calling forth complex patterns of social behavior. And, the work of Hall (1959; 1966), undertaken from an anthropological perspective, and that of Kuethe (1962a: 1962b), done in a laboratory context, were early illustrations of the role of personal space mechanisms in different social situations. These early efforts sensitized researchers to the role of the environment as an essential feature of social behavior. The result was a reaching out to disciplines who dealt with the environment-architecture, interior design, geography, urban planning. Thus, in the early 1960's a critical mass of professionals developed, who wanted to break away from the constrictions of their own disciplines.

During this initial period, spontaneous and organized interdisciplinary discussions took place, some under the sponsorship of formal organizations, and others as *ad hoc* meetings. From these meetings new channels of communication and more organized activities emerged, such as formal conferences and symposia, newsletters and informals journals, interdisciplinary organizations, and academic programs to train man-environment researchers and practitioners.

In the mid- to late 1960's it appeared as if the early honeymoon was over, as basic value systems and styles of behavioral scientists and practitioners began to clash. The criterion-oriented, problem-directed, unit/place strategy of the practitioner was not being satisfied by the researcher, and

vice versa. That state continues to exist to some extent, but one also has the impression that, having gone through a period of unreal expectations and subsequent disillusionment, a new stage of relationship now exists. Both sides seem ready to make a more realistic assessment of each others' points of view and mutual advantages and disadvantages. It is essential that continued efforts be made in this direction, else the study of man-environment relations will fragment, and once again be approached from the myopic view of individual disciplines.

A Models-of-Man View of the Field

The conduct of environmental research by practitioners and scientists has increased dramatically in the past few years—as evidenced in conference proceedings, technical reports, newsletters and journal articles. And, there is apt to be an even greater outpouring in the coming years. Aside from the question of which research topics are popular or desirable to pursue (see Craik, 1970; Proshansky, Ittelson & Rivlin, 1970; Sommer, 1967; 1969), there is the less tangible issue of which philosophical models underlie present-day research. What general conceptions or models of man seem to be implicit and are in vogue in existing studies? Do these represent historical, evolutionary stages of the man-environment field? Are there philosophical viewpoints which may be fruitful to pursue but which are not yet evident in current research? Even brief consideration of these questions may make salient guiding assumptions underlying current research. And, other perspectives about which researchers and practitioners are not yet wholly aware may evolve from such an analysis.

1. The mechanistic model of man

This model was one of the first applied to the study of man-environment relations. Its origin was in the human engineering, hardware-oriented systems work of the 1950's and 1960's, when it was a maxim that the design of complex systems had to include considerations of human users. The "man-machine systems" approach called for the design of equipment built around physical, sensory, motor and intellectual capabilities and limitations of man, with one motto being, "Fit the machine to man." The roots of this approach were in the early industrial psychology studies of time and motion, energy expenditure, etc. In modern times this approach has been translated into layout analyses, traffic flow systems, lighting, color, heating analyses of environments.

Several assumptions are implicit in this model. Man is viewed primarily as a *performing*, task-oriented organism. As a consequence, emphasis has been placed on his capabilities for sensing, processing, and interpreting inputs, and on his skills in evaluating and selecting action alternatives. Motivational and emotional states and interpersonal processes are either of secondary interest or are treated as factors which enhance or degrade man's system-like functioning. Such processes are not usually considered in and of themselves, but are cast in the context of efficient performance output.

Another feature of this approach is its extensive concern with environmental design, or the shaping of physical environments. The goal has been to insure that man's performance-related skills are maximized and that his limitations are not exceeded or unduly stressed. While training for maximum performance is often undertaken, emphasis has been placed on the design of physical environments, with man as one major constraint on that environment. Thus, environments are designed *for man*, often in a static sense and with relatively few options for him to alter environments or to function in them in a flexible fashion. In this sense, man is merely another system component with limited degrees of operating freedom.

While this approach achieved popularity in the 1950's and early 1960's, and still

has relevance today, current man-environment research does not appear to rely heavily on this model.

2. *The perceptual-cognitive-motivational model of man*

The major present-day approach in environmental research conceptualizes man in terms of a variety of internal processes. These include *perceptual reactions* to the environment (how he senses, perceives, and organizes environmental stimuli), *motivational and emotional states* associated with environmental stimuli (stress, negative and positive affect), *cognitive responses* to the environment (subjective estimates of the richness, complexity, meaning and evaluation of the environment). This model conceives of man as an internal processing organism, and is more concerned with subjective psychological processes in relation to the environment than with overt behavioral responses.

Historically, psychology has relied heavily on an "internal state" model of man. This has been especially true in clinical psychology which, stemming from the earlier Freudian tradition, emphasized man's emotional and motivational states. This model has also been prevalent in social psychology, with its emphasis on: (1) attitudes and belief systems, (2) personality-oriented social states such as need achievement, affiliation, and dominance, and (3) interpersonal psychological states involving cooperation and competition, interpersonal attraction, conformity and influence, etc.

Research-oriented practitioners have been quick to adopt this model, perhaps because there is a large body of available theory and measurement techniques. The goal has been to uncover how man sees, perceives, feels and reacts to aspects of his environment. Use has been made of questionnaire and rating procedures such as the semantic differential, where environments are rated on scales tapping *evaluative* (good-bad), *activity* (dynamic quality of environments), and *potency* (impact characteristics of environment) dimensions. Other approaches include "cognitive maps," where people are literally asked to draw their neighborhoods, streets, and cities, or are interviewed as they move through environments. The goal is to determine subjective perceptions of an environment, independent of its "objective" characteristics. One of the earliest examples of this approach involved taking people on a walk and asking them to give subjective impressions as they moved about (Lynch & Rivkin, 1959). Recently, Ladd (1970) asked black children to draw their neighborhoods and streets, and then content analyzed their responses. Various aspects of cognitive map research and techniques have been summarized by Stea and Downs (1972).

A massive body of data is building in this area and it seems that this model of man dominates research at the present time. It is also interesting to consider this approach from an extended historical perspective. Early in the history of modern psychology, during the last third of the nineteenth century, a substantial aspect of research involved "introspection," or the systematic analysis and self-reporting of internal cognitive and psychological events. In fact, there was an attempt by Wilhelm Wundt and his associates to establish a "mental chemistry." In many respects the cognitive map movement in man-environment research is analogous to the introspectionist movement of the 19th Century, as it also seeks to unravel how man cognizes, perceives and feels about the environment. It will be interesting to see how long this "inside the head" model of man remains prominent in man-environment research.

3. The behavioral model of man

This approach emphasizes study of *overt* behavior rather than internal, subjective states. What man *does* is stressed rather coming years will show a surge of energy in this direction.
than how he feels, perceives or cognizes. The work of Roger Barker and his associates (Barker, 1963; 1968; Barker & Gump, 1964; Barker & Wright, 1955) is representative of this approach, with detailed observations made of people's movements and activities as they function in various environments.

Behavioral analyses are not restricted to naturalistic observation. Much of the work of Sommer and others (Sommer, 1969) involves field experimentation coupled with behavioral measurement, e.g., how people overtly interact, protect spaces, occupy chair locations, and approach others at varying distances as a function of manipulated variables such as nature and degree of intrusion, status, etc. There is also an increasing volume of research in laboratory settings on such factors as personal space, crowding and territorial behavior, all of which deals with overt behavioral events. (See Altman, 1973; Lett, Clark, & Altman, 1969; Proshansky, Ittelson, & Rivlin, 1970; Sommer, 1969 for reviews of some of this literature.) While this approach generally emphasizes overt behavior, many studies also simultaneously examine internal motivational states.

The behavioral approach is beginning to have an impact on practitioners. Many early conferences were dominated by the cognitive map approach, as practitioners sought to gain better understanding of man's internal needs and perceptions. And it appeared as if everyone scampered about, armed with questionnaires, rating instruments and interview schedules designed to tap all manner of internal states. More recently the behavioral approach has begun to gain momentum. For example, Barker-type work occupies more and more time at conferences, sessions are increasingly crowded, students and practitioners now talk about committing themselves to behavioral observation. It is likely that the coming years will show a surge of energy in this direction.

4. A social systems, ecological model of man

This approach has not been well established in the behavioral and social sciences, although the present author and others have formulated some ideas in this direction (Altman, 1933; Altman, Nelson, & Lett, 1972: Altman & Taylor, 1973). A central theme underlying this model is that human interpersonal behavior is part of a complex ecosystem which has several features:

1. Environment and behavior are closely intertwined. This involves more than the accepted dictum that "environment affects behavior." It also states that behavior cannot be wholly understood independent of its intrinsic relationship to the physical environment, and that the very definition of behavior must be within an environmental context (Barker, 1968). To a great extent the social and behavioral sciences, especially psychology, have historically studied man almost as if he were separate from physical environments. What is now called for is recognition that man is at one with his environment and that the appropriate unit of study is a behavior-environment or organism-environment unit.

2. There is a mutual and dual impact between man and his environment. Not only does the environment act upon men, but man acts on environments, in a true ecological sense. Historically, researchers and practitioners have emphasized the environment as an independent variable—as something which acts on, determines, or causes behavior. Thus, one often encounters the view that environments must be designed for people to be placed in, to meet their needs and to satisfy their purposes. Implicit in this traditional notion is the idea that man's control over his environment is to be limited, that environments are tailored to him in somewhat of a static, nonmodifiable form.

More recently, however, increased emphasis has been given to the design of flexible, changing environments which men can manipulate, shape and alter. Here, man becomes an environmental change agent, not merely a recipient of environmental influences. And, according to this approach, the environment becomes an extension of man's being and personality. Concepts such as territory (the use and possession of places), privacy (control of input from others) and personal space (spatial distances from others) all refer to an active, coping use of the environment by people, not merely reactive responses to environmental stimuli.

3. A third feature of this ecological approach concerns the dynamic, changing quality of man-environment relations. These are not static, immutably fixed or intransigent relationships. Territories shift, functions alter, group composition changes. While a seemingly obvious truism, practitioners and researchers often act as if their products and knowledge were fixed and unchanging through time. Social systems adapt, cope and struggle, and both research and practice need to incorporate this idea.

4. A final theme of this approach is that man-environment relations occur at several levels of behavioral functioning, and as a coherent system. The man-machine, perceptual-motivational-cognitive and behavioral models emphasize different facets of human functioning, and almost presume that each is sufficient unto itself to understand man-environment relationships. It is proposed here that many such levels of behavior occur simultaneously and must be considered as a coherent set. Thus, perceptions, cognitions, feelings and emotional states serve as internal forces which eventually become translated into several levels of overt behavior, such as: (a) *verbal content* and *paraverbal behaviors*, including tone, pitch, interruptions and other stylistic features of speech; (b) *nonverbal behaviors*, including body postures and positions, and dynamic body behaviors such as eye contact, smiling, hand and feet movements

and gestures, (c) *environmentally oriented behaviors,* or active use of objects and areas in the environment, such as personal space or physical distance, arrangements of furniture and other objects, selection and use of environmental objects.

Explicit in this last theme is the idea that different levels of behavior fit together as a "system," with the various levels capable of substituting, complementing or amplifying one another. Thus, a verbal statement can substitute for a smile or a head nod, or vice versa, or can be combined with a particular body position or use of the physical environment. This results in a wide repertoire of behaviors which are coordinated in various patterns. While sole emphasis on one level of behavior may be necessary in a particular research study, continued particularistic analysis without integration of behavioral levels can lose sight of the system quality of man-environment relations.

From the perspective of this paper, the social systems approach is the most potentially fruitful "model" of man for several reasons. For example, it may be useful in establishing connections between the other models. Furthermore, it seems to fit more appropriately the complex nature of man-environment relationships. It also may help bridge the gap between the place-oriented approach of the practitioner and the process-oriented approach of the behavioral scientist. That is, a model based on several levels of behavior which function as a coherent system may permit a synthesis of a total organism—a person, group or person-environment unit—as separate levels of behavior are interrelated. If carried to its logical possibilities, this approach can be analogous to understanding and managing a symphony orchestra, in terms of simultaneous knowledge of separate instrument sections as well as the whole orchestral unit. If this can be achieved, then place-unit and process-oriented approaches can be bridged, as can analysis and synthesis strategies.

Summary and Conclusions

Progress in the man-environment area depends on the joining of forces by scientists and practitioners. However, barriers to mutual understanding exist, because of differences in styles of practitioners and researchers. Researchers are primarily analytic and independent variable-oriented, and less concerned with solving "real world" problems. Their efforts are directed toward behavioral processes, and less emphasis is placed on whole organismic units, i.e., places or people. The typical practitioner operates according to a goal-directed, criterion-oriented, place-focused strategy. He seeks to synthesize information, and deals with processes only if specific information is necessary to design a viable place or unit. Because of these different strategies, practitioners and scientists have often miscommunicated. To understand and solve man-environment problems, it is important that these differences be understood and bridged. For example, scientists and practitioners may find it useful to translate their knowledge into one another's frameworks—the scientist viewing his data in terms of its potential application, and the practitioners becoming more analytic, even at the expense of ignoring immediate applications of knowledge. It is not advocated that each should *become* the other, nor that they necessarily achieve total mutual consensus. Rather the goal should be to occasionally view a problem from the perspective of the other. In this way the strengths of each approach might generate new modes of attack.

Researchers and practitioners have implicitly adopted one of several theoretical "models of man." While none of the following models are "correct" in an absolute sense, they have served to guide research and practice:

1. A *mechanistic model,* with man viewed primarily as part of a complex man-machine system, and emphasis placed on

performance-related behaviors; 2. a *perceptual-cognitive-motivational model*, with man conceived of as an internal, subjective, inside-the-head processor. This model is presently popular in man-environment research, in the form of studies of cognitive maps and subjective reactions to environmental stimuli; 3. a *behavioral model*, which places emphasis on overt behavior rather than internal psychological processes. According to this position, man-environment relations are best understood through study of overt transactions between man and his physical environment; 4. an *ecological, social systems model*, which conceives of man-environment events as involving: (a) several behavioral levels, e.g., subjective internal processes, overt verbal, nonverbal and environmental behaviors, which (b) function as a coherent system of interrelated, substitutible and complementary behaviors and (3) where there is a mutual relationship between environment and behavior, each influencing and shaping the other, (d) in a dynamic time-linked sense.

The position was taken that no single model is complete, but that the ecological social systems approach held considerable promise for understanding man-environment relations for several reasons: 1. it treats man and environments as the central units, not men alone or environments alone; 2. it holds the potential for bridging between the approaches of practitioners and researchers. That is, it calls for scientists to synthesize separate behavioral events into total organismic units and calls for practitioners to examine social processes in an analytic fashion; 3. its emphasis on multi-level behaviors brings together several areas of the behavioral and social sciences and 4. it views man-environment relations in a way which stresses flexibility of environments and active organisms shaping environments.

The understanding and solution of man-environment problems cannot be approached from a dogmatic and doctrinaire perspective. What is most important, and the primary goal of this paper, is to point out alternative strategies and implicit assumptions underlying differences in styles of problem solving. In this way those interested in the field can pursue a line of attack consciously, with some perspective on its history and sociology.

3. Conceptualizations of Human Environments
RUDOLF H. MOOS

Current interest in the physical and social aspects of planning for both large (e.g., cities and "new towns") and small (e.g., industries, psychiatric hospitals, correctional institutions) environmental systems is remarkable. Jordan (1972) noted that more books treating man and his environment from a wholistic and ecological viewpoint have appeared within the past four years than had appeared during the prior three decades. Within the broader society, this interest is largely due to technological advances, whole "side effects" raise critical issues about the delicate ecological balance existing on "Spaceship Earth." Major human problems such as general environmental deterioration, particularly water, air, and noise pollution, the probable effects of increasing population and population density, and issues of resource depletion, specifically in relation to food materials, are being discussed extensively.

Psychology and the behavioral sciences have reflected these concerns and

From *American Psychologist*, Vol. 28, No. 8, August 1973, pp. 652–663. Copyright 1973 by the American Psychological Association. Reprinted by permission of the publisher and the author.

have also recently shown increased interest in the environment. This interest has arisen in part because of dissatisfactions with trait conceptualizations of personality, in part because of low correlations obtained between measures of personality traits and various validity criteria, and in part because of growing evidence that substantial proportions of the variance in behavior are accounted for by situational and environmental variables (Endler & Hunt, 1968; Moos, 1969). The literature criticizing the empirical legacy of several decades of work with trait models of personality has been most cogently summarized by Mischel (1968). In addition, many studies have demonstrated that substantial differences may occur in the behavior of the same individuals when they are in different milieus (e.g., Barker & Gump, 1964).

Although most current personality theorists subscribe to the belief that behavior is a joint function of both the person and the environment, they have until recently emphasized and studied person variables while paying relatively less attention to environmental variables. Kurt Lewin and Henry Murray have been the most influential psychological theorists; however, there are as yet few theoretical approaches that fully conceptualize a broad range of environmental variables and systematically relate these to behavior.

These issues raise the common problem of how human environments can be conceptualized and assessed. Six major methods by which characteristics of environments have been related to indexes of human functioning are presented here. These are (1) ecological dimensions, which include both geographical–meteorological and architectural–physical design variables; (2) behavior settings, which are the only units thus far proposed which are characterized by both ecological and behavioral properties; (3) dimensions of organizational structure; (4) dimensions identifying the collective personal and/or behavioral characteristics of the milieu inhabitants; (5) dimensions related to psychosocial characteristics and organizational climates; and (6) variables relevant to the functional or reinforcement analyses of environments. The six categories of dimensions are nonexclusive, overlapping, and mutually interrelated. The overview presented here is necessarily incomplete and sketchy, but it serves to illustrate the broad range of dimensions relevant to this area. The common relevance of these six types of dimensions is that each has been conceptualized and shown to have an important and sometimes decisive impact on individual and group behavior (Moos & Insel, 1974).

Ecological Dimensions

Down through the ages there has been the recurrent notion that geographical and meteorological characteristics (e.g., temperature, rainfall, topography, etc.) may significantly shape the culture, character, and activities of societies (e.g., Huntington, 1915). Environmental determinists believe that there are specific connections between environmental characteristics, such as mountainous terrain, soil conditions, humidity, etc., and personality traits, such as strength of character, assertiveness, bravery, and laziness. For example, one study (Barry, Child, & Bacon, 1959) found an association between different types of subsistence economy and differential importance given to the development of certain character traits. Societies whose economies entailed the accumulation and care of food resources tended to stress the development of such personal traits as responsibility and obedience, whereas hunting and fishing societies tended to emphasize achievement and self-reliance. Such conclusions are of course tenuous since intricate patterns of potential mediating factors are always present.

It has been suggested that climate may be one of the major factors in economic development throughout the world, the optimum climate being the temperate climate within which most of the world's current industrial powers lie. Further, many people feel that their efficiency is impaired by extremes of heat and cold, and one of the arguments in support of air conditioning is that it improves worker efficiency. Climate has been associated with gross national product per capita (Russett et al., 1964), with specific indexes of affective interpersonal behavior (Griffit & Veitch, 1971), and with variations in organizational participation among metropolitan housewives (Michelson, 1971).

Some of the other variables implicated in the determination of behavior include extreme cold, barometric pressure, cyclonic and anticyclonic storm patterns, and oxygen, nitrogen, carbon dioxide, and ozone concentrations in the atmosphere (Muecher & Ungeheuer, 1961; Sells, Findikyan, & Duke, 1966). For example, Mills (1942) reported that statistics for Tokyo show that people are more forgetful on days of low barometric pressure, as indicated by a higher frequency of packages and umbrellas left on buses and streetcars.

The weight of the evidence suggests that geographical and meteorological variables may be more important in the determination of group and individual behavior than has been thought to be the case. Man is increasingly creating his own geographical and meteorological environment, and trends in this area are thus concerned with the possible relationship of man-made variables, such as radiation and pollution, to mood changes and to mental and physical symptoms.

Other aspects of the man-made environment, especially dimensions relevant to architectural and physical design, are also important. Behavior necessarily occurs in a specific physical context, which may impose major constraints on the range of possible behaviors and serve to determine particular aspects or patterns of individual action. A substantial amount of research has been done in this area; for example, behavioral maps can be arranged in a matrix showing the frequency of different types of activities in different available locations. Psychiatric wards have been analyzed in terms of variables such as behavior density (the frequency of all types of activities at a particular place), diffuseness (the range of different activities occurring at a place), and activity profile (the frequency of specific types of activities occurring at a place). Research in ergonomics, human engineering, and human factors has been concerned with the relation of selected environmental variables, such as heating, lighting, noise level, ventilation, and the layout and design of machines, to behavioral measures of work efficiency, comfort, social interaction, interpersonal perception, and exploratory behavior. For example, Maslow and Mintz (1956) demonstrated that interpersonal perceptions could be highly sensitive to variations in the physical environment. They found that judgments of psychological states (weary, zestful, irritated) based on photographed faces differed in three physically different rooms. Basic reviews of this area may be found in Craik (1970), Kates and Wohlwill (1966), Proshansky, Ittelson, and Rivlin (1970), and Sommer (1969).

However, there is as yet no adequate dimensionalization or typology of architectural and physical design variables. Kasmar (1970) has developed an Environmental Description Scale which assesses perceptions of physical characteristics of rooms along dimensions such as physical organization, lighting, size, temperature, ventilation, etc. At a more global level, Lansing, Marans, and Zehner (1970) have characterized planned residential environments (e.g., Columbia, Maryland; Reston, Virginia) along dimensions such as dwelling unit density, accessibility of recreational facilities, percentage of homes with sidewalks nearby, etc. The next major advance in this area will probably be a creation of several alternative typologies of variables which will be used in order to systematically study social problems such as physical environmental factors affecting residential choice and migration, the adaptational cost of urban noise and urban ghettos, etc.

Behavior Settings

The work of Roger Barker (1968) in ecological psychology at the Midwestern Psychological Field Station is important and unique. Barker and his associates have worked in this area for over 20 years and have developed the concept of the behavior setting, which they consider to be the essential element in studies of the ecological environment. Behavioral ecology is conceptualized as being concerned with molar behavior and the ecological context in which it occurs. Barker carefully analyzed and categorized all of the behavior settings of a small midwestern community. He pointed out that these behavior settings (e.g., drugstore, garage, junior high school play, basketball game, etc.) are natural phenomena; that is, they are not created by an experimenter for scientific purposes. They have a space and time locus which is self-generated. They are a perceptual ecological entity. They have two sets of components: (a) behavior, for example, reciting, discussing, and sitting; and (b) nonpsychological objects with which behavior is transacted, for example, chairs, walls, a blackboard, paper, etc. The important characteristic of behavior settings is that they are stable extra-individual units which have great coercive power over the behavior that occurs within them.

Barker (1968) has presented in detail a methodology by which to identify and categorize behavior settings. The most important aspect of this work is that behavior settings can be shown to have pervasive

effects on individuals, not only in terms of the specific behavior which is "demanded" by the setting (e.g., reading and writing in classrooms) but also on both other behaviors and effects experienced by individuals. Barker and Gump (1964) have done an extremely intriguing analysis of the different demands of undermanned and optimally manned behavior settings and have shown that these produce characteristic differences in the strength, direction, origin, and termination of forces that impinge on their inhabitants. In comparison with the inhabitants of optimally manned behavior settings, the inhabitants of undermanned settings (a) engage in more and more varied program actions; (b) engage in more varied, stronger, and more deviation-countering maintenance actions; (c) have less sensitivity to and are less evaluative of individual differences in behavior; (d) see themselves as having greater functional importance within the setting; (e) have more responsibility and greater functional identify. For example, students in small schools with relatively few associates within behavior settings, in comparison with students of larger schools with relatively many associates, report twice as many pressures on them to take part in the programs of the settings, actually perform in more than twice as many responsible positions in the settings, and report having more satisfactions related to the development of competence, to being challenged, to engaging in important actions, to being involved in group activities, to being valued, to gaining moral and cultural values, etc. Some of these findings have been replicated in large and small churches (Wicker, 1969).

Thus, behavior settings are conceptualized as ecological units that have both an environmental and a behavioral component. It has been shown that these units have considerable importance in the determination of individual behavior and experience. Unfortunately, there has still been relatively little work utilizing this methodology aside from that of Barker and his students. Behavior setting analyses can and should be done in a variety of different types of institutions, for example, mental hospitals, correctional institutions, universities, and urban ghettos. The range and variety of behavior settings in central city, suburban, and rural areas must be very different, and from Barker's results it would be expected that this would have extremely important effects on the affect, behavior, and development of the inhabitants. While the behavior setting is probably the best conceptualized and most studied basic unit in this entire area, a systematic typology of behavior settings has yet to be developed.

Dimensions of Organizational Structure

Many investigators have attempted to assess and discriminate among organizations using relatively objective dimensions such as size, staffing ratios, average salary levels, organizational control structure, etc. (March, 1965). Organizations vary widely in their structural characteristics, and thus an important question is whether differences in organization structures are related to different behavioral and attitudinal indexes of the organization members. Porter and Lawler (1965) defined structure to mean the positions and parts of organizations and their systematic and relatively enduring relationships to each other. Within this broad definition, they identify seven dimensions of organizational structure, some of which are size of the overall organization, centralized or decentralized shape, number of organizational levels, span of control (the number of subordinates a manager is responsible for supervising), and size of organizational subunits. Porter and Lawler concluded that several of these dimensions are significantly related to one or more attitude or behavior variables, for example, morale, need satisfaction, absenteeism, and turnover. In general, the im-

pact of structural variables was clearer on attitudes than on behavioral variables. Porter and Lawler pointed out that much more attention needs to be given to the interrelationships between and among different dimensions of organizational structure. Organizations are probably too complex for any given variable to have a consistent effect across a wide variety of conditions. Recent articles that review various aspects of this work, most of it concentrating on industrial and business organizations, include Pugh (1966), Roberts (1970), and Lichtman and Hunt (1971).

Similar work has been done in colleges and universities. For example, Astin (1968b) used relatively objective indexes differentiating among universities and attempted to relate them to undergraduate achievement. The types of institutional quality dimensions he utilized included (*a*) selectivity (an estimate of the average academic ability of the entering student); (*b*) per-student expenditures for educational and general purposes; (*c*) number of books in the library per student; (*d*) faculty-student ratio; (*e*) percentage of faculty with PhD degrees; (*f*) total undergraduate enrollment; and (*g*) percentage of men in the student body. Astin concluded that these traditional indexes of institutional quality did not contribute much to student achievement, but there is some disagreement on this point.

In work outside of industrial and educational institutions, the three most well investigated dimensions are size, turnover rate, and population density (crowding). The literature on the effects of size is quite vast; however, a brief review may be found in Barker and Gump (1964). There is very little systematic knowledge about the effects of differential turnover rates in different institutions, although some studies are in progress (e.g., Kelly, 1971). Most of the important work on population density has been done in animal studies, but the potential applications to human environments seem clear. Increased population density and crowding in animals have been shown to be related to reproduction, aggressive behavior, drug toxicity, adrenomedullary function, adrenocortical function, blood pressure, brain amines, and immune responses. Attempts have been made to conceptualize crowding effects in human environments such as urban ghettos (Duhl, 1963) and cities (Milgram, 1970).

Personal and Behavioral Characteristics of the Milieu Inhabitants

Various factors related to the characteristics of individuals inhabiting a particular environment, for example, average age, ability level, socioeconomic background, and educational attainment, may be considered to be situational variables in that they partly define relevant characteristics of the environment (Sells, 1963). This general idea is based on the suggestion made by Linton (1945) that most of the social and cultural environment is transmitted through other people. It implies that the character of an environment is dependent in part on the typical characteristics of its members.

This approach may be illustrated by Astin (1968a), who has recently developed a new technique for characterizing environmental stimuli in colleges and universities —the Inventory of College Activities. The Inventory provides information about the average personal and behavioral characteristics of the college environment by the following kinds of items: (a) questions about activities in college, such as whether or not the individual flunked a course, became pinned or engaged, got married, participated in a student demonstration, or changed his or her major field; (b) the median number of hours per week the student spent in different activities, such as attending class, studying school assignments, reading for pleasure, watching television, watching athletic events, sleeping, and playing games; (c) the kinds of or-

ganizations in which the student was a member, such as fraternities or sororities, college athletic teams, marching bands, religious club, service organization, etc. Remarkable diversity was found among the environments of 246 colleges and universities included in this study. Thus, the proportion of students who engaged in any particular activity (e.g., dating, going to church, drinking beer, voting in a student election) often varied from no students in some institutions to nearly all students in others. Astin felt that this considerable diversity indicates that the college and university environment has great potential for differentially influencing the experience and behavior of the individual student.

For illustration, he assumes that a new student enrolls in an institution with high academic standards in which certain environmental stimuli occur relatively frequently: classroom examinations, discussions among students about grades, studying, intellectual arguments among students, and debates between faculty and students. The new student would be exposed to these and related stimuli and thus might feel anxiety about possible academic failure (a change in immediate subjective experience), experience increased fear of or hostility toward fellow students, or have increased feelings of competitiveness and/or feelings of inferiority. Presumably the student might be affected differently if he attended a different college. In terms of short-term behavioral effects, the student may increase the time he devotes to studying, reduce the time he devotes to social activities, and perhaps increase his intellectual aggression. He may consequently experience greater feelings of loneliness and isolation. Finally, there may be longer lasting alterations in his self-concept and/or relatively permanent changes in behavior which may persist beyond college (e.g., devoting a great deal of time to the job or competing constantly with others). Astin and Holland (1961) and Holland (1966) have done other highly relevant work in this area. Holland assumed that vocational satisfaction, stability, and achievement depend on the congruence between one's personality and the environment (composed largely of other people) in which one works. He has proposed six model environments to characterize the common physical and social environments in our culture and six personality types or personal orientations as identified by the type of vocation to which a person belongs. Since both the environmental models and the personality types are derived from the same six basic concepts (realistic, intellectual, social, conventional, enterprising, and artistic), it is possible to classify people and environments in the same terms and, at least theoretically, to assess the degree of person–environment congruence and its effects. Thus, there are some highly promising approaches in this area.

Psychosocial Characteristics and Organizational Climate

Until recently, most of this work involved rather detailed naturalistic descriptions of the functioning of different institutions, such as psychiatric wards, colleges, and universities. This work was valuable in that it indicated the importance of the immediate psychosocial environment in the determination of behavior and in that it suggested various types of dimensions along which psychosocial environments might be compared.

The newer organization theorists have also discussed various analyses of organizations that specifically imply certain dimensions along which these organizations might be compared. For example, Katz and Kahn (1966) presented certain defining characteristics of social organizations: (a) maintenance, production, and production-supportive structures; (b) elaborate formal role patterns; (c) authority structure; (d) regulatory mechanisms and adaptive structures which include feedback to the insti-

tution concerning its own operation and the changing character of its environment; and (e) explicit formulation of an ideology that provides system norms and that supports the authority structure. Some of the dimensions inherent in this type of analysis may be categorized as objective organizational structure dimensions; however, others are psychosocial or "event-structure" dimensions.

A number of perceived climate scales have been developed in the last few years in order to attempt to measure more systematically the general norms, value orientations, and other psychosocial characteristics of different types of institutions. For example, Stern (1970) followed the Murray (1938) need-press theory and stated that the "concept of environmental press provides an external situational counterpart to the internalized personality needs [p. 7]." Stern pointed out that descriptions of institutional press are based on inferred continuity and consistency in otherwise discrete events. If students in a university are assigned seats in classrooms, if attendance records are kept, if faculty see students outside of class only by appointment, if there is a prescribed form for all term papers, if neatness counts, etc., then it is probable that the press at this school emphasizes the development of orderly responses on the part of the students. It is these conditions that establish the climate or atmosphere of an institution.

Stern (1970) divided press into two basic categories: (a) anabolic press which is represented in those stimuli that are potentially conducive to self–enhancing growth, for example, press conducive to the development of cognitive mastery; and (b) catabolic press, which includes stimuli that are antithetical to personal development or are likely to produce countervailing responses, for example, press involving psychological constraints. Examples of developmental press include intellectual climate, personal dignity, and closeness and achievement standards; examples of catabolic press include orderliness and impulse control.

Another major scale used extensively in this area is the College and University Environmental Scale, which assesses five different dimensions of college environments, for example, scholarship (the emphasis on competitively high academic achievement and interest in scholarship), community (the cohesiveness, supportiveness, and sympathy of the environment as well as the feeling of group welfare and group loyalty), and practicality (concrete and realistic rather than speculative or abstract emphasis). A recent new technique, the Institutional Functioning Inventory, is most appropriate for faculty and administrators, although students may answer some of the items. This Inventory affords the opportunity for study of sources of disparate beliefs about the work of the college and is considered to be for the purpose of institutional self-study, carried out on behalf of institutional reform (Peterson, Centra, Hartnett, & Linn, 1970). Most relevant for present purposes is the fact that the Institutional Functioning Inventory yields scores on 11 different scales which are considered to be representative of basic dimensions differentiating among colleges and universities. Examples of these dimensions include (*a*) human diversity, which has to do with the degree to which the faculty and student body are heterogenous in their backgrounds and present attitudes; (*b*) concern for undergraduate learning; (*c*) concern for innovation, which refers to an institutionalized commitment to experimentation with new ideas for educational practice; and (*d*) institutional spirit, which refers to a sense of shared purposes and high morale among faculty and administrators. A substantial amount of work utilizing this general logic has also been carried out in elementary schools (Halpin & Croft, 1963), in high school classrooms (Walberg, 1969), and in industries (Likert, 1967).

Moos and his associates have studied nine different types of social environments relatively extensively and have developed perceived climate scales for each of these environments: (1) psychiatric wards (Moos, 1974); (2) community-oriented psychiatric treatment programs such as halfway houses, day hospitals, and community care homes (Moos, 1972a); (3) correctional institutions, including those for both adult and juvenile offenders (Moos, 1968); (4) military basic training companies; (5) university student residences, such as dormitories, fraternities, and sororities (Gerst & Moos, 1972); (6) junior high and high school classrooms (Trickett & Moos, 1973); (7) social, task-oriented, and therapeutic groups (Moos & Humphrey, 1973); (8) work milieus (Insel & Moos, 1972); and (9) families (Moos, 1974).

Moos conceptualized the following three basic types of dimensions which characterize and discriminate among different subunits within each of these nine environments:

1. Relationship dimensions, which are quite similar in all nine environments, assess the extent to which individuals are involved in the environment and the extent to which they support and help each other. The basic dimensions are involvement, support, and expressiveness.

2. Personal development dimensions assess the basic directions along which personal development and self-enhancement tend to occur in the particular environment. The exact nature of these dimensions varies somewhat among the nine environments studied, depending on their basic purposes and goals. For example, in psychiatric and correctional programs these dimensions assess the treatment goals, for example, autonomy (the extent to which people are encouraged to be self-sufficient and independent), practical orientation (the extent to which the program orients an individual toward training for new jobs, looking to the future, setting and working concrete goals), and personal problem orientation (the extent to which individuals are en-

couraged to be concerned with their feelings and problems and to seek to understand them). An autonomy or independence dimension is also identified in military companies. University residences (e.g., competition, academic achievement, intellectuality) and junior high and high school classrooms (e.g., task orientation, competition) include other dimensions which are conceptualized as belonging in the person development category.

3. System maintenance and system change dimensions are relatively similar across the nine environments studied. The basic dimensions are order and organizations and clarity and control. An additional dimension in work environments is work pressure, whereas a dimension of innovation is identified in educational, work, and small group environments. There is evidence that these types of dimensions are related to important criteria such as morale and indexes of coping behavior and to different objective indexes of treatment outcome (Moos, 1974).

Techniques by which to assess the organizational climate characteristics of social milieus are important in the identification of salient environmental dimensions. Their specific relevance here is that they identify dimensions that have demonstrable effects on individual and group behavior. They are useful in the measurement of personality-environment congruence, in cross-cultural comparisons (Moos, 1972b), and in helping to define directions for environmental change (Moos, 1973a). The striking similarity of the specific dimensions and their categorization across different investigators and organizational environments indicates that one or more widely useful typologies may soon emerge.

Functional or Reinforcement Analyses of Environments

The methodology of functional analyses of environments is an outgrowth of a social learning perspective (Bandura, 1969; Mis-

chel, 1968). The social learning theorist takes as a given that people vary their behavior extensively in different social and physical environments, mainly because the reinforcement consequences for particular behaviors vary extensively. People are expected to behave similarly in different settings only to the extent that those settings are alike (or perhaps are perceived to be alike) in their potential reinforcing properties.

Social learning theorists attempt to identify the exact controlling stimulus conditions for particular behaviors, for example, the specific models involved, the substantive reinforcers, and the precise discriminative stimuli. A social behavior assessment is thus highly idiographic. The assessment complexity of this analysis may be illustrated by the fact that essentially any stimulus or stimulus change may be a reinforcer. In addition, the patterning or sequencing of reinforcements is also important, as are internal cues which may be utilized for self-reinforcement. Very little is known about what the most important discriminative stimuli are for the maintenance of specific behaviors in different types of social settings.

Techniques for the assessment and identification of reinforcing stimuli have mainly included actual observations by independent observers and subject observations, for example, by preference ratings for different types of reinforcement (praise and social approval, money, information, etc.). Kanfer and Saslow (1965) have presented a detailed interview guide, and Wolpe and Lazarus (1966) have asked clients to keep detailed daily records of the exact conditions related to their specific anxieties. The recent construction of actuarial stimulus hierarchies for deconditioning phobias indicates that there may be some intersubject consistency in the important eliciting conditions. In this connection, Rotter (1954) has suggested classifying situations in terms of the major types of reinforcements which are likely to occur in them, for example, affiliative situations, academic status situations, etc.

Schoggen (1963) has developed highly relevant categories from naturalistic observations of the stream of behavior. He conceptualized the environment to be active and directed with respect to the developing child and identified environmental force units (EFUs), which were defined as any action by an environmental agent that occurred vis-à-vis the child and that was directed toward a recognizable end state with respect to the child. His results indicated that EFUs occurred at a very frequent rate, that mothers were more frequent sources of EFUs than fathers, and that there were wide individual variations between children in the percentage of EFUs initiated with the child and by agents in interaction with the child. Schoggen also identified conflict EFUs, which were any EFUs in which the agent's goal for the child was different than the child's own goal. Different behavior settings have quite different types and amounts of EFUs, presumably indicating that individual behavior is being differentially shaped in them. Since EFUs identify the directions in which behavior is to be shaped and also indicate the types of behaviors that are likely to be positively and negatively reinforced, this approach is essentially a functional analysis of settings.

Some investigators have attempted to identify aspects of a total environment that are thought likely to be related to the development of selected specific characteristics. For example, Wolf (1966) listed the conditions and processes in the environment that were likely to influence the development of general intelligence and/or academic achievement. The types of environmental variables which were identified included the climate created for achievement motivation, the opportunities for verbal development, the nature and amount of assistance provided in overcoming academic difficulties, the level of intellectuality in the environment, and the kinds of work habits expected of the individual. Wolf developed a technique for assessing these variables and found that the relationship between the total rating for the degree of intellectual "press" of the environment and measured general intelligence was .69. He stated that environments for the development and maintenance of such characteristics as dependency, aggression, and dogmatism could be delineated, measured, and systematically related to measures of that particular characteristic. Many investigators have presented analyses of institutional environments along these lines (Buehler et al., 1966; Cohen & Filipczak, 1971).

The functional analysis of environments has important implications. Behavior variability is treated as a given rather than as something which needs special explanation. Discriminative stimuli may be assessed both by subject perceptions and by more objective independent observations. The analysis is relevant to the prediction of behavior in the sense that one can attempt to discover whether environmental maintaining conditions for specific behaviors tend to change markedly. Also, the assumption is that behavior change can readily occur when there is environmental change. Generalization of behavior change should occur to the extent to which there is generalization of the reinforcement which induced the behavior change.

Other important problems may also be analyzed utilizing this theoretical orientation. For example, the relation between attitudes and behavior should depend on the similarity of the maintaining conditions and probable consequences for expressing a particular attitude and then actually carrying it out behaviorally. Factors affecting test performance may also be similarly studied, that is, an analysis of the probable consequences of answering a particular questionnaire in a particular manner. Most importantly, commonalities among stimulus conditions that evoke similar behaviors may be identified, and some evidence indicates that there may be substantial predictive increments based on specific knowledge about environmental conditions. On the other hand, there is still no accepted typology of variables in this area. Since any stimulus, including an internal stimulus, may have reinforcement and/or discriminative value, the resulting bewildering array of potentially relevant variables must of necessity eventually be cast into some relevant typologies. This will be a complex task, since, of course, the "value" of any stimulus depends in part on the specific social context in which it is embedded.

An Example of Aggression and Violence

This brief overview illustrates the many different assessment techniques, types of variables, and potential environmental typologies. The area is in its empirical infancy, and it is still unclear how the different methods will eventually relate to each other. In the broadest perspective, environmental and stimulus variables may be conceptualized as reducing and shaping the potential variability in human behavior. In this sense, all of the six types of dimensions mentioned above are related. The geographical and meteorological environment to some extent shapes the environment of architecture and physical design, which in turn has demonstrable effects on the types of available behavior settings. In their turn, behavior settings constrain the potential range of organizational structure, methods of institutional functioning, and the personal and behavioral characteristics of individuals who choose to inhabit the behavior settings. In turn, different behavior settings, organizational structures, and sets of milieu inhabitants give rise to different psychosocial characteristics and organizational climates. Finally, any of the above types of variables may, to some extent, affect the types of reinforcements that are likely to occur in a specific setting. Decisions about specific reinforcements which are valued may then in a feedback

loop have effects on the resulting geographical and architectural environment. Any of these levels of environmental variables may be influenced by any other level, although the relationship between some levels (e.g., personal characteristics of milieu inhabitants and organizational climates) may be closer than that between others (e.g., geographical and meteorological variables and organizational structure).

The categorization of environmental dimensions into six broad types may or may not have general utility. The categories are overlapping, and certain variables can as easily be placed into one category as another. On the other hand, the conceptualization identifies some initial directions for an overall organization of this field. The potential relevance of a coherent conceptualization of environmental and stimulus variables may be illustrated by utilizing aggression and violence as an example. The point is to illustrate a framework for the analysis of milieu effects, which is of critical importance not only for aggression but for the entire range of human behaviors.

There is substantial evidence that various attitudinal and behavioral indexes of anger, hostility, and aggression vary considerably over different settings, even for the same individuals. For example, Endler and Hunt (1968) found that consistent individual differences accounted for only between 15% and 20% of the variance in hostility, whereas setting differences accounted for between 4% and 8%, and the various interactions (e.g., Subjects X Situations) accounted for approximately 30%. The relevance of this and other similar work is that there is an upper limit to the accuracy of predicting aggressive behavior from knowledge of the individual alone and that different settings (all of which may have at least some anger-provoking elements in common) differentially elicit aggressive behavior from different individuals. For example, one cannot assume that individual differences in the strength of indexes of aggression which are obtained in experimental situations will necessarily generalize to real-life situations or even to other experimental situations.

Each of the six types of dimensions discussed above has an impact on the determination of individual and group aggressive behavior; for example, Wolfgang (1958) has reported that the peak months for the occurrence of homicide are the hot summer months. Berke and Wilson (1951) pointed out that most major political uprisings, rebellions, and revolutions begin during the hot months. Griffitt (1970) found that interpersonal attraction responses were significantly more negative under a "hot" condition (over 90 degrees Fahrenheit) than under a "normal" condition (about 68 degrees Fahrenheit). Lieber and Sherin (1972) analyzed over 1,900 murders occurring over a 15-year period in Dade County, Florida, and found that the murder rate began to rise about 24 hours before the full moon, reached a peak during the full moon, and then dropped back before climbing again to a secondary peak at the new moon.

The exact interpretation of these findings is unclear, although evidence for the effects of temperature on aggressive behavior is relatively consistent. There is less available evidence that architecture and physical design variables have effects on aggressive behavior, although they do generally have effects on interpersonal transactions (Osmond, 1957), and the body-buffer zone has been shown to be larger in violence-prone individuals (Kinzel, 1970).

Different types of behavior settings differentially elicit aggressive or hostile behavior. In an interesting clinical study, Raush, Dittman, and Taylor (1959) found that changes in hostility in hyperaggressive children were setting specific; for example, one child showed a marked reduction in hostile responses toward adults in a structured group setting, whereas another child showed these changes mainly during mealtimes. Gump, Schoggen, and Redl (1957) observed children in camp settings

and found that the quality of interaction of the same boys in swimming and craft settings was quite different. Assserting, blocking, and attacking behaviors were significantly higher in the swimming setting, whereas helping reactions were higher in craft settings.

Many organizational structure dimensions have been related to the frequency of aggressive behavior, most notably indexes of space and population density (crowding). For example, Swift (1964) concluded that conflicts between children are more numerous when play space is more restricted. Other studies have found correlations between high-population-density areas and high crime rates for both juveniles and adults (Schmid, 1960). Calhoun (1962) has presented experimental data linking population density and overly aggressive, conflict-oriented behavior in rats.

In an important article, Galle, Gove, and McPherson (1972) found that four different components of population density (e.g., the number of persons per room, the number of rooms per housing unit) showed highly significant correlations with asocial aggressive behavior, even when ethnicity and social class were controlled. Extensive data linking various indexes of anger, aggression, and conflict to organizational structure variables such as size, staffing, the heterogeneity and stability of personnel, etc., are also available (Corwin, 1969). Since measures of aggressive responses may be heavily affected by organizational structure dimensions, changes in these dimensions (e.g., an increase in amount of play space) may have dramatic effects.

Discussions of the effects of variables relevant to the last three methods of characterizing environments are particularly numerous, and only selected examples can be given here. In terms of the personal and behavioral characteristics of the inhabitants of the milieu, perhaps the most relevant example is that of the "interpersonal reflex" (Leary, 1957) or "behavorial reciprocity" (Raush et al., 1950). Aggression begets aggression, and the proportion of hostile actions "sent" by an individual often parallels the proportion he "receives." For example, Purcell and Brady (1964) found that the interpersonal response of affection was preceded by the interpersonal stimulus of affection 80% of the time and by the interpersonal stimulus of aggression 0% of the time.

In a particularly relevant study, Couch (1970) found that the response of interpersonal hostility was more highly correlated with the immediately preceding behavioral press than it was with a combination of personality need, concealment defense, and perceived press predictors. Thus, knowledge of the immediately preceding interpersonal stimulus was the best predictor of interpersonal hostility. This finding should give all of us who attempt to make predictions from personality needs alone significant pause. Holsti and North (1964), in careful analyses of documents authored by key European decision makers in the period from June 27 to August 4, 1914, indicated that these conclusions are not limited to individuals acting alone. They found that the correlation between the hostility expressed toward a nation and the hostility expressed by it was .46 for the Triple Entente (England, France, and Russia) and .68 for the Dual Alliance (Austria-Hungary and Germany). Perceived hostility and actual violent behavior (i.e., actual troop mobilizations, etc.) were also highly related.

There have been several demonstrations of social climate effects on aggression, particularly in groups and families. Perhaps the most intriguing work was done by Lewin, Lippitt, and White (1939), who found that the same group may change markedly (from apathy to aggression or vice versa) when it is changed to a new leadership atmosphere under a different leader. Lewin (1951) has also shown that an individual's conduct may change drastically in line with the social atmosphere of the group. He concluded that changing group climates should have important effects on changing individual aggressive behavior.

Finally, the potential effects on aggressive behavior of both positive and negative reinforcement procedures (including imitation and modeling) are well known (Bandura, 1969; Milgram, 1963, 1964). Milgram's studies have shown that subjects who are not usually aggressive can be made to behave very aggressively under experimenter- and group-pressure encouragement. Recent examples from world history seem to amply corroborate this finding. Bandura and Walters (1959) have also illustrated the specificity of aggressive behavior in their finding that parents who punished aggression in the home, but who simultaneously modeled aggressive behavior and encouraged it in their sons' relationships with peers, produced boys who were not aggressive at home but who were markedly aggressive at school.

Thus, the evidence indicates that ecological variables, behavior settings, dimensions of organizational structure, behavioral characteristics of milieu inhabitants, social and organizational climate, and reinforcement variables all have important impacts on various indexes of aggression and violent behavior. Similar analyses may be carried out, and similar conclusions probably hold for many other categories of behaviors. This analysis in no way minimizes the importance of individual dispositions, in the sense that it is obvious that some individuals are generally more prone to express certain behaviors (including aggressive and violent behaviors) than others. In addition, individual dispositions may have their effects in interaction with environmental conditions. On the other hand, the importance of this work on the development of taxonomies of environ-hand, the importance of this work on the mental variables can hardly be overemphasized, particularly in its implications for both behavior predictions and behavior change. Knowledge of the probable be-havioral and attitudinal effects of different environmental arrangements is at least as central an issue for psychologists as is knowledge about traditional personality theory and psychotherapy.

Implications

Thus, there are many different assessment techniques, types of variables, and potential environmental typologies. Even though it is not yet clear how these different levels of environmental description will eventually relate to each other, it is clear that they are all directly relevant to the central tasks of psychology. Psychologists and behavioral scientists are being asked to help design physical and social systems that will max-imize the probabilities of human growth and that will facilitate effective functioning and excellence. Different environments may facilitate different preparatory activities for coping in new environments, and thus dif-ferent cultural and social groups obtain dif-ferential preparation for environmental transitions. Disorders of human functioning are at least partially rooted in social sys-tems, and thus research toward effective modification of institutions to promote con-structive handling of life stresses must have high priority. Bergin (1966) has suggested that we actively study the naturally occur-ring therapeutic conditions in society. An-astasi (1967) has added the important point that environments must not be ordered along a simple favorable-unfavor-able continuum, since, for example, an environment favorable for the development of independence and self-reliance may differ significantly from one favorable for the development of social conformity or abstract thinking.

Further conceptualization and knowl-edge about environmental dimensions are essential for the central task of psychology, which is to understand, predict, and change behavior. The optimal arrangement of en-vironments is probably the most powerful behavior modification technique which we currently have available. Psychologists and other behavioral scientists are being asked to consult on the probable behavioral and attitudinal effects of environmental rear-rangements, precisely to the extent that human beings can control and change their environments. Essentially, every institution in our society is attempting to set up con-ditions that it hopes will maximize certain types of behaviors and/or certain vectors of development. Families, hospitals, prisons, business organizations, secondary schools, universities, communes, groups and, for that matter, entire societies are all engaged in setting up environmental conditions which will have certain effects. In this sense it may be cogently argued that the most important task for the behavioral and social sciences should be the systematic description and classification of environ-ments and their differential costs and benefits to adaptation.

These issues are also closely related to the more traditional concerns of clinical psychology. Rates of dysfunctional behav-ior (e.g., accidents, drug abuse, symptom expression, sickness) vary considerably in different social and physical environments. Environmental variables are closely related to health and illness (e.g., the extent of environmental change is related to both sickness and accidents), and indexes dif-ferentiating among social environments have been related to specific physiological reactions (e.g., Leiderman & Shapiro, 1964).

These issues are also relevant to the choice of environmental placement (e.g., Should a child go to this foster home or that one?) and to the development of an adequate information source on environ-ments. For example, it is well known that whereas college catalogs provide a certain amount of information about the formal organization structure and educational op-portunities of universities, they provide very little information about variables that importantly affect student development (e.g., different types of residence-hall groupings, amount of faculty–student contact that actually occurs, etc.). Finally, we cannot begin to systematically answer questions about the effects of various kinds of programs in hospitals, universities, schools, etc., unless we can somehow systematically assess and compare these programs.

It is well established that social milieus have important physiological and "health-related" effects (Cobb, French, Kahn, & Mann, 1963; Mason, 1968). A systematic conceptualization of environments makes it possible to test more differeniated hypotheses about the effects of specific environmental dimensions on specific physiological indexes. The potential importance of this area is indicated by the fact that the incidence of coronaries varies among environments as well as among types of individuals (Caffrey, 1969) and that the same psychopharmacological agent may have different therapeutic effects in different treatment settings (Klerman, Goldberg, & Davis, 1969). Finally genetic and developmental studies are in need of much more differentiated information about environmental characteristics. The fact that home environ-

ments of individuals with certain chromosomal abnormalities are or are not "disharmonic" (e.g., Nielsen, 1970) is simply no longer sufficient.

One last point deserves emphasis here. A number of environmental psychology programs have sprung up in different universities over the past few years (Wohlwill, 1970). Whereas this is encouraging in that it tends to highlight and emphasize important areas of inquiry, it is also disconcerting both because of the limited definition of environmental psychology which is currently in use and because separate programs to some extent become part of a communication-inhibiting social structure. Environmental psychology certainly cannot be limited to geographical and architectural variables as seems to be currently the case. We have learned from previous experience that behavior cannot be studied apart from the environment in which it occurs. Similarly, it is unlikely that either physical or social environments can be fully understood independent of each other. It is hoped that the classification scheme presented here may help direct fruitful effort into the eventual development of a robust and socially relevant environmental psychology.

4. Some Issues Facing a Theory of Environment and Behavior
WILLIAM H. ITTELSON

This conference is addressed to theory development, underlining a belief which is shared by many of us that our most difficult problems stem from the rather inadequate and shaky theoretical base from which we operate and that an adequate theory will quickly lead to the resolution of major issues both methodological and

Keynote address at a Conference on Theory Development in Environment and Aging, held at Kansas State University, Manhattan, Kansas, April 1974.

substantive. I have been asked to give a keynote address which, according to the dictionary, is intended to be a "presentation of issues of interest to the assembly." That is what I shall earnestly endeavor to do. This assembly is by definition interested in questions of environments and aging. I shall take this to be a special case of the larger question of environments and behavior and will address my remarks to that context, leaving the explication of specific implications for aging in the able hands of the speakers of the next two days.

Each of us lives and carries out our life's activities in a world which we experience as being separate from us and as having an existence independent of us, although we are in constant interaction with it. The phenomenological separation of self and environment is not an immediate given, but is rather an achievement of some magnitude. To students of human development the attainment of a fully autonomous sense of self is one of the significant features of at least the early stages of development. The mature adult sees himself as being separate from, although interdependent with, an environing world.

This dichotomous view of self and surround, so essential for the effective functioning of the individual, becomes a problem when it is uncritically accepted as a premise upon which scientific theories may be erected. Nevertheless, man-environment dichotomy has permeated most of Western thinking about social and scientific problems. It certainly underlies the history of thinking in the behavioral sciences, where the primary emphasis has been on the effect of environmental variables on behavior. In psychology both the person and the environment have been conceptualized in a variety of ways, although historically, psychology has tended to stress environmental variables, and the charge of excessive environmentalism is frequently made. Of course, the environment most commonly referred to is not the full-scale environment with which we are here concerned. Most commonly in psychology, at least until quite recently, environment has meant one of three things: it is either the social and interpersonal environment, with scant attention to the physical, or the environment as internally represented, or a set of discrete external stimuli. All of these aspects may be part of, but are not coextensive with, the full-scale environment toward which studies in environment and behavior are directed. In that context the environment has variously been looked upon as a source of information, as a set of limits or constraints, as a set of behavioral opportunities, as a setting within which behavior occurs, and in a variety of other ways.

My interest at this point is not in the various types of definitions and conceptualizations of the environment, but rather in the underlying assumption that behavior is a product of a complex function of variables related to the individual on the one hand, and variables related to the environment on the other hand. This is expressed in a variety of ways, sometimes verbally, sometimes symbolically. However, there is always an implied directionality, often explicitly represented with an arrow, that says that person and environment lead to behavior, and no other combination of the variables is acceptable.

Exactly how this equation is solved, of course, varies with the period and the investigator. At one extreme, for example, we find the complete environmental determinism which grew out of the work of a number of scientists, in particular, geographers and economists in the 20's, who held that a wide range of human behavior is directly and entirely determined by the environmental circumstances within which the behavior occurs. In effect, the person was ruled out of the equation, the environment became the sole determinant, and considerable supporting evidence was assembled. Partly in reaction to extreme environmental determinism, an equally extreme but diametrically opposed position developed, one that claimed that the environment makes absolutely no difference in human behavior and that man's apparently infinite adaptability to circumstances is all one needs to consider. There is probably at least as much plausibility to this position as there is to strict environmental determinism. One can cite masterpieces painted in garrets and treatises written in jail to convince oneself that, while other creatures may be subservient to their environments, man rises above it. But neither of these positions has in fact been acceptable to the majority of the investigators, and today one is much more likely to encounter a presumably more sophisticated approach which is dedicated to a careful analysis of the parameters, both personal and environmental, as they are encountered in the actual situation.

This brief survey of some of the ways in which environment has been seen as entering into the behavioral equation illustrates the fact that a single underlying assumption runs through them all. Whether one considers the environment to be a set of lifted weights in the psychology laboratories of late 19th century Germany or a set of complex environmental displays in the laboratories of late 20th century Berkeley, man and environment are seen as being separate, and behavior is the resultant of some complex relationship involving the two.

There is, however, another direction in which this process quite obviously operates, one which is of particular interest to architecture and the design professions, for example. While it may be true that environments produce behavior, it is certainly true that behaviors produce environments. Conceptions of man the builder are equally rooted in the assumption of a man-environment dichotomy, but they look at the process in terms of a different direction, at man's effect on his environment. In so doing they may be touching a characteristic that distinguishes man from all his fellow creatures of the earth. Man is, of course, not the only tool-making and tool-using animal, but the way he goes about doing it is qualitatively and quantitatively so different that it has frequently been suggested as one of the specifically defining characteristics of man. Recently a biologist has enlarged this concept and has explicitly stated that "what's human about man in his technology (Medewar, 1973)." Since earliest times, dimly seen through the lens of archeology and paleontology, man has always been the builder. The transformation of man the builder into man the maker of environments has come with such dramatic suddenness in our own time that most of us remain stunned, unable to grasp its significance or cope with its implications.

This, then, brings me to the first issue to which I would like to draw your attention. The necessary sense of an autonomous self translated into a world view which dichotomizes man and environment has been re-internalized as a dichotomous man, man the responder to environments on the one hand, and man the creator of environments on the other, both of whom stand separate from an external environment which itself is split into those aspects which are sources of responses and those which are products of human activity. Two rather different ways of thinking and talking have grown up around these two viewpoints. Man the responder and the environment to which he responds have been treated in what can loosely be labeled the scientific domain of thought, while man the builder and the environment that he builds are encompassed in the general approach of design and technology.

There have, of course, been attempts to bridge these gaps and to bring dichotomous man back into unity both with himself and with his environment. Thus, those concerned with man the maker of environments have conscientiously tried to make their technology more scientific, both by demanding and using more and better findings from the behavioral sciences and by directing themselves internally toward a more basic analysis of their problems. Bridging theories of great importance have emerged from technological considerations: for example, information theory and systems theory, as well as practices such as technology assessment which hope also to provide bridges into the presumed scientific study of man.

On the other side, from the behavioral sciences bridging attempts have stemmed from a variety of directions. The most straightforward has been a simple assertion by definition that man and environment are inseparable. Indulging oneself in holistic definitions of this sort is a favorite pastime of soft-headed psychologists such as myself and frequently calls forth the score of our more hard-headed colleagues. Along theoretical lines, bridging attempts most frequently take the form of turning the directional arrow back on itself. This view accepts the premise that person and environment lead to behavior, but then adds that behavior produces new person-environment situations which in turn lead to new behaviors. In this way it develops a feedback model which accounts for both directions of effect.

The study of environment and behavior represents the most recent and ambitious attempt conceptually and empirically to link the two halves of dichotomous man. It involves the joint efforts of behavioral scientists and environmental designers working together to forge out a new field of study. However, as I have already suggested, the two groups approach this task, implicitly accepting the assumption of dichotomous man, and each trying to provide bridging concepts out of ways of thinking which are in fact incompatible with each other. The second issue which I consider to be of interest to this assembly is that this effort is bound for failure, or at best, partial and limited success unless and until the two groups, that is, behavioral scientists and environmental designers, develop ways of thinking about their common problems which embrace both approaches and which are acceptable to both groups.

It would, of course, be comforting to think that this can be accomplished by simply adding the theories and concepts of the two, or perhaps putting them into a blender and coming out with a smooth amalgam which will cover all contingencies. Unfortunately, the behavioral sciences and the design professions will have to face up to the hard fact that such a solution is not available, that in very fundamental ways

their modes of thinking about problems are incommensurable. This is certainly not the place to elaborate in detail the relationships and conflicts between science and technology, or even in more limited terms, between behavioral science and environmental design. The scope of the problem can, however, be suggested simply by looking at contrasting criteria for acceptance of the solution to a problem. In the sciences it is generally agreed that an issue is resolved when an adequate theory is developed. This is no less true in the behavorial sciences, although the theories may be less general and less elegant than in other areas. In short, and skipping all questions of definition and precision, knowledge is expressed in terms of a theory which encompasses the phenomena in question. In contrast, in the design professions and in technology in general function is the ultimate criterion. If it works, it is successful, and successful working is taken as evidence that the designer possessed the requisite knowledge. In the same vein progress in science, insofar as it can be defined at all, is usually seen in terms of theory replacing theory—that is, a better theory replacing a lesser. In contrast, in the field progress is defined by practice replacing practice—that is, better practice replaces poorer practice. I raise these issues only to suggest that the problem of theory developing in our area is considerably more complex than simply learning to talk to each other and, indeed, touches upon some basic philosophical issues.

Let me illustrate how deep some of these issues run by reminding you of the traditional stance which both science and technology take toward the social uses to which their works are put. This is, of course, the very issue toward which this conference is directed. It is the supreme parodox of our time that science at the very peak of its power, achievement and success may well turn out to be the most unsuccessful of all human endeavors. From an evolutionary point of view, it is hard to imagine any other human activity which offers so clear and present a danger to the survival of the species as does contemporary science and its concomitant technology. While making life far better for some individuals, science is clearly raising the possibility of making life impossible for all humans and perhaps for all organisms of any kind. The threat, of course, lies not in a danger to individuals, but in the danger of producing an environment within which life cannot exist. Parenthetically, it is an interesting though rather futile exercise of the imagination to note that, if science does indeed accomplish this result, the fact will never be capable of scientific demonstration, nor indeed will it be a fact at all in any useful sense of the term.

We all know the familiar answer to this implied indictment of science and technology. First of all, the argument runs, one cannot charge science with its good or evil consequences, for science itself is value free—it is neither good nor bad. It deals only with the search for immutable truths, and if one must assign value to it, it will have to be the same value as truth itself, which most people agree is good. In any event, this charge is irrelevant, because the indictment should be aimed not at science, but at technology which is separate from science in the sense that science does not produce technology, although technology is dependent in part on science. But, the argument continues, technology is also value free; technology in itself is neither good nor evil. There may be poor technology in the technical sense, but never evil technology in the value sense. Only the human uses in technology result in value effects for better or for worse. And then, the capstone of the argument asserts that the human uses of technology are outside the realm of science or technology. They lie in the area of politics, of statesmanship, perhaps even of religion. But wherever they lie, if people choose to use technology for

worse rather than for better, that is the responsibility of neither science nor technology. Some such argument in essentially this form, I believe, is subscribed to by both the scientific and design and technological communities. It is also subscribed to by the great majority of statesmen in decision-making positions. Thus, for example, we find a noted biologist asserting that our environmental problems "are not biological. Neither are they scientific or even technological. They are social, and their solution depends on radical changes in social priorities (Luria, 1974)." A major sociologist writes that: "The task before us is to marshall more of technology to the service of human purposes . . . by carefully developing those tools which can be geared to advance our true values (Etzioni, 1973)." While a business man turned international statesman asserts: "We have the know-how to do almost anything. The real question is do we have the know-what and the know-why (Linowitz, 1972)."

These conclusions, attractive though they may be, are simply untrue because they are based on the false premise that we in fact know how to accomplish whatever we want to; the plain truth is that we do not. Even the relatively simple problem of choosing among alternative existing technologies frequently proves insurmountable. And the choice of what among possible alternative technologies should be developed in the future is made in almost complete ignorance as to the probable consequences of the various alternatives, except perhaps in the most limited and extreme cases. Of course, choices are made, decisions are taken, but in the absence of adequate knowledge they are inevitably based on short-term economic or political gain. All the changes in social priorities, all the decisions of what we want to accomplish are meaningless if we do not know how to produce environments which will achieve the desired ends and which will have the desired consequences for human behavior. And, therefore, the issue goes far beyond the question of deciding what to do and reorganizing social priorities in order to accomplish it. For example, social priorities have to a certain extent been altered, and society has given at least a limited mandate to develop adequate environments for the aging. And even in such a relatively restricted area as this, we simply do not know how to do it, although we are rapidly learning. With respect to larger scale issues we are barely scratching the surface. I think we all accept the proposition that a great deal more knowledge is necessary before we are minimally able to design environments which will within reasonable limits produce anticipated behavioral consequences, and that one of the necessary components of the subject matter for such study will be the very social, political and moral uses to which environmental design and technology can be applied. The third issue of interest to this assembly is that if we, as students of environment and behavior, push our investigation to its logical limit, we find that we are committing ourselves to a study which neither our scientific and professional colleagues nor our political and economic leaders want us to undertake. It is in fact a revolutionary undertaking in the scientific and perhaps even ultimately in the political sense. Since most of us are not revolutionaries, I see a danger that our field of study will not be pushed to its limits and may unfortunately settle for something far short of its potential.

One of the major arguments running throughout my remarks to this point is that current difficulties in the study of environment and behavior reduce essentially to questions of theory rather than of method or substance. An adequate theory will replace the concept of dichotomous man rather than attempt simply to bridge the chasm. Such a theory will take as its starting point the inseparability of man and environment and will recognize that neither man nor environment is ever encountered, nor can either be defined independent of the other. Such a theory will inevitably contain elements which are inimicable to current approaches both in behavioral science and in the design fields.

I do not mean to suggest that there are no current attempts at such theories. Indeed there are. One can list without any elaboration: ecological theory, systems theory, structural theory, and transactional theory—each of which has as one of its central assumptions the essential unitary nature of its subject matter. However, I do not believe that any of these or a combination thereof is adequately worked out yet for direct application to environment/behavior problems, although of course, my own prejudice is that transactional theory most closely approximates this. Nevertheless, I believe that none of these adequately deals with the fact already referred to that man has become the maker, the creator of his own environment, both on the individual level and on the social level. Recognition that the environment is a human creation, that the environment is artifact, is perhaps the major significant step needed for the development of an adequate theory. To say this, however, is not to imply a nature versus artifact, a natural versus artificial dichotomy. To be sure, the environment seen as artifact seems to stand in sharp distinction from the natural world. But as soon as one says this, the internal contradiction becomes apparent. If man and all his products, if technology and its artifacts, are not part of nature, what are they part of? The city may be inhuman, but it cannot be unnatural. Design and technology as human process and building and artifact as human product are part of the natural subject matter for study. They have no other place to go. So, to say that environment is artifact is tantamount to saying that environment is natural; man and his products are as much a part of nature as are the birds and their nests or the bees and their hives. To recognize man's environment as artifact is, therefore, simultaneously to deny the existence of a natural versus a man-made dichotomy, and at the same time to point out the particular directions which the study of human environment must take.

I will not attempt to elaborate the details of a theory approached from this point of view. It is clear, however, that considered as a subject matter for scientific study, the environment as artifact is a rather strange creature. Against the vast and unlimited reaches of nature, the supply of human environment is obviously definitely limited, a concept which has been popularized by the notion of Spaceship Earth. Not only is it limited, but the human environment is also transient and constantly undergoing fundamental change. The subject matter which we study today is not the same as that which we studied yesterday. That one never puts one's foot twice in the same stream we have long recognized. The constant change in the human environment raises a much more fundamental issue. There are no functionally equivalent replicas of yesterday's environment for today's study—the grandeur that was Rome, the peasant villages of Vietnam, the beauty of Glen Canyon—all are gone with the days of yesteryear, never to return. The causes of these changes are many and complex, but within the context of this discussion we can note that much of the change is brought about by the very fact that the environment is being studied and understood. In a very basic sense we cannot know the environment without changing it. The traditional subject matter of scientific study is natural, unlimited, unchanging and remote. In place of this the student of environment and behavior faces a subject matter which is man-made, limited, transient and close enough to be changed by the very process of studying it.

This final characteristic is perhaps the most significant and carries the greatest implications for our study. In contrast with traditional science searching for fixed and immutable laws underlying an eternal and unchanging nature, we are trying to understand a subject matter which is changed through the very process of our studying and knowing it. From the very outset, then, we are faced with a curious parodox—the more we learn about environment and behavior, the more we change it, and the less we know. Much has been said about the concept of the self-fulfilling prophecy within the behavioral sciences. In the present context, however, it may be profitable to consider a perhaps more difficult but potentially more powerful notion which might be called the self-falsifying hypothesis. To the extent that any hypothesis about the nature of environment and behavior contains elements of validity, it will also contain within it the possibility—indeed, the inevitability—of changing the environment in ways which will ultimately deny the applicability of the original insight. In a fully worked-out study of environment and behavior the ultimate test of the validity of a hypothesis may well be its falsification. The hypothesis which is eventually falsified by events contingent upon the existence of that hypothesis was in fact correct.

The reasons for this peculiar state of affairs follow from the fact that in trying to understand environment and behavior we are dealing with contingent rather than lawful relationships, with things that did not have to be the way they are, and with future states that cannot be predicted from present conditions. This is not to say that prediction is impossible, but to open for study the question of what kinds of predictions can be made. For example, prediction of future states is probably not possible in principle. Knowledge about environment and behavior cannot be achieved independent of human action, and the very knowledge thus obtained is itself contingent on the human activity it engenders.

The study of environment and behavior, then, is the study of choice, of action, and of change. As illustrations, I will briefly mention two of the many types of choices which can be informed through this study. All environmental changes are probably at least in part irreversible. Some are undoubtedly completely irreversible. At the present state of our knowledge we do not have the information necessary to tell us to what extent we are choosing chains of action which will lead to irreversible changes, except perhaps in the most extreme cases. As our study progresses, we will hopefully be able to make finer and finer discriminations of those choices which are forever irreversible from those which are at least potentially modifiable.

Environmental changes also have an impact on the range of possible future choices. Every change both expands and restricts future options. Again, we do not know yet how to tell those changes which result in a sharply restricted range of future possibilities from those which maximize future options. When we can do this, it will at least in principle be possible to develop a social model which will at regular intervals assess its current situation and redirect change by making choices which will predict the greatest range of alternatives at the end of the next assessment period, and so forth. Whether this or some other model will turn out to be the optimum arrangement, of course, would be one of the subjects of the study itself.

I have, then, suggested that among other things the study of environment and behavior will enable us to tell reversible from irreversible choices and to distinguish actions which will expand future options from those which will restrict them. These considerations lead us to the next issue which I would like to call to the attention of this assembly. What the body politic will choose to do will, of course, not be determined by our study. However, as our knowledge grows, it increasingly becomes our responsibility to inform decision makers of the probable consequences of specific solutions to problems, as well as to emphasize the importance of considering as wide a range as possible of alternative solutions. In this way we can bring into active consideration the long-term consequences of optional courses of action, as well as making known the nature and limits of predictions which can be made, and the areas in which long-term prediction is not possible. Our study will thus ensure that those individuals and groups who normally take action through social and political processes will be informed of the probable consequences of their choices in ways which go far beyond current concepts and which may alter the very concept of social responsibility.

The study of environment and behavior, then, is the study of change, change not imposed by some external and autonomous force, but change growing out of the natural process within which mankind plays a central role. Man alone of all the many faces of nature to be seen on this planet can deliberately and self-consciously choose and direct the process of environmental change. Most of what I have said today, and indeed the main thrust of most·studies of environment and behavior, is aimed at making those choices more informed and that direction more effective. We already have the capacity for self-destruction. The struggle to acquire the capacity to survive contains within it the necessity of developing new standards for decision, perhaps what Hardin has called "new ethics for survival." The ancient dilemma that the individual ethic may not serve the collective good and that the social ethic may violate individual canons of conduct has now been complicated by the recognition that neither may be conducive to global survival. The elaboration of an environmental ethic is a pressing need of our time. We in the field of environment and behavior cannot develop the details of such a system of ethics, but we can be aware of the major ethical implications of our work. This, then, is the final issue to which I would draw your attention. A system of ethics implies, indeed demands, knowledge of the consequences of behavior.

The work that we do, however small each piece of it may seem, will cumulatively over time provide the knowledge base requisite for the development of an informed environmental ethic, and it must be our hope and faith that such an ethic can exist harmoniously with the individual and social ethics to which we all so deeply subscribe.

I have now reached the end of the issues to which I wish to draw your attention. Let me close by quickly summarizing.

To the man-environment dichotomy, so directly derivable from phenomenal experience, has been added a dichotomous view of man, separating man the responder to environments from man the creator of environments. Around each of these views has developed a system of thought and action roughly paralleling the scientific and the technological which is inherited by the student of environment and behavior. Attempts to straddle these dichotomies by providing a variety of bridging concepts and theories offer an immediate and important first step but do not provide an adequate long-range solution which requires a theory which reunites these two diverse elements of human activity. However, if we pursue this direction to its logical conclusion, we find that we are undertaking a task which in general our fellow citizens have not asked for and do not want us to do. A fully adequate theory of environment and behavior will inevitably contain elements which go contrary to the prevailing views of the intellectual community, and the implications of such a theory both in terms of subject matter and of understanding move into areas presently considered more clearly political in the broad sense of that term. And finally, as knowledge of environment and behavior grows, we recognize the inevitability of developing an environmental ethic which potentially at least may come into conflict with already established ethical systems.

Perhaps these six issues really add up to one: the need for knowledge of environment and behavior is clear and pressing. If we in this field do not meet that need, future generations may no longer have the opportunity.

5. Environmental Psychology: A Methodological Orientation
HAROLD M. PROSHANSKY

The study of man's relationship to his physical world—and more particularly his built environment—is a relatively new field of scientific inquiry. Whether identifying themselves as "environmental psychologists," "behavioral ecologists," or even just plain "environmental researchers," these are professional and academic designations that were to all intents and purposes nonexistent two decades ago. During this twenty year period a great deal has taken place: books on environmental psychology have been written; courses of study at the graduate and undergraduate level have been established at an increasing number of colleges and universities; and a number of professional associations and societies have been established. The new field is not just on its way. It has arrived.

As one might expect, despite its infancy in comparison to other behavioral science fields and specializations, the questions concerning the origins have been asked and will continue to be asked. What are the underlying influences both within and external to the various behavioral science fields of endeavor that led to the development of this new field? Although still accepted by some, the general view of science as a value-free and unassailable approach to knowledge, has slowly and inexorably given way to the same reality of human, social, and physical events it continually seeks to order and explain. Not unlike other approaches to knowledge, it is now recognized that science is an organized human and social endeavor which is influenced by the social structure of which it is a part, as much as it serves to influence this same structure. Any attempt to trace the origins and roughly twenty-year development of environmental psychology will have to take these and related factors into account.

It is not the purpose of the present paper to attempt such an analysis. On the other hand even a cursory consideration of this two decade period immediately suggests the importance of such influences as the environmental crisis of the late 1960's, the increasing number of behavioral questions confronting designers, planners, and architects, the emergence of urban settings not as *a* way of life but *the* way of life, the demand for physical settings that would solve complex social problems, e.g. mental hospitals, and so on. But there can also be no question that the emergence of an environmental psychology was to no small degree a matter of "push from within" as well as "pull from without": as much a function of what was happening in the behavioral science disciplines, particularly those focussed on man as a social and cultural organism, as of the external factors noted above.

In this respect also, undoubtedly more than one factor contributed to the development of an interest by some psychologists in the relationship between behavior and human experience on the one hand and the design of physical settings on the other. Thus and by way of example, it seems

reasonable to assume that research and theoretical issues of this kind were so conspicuous by their absence in scientific disciplines purportedly dedicated not just to the task of establishing principles of human behavior but in the process of also solving complex social problems, that eventually such issues could no longer be ignored. To some extent this same "influence" probably underlies the only relatively recent research interest in such ubiquitous human behavior as jealousy, love and romance, altruism, and finally, the individual's fear of dying and death.

Yet, at root, particularly with respect to environmental psychology, there was a still more essential determinant that led to the emergence of the new field. The matter can be put very simply: among the various fields of psychology concerned with the behavior and experience of the individual and groups, the "payoff" or return from the *analytic-experimental* model of science increasingly failed to realize the promise it once seemed to offer. Although, highly critical of the atomistic, non-context oriented research of those psychologists in the experimental fields of psychology such as learning, perception, physiological, and psychophysics, those in the person-oriented fields enthusiastically borrowed this model of research and theory; the paradigm, of course evolved as the *sine qua non* of science because of its overwhelming success in advancing knowledge in many problem areas of the physical and natural sciences.

The model itself is well known in almost every field of psychology and needs no elaborate presentation here. It seeks to establish cause and effect relationships between specified independent (stimuli, situations, etc.) and dependent (behavior, experience) variables by means of rigorously controlled investigations in which all relevant events are either manipulated or controlled, or if not, their possible consequences are known or believed to be known to the researcher. Although the analytic-experimental paradigm emerged from and indeed defines the concept of "laboratory research," its use was and is by no means confined to that setting. In real-life settings or more complicated contrived human settings outside the laboratory the logic of the paradigm for acquiring knowledge or understanding remains the same. Of course, many problems of human behavior and experience cannot be experimentally manipulated or directly controlled. However, the intention of establishing cause and effect relationships through research strategies that permit inferences to be made that such relationships exist, merely casts the paradigm in a somewhat different form.

Standing in the towering shadow of the gains in knowledge produced by the analytic-experimental paradigm in the physical and natural sciences, the field of psychology sought and continues to seek to establish not just cause and effect relationships expressed in quantative terms. The eventual goals, of course, are that scientific fabric which has woven into it the strands of theory, principles, and facts that will constitute an organized body of knowledge for explaining the experiences.

If the analytic-experimental paradigm has failed to realize even a little of its original promise in most if not all of the person-situation fields of psychology (and in other behavioral sciences), it is not for want of trying. As Dan Katz (1972) has noted, some twenty thousand experimental studies in social psychology have provided very little return—if any—by way of established facts or explanatory principles. There is nothing wrong with the logic of the model itself, and indeed whatever its failure to date in the behavorial sciences, its value as a scientific method for many areas and problems of the sciences generally is unassailable. The difficulty lies not in the model itself but in its application; or perhaps better said, in its misapplication.

What lies at fault in its studies of complex human problems are the many untenable assumptions that are made about the nature and meaning of human behavior

and experience. At the root of these assumptions is the view of the individual as another "object" to be studied. His or her behavior and experience can be dealt with in terms of discrete components or properties that can be isolated, studied under pure conditions, and eventually be quantified. Indeed taking his cue from the natural or physical scientist, the behavioral scientist has subjected man's environment to the same kind of elemental analysis in the attempt to meet the specifications of the analytic-experimental mode. None of this is really difficult for the experimental or laboratory behavioral scientist because inherent and most fundamental in his conception of men in society—wittingly or unwittingly—is a reductionist conception of both: human events, behaviors and settings divisible and capable of study within the framework of the analytic-experimental model because there are a set of underlying irreducible and unifying principles that transcend differences between humans and infraorganisms, between one level of human organization and another, and between the simplicity of the laboratory setting and the complexity of the real-life settings of people.

There were those who raised doubts concerning the value of the analytic-experimental model for the study of human behavior long before environmental psychology came on the scene. Allport's emphasis on the idiographic approach to the study of human personality in contrast to an emphasis on a nomethetic methodology is a case in point (1937). Clinicians and other practitioners as well as those concerned with developmental processes also found the use of the experimental model highly questionable as an approach to understanding human behavior and experience even when the intention was to establish general laws or principles. While Lewin's emphasis was on the life-space or the world of real events as perceived by the individual, and while he rejected stimulus-response conceptions and Aristotelian methodology and in turn constantly referred to the necessary interplay between field and laboratory research, he and his associates were as much taken by the "scientific experiment" as other far less imaginative and creative theorists (1948). For this reason his own plea and the efforts of his students to make research "socially useful as well as theoretically meaningful," to a large extent produced little by way of concrete advances in knowledge. A laboratory contrived group process experiment did not do much better by way of meaningful advances for the understanding of social behavior and interaction process, than did the memory drum and nonsense syllables for the understanding of the nature of human learning.

It is rather paradoxical that social psychology and related fields of psychology should have fallen prey to the same methodological pitfalls for which they so consistently and righteously criticized other fields and/or theoretical orientations, e.g. S-R learning research, experimental perception, etc. Inspired by the thinking of Gordon Allport, Kurt Lewin, Solomon Asch, Gardner Murphy, and Muzafer Sherif, many social psychologists turned their backs on these conceptions in favor of holistic approaches in which complex human and social processes were to be studied in ongoing situational contexts that defined the existence of the individuals involved. But in the end insofar as a methodological orientation was concerned, social psychologists too succumbed to the analytic-experimental paradigm. Not unlike what happened in the areas of human and animal learning, the intense experimental or quasi-experimental studies by social psychologists of complex social attitudes, values, small group processes, social interaction, cognitive dissonance, helping behavior, social conflict, and still other problems led to a wealth of conflicting data, very few principles, if any, whose generalizability was not extremely limited,

conflicting theoretical conceptions, and a variety of highly specialized methodological techniques. To make matters even worse, the demand character of the many, many studies done with college students made it apparent that analogous to animal learning research, social psychology had produced its "laboratory rat" science based far more on factors rooted in implicit and explicit student-faculty member relationships than in the actual variables under study.

Of course, the move of some psychologists into environmental psychology in no sense took the form of researchers in search of a new field that would lend itself to a new methodological approach. Speaking for the writer and his colleagues, the dissatisfaction experienced in the midst of their earlier efforts with an approach whose potential was not being realized, undoubtedly added greater weight to the many other external factors that focused their individual attentions on questions of the relationships between the person's physical environment and human behavior and experience. Yet, the truth of the matter is that the real measure of the difficulties inherent in the analytic-experimental paradigm was thrust upon us not before we turned to problems of man/environment relationships but after, indeed, only after we had been involved for some years in studying them. Furthermore, the broad methodological orientation of environmental psychology to be described below did not burst forth full bloom. It evolved over a longer period of time. "Evolved" is clearly the appropriate term, for in fact when my colleagues and I left the respective fields we were trained in, it was one thing to reject the past and another to escape the socializing influence of previous training, research interests, and professional identity commitments. Said differently, we were no sooner involved with environmental problems, then we were already talking about experiments, controls, questionnaires, scaling models, after-only designs, and the like.

As it turned out we did not get very far with this approach. What happened was that every environmental problem we were confronted with, first, had very little if any previous research related to it, second, simply did not lend itself to the often quick and available methods and techniques we had all used before our "reincarnation," and finally and perhaps most importantly, was presented to us by architects, designers, administrators, and other non-behavioral scientists in ways that brought us face-to-face with the real world. Empirical dimensions and analytic concepts that social and other kinds of psychologists had to ignore because they don't fit the model of the "scientific investigation," could no longer be ignored.

In an earlier publication the writer and his colleagues have set forth in some detail the conceptual framework that has guided their formulation of problems in environmental psychology in a variety of physical settings, e.g. hospitals, schools, playgrounds, day care centers, senior citizen residences, housing projects, parks, and still others (Ittelson, Proshansky, Rivlin, Winkel, 1974). It is important to stress, however, that these conceptions and a host of stated assumptions about the nature of the environment, have inherent in them a series of methodological implications that in turn determined the definition and use of these concepts in the research we carried out. Elsewhere the writer has described these implications as "methodological requirements," requirements thrust upon us because as just indicated above inital research forays in environmental psychology merely confirmed the already experienced inadequacy of the analytic-experimental model in the study of complex human processes and problems in the traditional "social science" fields of psychology. Here we shall consider five of these requirements. Although they all have some interrelationship to each other, they each impose their own consequences on the broad research methodology of the environmental psychologist.

It is best to begin with perhaps the most critical of the five methodological requirements inherent in the problems to be studied by the environmental psychologist. It can best be described as the *absolute integrity of person/physical setting events*. Whatever the possibilities of maintaining at least some of the integrity of such psychological or group phenomena as interpersonal conflict, task competition, small group process, or ethnic prejudice while studying them in the laboratory or under contrived conditions, the very nature of man/physical setting relations makes this virtually impossible. Since at a very minimum the person's awareness of his being in a given physical setting is a requirement for his behaving and coming to terms with that setting, no laboratory or other artificial setting, no matter how contrived, can serve as a substitute for such a reality. No matter how well a research setting duplicates the real physical world of the individual, his knowledge that it is not the actual setting immediately invalidates the integrity of any person-environment phenomenon being studied in relation to that real-world setting, whether it is a classroom, living room, apartment, hospital ward, railroad station, crowded elevator, and so on.

For the environmental psychologist there is only the real world to be studied. Understanding the mutual relationships between human behavior and experience and the dimensions of physical settings, is necessarily rooted in a methodology which preserves the *integrity* of these events. It would be easy enough to conclude that all that follows from this prescription for environmental research is an emphasis on field research. Properly qualified, one would suppose, the use of the term "field research" would be appropriate. However, because the term itself grew out of the distinction between laboratory research vs. research in more complex realistic settings, and inasmuch as so much field research in the traditional areas of psychology simply moved the laboratory scientist paradigm into the field, it is less than useful for our purposes.

The need to preserve the integrity of person/physical setting events in attempting to investigate problems of this kind has implicit in it at least three other methodological requirements. First, the analytic concepts and empirical dimensions employed in studying individual/physical setting relationships in their natural context, must themselves be of such a nature that they preserve the integrity of such relationships. It is the total individual acting upon and being acted upon by a circumscribed and patterned environmental context that also constitutes this integrity, and therefore the study of isolated, piecemeal "stimuli" or "responses" has no validity in this approach. Second, to arrive at the appropriate analytic dimensions and concepts for investigating some person/physical setting phenomenon, requires the continuing study of this phenomenon in its natural context just to establish its defining properties and boundaries. In this respect, given the complex nature of person/physical setting phenomena and the inchoate state of development of this new field called environmental psychology, it is crucial that we emulate the ethologist who studies animal behavior in its natural setting by means of continued and extensive observation, rather than adopting the paradigm of the experimental psychologist or the organic chemist.

The final and third implication is that it is not enough to say that the research process must minimally intrude or have an impact on the environmental event being studied. New and yet to be discovered methods and techniques will have to be employed, and indeed it may be necessary to do this as the nature of the phenomenon being considered varies. In my judgment, the days of subject deception and manipulation in social research are over, if not for ethical and human reasons, then at least for the fact that in both explicit and implicit ways they distort the phenomena being studied. From our point of view, the study of person/physical setting relationships must necessarily involve the cooperative involvement of those being investigated in the study or research process itself.

A second methodological property of individual/physical setting phenomena requires that a distinction be made between *behavior system reactions* and *psychological system reactions*. It is important to distinguish between behavior and experiences of the individual of which he is not consciously aware, that is, *behavior system reactions;* and those which we refer to as psychological system reactions characterized by behavior or responses in which the individual is consciously aware of what he is experiencing and doing. But if you examine the vast array of research literature in developmental, social, personality and other related fields of psychology, except for concerns with personality dynamics and motivational process, the assumption is made that conscious awareness is at the core of what the person does and feels most of the time. The assumption is probably a correct one for many of the human problems being investigated. If it were not, then the use of such measurement techniques as interviews, attitude scales, or other verbal techniques that depend on the individual's awareness of his own behavior and experience would be in question.

What our first years of environmental research revealed to us in no uncertain terms was that to a large extent the individual is not aware of his or her behavior and experience in the continuing process of responding to the kaleidoscope of physical settings that one enters and leaves in the course of a person's day-to-day existence. Of course, the individual knows where he or she is and indeed can even describe the setting (although not always), but what one often doesn't know is how he or she uses the physical setting—the movement patterns, locational preferences, sensory adaptations, and even inner feelings (such as stress produced by noise). More significant, is the fact that in most instances the assumed constellation of likes and dislikes, preferences and rejections, positive and negative attitudes about these physical settings usually do not exist; they have not and indeed may not be crystallized. In most instances, awareness of one's own behavior and experience in given physical setting, and the buildup of attitudes, values, preferences, and likes and dislikes about the setting, occurs when a setting fails to work for the person. The implication in the distinction between behavior systems and psychological systems for the use of interviews, attitude scales, semantic differentials, opinion questionnaires, and other survey forms is obvious. You cannot measure behavior systems with techniques based on the assumptions involved in measuring psychological systems. In our very early research, individuals were always ready to say either "I never thought about it," or when they didn't say this and gave us an immediate response, it was not consistent with what was seen in repeated observation.

Still another implication follows, but not so much a methodological one as a theoretical one. Not only must person/physical setting events be observed intact so that the integrity of these events is maintained, but in that observation will be revealed patterns of movement, gestures, postures and feelings that constitute that process we call the continuing adaptation of the person to his physical world. But in no sense do we mean to underestimate the significance of psychological system reactions in environmental psychology. There is much to be done with respect to self-identity in relation to place-identity as well as with respect to the issues of privacy,

territoriality, aesthetic preference, physical setting role and status, and so on. In many ways and under many circumstances individuals know about, think about, fantasize about, and make judgments about their physical settings. But one cannot plunge in with the usual array of methodological techniques which assume that there is awareness. And even where such awareness exists, the words and concepts necessary for the individual to communicate about places and spaces may not be available to him.

Let us turn now to the third methodological requirement inherent in any attempt to understand the relationships between people and their built environment. It can be referred to as the *content orientation* of environmental psychology. By this is meant the rather simple and direct notion that it is essential that we identify what physical settings, for what purposes, eliciting what specific forms of behavior and experiences in the person. In other words, the actual character of a physical setting, namely, is it a bedroom, schoolroom, living room, playground, city street, or in fact main street or side street, are important determinations for the environmental psychologist. It is no less important to identify what actual behaviors occur, what activities are going on, and indeed exactly what kinds of people are involved in them.

Are we being obvious? I think not. Let me remind you—and McClelland made this point in a rather obscure article in the *American Scientist* almost twenty years ago —psychological theory and research is obsessed with process and almost very little with content. Thus, the concern is with motivational process, cognitive process, affective process and the like. In part this is understandable when we consider that all of psychology has been consumed with the question of what are the basic psychological processes of man. So much involves and indeed continues to involve questions of how motives develop and operate or how we learn and perceive, that no matter how we tried, the significant motivations, attitudes, values, and other psychological structures never seem to become the focus of our theoretical orientations. Of course we had our lists of motives, values, and needs, but in the case of McClelland, for example, it is hard to believe that all that is involved in Americans is the needs for achievement, recognition, and affiliation. In the case of social attitudes far more time has been spent on the questions of attitude structure and function in relation to attitude change, than on—except in the case of ethnic prejudice—the specific attitudes themselves.

The situation in environmental psychology is quite different. As we have already suggested content counts a great deal. If as we have already indicated, the integrity of person/environmental setting events must be maintained in the process of research, then this must include the meaning and nature of these events as they are defined by geographical locations, designed purposes, intended and actual activities, and the character of the actors involved. To take but one example, the longer my colleagues and I consider the problem of human privacy, the clearer it becomes that this is not one phenomenon but many, and that the difference in the types and forms of human privacy may far outweigh any common underlying need or attitude—if it exists at all. Furthermore, we are continually confronted with specifying what kind of privacy, involving what kind of setting, with what kind of individuals, for what kinds of purposes.

The methodological requirement we turn to now imposes great problems on the environmental psychologist. Oddly enough, it is clearly inherent not just in the study of the individual's relationship to his physical world, but in the problems of developmental psychology, social psychology, personality psychology, and actually all areas of psychology focused on the behavior and experience of the person in complex social settings; said differently, focused on the actual problems of people when they are conceived of as goal directed and cognitively oriented organisms involved in complex activities. It is a methodological and theoretical requirement that has almost been ignored in the formulation of problems by psychologists. I am referring here to *time orientation*. Whether we deal with individuals or groups, if you examine the research literature you will find without exaggeration that the analysis of behavior and experience seldom involves the dimension of time. Our research is here-and-now oriented, and what we have done in the name of longitudinal research is miniscule compared to the timeless study of people of cross-sectional research. We talk about childhood influences, changes over time, the life cycle and other time-oriented conceptions but they seldom take shape in our research.

This brings us back to our first methodological requirement, namely, the integrity of person/physical setting events. It is not enough to study them in their natural context with a minimum intrusion of the research process or with conceptions that do not violate the integration of the totality that we call man and his adaptation to his physical setting. They must be studied over time, for in fact part of the integrity of human events is that they have a beginning and an end; they have a unity over the dimension of the time as well as at any point on that dimension. In saying this, it may well be that an insurmountable problem may be involved, for the fact of the matter is that it is not only not easy to carry out research with a time dimension, it may be in many instances virtually impossible.

Yet we must approximate as best we can. The preservation of the integrity of any human event must involve its history —its beginning—what happened—and its end. If it is patently true that the individual has a history, then it is no less patently true that human interactions and relationships with their built environment also have a history. The use and meaning of physical settings is not just a here and now phenomenon; it extends over time. Thus, in our observation—or more generally said—in our studies of problems of the relationships between individuals and their physical settings, repeated if not continuous recording is the order of the day. Spaces and places like people change, and these changes in turn induce change in the behavior and experiences of the people who brought about these changes in the physical environment in the first place. Time, of course, is not merely a methodological requirement; it is a theoretical necessity. Our understanding of the nature and meaning of various forms of privacy, of how individuals express themselves in or in turn internalize their physical and geographical worlds, or any other human/space related phenomenon, must include the factors of what happens over time.

The final methodological requirement for the study of personal–physical setting relationships raises even more difficult problems in our research. Yet, there is no turning away from it. There is much to be said here but limited space requires it be said briefly and directly. It turns out—as you clearly may have known from the beginning—that there is no physical setting that is not also a social and cultural setting. What this means in effect is that however we conceptualize and describe the physical setting of the person in relation to how he acts upon it, and vice versa, that setting has a social definition and purpose, such that its use, function, and consequences are as much a result of these definitions and purposes as they are of its actual physical properties; perhaps even more so. The simple administrative decision that there shall be four patients in a hospital room rather than two, or that no lights are to be on in a college dormitory after nine o'clock, has its obvious consequences

for the interrelationships between the behavior and experience of the person and his given physical setting. Thus, not only is a content and time orientation important, but also a *context orientation*, our final methodological concern.

The study of how people use space must not only include from the beginning a description of what space for what purpose, but also a description of the larger context of this space in terms not only of its physical properties but its social, organizational, and cultural properties as well. Does this methodological requirement need emphasis if not espousal? We think so. The fact is that so many of the traditional fields of psychology talk about the social context—whether it is the family setting, school setting, or community setting —without actually including it as part of their conceptual analysis of the behavior of the person. These fields have done better in recent years, but much of scientific research in the so-called "Soft Science" fields of psychology are still haunted by the one independent variable—one independent cause and effect analysis of behavior. In one way or another, problems seem to become isolated from their broader defining contexts.

In environmental psychology we have no choice. How children, for example, use a playground with a given design and equipment and in a given setting, forces us to consider who runs the playground, what rules are set, how is it governed, how does it relate to the immediately surrounding area, of what other broader institutional context is it a part, and so on. The same is true of a schoolroom, shopping area, hospital ward, secretary's office, college study hall, library or reading room. It is only by considering the pattern of social, organizational, and cultural factors that define an observed physical setting that one is able to define the question of the use and consequences of that space in relation to the behavior and experience of the people who occupy it. Such a contextual analysis does more than help to define the questions to be answered; it becomes the basis for understanding the data that emerge in investigating these questions.

It should not be assumed that because we assert as easily as I have done here the principles or assumptions involved in our approach, that our problems are over. On the contrary, they haven't really yet begun. We grope in all respects: in just how to define our problem; in how to observe the natural flow of behavioral events in an environmental setting; in how to introduce a research process that has minimum impact; and so on. Our research is slow and ponderous, because in effect we are not only new at it but we have given ourselves a set of requirements—the methodological properties I described above—that do not permit it to be otherwise. From our point of view there are no short-cuts.

However, if you carefully consider the methodological approach I have elaborated here today, certain other implicit assumptions are involved which free us from other kinds of problems that constantly plague our colleagues in the traditional fields. First, we not only reject the laboratory physical-science model for our research, but we reject the conception of simple cause and effect relationships in understanding how the built environment and human relationships are related. We worry far less about experimental controls in doing our research and far more about what, when and how to describe ongoing events. This is because we are not looking for the usual independent-dependent variable relationships. We are looking for that pattern of relationships between the observed and described properties of physical settings and the similarly observed and described reactions of people in these settings. Since the influences are mutual, it is these patterns of relationships which are critical and not the isolation of how one variable causes effects in another.

But given this approach which is more descriptive than explanatory, more qualitative than quantitative, it leaves us free in still another way. We are not looking for immutable general principles with respect to how people respond to their physical settings. Whatever general principles of perception, learning, emotion, and motivation are revealed by our colleagues in the laboratory or basic properties fields of psychology, will be useful. Of course such principles undoubtedly include all human response systems, but at the non-reductionist level of analysis that has been emphasized, they are of little value for the kinds of problems that concern the environmental psychologist. Besides, like Ken Gergen we do not believe in a fixed set of universal principles for complex human behavior. We take the view that social, personality, environmental and still other fields of psychology are historically contained endeavors in the sense that it is *time* as well as *place* that governs behavioral influences. Whether it is a concern with attitude development, praise and punishment of the child, cooperation and competition, need achievement and need abasement, etc., whatever generalizations emerge must be viewed in the context of the social structure and social process that defines our society at the present time. As that context changes over time, not only will those so-called general principles no longer be applicable, but the researchers of that period will have to identify the essential characteristics of that new society in order to derive a new set of principles. For us, environmental psychology is a socio-historical behavioral science. What it finds today may have little consequence for our society a hundred years from now.

Finally, the methodological approach that has been described frees my colleagues and myself from another difficulty. These properties make it evident that environmental psychology is not just problem oriented rather than principle oriented, but it is interdisciplinary in character. After ten years of having given lip-service to the great interdisciplinary approach that was necessary for studying social man, one finally had to stop talking and begin doing. The fact is that there is actually no way of dividing the problems in environmental psychology into psychological, sociological, organizational studies or studies at other levels of analysis. Our emphasis on the real-life physical setting in the context of the broader sociocultural boundaries which defines such a setting, constantly forces us to integrate our efforts with those of other behavioral scientists. In our own program, there are architects, planners, a geographer, as well as the other behavioral scientists.

This completes the discussion. Where this new approach will take us and how it will end we don't know. However, we do know that we are happy to be in the real world. That's where we began and that is where one must stay if it is complex human social problems and issues that one seeks to understand and perhaps to solve.

6.   Knowledge and Design
BILL HILLIER, JOHN MUSGROVE, AND PAT O'SULLIVAN

This paper is about knowledge and design. Before you reach for your hats, we should add that it is intended to be a technical not a theological contribution to the subject. We offer it, not because we have no research to report, or because we think this conference is in need of philosophic homilies, but because we believe we are up against some fundamental limitations in the arguments which have been used to justify research and to define its tasks.

Research of one kind or another has

Reproduced from W. J. Mitchell (Ed.), *Environmental design: Research and practice.* Proceedings of the EDRA 3/AR 8 Conference: University of California at Los Angeles, January 1972.

In this paper the words 'architecture' and 'architectural' are used as shorthand for the built environment and its action systems, as a sub-system of environmental action and modification as a whole. It is not intended to refer to the activities or ideology of a particular professional group. We apologise for any confusion this may cause.

The analysis in the early part of the paper refers principally to the UK situation as it has developed in the last fifteen years or so, but we hope that the arguments will retain most of their validity when applied elsewhere.

now a longish history in building. By and large, this increased investment in research has proceeded side by side with a marked deterioration in the quality of building. A serious 'applicability gap' appears to exist. Regardless of the quality of research work itself, the history of attempts to link research to improvements in environmental action is largely one of confusion and failure (Royal Institute of British Architects, 1970).

When the concepts of 'environmental research', as opposed to technologically oriented building research, began to emerge a decade or so ago, there seemed to be good reasons for hoping that these new concepts in research would lead to new relationships between research and action. At that stage, when the ground was being cleared for the expansion of environmental research, programmatic statements took a clear line.

Ten years ago, when the ground was being cleared for great expansion of architectural research activity, programmatic statements took a clear line. Design was a problem-solving activity, involving quantifiable and non-quantifiable factors. Research, it was thought, should bring as many factors as possible within the domain of the quantifiable, and progressively replace intuition and rules of thumb with knowledge and methods of measurement. This process would never be complete. Non-quantifiable elements would remain. In order to assimilate such knowledge and use such tools as we were able to bring to bear on design, the procedures of designers would have to be made more systematic. Because the education of architects was broad and shallow, and because they were concerned with action rather than knowledge, they could not be expected to generate new knowledge for themselves. This was the job of 'related' disciplines, whose concern was the advancement of knowledge. Architects, on the other hand, knew about design, and should make systematic design their research focus. Otherwise their contribution to research lay in technological development, or as members of multi-disciplinary terms, in defining the problems for others to solve.

The educational consequences of these notions were that schools of architecture and planning were to be located in an educational milieu containing a rich variety of related disciplines, and students were to be well grounded in each of them. The core of the architectural course would still be design, and, at the academic level, this meant increased concentrations upon systematic methods. Students would be taught to analyse problems, and to synthesise solutions.

A few voices crying in the wilderness that architecture contained its own fundamental disciplines could not stop the onward march of these simple and powerful ideas, and by and large, they still hold the stage today. But if these are to be the paradigmatic ideas by which we define our subjects and link them to action, then today's landscape, (although promising in that other disciplines are developing their latent 'environmental' interests), must appear depressing. Systematic design studies are in disarray. Increasing numbers of research workers, including architects, are moving into the areas previously called 'unquantifiable'. There is a widespread feeling that an 'applicability gap' has developed between research and design. Design is still led by the nose by technology, economics and imagistic fashions. The human sciences and architecture are still at loggerheads. Education, with few exceptions, has not managed to develop a radically new capability in the problem-solving power which students bring to design.

In fact, we are far from pessimistic about the progress of architectural research, because a great deal is now happening that cannot be explained in terms of the ideas we have outlined above. The situation has outstripped the paradigm which gave birth to it. But the intelligibility of the situation is poor, perhaps because it is inconsistent with the paradigm. We require some radical overhaul of its assumptions—particularly those to do with the relationships between knowledge and design, and the presupposed polarities (e.g. rationalism/intuitionism) along with a new effort to externalise the dynamics of the new situation. To us this seems to be an essential step before the 'applicability gap' is compounded by a 'credibility gap' arising from the gulf between what is expected of research, and what research appears to be offering.

Perhaps the simplest way of introducing what we have to say is by drawing an analogy with the slow but decisive shift in philosophy and scientific epistemology over the past half-century or so. Implicit in both the rationalist and empiricist lines of thought was the notion that in order to get at truth, preconceptions must be eliminated or at least reduced to the minimum. Rationalism began its long history by proposing *a priori* axioms whose truth was supposed to be self evident; empiricism relied on the neutrality of observation. Since the early part of this century, developments in such areas as psychology, meta-mathematics, logic, and the philosophy of science have combined to show that both of these are impossible and unnecessary to an account of scientific progress. Far from being removed from the field of science, the cognitive schemes by which we interpret the world and pre-structure our observations are increasingly seen to be the essential subject matter of science. The question is not whether the world is pre-structured, but how it is pre-structured.

Too often these developments appear to have escaped the attention of scientists working in the environmental field and designers interested in research and looking to research for solutions to problems. This is particularly unfortunate, because the idea of pre-structuring has immediate and fundamental applications in design. We cannot escape from the fact that designers must, and do, pre-structure their problems in order to solve them, although it appears to have been an article of faith among writers on design method (with a few exceptions—for example, Coloquhoun, 1967) that this was undesirable because unscientific. The nub of our argument is that research in the field of the built environment and its action systems should see as its eventual outcome and point of aim the restructuring of the cognitive schemes which designers bring to bear on their tasks, not in terms of supplying 'knowledge' as packaged information to fit into rationalised design procedures, but in terms of redefining what those tasks are like, and using the heuristic capability of scientific procedures to explore the possible through a study of the actual. It is our view that the notion that well-packaged knowledge coupled with a logic of design can lead to radically better artifacts, on the evidence we have, should be relegated to the realm of mythology. But in arguing our case we would like to say a little more about why we think modern scientific epistemology has an important bearing on design and meta-design (which we will argue is probably the simplest and most adequate

characterisation of design research) and why it can help us reconstitute our paradigmatic notions about the subject.

Fifty years ago, it was still possible to think of science as ultimately constituting a set of signs which at the most rudimentary level, would bear a one to one correspondence with atomic facts, and that these could eventually be combined by the laws of induction and verification into a pyramid of laws of greater and greater generality. Scientists on the whole believed this to be the case, and philosophers concerned themselves to show how it would be accomplished.

The overthrow of the Newtonian account of the universe, previously taken as the paradigm of positive knowledge arrived at by observation and induction (as described by Newton himself), threw scientific epistemology into a crisis, the effects of which are still with us. We will give a brief account of this later on. Shortly afterwards, even more remarkable and undermining developments took place in the foundations of mathematics and logic. Gödel showed, by his incompleteness theorem, that 'the construction of a demonstrably consistent relatively rich theory requires not simply an 'analysis' of its 'presuppositions', but the construction of the next higher theory with the effect, to continue quoting Piaget, that 'Previously it had been possible to view theories as layers of a pyramid, each resting on the one below, the theory at ground level being the most secure because constituted by the simplest means, and the whole poised on a self sufficient base. Now however 'simplicity' becomes a sign of weakness and the fastening of any story on the edifice of human knowledge calls for the construction of the next higher theory. To revert to our earlier image, the pyramid of knowledge no longer rests on its foundations but hangs by its vertex, an ideal point never reached and, more curious, constantly rising (Keen, 1959; Nagel & Newman, 1959; Piaget, 1971).'

This is of vital importance, not simply because it demonstrates the inherent limitations of formalism, and the impossibility of such notions as the class of all classes, or the single unified science, but because it demonstrates that there is a necessary hierarchy which limits what we can mean by knowledge—the hierarchy of meta-theories and meta-languages, independent of (we can think of it as orthogonal to) the hierarchy of levels of integration of phenomena in the 'real' world, which constitutes the formal basis of most scientific disciplines. Any cognitive formalisation takes a lower-order formalism for its object and can itself become the object of a higher formalism. To quote Piaget again: 'The limits of formalism can, more simply, be understood as due to the fact that there *is* no 'form as such' or 'contest as such', that each element—from sensory motor acts through operations to theories—is always simultaneously form to the content it subsumes and content for some higher form' (Piaget, 1971).

If we accept that the idea of a monumental edifice of knowledge, descriptive of the world in its account of facts and explanatory of them in terms of theories of increasing generality, has to be given up, what have we left? Have we not effectively debunked the idea of knowledge? Having got rid of positivism, are we left with pure relativism? Intuitively, we feel that such a retreat cannot account for the success of science in improving our understanding of the world and our capacity to modify it. If we adopt a position of pure philosophic relativism then relativity (in theoretical physics—we are short of terms here) and the atomic bomb appear as a kind of epistemological paradox. If on the other hand, we accept that there are strong reasons for rejecting both positivism and pure philosophic relativism, then where do we go? It seems that, as with Scylla and

Charybdis, we cannot escape the one without falling into the other.

It is against this background that the achievement of scientific philosophers like Karl Popper, Thomas Kuhn and Imre Lakatos take on their full stature. Popper has demonstrated that a logic of induction and the principle of verification, previously the twin pillars of positivist science, were both unattainable and unnecessary, and that science could be contained within a hypothetico-deductive scheme (Popper, 1959, 1963): Kuhn suggests a changing epistemological paradigm, within which science can operate as a puzzle solving activity until the next revolutionary 'paradigm switch' (Kuhn, 1962). Lakatos reconstructs science as conflicting sets of inter-related theories (on a smaller scale and more volatile than Kuhn's paradigms), retaining the idea of a 'negative heuristic theoretical core' and a 'positive heuristic' puzzle solving area, each of which exhibits at any time either a 'progressing' or 'degenerating' problem shift according to whether or not it is able to predict new phenomena within its basic theories without having to add *ad hoc* hypotheses to account for newly discovered phenomena (Lakatos, forthcoming: Lakatos & Musgrave, 1962). Then we have a reconstruction of science which is able, in a highly non-linear way, to account for its own continuity, as well as offering some rational justification for using the word 'knowledge' perhaps, to use Popper's expression, as 'piles in the swamp', the swamp being essentially the infinite regress of meta-theories and meta-languages.

The simplest reconciliation of these lines of thought in meta-mathematics and the philosophy of science is to state frankly that the object of science is cognition, and that it is the stratagems of science that are directed towards the real or empirical world. More precisely, we could say that science is about 'remaking cognition', it being clear that if we were satisfied with our cognitive codes for deciphering the world, we would not have science. This seems to us an adequate resolution of the old philosophical problem of whether the 'world out there' or our perception of it is the more real. Such a definition is implicit in the work of psychologists like Kelly, who characterise everyday behaviour by analogy with scientific behaviour (Kelly, 1964). It is a small step to reverse the argument, and it allows us to account not only for the preoccupation of science with the empirical, but also for the fact that some advanced areas of science—notably certain branches of theoretical physics—have had no means of contacting the empirical world for about forty years. We would hardly be satisfied with a characterisation of science which relegated theoretical physics to the realm of metaphysics.

How does all this help us with architectural research? First, it should be clear that once we move away from the establishment of basic criteria set up with a view to avoiding physical discomfort (which we knew how to do anyway in pre-scientific days) then we can avoid a lot of misconception about the status of "knowledge' in design. Secondly, we can begin to see the problems raised by the paradigm for research in architecture that we outlined at the beginning of the paper. Thirdly, it provides us with a better method of making fertile analogies between and thus in connecting the activities of scientists and designers.

The paradigm we suggest as underlying most current research activity in architecture appears to be based on two notions about science that take no account of the developments we have outlined: the notion that science can produce factual knowledge, which is superior to and independent of theory; and the notion of a logic of induction, by which theories may be derived logically from an analysis of facts. In the paradigm, these two notions appear to constitute the fundamental assumptions on which the whole set of ideas is founded: first, that the role of scientific work is to provide factual information that can be assimilated into design; second that a rationalised design process, able to assimilate such information, would characteristically and necessarily proceed by decomposing a problem into its elements, adding an information content to each element drawn as far as possible from scientific work, and 'synthesising' (i.e. inducting) a solution by means of a set of logical or procedural rules.

So far we have suggested very theoretical reasons why such ideas would not be viable or realisable. But equally, from the more practical point of view of the designer or the student, the ideas—or more precisely the operational consequences that flow directly from them—appear even more unviable. Designers are left to make their own links with research by assimilating 'results' and quantification rules, and to evaluate them as they appear without guidance on priorities or patterns of application. The designer's field thus becomes *more* complex and *less* structured. It follows that if a designer cannot make use of this 'information' he is forced to the conclusion that it is because his procedures are not systematic enough, with the result that if he tries to improve himself, he immediately becomes preoccupied with means at the expense of ends.

Similar consequences flowed from these twin paradigmatic assumptions in architectural research itself. For example, building science as a university discipline tended to remain separate and independent of the design disciplines, usually as a research-oriented service-teaching department, sometimes even generating the packages of knowledge that were to fit into the rationalised design procedures. In trying to formalise the process, designers were forced into developing concepts like 'fit' and 'optimisation' simply in order to complete the line of logic by which a 'synthesis' could be accomplished, even though such notions are highly artificial in terms of what buildings are really like and are actually refuted by considering buildings as time-dependent systems rather than as once-and-for-all products.

Our negative aim in this paper was to try to show why the advance of research related to design has so far appeared to progress in parallel with deterioration in the acceptability of the designed product—and this, in the UK, in spite of two decades of excellent work by such bodies as the Building Research Station and government departments, well disseminated in intelligible form and often containing mandatory requirements. We hope that we have shown that there are both theoretical and practical reasons why such a state of affairs should not surprise us. If the present paradigm is unworkable in its essentials, what can we put in its place? We have to preface our proposals with some suggestions about the nature (the actual nature as well as the desirable nature) of design activity.

It is not hard to see why the analysis-synthesis, or inductive, notion of design was popular with theorisers and even with designers as a rationalisation of their own activities. The architectural version of the liberal-rational tradition was that designs should be derived from an analysis of the requirements of the users, rather than from the designer's preconceptions. It is directly analogous to the popularity of induction with scientists who were anxious to distinguish their theories as being derived from a meticulous examination of the facts in the real world. The point we are making in both cases is not that the ideas are immoral or fundamentally deceptive—scientists *do* describe meticulously the 'facts' of the situation, and designers *do* pay attention to the details of user needs—it is that they are theoretically untenable and unnecessary, and as a result, practically confusing.

The first point we would like to make

about our version of science in relation to design, is that if scientists really operate by a kind of dialectic between their prestructuring of the world and the world as it shows itself to be when examined in these terms, then why should such a procedure be thought unscientific in design? Why not accept that only by prestructuring any problem, either explicitly or implicitly, can we make it tractable to rational analysis or empirical investigation?

The second point is also in the form of a question. If rationality in design is not to be characterised in terms of a procedure that allows the information to generate the solution, then in what terms can it be characterised? Is it a redundant notion? Is there any alternative to the mixture of intuitive, imitative and quasi-scientific procedures which appear to characterise design as it is carried out? We would like to work towards answers to both of these questions by using some of the ideas we have discussed in a kind of thought experiment about the nature of design.

First, some observations about reflexivity (cognitive activity making itself its own object, or part of its object) and meta-languages and meta-theories (cognitive activity making other cognitive activity its object.) These, it would appear, have clear parallels at the social level, in terms of the progressive differentiation of roles, especially in areas like design where physical activity is preceded by cognitive and reflective activities. For example, if we start with a simple picture of a man making an object, then it would be reasonable to argue that in as much as he has a definite cognitive anticipation of the probable object (i.e. he is not simply experimenting by trial and error with the latencies of his tools and raw materials) then he is acting analogously to a designer as well as being a maker. His cognitive anticipation of the object is part of the field of tools and raw materials that constitute his 'instrumental set'. Design as we know it can be seen as the socially differentiated transformation of the reflexive cognition of the maker in terms of the latent possibilities of his tools, materials and object types. Its object is not the building, but at one remove, sets of instructions for building. The activity called architectural research can be derived by an exactly similar transformation, namely a socially differentiated transformation of the reflexiveness of the activity of design upon itself, i.e. its object is design, and its product takes the form of rules or rule-like systems for design which stand in the same relation to design as design does to building. As in other sciences, it finds the best way of doing this is by addressing most of its strategies to the 'real' world, and if we are not careful this coupled to the fact that the activity is necessarily multi-disciplinary, tends to conceal the 'deep structure' of the activity. This is why we suggested earlier that we should call the research activity meta-design. At least this might begin to emancipate us from the silly (but pervasive) idea that the outcome of research is 'knowledge', to be contrasted with the absence of such 'knowledge' in design.

We can perhaps clarify the characteristics of design as a cognitive activity by going back to the very simplified situation we have just referred to, to see if we can discover what there is in the maker/designer's field, and go from there to see how it differs today. Here we owe some debt to Levi-Strauss' discussion of 'bricolage' as an analogy to myth making (Levi-Strauss, 1966).

We can imagine a man and an object he will create as though separated by a space which is filled, on the one hand, with tools and raw materials which we can call his 'instrumental set', (or perhaps technological means) and on the other, a productive sequence or process by which an object may be realised. If time is excluded from the space, we can conceive of the 'instrumental set' as though laid out on a table, and constituting a field of latencies and preconstraints. If time is in the space,

then the instrumental set is, as it were, arranged in a procedure or process.

The total field thus exhibits two types of complexity, and we may allow that the maker is capable of reflexively making both types of complexity (the latencies of the instrumental set, and the distribution in process-time) the objects of his attention.

Two basic strategies appear to be open to him. He can either distribute the latencies of the instrumental set in process-time according to some definite cognitive anticipation of the object he is creating, i.e. pursue a definite design or plan, which may be based on an analogy or on pure imagination, as it may be conceived in terms of the familiar products of the instrumental set. Or he can, as it were, interrogate his instrumental set, by an understanding of its latencies in relation to general object types. In both strategies an understanding of the latencies of instrumental sets and a general knowledge of solution types is of fundamental importance. In other words, the maker's capability in pre-structuring the problem is the very basis of his skill, even if he wishes to proceed heuristically by interrogating his instrumental set and exploring unknown possibilities by a dialectic between his understanding of the latencies and limitations of the instrumental set and his knowledge of solution types. On this basis we would argue that design is *essentially* a matter of pre-structuring problems either by a knowledge of solution types or by a knowledge of the latencies of the instrumental set in relation to solution types, and that this is why the process of design is resistent to the inductive-empiricist rationality so common in the field. A complete account of the designer's operations during design, would still not tell us where the solution came from.

But there is an escape clause. As with science, it is not a matter of *whether* the problem is pre-structured but how it is pre-structured, and whether the designer is prepared to make this pre-structuring the object of his critical attention. From here we would go on to suggest that the polarisation we have assumed between rational and intuitive design should be reformulated as a polarity between reflexive design (i.e. design which criticises its understanding of the latencies of instrumental sets and solution types) and non-reflexive design (i.e. design which is simply oriented towards a problem and which therefore operates within the known constraints and limits of instrumental sets and solution types). To equate rationality with a certain type of systematic procedure appears therefore, quite simply, as a mistake.

It is obvious that today the designer operates in a field which is considerably more complicated than the one we have described, based on a man making an object. The notion of pre-structuring is *necessary* to any conceptualisation of design, but not *sufficient* in itself. We have to look at the complications and how they have evolved, in order to complete our conceptualisation of the designer's field and his operations in it.

The most obvious difference is that design is not simply the reflective/cognitive aspect of making an object, but a separate, socially differentiated activity with its own internal dynamic and its own end product, namely sets of rules for making artifacts. It is also a highly specialised activity, carried out by a clearly defined social group. There is therefore no direct link between interrogating the instrumental set and the result as it is likely to be experienced by those who use it. We thus require a great deal of information about the latter in order to interrogate the instrumental set.

We can explore the consequences of this development by trying to imagine what life was like when we had designers, but not user requirement studies. How did we live without them? The answer seems quite simple. Notions about the user were built into the instrumental set and the solution types. The instrumental set was compara-

tively unsophisticated and had in any case been developed mutatively over a long period. It was already an expression of the basic physiological requirements of users in terms of available technology, and probably a reasonable approximation of their psychological and other expectations. The solution types had been similarly evolved, and contained already the notions of use and activities within the building. We could say that, contained in the instrumental set and the solution types was an implicit, historically evolved code, which linked the means to the ends. It would be difficult to decipher and reconstruct, but we can see that it was there, and, in principle, how it got there.

Since those days we have seen developments like the proliferation of building types, and the proliferation of instrumental sets (technological means) and a formal organisation of the process which results in most activity being of a on-off kind with the simple effect that the users' needs in terms of activities, physiological requirements and cultural expectations are no longer contained, as it were, in the instrumental sets and solution types. A much freer, more indeterminate situation appears to exist. This deficiency is made up in terms of information which is expressed in terms of the users rather than in terms of buildings, and the designer operates a kind of *informal code* for linking one to the other. Part of the outcome of research in the past has been a piecemeal and atomistic partial replacement of the codes, by formal rules which when implemented often have the unfortunate effect of dictating the whole design (the 2% daylight factor is a classic example). The designer's task becomes something like the utilisation of these codes in order to link the information he gathers about the project to his interrogation of the increasingly prolific instrumental sets, or his manipulation of solution types. He has to deal similarly with the proliferation of information extraneous to the particular problem relating to standards, constraints, quantification rules etc. In this situation it is perhaps no wonder that the designer (unless his ambitions are frankly artistic) welcomes the prospect of a logic whereby solutions can be synthesied out of information. It offers him the prospect of eventual escape from the contradiction of actually working by the interrogation of instrumental sets or the adaptation of solution types, as he always did, but being expected to utilise a procedure of optimising information which bears little relation to building, except where piecemeal atomistic rules have been developed. Perhaps we should add one more point to this analysis: that the informal codes the designer must use to link information to built outcomes are also instances of problem prestructuring.

If this is a reasonable characterisation of the principal elements in the designer's field, then at least we are some way to understanding why designers do not produce better buildings out of the information research provides, and why, with expanding technological means and user requirements the theoretical open endedness of architectural problems lead to so little fundamental variety in the solutions proposed. With a proliferation of poorly understood instrumental sets, increasingly masked by unrelated information, we would expect that a retreat to the most basic form of pre-structuring—the adaptation of previous solutions—would become the only viable way through the morass. Far from helping the designer escape from his preconception, the effect of proliferating technology and information, is to force the designer into a greater dependence on them. Innovation becomes more rather than less difficult, but the diffusion of uncritical innovation would become more rapid. A situation develops in which a few experiment and others adapt solution types, without understanding or evaluating the rationale of the original experiment. The net result is unstructured innovation, with slow and piecemeal feedback, giving the impression of arbitrary shifts in fashion. This seems a not

unreasonable account of the situation we have, and would explain why even well disseminated and well presented information—such as widely exists in the UK from BRS and government departments—either does not lead to an improvement in the product or does so only in a haphazard way.

We would also suggest that this leads to a situation in which students are learning two different and largely unrelated strategies: methods of analysing a problem into its elements; and a knowledge of informal codes and solution typologies, which they pick up almost as by-products of architectural education, and which act as the pre-structuring that enables them actually to design buildings.

We have argued that the chief elements present in the designer's field are *knowledge of instrumental sets, knowledge of solution types, informal codes, and information.* These cannot usefully be reduced to homogenised 'information', although it is possible at a theoretical and formalised level. Now we would like to use these ideas to try to construct a likelife conceptualisation of design as an activity.

These elements constitute the designer's field, his set of latencies and preconstraints. Somehow these are to be distributed in a process time. We will need to introduce one or two further basic ideas as we proceed, but we hope that these will either be from those we have already discussed, or simple logical statements of an unproblematical kind.

For example, it seems unproblematic to say that when a design problem is stated there are, theoretically at least, a number of solutions open, probably a very large number. Yet only one of these possible solutions will be the final one that is built. We may reasonably say that some process of *variety reduction* has taken place. The variety of possible solutions has been reduced to one unique solution by some means. The succession of documents produced during design reflect this progressive reduction of variety. More and more specific drawings for example exclude more and more detailed design possibilities. We would like to introduce this as a basic idea in our conceptualisation of design.

A second idea we would like to introduce is that of *conjecture*. Here we would like to go to science. It was once thought that conjecture would have no place in a rigorous scientific method. It was thought to be akin to speculation, and science sought to define itself in contradistinction to such notions. Since Popper we know that science cannot progress without conjecture, in fact that together with rigorous means of testing, conjectures constitute the life blood of science. Conjectures come from anywhere, and because they are not derived from the data by induction, it does not mean that the process of thought of which they form part is any the less rational or rigorous. What is irrational is to exclude conjecture. So we will include it in design.

How does the reduction of variety from many possible to one actual solution take place? Obviously anything we can say here will only be an approximation of any particular case. But our aim is to try to understand the process of design as it exists in the real world, in order to try to define the contribution of meta-design. What we are aiming at is some more or less true to life approximation of the psychology of design, bearing in mind that design is a practical as well as a cognitive activity, and that design problems do not happen in a social vacuum, but are socially constructed.

Beginning with a theoretically open problem, with an unlimited number of solutions, it should be clear that the variety of possible solutions is already reduced before any conscious act of designing begins by two sets of limiting factors, one set external to the designer, the other internal. The first set we can call 'external variety reducing constraints' and these can often be quite powerful, or even totally deterministic of the design. For example a client who says

categorically 'I want one like that' has already reduced the number of possible solutions to one. More often the external constraints will be of a less overt, but still powerful, kind, such as norms of appearance, availability of technological means, costs, standards and so on. Some of these will not be fully understood by the designer at the outset, but as he specifies them their role as variety reducers will become clearer.

The second set we can call the 'internal variety reducers' and these are an expression of the designer's cognitive map, in particular his understanding of instrumental sets and solution types. This notion of the pre-existing cognitive map is very important indeed, because it is largely through the existence of such maps that any cognitive problem-solving activity can take place. They are, and must be, used by the problem-solver in order to structure the problem in terms in which he can solve it. It acts as a kind of plan for finding a route through problem material that would otherwise appear undifferentiated and amorphous. Its role is equivalent to the role of theory and theoretical frameworks in science. Data is not collected at random. What is to be called data is already determined by some prior theoretical or quasi-theoretical exercise, implicit or explicit.

We have to recognise, therefore, that before the problem is further specified by the gathering of data about the problem, it is already powerfully constructed by two sets of limiting factors: the external constraints (although some of these may still be poorly understood) and the designer's cognitive capability in relation to that type of problem. It is quite likely that these latent limitations are already being explored right from the beginning, if the designer is conjecturing possible solutions, or at least approximations of solutions, in order to structure his understanding of the problem, and to test out its resistances. There is also a very practical reason why conjectures of approximate solutions should come early on. This is that a vast variety of design decisions cannot be taken—particularly those which involve other contributors—before the solution in principle is known.

As the designer collects and organises the problem data, and data about constraints, his conjectures acquire sharper definition. Previously he was not able to test them out in a very specific way. Now he has an increasing fund of information against which to test them. He will also be using this information heuristically by using it in relation to his informal codes (see above, p. 76) by which abstract requirements are linked to built outcomes, and conjecturing further specifications within his roughly conjectured solutions. Information which has been used heuristically, can also be used to test the new conjectures. Conjecture and problem specification thus proceed side by side rather than in sequence. Moreover conjectures do not, on the whole, arise out of the information although it may contribute heuristically. By and large they come from the pre-existing cognitive capability—knowledge of the instrumental sets, solution types, and informal codes, and occasionally from right outside—an analogy perhaps, or a metaphor, or simply what is called inspiration. At least within this conceptualisation of design we do not have to say that designers who use these last three types of source for conjecture are acting in a way that is markedly different to the architect with more modest ambitions. He has simply widened the scope of his conjectural field, sometimes moving right beyond the limits of the instrumental sets that are available.

When a conjectural approximation of a solution stands up to the test of the increasingly specific problem data (bearing in mind that it is always possible to collect more data and to produce more conjectures) a halt is called to both conjecturing and data-gathering, and a solution in principle is agreed to exist. Further specification then

takes place (i.e. further variety reduction) by completing a full design, and this is followed by a further refinement when the final production drawings are made. Unless the designer has great foresight, it is likely that further refinements will be made at the building stage.

We believe that this is more or less how design happens in most situations, and we believe moreover that it is as rational a process as is possible in the complex circumstances, not sub-rational because it is not 'systematic' and because so much depends on how the designer pre-structures the problem. This outline model differs from the analysis-synthesis model (which we take to be the dominant notion in design method studies, hitherto) in several important ways. First, its core strategem is conjecture-analysis rather than analysis-synthesis. Secondly, the purpose of analysis is primarily to test conjectures rather than to optimise by logical or magical procedures. The notion of optimising which architects believe they carry out can be easily contained within a conjecture-test psychology of design. Thirdly, the solution in principle is allowed to exist at a much earlier stage than in the analysis-synthesis model. Fourth, the model shows the path of convergence on a unique solution without introducing notions like the optimisation of information which, while attractive theoretically, are largely unlifelike and unworkable. Fifth, the model suggests *within its basic concepts* the possible origins of solutions in principle, a matter on which the design methodologists are notoriously silent or mysterious. Sixth, the model corresponds to the observed sequences of products of design, namely a set of descriptive documents of increasing refinement and specificity. Seventh, it recognises implicitly that both information and conjectured solutions are inherently incomplete, but a stop has to be called somewhere. This is precisely equivalent to the situation in science. Eighth, and perhaps most important, the model emphasises the importance of the designer's pre-structuring of the problem, rather than denigrating it. It recognises that architects' approach—and should approach—design holistically and not piecemeal.

What does this have to say about research? We have already argued that presenting the 'results' of research in the form of packaged information or quantification tools does not seem to lead easily to better solutions. Perhaps the model will help to explain why. It is largely because unless research can influence designers at the stage of pre-structuring the problem in order to understand it, then its influence on design will remain limited.

To explore this further, we might usefully examine the outcomes of research in terms of the four main types of elements which characterise the designer's field, namely instrumental sets, solution types, codes and information. It can be seen than much research of a purely technological kind (still by far the largest investment in building research) has its outcomes in terms of instrumental sets. Development work extends this into solution types by proposing exemplars. Research which aims to provide a method of checking design proposals against abstract requirements can be seen as a partial formalisation of codes (partial because it is concerned with testing rather than generation and it is piecemeal). And research which has its outcome in the form of 'results', rather than a tool, falls into the field of information.

It can easily be seen that the first and last of these do not really help the designer to design. They normally increase the complication of the field and obscure its structure. Certainly they do not help the designer much at the stage of pre-structuring the problem, and if they do so, it can only be in a haphazard way. The exemplars and prototypes that are the outcomes of development work certainly help the designer to pre-structure his problem, but only if he proceeds in a largely imitative way. If the

development is inadequate in any respect, it leads to a proliferation of these inadequacies.

Over and above this, the prototype may be poorly understood, or badly adapted. Research in the third category is similarly unhelpful at the crucial stage of pre-structuring. It may provide a means of eliminating errors at the design testing stage, given that the designer is able to use them properly, but we can hardly conceive of the designer being able to effectively utilise the full panoply of such techniques that would be required to cover all aspects of the design.

Of the four, only the development model can demonstrate to the designer new ways of pre-structuring his problem. In spite of its disadvantages, its potential usefulness should not be under-estimated. We could say that it suggests an organisational solution to the problem of linking research effectively with design. If research workers work with designers in producing experimental prototype solutions, which are intensively monitored and improved, then explained and publicised, then research itself benefits by becoming part of a dynamic process from which it can continuously learn and develop its concepts. In the past, development work in building has tended to lack both the deep involvement of research workers, and a properly developed monitoring function linked to a building programme. If both of these are provided for, there is at least an opportunity for sustained development over a period. By the quality and conviction of its exemplars, it can lead quite rapidly to a diffusion of real improvements in solutions.

On the other hand, the disadvantages of relying wholly on this fail-safe means of linking research with design are strong. The individual designer becomes severely constricted, problems of poor interpretation and debasement are likely to arise, creative innovation may be cut off or inhibited. Is there not some way in which research may help the designer to pre-structure his problems more effectively without pre-determining the solutions?

We believe there is, and that it lies in the notion of codes, the third element in the designer's field. Informal or implicit codes, we suggested, were used by the designer to link abstract functional requirements with instrumental sets, which no longer contained such codes. Taken together as a system, they constitute a kind of quasi-theory by which the designer structures his problem and finds a route through it—or through as much as is left of the problem after other external and internal constraints, including solution types, have had their say. Sometimes these codes are formalised and externalised in a rather pragmatic and programmatic way as 'architectural theory'. The influence and rate of diffusion of such externalisations is often very considerable (Le Corbusier, 1927/1946). On occasion their impact is such as to have a marked effect on the development of instrumental sets.

The idea we are working towards, stated simply, is that research should aim (and already is beginning to aim) at the progressive reconstitution of the codes on a conceptual base by studies of people and their built environment which are oriented towards theory rather than 'results'. This is a complex and long-term aim, but it is entirely consistent with the normal impact of scientific work on human activities. The difference between a craft and a technology is not research results, but theory which brings structure and classification into phenomena, and allows the possible to emerge from an understanding of the actual. In any problem-solving activity, theory is the essential link between science and action. Without theory and its classificatory and route-finding possibilities, design is likely to remain, even in a field of endlessly proliferating scientific 'information', a kind of craft without continuity.

Here we come back to the reasons for optimism about architectural research. It seems to us, that we are seeing the devel-opment of strong research programmes which are architectural in that they deal with broad bands of connected factors in design, and fundamental in that they are concerned with theories which actually relate to these levels of integration, rather than theories about isolated factors in environment. We would therefore like to try to explain what we see as the emerging structure of architectural research, why it is theoretical in a design as well as a scientific sense, and why it appears capable in the long run of affecting the ways in which problems are pre-structured by designers.

We can best explain this by asking a question. What, in theoretical terms, is a building? On the grounds that buildings are not gratuitous but entirely purposeful objects, we would define a building as a realisation of a number of social functions with an effect of ecological displacement. By specifying these functions and displacement effects in sufficiently abstract terms, we can formulate an adequate theoretical description of what a building is (such that anything which lacks one of them is not a building, and that if an object is a building, it will fulfil all these functions whether by intention or as a by-product) and what its displacement effect is in terms of a four-function model. These are not true for all time, but are an historically accumulative set which define more or less what a building is at this point in time.

First, a building is a climate modifier, and within this broad concept it acts as a complex environmental filter between inside and outside, it has a displacement effect on external climate and ecology and it modifies, by increasing, decreasing and specifying, the sensory inputs into the human organism.

Second, a building is a container of activities, and within this it both inhibits and facilitates activities, perhaps occasionally prompting them or determining them. It also locates behaviour, and in this sense can be seen as a modification of the total behaviour of society.

Third, a building is a symbolic and cultural object, not simply in terms of the intentions of the designer, but also in terms of the cognitive sets of those who encounter it. It has a similar displacement effect on the culture of society. We should note that a negatively cultural building is just as powerful a symbolic object as a positively, (i.e. intentionally) cultural one.

Fourth, a building is an addition of value to raw materials (like all productive processes), and within this it is a capital investment, a maximisation of scarce resources of material and manpower, and a use of resources over time. In the broader context of society, it can be seen as a resource modifier.

In brief a building is a *climate modifier, a behaviour modifier, a cultural modifier and a resource modifier,* the notion of 'modification' containing both the functional and displacement aspects.

Each of these functions can be conceived of separately as a people-thing relationship and each, in contrast to research orientated towards the 'atom of environment' deals with a holistic set which constitutes *one way* of looking at a design problem. Each is capable of developing theory about people and their built environment. We would argue that research is gradually organising itself within these foci as a set of interdependent, theory-oriented and largely structural studies, and that these are emerging as the fundamental disciplines of architectural research, and providing the base within which various disciplines become integrated and lose their identity.

It is notable, by the way, that the emphases implicit in this model shift architectural research right away from the study of procedures of design and into the study of buildings and their occupants, as well as away from 'results' and towards theory. We are beginning to look again at ends rather than means.

How will such research contribute to design? We have argued at the general level that it will progressively enable us to reconstitute codes from a theoretical base concerned with the relations between physical environments and those who experience them. We may add first that we conceive of this happening not in a positivistic and piecemeal way, but, because of the theoretical base, in a more holistic, non-deterministic and heuristic way. But this is too general a statement to be useful. We must specify further what we mean, and show why we can use this idea to escape from the idea of once-and-for-all 'knowledge' and allow for fundamental shifts in the theoretical bases by which we define 'knowledge' which will undoubtedly occur. We appeal again to the lessons of science.

In spite of periodic epistemological crises, paradigm switches and the progression and degeneration of research programmes, science continues to build its usefulness (as it has always done) on the strength of precise descriptions of the world. The theories on which these precise descriptions are based may be incomplete and even wrong, but they enable us to organise more and more of the world into useful cognitive schemes which, among other outcomes, enable us to conceive the possible out of a study of the actual. It might not be going too far to characterise the history of science as a series of immensely fertile delusions.

We do not therefore need to invoke the idea of 'knowledge' in order to propose that out of the notion of a building as a multi-functional object, and design as a multi-theoretical activity, we can begin to build up theory-based descriptions of the basic elements in design. These basic elements include ranges of activities, movements, perception-motivated actions, social-intercourse patterns, spaces and the environmental criteria that will satisfy a classified range of possible uses, coded and described in terms of the technologies which make them possible. Such a breakdown we might call a *base component classification* for environmental action, which would shift both in response to theoretical changes and also in response to changes in the environmental objectives of society. From the point of view of the designer, such classifications and code formalisations would not be deterministic or constitute a set to be specified in relation to problem information, but would constitute an extension of the designer's basic cognitive capability, and provide him with—and this is really the point about science—*a position of strength from which to make his conjectures.* In other words he would be using theories operationalised and specified as far as possible in terms of externalised codes, linking instrumental sets to human usage, as a basis for proposing his own further modifications to the environmental field.

The implications of this for the current formal structure of design activity—particularly those concerned with briefing, on-off user studies, and the designer's ability to reinterpret the 'client's requirements' —are enormous, and to examine them in detail would require another paper. To give one example, in the area of activity-space relations, we can foresee the possibility of moving from the 'activity-space fit' notion which is implicit in current practice, towards much more fundamental theories about the capability of certain types and configurations of space to contain an unpredictable variety of activities, perhaps with consequences for the idea of building types, and even for the size of cities. Such

theories are not pseudo-deterministic ways of telling the designer what will be the outcome of his design, but strong and cumulatively developing bases for conjecturing possible futures.

If we are right in thinking that this is the underlying direction of the new lines in environmental research, then the notion of research simply as a service to design and the by-product of an eclectic variety of disciplines has to go by the board. Research is of course necessarily multi-disciplinary. In fact in the environmental field there appear to be no limits to the disciplines that could contribute to the advancement of the subject. But the contributions of the wider areas of science will only become effective through the integrative theories which will increasingly form the fundamental disciplines of environmental action itself, and these disciplines are not separate from design, but extensions of it in that their subject matter is design just as the subject matter of design is sets of instructions for building.

This is not a strange or unique arrangement. In fact it is very similar to science itself, seen in its broadest terms as one of the activities of society. Through science we continuously modify the world we live in and our understanding of—that world and that understanding that it is the aim of science to study.

7. Undermanning Theory and Research: Implications for the Study of Psychological and Behavioral Effects of Excess Human Populations
ALLAN W. WICKER

Interest among social psychologists in problems related to population growth, crowding, and population density appears

From *Representative Research in Social Psychology*, Vol. 4, No. 1 (1973), pp. 185–206. Reprinted by permission of the author and the publisher.

to be greatly increasing. However, this interest has not yet generated any substantial body of knowledge regarding the effects of excess populations; indeed, the scientific literature on the problem, particularly for the case of human populations, is extremely sparse and inconclusive (Freedman, Klevansky, & Ehrlich, 1971; Galle, Gove, & McPherson, 1972; Sommer, 1966; Zlutnick & Altman, 1972).

A major impediment to the development of this problem area appears to be the lack of either theoretical or empirical guidelines for future research. The few available studies[1] certainly are not very helpful in this regard. They are conceptually and empirically isolated from one another, and in most cases have not been guided by explicit theory.

There is, however, a body of research and a developing theory which have not yet been directly applied to problems of excess populations, but which should prove to be a useful guide for that study. This is the ecological psychology literature initiated by Barker and Wright and extended by them and their colleagues. It provides a theory, concepts and measures which have been developed in the course of 30 years of research on human behavior in natural (uncontrived) environments (e.g., Barker & Wright, 1955; Barker, 1960, 1963, 1965 1968). Before making the case for the relevance of this research to problems of excess populations, the basic concepts, theory and research will be briefly summarized.

Ecological Psychology Concepts, Theory, and Research

Behavior Settings

The behavior setting is the basic environmental unit in ecological psychology. As conceived and studied by Barker, behavior settings are public places and activities, such as banks, piano lessons, church worship services, Lions Club meetings, paper routes, and baseball games. More precisely, behavior settings have the following characerics: (a) One or more standing pat-

[1] These studies have been reviewed by Freedman, et al. (1971), Galle, et al. (1972), Sommer (1966), and Zlutnick & Altman (1972) and will not be cited here. A recent study not cited in the reviews is Desor (1972).

terns of behavior, that is, regularly occurring human activities. For example, at a church worship service, these activities would include ushering, giving the sermon, and singing. (b) Coordination between behavior patterns and the inanimate objects nearby. Behaviors at a worship service are coordinated with the location and physical characteristics of the pews, altar, hymnals, and offering plates for example. (c) Definite time-place boundaries, such that the behaviors outside these boundaries are readily discriminable from those within. The boundaries of the worship service, say, would be between 10 and 11 a.m. on Sundays, and within the walls forming the church sanctuary. Behaviors outside the walls at that time, or within the walls at a different time, would differ from those at the specified time and place. A more complete description of behavior settings, and rules for determining whether two or more possible settings should be considered as a single setting or as distinct settings, are given in Barker (1968).

Barker and his co-workers have catalogued and described behavior setting in terms of such variables as their frequency of occurrence and duration; the numbers and ages of people who occupy them; the degree to which setting occupants have positions of involvement and responsibility; and the kinds of behavior patterns which occur within them, such as whether they involve recreation, education, and so on. Of particular interest here is the distinction between setting occupants who have assumed some responsible job in a setting (for example, the manager, player, or concessionaire at a baseball game, the proprietor or janitor in a grocery store) and those who have not (for example, the baseball fan in the stands or the shopper). The former set of occupants are called *performers*, the latter set, *non-performers*.

Theory of Undermanning

Barker (1960) proposed a theory of undermanning based on his extensive observations of all of the public behavior settings occurring in two small towns: "Midwest," Kansas, U.S.A., and "Yoredale," Yorkshire, England. He had found that Midwest, although it had only half as many residents as Yoredale in a given survey year, had 1.2 times as many public behavior settings and 1.7 times as many *performances*; i.e., instances of people serving as performers. On the average, Midwest residents were performers in the settings 3 times as often as Yoredale residents. An even greater spread in performance rates was found for the adolescents in the two communities: Midwest adolescents served in 3.5 times as many positions of responsibility as did their Yoredale counterparts. It was also reported that nearly 8% of all the public behavior settings in Midwest depended upon adolescents to an important degree, compared to 2% for Yoredale.

Barker's interpretation of these data was as follows: The behavior settings in the towns provided satisfactions to the persons who occupied them (albeit different kinds of satisfaction were undoubtedly experienced by different occupants), and thus the occupants had an active interest in keeping the settings functioning. However, in order to maintain their more numerous settings, residents of Midwest had to occupy more positions of responsibility, and to accept larger numbers of marginally qualified persons into the settings, than did Yoredale residents. The settings in Midwest were viewed as *undermanned*[2] relative to those in Yoredale.

More generally, Barker proposed that behavior settings could be viewed as ecobehaviorial systems capable of generating forces necessary for their own maintenance. He suggested that the condition of under-

² Apologies are herewith extended to those for whom the term, manning, has sexist connotations. No such meaning is implied either by the originator of the term or by the present author. Other terms, such as staffing, seem now to be more suitable; however, since the present paper is in part a historical review, the original term will be retained here.

manning; i.e., of having insufficient or barely sufficient personnel in a setting to carry out the essential tasks or functions, represents a threat to the behavior setting system and thus results in the generation of forces or pressures on the occupants to maintain the setting. In Barker's terminology, the *claim* of the behavior setting on its inhabitants is greater in conditions of undermanning than when the number of persons available is at or above the optimal level.

Barker asserts that the greater claim of undermanned settings results in the following consequences for the setting occupants:

1. Greater effort to support the setting and its functions, either by "harder" work or by spending longer hours
2. Involvement in more difficult and more important tasks
3. Participation in a greater diversity of tasks and roles
4. Less sensitivity to and less evaluation of differences between people
5. A lower level of maximal or best performance
6. Greater functional importance of individuals within the setting
7. More responsibility in the sense that the setting and what others gain from it depend on the individual occupant
8. Viewing oneself and others in terms of task-related characteristics, rather than in terms of social-emotional characteristics
9. Setting of lower standards and fewer tests for admission into the setting
10. Greater insecurity about the eventual maintenance of the setting
11. More frequent occurrences of success and failure, depending upon the outcome of the setting's functions.

Research on the Theory of Undermanning

Most of the research stimulated by the above set of suppositions has compared the experiences and behaviors of members of organizations (high schools and churches) which differed in size of membership. In this research, it has generally been assumed that degree of manning of the behavior settings in the organizations studied varied directly with organization size, i.e., that the settings in the smaller organizations were undermanned relative to the settings in the larger organizations. Consistent with this assumption, the ratio of number of members to the number of behavior settings in an organization has been found to increase with organization size: there tend to be fewer people per behavior setting in smaller organizations than in larger ones (Barker & Barker, 1964; Gump & Friesen, 1964a: Wicker, 1969b; Willems, 1967). Another way of stating this finding is that number of behavior settings does not increase at the same rate as number of members in an organization.

Studies of school behavior settings have been primarily of extracurricular activities, e.g., sports and dramatics events, while studies of churches have included all organization behavior settings, e.g., worship services, business meetings, dinners, parties. Consistent with the theory, most of the research has shown that the behaviors and experiences of members of small organizations, whose behavior settings are apparently undermanned, differ considerably from the behaviors and experiences of members of large organizations, whose behavior settings are apparently not undermanned. Members of all schools and churches, compared to members of large schools and churches, (a) entered more different kinds of organization behavior settings, (b) had more performances in the settings (Baird, 1969; Barker & Hall 1964; Campbell, 1964; Gump & Friesen, 1964a; Wicker, 1969a, 1969b; Wicker & Mehler, 1971), and (c) reported more experiences of challenge, involvement, and felt obligation to participate (Campbell, 1964; Gump & Friesen, 1964b; Wicker, 1968; Wicker & Mehler, 1971; Willems, 1964, 1967). Members of a small church contributed more money, attended Sunday worship service more frequently, spent more time in church behavior settings, and were more

approving of high levels of support for church activities than members of a large church (Wicker, 1969b). Moreover, new members of the small church were more readily assimilated into church activities than were new members of the large church (Wicker & Mehler, 1971).

Using archival data, Wicker (1969b) found significant negative correlations between organization size and the percentage of members who attended and participated in church activities. However, using a larger and more representative sample of churches, Wicker, et al. (1972) found a linear relationship between each of three measures of participation and size of membership, rather than the predicted negatively accelerated relationship. Finally, in a study of the effects of a merger of two churches differing in size, Wicker and Kauma (1972) found that members from the smaller church showed a greater decline in participation and reported feeling less close to the church as a consequence of the merger than did members from the larger church.

At this point, it should be noted that the research discussed above has focused primarily on aspects and consequences of insufficient populations, rather than excess populations. Barker, in his theorizing, has generally contrasted undermanning with optimal manning (e.g., Barker, 1968). He has not offered a clear conceptual distinction between optimal manning and overmanning, nor has he said anything about differential consequences of the two conditions. Such distinctions are obviously necessary, however, if research is to be conducted on the overpopulated end of the manning continuum.

A More Complete Specification of Degrees of Manning

Recently, Wicker, et al. (1972) have sought to provide more complete and precise definitions of the various conditions of manning of behavior settings, including overmanning. Degree of manning is examined separately for two mutually exclusive sets of setting occupants, performers and non-performers: thus there can be differential degrees of manning of the same setting. For example, a one-man barber shop having insufficient customers can be adequately manned at the level of performers but undermanned at the level of non-performers. And a crowded physician's office can be undermanned at the level of performers yet overmanned at the level of non-performers.

In determining the degree of manning of a setting, the following basic concepts are applied to each class of potential setting occupants (i.e., to performers and to non-performers): the minimum number of persons required in order for the setting to be maintained (the *maintenance minimum*); the maximum number of persons which the setting can accommodate (*capacity*); and the total number of persons who both seek to participate and meet the eligibility requirements (*applicants*). As will be seen in the following discussion, addition of the capacity notion to the definition of manning permits a distinction between adequate manning and overmanning. According to Wicker, *et al.* (1972):

The maintenance minimum of performers in a behavior setting is the smallest number of functionaries required by the setting; this number depends upon the *program* of the setting, i.e., the time-ordered sequence of events which must occur in the setting; and the temporal-spatial limitations which the program impresses (Barker, 1968). It may be noted that, in contrast to the earlier conception of degree of manning, the present concern is not with the absolute number of tasks or amount of work to be done, but with the number of persons required to carry out the tasks in their proper sequence.

In the case of non-performers, the maintenance minimum is the smallest number of persons who must be present as consumers (audience, members, customers) in order for the setting to continue. A quorum is the maintenance minimum for a business meeting, for example.

A behavior setting's capacity for performers may be constrained both by physical and social structural factors. The backstage area of a theater may limit the number of persons who can serve on the stage crew, and the size of the choir loft in a church may effectively limit the size of the choir. But the program of the setting may also limit capacity. Examples would include rules specifying the size of the roster of athletic teams, scripts specifying the number of actors in a play, by-laws of organizations, and the like.

The capacity for non-performers in a setting is largely constrained by physical factors [such as number of seats and available floor space], but social structural factors may operate as well. For example, safety regulations may limit the number of persons who can be admitted to an auditorium to a figure below the absolute physical capacity.

The applicants for performer roles in a behavior setting are those persons who are both eligible to participate at the performer level and who wish to do so. A person is eligible for a setting if he can attend at its specified time and place and if he meets all admission standards. This view of potential performers differs from the earlier one in that a person, in order to be considered an applicant, must desire or at least be willing to accept a position of responsibility: persons who are eligible but unwilling are not included.

Applicants for non-performer roles are simply those people who meet the admission requirements and who can and wish to enter (Wicker, *et al.*, 1972, pp. 511–512).

These concepts can be more clearly understood by relating them to a particular kind of behavior setting. For example, in a high school play, the maintenance minimum for performers would include the director, members of the cast, persons to handle lighting, props, and costumes, a ticket seller, and possibly a few others. The maintenance minimum for non-performers would be the smallest audience size which would be tolerated before the setting would be altered or eliminated. Capacity of performers would be the total number of persons who could be accommodated in all functional roles, including in addition to those listed above, ushers, a house manager, an assistant director, understudies, concessions sellers, and others. Capacity of non-performers would be the number of persons who could be seated in the auditorium. Applicants at the performer level would be the number of people who sought to or at least were willing to serve as a functionary in the settings, i.e., to direct, act, usher, serve on the stage crew, and so on. Applicants at the non-performer level would be the number of persons who have the admission fee and seek to enter the play performance.

It is now possible to specify three major conditions of manning, which, it should be recalled, may exist with respect either to the performer roles or the non-performer roles in a behavior setting. The condition of manning of a setting depends upon where the number of applicants falls relative to the maintenance minimum and capacity, as illustrated in Figure 7–1. If the number of applicants is below the maintenance minimum, e.g., at point *a*, the setting is undermanned. If the number of applicants falls between the maintenance minimum and capacity, e.g., at points *b*, *c*, or *d*, adequate manning exists. When there are more applicants than capacity, e.g., at point *e*, *overmanning* is present. Although Wicker, *et al.* (1972) do not make this distinction,

it seems useful to suggest two subdivisions of adequate manning: *poorly manned,* when applicants barely exceeds the maintenance minimum, e.g., at point *b*, and *richly manned*, when applicants approaches capacity, e.g., at point *d*.[3]

Adequate manning is assumed by Wicker, *et al.* (1972) to be a quasi-stationary state with no strong pressures toward change. However, in the poorly manned and richly manner regions, it seems likely that the pressures described below would begin to increase as the number of applicants approaches the maintenance minimum and capacity, respectively.

Both undermanning and overmanning are postulated to be unstable and to generate forces toward adequate manning. Undermanning, whether it exists at the performer level or non-performer level, results in "pressures to increase the number of applicants, perhaps by recruiting from among the eligibles or by lowering eligibility standards, and/or to reduce the maintenance minimum, perhaps by reducing the scope of the setting or by reorganizing it (Wicker, *et al*, 1972, p. 512)." Overmanning (again at either the performer or non-performer level) results in "pressures to reduce the number of applicants, perhaps by reducing recruiting efforts or by raising eligibility standards, and/or to increase the setting capacity (Wicker, *et al.*, 1972, p. 512)."

[3] I am indebted to Stuart Oskamp for this suggestion.

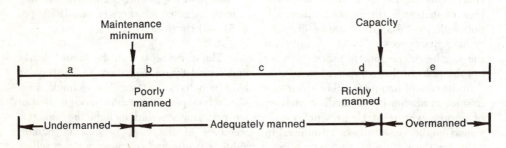

FIGURE 7–1. The continuum of degrees of manning.

In the example of a high school play, overmanning at the performer level would exist if more students sought to be in the cast than there were acting parts available. In this case, the eligibility standards might be raised so that only the best actors would be selected. Or an additional cast might be set up ("double casting") to perform on a different night so that twice as many people could serve as actors. At the non-performer level, the capacity of the play behavior setting might be increased by either dealing with physical features of the setting (adding more chairs, allowing people to stand at the back of the theater, finding a larger theater) or by repeating the performance.

The rationale for calculating degrees of manning separately for performers and non-performers might in some cases profitably be extended to different performance roles. Just as it is possible for a behavior setting to be undermanned at the performer level and overmanned at the non-performer level (the example cited earlier was a crowded physician's office), it is also possible for one performer role in a setting to be overmanned while a different role is undermanned. An example would be a high school operetta for which many more girls wanted to participate than could be accommodated (applicants exceeded capacity) but fewer boys appeared for "try-outs" than there were parts (applicants below maintenance minimum). Or the nurse role in a physician's office might be adequately manned, while the physician role is undermanned. The critical issue here, of course, is the permeability of the roles. In instances where roles cannot be readily crossed (e.g., girls cannot sing bass, nurses cannot make diagnoses), calculation of degrees of manning for each role is desirable.

Relevance of Ecological Psychology to the Study of Psychological and Behavioral Effects of Excess Human Populations

How can the concepts, theory, and research of ecological psychology be helpful in the study of overcrowding and overpopulation? For one thing, ecological psychology provides a workable, "medium-sized" unit of the natural environment. The behavior setting is larger and more complex than the notion of personal space, for example, yet smaller and less complex than the residential neighborhood or apartment building. Moreover, behavior settings, as they are defined, are ubiquitous. A person cannot choose to be in no behavior setting, only to move from one setting to another. Another advantage of the behavior setting unit is that it includes behavioral, physical, and temporal aspects, and does not rely only on one or two of these facets. A behavior setting is not a creation of an investigator: it has substance and meaning—that is to say, it exists—independently of him. Finally, as will be seen more clearly in a subsequent section, the behavior setting is viewed as a functional, dynamic system, not as a static object.

The theory of undermanning, and the revised formulation for defining degrees of manning, point to some additional factors which need to be considered in dealing with consequences of excess populations. They stress the need to consider not merely the number of persons present in a setting, but rather how that number relates to the personnel requiremets of the setting, and to the number of persons the setting can accommodate. It follows from this view that population density, in terms of number of people per acre, household, or square yard of floor space, at least within the range in which they naturally occur, may not be crucial in determining human experiences and behavior. What one needs to know is what are the maintenance minima and capacities of the settings which are located within the physical spaces.

There is another, more subtle, consequence of thinking of exeess populations in terms of behavior setting characteristics rather than in terms of population density. As Zlutnick and Altman (1972) suggest, how one defines excess population constrains how he will seek to deal with it. Thinking in terms of population density implies the solutions of reducing the number of people or increasing the amount of space. Thinking in terms of behavior settings implies a broader range of strategies. Too many people in a setting might suggest increasing the physical capacity of the setting, but as noted above, it might suggest a number of other alternatives as well, such as scheduling an additional performance of the setting or altering the setting program so that more people could be accommodated. An example of the latter would be a chamber music group which reorganizes to become an orchestra.

Barker (1968) has argued the "immediate practical significance" of the research on undermanning for problems of excess populations:

The increase in population is usually considered in connection with economic and nutritional problems, but its more direct effects upon behavior deserve consideration, too. Undermanned behavior settings are without doubt becoming less frequent, and optimally manned (and overmanned) settings more common. This change within the United States has relevance for theories of American culture and character. The United States has been known as a *land of opportunity* and its inhabitants have been called a *people of plenty*; its environment is said to have been dominated by the *free frontier*. Involved in the complex of ideas behind these aphorisms is the idea that there has been a superabundance of goals to be achieved and an excess of tasks to be done in relation to the nation's inhabitants, and that these have been important influences on the American society and people. This is, in important respects, a theory by historians of the influence of undermanned behavior settings upon a society and the characteristics of its members. An eco-behavioral science should have something to say about this theory, and about the consequences of the change

from a society of undermanned settings to one of optimally manned and overmanned settings (Barker, 1968, p. 189).

Basic Issues in the Study of Manning of Behavior Settings

If the work by ecological psychologists is relevant to and useful for the study of problems associated with excess populations, then it should be possible to formulate a number of concrete suggestions for future study of overmanning. The present approach has been first to identify the issues which appear to be most important in the study of manning, and for each issue, to review critically the existing literature in a search for guidelines for future study.

The basic issues to be discussed are the following:

1. Do differential degrees of manning of behavior settings result in differential behaviors and experiences by setting occupants? The issue here is essentially whether manning conditions can be viewed as sufficient causes for certain behaviors and experiences.
2. Do intra-setting events (interpersonal and person-task interactions) differ in settings which themselves differ in degree of manning? This issue has to do with the processes which occur throughout the duration of a behavior setting, and not merely what are the outcomes of those events.
3. Does a history of participating in behavior settings at a given level of manning produce effects in the participant which transfer to other situations? Put slightly differently, this issue is how one's current behavior and experiences in settings are affected by the conditions of manning in the settings he has previously occupied.

These three questions represent essentially the same three directions for future research on crowding proposed by Zlutnick and Altman (1972): crowding as a determinant of behavior, coping and adaptive responses to crowding, and historical antecedents and responses to crowding.

Behavior and Experimental Consequences of Manning Conditions

Evidence from studies of undermanning. As indicated earlier, investigations of Barker's theory have generally employed the following rationale: Undermanning is more characteristic of the behavior settings of small organizations than of large organizations, therefore the members of small organizations should show the consequences of occupying undermanned behavior settings, e.g., higher levels of participation and stronger feelings of involvement, than members of large organizations. Data consistent with this expectation have been interpreted as confirming the proposition that the condition of undermanning is a sufficient cause for the consequences outlined.

However, the empirical evidence cited earlier is not sufficiently compelling that unqualified statements can be made regarding the *effects or consequences* which undermanned behavior settings *produce* or *cause* in setting occupants. Since all of the research cited involved correlational designs, it can be argued that the obtained differences between members of small and large organizations are due to some correlate of organization size other than degree of manning.[4] Moreover, there is some basis for questioning the adequacy of the data which have been interpreted as showing a direct relationship between degree of manning of organization behavior settings and organization size. Barker's (1960) conception of degree of manning is that of the relationship between number of available personnel and the number of essential tasks in a

behavior setting. However, the traditional operational definition of degree of manning of settings in an organization, the ratio of number of members to number of behavior settings, does not reflect this concept particularly well. Use of the number of members as the numerator presumes that all members are eligible for all settings, or at least that members do not differ in eligibility for the settings, when in fact most organizations have settings which are restricted to subsets of the membership and most also have some settings which are scheduled simultaneously. The denominator of the index, number of behavior settings, presumes that settings do not differ in their task requirements, when they undoubtedly do. Thus, conclusions regarding degree of manning of different organizations based on the traditional index may be inaccurate, since the index is not sensitive to organizational differences in eligibility requirements, temporal scheduling of settings, or task requirements within the settings (Wicker, *et al.*, 1972).

Another difficulty with the index is the fact that it provides only a single, overall statistic for an organization. Investigators using it are therefore forced to make comparisons of organizations rather than comparisons of behavior settings per se, in spite of the fact that the theory clearly deals with phenomena at the level of behavior settings. In most studies, investigators have summed across members' behaviors and experiences in diverse settings, implicitly assuming that all settings were equivalent. To the extent that this assumption is not true, i.e., to the extent that the behavior settings within organizations vary in degree of manning, comparisons at the organizational level provide only imprecise tests of the theory.

Only two studies, one conducted in the field and one conducted in the laboratory, have examined the theory of undermanning using finer levels of analysis than the organization. The field study (Wicker, 1968) compared subjective experiences of high school students in six different kinds of school be-

---

[4] At least one alternative explanation, that of rural-urban differences, has been discredited, however. See Baird (1969) and Wicker (1968, 1969b).

havior settings (varsity basketball games, organization business meetings, plays, dances, money-raising projects, and school-sponsored trips); comparisons were made both across and within schools of different size. There were four small high schools from which data were pooled and compared with one large high school. The experiences studied were derived from the theory of undermanning, and included feelings of developing competence, being challenged, working hard, having a responsible position, being needed, and others. Degree of undermanning was calculated for each kind of activity in both small and large schools by dividing the number of performers in behavior settings of a given kind by the number of attenders.

Major findings were: (a) Undermanning was greater in the small schools than in the large school for five of the six kinds of behavior settings (with the exception of school-sponsored trip). (b) Within both small and large schools, the kinds of activities varied greatly in degree of manning. (c) The kinds of activities for which there were the largest differences between small and large schools in degree of manning (basketball games and plays) showed the greatest numbers of large school-small school differences in students' experiences. The direction of the differences was as expected, with students from the small schools reporting greater feelings of competence, challenge, and so on. (d) Within the same school size, whether large or small, students' experiences varied greatly, depending upon the degree of manning of the setting; feelings of competence, challenge, and so on were more prevalent in the kinds of settings which were relatively undermanned. (e) When performer-non-performer differences between students of the large and small schools were controlled for, the differences in experiences of the two groups largely disappeared. Wicker's study thus confirms the need for investigation of manning on sub-organizational levels. Degree of manning within organizations was not uniform across all types of settings as had been assumed, and undermanning was not always greater in small schools than in the large school.

In the laboratory study (Petty & Wicker, 1971) degree of manning was investigated by randomly assigning subjects to work on a task in groups of two (under-manned condition) or three (adequately manned condition).[5] The task consisted of running a miniature car (a "slot-car") around a circular race track. It was designed for three persons, but two could perform it with difficulty. After working on the task, the group members completed a questionnaire based on a number of the consequences of occupying undermanned settings. While subjects were completing the questionnaire, a confederate arrived at the experimental room posing as a late experimental subject. The newcomer was allowed to enter and to practice driving the car with other members. During this practice session, the confederate performed the task rather clumsily. The original members were then asked to indicate by secret ballot whether they wished the newcomer to remain in the group for a subsequent trial on the task.

Consistent with the theory, members of undermanned groups, compared to members of adequately manned groups, reported greater feelings of involvement, importance, and so on, and more of them voted to accept the inept newcomer. Contrary to expectation, however, subjects in the two conditions did not differ in the standards they set for admission of a newcomer into their groups (based on ratings of minimal qualifications for the group task), or in their confidence in rating other group

[5] It should be noted that clear inferences about the effects of degrees of manning cannot be made from this study, since manning was confounded with group size. A more adequate design would have varied *both* the nature of the task requirements (in terms of number of persons) and the number of persons who actually worked on the task.

members on task-related and personality-related characteristics.

Implications of the evidence for future research on overmanning. The following specific suggestions may be derived from the preceding discussion:

1. Degrees of manning of behavioral settings must be more precisely specified in future research either by creation or measurement of the critical setting characteristics (maintenance minimum, capacity, applicants). If a summary measure of manning for the behavior settings of an entire organization is to be used, it should be based on a summation of the available personal, task, and capacity data from individual settings.
2. Research on overmanning needs to be conducted both in the laboratory (to facilitate making causal inferences) and in the field (to provide information on the distribution of manning conditions in the "real world").

Intra-Setting Processes Associated with Manning Conditions

Barker's behavior setting theory. In his 1960 statement of the theory of undermanning, Barker suggested that behavior settings which are threatened by undermanning, generate forces which act on setting occupants to maintain the setting. He did not specify in detail the nature of these forces, nor the mechanisms by which they are generated. More recently, however, Barker (1968) has proposed an information processing, feedback model to describe the events which occur in behavior settings to deal with any potential threat,[6] including undermanning, which he dis-

cusses (also presumably overmanning, although he does not discuss it). In the following paragraphs, Barker's model is presented and related to undermanning. Relevant research is then discussed, followed by a listing of the implications of the revised theory and the research for the study of overmanning.

Barker proposes that setting occupants act as if they have a *sensory mechanism* which receives and transmits information about the setting to an *executive mechanism*, which tests the information against the occupants' criteria of adequacy for the setting. If the perceived events, whether social or physical in origin, are judged adequate (not disruptive or dangerous to the setting), occupants employ *operating mechanisms,* that is, they continue to show the standing patterns of behavior in the setting (*program mechanism*) and continue to receive satisfactions (*goal mechanism*). However, if the events are judged to be disruptive or potentially dangerous to the setting, occupants will employ *maintenance mechanisms* to bring about changes to restore the setting to a condition which permits their goals to be pursued. Two forms of maintenance are proposed: *deviation-countering mechanisms,* by which the occupant takes steps to *counteract or alter* the interfering conditions, and *veto mechanisms,* by which the person eliminates the interfering conditions. The effectiveness of the maintenance mechanism is then evaluated via the sensory and executive mechanisms. If the maintenance mechanism proves successful, occupants switch to operating mechanisms ("business as usual"). If the maintenance mechanism proves unsuccessful, they continue to employ maintenance mechanisms until the potential threat is corrected.

Barker is saying that people are sensitive to environmental events (such as an unruly student or a broken light fixture) which may disrupt their present behavior or future goals in a behavior setting. When they see such an event occurring, they seek

---

[6] For a discussion of other mechanisms which seem to operate in behavior settings to assure that behaviors are congruent with the immediate environment, see Wicker (1972).

to correct the situation either by modifying the disruptive condition (quieting the student, repairing the light fixture) or by removing it from the setting (expelling the student, discarding the light fixture). If their attempts to correct the situation succeed, they proceed with their original plans. If their attempts fail, they will continue to deal with the disruptive condition until it is corrected.

Maintenance mechanisms in behavior settings may involve one person's actions toward a single other setting component, as when a teacher ejects an unruly child from a classroom, or they may involve induction of maintenance forces to other inhabitants. Barker gives the following example of the latter process:

The director of a play notes (sensory mechanism) that the behavior setting Play Practice is not going well, that it is inadequate for the program of the setting and for his goals within it (executive mechanism): the sets are not ready, the lines are not learned. One deviation-countering course he could take (executive mechanism) would be to construct the sets and drill the cast himself (maintenance mechanism). Another would be to bring the state of the setting as he sees it to the attention of some deviant members of the cast, e.g., provide input about the state of the setting to member A and member B. If A and B were to agree with the director's observations (sensory mechanism), and with his evaluation (executive mechanism), actions (maintenance mechanisms) along maintenance circuits would increase, and three members would exhibit increased activity via maintenance mechanisms, rather than one (Barker, 1968, p. 175).

Barker further points out that all occupants are not equally sensitive to all possible deviations in a setting. People who hold positions of responsibility and authority (i.e., setting performers) are prob-

ably more sensitive to potential threats to the setting, and to a broader range of threats, than those who are less centrally involved. For example, the chairman of a business meeting would probably be more sensitive to deviations from the rules of order than would the average member. Also, centralization of function may occur, so that certain individuals are charged primarily with monitoring setting activities, while others carry out the operating and/or maintenance activities. For example, the person monitoring an examination in a college classroom has essentially the sensory function; the sergeant-at-arms of a legislative body may primarily serve the maintenance function. Another type of specialization which occurs is the assignment of different kinds of potential deviations to different people. Thus, for example, the janitor in a business office may be sensitive to and deal with only a small number of the possible threats to the setting.

Relating these notions to degrees of manning, Barker suggests that, by definition, undermanned and optimally manned behavior settings[7] of the same kind (e.g., baseball games) have the same behavior patterns and programs (e.g., rules of the game), but undermanned settings have fewer people available to carry out the required behaviors (e.g., seven players on a team instead of nine). As undermanned behavior settings progress over time (e.g., as the baseball game is played), more frequent and more serious instances of inadequacy arise than is the case in optimally manned settings (e.g., balls are hit to areas not covered by any fielder, batters hit safely because infielders must run and throw further distances). These events are noticed by setting occupants (sensory mechanism), evaluated as deficiencies

[7] In this section, Barker's term, optimal manning, is employed rather than Wicker, et al.'s (1972) term, adequate manning. For the present purposes, the two concepts may be viewed as basically interchangeable, however.

(executive mechanism), and reacted to (maintenance mechanisms, e.g., giving advice or encouragement, demanding greater speed or alertness). Often the maintenance behaviors by setting occupants are multiplied and increased in strength by induction (e.g., a player failing to catch a fly ball may resolve to perform better, he may be charged by the coach, other players, and the fans to do so). In contrast, optimally manned settings are postulated to have fewer inadequacies and therefore, generally fewer and weaker maintenance mechanisms (except for vetoing mechanisms, as explained below), and fewer induced maintenance mechanisms.

Barker also proposes that the degree of manning of behavior settings affects the kinds of maintenance mechanisms which are employed. In optimally manned settings, occupants whose characteristics (e.g., motor skills, physiques, interest levels) make them perform at levels below what is required or expected by other setting occupants, are often dealt with by vetoing mechanisms, i.e., by removing them from the setting. This is because the costs involved in replacing deviant persons are generally less than the costs of modifying the deviants' behaviors. However, in undermanned settings, the costs of replacing deviants or of maintaining the setting with an even smaller number of persons are generally greater than the costs of countering or shaping the deviants' behaviors. Thus, deviation-countering mechanisms are more prevalent and vetoing mechanisms are less prevalent in undermanned than in optimally manned settings.

One consequence of the differential occurrence of deviation-countering and vetoing circuits in undermanned and optimally manned settings noted by Barker is a difference in the "prevailing direction of forces within them." In undermanned settings, the forces are inward, in that the deviant components (people) are retained, and their behaviors modified. "Deviation-countering circuits are discriminating; they

are 'against' the deviant *attributes* of behavior setting components, they are 'for' the deviant *components*." In this case, the message to the deviant is that his behavior is unacceptable, but he is accepted. In optimally manned settings, the forces are often directed outward, in that deviant components (people) are shunted out of the setting. "Vetoing forces are not discriminating; they are against the components, too." Here, the message to the deviant is simply that he is not accepted[8] (Barker, 1968:182).

Barker (1968) summarizes these differences as follows:

In comparison with the inhabitants of optimally manned behavior settings, the inhabitants of undermanned settings.
(1) engage in *more program actions,* and
(2) in *more varied program actions;* they
(3) engage in *more maintenance actions,*
(4) in *more varied maintenance actions,* and
(5) in *stronger maintenance action;* they
(6) engage in *more deviation-countering maintenance actions,* and in
(7) *fewer vetoing maintenance actions;* they
(8) engage in *more induced [maintenance] actions* (Barker, 1968: 189–190).

These eight differences are described by Barker as "the primary behavior differences between undermanned and optimally manned behavior settings" (p. 192), in that they are based on direct chains of events which must occur under the conditions of manning specified; they are not seen as probabilistic statements which depend

[8] It is tempting to speculate that the current youth culture emphasis on acceptance and love may be partially a reaction to dehumanizing vetoing mechanisms, which stem from increasing overmanning in our society (Oskamp, personal communication).

upon factors not present in the setting. The primary behaviors referred to above are classes of discrete, molar, observable behaviors by setting occupants which occur throughout the duration of behavior settings. These actions represent *processes* which occur within behavior settings, rather than the experiential *outcomes* of settings.

Barker continues to maintain that in addition to these basic process differences, there are also differences in behavioral and psychological outcomes associated with optimally manned and undermanned behavior settings. These include the variables specified in the presentation of the theory of undermanning earlier in the paper: importance and diversity of roles assumed, feelings of responsibility, insecurity, and so on. However, in his 1968 presentation, Barker stresses that these outcomes are less certain, since they depend in part upon conditions external to the settings, such as the prior experiences and personalities of the setting occupants.

Evidence from studies of undermanning. The research on undermanning provides only indirect data on the primary differences between undermanned and optimally manned behavior settings postulated by Barker. The kinds of events which Barker discusses can best be studied by direct observation of setting events, and no such study has been conducted. The available evidence is restricted to differences between retrospective reports of members of small and large organizations.

Willems (1964) gave high school students a list of five extra-curricular behavior settings which had occurred in their school and then asked them to report any "reasons for or pulls toward" attending the activities. The list included basketball games, dances, plays, and other activities. Subjects were from several small schools and one large school and had been selected on the basis of their being "regular" or "marginal" students. Regular students had average or better IQ's and grades, and were from

middle social class families. Marginal students had below average IQ's and grades and were from lower social class families.

Willems found that students from the small schools reported twice as many external pressures to participate (e.g., "my teacher talked me into it," "they needed girls in the cast") as did students from the large school. Moreover, in the small schools, marginal students reported nearly as many pressures to participate as regular students. But in the large school, the marginal students reported only one-fourth as many pressures as regular students.

If it is assumed that the behavior settings in the small schools were undermanned relative to those in the large school, then Willems' data are compatible with Barker's contention that deviation-countering behaviors are more prevalent in undermanned settings, and that vetoing mechanisms are selectively applied in optimally manned behavior settings. Also consistent with this view are the findings by Wicker & Mehler (1971) that new members of a small church, compared to new members of a large church, reported receiving twice as many offers to take or accompany them to three kinds of church activities (choir practice, social club meetings, religious study groups), and also reported three times as many instances of themselves asking other members to participate in the activities.

Implications of the revised theory and the evidence for future research on overmanning. Barker's revised theory provides a conceptual focus for research on intrasetting events associated with different degrees of manning. He has again dealt with differences between conditions of undermanning and optimal manning, and has not considered overmanning. A review of the "primary differences" he has postulated suggests that in some instances, the direction of undermanning-optimal manning differences would be the same as adequate manning-overmanning differences, while in other instances the direction would be the opposite. That is, it might be expected that inhabitants of adequately manned settings, due to their smaller number, will engage in more program actions, more varied program actions, more deviation-countering maintenance actions, and fewer vetoing maintenance actions than inhabitants of overmanned settings. These differences parallel those proposed by Barker for undermanning versus optimal manning. But it might also be expected that occupants of adequately manned settings, due to the fact that their number can be accommodated by the setting and does not constitute a threat, will engage in fewer, less varied, and weaker maintenance actions, and fewer induced maintenance actions, than occupants of overmanned settings. These differences are divergent from those proposed by Barker for undermanning versus optimal manning.

Turning from these primary process variables to outcome variables, it seems likely that the adequate manning-overmanning differences in levels of participation and subjective experiences regarding participation will parallel the undermanning-optimal manning differences.

The above discussion suggests the following guidelines for research on overmanning:

1. Direct observation of events in behavior settings is necessary in order to focus on the postulated primary differences associated with differential degrees of manning. This will require the development of an observational scheme to operationalize the concepts of behavior setting theory.
2. In creating or selecting behavior settings for the study of intrasetting events, careful consideration must be given to the particular authority systems and task structures of the settings. For example, the degree to which setting occupants engage in program and maintenance actions will very likely depend upon whether their role in the setting involves supervision of others and whether the task imposes or permits a division of labor. The importance of these factors is suggested not only by the research on behavior settings, but also by the group dynamics literature (see, for example, Shaw, 1971).

Related to the issue of authority systems is the question noted earlier of the permeability of the boundaries among performer roles in a behavior setting, as well as the permeability of the boundary between performers and non-performers. In many voluntary activities, the boundaries between performers and non-performers and among different performer roles can be easily crossed, e.g., a member or the treasurer may become the presiding officer of an organization business meeting if necessary. However, in settings where the performers are paid professionals, such as attorneys' offices, the boundaries are not so permeable: neither clients nor legal secretaries can readily assume the role of an attorney. It seems likely that role permeability will interact with the degree of manning of a behavior setting to affect the kinds of events which occur within the setting. For example, undermanning in a role with a non-permeable boundary will stimulate a search for qualified personnel outside the setting, while undermanning in a role with a permeable boundary will involve selection of one of the present setting occupants to fill the role.

Transfer Effects of Manning Conditions

Evidence from studies of undermanning. A question which is often raised regarding the studies of undermanning in schools is whether the differential rates of participation and kinds of experiences associated with school size produce changes in students which carry over to other settings. A study by Baird (1969), conducted using data from the American College Testing

Program, examined this question. Over 5000 college freshmen from 29 colleges reported their high school non-academic achievements, and then the following year, reported their college non-academic achievements. Questions on achievements focused on six different areas: science, leadership, drama, art, writing, and music. Baird found that while high school size was generally negatively related to *high school* achievements, particularly in the area of leadership and drama, there was little relationship between high school size and *college* achievements. Moreover, correlations between college size and number of college non-academic achievements in several areas were generally negative.

Wicker and Kauma's (1972) study of the merger of two churches provides additional data on the residual effects question. They found that members formerly from the smaller church did not differ from members formerly from the larger church in their levels of participation in activities in the merged church. However, the members formerly from the small church reported feeling less close to the merged church, and fewer feelings of being welcome and obligated to participate in the activities of the merged church.

The two studies cited provide direct evidence on carry-over effects of occupying organizations of different sizes, but only suggestive evidence on transfer effects of manning conditions of behavior settings. Nevertheless, the data are consistent with the view that *overt behaviors* in settings are primarily a function of the immediate setting conditions. Levels of participation seem to be most readily predictable from the current situation, and not from the occupants' histories.

Subjective experiences in settings, however, may be more influenced by historical factors which help to establish an individual's *adaptation level* (Helson, 1964) or *comparison level* (Thibaut & Kelley, 1959) for outcomes in settings. Helson's notions seem particularly revelant to the present question of carry-over effects of settings. Helson proposed that stimuli are evaluated or judged on the basis of the respondent's adaptation level, which is in turn dependent upon the interaction of three types of stimuli: the immediately present stimuli, called *focal* stimuli; the immediately preceding series of stimuli in an experiment, called *contextual* stimuli; and the stimuli which the respondent has previously experienced outside the experimental setting, called *residual* stimuli. Inhabitants of behavior settings may evaluate their present experiences in terms of the three kinds of factors suggested by Helson, i.e., the conditions of the present behavior setting, the conditions of the settings which they occupied just prior to the present setting, and the conditions of the much larger number of behavior settings which they occupied in the more distant past.

Implications of the evidence for future research on overmanning. The above discussion suggests that investigations of the effects of prior conditions of manning on present behavior might profitably do the following:

1. Consider not only longer-term, residual aspects, but also the more recent, contextual aspects. While residual effects can probably only be determined by measurements, effects of the immediately prior setting conditions can most efficiently be studied by systematic manipulation of manning conditions. For example, some persons might be exposed to adequately manned and then to overmanned setting conditions, while other persons experienced overmanned setting conditions the entire time.

2. Examine and compare both subjective experiences and overt behaviors in settings.

3. Utilize measures and/or experimental variations which reflect manning conditions and not merely organization size.

Conclusion

A marriage of ecological psychology and research on excess population effects could benefit both. Ecological psychology provides a pretested unit of the natural environment of human behavior, theoretical guidelines for what effects to look for, and a research literature which provides suggestions on how future research might proceed. Study of the effects of excess populations using ecological psychology-derived guidelines could provide new inputs into an orientation which has heretofore been preoccupied with the benefits of small, underpopulated institutions (towns, schools, churches).

Part II

Environment Perception and Cognition

Perception and cognition have always been focal points around which philosophers and psychologists have organized their views about human psychology. Although there are strong logical reasons for this, it is probably more fundamentally based on the nature of individual experience. It seems intuitively obvious that how we perceive the world and how we think about it are crucial factors in influencing all other aspects of our complex relationships with the people and things that make up our world. To this intuitive feeling, common to all of us, can be added strong intellectual reasons to give primacy to perceiving and cognition. Many theorists have pointed out over the ages that what we do in the world is logically inextricably related to how we perceive and how we think about the world. It is this close relationship between perceiving, thinking and doing which has proved so attractive to theorists throughout history and which ultimately accounts for the primary significance accorded in most psychologies to perception and cognition. It is, therefore, not surprising that environmental psychology has already, in its very short history, chosen these two topics as representing areas for intensive study and thought. Work in this area has progressed so rapidly that a special section seems necessary. These are the most "psychological" aspects of environmental psychology, and an examination of how they are treated in contemporary work may provide some clues to the probable direction of future research and theory in environmental psychology.

Although perception and cognition are at the core of most psychological theories, they have, of course, been treated in vastly different ways, both over the course of history and by different contemporaneous psychologists. Diametrically opposed and totally incompatible psychologists each takes as the starting point a particular view about perception and cognition. To say that environmental psychology has given a central position to these two psychological functions tells us very little about the specific nature of thinking or theoretical details within the field of environmental psychology. It is, however, instructive to compare environmental psychology with the most common approaches to perception and cognition in other areas of contemporary psychology. If we do this, both similarities and differences are immediately apparent. The most obvious similarity is a general recognition of the lack of sharp boundaries between these two psychological functions. Historically, psychology started with perception and cognition sharply defined and clearly differentiated into two separate and distinct fields of study. Gradually and painfully it has become clear that these distinctions are difficult to maintain under closer and closer empirical and theoretical scrutiny. Increasingly, the differences have become blurred or irrelevant. Environmental psychology seems to have accepted this trend as an accomplished fact. Although the terms *perception* and *cognition* are indeed to be found in much current environmental work, they frequently appear to be used interchangeably. Some writers use one term, some the other, and many use both, but the specific nature of the work done is relatively unrelated to the term chosen to describe it. Most writers in environmental psychology are not particularly concerned with asking whether they are in fact talking about perception or cognition, but use the terms almost interchangeably and have developed a tacit agreement that the two are, in some sense, very largely synonymous. In doing this, environmental psychologists are, as we have suggested, following or perhaps in some sense going ahead of, trends already well established in other areas of psychology.

There is, however, at the same time an equally important and interesting divergence between the way in which environmental psychology approaches these topics and the way they are approached by other sectors of current psychological research. This difference can probably most adequately be described by the familiar distinction between process and content. In most psychology today, research in the areas of perception and cognition is primarily directed toward the underlying processes. Much, but by no means all, of this work has been organized around the notion of information processing. However, structural approaches are also process-oriented as is the important current physiological research. Whatever the particular approach, the emphasis is on looking at recognized aspects of perception and cognition in order to illuminate the underlying processes. Whether the specific topic is a simple discrimination or a complex decision, the direction of attention or the nature of memory, the solving of a problem or the masking of a sound, interest has been aimed at finding out what is actually going on, either directly in the nervous system or hypothetically in some proposed model. In contrast, the studies in environmental psychology are almost entirely concerned with specific content areas. We find studies of urban perception, wilderness perception, the perception of hazards, the perception of environmental quality, to mention a small sample of the currently popular environmental perception research. To balance this strong content orientation, relatively little work is addressed to the question of what, if any, underlying processes link or differentiate these subject matters. In this, emphasis on content research in environmental perception and cognition has diverged fairly markedly from the main lines of approach in the rest of psychology.

This interest in content as opposed to process may be nothing more than a reflection of the current state of theory in environmental psychology. We have already seen that determined and important efforts are being made to develop such a theory. However, as was pointed out earlier, it cannot yet be said that there is anything approaching a comprehensive and general theoretical approach to environmental psychology. In the absence of theory most researchers are forced into a more or less straightforward empiricism which is reflected in the field of perception and cognition by a proliferation of studies of different content areas.

There is undoubtedly considerable truth in this explanation. But we would like to close with the suggestion that there may be a more fundamental and more significant factor underlying this trend in the study of perception and cognition in environmental psychology. We have already mentioned the almost complete disappearance of clear distinctions between perception and cognition and have related this to similar trends in other areas of psychology. But perhaps there is an additional consideration that is specific to the study of environmental psychology. The question arises of whether any of the traditional distinctions among subtopics within psychology are useful or meaningful when one is thinking in terms of large-scale environmental phenomena. These analytic categories were, after all, developed in a system of thought that for the most part ignored the existence and the relevance of the environment. In contrast, thinking on an environmental scale seems almost to force one away from an analytic attitude and toward the study of the total experience of the environment. If this is true, the trend within environmental psychology can best be stated, not negatively, as a failure to distinguish between various psychological processes, but positively, as a trend toward the consideration of environmental experience as a single and unitary phenomenon worthy of identification and study in its own right. If this trend continues, and the total human experience of the environment becomes a recognized and defined area of study, it may turn out that environmental psychology has moved into the forefront of psychological thinking and is establishing a direction for research which the other areas of psychology will follow in years to come.

8. *Psychological Maps of Paris*
STANLEY MILGRAM
with the collaboration of DENISE JODELET

In this report we shall explore the way in which Parisians mentally represent their city. It is not an examination of Paris as a geographic reality, but rather of the way that reality is mirrored in the minds of its inhabitants. And the first principle is that reality and image are imperfectly linked. The Seine may course a great arc in Paris, almost forming a half circle, but Parisians imagine it a much gentler curve, and some think the river a straight line as it flows through the city.

Paris, the city of stone, is the template from which the mental map draws its structure, but it is not the same as the map. The person harboring a mental model of Paris may die, but the city endures. The city may vanish through flood or nuclear holocaust, but the maps encoded in millions of human brains are not thereby destroyed.

The main problem in investigating a mental entity is to learn how to render it observable. The person's mental image of Paris is not like his driver's license, something he can pull out for inspection. Rather, we shall have to tease the information from

The research was supported by a fellowship to the senior author from the John Simon Guggenheim Memorial Foundation, and by a grant from the Délégation Générale à la Recherche Scientifique, an agency of the French Government. Grateful acknowledgment is made to Professor Serge Moscovici for his generous aid, and to Anne André, Ben Zion Chanowitz, Alexandra Milgram, and Judith Waters for research assistance. The services of the Institut Français d'Opinion Publique were employed in interviewing the working-class segment of our sample and in computer analyzing the data from all subjects. The assistance of Paris MENSA is gratefully acknowledged.

the subject, using whatever means psychology can offer to inspect the contents of the mind (Downs and Stea, 1973).

It is not quite as easy as simply asking the person. First, many of the concepts people have about cities are nonverbal, spatial ideas. They are not easily translated into words, particularly on the part of subjects of limited education. Moreover, Parisians are all exposed to stereotypes about their city, readily available clichés, which do not so much tap their personal ideas of the city, as their immersion in a world of prepackaged platitudes. We want to get at something more personal and more closely tied to direct experience.

Handdrawn Maps

To begin, our 218 subjects, drawn from each of the 20 arrondissements (i.e. administrative sectors) of Paris in proportion to their numbers, were asked to draw a map of Paris in which they were to mention all of the elements of the city that came to mind; they could illustrate their maps with monuments, squares, neighborhoods, streets, or whatever elements spontaneously occurred to them. They were told further that their sketch should not resemble a tourist map of Paris, but ought to express their personal view. Let us now consider the maps of some of the subjects:

Map 108 (Fig. 8.1). The subject is a 25-year-old commercial agent, with university degrees in physical chemistry. His first entries on the map were Boulevard St. Germain and St. Michel, then the Faculté des Sciences at Jussieu, suggesting that his student experience remains dominant. The modern structures of the Zamanski Tower at the Faculté des Sciences and the 50-story Maine-Montparnasse office tower are prominently shown. Youthful subjects, more often than their elders, include these

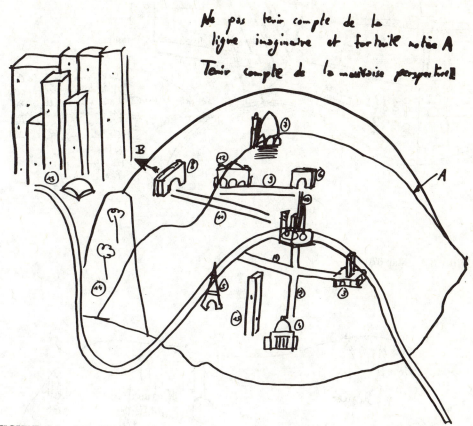

FIGURE 8.1. Map 108

contemporary elements as if the mental maps of the old were internalized a long time ago and cannot admit these recent additions. Rising in the northwest, the massive office complex, La Défense, is given an almost projective significance, as it hovers menacingly alongside the city. The map expresses the central dilemma of contemporary Paris: how can it preserve its distinctive character, formed in earlier centuries, while coming to grips with modernity?

Map 070 (Fig. 8.2). Map 070 is drawn by a 50-year-old woman who, at the time of the interview, lived in the 12th arrondissement; however, for 15 years she had resided in the 4th, which she maps with scrupulous detail, even to the point of indicating the one-way street directions for automobiles. She centers her map not on Paris as a whole, but on a segment of it that has special meaning to her. Yet she is able to link her personal experience to highly public landmarks such as the Louvre and the Palais Royale. Perhaps it is characteristic of Paris that one can readily fuse private and public aspects of life through the network of streets and landmarks.

Map 215 (Fig. 8.3). This subject is a 33-year-old butcher who lives in the 11th arrondissement. At first the map looks confusing, but we begin to discern the elements of a set of life circumstances when we examine it closely. He does not forget

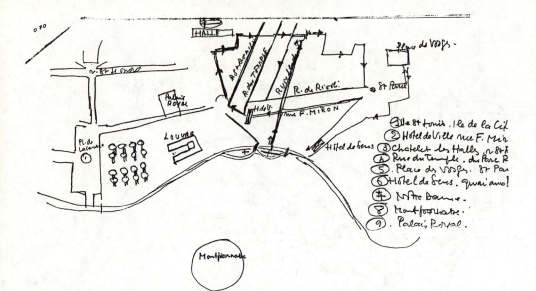

FIGURE 8.2. Map 070

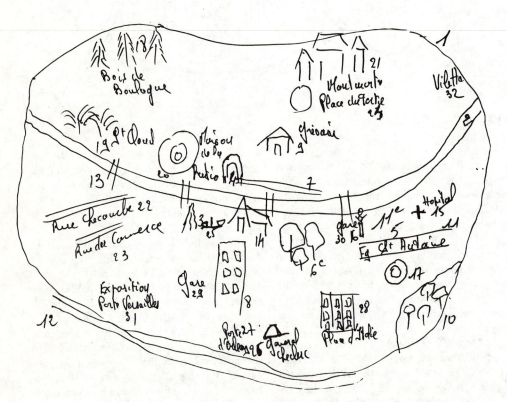

FIGURE 8.3. Map 215

to include his home arrondissement, which is something of a hidden one to most subjects. Nor does he neglect La Villette, where the major stockyards and slaughterhouses of Paris are to be found. One can imagine his visits to the great exposition hall at the Potre de Versailles, to see displays of meat cutting equipment, motorcycles, and perhaps automobiles. Faubourg St. Antoine, of revolutionary significance, is placed on the Left Bank, where it would seem to belong politically.

We are most confused, perhaps, by the inverted curvature he has given to the Seine; the disposition of elements along the river seem all out of line with reality. Yet if Etoile, Maison de la Radio, and the Porte de St. Cloud deviate from their true spatial coordinates, they do preserve a meaningful topological sequence.

Map 037 (Fig. 8.4). A mental map is not limited to reality, but may incorporate visions of how a city ought to be. This subject, an architect, organizes the city around the Place de la Concorde. He envisages a major avenue stretching south from the Place, over the Seine, piercing the Chambre des Députés, and continuing south into the heart of the Left Bank, terminating in an impressive structure (as yet unrealized). From that point, a broad avenue would sweep northwest to reveal the Eiffel Tower, and another northeast leading to the colonnade of Madeleine (displaced from its present location). Such mental maps are fanciful. Yet Paris as it exists was born first as a set of ideas, and the Paris to come is also germinating in the minds of architects and city planners. The subject's concern with problems of auto-

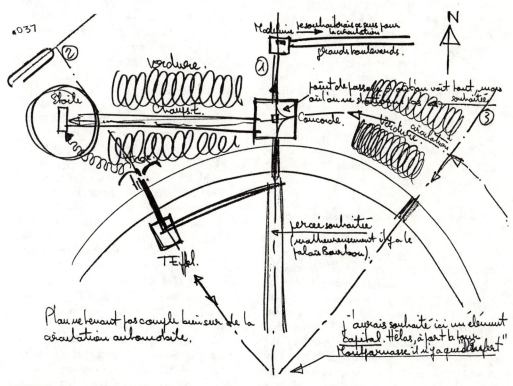

FIGURE 8.4.   Map 037

mobile traffic represents a realistic attention to the city's most severe environmental problem.

It is clear the subjects did not merely derive their maps from personal, direct experience with the city. They learned them, in part, from other maps. Street maps of Paris, prepared by technically skilled cartographers, are an inherent part of contemporary Parisian culture. Probably not a single subject could have generated a map of the city accurately showing its form and basic structure without reference in his own mind to maps he has already seen. But through processes of selectivity, emphasis, and distortion, the maps become projections of life styles, and express emotional cathexes of the participants.

Second, neither the city, nor the mental maps of the city, are simple agglomerations of elements; they are structures. It is the essence of structure that displacement of one element is not an isolated event, but has consequences for the other elements with which it is linked.

Finally, a map that a person draws of his city is not his mental map, but is only a clue to it. He may not be able to draw very well; he may have images in his mind which he cannot put on paper. He may make errors in his initial strokes that complicate his later completion of the map. But still, the sketch is an opening into his conception of the city.

Paris as a Collective Representation

A city is a social fact. We would all agree to that. But we need to add an important corollary: the perception of a city is also a social fact, and as such needs to be studied in its collective as well as its individual aspect. It is not only what *exists* but what is *highlighted* by the community that acquires salience in the mind of the person. A city is as much a collective representation as it is an assemblage of streets, squares, and buildings. We discern the major ingredients of that representation by studying not only the mental map in a specific individual, but by seeing what is shared among individuals. Toward this end, we turn from the clinical use of individual maps to an actuarial analysis of the entire group of maps provided by the subjects.

Emerging Elements

The sequence that spontaneously emerges as subjects sketch their maps of Paris may tell us what is uppermost in their minds when they think of the city. What is most salient is probably what comes out first. With this point in mind, from the outset we had asked our subjects to number each element as they drew it, emphasizing that the numbering process is to accompany their process of drawing, and not be applied afterward.

Most subjects begin their maps of Paris by drawing a rough ellipse designating the city limits. Unlike many cities in the United States, such as Los Angeles, which do not possess a strong form and whose boundaries bleed off into surrounding areas, Paris possesses a clear boundary and its form impresses itself on the inhabitants. The boundary is sharply etched by the *périphérique,* a highway wrapped around the city, separating the city from the densely populated suburbs, and providing a contemporary moat-in-motion to replace the historic walls.

Within the city there are almost a thousand different elements included in the maps of our subjects, but only one feature is the first entry of a large number of participants, the Seine. After the city limits are sketched, it is the element that far and away is drawn first. It is not only a basic geographic fact of the city, but its most salient psychological fact as well, and much of the subjects' subsequent mapmaking is organized around it.

But there is a serious distortion in the way the Seine is represented. In reality the path of the Seine resembles a wave that enters Paris at the Quai Bercy, rises sharply northward, tapers slightly as it flows into separate streams around the islands, initiates its flat northernmost segment at the Place de la Concorde, then turns sharply in a great 60° bend at the Place d'Alma to flow out of the southwestern tip of the city. But in their drawings, 91.6 percent of the subjects understated the river's degree of curvature. Several subjects pulled it through the city as a straight line, and the typical subject represented the Seine as a gentle arc of slight but uniform curvature.

Because the course of the river is made to resemble an arc of gentle convexity, some subjects find it necessary to force the river through the Bois de Boulogne, and there is no space for the Auteuil and Passy districts. Accordingly, these districts are eliminated or displaced to the Left Bank.

Figure 8.5 compares the actual course of the Seine to the average curvature imparted by the subjects.

Why does this systematic distortion occur? Quite clearly it reflects the subjects' experience. Although the Alma bend of the Seine is apparent in high aerial views of the city, it is not experienced as a sharp curve in the ordinary walk or drive through the city. The curve is extended over a sufficient distance so that the pronounced turn of the river is obscured. Such long, slow curves have, in almost all studies of orientation in cities, proved to be the most confusing, and difficult to reconstruct (Lynch, 1960).

We return now to the general question of the sequence with which the elements are set down. After the Seine, Notre Dame and Île de la Cité are set down most often as the first entries. The three elements of

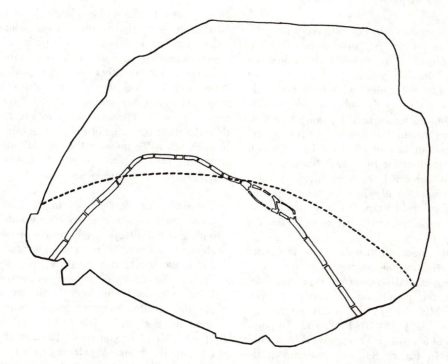

FIGURE 8.5.   Perceived curvature of the Seine. The dotted line represents the median curvature imparted to the Seine in the subjects' hand-drawn maps. It is superimposed on the actual course of the river.

the Seine, Ile de la Cité, and Notre Dame are at the very heart of the idea of Paris. Lutèce was born on the Île de la Cité; Notre Dame was constructed there 800 years ago. The sequence with which subjects enter their elements in the handdrawn maps recapitulates this history.

Unlike a city such as New York, whose psychological core has shifted continuously northward (and now focuses on the area between 34th and 86th Streets), the psychological center of Paris has remained true to its origins, building outward from the Seine, never shifting its center away from its historic root. The remarkable stability of the "heart of Paris" confers a dimension of permanence to the city's psychological structure.

The Major Elements

Altogether our subjects entered 4,132 elements in their maps, an average of 19 for each subject. If the city did not impress on its inhabitants a sense of its structure, its highlights and nodes, we would find little agreement among the subjects. But, in fact, time and again we find the same locations, showing up in the handdrawn maps. Indeed, about half of all the 4,132 elements are accounted for by only 26 locations.

In Table 8.1 we have listed by rank, and irrespective of when the items appeared in the subject's map, the fifty elements of the Paris cityscape listed most frequently by the subjects.

We need to translate the frequency of information into cartographic form. Perhaps we can take a cue from Rand McNally. When the population of a city is large, Rand McNally translates this information into BOLD TYPOGRAPHY, and the population of a small city is expressed by smaller print. In Figure 8.6 we have shown the names of the locales, streets, and monuments in a size proportional to the number of people who cited them; that is, in proportion to their salience to the Parisians.

Parisians like to say that there is a tourist Paris, but the real Paris is something quite apart. But if we examine the maps produced by the subjects, we see that time and again tourist Paris—the famous monuments and landmarks—reappears as the basic structuring devices in their own productions of the city. Paris is integral, and it is not possible to efface l'Etoile, the Louvre, and others from any intelligent representation of the city.

In scoffing at tourist Paris, Parisians imply they have access to a much deeper treasure, and choose to dissociate themselves from the city's public aspect. But, of course, the very greatness of Paris and its attraction to millions reside in its very availability as a city.

Links

No city consists of a set of isolated elements floating in an urban vacuum, but some cities possess a dense set of pathways tying its varied monuments and squares together. A city is either barren or fertile, depending on the degree to which its varied elements are woven into an interconnected web. The sum becomes greater than the parts by virtue of their relationship to each other. To uncover the associational structures of Paris, we posed the following problem to our subjects:

We shall name an element in the Paris scene, then we would like you to wander with the mind's eye to the next specific element in your own mental imagery, which we would then like you to write down. For example, if we say "Tour Eiffel" you might summon up the scene in your mental imagery, probe around mentally, and say "Palais de Chaillot" or "Pont d'Iéna," or you might think of the Champ de Mars. Whatever comes to mind as forming a natural connection is what interests us.

In this way we hoped to see how the varied elements in the subject's mental structure

TABLE 8–1.   *The Fifty Elements Most Frequently Included in the Handdrawn Maps of Paris*

Rank	Name of Element	Percentage of maps in which this element appears	Rank	Name of Element	Percentage of maps in which this element appears
1.	Seine	84.3	26.	Bastille	22.1
2.	Limites de Paris	81.5	27.	Quartier Latin	20.7
3.	Etoile, Arc de		28.	Panthéon	20.7
	Triomphe	61.9	29.	Place des Vosges	18.4
4.	Notre Dame	55.5	30.	Gare de Lyon	18.4
5.	Tour Eiffel	54.6	31.	Champ de Mars	17.9
6.	Bois de Boulogne	49.1	32.	Madeleine	17.9
7.	Louvre	45.4	33.	Parc Monceau	17.0
8.	Concorde	45.4	34.	Parc de Montsouris	16.6
9.	Champs Elysées	40.4	35.	Gare St. Lazare	16.6
10.	Jardin du Luxembourg	38.5	36.	Jardin des Plantes	16.1
11.	Bois de Vincennes	38.1	37.	Gare de l'Est	15.6
12.	Gare et Tour Montp.	35.3	38.	Palais Royale	15.2
13.	Île de la Cité	33.9	39.	Gare du Nord	14.7
14.	Tuileries	33.5	40.	Place de la République	14.3
15.	Butte Montmartre	32.1	41.	Gare d'Austerlitz	13.8
16.	Chaillot, Trocadero	32.1	42.	Père Lachaise	12.9
17.	Île de St. Louis	31.7	43.	Porte, Place d'Italie	12.4
18.	St. Germain	31.2	44.	Place de la Nation	12.0
19.	Opéra	30.7	45.	Chambre des Députés	11.5
20.	Boulevard St. Michel	30.1	46.	École Militaire	11.5
21.	Invalides	29.8	47.	Les Halles	10.1
22.	Marais	26.2	48.	Grand, Petit Palais	9.7
23.	Buttes Chaumont	24.4	49.	La Défense	9.7
24.	Sacre Coeur	23.4	50.	Grands Boulevards	9.2
25.	Quais, Berges	22.5			

of Paris were held together. The 20 stimulus locales that we provided the subjects are listed in Table 8.2.

In Column *A* we have indicated the number of links forged between each stimulus location and some other location by at least 10 percent of the subjects. For example, there are six such links for the Arc de Triomphe, five links for the Tour Eiffel, and so on. There is a great difference in the degree to which the different stimulus locales are embedded in a context of mental associations. Among the most richly embedded sites are Arc de Triomphe, l'Opéra, Notre Dame de Paris, and Panthéon. The most weakly embedded are Buttes Chaumont and Père Lachaise.

The structure of associations for two of the stimulus locales is shown in the "molecules" in Figure 8.7.

By linking up the separate molecules at points of overlap, one may map the entire network of associations for the city, the reticulate structure of its images.

A related measure of the "embeddedness" is the proportion of subjects who are unable to give any association whatsoever to a stimulus location. As Column *B* of Table 8.2 shows, this varies greatly from one location to the next. Fewer than one

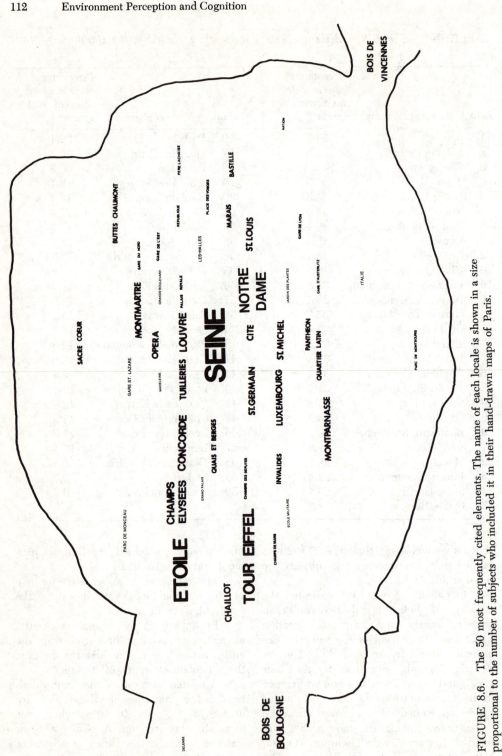

FIGURE 8.6.   The 50 most frequently cited elements. The name of each locale is shown in a size proportional to the number of subjects who included it in their hand-drawn maps of Paris.

TABLE 8–2.   *Mental Links to Twenty Stimulus Locales*

Stimulus locales	A Number of locales with which stimulus locale is linked by 10% of the subjects or more	B Percentage of subjects who fail to link stimulus locale with any other locale
Arc de Triomphe	6	.5
Notre Dame	6	1.8
Place de la Concorde	6	1.8
L'Opéra	6	2.3
Sacre Coeur	2	2.3
Le Louvre	4	3.7
Tour Eiffel	5	5.1
Gare St. Lazare	1	5.5
Bois de Vincennes	3	6.9
Porte St. Martin	2	11.0
Le Panthéon	6	11.5
Tour St. Jacques	4	12.4
Place de la Nation	2	13.3
École Militaire	3	13.8
Place de la République	2	16.1
Lion de Belfort	3	18.4
Parc des Buttes Chaumont	0	20.2
Place d'Italie	3	22.5
Père Lachaise	0	27.0
Parc de Montsouris	1	34.0

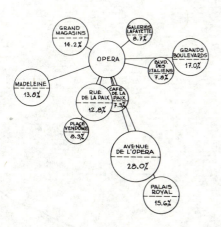

Figure 8.7a: Associations to *Opéra*. Shows all associations to the stimulus locale *Opéra* made by at least 5 percent of the subjects.

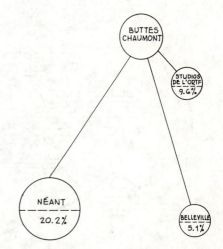

FIGURE 8.7b: Associations to *Buttes Chaumont*. Shows all associations to the stimulus locale *Buttes Chaumont* made by at least 5 percent of the subjects.

percent of the subjects were unable to provide an association to the Arc de Triomphe, while 34 percent were unable to provide any association for the Parc de Montsouris. The former is a well-embedded element, while the latter is poorly articulated with the main structure of the city.

Although we asked our subjects to concentrate on geographic, visual elements, they often included purely social or historical features such as "La Guillotine" or "clochards," as if these elements could simply not be excluded from the meaning of a particular locale. We used this information to create an additional map (Fig. 8.8); one in which each locale is surrounded by the verbal associations it stimulated.

Recognition of Parisian Scenes

There are numerous representations of things that a person cannot externalize

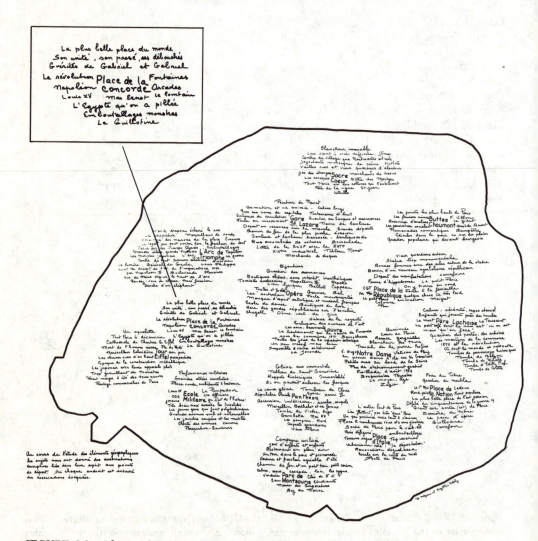

FIGURE 8.8.   Ideational associations to several stimulus locales.

through drawing or verbal recall. He may be able to see a loved one's face in his mind's eye without being able to draw it. But he is likely to recognize it if shown a photograph. And the same is true of cities. A person may have encoded visual aspects of the city that can be most sensitively uncovered through recognition, that is by seeing if the person can match an external stimulus to some memory of it. Accordingly, to supplement the method of "free recall" used in drawing maps of the city, we presented subjects with 40 photographed scenes of Paris, which they were asked to identify. Correct recognition shows that a scene is an active part of the subject's representation of the city, even if he did not sponstaneously include it in his map.

We scored recognition by noting the percentage of subjects who correctly identified the scene, and as Table 8.3 shows, this ranged from 100 percent for Etoile to under 5 percent for Rue de Cambrai and Place d'Israël. We may touch briefly on four aspects of the recognition data: *icons of the city, confusions, class differences,* and *paradoxical unknowns.* (See Figure 8.9.)

Icons of the City

All of the groups shown the photographs, whether professionals or workers, recognized the same four scenes with the great-

TABLE 8–3. *Recognition of Parisian Scenes*

Scenes Shown to Group I[a]	Percentage of S's who correctly identified scene	Scenes Shown to Group II[a]	Percentage of S's who correctly identified scene
Etoile	100.0	Place Denfert	
Notre Dame	98.5	Rochereau	94.4
Place de la Concorde	97.0	Place Vendôme	90.8
Palais de Chaillot	93.3	Place de la République	81.6
Mosque	82.8	Parc Monceau	80.5
Louvre (Porte la Tremoille)	79.0	Place du Tertre	79.3
Places des Vosges	70.1	Porte de St. Cloud	61.0
Porte St. Martin	67.0	Square du Vert Galant	59.8
UNESCO (Place Fontenoy)	52.0	École des Beaux Arts	58.7
Musée des Arts		Place des Victoires	56.3
Africains	46.4	Arène de Lutèce	55.2
Place Furstenberg	44.8	Fontaine Molière	55.2
Parc de Montsouris	44.8	Eglise d'Alésia	54.0
Eglise Orthodox	44.8	Fontaine des Innocents	49.4
Place Félix Eboué	39.6	Place St. André des Arts	31.0
Avenue d'Italie	36.6	Mémorial du Martyr Juif	23.0
Monument de la		Passage Dellesert	20.7
Déportation	30.6	Avenue Clichy	16.1
Fontaine Cuvier	37.7	Place Rodin	12.6
Avenue des Gobelins	7.5	Pont Bir Hakeim	12.6
Place d'Israël	4.5	Place de Santiago	6.9
Rue de Cambrai	4.5		

[a] Twenty scenes were shown to each of two groups of subjects, studied at different times.

Icon: Etoile, 100% correct Identification

Confusion: Porte St. Martin, 67.0% identification. Often misidentified as Porte St. Denis.

Class Differences: UNESCO at Place Fontenoy. 52% correct overall. Professionals: 67%; Workers: 24%.

Unknown: Place D'Israël, identified by 4.5% of the S's.

FIGURE 8.9.   Representative photographs used in the recognition test.

est degree of accuracy: Etoile, Notre Dame, Place de la Concorde, and the Palais de Chaillot. What distinguishes these scenes is not so much their beauty, as their monumentality, special historic significance, and scenic grandeur. (To this group one could, without doubt, add the Eiffel Tower, and Sacre Coeur [Sondages, 1951]). Each of these scenes has come to be indelibly associated with Paris, not merely within the city, but abroad as well. One might conclude, therefore, that those sites which are universally identifiable among residents serve as internationally circulated symbols of the city. This formula is, however, too simple: Denfert Rochereau, with its imposing Lion de Belfort, though recognized by 94 percent of the subjects, in no way functions as an international symbol. (This raises questions of urban iconography too complex to discuss here. We may also ponder why Paris is so richly endowed with exportable symbols, while such great urban centers as São Paulo and Chicago lack them entirely.)

Confusions

In the mental representation of a city, two quite separate geographic locales may be collapsed into a single imagined site. Thus, many Parisians mentally combined the nonsectarian Monument de la Déportation (located on Île de la Cité) and the Mémorial du Martyr Juif (located in St. Paul) into a single locale, believing there is only one such monument, rather than the two that actually exist. Porte St. Martin was frequently misidentified as Porte St. Denis, highlighting the psychologically interchangeable character of the two arches.

Class Differences

Class factors shape the maps of the subjects by segregating rich and poor residentially, and also by transmitting a class-linked culture to various segments of the

population. Thus, Place Furstenberg is recognized by 59 percent of the professional subjects, but only 17 percent of the workers; UNESCO headquarters by 67 percent versus 24 percent. The icons of the city, however, are recognized equally by all groups, serving as integrative elements in the urban culture.

Paradoxical Unknowns

When a city is deficient in fine squares and architecture, mediocre locales may be widely publicized because they are the best of what is available. But in Paris, a surfeit of riches creates an opposite situation. Competition for a place in the mind is fierce; many worthy locales are excluded. Thus Place Felix Eboué, which displays an impressive and monumental fountain, is recognized by less than half of the Parisians, while 87 percent of the subjects cannot identify Place Rodin. Place d'Israël, which could serve as an architectural showpiece, sinks to virtual obscurity—identified by only 4.47 percent of the subjects. Locational factors play some part. But more critically, the data highlight how the mental maps which Parisians internalize are not only individual products, but are in an important degree social constructions. Any one of these last scenes possesses sufficient aesthetic value to serve as a widely known feature of the Parisian environment. If society chose to publicize Place Rodin, the square could become as famous as (God forbid) the urinating statue of Brussels. Social definition determines, through selectivity and reiteration, which features of the city acquire salience in the mental maps of the inhabitants.

Paris, Known and Unknown

The photographic recognition test tells us about the knowledge of specific landmarks, but we wanted a more general picture of the known and unknown parts of the city.

Accordingly, we provided each subject with an illustrated map of the city, which we overprinted with the boundaries of the 80 administrative districts (*quartiers*). We asked each subject to study his map and indicate the ten quartiers with which he was most familiar, and those that were least familiar to him. By combining the response for all subjects, we generate a gradient of asserted familiarity across the entire city.

The five most familiar quartiers are contiguous and center on the Quartier Latin and Île de la Cité. The next five choices accrete to this cluster, but also extend to the Champs Elysées and Etoile. When subjects are asked to list the quartier they know least well, we find a striking movement away from the center of Paris to the peripheral arrondissements.

Figure 8.10 shows how these data, translated into respective arrondissements, delineate a ring of unknown areas around the core of Paris. Curiously, in this map the boundary between known and unknown parts of the city retraces part of the route of the last wall of Paris, the Férmiers Généraux. Although the wall was torn down in 1859 its effects endure in the mental maps of contemporary Parisians, with the least familiar parts of the city lying outside the boundary where the wall once stood.

The residential patterns of Paris create a class basis to known and unknown parts of the city. Generally speaking, the wealthier segments of the population live in the western part of the city, and the poorer classes live in the east. It is not surprising, therefore, that the areas least known to the working-class subjects should differ from those of the middle-class professionals, as Table 8.4 shows. While all of the least-

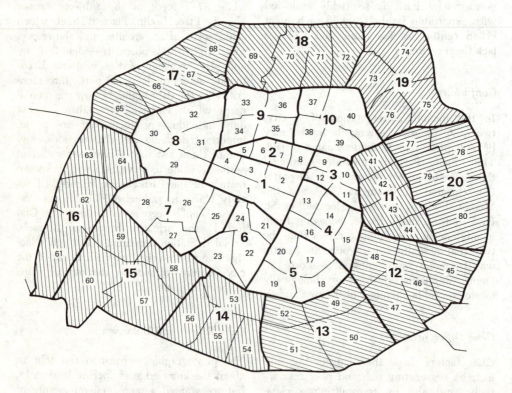

FIGURE 8.10.   Least known areas of Paris, by arrondissement. The shaded portion of the map indicates the ten arrondissments that contain areas subjects indicate they know least well.

TABLE 8–4. *Least Familiar Arrondissements by Social Class*

| | Middle Class | | Working Class | |
Rank	Arrond.	Percentage of Ss indicating a quartier in this arrondissement to be among the least familiar	Arrond.	Percentage of Ss indicating a quartier in this arrondissement to be among the least familiar
1	20	69.3	15	61.0
2	19	68.2	13	58.5
3	12	62.5	17	53.7
4	18	61.4	16	51.2

known arrondissements are on the periphery of Paris, there is no overlap between the class-linked perceptions. It is only a knowledge of the central arrondissements of Paris that is claimed by both groups.

Social Perceptions

While ethnic turfs have a salient place in the representation of New York, with exception of the North African districts, and the Jewish quarter around St. Paul, they do not figure greatly in the mental maps of Paris. The city does not have the multiple ethnic concentrations found in New York, and areas are not selectively highlighted and affixed with an ethnic label, a process Suttles (1972) has shown to be important in the definition of ethnic neighborhoods. In pre–World War II Paris, areas of the city were rich in residents from particular provinces, and subjects continue to identify the quartiers around Gare de Montparnasse as *Paris des Bretons*. On the other hand, the Chinese community that once flourished behind the Gare de Lyon receives no prepresentation in the maps of contemporary Parisians.

Subjects locate the very poor in the northeastern districts; while the wealthy are overwhelmingly situated in the 16th arrondissement, at the western edge of the city (Table 8.5). This is a sharply differentiated perception, with no geographic overlap between the two groups. The criminally dangerous areas of Paris are identified with the 18th and 19th arrondissements, with the greatest threat to personal safety ascribed to the Goutte d'Or quartier, which houses many North African immigrants.

The responses to several purely personal questions appear to derive from this rough socioeconomic map. When subjects are asked if there is a quartier they would refuse to live in under any circumstances, they cite the quartiers around Goutte d'Or (quartiers 71, 72, 73, 74).

The deepest affection for the city is reserved for its central historic areas, with the best-liked quartiers falling out in the 6th, followed by 4th, 1st, and 5th arrondissements. Along related lines, subjects were asked to engage in a pleasant financial fantasy: *Suppose you came into a great deal of money, and could afford to live anywhere in Paris. Where would you move to?* The arrondissements exerting the greatest residential attraction are, in order of popularity, 6th, 4th, 7th, and 16th. The single most desired location is the Île de St. Louis. Popular with all groups, and particularly so with younger Parisians, 36.2 percent of those under 30 speculated that if they had a financial windfall they would move there, to the island in the middle of Paris, but removed from the bustle.

The subjects' attachment to "le vieux Paris" is expressed in a somewhat different form when they responded to the following

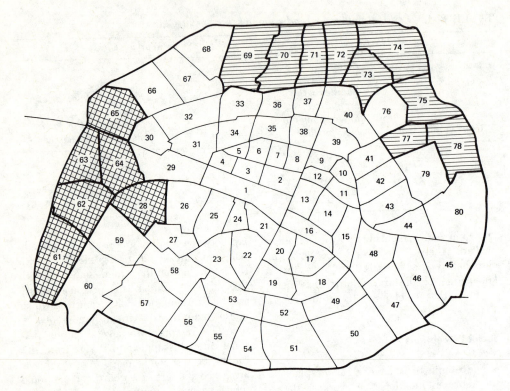

FIGURE 8.11. Perception of rich and poor areas. Shows all quartiers which at least 10 percent of the subjects indicated as among the rich (grating) or poor (stripes) areas of Paris.

hypothetical problem: *Suppose you were about to go into exile, and had a chance to take only one last walk through the city. What would be your itinerary?* Each subject was given an unmarked street map and was asked to trace a final itinerary of not more than three kilometers. Many idiosyncratic routes appeared as subjects traced paths through childhood neighborhoods, sites of romantic encounters, and so on. But when we focus on the commonly selected paths (any street segment tranversed by at least five of the subjects) a definite pattern is revealed (Fig. 8.13). The densest network of walks are along the quais of the Seine, on the Île St. Louis, Île de la Cité and the Quartier Latin. (Smaller numbers of subjects chose to stroll through Place des Vosges, Palais Royale, and Montmartre.) And a considerable group chose

to walk along the Champ Elysées. Paris contains more than 3,500 streets within its limits (Hillairet, 1964), but the concentration of choices on only a score of these reveals the few which have a shared emotional significance.

Intuitions and Secrets

Before drawing the report to a close, we wish to make a few additional observations about Paris and the processes of its mental representation. A person may know many things about a city while not being aware that he possesses such knowledge; and such implicit knowledge may be widely shared. Consider the following hypothetical situation we presented to the subjects:

Suppose you were to meet someone in

TABLE 8–5. *Qualities Ascribed to Different Areas of Paris*

| Qualities | The arrondissements in which the quality on the left is most frequently located, ranked 1–4, and the percentage of all subjects locating the quality within this arrondissement.[a] (N=218) | | | |
	1	2	3	4
Paris of the rich	16	17	8	7
	87.6%	20.6%	18.3%	17.0%
Paris of the poor	18	19	20	13
	38.5%	31.7%	29.8%	11.0%
Dangerous Paris	18	9	10	19
	38.5%	31.7%	29.8%	11.0%
Areas you like best	6	4	1	5
	70.6%	65.1%	57.8%	51.4%
Areas in which you would refuse to live under any circumstances	18	19	10	8
	37.2%	27.1%	18.3%	17.0%
Areas you know best	6	1	5	8
	73.9%	61.5%	58.3%	57.8%
Areas you know least well	20	13	19	18
	60.1%	58.7%	57.3%	55.0%
Snobbish Paris	16	6	8	17
	49.1%	15.1%	14.7%	9.6%
"Paris des Bretons"	15	4	6	—
	50.0%	34.9%	23.4%	—
Where you would move if you became wealthy	6	4	7	16
	33.9%	31.2%	24.8%	21.6%
Friendlier, more relaxed atmosphere	6	5	4	7
	30.3%	22.5%	18.3%	14.7%
Greatest loss of pleasant qualities because of urban renewal	15	1	13	6
	43.1%	14.2%	13.8%	10.1%

[a] Subjects were instructed to give all responses in terms of quartiers and not arrondissements. (There are four quartiers in each arrondissement.) But we have integrated the results and presented them in terms of arrondissements for ease of comprehension, particularly for those familiar with the city.

Paris, a person whom you had never met before, and you knew the exact date and time of the meeting, but not the place. Assume the person you were to meet operated under the similar handicap of not knowing where you would wait for him. Where in Paris would you wait so as to maximize the chances of encountering the person?

Subjects were encouraged to use their intuition in answering the question, but this did not prevent many of them from denouncing the question as illogical, stupid, and unanswerable. But those who responded (N = 188) demonstrated that a set of appropriate—even intelligent—responses was possible. (An answer to this question may be considered "appropriate" if it is selected by a large number of other respondents, and thus represents a shared intuition of where others are likely to wait.) Two principles governed the choice of locales (a) some subjects selected a location

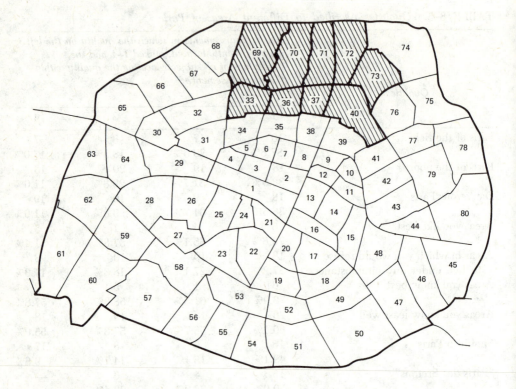

FIGURE 8.12.   *Paris dangereux*. Indicates the quartiers perceived as being the most dangerous, from the standpoint of criminal activity.

that was unequivocally representative of the city, (b) other subjects chose locales that by custom and practice had become institutionalized waiting places (much as the clock at Grand Central Station in New York serves this function).

Six locations accounted for more than 50 percent of all answers, as Table 8.6 shows. The largest number of Parisians indicated they would wait by the Eiffel Tower, the preeminent symbol of Paris in modern times. (What would the dominant response have been prior to its construction in 1889? We have no psychological maps to tell us.) The second most popular choice was the Monument des Morts at the Gare St. Lazare. The consensus generated by this question shows that the inhabitants share an implicit, intuitive knowledge of the city that can be crystalized given the proper stimulus.

A second observation is that even poorly known areas of a city may exercise a fascination for the inhabitant: thus, three-fourths of the subjects answered affirmatively when asked if there was any part of Paris they did not know well but were attracted to. (The most popular choice was *le Marais*, a once unfashionable area that has recently experienced a renaissance.) And subjects generated the names of 155 different locales when asked if they had come across any places of particular beauty or interest that were unknown to the general public. Among their responses were: quaint provincial streets off the Parc de Montsouris; Villa Montmorency, a rustic residential enclave of several acres into which the noise of the surrounding streets scarcely penetrates; the courtyards off the Rue de Sèvres, which represent the inner folds of the convoluted brain of Paris, providing a great deal more surface area than

Promenades à pied. La carte combine
les réalisés obtenus de 177 participants.
Elle nous montre, en noir, toutes les rues
et segments de rues choisis par au moins
cinq sujets. La largeur de chaque rue
est proportionnelle au nombre de gens
qui ont choisi cette rue pour s'y promener.

FIGURE 8.13. Last walks before going into exile. The black paths indicate all street segments chosen by at least five subjects. The width of each segment is proportional to the number of subjects who traverse the segment during his last walk.

TABLE 8–6. *Meeting Places Chosen to Maximize Encounter*

Location	Percentage of Subjects Selecting This Location (N = 188)
Tour Eiffel	16.5
Monument des Morts (Gare St. Lazare)	8.0
Etoile	7.4
Opéra	7.4
Blvd. St. Germain	6.9
Notre Dame	6.9
Blvd., Pl. St. Michel	6.9

a mere skimming of the surface would suggest; Canal St. Martin; Place des Peupliers; Cour du Rohan, and numerous others. Many of the so-called "secret places of beauty" were actually cited by a large number of subjects, yet more important is the

subject's attitude that the city yields some secrets to him alone, and that Paris is intricate, variegated, and inexhaustible in its offerings.

But it is false to end this report as a panegyric. For many Parisians assert that the city is declining in quality, succumbing to vehicular pollution, noise, and the flight of artisans from the city; they assert that urban renewal is destroying a good deal of the beauty of Paris, and they locate its worst effects in the 15th, 1st, and 13th arrondissements, where modern apartment buildings and office towers have replaced the greater charm, but also the greater decrepitude, of the older structures.

The problem for modern Paris, then, is to learn something about the transmutation of charm into its contemporary forms, and to learn it quickly, before the old is brutally replaced by the new, and only the street patterns remain.

Appendix

Distribution of subjects by Sex and Arrondissement

Arrondissement	Percentage of Subjects in Study (N = 218)			Percentage Distribution According to 1968 Census
	Men	Women	Total	
1	1.6	2.2	1.8	1.3
2	0.8	2.2	1.4	1.4
3	3.2	1.1	2.3	2.2
4	4.8	1.1	3.2	2.2
5	4.0	4.3	4.1	3.2
6	2.4	1.1	1.8	2.7
7	4.8	2.2	3.7	3.4
8	2.4	3.3	2.8	2.7
9	2.4	5.4	3.7	3.4
10	4.8	4.3	4.6	4.5
11	6.3	4.3	5.5	7.0
12	8.7	4.3	6.9	6.1
13	4.0	4.3	4.1	5.8
14	7.1	6.5	6.9	6.2
15	8.7	12.0	10.1	9.1
16	8.7	5.4	7.3	8.4
17	7.1	8.7	7.8	8.3
18	7.1	14.1	10.1	9.4
19	6.3	5.4	6.0	5.5
20	4.8	7.6	6.0	7.2

9. Ecological and Cultural Factors in Spatial Perceptual Development
J. W. BERRY

It is once again a legitimate enterprise for behavioural scientists to investigate the possible role of ecology in shaping human behaviour. Long gone is the environmental determinism which was so easily discarded; workers in both psychology and anthropology have returned now to an ecological perspective, taking care, however, to detail their inquiry and to avoid generalizations. For psychology, Brunswik (Hammond, 1966), Barker (1965, 1968) and Wohlwill (1966, 1970), and for anthropology, Steward (1955), Helm (1962), Rappaport (1967) and Vayda (1969) have all attempted to comprehend the nature of ecological-behavioural interactions.

In its weakest form the approach merely asserts that behavioural and ecological variables interact in some systematic way (cf. Vayda and Rappaport, 1968), and in its strongest (not currently espoused), it would assert some ecological determination of behavior. In its moderate forms, it asserts

Reprinted from *Canadian Journal of Behavioural Science*, 1971, 3 (4), 324–336, by permission of the author and the Canadian Psychological Association.

Paper delivered at a Symposium on Cross-Cultural Research held by the Centre for the Study of Human Abilities, Memorial University, St. John's, Newfoundland, 29 and 30 October 1970.

The paper is an empirical and theoretical extension of work originally published in 1966, and includes data and ideas stemming from recent fieldwork in Australia and New Guinea. A further extension is being made in the form of a monograph, exploring more fully than is possible here the interaction in the data and their theoretical implications.

The research was made possible by grants from the Canada Council, the Government of Quebec, University Research Committees of the University of Sydney and of Queen's University, and by the Australian Research Grants Committee.

the ecological limitation of behavioural development (e.g. Meggars, 1954), the ecological source of the probability of behaviour (e.g. Brunswick, in Hammond, 1966) or the behavioural adaptation to ecological pressures; it is this latter version which will be explored in this paper.

For psychologists the role of ecological factors is basic to our science (e.g. in Stimulus-Response theory); however, we have usually explored these ecological-behavioural interactions from a molecular point of view. The molar approach, which characterizes the present study, examines not only the fleeting ecology (the Stimulus) but also the long-term impact on the development of the organism of the persistent and surrounding ecology, more usually termed the physical environment.

The model in Figure 9–1 exemplifies this molar approach. The overriding arrow indicates the conventional stimulus impinging on the individual, as well as the culturally unmediated expectancies based on previous interactions with the environment. The underriding arrow illustrates the potential transformation that the organism can make on his physical surrounds, either through the conventional Response or through group activity such as Technology. The intermediate bonds indicate four of the numerous possible mediating factors present in all mankind:

(i) Culture: within this model, culture is viewed as a group's adaptation to recurrent ecological pressures (cf. Vayda, 1969) and as a contributor to the direction of development of individual human beings. It is also considered to act as a mediator (filter) of the ecology for individuals. In this study particular attention will be paid to language and technology.

(ii) Socialization, although technically a part of culture, is singled out for special attention because of its dominant role in

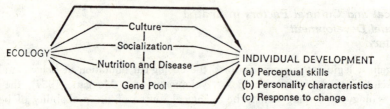

FIGURE 9–1. Model relating individual development to ecological and other variables.

shaping human behaviour, and because of its known adaptive relationship (in subsistence-level societies) to ecological variables (Barry, Child and Bacon, 1959). Both techniques of socialization and its content will be considered in this study.

(iii) and (iv) Nutrition, Disease and Gene Pool are included in the model because of their generally-accepted role in mediating ecology and individual development. Aspects of nutrition and disease considered most important include protein availability and parasites (Cravioto, 1968), while the gene pool is held to be adaptive to the ecological pressures, and in turn a contributor to group and individual differences.

This model is unabashedly *functional*, emphasizing as it must *interactions* rather than *causal sequences*. It of course shares the accepted deficiencies of all functional analyses (Collins, 1965), but gains as a relatively powerful heuristic device for exploring ecological, cultural and behavioural interactions.

It is not possible in a single paper to explore all the possible varieties of individual development; to illustrate the model then, one aspect only has been chosen—visual spatial skill development. Other data are also available on selected value and personality attributes, and on predisposition to acculturative stress, but these will be reported elsewhere.

The Argument

Originally (Berry, 1966b) the argument was that the 'ecological demands' placed on a group of people, plus their cultural adaptation to this ecology ('cultural aids') would lead to the development of certain perceptual skills. Specifically, it was argued, persons who inhabit ecologies where hunting was the mode of sustenance should develop perceptual discrimination and spatial skills adapted to the ecological demands of hunting:

1. He must first of all in order to hunt effectively develop the ability to isolate slight variation in visual stimulation from a relatively featureless array; he must learn to be aware of minute detail.

2. Secondly, in order to navigate effectively in this environment he must learn to organize these small details into a spatial awareness, an awareness of his present location in relation to objects around him. (Berry, 1966b, p. 212)

Further it was argued that 'cultural aids' such as language coding, arts and crafts, and socialization would be adapted to these ecological demands, and assist in the development of the requisite skills.

The strategy was to test for differences between two cultural groups (Temne and Eskimo) which were greatly ecologically discrepant, the Eskimo experiencing to a large degree the demands of a hunting ecology while the Temne did so not at all. Visual Discrimination and Spatial Test results were so divergent (all differences were significant beyond the 0.01 level) that an overall relationship was difficult to comprehend; were the data on the same dimension at all? Further, considerations of 'functional equivalence' (Berry, 1969a) led to the doubting of the usefulness of the original strategy, where ecological divergence was so great. Hence the present strategy is to seek out and rank a number of samples from cultural groups on the ecology dimension, and to examine the nature of the relationship between the ecological and behavioural (perceptual) variables.

The original procedure of analysing the cultural aids as adaptive to the ecology and mediating perceptual skill development has been retained. For language aids, it is argued that the presence of 'geometrical spatial' terms would assist in transmitting spatial and orienting concepts and information, and that their presence in a language would be consistent with the spatial demands placed on that group by their ecology (cf. Whorfian hypothesis). For arts and crafts aids, it is argued that their use would assist the early learning of spatial manipulations and the discrimination of detail, and the development of these techniques would be consistent with the ecological demands.

For socialization, the argument is necessarily more complex, since a somewhat arbitrary distinction is made between *content* and *technique* (although it will be argued later that they are functionally related).

With regard to the *content* of the socialization process, Barry, Child and Bacon (1959) have shown that there is a significant tendency for child-rearing practices to relate to a specific economic variable: the degree to which food is accumulated at the subsistence level. In detail, they were able to demonstrate that in high food accumulation societies (agricultural and pastoral), there was a strong tendency to emphasize responsibility and obedience during socialization, while in low food accumulation societies (hunting and gathering), achievement, self-reliance and independence were emphasized. Their rationale centred on the functional adaptation of child-rearing practices in order to mould adults with personality characteristics best suited to their particular economic pursuits. Despite criticism (Whiting, 1968) of this study, Barry (1969)

was able to confirm these relationships while meeting the criticisms.

With regard to the *technique* of socialization, Witkin and his coworkers (1962) have been able to demonstrate consistent relationships between methods of child-rearing and 'cognitive style'. Generally, techniques employed to achieve mother-child separation and to control aggressive behaviour are related to the 'psychological differentiation' attained by a growing child. Specifically, for our perceptual concerns, 'field-independence' has been shown to stem from the encouragement of responsibility and self-assertion and by parental stimulation of the child's curiosity and interests, and is characterized by an 'analytic' approach to a perceptual field. At the opposite pole, 'field-dependence' stems from a stress on conformity, from arbitrary or impulsive discipline, and from the use of irrational threats to control aggression, and is characterized by a 'global' approach to a perceptual field.

Within a functional model, one would expect to find content and technique related to the socialization goals of a particular cultural group. That is to say, one would not expect to discover a society in which independence and self-reliance are conveyed as goals by a harsh, restrictive method of socialization. Nor, conversely, would one expect to discover societies in which conformity is taught by a method characterized by a stimulation of the child's own interests and of his curiosity. This functional expectation is open to empirical check and will be examined for each society in this study.

With respect to the role of genetic factors, no data have been collected in this study. Since it is proposed however that cultural and genetic factors are functionally adapted to ecological demands, no opposition is envisaged between these two variables in their mediation of perceptual development. That is to say, for the purposes of the model, it is not necessary to assess the relative operation of these two variables, although for broader purposes one might wish to do so. The focus upon sociocultural variables (to the exclusion of the genetic) in this study reflects the lack of competence, but not necessarily the bias, of the investigator. Sample characteristics pertaining to the nutrition and disease variables were observed within the communities, although no individual data were taken. Generally data on the adequacy of nutrition (especially of protein) and on the presence of disease (especially of eye problems and parasitic infections) are used to predict performance on tests of perceptual development.

The argument may now be summarized: hunting peoples are expected to possess good visual discrimination and spatial skill, and their cultures are expected to be supportive of the development of these skills through the presence of a high number of 'geometrical spatial' concepts, a highly developed and generally shared arts and crafts production, and socialization practices whose content emphasizes independence, and self-reliance, and whose techniques are supportive and encouraging of separate development. Implicit in this argument is the expectation that as hunting diminishes in importance across samples ranked in terms of this ecology dimension, the discrimination and spatial skills will diminish, as will each of the three cultural aids.

Method

To assess this argument, eight samples of subsistence-level peoples were studied: four were termed 'traditional', living as close to traditional ways as could be found, while four were termed 'transitional', comprising samples undergoing Westernization. In general the two kinds of samples were employed to assess the impact of acculturation; in two of the four areas (Sierra Leone and Baffin Island), the traditional and transitional samples were of the same culture, allowing a further assessment—that of persistence of psychological and cultural characteristics beyond the subsistence level. Table 9-1 indicates the area, culture and numbers in each of the eight samples. Two groups of Scots were also administered the tests in order that the battery data might be related to scores from better-known Western samples.

The data were collected in communities considered to be representative of their societies, and in each community, samples were drawn so that males and females were approximately equally represented. The age range 10 to 70 years was also sampled, with approximately equal proportions in age ranges: 10–15, 16–20, 21–30, 31–40, and over 40. These two sampling aims were set so that sex and age differences could be adequately examined. In all communities, interpreter/assistants were employed to assist in the sampling, interviewing and testing. This was carried out largely in the traditional language, in an attempt to establish and maintain adequate communication.

In addition to the main dependent variables (tests of discrimination and spatial skills) individual data were collected on severity of socialization, years of education (if any), religion, language, near and far

TABLE 9–1.   *Sample Locations*

Area and culture	Rural/traditional	n	Urban/transitional	n	Total
Sierra Leone (Temne)	Mayola	90	Port Loko	32	122
New Guinea (Indigene)	Telefomin	40	Hanuabada	30	70
Australia (Aborigine)	Santa Teresa	30	Yarrabah	30	60
Bafflin Island (Eskimo)	Pond Inlet	91	Frobisher Bay	31	122
Scotland	Inverkeilor	62	Edinburgh	60	122
Total n		313		183	496

visual acuity and colour blindness; other dependent variables in the same battery have been reported on previously (Berry, 1967, 1968, 1969b). Community data were also gathered to assess degree of Westernization (to ensure correct Traditional v. Transitional placement), ecology (to ensure correct placement on the ecology dimension), typical socialization (as a check on self-reported experiences), arts and crafts, linguistic distinctions made about 'geometrical-spatial' concepts, and typical diet and disease (to assess the other mediating variables). Analyses of these individual and group data are too detailed to report here, and have been prepared as part of a monograph (Berry, n.d.). In general, the contextual (both individual and group gathered) data are internally consistent and are supportive of the proposed model. That is to say community observations support the individual reports with respect to socialization. Further, all mediating variables vary consistently with the ecological setting: rank orderings of these variables for the four samples within the Traditional and Transitional community groups are identical with the rank ordering on the ecological dimension (degree of food accumulation and its concomitant, the presence of hunting).

The major dependent variables were a tachistoscopic test of visual discrimination ability and three tests of spatial skill. The discrimination test consisted of a series of cards with india-ink figures on them, each with increasingly large gaps (from 1 mm to 15 mm) placed randomly in their sides. The smallest gap detected and drawn on paper was taken as the measure of discrimination ability, and the score is expressed in millimetres of gap detected. For all Ss, tests were conducted in a portable tachistoscope (mercury-cadmium battery operated, with a camera shutter set at 20 milliseconds) and the target was 25 cm from the eyes. Since visual acuity (tested by the Landolt Rings) did not differ across samples, ability to detect these random gaps was taken as a measure of discrimination ability, similar to that demanded in a hunting ecology.

The three tests of spatial skills were Kohs Blocks (Original 17 design series), a short form (six items) of the Embedded Figures Test (Witkin, 1950): and the Ravens Matrices (Series A, Ab, B; Raven, 1956). Although all these tests undoubtedly have characteristics other than spatial, it is contended that these are largely spatial in nature. In the case of Kohs Blocks, time limits were extended 30 seconds for each design 1 to 10, while the Matrices were untimed.

Results

Discrimination skill results are presented in Figure 9–2, while spatial scores are given in Figures 9–3, 9–4 and 9–5. A low score on the discrimination test indicates that a small gap (expressed in millimetres) could be detected, while a high score indicates that only larger gaps were noticed. For the three spatial tests, a high score indicates high spatial skill. In each table Traditional sample scores are given on the left, while the Transitional scores are on the right. The ranking on the ecology dimension is of course standard throughout the four tables with Mayola and Pond Inlet designating the high and low food accumulating extremes within the Traditional samples, and Port Loko and Frobisher Bay in the same respective positions within the Transitional samples. Telefomin (New Guinea) and Santa Teresa (Arunta Aboriginal) are high-medium and low-medium respectively in the former samples, while Yarrabah (coastal Aborigine) and Hanuabada (coastal New Guinea) are high-medium and low-medium respectively for the latter samples. Note that the Traditional and Transitional Aborigine and New Guinea samples reverse their positions on the ecology dimension, there being little ecological continuity between central and coastal peoples in these two culture areas. In each figure the scores of the comparison (Scottish) samples appear adjacent to the y-axis.

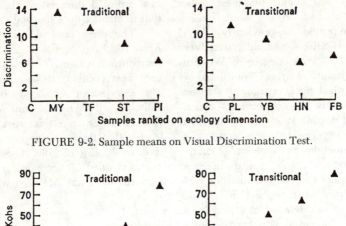

FIGURE 9-2. Sample means on Visual Discrimination Test.

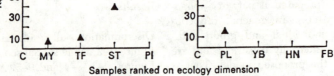

FIGURE 9-3. Sample means on Kohs Blocks Test.

Traditional		Transitional	
MY	Mayola	PL	Port Loko
TF	Telefomin	YB	Yarrabah
ST	Santa Teresa	HN	Hanuabada
PI	Pond Inlet	FB	Frobisher Bay
C	Comparison (Inverkeilor)	C	Comparison (Edinburgh)

Sex differences, especially in spatial ability, have received previous attention (Berry, 1966b; MacArthur, 1967). Table 9–2 provides mean scores for each sex and level of significance for three tests of spatial skill. It is apparent that, contrary to usual findings stemming from Western or industrialized samples, there is no general superiority of males in tests of spatial ability in these data. The most that may be said is that a pattern of superiority emerges either where male-female role separations are strong (as in urban-industrial society) or where there is no high development in these skills generally, as among the Temne and Telefomin peoples.

Age trends were also previously examined for the Temne and Eskimo data (Berry, 1966b, pp. 226–7) and may be further ex-

plored here. It was considered that where ecological demands for these skills is low, relatively flat developmental curves (from ages 10 to 70) would appear for the three spatial tests. This expectation (which had previously been expressed by Ferguson, 1954, p. 107) is borne out in both Temne and Telefomin samples: they have relatively little growth of these skills with age, past a basic ability to produce a numerical score on these tests. For the other samples, however, the usual inverted U curve appears across this age range.

Discussion

The original strategy was to test for the significance of differences between the eco-

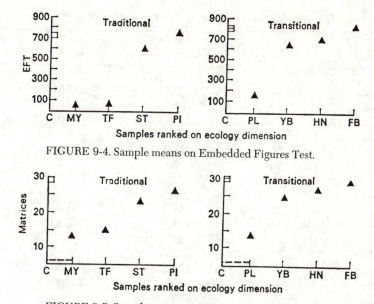

FIGURE 9-4. Sample means on Embedded Figures Test.

FIGURE 9-5. Sample means on Raven Matrices Test.

	Traditional		Transitional
MY	Mayola	PL	Port Loko
TF	Telefomin	YB	Yarrabah
ST	Santa Teresa	HN	Hanuabada
PI	Pond Inlet	FB	Frobisher Bay
C	Comparison (Inverkeilor)	C	Comparison (Edinburgh)

logical extremes within the traditional and transitional groups (Temne and Eskimo); in all tests (*t* tests for discrimination and spatial ability) the Eskimo scored significantly higher at the 0.01 level (Berry, 1966b, pp. 216, 220). The present approach to the data is merely to note firstly that these extremes are significantly different, and secondly that when samples which are ecologically intermediate are included, the pattern of the data displays only a single error in the rank ordering of the dependent variables (Hanuabada and Frobisher Bay on discrimination ability). Such a patterning of data is taken to confirm, without statistical appraisal, the general expectation that across a grading of food accumulation and hunting, peoples will attain the levels of visual discrimination and spatial ability appropriate to the ecological demands.

Comment upon specific characteristics of each graph must await specific analyses of the contextual data; however the single error in ranking should receive some attention now. The major predicted determinant of discrimination ability lies in the hunting demands typically placed on persons; however, transitional groups typically perform slightly better on this test than traditional peoples (even though hunting activity usually is diminished), and this may be attributable to the effects of Western education, especially literacy. Given the much higher average education of the Hanuabadans in relation to the Frobisher Bay Eskimo (7.3 *v.* 3.0 years), the reversal in the rank ordering is not so surprising.

To what extent do these data support the proposed model? Mediating variables of socialization, arts and crafts and language

TABLE 9–2 *Sex differences in three tests of spatial ability*

Traditional	N	Kohs mean	EFT mean	Matrices mean
Mayola				
males	45	8.8	55.5	13.7
females	45	3.9	0	11.4
p <		0.01	0.01	0.01
Telefomin				
males	20	11.9	56.4	15.7
females	20	7.1	0	13.7
p <		0.05	0.01	NS
Santa Teresa				
males	20	41.8	595.6	22.3
females	10	35.9	575.8	25.0
p <		NS	NS	NS
Pond Inlet				
males	46	76.8	720.0	27.0
females	45	80.6	754.1	26.6
p <		NS	NS	NS
Inverkeilor				
males	27	91.7	756.0	29.7
females	35	89.1	738.7	29.4
p <		NS	NS	NS
Port Loko				
males	20	17.9	228.8	14.1
females	12	11.8	15.6	13.6
p <		NS	0.01	NS
Yarrabah				
males	15	48.6	718.2	26.4
females	15	53.5	529.7	23.0
p <		NS	NS	NS
Hanuabada				
males	18	62.2	661.9	24.8
females	12	63.3	716.1	28.1
p <		NS	NS	NS
Frobisher Bay				
males	16	92.8	794.0	29.1
females	15	86.9	797.7	28.7
p <		NS	NS	NS
Edinburgh				
males	31	98.4	881.4	31.8
females	29	82.6	745.1	29.9
p<		0.05	0.01	NS

are considered to be related to the ecological dimension in the predicted rank orderings. This conclusion has resulted from field observation and from ethnographic or linguistic reports, and is supported, in the case of socialization, by self-reporting from subjects in the various samples. That is, the Temne and Telefomin respondents report (and are reported in the literature as having) harsh techniques of socialization, emphasizing conformity and reliance upon the group; at the other extreme the Eskimo and Arunta have decidedly lenient and individually supportive socialization, while the other samples are rank ordered as they are on the ecological dimension. Further, within each sample, both individual and group data on socialization content and technique betray no gross inconsistences between these two aspects of the socialization process. In each sample observed and reported content (including aims) of child-rearing are consistent with the techniques employed. For arts and crafts practices, Eskimo and Arunta peoples generally are well-known internationally for exhibiting skill in artistic design and execution, while Temne and Telefomin output is of relatively poor quality and tends to be produced by only a few specialists among these peoples. Finally, the possession of geometrical-spatial terms in the languages of these samples is rank ordered consistently with the ecological dimension. It is therefore considered that these mediating variables are adapted to the ecological demands made upon these groups, and are available to the appropriate extent for the nurturing of the discrimination and spatial skills demanded by the group's ecology.

Although no data have been collected on disease, nutrition or gene pool, the functionally adaptive nature of protein nutrients may be illustrated. We know that a sufficient level of protein is necessary for perceptual/cognitive development (Cravioto, 1968; Dawson, 1966, 1967a), and from our hypothesis, we expect that there is a stronger requirement for perceptual development among some peoples than among others. Specifically, we would expect from the model that to hunt effectively, sufficient proteins should be available, and we note that within the ecological dimension as proposed, it is precisely the hunters who get the protein. In a sense then those who need the protein most to exist in a particular ecology have it available through hunting (Eskimo and Arunta), while those who need it least have lesser amounts available through reliance on rice or cassava farming (Temne and Telefomin).

With respect to the dependent variables, visual discrimination and spatial skills, it is apparent from the data that the visual skills are developed to a degree predictable from an analysis of the ecological demands facing the group, and the cultural aids developed by them. Further it is apparent that there are relationships between the ecological and psychological variables which are more than dichotomized ones; they appear to covary in a systematic way (cf. weak version of ecological-behavioural interaction) and can be demonstrated to be adaptive to the ecological demands placed on the group (cf. moderate version of ecological-behavioural interaction). Finally, the psychological underpinnings of technological development, often isolated as spatial ability, are shown to develop in relation to an ecology, which by way of technological change is open to change itself.

10. Structuralism, Existentialism, and Environmental Perception
YI-FU TUAN

Structuralism and existentialism are two relatively new perspectives on man. They add something to our understanding of human perception and behavior. In this short paper, I cannot try to establish the validity of structuralism and existentialism. I shall limit myself to stating a few of their findings, those which contribute to our knowledge of how people perceive and organize their worlds and behave in them. These new approaches should complement those which are better established.

The "individual" and "culture" are two well-established concepts that humanists and social scientists have used to examine man and his world, including his perception and evaluation of the environment. The individual is, from one point of view, a human organism that has basic needs and reacts to external stimuli in definable ways; from another, he is a being with a unique genetic makeup, unique experiences, and unique world view. The second sense is the more important when we differentiate the individual from his culture. Novelists describe distinctive personal worlds within the shared value system of society. Social scientists describe that society and note how individuals tend to behave alike within it. Yet, if we take the first sense of the individual, we can say, with Walter Goldschmidt (1966), that "people are more alike than cultures." This is because social demands are normative, while the average behavior under any culture tends toward the center of the range for humans as a whole. Goldschmidt suggests, for instance, that the average Zuñi and the average Kwakiutl man behave a good deal more alike than the normative patterns of the two cultures are alike. The

Reprinted from *Environment and Behavior*, Vol. 4, No. 3 (Sept. 1972), pp. 319–331, by permission of the Publisher, Sage Publications, Inc., and the author.

suggestion points to the limitations of culture as a force making for human adaptiveness; it recognizes the existence of a human nature to which culture must adapt.

Social scientists study group behavior and group attitudes. They want to know, for instance, how low-income people living in slums perceive their neighborhood, and how professional middle-class people perceive downtown. The assumption is that each culture, and each class in a complex culture, will have its own set of values, attitudes, and behavioral routines. In general, this is indeed the case. It is true that social organizations and institutions do not completely determine the attitudes and values of their members. For one thing, even in a homogeneous and simple culture, the social order is never a completely integrated functioning whole, generating common ideals and values. The social order contains in itself elements that make for malfunctioning: dysfunctions can perhaps be viewed as the tears in the fabric of society which allow contrary values to emerge. We are, however, still explaining individual and group predilections within the conceptual frame of culture and society: for it is only a small step to extend functionalism to the fact and consequences of malfunctioning. To the extent that social processes have their limits in enforcing human adaptation, these limits are placed by two polar attributes of man: his uniqueness and his participation in universal human nature.

As social scientists, we tend to regard uniqueness as mere eccentricity or perturbation in the cultural norm: as full-bodied human beings, on the other hand, we tend to judge the recognition of individuality, in all its multifaceted richness, as an achievement beyond the mere characterization of the cultural norm. But I wish to put aside the question of uniqueness and turn instead to its opposite pole, the question of human nature. The way a person evaluates his work can be explained almost fully by his upbringing and education, by the social, economic, and physical conditions under which he lives. These processes and operations can be observed: they are the functioning parts of society. Structuralism and existentialism reveal those dimensions of man, including his response to the world, which cannot be directly observed. They lie outside the tradition of functionalism, and hence—until recently—the purlieu of social science.

Structuralism

The structuralist, as exemplified by Claude Lévi-Strauss, is ultimately concerned to establish facts that are true of the "human mind" rather than facts about the organization of any particular society or class of societies. The approach is not phenomenological. Its vocabulary is devoid of such expressions as personal experience, lived-space, and lived-time. The language of the structuralist is at times forbiddingly objective, steeped in the vocabulary of linguistics, cybernetics, and matrix algebra. It seems to ring the death knell of the *subject* and its activities. The individual or *existential* subject does not in fact have a role in structuralism; but what Jean Piaget (1970) calls the *epistemic* subject does. The epistemic subject is that cognitive nucleus which is common to all subjects at a certain level of abstraction. It is clear at this point that structuralism and existentialism offer distinct, though not necessarily contradictory, perspectives on man. I intend to show how each throws additional light on man's place in the world.

What is structuralism about, and how does it contribute to our understanding of perception? For a start, I can do no better than to quote and paraphrase Edmund Leach (1970), the noted English interpreter of Lévi-Strauss. The general argument, Leach says, runs something like this. What

we know about the external world we apprehend through our senses. Phenomena have the characteristics we attribute to them because of the way our senses operate and the way the human brain is designed to order and interpret the stimuli that are fed into it. One very important factor of this ordering process is that we cut up the continua of space and time into segments; we are predisposed to think of the environment as consisting of a vast number of separate things belonging to named classes, and to think of the passage of time as consisting of sequences of separate events. Nature is perceived to consist of things and events; correspondingly, the artificial world we construct is segmented and ordered in the same way that we suppose nature to be segmented and ordered.

Leach illustrates the process of ordering with the simple example of the color spectrum. The color spectrum is a continuum, which the human brain breaks up into segments, so that we feel that blue, green, yellow, and red are quite "different" colors. A further proclivity of the brain is to discern opposite pairs: red is perceived to be the opposite of green, of white, or of yellow, in the same sense that black is the opposite of white. The actual colors chosen as opposite pairs may be somewhat arbitrary, since the selection can vary with culture. In fact, red is interpreted to mean danger in several cultures in addition to the Western, perhaps because of a natural tendency for people to associate it with blood. The important point here, however, is not the universality of a particular color symbolism, nor of a particular binary opposition; it is rather man's proclivity to set up polar oppositions and, once having set them, his tendency to be dissatisfied with the discontinuities, which lead him to search for intermediate positions. In Western culture, red and green are recognized as plus and minus signs. Red signals danger. It is the color for debit entries in account books and for stop signs on roads and railways. With traffic lights, red means stop and green means go. The brain is able to perceive yellow as the intermediate segment lying between red and green in the color spectrum. Therefore, when we want to devise a further signal with an intermediate meaning—*about to stop/about to go*—we choose the color yellow.

To summarize, the characteristic structuralist elements of this illustration are (1) the recognition of discontinuous segments in nature's continua; (2) the recognition of binary oppositions among the segments; (3) dissatisfaction with the discontinuities of the polar oppositions and the search for mediating terms; and (4) the transformation of one structure to another; in this case, the green-yellow-red color system is transformed to the go-caution-stop signal system. The two are said to display the same structure. The three-color traffic signal, a cultural product, is an imitation of nature as apprehended by the human brain.

This simple illustration of the structuralist approach barely hints at the ramifying relationships that appear when Lévi-Strauss applies it to the study of culture. In an early paper, "The Story of Asdiwal," he demonstrates how the structuralist approach to myth can open up worlds hidden from the observation of society's manifest acts, including its stated ideals and values (Lévi-Strauss, 1967). Myth is a kind of collective dream, containing subconscious wishes that are at odds with conscious experience. Experience leads to unresolved oppositions. At a fundamental level, these oppositions include the universal polarities of self and society, life and death, male and female. More culture bound are such unresolved oppositions as these: in society, between endogamy and exogamy; in livelihood, between mountain-hunting and sea-hunting; in geography, between water and land, peak and valley.

Now, if we are to study the culture directly, we shall learn of its geography, livelihood, kinship system, rituals, and myths. Each can be known in great detail but how they essentially interrelate escapes us. It also escapes the native philosopher: his way of interpreting his world is to tell a story, more or less elaborate, that we call myth. This myth has obvious chronological sequences. But the structuralist can discern in it also sequences which occur simultaneously, superimposed one on another at different levels of abstraction. In the Asdiwal myth, for example, Lévi-Strauss discerns four interpenetrating, contrapuntal schemata: the cosmological, the geographical, the sociological, and the techno-economic. A sequence in one schema can be transformed to a sequence in another because they display the same structure or because the one is the mirror image of the other (Figure 10–1).

Myths serve as a charter for social action; they also serve to mask the inconsistencies between what is postulated and what is experienced. They are in this sense "problem-solving," but the process operates at a subconscious level. Certain mythical themes are believed to be universal: those, for instance, which answer questions such as whether death is final; how humanity began. There is also a language of myth: its structure, expressed in binary oppositions, is generated by mechanisms intrinsic to the human mind. Indeed, any description of the world must discriminate among categories; and discrimination, at least in its initial steps, seems to take the form that "p is what not-p is not."

The perceived world is almost infinitely complex, varying as it does with differences in individual physiology, experience, and intention. At a higher level of abstraction, we learn to see similarities in the personal worlds, for they reflect the constraints placed on individuals by a common culture. The values and beliefs of cultures vary greatly, and yet they appear to share certain themes. It is nature that places limits on the range of cultural varia-

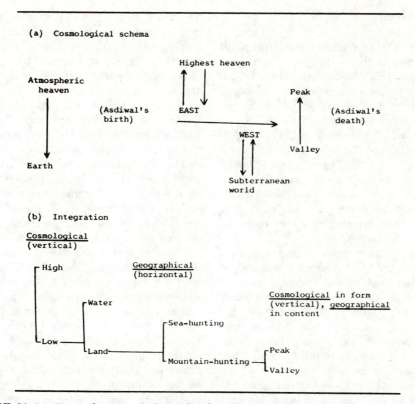

FIGURE 10–1. Two schemata of the Asdiwal myth. (a) Cosmological schema—the cosmo-logical framework of Asdiwal's life. (b) The integration of the cosmological and geographical schemata. The integration consists of a series of oppositions, none of which the hero can re-solve, although the distance separating the opposed terms diminishes (after Lévi-Strauss).

tion; and, by nature, the structuralist means not only external reality and not only the biological needs for food and procreation common to all mankind, but also the char-acter of the human mind, which appre-hends reality.

Here is a simple illustration. Some five years ago, at a symposium on environmen-tal perception, Robert Beck (1967) read a paper on spatial meaning and the prop-erties of environment. Among his findings is that geographers exhibit very strong preferences for the categories "diffuse," "de-lineated," and "right" but are rather am-bivalent with regard to "up versus down" and "horizontal versus vertical." This find-ing demonstrates the constraints that the geographer's milieu (his education, profes-sional experience, and the like) imposes on him. To the structuralist, however, the real interest of the paper lies not so much in this result as in the dichotomous variables that Beck used to determine it. The dichotomous variables, far from being sim-ply an "experimental convenience," reveal a proclivity of the human mind. Given this type of data, I can imagine the structuralist wanting to see whether spatial binary pairs, such as diffuse and compact, are trans-formable into paired oppositions revealed in other spheres of life: for instance, the raw and the cooked.

Existentialism

A common charge against the structuralist perspective is that it neglects history and development. Lévi-Strauss himself has avoided the application of his techniques to history. In *The Savage Mind,* he reverses Bergson's criticism of science by saying that philosophers, Sartre in particular, tend to give "time" a privileged status as compared with "space" (Lévi-Strauss, 1966). The charge is unanswerable if we but look at the existentialist classic, *Being and Nothingness,* which contains a long chapter on "temporality" but none on "spatiality" (Sartre, 1966).

Certain concepts in Sartrean existentialism contribute to our understanding of perception and to the ethics of environmental behavior. They center on the words "freedom," "future," "nothingness," and "bad faith"; we may view them as burdens placed on man, as distinct from things. A thing exists in full plenitude; it is solid, and its future is completely determined by what it is—for instance, an inkwell or a tree. Man, by contrast, has consciousness, which makes it possible for him to see himself as separate from things. The word "separate" suggests gap or space. It is the emptiness or nothingness which divides man from his world. Another aspect of nothingness Sartre takes as internal to man. It is the emptiness within him, which he aims to fill by his own actions, thoughts, and perceptions. Man is directed to an imagined future. Lacking an essence, he is free to fill the internal gap in whatever way he chooses. This is his freedom.

The existentialist concept of freedom and the future helps us appreciate why attitudes to environment are often difficult to pin down or express. In biography and psychoanalysis, it is usual to explain a person's hold on the present by his past. In cultural geography, we habitually note how the past experiences of a people affect its response to a new world; although we could treat the data from another perspec-tive and say with the existentialists that a people, in moving to a new world, was fulfilling projects that it placed in the future. We cannot, of course, literally live in the past; nor do we live entirely in the present. Consider a lecture hall. The audience is subject to its influences, including the droning voice of the speaker. What the audience receives from the environment is highly selective, varying not only with individual differences in background but also with differences in future projects. The point is that there are these future projects. At any instant, members of the audience are thinking of the next program and of the martinis beyond. But I do not wish to say merely that human beings can daydream. Daydreaming does free a person from the immediate present. A more basic and general statement is that although a person can perceive only what is before him, in perceiving he has actually gone beyond what actually exists. Likewise, in action he goes beyond what he would do if he were totally committed or determined by his environment. Except in sleep and in death, the human being never arrives at a point when he simply is.

Nothingness has another aspect which, in Sartrean thought, connects it with the concept of negation. Negation appears to man in several ways. For instance, man is prone to ask questions; in asking them, he risks replies that may be negative as well as positive. People also encounter the notion of not-being in thought: the most rudimentary attempt at classification entails thinking, for instance, that evergreen trees are those which are *not* deciduous. But people actually experience not-being directly. Sartre (1966) describes a situation in which a person goes into a cafe expecting to see his friend, Pierre, and perceives immediately that he is not there. The different parts of the cafe and the people in them drop into the background as he measures each in turn against the nonexistent figure of his friend. Of course, many other people beside Pierre are *not* in the cafe at that patricular moment, but that they are *not* is something which he may *think*, rather than perceive. The absence of someone whom a person had expected to see is a *perceived* absence, an actual experience of negation and nothingness, despite the fact that the cafe, with its tables, coffee cups, and bustling clientele, is a plenitude of being.

Human reality is a lack. The existence of desire proves it. The relation between conscious beings and the world is not simply perceptual and cognitive: it is also emotional. Consciousness yearns to be something it cannot be. A man desires to become in some sense thing-like. He not only observes and uses things but also loves, hates, and envies them. Emotion is, in fact, a particular kind of perception: it is a way of apprehending the world. Love sees beauty in a plain face or in a plain landscape. Disappointment leads one to apprehend things in another light: for example, grapes that one cannot reach are perceived as green and unripe; residences wholly beyond one's socioeconomic means are judged cold and sterile. Do we speak here simply of cultural bias? But bias implies emotion. Yearning, desire, and other emotional states do not merely color perception; they *are* a way of perceiving, and they are also incipient actions. We may indeed find it hard to explain how perception and cognition can lead human beings to act on the world without emotion and directed energy. As Mary Warnock (1970), interpreting Sartre, puts it, "We operate upon the world, we feel moved by the world, we perceive the world. All these happen together."

Bad faith or inauthenticity describes man's tendency to fill the void of his being with thing-like traits and thus avoid the anxiety of freedom and the necessity for choice. There are several ways for a person to mask his responsibility for choice. One is to seek refuge in identity with a status that society assigns him. For instance, a person tells himself that he is a glutton, a miser, or a nature-lover, as though he can no more choose his being than can a beech tree decide to be a sycamore. Having gained a measure of thing-like solidity, the person is then removed from the burden of creating his own nature. He is a miser because of certain traumatic childhood experiences; he buys a summer home because society expects people of his income group to consume conspicuously. The one is a species of historical determinism, the other, socioeconomic determinism. The excuses that we make for what we are and do are of the same general type as those that scientists use to explain the movements and behavior of things and dimly conscious organisms. To the extent that science can explain human behavior, it is first because real constraints exist to limit our freedom and second because bad faith prevails—that is, we tend to deny the freedom we have.

There are other occasions of inauthenticity: for instance, when we claim that the family enjoys annual excursions to the Everglades, we surely do not pause to examine our real motives. What in fact is the tie between a kind of satisfaction and the reality of the Everglades? More generally, the belief is widespread that there exists a human nature which requires that man, to maintain his health, undergo certain environmental experiences such as worshipping in the cathedral of nature or snowmobiling in the countryside. Existentialists doubt that man has an essence in the sense that things do and would deny that human life, for fulfillment, must submit to any specifiable course of action. Moreover, what is "experience," particularly "nature experience," and how do we define "health"? Is personal experience necessary to knowledge, and are the fruits of experience additive so that two trips to Yosemite National Park are twice as enriching as one?

I have noted earlier in this paper that man has the desire to become thing-like, to fill the lack at the center of his being with an unvarying essence. This is one teaching of existentialist thinkers. Yet they also believe that man dreads the reduction of his being from a subject able to command a world to a worldless object in the presence of others. To illustrate: a man, believing himself to be alone in the room, is suddenly aware of someone looking at him. At that instant he becomes self-conscious; that is to say, he sees the room and the things in it, including himself, from another's viewpoint. He has suddenly been deprived of his subjectivity and has become an object in someone else's world. The result is embarrassment mixed with irritation. To give another example, in an elevator, we are discomfited by having our backs exposed to the gaze of other passengers; hence the maneuvering for a place where we can see and not merely be seen.

In *Being and Nothingness,* Sartre (1966) takes a rather grim view of human relationships. Even in a casual and friendly encounter, one person is either reducing the other to an object in his world or being so reduced in the fleeting awareness of the other's subjectivity. Conflict, in this sense, lies at the heart of human reality. Our attitude and behavior toward things are extrapolations from our more intense experience with people. Things do not challenge man's subjectivity: they are domesticated, comfortable objects, barely heeded because they have no existence outside the human purview. Man's abuse of nature, whether it is to smother an animal in affection or to kill it for science, is easily understandable from the position of existentialism. However, existentialist thinkers (Sartre, in particular) also recognize a more unusual state, which is man's occasional awareness of the contingency and superfluity of things. A pebble on the beach, a bench in the park, one's own hand may seem grotesquely *real,* stubbornly *other,* and irreducible to the categories of meaning that we take so much for granted in our rationalizing and mundane lives. For Sartre, the feeling associated with this awareness is nausea (Sartre, 1938). For others, it could also be mystical joy, the sense of a thing that is utterly real and capable of piercing the cocoon of human subjectivity. People under the influence of drugs such as mescalin have known both experiences.

Concluding Remarks

Only a few themes on environmental perception are broached in this paper. I shall conclude by restating its modest purpose, which is to introduce two perspectives in addition to the one with which social scientists are familiar. Functionalism is our basic model for explaining man as a socioeconomic being. Structuralism and existentialism supplement this model from opposite sides. Their importance is that they are able, from quite different perspectives, to reveal the human being and his response to the world, beyond the relativism of culture. The social man behaves predictably within the norms of society; the epistemic subject structures the world a certain way without his being aware of it; the existential being experiences anxiety because he is aware. All three are facets of the same complex person. Thus, as a social man, I feel compelled to attend the meetings of a profession in which I am a member in good standing; as epistemic subject, I find myself writing on structuralism and existentialism, a paired opposition I had not originally recognized; and, as an existential being, I may yet hope to transcend these limitations to my freedom.

11.   Environment Perception and Contemporary Perceptual Theory
WILLIAM H. ITTELSON

The study of perception has been called the weather vane of psychology, suggesting that it points the direction in which future studies in other fields will follow. None of us is likely to quarrel with the assignment of perception to such a central position, if we pause for a moment to consider the role that perception plays in our lives. Cultural as well as individual existence depends on perceiving, and modes of thinking about perceiving are central in setting the intellectual climate of any time. In fact, to be alive is to be sentient. If we did not perceive, each one of us would be alone in a deeply profound sense of the term, if indeed we could be considered to exist at all. In a word, the study of perception touches on the very essence of human existence.

Periods of turmoil in human thought are likely to be accompanied by periods of reassessment of ideas about perception. Psychology is in such a period today. Consider the contrast with an earlier, but not too distant, time. One hundred years ago, Helmholtz (1962) wrote the *Treatise on Physiological Optics,* that magnificent summary and systematization of all that was known of visual perception. In 1878, he delivered his famous address on the "Facts of Perception" (1968). Of perhaps greater significance than the context of these summary works, is the fact that a single man wrote them. Today no one man would be so foolhardy as to undertake a similar endeavor. This might be dismissed as merely a reflection of the so-called information explosion, with its implication that the

From W. H. Ittelson (Ed.), *Environment and Cognition* (New York: Seminar Press, 1973).

Portions of this article have previously appeared, in somewhat modified form, in *Transactions of the New York Academy of Sciences,* 1970, **32** (7), 807–815, Series II.

Renaissance man is forever gone, and that today no single mind can encompass all there is to know about any subject. Or perhaps it has no deeper significance beyond the self-evident fact that there are no Helmholtzes around today. However, there are men of great intellect working in the field of perception at present, and knowledge has not passed the limits of one man's comprehension. Thus, in all probability there is something more fundamental at issue.

The study of perception has become fragmented into a number of loosely connected subproblems which cannot, as presently formulated, be joined together into a larger whole. We may speculate briefly as to some of the historical reasons for this particular research strategy. The atomistic and structuralist psychology of the 19th century, developed in the image of a then universally successful Newtonian atomism, had no alternative. The study of irreducible elements and the laws of their combination was the only acceptable scientific strategy, and the context within which these laws were derived was ruled out as containing any relevance, other than experimental contamination. In the Gestalt reaction, with its explicit interest in the behavioral environment and its recognition of the importance of context, one had the possibility of a study which might truly be called environment perception. That this did not occur is traceable to certain assumptions at the heart of the Gestalt approach. Perception was seen as a single, unitary, and immediate response of a nervous system whose complete workings could be elucidated in any specific example. The same principles of perception would apply in every individual case. While these presuppositions would not necessarily rule out the study of environment perception, the historical fact is that Gestalt perceptual theory was primarily developed through the study of form and object perception.

Over the same period of history, that is, the past half century, a strong current has also been running in the opposite direction. Paradoxically, this has had the same effect of eliminating the larger environmental context as subject matter for perceptual investigation. This trend has been characterized by a strong antimentalistic approach which has tended to rule out as proper subjects for study most of the more fascinating and more complex problems which arise in the larger context. At the same time, the extremely narrow definition of behavior and rigid concept of experimental procedures characteristic of this approach has driven the study of perception almost exclusively into the highly contrived laboratory situation, where object perception is virtually the only avenue open for study.

Thus, in the history of experimental psychology the overwhelming bulk of perception research has been carried out in the context of object perception, rather than environment perception, with the findings of the former providing the basis for understanding the latter. Virtually every major school of psychology in the past 100 years has investigated its perception problems in the context of object perception; has developed its theory of perception from the results of these studies; and has then transferred the explanatory system thus derived into the context of environment perception. As a result, the investigation of perception has lost the essential esthetic unity without which any pursuit leads to chaos, rather than resolution.

When all the historical trends are taken into account, there still remains an explanatory gap which can be accounted for only by paraphrasing Whitehead's famous comment, that it takes an uncommon mind to undertake the study of the obvious. There is nothing more obvious than the environment, and with few exceptions psychologists have not possessed

minds uncommon enough to undertake its study. However, the revolution in perceptual studies, which took form in the postwar decade and has accelerated with such remarkable consequences in the past 5 or 10 years, has demonstrated the inadequacy of the old assumptions and has pointed out clear trends for future work. The unity which is needed in the study of perception will be accomplished in psychology only if its concepts of the nature of the environment and man's role in it are reconsidered. Thus, psychologists need to reexamine carefully what is meant by perception and its role in the overall functioning of the individual.

Perceiving is both phenomenal experience and directive for action. Both aspects are crucial. Until quite recently, students of perception have been guided by Aristotle and have approached perception as the conscious experience of sensory input. But perceiving is actually a much more complex process. If this suggestion were offered as mere personal evaluation, it would be neither very startling, nor very helpful. However, the complexity of perceiving stands as one of the most important empirical findings of contemporary work.

The adjective "complex" is not used here to mean extremely complicated and difficult to understand, although these qualities are certainly true of perception. Such a statement would scarcely qualify as a great new insight and certainly would not present major obstacles. Nor is "complex" used in the quantitative sense of having numerous components, although, again, this is quite true of perception and strikes somewhat closer to the intended meaning. Certainly the number of separate and unique perceptual situations one individual encounters in a lifetime is huge, of the order of magnitude of the number of waking seconds in his life. But this staggering quantitative complexity is not, in and of itself, a source of great difficulty. Within the framework of a few general principles, divers special cases can be encompassed: That is one of the central features of science—one of the foundations of its strength. The need for reassessing the understanding of the complexities of the problem arises precisely because general explanatory principles for perception have not been found. It is not the magnitude of the complexity which has not been grasped, but rather the nature of the complexity—to borrow a term from Chomsky (1968), the quality of the complexity. That is, the quality of the explanatory systems used has not matched the quality of the phenomenon to be explained. It is not that perception is too complex; it is, rather, that perception is complex in a different way.

If perception, considered as experience, is complex, so is it complex when viewed as directive for action. An understanding of the total environmental network within which perceiving takes place, both as a source of information and as an arena for action, is an essential first step in unraveling this complexity.

Every organism lives out its day in relation to, and as part of, a larger environmental context. All but the most primitive organisms receive information from this context through sense organs and process it, together with information from other sources, in a nervous system. The reception and processing of information from the environment constitutes the area of study designated as perception. Even within the narrow confines of experimental psychology the problem has been formulated in many ways and has been studied using diverse methodologies. But whatever the specifics of their approach, all investigators recognize, sometimes explicitly, but more frequently implicitly, that perception is important as an area of study because it is the source of information about the environment—which is intimately related to the adaptive functioning of the organism.

To start with a teleological question: Why do organisms have sensory receptors? This question can be translated into more acceptably scientific formulations. From an evolutionary perspective, the question is: What adaptive advantages accrue from the possession of sensory receptors? In psychological terminology one might ask: What is the function of sensory reception in the total behavior of the organism?

The answers to these questions become important because they determine, to a very large extent, the way in which the problem of perception is formulated, and the variables which are considered relevant to this problem. For example, considered from an evolutionary point of view, it is evident that the reception, the transformation, and the utilization of stimuli from the environment cannot be separated. It is true that in a limited sense one can study the receptor mechanisms and the response mechanisms independently. However, to understand any specific instance, we must know the interrelationships among the receptor potentials, the response repertoire, and the environmental opportunities.

The very fact that a particular organism has survived presupposes some degree of compatibility among these three features. We rarely, if ever, find receptor capabilities far beyond the response potentials of the organism. Similarly, the response repertoire of the organism is geared to the particular range of environmental stimuli with regard to which the receptor provides information. Simpson has suggested that if a protozoan were to receive an image by its sensory apparatus it is, so to speak, difficult to see what it could do about this. Following this lead one can ask: Would a theory of perception of the protozoan have to be significantly modified if the protozoan were suddenly granted an image-forming eye? If the answer to this question is no, as indeed it must be, at least one particularly far reaching implication follows: An adequate theory of perception must be, to a certain extent, specific to the particular organism being examined.

As one considers different levels of evolutionary development, there are certain well-established trends revelant to the discussion—the increased modifiability of processes, the difference between fixed receptor–response sequences and "data processing" mechanisms for handling receptor information, the number of other processes interrelated to the particular one being considered, and the areas of functioning relevant to the particular process. These trends, although developing at different rates, tend to be common characteristics of the growing complexity of the total organism. In man, increased freedom from fixed sensory-motor pathways has made the interrelationship among diverse psychological functions increasingly more possible.

At lower levels, sensory reception is limited largely to the avoidance of noxious situations and the approach to nurturant ones. As organisms grow more complex, sensory reception enters into many other functions: distance reception, identification, communication, sexual attraction, and more complex social interrelationships. In man, this trend is accentuated and perception, in addition to these functions, acquires relevance to many other processes far removed from the adaptive significances observable at lower levels—for example, language and esthetic experience.

Furthermore, the predictive function of perception becomes quite explicit. A quarter of a century ago, Ames (Cantril, 1960) recognized this in describing perceptions as "prognostic directives for action." Bruner (1970) has more recently noted that:

What holds together the structure of sensory organization and the structure of action, is in effect, a signalling of intended action, against which the feedback of the senses during action is compared in order to provide discrepance information and the basis of correction. There is now much evidence that biological systems do in fact operate in some manner close to this [p. 83].

One characteristic which the evolutionary and the psychological questions have in common is their focus on the relationship between perception and the external environment. The evolutionary implication that this relationship must in some sense be adaptive is related to the psychological implication that the relationship has something to do with the behavior of the organism. In very general terms, one fundamental feature of perceiving is that it is relevant or appropriate to the situation in which it occurs. While few would be inclined to argue with this statement, differences emerge as soon as attempts are made to specify what is meant by relevancy or appropriateness.

In psychology, these terms have traditionally been translated to mean accuracy or correctness considered as a match between reality and appearance. This view is also the everyday, common sense view. Yet it is deeply rooted in experimental psychology as exemplified by Wundt (1912), its founder, who wrote, "for every piece of knowledge two factors are necessary—the subject who knows and the object known, independent of this subject [p. 197]."

In contrast, Whitehead (1957) has written that "we must not slip into the fallacy of assuming that we are comparing a given world with given perceptions of it [p. 47]." Bridgman adds "that it is in fact meaningless to try to separate observer and observed, or to speak of an object independent of an observer, or, for that matter, of an observer in the absence of objects of observation [1954, p. 37]."

The relative philosophical adequacy of these contrasting formulations is a matter of continuing debate. Suffice it to say that experimental studies of perception use the traditional criterion for assessing relevance to the situation—the comparison of a psychological reponse with a physical measure. Whether this procedure is useful, and indeed whether it is philosophically sound, is a function of its appropriateness to the problem, and not of the method itself. The intention here is not to examine the vast body of work in which this criterion has been used, but rather to suggest that there are other criteria for assessing relevancy of perceiving to a situation—criteria which have come to be recognized as at least equally valid, and perhaps applicable to other classes of phenomena.

One such criterion is that of consensual validation. The appeal to the consensus of a large group of equally involved individuals is perhaps the most frequently used criterion of relevancy. What everyone agrees upon is considered relevant, and deviations from this become irrelevant or inappropriate. The consensus is usually, though not necessarily, made explicit through verbal statements with phenomenological referents. The criterion of consensual validation is increasingly important as the situation becomes increasingly complex. If, on the one hand, I wish to study the apparent size of a piece of paper, I can usefully resort to comparisons with physical measurements. If, on the other hand, I am interested in the sense of size of a room, what the architects call its scale, I find some form of consensual validation the only useful criterion to apply.

There are still other types of problems and situations in which a third criterion of relevancy must be applied. Indeed, the most obvious and common sense approach to the question is the pragmatic one. Is behavior effective? Is it adaptive to the situation? If so, then the perception can be labeled appropriate. However, the pragmatic criterion implies some knowledge of the goal, or intent, of the perceiver. Here lies the difficulty in applying this seemingly self-evident test. The predictive function of perception is thus central to any pragmatic approach to perceptual relevance. Effectiveness can be evaluated only in term of intent, which raises extremely difficult problems.

There are, then, at least three useful criteria for assessing the appropriateness of perception to the situation. One can compare some identifiable aspect of the response to some identifiable physical characteristic of the situation; one can compare the response of one individual to the responses of others in the same situation; one can evaluate the effectiveness of behavior in the situation. An examination of these three criteria for relevancy suggests two conclusions: first, that relevancy has no meaning apart from the criteria used to evaluate it; and second, that the applicable criteria will vary from situation to situation, and from problem to problem.

There is, however, in addition to the procedures just discussed, a quite different direction from which experimental psychology has approached the question of the relation between perceiving and the situation; namely the role of the stimulus. Here the traditional position has been to assert the complete control of the stimulus over psychological events.

Instead of examining the history or the evidence concerning this belief, I shall simply assert that the notion of perceiving being relatively free from control by the external stimulus is an inescapable conclusion at present. From the viewpoint of the perceptual theorist, this means that perception cannot be understood by reference to the stimulus alone. On the face of it, this represents an unbelievable state of affairs regarding a process which, for millenia, has been thought of in terms of the direct consequences of sensory stimulation. And yet, the relative independence of perceiving from the stimulus is one of the most remarkable conclusions of contemporary studies.

Note, however, that freedom from stimulus control does not imply that the stimulus is in no way involved in the perceptual process. Clearly it is. It would be difficult to find a writer who claims otherwise. The questions are, rather, how the stimulus has come to be defined and what its role is seen to be. Traditionally in psychology the stimulus has had a very specific and limited meaning. It is physical energy outside the organism which, when it impinges on the organism, initiates processes, the end product of which is a response wholly determined, and predictable from the nature of the stimulus. This may be an oversimplification, but it is not a distortion. It is certainly what Stevens (1966) meant when he said that "there is only one problem in all of psychology—the definition of the stimulus [p. 31]."

The evidence against a stimulus determination approach to perception has accumulated slowly and from many directions. In the years immediately following World War II, this work began with great fanfare; and while the rejection of a stimulus determination approach has not taken place suddenly or dramatically, it is virtually complete.

The intention here is not to catalog evidence leading to the change in conceptualization of "stimulus." However, a rather subtle change in terminology which has been gradually manifesting itself illustrates the fact that the change has indeed taken place. Today one regularly encounters references to "stimulus information" in contexts where "stimulus" would have been used in the very recent past. Gibson (1966), for example, has devoted most of his recent book to spelling out his notion of stimulus information. Contrast, for example, the statement made in 1950 that, "the term 'stimulus' will always refer to the light change on the retina [p. 63]," with his affirmation in 1966 that this kind of definition "fails to distinguish between stimulus *energy* and stimulus *information* and this difference is crucial [p. 29]."

The concept of stimulus information is not always carefully defined and explicitly stated. "The first problem in the study of visual perception is the discovery of the stimulus [p. 204]," Neisser wrote (1968). A comfortable traditional view, one thinks. He then asked, "What properties of the incoming optic array are informative for vision [p. 204]?" The concept of stimulus

turns out to be obliquely, but nonetheless firmly, tied to the concept of information. One could multiply examples. At present, the term "stimulus information" is at best a loose one, with probably as many uses as there are writers. Conceptual clarification and agreement will come as the concept proves its value; here the fact that the terminology has gained widespread use is itself sufficient.

The stimulus considered as a source of information, then, is quite a different proposition from the stimulus considered as a source of stimulation. For one thing, stimulation can be understood in the immediate context of physical and physiological reactions: Information refers to a much larger context. The stimulus information referred to by students of perception is information from, and about, the environment within which the individual lives and functions. This position was made quite explicit 30 years ago by Tolman and Brunswik (1935) when they put forth the notion of environmental probabilities. For Brunswik (1956), as he later amplified his views, the information coming from the environment is never perfectly correlated with the source of the information, that is, some information is more valid than other information. The process of extracting information from the environment thus also involves the extraction of the probability factors or validity coefficients of the information. Similarly, Gibson (1966), today, although differing in almost every detail, is emphatic in asserting the same underlying postulate, that a detailed understanding of the environment as a source of information is an essential and necessary part of the study of perception. Many other writers, spanning both the temporal and the conceptual distance between these two, attest to the interest of students of perception in the total environmental context within which the perceiver functions. For example, one consequence of what might be called the environment corollary of the stimulus-information hypothesis, is the prediction that environments which differ in significant ways will lead to perceivers who perceive in significantly different ways. Considerable experimental effort in recent years has been devoted to examining this proposition, with generally affirmative results. Most important, the studies have strengthened, rather than weakened, acceptance of the importance of the environmental context as a source of stimulus information.

Consider the studies using environments which differ naturally—as in cross-cultural studies of perception (Allport & Pettigrew, 1957; Segall, Campbell, & Herskovits, 1966), or artificially—as in the long series of studies using distorting lenses of various kinds (Rock, 1966).

A second consequence of the stimulus information hypothesis has been the gradual breakdown of the traditional, conceptual compartmentalization of the various, so-called basic psychological processes. Stimuli considered as stimulation are quite specific. This statement reached its classic expression in the specific energy of nerves which provided the final link in an apparently immutable sequence. Light stimulates photoreceptors; photoreceptors stimulate optic nerves; optic nerves produce visual experience. This, and no other sequence is allowable to the student of perception. The concept of stimulus information is one of many influences which have led to a reevaluation of the traditional approach. Information is nonspecific with regard to the channel through which it is transmitted, the form, or locus of its storage.

The power of the information concept lies in the generality of information. At most, one may postulate that information can enter the system from various sources; but once in the system, one unit of information is fully on par with all other units. For example, a narrow definition of "visual information" has no place in such a system and is replaced by a broader notion of all information which has relevance to visual perception. This latter is both theoretically and empirically shown to be a much larger category. The result has been a breakdown of the rigid compartmentalization of psychological processes and a recognition that many processes which had previously been sharply distinguished from perception are, in fact, concurrently and actively involved in every act of perceiving.

The study of the relationship between perception and cognition can serve as an illustration. For a sizable part of its history, psychology, with few exceptions, handled this problem by refusing to recognize its existence. Perception was studied from the standpoint of what one might call, with some license, the external mechanics of the process according to the stimulus-determination tradition. Insofar as cognition was considered in relation to perception, it was summed up by the ancient dictum, "seeing is believing." The road to the cognitive or belief system lay through the perceptual process.

Approximately two decades ago psychology, in a burst of self-conscious sophistication, challenged the wisdom of the ages and rewrote that law. "Believing is seeing" became the keynote of a generation of perceptual studies. No longer did perception mirror an external world which we believed precisely because we saw it. On the contrary, perception mirrored our innermost values and produced a world which we saw precisely because we believed in it. Today, of course, it is known that neither of these views is correct because both are predicated on the inadequate assumption that two separate and isolated systems are involved—perception and cognition, with certain fixed and unidirectional contacts between them.

A large body of work has led to a growing acceptance of an approach which considers the whole perceptiocognitive system as part of a larger system whose fundamental function is the processing of information. More and more activities formerly considered to be exclusively the province of cognitive functioning are being shown to be inseparably a part of perceiving as well. What used to be considered simple sensory discriminations are now considered in detection theory to involve complex judgments subtly influenced by such apparent features as the individual's value hierarchy. Or consider from another point of view, continuing studies of the reticular system show the involvement, even in a direct sensory level, of such previously considered remote processes as attention and concomitant needs.

Perhaps nowhere is the interconnection between perceiving and other psychological processes more clearly shown than in relationship to memory. Some of the examples of this interrelationship do not correspond to the common sense, everyday concept of memory. The term is used here in the very general sense of the storage and later utilization of information. Two general types of memory have been studied in connection with perceiving: long-term and short-term memory, each of which operates in a quite different way from the other. Within each of these categories, two subtypes of memory have been revealed: one involved in the processing of visual information, and the other in the retention of visual information. Whether these distinctions will hold up with further study, or will prove to be merely different ways of looking at a single process, we cannot yet know. However, the four roles of memory are easily illustrated.

The function of short-term memory in the processing of visual information is immediately suggested by the fact that our perceptual experience has a form, a structure, and a continuity over time.. Discrete and erratic sensory input emerges as continuous and ordered perception. Even more compelling evidence is provided by experiments which demonstrate that sequences presented over fairly long periods of time, in the order of seconds, determine the nature of the immediate perceptual experience. Short-term memory thus provides not only a continuity of perception, but also a continuous monitoring of the actual processing of information.

Long-term memory in the processing of visual information leads into an area which has probably been mislabeled "perceptual learning." It is clear that there are long-term changes over time in the ways whereby perceptual information is processed. The role of the environment as a source of information and the acquisition over time of this information has already been noted. Perceptual adaptation, sensory deprivation, and a variety of other procedures can probably all be subsumed in this general context. Perceptual experience, in short, has been shown to influence, in a variety of ways, the later processing of perceptual information.

The direct retention of perceptual information is less clearly differentiated into two different processes involving short-term and long-term memory; but in the extremes, the differences are quite clear—short-term memory might be termed "photographic," and long-term memory, "symbolic." The distinction between these processes, as well as the confusion between them, is well illustrated by studies in the memory of color. If, for example, a color is presented and the subject is asked immediately afterward to match it from a color chart, he can typically do so almost as if the color were still in front of him. However, if an extended period of time elapses after showing the color, the subject can, in general, match it only if he has already provided himself with a symbolic label or name for the color. These distinctions are obscured, however, by the possibility of long-term eidetic imagery, a subject in need of further study.

This telescoped summary of relationships between perception and memory reiterates that the distinction between what formerly had been considered separate and discrete processes is arbitrary and archaic. At the one extreme perception and memory are, if not synonymous, at least equivalent and necessary components of the same process; while at the other extreme, perceptual memory and symbolic processes are inextricably interwoven. The precarious state of memory as a separate psychological process was noted by Kiss (1971) who, in reviewing a book on the subject, suggested that it may be the last.

If all that has been said to this point is to be taken seriously, three very general conclusions can be offered on the nature of perceiving. First, perceiving is relatively free from direct control by the stimulus. Second, it is inseparably linked to, and indeed indistinguishable from, other aspects of psychological functioning. Third, and perhaps paradoxically, perceiving is relevant and appropriate to the environmental context in which it occurs.

The foregoing discussion points to the necessity of considering the environment as a subject for perceptual studies, while at the same time suggesting why this topic has been largely neglected. This neglect has even been apparent in studies logically quite close to the environment, such as space perception. The space studied in traditional space perception is quite different from the environment as considered in the present context. Most space perception is in fact concerned quite explicitly with objects in space, their distance, orientation, movement, and the like. Space perception, as usually conceived, and in spite of its name, is closely linked to the more obviously object-oriented approaches.

The distinction between object and environment is crucial. Objects require subjects—a truism whether one is concerned with the philosophical unity of the subject–object duo, or is thinking more naively of the object as a "thing" which becomes a matter for psychological study only when observed by a subject. In contrast, one cannot be a subject of an environment, one can only be a participant. The very distinction between self and nonself breaks down:

the environment surrounds, enfolds, engulfs, and no thing and no one can be isolated and identified as standing outside of, and apart from, it.

Environments surround. Perhaps that statement says no more than the dictionary has already told us. Nevertheless, it will be considered more closely, after first looking at the question of scale. Perceptual objects may be very large in scale; anyone who has flown over Manhattan Island on one of its rare clear days knows that Manhattan can be a beautiful object indeed. But object it is under these conditions, apart from, and observed by, the subject. Environments are necessarily larger than that which they surround, and the environments under discussion here are large in relation to man. In a very general way this means large enough to permit, and indeed require, movement in order to encounter all aspects of the situation—at least the size of a small room and generally much larger. (Telephone booths, elevators, closets, or even automobiles and space capsules are environments, but one intuitively senses that they are special cases and perhaps involve different processes than do larger environmental contexts.) Large-scale environments, extending from rooms through houses, neighborhoods, cities, countrysides, to the whole universe in size, necessarily possess many properties which objects almost always do not, and usually cannot, have. And these characteristics, to a large extent, determine the nature of the problem posed by environment perception.

The quality of surrounding—the first, most obvious, and defining property—forces the observer to become a participant. One does not, indeed cannot, observe the environment: one explores it. If the observation is the object, then the exploration is the environment. The problem of exploratory behavior, its nature, function, and its relation to the individual's larger purposes, becomes central to the study of environment perception. The limits of the exploration, moreover, are not determined; the environment has no fixed boundaries in space or time, and one must study how the explorer himself goes about setting boundaries to the various environments he encounters. The exploratory aspects of environment perception can thus extend over large spaces and long time spans, and require some process of spatial and temporal summation; both long- and short-term memory are essential.

Environments, in addition, are always multimodal. It may be possible to conceive of an environment which offers information through only one sense modality, but it probably would be impossible to build. In any event, it would be a curiosity. Perceptual experiments have been notably deficient in their study of multimodal processes, and yet these are essential for understanding environment perception. We need to know the relative importance of the various modalities, the kinds of environmental concepts, and sets of environmental predictabilities associated with each modality. But more important, we need to know how they function in concert: what processes are involved when supplementing, conflicting, and distracting information is presented through several modalities at once.

A third necessary characteristic of environments is that peripheral, as well as central, information is always present, peripheral in the mechanical sense—the area behind one is no less a part of the environment than that in front—and peripheral in the sense of being outside the focus of attention. Both meanings are important and raise questions concerning the process underlying the direction of attention.

Fourth, environments always provide more information than can possibly be processed. Questions of channel capacity and overload are inherent in environmental studies. However, the mere quantity of information does not tell the whole story. Environments always represent simultaneously, instances of redundant information, of inadequate and ambiguous information, and of conflicting and contradictory information. The entire mechanism of information processing in the nervous system, about which psychologists are only beginning to learn, is brought into play.

The four characteristics of environments which objects either cannot or usually do not possess (their surrounding quality; their multimodal property; the presence of periphereal stimulation; and the presence of too much information which is simultaneously redundant, inadequate, and contradictory) already suggest that findings in object perception can be applied only with great caution to environment perception. But these characteristics are nevertheless, rather traditional in perceptual studies in that they refer to what can very broadly be called stimulus properties. Beyond these properties, however, there is another group of properties of the environment which must be taken into account in any study of environmental perception, and which are almost completely foreign to the field of object perception.

The first of these, or a fifth characteristic of the environment, is that environment perception always involves action. Environments, as we have seen, are not and cannot be passively observed; they provide the arena for action. They define the probabilities of occurrence of potential actions, they demand qualities which call forth certain kinds of actions, and they offer differing opportunities for the control and manipulation of the environment itself.

Environments call forth actions, but not blind, purposeless actions. Of course, what an individual does can be expected to be largely influenced by the particular purposes which he brings to the situation; at the same time, however, the environment possesses the property, a sixth characteristic, of providing symbolic meanings and motivational messages which themselves may effect the directions which action takes.

Meanings and motivational messages are a necessary part of the content of environment perception.

Finally, and perhaps most important of all, environments always have an ambiance, an atmosphere, difficult to define, but overriding in importance. One can at this point only speculate on some of the features of the environment which contribute to this ambiance and which, thereby, become of central significance for the study of environment perception. First of all, environments are almost without exception encountered as part of a social activity; other people are always a part of the situation and environment perception is largely a social phenomenon. Second, environments always have a definite esthetic quality. Esthetically neutral objects can be designed; esthetically neutral environments are unthinkable. Last, environments always have a systemic quality. The various components and events relate to each other in particular ways which, perhaps more than anything else, serve to characterize and define the particular environment. The identification of these systematic relationships is one of the major features of the process of environment perception.

Thus, to the first four characteristics dealing roughly with stimulus properties, three others must be added: the role of action and purpose as defined, delimited, and called forth by the environment; the presence of meanings and motivational messages carried by the environment; and the concept of ambiance, related to the esthetic, social, and systemic qualities of the environment. This list represents a minimum set of considerations which must be taken into account in any adequate study of environment perception. But how is this to be accomplished? The separate study of the various processes in isolation is likely to yield a sum substantially smaller than the whole it seeks to explain, and a more fruitful approach is likely to involve investigations carried out in the context of the full-scale environment. That is, one can either make use of already existing environments and/or construct experimental environments.

The existing, everyday environment has, of course, the advantages of being readily available, obviously relevant, and usually inexpensive to study. It has the disadvantage of being approached by the participant with a vast amount of information already in hand, which may serve to mask important aspects of the process involved in the acquiring of that information. The novel environment, particularly the constructed laboratory environment, has the disadvantages of seeming unreal and contrived as well as being quite expensive. Yet to the extent that it is in fact novel, it can elucidate the process of acquiring information in ways which cannot be accomplished in familiar surroundings. Unfortunately, experimental environments for the study of environment perception have so far been almost nonexistent.

The perception of the everyday environment, in contrast, has been studied by a number of investigators, principally geographers, architects, and others outside the field of psychology. They have undertaken the study of mental maps of large environments, the identification of salient characteristics contributing to one's awareness of the city, and the analysis of meanings attributed to specific environmental contexts, for example. The general aim of these studies is to identify environmental search, or exploratory strategies, and the cognitive strategies used in conceptualizing the environment, with the ultimate aim of developing a comprehensive theory of the acquisition and utilization of information about environmental systems and subsystems.

Answers to these questions will be long in coming, but some findings, tentative and preliminary to be sure, are available which do command some degree of confidence. Most immediately obvious is the evidence of individual differences. But regardless of individual differences, people seem to organize perceptual responses to the environment around five identifiable and interrelated levels of analysis. These are: affect, orientation, categorization, systematization, and manipulation. The comments which follow about each of these levels are quite general; the details need further study and will vary with the nature of both the physical situation and the social relationships involved.

The first level of response to the environment is affective. The direct emotional impact of the situation, perhaps largely a global response to the ambiance, very generally governs the directions taken by subsequent relations with the environment. It sets the motivational tone and delimits the kinds of experiences one expects and seeks. The importance of the immediate affective response is sharply etched in the novel environment; it can be seen in the laboratory, the city, the school, and the hospital. It is gradually blurred and glossed over by familiarity, but its consequences are indelible.

The establishment of orientation within the environment is a second level of response. The identification of escape routes is perhaps the most primitive form of orientation and is particularly compelling in novel environments with negative affect. Generally the location of positive and negative features, including other people, results in an initial mapping of the situation which provides a base for more detailed exploration.

Along with a satisfactory level of orientation, the process of developing categories for analysis and understanding is undertaken; the first steps are made toward developing a taxonomy which in a sense is never to be completed. The initial categories probably have to do with events from which objects are ultimately distilled in more and more detail. The process of concept formation and the nature of conceptual categories require careful study in this context. It is already known that conceptual categories are not imposed by the external situation, but are largely governed by goals, predispositions, and generalized expectations which the individual has already internalized. The path to unique and idiosyncratic categories is open.

A fourth level in the process of environment perception is the systematic analysis of relationships within the environment. Predictable sequences of events are identified and separated from random or unique occurrences. Causal connections are postulated and verified. The complex set of interrelationships which characterizes any particular environment is gradually brought into order and harmony. This order, or system, in the environment is analogous to constancy in objects. Properties of the system remain constant in the presence of continually changing events, in much the same way that properties of objects remain constant in spite of ever-changing stimulation. Or perhaps it may prove more correct to say that object constancy is a special case derived from the more general continuity of the environmental system.

Throughout this process the individual is never passive. He acts within, and as part of, the situation. He learns both the kinds of interventions he can bring about and their consequences, generally in terms of environmental change and, more important, in relation to his own needs and purposes. In this context, the relevance of perception to the situation in which it occurs can be defined for the individual as the mutually supporting construction of action and perception in the service of purpose.

Affect, orientation, categorization, systemization, and manipulation are the processes involved in environment perception. They do not function sequentially, but continuously interact with each other. Each aspect calls for its own set of strategies which are probably characteristic of the individual. The identification and study of these strategies is just beginning, and any statements are speculative. However, it does seem clear that the individual cannot be separated from the environment. He is part of the system he is perceiving, and the strategies he chooses become part of the environment he in turn experiences as being external to himself.

The way one views the environment thus is, in a very general sense, a function of what one does in it, including what strategies are used in exploring and conceptualizing it. And what is done in the environment represents, in turn, a choice among many alternatives, the nature and scope of which are progressively restricted by previous, frequently irreversible decisions. It is not unreasonable to say that the environment is experienced the way it is because one chooses to see it that way. In this sense the environment is an artifact created in man's own image.

This approach is clearly in sharp contrast to a "common sense" view which dichotomizes the situation into man and environment and assumes simple, direct, causal sequences: the environment acting on man, or man acting on the environment. In practice these sequences do not exist; and one deals empirically with a situation involving complex interdependencies. In any concrete situation, one does not encounter man and his environment as separate but interacting; instead, one finds a total situation which can be analyzed in a variety of ways. What is environment under one mode of analysis may not be environment under another. The conclusion is reached that the common sense view must be completely reversed. Rather than defining the situation in terms of its components, the components, including man himself, can be defined only in terms of the situation in which they are encountered. Man and his environment are never encountered independently: they are encountered only in a concrete situation, and they can be defined only in terms of their modes of participation within the situation.

The "environment" is thus seen as a total, active, continuous process involving the participation of all aspects. All the components of the environment are defined in terms of their participation in the total process; no component is seen as an entity existing in an environment composed of other entities. Man and his environment are inseparable, and both are defined in terms of their participation in the total environmental process. In any concrete situation, the "environment" has no fixed boundaries in either space or in time. Perhaps the best way of conceptualizing this is to view the environment as an open, rather than a closed, system. Within this system it is clear that the process exhibits stable patterns which resist change and which may be common from one situation to another, and from one time to another. At the same time, the situation is constantly changing. The very participation of the various aspects, or components, of the process produces disequilibria which, in turn, alter the mode of participation of the various aspects and thus change the total environmental situation in a continuing process.

In summary then, the environment involves the active participation of all aspects. Man is never concretely encountered independent of the situation through which he acts, nor is the environment ever encountered independent of the encountering individual. It is meaningless to speak of either as existing apart from the situation in which it is encountered. The word "transaction" has been used to label such a situation, for the word carries a double implication: one, all parts of the situation enter into it as active participants; and two, these parts owe their very existence as encountered in a situation to such active participation—they do not appear as already existing entities which merely interact with each other without affecting their own identity.

The term "transaction" was first used in this general context by Dewey and Bentley (1949) for whom it took on far-reaching philosophical significance. It may be best to close by stating, in their own words, Dewey and Bentley's understanding of this term.

"Observation of this general [transactional] type sees man-in-action, not as something radically set over against an environing world nor yet as something merely acting 'in' a world, but as action *of* and *in* the world in which man belongs as an integral constitutent [p. 52]." Under this procedure we treat "all of [man's] behavings, including his most advanced knowings, as activities not of himself alone, nor even as primarily his, but as processes of the full situation of organism-environment [p. 104]." "From birth to death every human being is a *Party*, so that neither he nor anything done or suffered can possibly be understood when it is separated from the fact of participation in an extensive body of transactions—to which a given human being may contribute and which he modifies, but only in virtue of being a partaker in them [p. 271]."

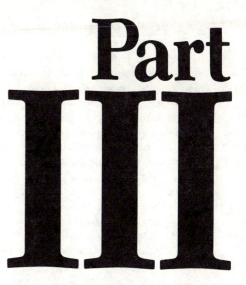

Part III

Social Processes and the Environment

The Introduction to this book pointed out that there really can be no understanding of the physical environment apart from human experience and social organization. Physical settings, as they have been presented throughout this book, are more than the context of behavior. They are active components of that behavior, but most important, from the perspective of this section (Part III), settings are expressions of a particular culture and its values.

This expression takes different forms, affecting many aspects of those settings, including their design, their function, and the meanings they communicate. First, both the design and the organization of settings are rooted in a particular social milieu—there is no single model for a home or school or city. Each will owe its form to a particular social organization. The variety that these structures take may not be infinite but certainly is considerable. The function of the setting will also depend on its cultural roots. It would be impossible to predict the activities ob-

155

served in a Japanese bathhouse, for example, without understanding its cultural context. Settings can be used, moved through, and altered in many different ways and the how and why is derived from the milieu. Still other components of the social and cultural roots of environmental behavior are the symbolic meanings associated with spaces. A church, in Western culture, is more than a specific architectural form, although the architecture ordinarily expresses its meaning. It is more than the context for specific behaviors, although its function defines what would be appropriate and inappropriate behaviors. More than both, it offers a total impression, partly a heritage of the past but capable of evoking from occupants an experience that goes beyond the moment. Along with the demand for socially appropriate activities to be performed is an affective reaction that is inseparable from the behaviors. This symbolic and affective component characterizes large- and small-scale settings, rooms, buildings, outdoor areas, and even cities. Walter Firey (1947) has identified cultural values that help explain the durability of the Beacon Hill area of Boston as well as other sites, where the symbolic meanings associated with these areas transcend pure economics. It is impossible to understand what these areas represent to Bostonians without understanding their past history.

How are we affected by these many social components of settings—their design, function, and meaning attributes? Central to this understanding is socialization, the learning processes through which we acquire the means of dealing with physical settings and the persons within them. Becoming socialized to a particular group involves internalizing its rules and regulations for behavior, and all of this learning takes place within specific environmental contexts. We learn how to relate to others, we learn particular roles we must play, we learn that these may be time-specific, but we also learn complex sets of rules about the setting. Some of this involves postures and locations within the area, appropriate and inappropriate behaviors with regard to people in that setting and what to expect from others, as well. This reciprocity, which underlies social activity, makes for smooth movement through various situations and settings in life.

All organisms move within and act upon their settings, but obviously other species do not draw on this cultural heritage. This emphasis on socialization does not deny the fact that human physical attributes set some limits to the social processes of which they are a part. In fact, our biological makeup does constrain social activity. Visual, auditory, and tactile capacities define, to a considerable degree, how interpersonal relationship can proceed. Conversation distances among people may vary over different cultures but they are constrained by visual acuity and the extent to which voices can carry. Biology thus places rough limits to social processes, and these limits should not be overlooked. The component added to behavior, which is unique to humans, is the cultural heritage that is part of spatial behavior. Many species communicate with one another, distance themselves, assume a variety of postures, and crowd together. What they do not share is the cultural backgrounds that underlie socialization among humans. Although many of the constructs to be considered in the selections that follow grow from ethological studies of animals, we must bear in mind the unique human qualities that make such concepts as territoriality, crowding, and isolation different when applied to human affairs. The culture and tradition with which our behavior is imbued move these space-related behaviors into a different realm from those of other species.

The concepts and themes covered by the readings range from the effects of varying degrees of population, behavior in groups, to those involving individuals. All of these themes were addressed in the earlier edition. Their presence in this section, elaborated and extended, is testimony to their usefulness in defining spatial behavior. In the absence of more comprehensive theories these constructs provide a means of organizing our thinking regarding social influences on spatial behavior and have generated considerable research efforts in the years since they were introduced.

The articles in Part III, as numerous and varied as they may appear, do not pretend to encompass the full range of issues dealing with social processes. They have been selected to highlight a few major topics, ones that, as we have indicated, have borne the test of time, at least in the six years since the first edition. But they represent more than themes that have persisted; they also represent areas of current work and thinking. Although crowding is an issue that has been addressed throughout history, it is the subject of much work in environmental psychology and related disciplines today. Yet what is being studied now differs from earlier research, both in its urgent connections to current environmental problems and in the concern with both social and spatial parameters. Although definitions may differ and research strategies may vary, current efforts tend to address many more variables, including the spatial. In time, it may be possible to fit the individual constructs covered into a more comprehensive theoretical structure. However, it would not be surprising to find the next edition of this book of readings (if one should ever be undertaken) covering many of the same themes.

Three major groupings cover the issues relevant to social processes. The first involves spacing behaviors, the distances maintained under different social conditions, the projection of the self into space sometimes labeled personal space and territoriality. The second deals with the effects of groups of people on each other. These cover a broad range from people alone to the presence of many others. Under this broad rubric falls work on isolation, confinement, privacy, density and crowding, and many but not all are included in this section. The final grouping of studies places major emphasis on people in specific settings, examining the culturally based behaviors that emerge as we move through different types of places. The way we use space in houses and relate to family members and friends within the home has one set of normative demands. The same person in an office, school, church, bus or subway will reflect another set of expected behaviors. One can think, for a moment, of how we might read or talk to another person under each of these conditions, to appreciate the range of different ways of dealing with both people and objects in these settings. And if we shift our focus across cultural groups, another set of potential differences appears. In reality, if our understanding of spatial behavior is only in the beginning stages, our view across cultures is even more impoverished. This is a gap that is slowly being filled. The major focus within this book is on Western cultures. However, the increased interest throughout the world in the study of environmental issues may provide a source for selections in the future.

A final caution should be added. There is a major difficulty residing within the definitions provided in the various pieces. The reader will quickly discover that there is a variety of definitions held for each concept, and many ways of studying them. It is essential to reflect on each conception whatever its name and critically evaluate where it fits into the larger scheme of social norms for spacing behaviors. Only then can an understanding of this area be approached. The large number of selections, with many addressing the same nominal concept, make it possible to consider the many conceptions held by researchers and other writers. It is left to the reader to review them, consider how well or poorly they predict, and perhaps how they may eventually fit into a more overarching and comprehensive view of sociospatial behavior.

12. The Anthropology of Space: An Organizing Model
EDWARD T. HALL

The term proxemics is used to define the interrelated observations and theories of man's use of space. His use of space, however, can only be understood in terms of a multilevel analysis of its manifestations and related determinants. Thus, *infraculture* applies to behavior on lower organizational levels that underlies culture and is rooted in man's biological past. It is a part of the proxemic classification system and implies a specific set of levels of relationships with other parts of the system. A second proxemic manifestation, the *precultural*, refers to the physiological base shared by all human beings, to which culture gives structure and meaning, and to which the scientist must inevitably refer in comparing the proxemic patterns of Culture A with those of Culture B. The *precultural* is very much in the present. The third, the *microcultural* level, is the one on which most proxemic observations are made. Proxemics as a manifestation of microculture has three aspects: fixed-feature, semifixed-feature, and informal.

Fixed-feature Space

Fixed-feature space is one of the basic ways of organizing the activities of individuals and groups. It includes material manifestations as well as the hidden, internalized de-

This selection is a slightly condensed version of Chapters 9 and 10 from *The Hidden Dimension* by Edward T. Hall. Copyright © 1966 by Edward T. Hall. Reprinted by permission of Doubleday & Company, Inc.

signs that govern behavior as man moves about on this earth. Buildings are one expression of fixed-feature patterns, but buildings are also grouped together in characteristic ways as well as being divided internally according to culturally determined designs. The layout of villages, towns, cities, and the intervening countryside is not haphazard but follows a plan which changes with time and culture.

Even the inside of the Western house is organized spatially. Not only are there special rooms for special functions—food preparation, eating, entertaining and socializing, rest, recuperation, and procreation—but for sanitation as well. *If*, as sometimes happens, either the artifacts or the activities associated with one space are transferred to another space, this fact is immediately apparent. People who "live in a mess" or a "constant state of confusion" are those who fail to classify activities and artifacts according to a uniform, consistent, or predictable spatial plan. At the opposite end of the scale is the assembly line, a precise organization of objects in *time* and *space*.

Actually the present internal layout of the house, which Americans and Europeans take for granted, is quite recent. As Philippe Ariès (1962) points out in *Centuries of Childhood*, rooms had no fixed functions in European houses until the eighteenth century. Members of the family had no privacy as we know it today. There were no spaces that were sacred or specialized. Strangers came and went at will, while beds and tables were set up and taken down according to the moods and appetites of the occupants. Children dressed and were treated as small adults. It is no wonder that the concept of childhood and its associated concept, the nuclear family, had to await the specialization of rooms according to function and the separation of rooms from each other. In the eighteenth century, the house altered its form. In French, *chambre* was distinguished from *salle*. In English, the function of a room was indicated by its name—bedroom, living room, dining room. Rooms were arranged to open into a corridor or hall, like houses into a street. No longer did the occupants pass through one room into another. Relieved of the Grand Central Station atmosphere and protected by new spaces, the family pattern began to stabilize and was expressed further in the form of the house.

Goffman's *Presentation of Self in Everyday Life* (1959) is a detailed, sensitive record of observations on the relationship of the façade that people present to the world and the self they hide behind it. The use of the term façade is in itself revealing. It signifies recognition of levels to be penetrated and hints at the functions performed by architectural features which provide screens behind which to retire from time to time. The strain of keeping up a façade can be great. Architecture can and does take over this burden for people. It can also provide a refuge where the individual can "let his hair down" and be himself.

The fact that so few businessmen have offices in their homes cannot be solely explained on the basis of convention and top management's uneasiness when executives are not visibly present. I have observed that many men have two or more distinct personalities, one for business and one for the home. The separation of office and home in these instances helps to keep the two often incompatible personalities from conflicting and may even serve to stabilize an idealized version of each which conforms to the projected image of both architecture and setting.

The relationship of fixed-feature space

to personality as well as to culture is nowhere more apparent than in the kitchen. When micro-patterns interfere as they do in the kitchen, it is more than just annoying to the women I interviewed. My wife, who has struggled for years with kitchens of all types, comments on male design in this way: "If any of the men who designed this kitchen had ever worked in it, they wouldn't have done it this way." The lack of congruence between the design elements, female stature and body build (women are not usually tall enough to reach things), and the activities to be performed, while not obvious at first, is often beyond belief. The size, the shape, the arrangement, and the placing in the house all communicate to the women of the house how much or how little the architect and designer knew about fixed-feature details.

Man's feeling about being properly oriented in space runs deep. Such knowledge is ultimately linked to survival and sanity. To be disoriented in space is to be psychotic. The difference between acting with reflex speed and having to stop to think in an emergency may mean the difference between life and death—a rule which applies equally to the driver negotiating freeway traffic and the rodent dodging predators. Lewis Mumford (1961) observes that the uniform grid pattern of our cities "makes strangers as much at home as the oldest inhabitants." Americans who have become dependent on this pattern are often frustrated by anything different. It is difficult for them to feel at home in European capitals that don't conform to this simple plan. Those who travel and live abroad frequently get lost. An interesting feature of these complaints reveals the relationship of the layout to the person. Almost without exception, the newcomer uses words and tones associated with a personal affront, as though the town held something against him. It is no wonder that people brought up on either the French radiating star or the Roman grid have difficulty in a place like Japan where the entire fixed-feature pattern is basically and radically different. In fact, if one were to set out to design two systems in contrasts, it is hard to see how one could do better. The European systems stress the lines, which they name: the Japanese treat the intersecting points technically and forget about the lines. In Japan, the intersections but not the streets are named. Houses instead of being related in space are related in time and numbered in the order in which they are built. The Japanese pattern emphasizes hierarchies that grow around centers; the American plan finds its ultimate development in the sameness of suburbia, because one number along a line is the same as any other. In a Japanese neighborhood, the first house built is a constant reminder to the residents of house #20 that #1 was there first.

Some aspects of fixed-feature space are not visible until one observes human behavior. For example, although the separate dining room is fast vanishing from American houses, the line separating the dining area from the rest of the living room is quite real. The invisible boundary which separates one yard from another in suburbia is also a fixed-feature of American culture or at least some of its subcultures.

Architects traditionally are preoccupied with the visual patterns of structures—what one sees. They are almost totally unaware of the fact that people carry around with them internalizations of fixed-feature space learned early in life. It isn't only the Arab who feels depressed unless he has enough space but many Americans as well. As one of my subjects said: "I can put up with almost anything as long as I have large rooms and high ceilings. You see, I was raised in an old house in Brooklyn and I have never been able to accustom myself to anything different."

The important point about fixed-feature space is that it is the mold into which a great deal of behavior is cast. It was this feature of space that the late Sir Winston Churchill referred to when he said: "We shape our buildings and they shape us." During the debate on restoring the House of Commons after the war, Churchill feared that departure from the intimate spatial pattern of the House, where opponents face each other across a narrow aisle, would seriously alter the patterns of government. He may not have been the first to put his finger on the influence of fixed-feature space, but its effects have never been so succinctly stated.

One of the many basic differences between cultures is that they extend different anatomical and behavioral features of the human organism. Whenever there is cross-cultural borrowing, the borrowed items have to be adapted. Otherwise, the new and the old do not match, and in some instances, the two patterns are completely contradictory. For example, Japan has had problems integrating the automobile into a culture in which the lines between points (highways) receive less attention than the points. Hence, Tokyo is famous for producing some of the world's most impressive traffic jams. The automobile is also poorly adapted to India, where cities are physically crowded and the society has elaborate hierarchical features. Unless Indian engineers can design roads that will separate slow pedestrians from fast-moving vehicles, the class-conscious drivers' lack of consideration for the poor will continue to breed disaster. Even Le Corbusier's great buildings at Chandigarh, capital of Punjab, had to be modified by the residents to make them habitable. The Indians walled up Corbusier's balconies, converting them into kitchens! Similarly, Arabs coming to the United States find that their own internalized fixed-feature patterns do not fit American housing. Arabs feel oppressed by it—the ceilings are too low, the rooms too small, privacy from the outside inadequate, and views non-existent.

It should not be thought, however, that incongruity between internalized and externalized patterns occurs only between cultures. As our own technology explodes, air conditioning, fluorescent lighting, and soundproofing make it possible to design houses and offices without regard to traditional patterns of windows and doors. The new inventions sometimes result in great barnlike rooms where the "territory" of scores of employees in a "bull pen" is ambiguous.

Semifixed-feature Space

Several years ago, a talented and perceptive physician named Humphry Osmond was asked to direct a large health and research center in Saskatchewan. His hospital was one of the first in which the relationship between semifixed-feature space and behavior was clearly demonstrated. Osmond had noticed that some spaces, like railway waiting rooms, tend to keep people apart. These he called sociofugal spaces. Others, such as the booths in the old-fashioned drugstore or the tables at a French sidewalk café, tend to bring people together. These he called sociopetal (1957). The hospital of which he was in charge was replete with sociofugal spaces and had very few which might be called sociopetal. Furthermore, the custodial staff and nurses tended to prefer the former to the latter because they were easier to maintain. Chairs in the halls, which would be found in little circles after visiting hours, would soon be lined up neatly in military fashion, in rows along the walls.

One situation which attracted Osmond's attention was the newly built "model" female geriatrics ward. Everything was new and shiny, neat and clean. There was enough space, and the colors were cheerful. The only trouble was that the longer the patients stayed in the ward, the less they seemed to talk to each other. Gradually, they were becoming like the furniture, permanently and silently glued to the walls at regular intervals between the beds. In addition, they all seemed depressed.

Sensing that the space was more sociofugal than sociopetal, Osmond put a perceptive young psychologist, Robert Sommer, to work to find out as much as he could about the relationship of furniture to conversations. Looking for a natural setting which offered a number of different situations in which people could be observed in conversations, Sommer selected the hospital cafeteria, where 36- by 72-inch tables accommodated six people (1959). As Figure 12–1 indicates, these tables provided six different distances and orientations of the bodies in relation to each other. Fifty observational sessions in which conversations were counted at controlled intervals revealed that: F–A (cross corner) conversations were twice as frequent as the C–B (side by side) type, which in turn were three times as frequent as those at C–D (across the table). No conversations were observed by Sommer for the other positions. In other words, corner situations with people at right angles to each other produced six times as many conversations as face-to-face situations across the 36-inch span of the table, and twice as many as the side-by-side arrangement.

The results of these observations suggested a solution to the problem of gradual disengagement and withdrawal of the old people. Both Osmond and Sommer had noted that the ward patients were more often in the B–C and C–D relationships (side by side and across) than they were in the cafeteria, and they sat at much greater distances. In addition, there was no place to put anything, no place for personal belongings. The only territorial features associated with the patients were the bed and the

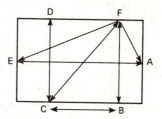

FIGURE 12–1.   F–A, across the corner; C–B, side by side; C–D, across the table; E–A, from one end to the other; E–F, diagonally the length of the table; C–F, diagonally across the table.

chair. As a consequence, magazines ended up on the floor and were quickly swept up by staff members. Enough small tables so that every patient had a place would provide additional territoriality and an opportunity to keep magazines, books, and writing materials. If the tables were square, they would also help to structure relationships between patients so that there was a maximum opportunity to converse.

The small tables were moved in and the chairs arranged around them. At first, the patients resisted. They had become accustomed to the placement of "their" chairs in particular spots, and they did not take easily to being moved around by others. The staff kept the new arrangement reasonably intact until it was established as an alternative rather than an annoying feature to be selectively inattended. When this point had been reached, a repeat count of conversations was made. The number of conversations had doubled, while reading had tripled, possibly because there was now a place to keep reading material. Similar restructuring of the dayroom met with the same resistances and the same ultimate increase in verbal interaction.

At this point, three things must be said. Conclusions drawn from observations made in the hospital situation just described are not universally applicable. That is, across-the-corner-at-right-angles is conducive *only* to: (a) conversations of certain types between (b) persons in certain relationships and (c) in very restricted cultural settings. Second, what is sociofugal in one culture may be sociopetal in another. Third, sociofugal space is not necessarily bad, nor is sociopetal space universally good. What *is* desirable is flexibility and congruence between design and function so that there is a variety of spaces, and people can be involved or not, as the occasion and mood demand. The main point of the Canadian experiment for us is its demonstration that the structuring of semifixed features can have a profound effect on behavior and that this effect is measurable. This will come as no surprise

to housewives who are constantly trying to balance the relationship of fixed-feature enclosures to arrangement of their semifixed furniture. Many have had the experience of getting a room nicely arranged, only to find that conversation was impossible if the chairs were left nicely arranged.

It should be noted that what is fixed-feature space in one culture may be semifixed in another, and vice versa. In Japan, for example, the walls are movable, opening and closing as the day's activities change. In the United States, people move from room to room or from one part of a room to another for each different activity, such as eating, sleeping, working, or socializing with relatives. In Japan, it is quite common for the person to remain in one spot while the activities change. The Chinese provide us with further opportunities to observe the diversity of human treatment of space, for they assign to the fixed-feature category certain items which Americans treat as semifixed. Apparently, a guest in a Chinese home *does not move his chair* except at the host's suggestion. To do so would be like going into someone else's home and moving a screen or even a partition. In this sense, the semifixed nature of furniture in American homes is merely a matter of degree and situation. Light chairs are more mobile than sofas or heavy tables. I have noted, however, that some Americans hesitate to adjust furniture in another person's house or office. Of the forty students in one of my classes, half manifested such hesitation.

Many American women know it is hard to find things in someone else's kitchen. Conversely, it can be exasperating to have kitchenware put away by well-meaning helpers who don't know where things "belong." How and where belongings are arranged and stored is a function of microcultural patterns, representative not only of large cultural groups but of the minute variations on cultures that make each individual unique. Just as variations in the quality and use of the voice make it possible to distinguish one person's voice from another, handling of materials also has a characteristic pattern that is unique.

Informal Space

We turn now to the category of spatial experience, which is perhaps most significant for the individual because it includes the distance maintained in encounters with others. These distances are for the most part outside awareness. I have called this category *informal space* because it is unstated, not because it lacks form or has no importance. Indeed informal spatial patterns have distinct bounds, and such deep, if unvoiced, significance that they form an essential part of the culture. To misunderstand this significance may invite disaster.

Birds and mammals not only have territories which they occupy and defend against their own kind but they have a series of uniform distances which they maintain from each other. Hediger (1955) has classified these as flight distance, critical distance, and personal and social distance. Man, too, has a uniform way of handling distance from his fellows. With very few exceptions, flight distance and critical distance have been eliminated from human reactions. Personal distance and social distance, however, are obviously still present.

How many distances do human beings have and how do we distinguish them? What is it that differentiates one distance from the other? The answer to this question was not obvious at first when I began my investigation of distances in man. Gradually, however, evidence began to accumulate indicating that the regularity of distances observed for humans is the consequence of sensory shifts.

One common source of information about the distance separating two people is the loudness of the voice. Working with the linguistic scientist George Trager, I began by observing shifts in the voice associated with changes in distance. Since the whisper

is used when people are very close, and the shout is used to span great distances, the question Trager and I posed was, How many vocal shifts are sandwiched between these two extremes? Our procedure for discovering these patterns was for Trager to stand still while I talked to him at different distances. If both of us agreed that a vocal shift had occurred, we would then measure the distance and note down a general description. The result was the eight distances described in *The Silent Language* (1959).

Further observation of human beings in social situations convinced me that these eight distances were overly complex. Four were sufficient; these I have termed intimate, personal, social, and public (each with its close and far phase). My choice of terms to describe various distances was deliberate. Not only was it influenced by Hediger's work with animals (1955) indicating the continuity between *infra*culture and culture but also by a desire to provide a clue as to the types of activities and relationships associated with each distance, thereby linking them in peoples' minds with specific inventories of relationships and activities. It should be noted at this point that *how people are feeling toward each other* at the time is a decisive factor in the distance used. Thus people who are very angry or emphatic about the point they are making will move in close, they "turn up the volume," as it were, by shouting. Similarly—as any woman knows—one of the first signs that a man is beginning to feel amorous is his move closer to her. If the woman does not feel similarly disposed she signals this by moving back.

The following descriptions of the four distance zones have been compiled from observations and interviews with non-contact, middle-class, healthy adults, mainly natives of the northeastern seaboard of the United States. A high percentage of the subjects were men and women from business and the professions; many could be classified as intellectuals. The interviews were affectively neutral: that is, the subjects were not noticeably excited, depressed, or angry. There were no unusual environmental factors, such as extremes of temperature or noise. These descriptions represent only a first approximation. They will doubtless seem crude when more is known about proxemic observation and how people distinguish one distance from another. It should be emphasized that these generalizations are not representative of human behavior in general—or even of American behavior in general—but only of the group included in the sample. Negroes and Spanish Americans as well as persons who come from southern European cultures have very different proxemic patterns.

Each of the four distance zones described below has a near and a far phase. It should be noted that the measured distances vary somewhat with differences in personality and environmental factors. For example, a high noise level or low illumination will ordinarily bring people closer together.

Intimate Distance

At intimate distance, the presence of the other person is unmistakable and may at times be overwhelming because of the greatly stepped-up sensory inputs. Sight (often distorted), olfaction, heat from the other person's body, sound, smell, and feel of the breath all combine to signal unmistakable involvement with another body.

Intimate Distance—Close Phase. This is the distance of love-making and wrestling, comforting and protecting. Physical contact or the high possibility of physical involvement is uppermost in the awareness of both persons. The use of their distance receptors is greatly reduced except for olfaction and sensation of radiant heat, both of which are stepped up. In the maximum contact phase, the muscles and skin communicate. Pelvis, thighs, and head can be brought into play; arms can encircle. Except at the outer limits,

sharp vision is blurred. When close vision is possible within the intimate range—as with children—the image is greatly enlarged and stimulates much, if not all, of the retina. The detail that can be seen at this distance is extraordinary. This detail plus the cross-eyed pull of the eye muscles provide a visual experience that cannot be confused with any other distance. Vocalization at intimate distance plays a very minor part in the communication process, which is carried mainly by other channels. A whisper has the effect of expanding the distance. The vocalizations that do occur are largely involuntary.

Intimate Distance—Far Phase (distance: six to eighteen inchese). Heads, thighs, and pelvis are not easily brought into contact, but hands can reach and grasp extremities. The head is seen as enlarged in size, and its features are distorted. Ability to focus the eye easily is an important feature of this distance for Americans. The iris of the other person's eye seen at about six to nine inches is enlarged to more than life-size. Small blood vessels in the sclera are clearly perceived, pores are enlarged. Clear vision (15 degrees) includes the upper or lower portion of the face, which is perceived as enlarged. The nose is seen as over-large and may look distorted, as will other features such as lips, teeth, and tongue. Peripheral vision (30 to 180 degrees) includes the outline of head and shoulders and very often the hands.

Much of the physical discomfort that Americans experience when foreigners are inappropriately inside the intimate sphere is expressed as a distortion of the visual system. One subject said, "These people get so close, you're cross-eyed. It really makes me nervous. They put their face so close it feels like they're *inside you*." At the point where sharp focus is lost, one feels the uncomfortable muscular sensation of being cross-eyed from looking at something too close. The expressions "Get your face *out* of mine" and "He shook his fist *in* my face" apparently express how many Americans perceive their body boundaries.

At six to eighteen inches the voice is used but is normally held at a very low level or even a whisper. As Martin Joos (1962), the linguist, describes it, "An intimate utterance pointedly avoids giving the addressee information from outside of the speaker's skin. The point ... is simply to remind (hardly 'inform') the addressee of some feeling ... inside the speaker's skin." The heat and odor of the other person's breath may be detected, even though it is directed away from subject's face. Heat loss or gain from other person's body begins to be noticed by some subjects.

The use of intimate distance in public is not considered proper by adult, middle-class Americans even though their young may be observed intimately involved with each other in automobiles and on beaches. Crowded subways and buses may bring strangers into what would ordinarily be classed as intimate spatial relations, but subway riders have defensive devices which take the real intimacy out of intimate space in public conveyances. The basic tactic is to be as immobile as possible and, when part of the trunk or extremities touches another person, withdraw if possible. If this is not possible, the muscles in the affected areas are kept tense. For members of the non-contact group, it is taboo to relax and enjoy bodily contact with strangers! In crowded elevators the hands are kept at the side or used to steady the body by grasping a railing. The eyes are fixed on infinity and are not brought to bear on anyone for more than a passing glance.

It should be noted once more that American proxemic patterns for intimate distance are by no means universal. Even the rules governing such intimacies as touching others cannot be counted on to remain constant. Americans who have had an opportunity for considerable social interaction with Russians report that many of the features characteristic of American intimate distance are present in Russian social distance. However, Middle Eastern subjects in public places do not express the outraged reaction to being touched by strangers which one encounters in American subjects.

Personal Distance

"Personal distance" is the term originally used by Hediger (1955) to designate the distance consistently separating the members of non-contact species. It might be thought of as a small protective sphere or bubble that an organism maintains between itself and others.

Personal Distance—Close Phase (distance: one and a half to two and a half feet). The kinesthetic sense of closeness derives in part from the possibilities present in regard to what each participant can do to the other with his extremities. At this distance, one can hold or grasp the other person. Visual distortion of the other's features is no longer apparent. However, there is noticeable feedback from the muscles that control the eyes. The reader can experience this himself if he will look at an object eighteen inches to three feet away, paying particular attention to the muscles around his eyeballs. He can feel the pull of these muscles as they hold the two eyes on a single point so that the image of each eye stays in register. Pushing gently with the tip of the finger on the surface of the lower eyelid so that the eyeball is displaced will illustrate clearly the work these muscles perform in maintaining a single coherent image. A visual angle of 15 degrees takes in another person's upper or lower face, which is seen with exceptional clarity. The planes and roundness of the face are accentuated; the nose projects and the ears recede; fine hair of the face, eyelashes, and pores is clearly visible. The three-dimensional quality of objects is particularly pronounced. Objects have roundness, substance, and form unlike that perceived at any other distance. Surface textures are also very prominent and are clearly differentiated from each other.

Where people stand in relation to each other signals their relationship, or how they feel toward each other, or both. A wife can stay inside the circle of her husband's close personal zone with impunity. For another woman to do so is an entirely different story.

Personal Distance—Far Phase (distance: two and a half to four feet). Keeping someone at "arm's length" is one way of expressing the far phase of personal distance. It extends from a point that is just outside easy touching distance by one person to a point where two people can touch fingers if they extend both arms. This is the limit of physical domination in the very real sense. Beyond it, a person cannot easily "get his hands on" someone else. Subjects of personal interest and involvement can be discussed at this distance. Head size is perceived as normal and details of the other person's features are clearly visible. Also easily seen are fine details of skin, gray hair, "sleep" in the eye, stains on teeth, spots, small wrinkles, or dirt on clothing. Foveal vision covers only an area the size of the tip of the nose or one eye, so that the gaze must wander around the face (*where the eye is directed* is strictly a matter of cultural conditioning). Fifteen-degree clear vision covers the upper *or* lower face, while 180-degree peripheral vision takes in the hands and the whole body of a seated person. Movement of the hands is detected, but fingers can't be counted. The voice level is moderate. No body heat is perceptible. While olfaction is not normally present for Americans, it is for a great many other people who use colognes to create an olfactory bubble. Breath odor can sometimes be detected at this distance, but Americans are generally trained to direct the breath away from others.

Social Distance

The boundary line between the far phase of personal distance and the close phase of

social distance marks, in the words of one subject, the "limit of domination." Intimate visual detail in the face is not perceived, and nobody touches or expects to touch another person unless there is some special effort. Voice level is normal for Americans. There is little change between the far and close phases, and conversations can be overheard at a distance of up to twenty feet. I have observed that in overall loudness, the American voice at these distances is below that of the Arab, the Spaniard, the South Asian Indian, and the Russian, and somewhat above that of the English upper class, the Southeast Asian, and the Japanese.

Social Distance—Close Phase (distance: four to seven feet). Head size is perceived as normal; as one moves away from the subject, the foveal area of the eye can take in an ever-increasing amount of the person. At four feet, a one-degree visual angle covers an area of a little more than one eye. At seven feet the area of sharp focus extends to the nose and parts of both eyes; or the whole mouth, one eye, and the nose are sharply seen. Many Americans shift their gaze back and forth from eye to eye or from eyes to mouth. Details of skin texture and hair are clearly perceived. At a 60-degree visual angle, the head, shoulders, and upper trunk are seen at a distance of four feet; while the same sweep includes the whole figure at seven feet.

Impersonal business occurs at this distance, and in the close phase there is more involvement than in the distant phase. People who work together tend to use close social distance. It is also a very common distance for people who are attending a casual social gathering. To stand and look down at a person at this distance has a domineering effect, as when a man talks to his secretary or receptionist.

Social Distance—Far Phase (distance: seven to twelve feet). This is the distance to which people move when someone says, "Stand away so I can look at you." Business and social discourse conducted at the far end of social distance has a more formal character than if it occurs inside the close phase. Desks in the offices of important people are large enough to hold visitors at the far phase of social distance. Even in an office with standard-size desks, the chair opposite is eight or nine feet away from the man behind the desk. At the far phase of social distance, the finest details of the face, such as the capillaries in the eyes, are lost. Otherwise, skin texture, hair, condition of teeth, and condition of clothes are all readily visible. None of my subjects mentioned heat or odor from another person's body as detectable at this distance. The full figure—with a good deal of space around it —is encompassed in a 60-degree glance. Also, at around twelve feet, feedback from the eye muscles used to hold the eyes inward on a single spot falls off rapidly. The eyes and the mouth of the other person are seen in the area of sharpest vision. Hence, it is not necessary to shift the eyes to take in the whole face. During conversations of any significant length it is more important to maintain visual contact at this distance than it is at closer distances.

Proxemic behavior of this sort is culturally conditioned and entirely arbitrary. It is also binding on all concerned. To fail to hold the other person's eye is to shut him out and bring conversation to a halt, which is why people who are conversing at this distance can be observed craning their necks and leaning from side to side to avoid intervening obstacles. Similarly, when one person is seated and the other is standing, prolonged visual contact at less than ten or twelve feet tires the neck muscles and is generally avoided by subordinates who are sensitive to their employer's comfort. If, however, the status of the two parties is reversed so that the subordinate is seated, the other party may often come closer.

At this distant phase, the voice level is noticeably louder than for the close phase, and it can usually be heard easily in an adjoining room if the door is open. Raising the voice or shouting can have the effect of reducing social distance to personal distance.

A proxemic feature of social distance (far phase) is that it can be used to insulate or screen people from each other. This distance makes it possible for them to continue to work in the presence of another person without appearing to be rude. Receptionists in offices are particularly vulnerable as most employers expect double duty: answering questions, being polite to callers, as well as typing. If the receptionist is less than ten feet from another person, even a stranger, she will be sufficiently involved to be virtually compelled to converse. If she has more space, however, she can work quite freely without having to talk. Likewise, husbands returning from work often find themselves sitting and relaxing, reading the paper at ten or more feet from their wives, for at this distance a couple can engage each other briefly and disengage at will. Some men discover that their wives have arranged the furniture back-to-back—a favorite sociofugal device of the cartoonist Chic Young, creator of "Blondie." The back-to-back seating arrangement is an appropriate solution to minimum space because it is possible for two people to stay uninvolved if that is their desire.

Public Distance

Several important sensory shifts occur in the transition from the personal and social distances to public distance, which is well outside the circle of involvement.

Public Distance—Close Phase (distance: twelve to twenty-five feet). At twelve feet an alert subject can take evasive or defensive action if threatened. The distance may even cue a vestigial but subliminal form of flight reaction. The voice is loud but not full-volume. Linguists have observed that a careful choice of words and phrasing of sentences as well as grammatical or syntactic shifts occur at this distance. Martin Joos's choice of the term "formal style" is appropriately descriptive: "Formal texts ... demand advance planning ... the speaker is correctly said to think on his feet" (1962). The angle of sharpest vision (one degree) covers the whole face. Fine details of the skin and eyes are no longer visible. At sixteen feet, the body begins to lose its roundness and to look flat. The color of the eyes begins to be imperceivable; only the white of the eye is visible. Head size is perceived as considerably under life-size. The 15-degree lozenge-shaped area of clear vision covers the faces of two people at twelve feet, while 60-degree scanning includes the whole body with a little space around it. Other persons present can be seen peripherally.

Public Distance—Far Phase (distance: twenty-five feet or more). Thirty feet is the distance that is automatically set around important public figures. An excellent example occurs in Theodore H. White's *The Making of the President 1960* when John F. Kennedy's nomination became a certainty. White is describing the group at the "hideaway cottage" as Kennedy entered:

Kennedy loped into the cottage with his light, dancing step, as young and lithe as springtime, and called a greeting to those who stood in his way. Then he seemed to slip from them as he descended the steps of the split-level cottage to a corner where his brother Bobby and brother-in-law Sargent Shriver were chatting, waiting for him. The others in the room surged forward on impulse to join him. Then they halted. A distance of perhaps 30 feet separated them from him, but it was impassable. They stood apart, these older men of long-established power, and watched him. He turned after a few minutes, saw them watching him, and whispered to his brother-in-law. Shriver now crossed the separating space to invite them over. First Averell Harriman; then

Dick Daley: then Mike DiSalle, then, one by one, let them all congratulate him. Yet no one could pass the little open distance between him and them uninvited, because there was this thin separation about him, and the knowledge they were there not as his patrons but as his clients. They could come by invitation only, for this might be a President of the United States (1961, p. 171).

The usual public distance is not restricted to public figures but can be used by anyone on public occasions. There are certain adjustments that must be made, however. Most actors know that at thirty or more feet the subtle shades of meaning conveyed by the normal voice are lost as are the details of facial expression and movement. Not only the voice but everything else must be exaggerated or amplified. Much of the nonverbal part of the communication shifts to gestures and body stance. In addition, the tempo of the voice drops, words are enunciated more clearly, and there are stylistic changes as well. Martin Joos's *frozen style* is characteristic: "Frozen style is for people who are to remain strangers" (1962). The whole man may be seen as quite small and he is perceived in a setting. Foveal vision takes in more and more of the man until he is entirely within the small circle of sharpest vision. At which point—when people look like ants—contact with them as human beings fades rapidly. The 60-degree cone of vision takes in the setting while peripheral vision has as its principal function the altering of the individual to movement at the side.

Why "Four" Distances?

In concluding this description of distance zones common to our sample group of Americans a final word about classification is in order. It may well be asked: Why are there four zones, not six or eight? Why set up any zones at all? How do we know that this classification is appropriate? How were the categories chosen?

The scientist has a basic need for a classification system, one that is as consistent as possible with the phenomena under observation and one which will hold up long enough to be useful. Behind every classification system lies a theory or hypothesis about the nature of the data and their basic patterns of organization. The hypothesis behind the proxemic classification system is this: it is in the nature of animals, including man, to exhibit behavior which we call territoriality. In so doing, they use the senses to distinguish between one space or distance and another. The specific distance chosen depends on the transaction: the relationship of the interacting individuals, how they feel, and what they are doing. The four-part classification system used here is based on observations of both animals and men. Birds and apes exhibit intimate, personal, and social distances just as man does.

Western man has combined consultative and social activities and relationships into one distance set and has added the public figure and the public relationship. "Public" relations and "public" manners as the Europeans and Americans practice them are different from those in other parts of the world. There are implicit obligations to treat total strangers in certain prescribed ways. Hence, we find four principal categories of relationships (intimate, personal, social, and public) and the activities and spaces associated with them. In other parts of the world, relationships tend to fall into other patterns, such as the family/non-family pattern common in Spain and Portugal and their former colonies or the caste and outcast system of India. Both the Arabs and the Jews also make sharp distinctions between people to whom they are related and those to whom they are not. My work with Arabs leads me to believe that they employ a system for the organization of informal space which is very different from what I observed in the United States. The relationship of the Arab peasant or fellah to his sheik or to God is not a public relationship. It is close and personal without intermediaries.

Until recently man's space requirements were thought of in terms of the actual amount of air displaced by his body. The fact that man has around him as extensions of his personality the zones described earlier has generally been overlooked. Differences in the zones—in fact their very existence—became apparent only when Americans began interacting with foreigners who organize their senses differently so that what was intimate in one culture might be personal or even public in another. Thus for the first time the American became aware of his own spatial envelopes, which he had previously taken for granted.

The ability to recognize these various zones of involvement and the activities, relationships, and emotions associated with each has now become extremely important. The world's populations are crowding into cities, and builders and speculators are packing people into vertical filing boxes—both offices and dwellings. If one looks at human beings in the way that the early slave traders did, conceiving of their space requirements simply in terms of the limits of the body, one pays very little attention to the effects of crowding. If, however, one sees man surrounded by a series of invisible bubbles which have measurable dimensions, architecture can be seen in a new light. It is then possible to conceive that people can be cramped by the spaces in which they have to live and work. They may even find themselves forced into behavior, relationships, or emotional outlets that are overly stressful. Like gravity, the influence of two bodies on each other is inversely proportional not only to the square of the distance but possibly even the cube of the distance between them. When stress increases, sensitivity to crowding rises—people get more on edge—so that more and more space is required as less and less is available.

13. Freedom of Choice and Behavior in a Physical Setting

HAROLD M. PROSHANSKY, WILLIAM H. ITTELSON, AND
LEANNE G. RIVLIN

For the social sciences, particularly those concerned with man's relations to other men, the physical environment has been conceived as a given, rather than as a source of parameters for understanding human behavior. Urban settings, for example, are distinguished from suburban or rural settings, or the "ghetto" from the more affluent areas of a community, but more for their contrasting properties as social systems or complex social contexts than for the differences between them as organized physical settings. The scientific literature abounds in descriptions of ghettos as a prelude to examining them as sociocultural systems generating given sets of values and relevant behaviors. But systematic studies of the behavioral consequences of ghettos as physical settings are rare indeed.

Even at a more circumscribed level of analysis—a neighborhood, an apartment, or a business office—the physical setting is no less taken for granted. It is assumed to set the stage for and perhaps define the actors' roles with respect to particular human relationships and activities; but for any given setting there are countless variations in design and substance that are generally ignored in the attempts to establish the factors that facilitate or hinder the prescribed behaviors.

It is reasonable to ask why physical setting has been neglected in the theory and research of social scientists. In our judgment, it is rooted in more fundamental considerations than those of priority or theoretical predilection. Increasingly the term "physical environment" is used to refer to the man-made environment: to the physical environment that is planned, constructed, and changed by man on the basis of a continually evolving scientific technology whose limits are by no means in sight. To the social scientist no less than to the casual observer,

the success of this technology has suggested, at least until the last decade, that the problem of man's control of his physical environment was solved and that each planned technological advance would produce corresponding favorable changes in man's existence. From the social scientist's point of view, the ability of modern technology to plan and construct a large variety of physical settings to meet the specification of any number of human functions, activities, and relationships meant that the effects of the physical environment were predictable and controllable. An appropriately designed physical setting could be expected to evoke, or at least to serve as the locus of, a range of expected behaviors whose variations could be studied as a function not of physical parameters but of those complex social and psychological determinants that are rooted in all human activities and relationships. Thus, for the child to learn, he needs to feel at ease, comfortable, and secure. It follows, therefore, that schools must be light, airy, colorful, and roomy, and beyond that how and whether the child learns will depend on psychological and social determinants.

During the past ten years both the citizen and the scientist have been compelled to take a second look at their man-made world. The physical environment assumes a new significance once it is viewed against the backdrop of pressing and urgent problems created by the inexorable progress of modern technology. The fruits of this progress are bitter as well as sweet, as evidenced by the existence of urban slums, water and air pollution, depletion of natural resources, congestion and crowding in the city, and any number of other contemporary evils. For the first time scientists of all persuasions are being asked to reexamine the physical world that they have in part created. Yet they are being asked to do more than simply provide solutions to these environmental problems.

To solve one set of environmental problems does not preclude the emergence of others as still greater technological advances are made. The concern with solving problems of a man-made environment has increasingly led to the more fundamental questions of why did it happen and what can be done to prevent new problems from occurring. What has emerged is an emphasis on predicting and understanding the consequences of the physical environment for the behavior of the individual, and this emphasis in turn has called attention to the social scientist, his theory, concepts, and methods. The result has been the new interdisciplinary field of inquiry, environmental psychology. The definition of this field and the conceptual and methodological problems inherent in its interdisciplinary character need not concern us here. What is of immediate interest is a consideration of some of the major concepts made prominent by the recent interest in the relationship between the physical environment and the behavior of the individual.

The concepts of privacy, territoriality, and crowding are used frequently and interrelatedly to describe a class of environmental problems or to explain behavior in relation to these problems. Their frequent use, however, is not evidence of a theoretical viability evolved in a context of sustained systematic research, but rather of the preliminary attempts of a new field of inquiry to define its problem areas and establish its conceptual structure. Since little if any systematic research with respect to these phenomena exists, we are not even afforded empirical definitions in the form of the conceptual restraints that emerge from specified operational procedures.

It is our purpose in the discussion that follows to consider briefly the status and meaning of the concepts of privacy, territoriality, and crowding as reflected in their use in the current literature and to suggest the value of introducing "freedom of choice" as a unifying concept that can help to organize and make clear the definitions of the other terms. Our concern is with concepts used in discussing the behavior and experience of the individual in relation to the nature and organization of the physical environment. Whether privacy is a "right of the individual," whether cities are growing more or less crowded, and whether individuals are seeking autonomy through territoriality are not of immediate interest. Furthermore, whether these processes can function as motivations, and whether freedom of choice can be used as a superordinate motivational concept, as Brehm has suggested, are not within the province of this discussion. Before more complex questions can be approached, the underlying concepts must be clarified.

We begin this conceptualization with three propositions.

1. *Man, in almost all instances and situations, is a cognizing and goal-directed organism.*

This proposition is generally accepted by behavioral scientists; indeed, it lies at the root of all modern theories that attempt to explain man's behavior either generally or in terms of specific social settings. While the proposition is obvious, it is important to stress the fact that the individual's behavior is guided not only by the goals he seeks, but also by his cognitive processes, that is, by the way he reads and interprets or even imagines his environment. Each individual interprets and gives meaning to his environment, and to this extent the real differences among individuals and groups lie not in how they behave but in how they perceive.

2. *Man's attempts at need satisfaction always involve him in interactions and exchanges with his physical environment.*

Since man himself is one physical component of a total environment in any given setting, it follows that any attempt on his part to change his state must involve him, because he is also a goal-directed and cognizing organism, in an interchange or interaction with other physical components of the environment. However obvious this statement, it has been virtually ignored in attempts to understand the behavior of the individual. Social scientists have taken the physical environment for granted. It has served merely as a mediating context in which need satisfaction and social interaction take place, rather than as a source of influence in its own right. In modern psychological and sociological research literature, not only are physical settings seldom described, but the individual does not seem to have the capacity to move or to change his physical environment. It appears that man is not a motor animal.

We can state Propositions 1 and 2 in somewhat different fashion. Taken together they tell us that the individual in most instances is an aroused and active organism who defines, interprets, and searches his physical environment for relevant ways of achieving his goals. He must often first seek subsidiary goals in order to achieve primary ones. To achieve solitude, he may first have to find the right place at the right time. To read a book in a library, he may first have to find the book, then find a place to sit, and then position himself so that he can read effectively. Trite as these examples seem, they illustrate quite accurately the goal-directed, cognizing character of man in transactions with his physical environment. Furthermore, even in the instance of the individual seeking to achieve complex social goals, the achievement of any one of them involves a myriad of subsidiary need satisfactions depending on the kinds of mundane transactions with the physical environment we have described. It is this view of man that leads us to our third and final proposition.

3. *In any situational context, the individual attempts to organize his physical environment so that it maximizes his freedom of choice.*

Freedom of choice is a critical aspect of man's behavior in relation to his physical environment. Whatever the primary purpose that brings the individual to a given physical setting, the setting must not only have the capacity to satisfy the primary need and other relevant subsidiary needs, but it must also allow for goal satisfactions that are only remotely related to the major purpose. The individual who comes to the library to read needs not only the particular books and the appropriate facilities; he may also need a water fountain, a toilet, and perhaps a place to smoke. Any physical setting that provides many alternatives for the satisfaction of a primary purpose and the satisfaction of related and unrelated subsidiary purposes obviously provides considerable freedom of choice.

In an established physical setting the individual will position himself so that he can both accurately cognize and move freely in it in order to achieve goal satisfactions. The individual must know his environment in order to search in it and use it appropriately in the pursuit of particular goals or objectives. Of course, a familiar setting in which the individual routinely satisfies particular needs is less likely to reveal the person's continuing adaptation in these respects. On the other hand, in any new setting or where a familiar setting changes, the person will in some implicit fashion reorganize his relationship to the physical environment so that his freedom of choice is maximized.

The extent of the person's freedom of choice in a given physical setting depends not only on the enduring structure and design of that setting, but on what happens in it from one moment to the next. Changes in light, sound, and temperature may either increase or decrease freedom of choice in, for example, a library, recreation room, living room, or office. If a hospital room is improperly lighted, the patient may be unable to read; and if the other patient in his semiprivate room is too noisy, he may not be able to concentrate on writing a letter. The mere presence of other people may reduce freedom of choice if the individual either cannot or will not carry on particular activities in the presence of others.

If the structure of the physical setting precludes the possibility of a desired behavior or range of behaviors, relatively permanent alterations in the physical surroundings may be undertaken. In this way the range of choices available is expanded. Of course, every expansion of possibilities through environmental manipulation at the same time precludes other choices, setting in motion the never-ending effort to organize the environment in ways that will maximize freedom of choice within the range of existing purposes and needs.

Freedom of choice involves much more than freedom from environmental constraints, but we are here concerned with the environmental context and particularly with freedom of choice in relation to the concepts of privacy, territoriality, and crowding. Our thesis is easily stated. We start with Westin's (1967) definition of privacy as "the claim of individuals, groups or institutions to determine for themselves when, how, and to what extent information about them is communicated to others." These are the objective defining conditions for privacy; if an individual believes these conditions are met, he will experience a sense of privacy. Clearly the specific circumstances under which this sense of privacy is experienced vary widely, but in all cases psychological privacy serves to maximize freedom of choice, to permit the individual to feel free to behave in a particular manner or to increase his range of options by removing certain classes of social constraints.

Anecdotal evidence of the importance of privacy in the daily existence of individuals in a complex society is readily available. Descriptions of the lack of privacy—and its consequences—among those who live in a ghetto are reported by Lewis (1961; 1965), Goodwin (1964), and Schorr (1966). There are, of course, many other situations in which crowding combined with social isolation evokes a strong sense of the loss of privacy. Vischer (1919) reports that the main complaint of French and German pris-

oners during World War I was that constant contact with other prisoners engendered a lack of privacy. From Vischer's account it is clear that the prisoner's response to the continual presence of others, irritability and resentment, revealed in excessive criticism of others and boasting about themselves was an attempt to maintain identity in the face of a complete lack of privacy. In a very different setting, the *kibbutz* or communal settlement, Weingarten (1955) reports that some smaller settlements did not survive because a small number of individuals were unable to continue living with each other in an isolated setting. Communal life can lead to frustration and tension if the continual awareness of other persons in the setting and the constant exposure to public opinion result in a sense of loss of privacy.

The crucial role of privacy in any attempt to understand man's relationship to a man-made world is not to be disputed. However, as Pastalan suggests (1968), this concept has not been examined in a systematic attempt to generate theoretical and empirical data. Privacy, as it is currently treated in the literature, is not a simple, unidimensional concept with an easily identifiable class of empirical referents. Indeed the question, "What is privacy?" can evoke a wide range of conceptions, not all of which are directly relevant to questions concerning the design and organization of the physical setting. And for those conceptions that are directly relevant, differences in emphasis and approach still remain. Yet with all this, decisions involving the design, organization, and use of space are still made as if the meaning of privacy was clear, and its implications for the development and functioning of the individual and groups of individuals in a variety of physical settings were fully understood.

Westin's discussion of privacy reveals the full complexity of the uses of this concept. As a political scientist sensitive to the changing nature of American sociopolitical structure in relation to the freedom of the individual, he states his definition in normative value terms. To speak of privacy as a claim of the individual is meaningful primarily in a democratic society, and this fact, for the political scientist, raises a host of questions: To what extent does the individual in America actually enjoy this right? What factors in American society facilitate its expression? What factors inhibit it? Considering the design and organization of the physical environment in the light of the changing character of the urban setting, we may even ask if, given this right, people can achieve privacy.

For the environmental psychologist and sociologist, the question of the individual's right to make decisions about his privacy is less important than the question of the function of privacy for the individual. To understand the relationship between the individual's behavior and the physical environment, it is important to establish what his needs are with respect to privacy and what he expects his physical world to be like in the light of these needs. Experience already tells us that cultural and subcultural factors play a role in what individuals want and expect in the realm of privacy. Whatever the needs of individuals in this respect, still another task for the environmental psychologist is to specify by means of theory and research the conditions under which these needs are aroused and satisfied. Finally, there remains the no less crucial question of what consequences follow from persistent frustration of human needs for privacy, or whether there are any conditions under which privacy ceases to be important?

The significance of questions concerning individual needs and expectancies in privacy is revealed by Westin's analysis of privacy into four basic states and four related functions. As we have already suggested, privacy subsumes various classes of empirical events, and Westin's analytical schema bears this out. The four basic states he suggests are solitude, intimacy, anonymity, and reserve.

Solitude is the state of privacy in which the person is alone and free from the observation of other persons. The key words here are "observation of other persons," for the person is still subject to auditory, olfactory, and tactile stimuli as well as to other sensations in the form of pain, heat, and cold. Solitude, then, is a state of complete isolation from the observation of others, and is almost identical with privacy as defined by Chermayeff and Alexander (1963).

Intimacy refers to the type of privacy sought by members of a dyad or larger group that seeks to achieve maximally personal relationships between or among its members, who are, for example, husband and wife, family members, peers, and so on. Here the requirements for privacy go beyond mere freedom from external observation. There is an attempt to minimize all sensory input from outside the boundaries of an appropriate physical setting.

Anonymity is a state in which the individual seeks and achieves freedom from identification and surveillance in a public setting, for example, in the street, in a park, on the subway, or at an artistic event. To be self-consciously aware of direct and deliberate observation in public is to lose the ease and relaxation that is often sought in such a setting.

Reserve, Westin's final state of privacy, in a sense is not only the most complex of the four states psychologically but its requirements lie more in the nature of interpersonal relationships than in the nature and organization of the physical setting. Stated simply, reserve is the state of privacy allowing each person, even in the most intimate situations, not to reveal certain aspects of himself that are either too personal, shameful, or profane. To achieve reserve, individuals in group situations must each claim it for himself and respect it in others.

In discussing functions of the various states of privacy, Westin again establishes a fourfold classification. A basic function of privacy is to protect and maintain the individual's need for *personal autonomy*, which is a sense of individuality and conscious choice in which the individual controls his environment, including his ability to have privacy when he desires it. Privacy, whether through solitude, intimacy, or anonymity, may serve the function of *emotional release*. Both social and biological factors create tension in everyday life, so that from the point of view of physical and mental health, people need periods of privacy for various types of emotional release.

Privacy affords the individual the opportunity for *self-evaluation*. To take stock of himself in the light of the continuing stream of information received in his day-to-day experience, the person must remove himself from these events so that he can integrate and assimilate the information they present. Indeed, in a state of solitude or withdrawal during reserve, the individual not only processes information but also makes plans by interpreting it, recasting it, and anticipating his subsequent behaviors. Finally, Westin sees privacy serving the function of *limited and protected communication*, which in turn serves two important needs for the individual. First, it meets his need to share confidences and intimacies with individuals he trusts, and second, it establishes a psychological distance in all types of interpersonal situations when the individual desires it or when it is required by normative role relationships. Clearly in many role relationships psychological distance or limited communication is required and may be achieved through physical arrangements such as private offices, "for teachers only," or "for officers only."

Westin's analytical schema for privacy is both provocative and useful, if only because it asks what privacy is and what its critical dimensions are. On the other hand, like other preliminary analytical schemes, it can be criticized. For example, the four states of privacy are not always conceptually clear or consistent with each other. "Solitude" describes the state of the individual's relationship to the physical environment—that is, he is not observed by others—rather than his experience of soli-

tude. On the other hand, "intimacy" defines a very close relationship between people in terms of psychological distance, which is achieved by seclusion from others. Yet this classification overlooks certain kinds of small groups, such as juries, in which members are only formally related to each other because of their involvement in a common task and in which privacy is a necessity and intimacy frowned upon.

Still another problem in Westin's states and functions of privacy is the fact that the relationships among the four states are not considered. It might be useful to distinguish between individual states of privacy (solitude and anonymity) and group states of privacy (intimacy and reserve). It is also apparent that intimacy and reserve are closely related forms of privacy, intimacy is a state of privacy achieved by two or more individuals, whereas reserve is a limiting condition placed on that privacy by each of the "intimate" members of the group. Both intimacy and reserve not only involve the group as the unit of analysis, but in each instance privacy can only be achieved if all members of the group agree to achieve it. An intimate state of privacy involving two individuals depends on both agreeing to exercise the right to exclude others, and without such mutual consent intimacy does not exist. Similarly reserve is a form of privacy that depends on the consensus of the members of the group to accept a limitation on the information about self provided by the others. As with other social-psychological conceptions, the application of a concept mainly derived from an individual level of analysis to phenomena at the group level of analysis can lead to conceptual confusion.

The conceptualization of the psychological function of privacy as increasing the individual's freedom of choice in a particular situation by giving him control over what, how and to whom he communicates information about himself offers a starting point for the resolution of some of the issues in the study of privacy. This approach takes into account, for example, the paradoxical fact that privacy is essentially a social phenomenon and that it includes the freedom to communicate differently with different individuals and groups. Westin's states of privacy specify certain socially prescribed conditions under which various types of behaviors become acceptable. Although the conditions and the behaviors vary widely, they all have in common the property of maximizing the choices open to the individual.

The functions of privacy that Westin lists—autonomy, emotional release, self-evaluation, and protected communication—similarly have in common the function of providing conditions under which the individual is able to behave in ways that produce these consequences. The overall function of privacy thus is to increase the range of options open to the individual so that he can behave in ways appropriate to his particular purposes. In this context, the "need for privacy" is seen as the need to maximize freedom of choice, to remove constraints and limitations on behavior, of which those social constraints subsumed under the heading "lack of privacy" represent an important segment.

One way to achieve this desired freedom of choice is through the ability to control what goes on in defined areas of space that are significant for the behavior of the individual. In recent years the concept of territoriality has been very much in vogue in discussions of man's relationship to his physical environment. Drawing heavily on the work of animal psychologists or ethologists, it has been assumed, implicitly if not explicitly, that man too lays claim to his piece of ground, which he will defend against intruders. Because he occupies it, he has the right to determine who may or may not enter "his" physical domain.

There is no need for us to review the growing literature on territoriality in lower organisms. The volumes by Lorenz (1966) and Ardrey (1966) and the papers by Leyhausen (1965) and others answer this purpose. What emerges from all of the existing research, both systematic and informal, is clear and unassailable evidence that various species of infrahumans stake out a territory that they will defend against intruders in order to protect their young, obtain food, carry out mating patterns, and generally preserve the species by establishing appropriate ecological balances. The question that arises, of course, is where man fits into this picture.

Man too gives clear evidence of territorial behavior. Human beings no less than lower organisms define particular boundaries of the physical environment and assume the right to determine who can and who cannot move across these boundaries. Whether we speak of a man's home, the turf of the streetcorner gang, a secretary's desk in an administrative office, or the locker given to an elementary school teacher for her belongings, we find evidence of behavior that can be subsumed by the concept of territoriality. On the other hand, the analogy with territorial behavior in infrahuman species quickly reaches its limit. For example, much apparently territorial behavior in humans involves the concept of private property. To assume that such behavior serves the same functions in man as in lower organisms, or that it is rooted in man in innately determined biological mechanisms, simply ignores the properties that distinguish man from all other groups of living organisms. Whatever the complex social behavior of man under consideration, and regardless of its essential origins in biology, in every instance it has been so inextricably tied to man's direct socializing and broader cultural experiences that the biological or animal analogy must necessarily be discarded.

What function does human territoriality serve? Another way of putting this question is to ask under what conditions territorial behavior may arise. Man is both a living organism and a physical object. To exist and survive as a living organism, indeed to be free of physical discomfort or pain, he requires a minimum amount of physical space. Under conditions that threaten to eliminate or reduce this mini-mum, we can expect territorial needs to be aroused and expressed. Thus, under condi-tions of severe spatial restriction, the tend-ency to push others away and to arrange oneself properly may be basic expressions of territoriality as a means of reducing pain and discomfort.

The functioning individual, however, requires another kind of minimum space in order to survive. The individual needs more than the minimum space that guarantees that others will not touch him and that allows him to breathe, move, and carry on in recurrent transient situations. He must be able to move freely within and between physical settings to satisfy not only his hun-ger, thirst, sex, and other biological drives, but also his needs for affiliation, achieve-ment, success, and other complex social mo-tives. In this sense, then, and under given circumstances, the individual may have to define a large enough space for himself to permit the satisfaction of these drives and motives, including those that are socio-spatial in nature.

Such a need may explain, for example, the findings of studies of territoriality in two very different settings. In a study of psychiatric patients in a hospital ward, Esser et al. (1965) found many specific instances of territoriality. Some patients claimed particular seats in a dayroom as theirs and they regarded them as off-limits for all other patients. In another investiga-tion, reported by Altman and Haythorn (1967), nine pairs of sailors who were ini-tially strangers to each other, were studied over a ten-day period during which each pair lived in a small room and had no out-side contacts. The men showed a gradual increase in territorial behavior and a tend-ency toward social withdrawal. At the be-ginning, the observed territoriality was ex-pressed by fixed geographical areas, for example, part of a room, and highly per-sonal objects, such as a bed or the side of a table. Later it extended to more mobile and less personal things, such as chairs.

Territoriality of this kind was more rig-idly maintained in the case of pairs of sail-ors who both were either high or low in dominance characteristics than among pairs of sailors who were compatible in this re-spect, that is, one was high and the other low in dominance. In the study by Esser and his associates, dominance tendencies were also found to determine territoriality, but in this case, territoriality both reflected and maintained a relatively stable domi-nance hierarchy.

In both settings, it should be remem-bered, individuals were confined to a single area (a room or a ward) and were socially isolated from other settings and groups of people. Need satisfactions of all kinds, social as well as biological, were necessarily lim-ited to whatever resources existed within the confines of the restricted physical setting. To be dominant or to be high in the domi-nance hierarchy of these settings was to have potential control of these resources. However, the actual realization of these re-sources depended on the instrumentality of behaviors which guaranteed that defined spaces and objects would always be avail-able, what we have called territoriality. Indeed, territoriality, whether achieved through dominance, mutual consent, aggres-sion, or administrative authority, establishes which individuals have access to what areas of a physical setting, and therefore, to what extent the needs of each will be satisfied.

Territoriality in man is not limited to situations involving social isolation and con-finement. On the contrary, it is a ubiquitous phenomenon, although its manifestations may be less apparent in everyday physical settings. Territorial behavior is instrumental in the definition and organization of vari-ous role relationships. The prescriptions for social and occupational roles often include the meaning and use of particular objects and spatial areas for carrying out these role assignments. In many instances a social or occupational role establishes exclusive or near-exclusive use and control of a given space or setting. Only doctors and nurses—

not patients—have access to the drug cabinet in a hospital; the boss's office is off-limits to everyone except his secretary and his executive assistant when he is not in it; the high school teachers' cafeteria is not open to students. Control of specific territories and the role relationships between people are closely interrelated.

The development and maintenance of an identity in the individual does not depend entirely on how others react to his behaviors, skills, and achievements. It is also a matter of places and things, and the acquisition of both serves to define and evaluate the identity of the person for himself and for others. The loss of valued objects or places, or unwilling separation from familiar physical settings for long periods of time, may contribute to a blurring or even a loss of identity.

Territoriality is thus one means of establishing and maintaining a sense of personal identity. This fact may in part explain why, under conditions of social isolation, territorial behavior will in time manifest itself. The socially isolated pairs of sailors in the Altman and Haythorn (1967) study may have laid claim to particular places, beds, and chairs not merely to guarantee the satisfaction of biological and social needs, but also to preserve a sense of personal identity. Removed from their usual physical setting and confined to a single setting in which social interaction was severely curtailed, these men may have needed a more or less primitive and continuing definition of self through ownership of places and things. Not unrelated is the unprovoked declaration by the pre-nursery or nursery school child that a friend can no longer play with his toys. The young child is likely to behave in this fashion even when his self-esteem or personal identity is threatened by events unrelated to his interaction with the other child.

These considerations suggest that territoriality in humans is probably quite different from the primitive, biologically determined behavior observed in many animal studies. Territoriality in humans, defined as achieving and exerting control over a particular segment of space, seems always to be instrumental to the achievement of a more primary goal. We have suggested that the inner determinant of territorial behavior in the individual is his desire to maintain or achieve privacy. Territoriality thus becomes one mechanism whereby he can increase the range of options open to him and maximize his freedom of choice in the given situation.

Under conditions commonly described as "crowded," control over one's territory may be severely limited. "Crowding" is a ubiquitous phenomenon of modern urban life, and it is not always evidence of a major social ill. Indeed, crowding is an inherent quality of the urban setting that may lend excitement and a sense of participation for those within it.

When does crowding represent a significant social problem? Given the population explosion and the urban crisis, discussions of the crowded city, home, ghetto, school, highway, hospital, mental institution, and subway have become commonplace. In these instances it is clear enough why crowding is a problem. Some settings chronically contain excessive crowd densities that have immediate and long-range detrimental effects on individuals within them. There is no need to document the already extensive anecdotal literature on the effects of crowding in the ghetto (Lewis, 1961, 1965) and elsewhere (Biderman et al., 1963).

To the extent that the optimum number of individuals in a physical setting can be maintained or achieved by increasing or redesigning the available space, we can expect the negative effects of crowding to be reduced. What, however, is the optimum number of individuals for a neighborhood, community, school, classroom, hospital ward, or any other physical setting? For an institutional setting that is currently in use, it would be easy to assume that the optimum number of individuals equals the number of available facilities—for example, the seats in a classroom, the beds in a hospital ward, and so on. But such an approach really begs the question, although a classroom with 35 seats provides a less desirable learning atmosphere for 50 students than for 35.

The problem of crowding, however, goes beyond this oversimplified, objective approach. A setting may be crowded even when individuals and facilities are equal in number. What our previous discussion suggests is that crowding must be seen as a psychological as well as an objectively-viewed social phenomenon. Its conceptualization as both a cause and a consequence of modern urban life must go beyond the question of the number of persons in a given space. How a space is organized, for what purposes it is designated, and what kinds of activities are involved—all are factors that contribute to the phenomenology of crowding.

Crowding may be pleasurable as well as painful. Some people thrill to the excitement of the crowded city. Other things being equal, a large crowd is a good indication at the theater, stadium, beach, or party. An office area intended to induce a sense of belonging among its occupants may require more clerical desks than is desirable from the point of view of maximum task efficiency. Of course, crowded areas that have positive effects, or that are enjoyed because they are crowded, are often described in terms that avoid the word "crowded." In most cases physical settings described as crowded are meant to have negative connotations. They are experienced as unpleasant or even painful.

For purposes of conceptual analysis it is important to ask under what circumstances the individual experiences a sense of being crowded. Physical settings have normative properties. Whether or not the individual experiences them as crowded depends on what he has experienced in the past and therefore expects in the present. Regardless of apparent discomfort or frustration because of the numbers of persons involved, the individual may experience no

sense of being crowded because this is what he expects and regards as desirable. Cultural and subcultural differences in the use and organization of space, including differences in acceptable levels of crowd density, have only recently been emphasized (Hall, 1966; Rivlin et al., 1968; Lucas, 1964). The very great density of crowds that characterizes the Tokyo subways, with "slick" coats sold to passengers to facilitate their progress through the hordes of other riders—suggests that the normative adjustments in the use of space are indeed unusual. Similarly, disconfirmation of culturally established expectancies in the use of space may induce a sense of crowding. If custom prescribes that a task should be performed in a given setting with a given number of individuals, any increase in this number may be experienced as crowding by each person in the situation.

It is important to note, however, that failure to confirm normative expectations with respect to space never contributes to a sense of crowding alone, but always changes other aspects of the situation as well. To find that space cannot be used as one expects means more to the individual than just a lack of expectancy fulfillment. The addition of a second person to an office may mean many other things for the original occupant: that he can no longer behave in exactly the same fashion; that he must accommodate his working habits to those of another; and that in fact what was once his must be shared with another.

This suggests that perhaps a more significant factor underlies the individual's sense of being crowded. He may feel crowded to the extent that he is frustrated in the pursuit of his goals in a given physical setting by simply the presence of others. For the patient hospitalized in a double room, the presence of one other patient who disturbs his sleep may cause him to regard his room as crowded. For those waiting in line to eat at their favorite restaurant, the sense of being crowded may be much less if 20 people before them are seated within 15 minutes than if only two or three people ahead of them are not seated for an hour.

Of course we should not overlook the obvious. The phenomenology of crowding must take into account sheer physical discomfort or pain under circumstances in which people are in fact packed like sardines in a can. The jammed rush-hour subway in many urban centers or even the crowded shopping centers during particular holiday seasons are cases in point. The fact that crowdedness has become the norm for these settings doesn't mean that they do not cause the individual to feel crowded when he is in them. His acceptance of these situations should not be construed as absence of discomfort or pain. Acceptance is a form of adaptation to negative situations in which the individual's willingness to act to change the situation is neutralized; his ability to experience the pain and discomfort they induce is not, although over long periods of time the intensity of these feelings may be reduced.

Crowding as a psychological phenomenon, then, is only indirectly related to mere numbers or densities of people. It is possible to feel crowded in the presence of few people or not crowded in the presence of many. The significant element appears to be frustration in the achievement of some purpose because of the presence of others. Crowding is thus directly related to privacy and territoriality. Crowding occurs when the number of people an individual is in contact with is sufficient to prevent him from carrying out some specific behavior and thereby restricts his freedom of choice.

Freedom of choice then becomes a key concept in understanding privacy, territoriality, and crowding. We have suggested that the psychological significance of privacy, whether it is achieved by structuring the physical environment or by learning to relate in specific ways to others who are continuously present, is its capacity to maximize the individual's freedom of choice. Whether for reasons of personal autonomy,

emotional release, or self-evaluation, the individual in privacy can satisfy these needs on his own terms. The presence of others is not merely distracting but inhibiting. Other things being equal, privacy affords the individual the opportunity, in both thought and action, to attempt any and all alternatives and to make his choice accordingly. The significance of freedom of choice in the individual's relation to his physical environment is no less evident with respect to territorial behavior. To the degree to which the individual can lay claim to and secure an area or an object, he maximizes his freedom of choice to perform any behavior relevant to that area or object. When he controls the available alternatives and the means to these alternatives, he can achieve privacy and satisfy other relevant needs. Invasion of his territory reduces his freedom of choice. Similarly, the number of persons in a physical setting is experienced by an individual as crowding when it results in the perhaps less than conscious realization that his freedom of choice is reduced by the presence of others, or even of one other person.

The importance of these considerations for anyone concerned with physical space and man's behavior in the most general terms is clearly and succinctly expressed by Doxiadis (1968), who sees the individual's freedom of choice as an essential determinant in the planning and organization of cities.

We must learn how to plan and build our cities in such a way as to give all of us the maximum choices. Since our cities restrict, because of their structure, the total number of our choices . . . we must study the type of structure that eliminates the smallest number of alternatives. To achieve this we must conceive the best type of life and then build the structure that allows the best function in the sense of a maximum of choices [p. 22].

Whether the individual's freedom of choice

represents a decision to use the least crowded of a variety of routes, to read in his bedroom rather than the living room, or to formulate any of many other decisions that he faces each day, broadening the available possibilities open to him can only enhance his dignity and human qualities, making him less an automaton and more a fulfilled individual.

14. The Role of Space in Animal Sociology
JOHN B. CALHOUN

The distribution of resources through the environment, the localization of objects eliciting responses, and the presence of barriers to movement or perception at a distance, represent primary circumstances moulding the evolution and maturation of social behavior. I shall summarize the formulations of the role of such variables, which have developed from my research (Calhoun, 1956a, 1956b, 1958, 1962, 1963, 1964, 1966) over the past 20 years, and place in perspective to them a few insights apparent from the wide literature on the ecology and evolution of mammals.

From any point, such as where there occurs a concentration of food, it often happens that some other kind of object may be distributed at varying distances from this primary locus of orientation. Such situations are common to the experience of anyone observing animals in their native habitats. However, despite such extensive experience, it was only after reading Stewart (1948) and Zipf (1949) that I was able to conceive of a more rigorous approach to this general problem. I constructed a very simple environment (Figure 14–1) in which several groups of domesticated inbred house mice were permitted to reside, each group separately.

At one side of a 225 sq. ft. pen a single opening gave access to a smaller pen containing an abundant supply of food,

From *The Journal of Social Issues*, Vol. 22, No. 4 (1966), pp. 46–58. Reprinted by permission of the author and publisher.

water, and nesting material. This became the primary center of orientation. On the opposite side of the room there stood a stand with shelves at four levels above the floor. A single ramp connected one end of each shelf to the floor. From the ramp end of each shelf four nest boxes were equally spaced along its length.

On each shelf five kinds of data were recorded which reflected single responses, groups of related responses, or physiological states. These were (1) defecation in boxes, (2) defecation beside boxes, (3) boxes entered during periods of activity, (4) mouse found "sleeping" in box, and (5) grams of nesting material deposited in box. These categories are here simply designated as behaviors. Regardless of type of behavior, it took place most frequently on the shelf nearest the floor, or near the next box at the ramp end of shelves. Toward higher shelves, or toward boxes farther out from the ramp end, the frequency of behaviors declined. An exception to this rule applied to the highest shelf or to the farthest box along a shelf from its ramp end. The increase in behaviors taking place at these more distant points included the sum of behaviors which would have taken place at even more distant points had not this absence of opportunity, or barrier effect, been present. Heightened goal orientation, such as when sleep follows entering a nest box as opposed to merely brief visits during periods of exploration, caused accentuated use of boxes on lower shelves or near the ramp end of shelves, with con-

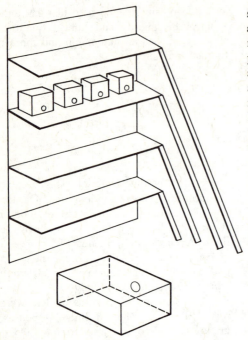

FIGURE 14–1. Diagrammatic representation of mouse-habitat. A four shelf stand, with four boxes on each shelf, formed the two-dimensional space over which mice spread their activities after visiting the small pen in the foreground in which were located the sources of food, water, and nesting material.

comitant more rapid decline in use of more distant boxes.

This influence of distance upon behavior alters social contact. The mean group size per box in the 2nd, 3rd, and 4th box from the ramp along shelves was respectively only 0.84, 0.65, and 0.56 of that in the box nearest the ramp. Likewise, the mean size of groups per box on the 2nd, 3rd, and 4th shelves were respectively only 0.46, 0.43, and 0.57 that per box on the lowest shelf. Furthermore, as groups of mice residing in such systematically structured habitats in turn became socially structured, the more dominant members concentrated their activities in areas nearer to the primary site of orientation, the food-water nesting material pen enclosure, while

still retaining their basic pattern of visiting all points but with fewer visitations to more distant points. In contrast, this normal pattern becomes partially disrupted for subordinate individuals; they tended to spend a disproportionate amount of time in places more distant from the major locus of orientation. This process accentuates the probability of associations among higher ranking individuals or among lower ranking ones. Very comparable results have been obtained with both wild and domesticated Norway rats.

It became imperative to gain more precise insight into the behavior of single individuals with regard to distance before it was possible to understand how this could affect social behavior. The basic tool in such study has been a long narrow alley with a starting compartment at one end containing food and water. Automatic recording provided a history of each trip out and back. Even when the alley was barren of structures except its walls, roof, and floor, and the rat introduced into it had a prior life history of living only in a smaller barren cage, it would, nevertheless, make a number of trips out into the alley. For each unit of distance more trips terminated nearest the starting compartment, with successively fewer at each farther location. A negative exponential equation of the form $\log_e y = a - bx$, where y is number of trips and x is distance of termination adequately describes the data (see Figure 14–2).

Furthermore, examination of long sequences of terminations of trips reveals that the distance at which any specific one is terminated is independent of that of the prior or succeeding one. This strongly indicates that in such constant surroundings the length, in effect the duration, of any trip is solely determined by some random signal from the central nervous system such that, no matter how long a trip has already continued, the same probability still exists that it will terminate within a fixed further amount of time.

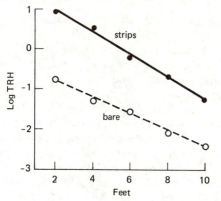

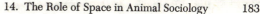

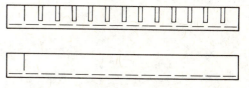

FIGURE 14–3. Cross-section side views of activity alleys. The lower represents a bare alley, while the upper one represents an alley structured with a pad of paper at each foot interval from the home compartment. The starting or home compartment is at the left of each.

FIGURE 14–2. Frequency of trips of varying lengths in structured and unstructured alleys. (Ordinate: TRH=trips per rat per hour. Abscissa: Distance of termination of trips. Mean trips per hour=6.31 in the structured alley vs. 1.17 in the bare alley.)

Such a barren alley can be structured by placing pads of paper strips at regular intervals (Figure 14–3). When this is done, the rat will make repeated trips out into the alley for paper with which it constructs a nest. Everything said above about the behavior of a rat in a barren alley applies to that in the structured one. However, many more trips are made and the probability of terminating trips increases (Figure 14–2). Thus, relevantly structuring the environment must modify central nervous system activity by increasing the probability of initiation of an appropriate behavioral state, while at the same time increasing the probability of it terminating. This latter effect results in the rat spending more time near its major point of orientation, its "home" cage compartment.

Now, we may turn from this one-dimensional environment to that of the normal, essentially two-dimensional one of such small mammals as mice and shrews in their field or forest habitat. Most such mammals have a single nest or burrow, or a few closely neighboring ones. From such a region the individual roams out and back for the various resources it needs for its daily life. Ecologists designate as the ani-

mal's *"home range"* the total space encompassed by such wanderings from and back to such a home base. Over most such home ranges every object meeting some need has roughly the same probability of being encountered within each relatively smaller subunit of space. In this general sense, resources can be said to be uniformly distributed over the range on the average.

When one records the places at which an individual makes specific responses and plots them, it is found that the number of responses per unit area declines with distance from home (Figure 14–4). Interestingly enough this distribution over space is quite adequately described by the bivariate normal distribution function. (See Calhoun, 1964, for proof that the distribution of responses in two-dimensional space conforms to the bivariate normal distribution function rather than to the univariate normal distribution function.) That is to say: 39 percent of the responses will occur within a 1σ distance from the home range center, 86 percent within a 2σ distance, and 99 percent within a 3σ distance. Sigma here in terms of the equation for the bivariate normal distribution function is merely some appropriate measure of distance in feet or meters.

How, then, do we make the insights developed in the one-dimensional environment helpful in appreciating an animal's use of space in a two-dimensional one? It will be helpful to clarify a conclusion relating to obtaining and transport of nesting

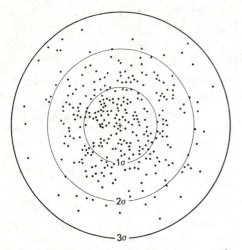

FIGURE 14–4. Diagrammatic representation of the distribution of responses in two-dimensional space about a central home site, marked by a +. Response points are normally distributed with reference to both their x and y coordinate dimensions and thus fit the bivariate normal distribution.

material mentioned above for one-dimensional environments. In such activity a single rat may make several hundred trips with only a few seconds intervening between successive trips. Three consecutive trips might terminate with strips taken from the 7th, 3rd, and 10th distance, respectively. In each case the rat will have passed by two or more opportunities to stop and get a piece of paper to take back to its nest-in-process-of-construction. Obviously, the rat is highly motivated, as evidenced by the many consecutive transport trips without much time for other behaviors intervening between trips. In fact, motivation here becomes synonymous with the probabilities of starting and continuing trips. It may only be concluded that as long as the stimuli in the environment—here the paper strips—remain essentially unvarying, the rat is blind to them in the sense of not being able to respond to any specific pad it passes until the central nervous system sends out the signal which terminates the

outward trip. Only then can it attend to the neighboring relevant stimuli.

Furthermore, it was observed in the alley that the amount of time a rat vacillated back and forth about the point where its trip terminated, was proportional to the distance (duration) at which the trip terminated. Now, taking only these two conclusions, (1) that there is a constant probability of a trip terminating no matter how long it has already persisted, and (2) that amount of wandering at the end of a trip is proportional to the length of the trip before it terminates, it is possible to develop from them an equation for the distribution of responses about a home site in a two-dimensional environment that is so similar to the bivariate normal distribution function that we are never likely to get any empirical set of data that would permit us to decide which one describes home range best. Because of this agreement one is then led to the conclusion (despite the inherent circular reasoning necessary until other more direct experimental confirmation is available) that mammals are perceptually "blind" to constant stimuli during outward excursions, and perceptually "cognizant" of them during the wanderings about at the end of trips.

This is not to say that a domesticated rat couldn't react to a flashing light, suddenly facing it on an outward trip, or a wild mouse or shrew couldn't detect a relatively unusual or foreboding stimulus, such as a weasel, if it were to encounter one.

You will also note that I am jumping back and forth from data relating first to domesticated mice or rats and then again to wild mice or shrews. The inherent assumption is that we are here dealing with processes equally applicable to mice or men, or to cats or bats, for that matter. But I shall actually, in the next few paragraphs, be concerned rather specifically with small mammals, such as mice and shrews, which in terms of the ecological situations they face are the closest we can come to the types of primitive mammals from which most mammals, including ourselves, trace their ancestry.

Here, we return to the two-dimensional home range. Over the course of evolution the "metronomes" of the central nervous system which normally control the start of excursions, their termination, and the cutting in of periods of heightened awareness, must be attuned to opportunities for relevant behavior provided by the environment. Otherwise animals would die of starvation. This whole built-in process of the central nervous system is reflected in the measure of its home range. Animals having more scattered resources will evolve the CNS function which reduces the probability of terminating trips, and in other ways increases their home range; thus they will be assured of adequate resources.

However, if we take the circular area encompassed by a 3σ radius about an animal's home as its home range, for at least 99 percent of its responses are included within this area, it is apparent that, were any individual alone in a habitat, it would make very effective use of its home range. Resources toward the periphery would be very ineffectively utilized simply because the individual rarely gets there. Evolution tends to produce species whose behavior makes more optimal use of avenues for behavior—including use of resources—available to them. More effective use of resources can most readily come about, in the early stages of evolution, by the several members of a population shifting their homes close together so that their home ranges overlap.

It may be shown that when homes of neighbors are 2σ apart, and when all homes are uniformly distributed over the available space, that the accompanying overlapping will produce a nearly equivalent impact on every unit of space, while still providing the maximal separation of individuals compatible with such effective use of space.

Studies of small mammals in their natural habitat provide fairly good substantiation of the above concepts about home range. If the ideal pattern of distribution of

home sites for such fairly asocial small mammals is as described above, some very interesting social relationships between any individual and his associate become apparent. Take any such individual. He will have six nearest neighbors, and lines connecting their homes form a hexagon. Due to the considerable overlapping of their home ranges, he will, by chance alone, fairly frequently encounter them. Likewise, he will have 12 next-nearest neighbors, and lines connecting their homes will form a larger hexagon about the central animal's home. Due to the much lesser overlapping of ranges of these 12 with the one central individual we are considering, they will encounter him less frequently, and so know him less well than do his six nearest neighbors.

At this level of social evolution each individual is sufficiently antagonistic to his neighbors to assure that neighboring home sites are approximately 2σ distance apart. Yet this force of dispersal becomes counteracted by the opposite one of attraction, in proportion to the probability of neighbors contacting each other by chance. This causes animals to shift their homes slightly toward each other. Some few individuals in a large population will each have attracted toward their own home site the home sites of all of their six nearest neighbors. This represents the first basic tendency toward group formation. The central animal will become the dominant member of this dispersed group of seven individuals. He will also have attracted toward him some of his next-nearest neighbors, but some of them will shift their home away from his toward the home of some other individual who, by a comparable process, is also gaining dominance. In this stochastic process of attraction, each animal becoming a dominant center will, on the average, attract toward him 5 of his 12 next-nearest neighbors, in addition to all of his 6 nearest neighbors. Thus, on the average, each of these primordial dispersed groups, which I have designated as a "constellation," will contain 12 individuals, consisting of a socially dominant individual and eleven associates who shift the sites of their homes toward his.

From this stage of loose aggregation of slightly clumped, but still quite dispersed homes sites, there is an abrupt transition to species customarily living as compact groups of about 12 adults. This number applies to a host of species as divergent as the Norway rat, howler monkeys, or man in his more primitive state as represented by the bushmen of the Kalahari Desert. My essential thesis thus holds that the stochastic process involved in developing the most effective use of resources by relatively asocial species will normally favor the evolution of species living as compact groups averaging 12 adults.

Professor Glen McBride of the University of Queensland (in a discussion with him during February 1964) has pointed out that other optimum group sizes can evolve by this process. If a species with dispersed home sites suddenly comes to live in an environment with a much greater density, or abundance of resources, home sites will tend to approach each other more closely and thus there will develop much more overlap of home ranges. Any one animal will encounter more associates. Related to the extent of such new abundance of resources, the optimum group size characterizing the evolving species will become one of the expanding series of 27, 48, 75, 108. . . . Domestication of the chicken has thus changed its heredity to be most nearly compatible to living in groups of 48.

Once a species has developed the capacity to live as members of a compact group, they then become subject to being further influenced by another change in their physical environment. The members of most such compact groups do not always remain together. Individuals make independent excursions away from the group or away from the site to which all return to sleep. During such excursions an individual may encounter some locally abundant resource, which in fact may be found in only a few places of the now-shared home range of the group. Even by chance, two individuals may find themselves simultaneously at the same such site, while responding to the resources available at it. Whenever this happens, there is the opportunity for each individual to become a secondary reinforcer for the other. As such secondary reinforcement becomes established, animals actively seek out places for satisfying such primary drives as hunger or thirst where others of their kind have already assembled.

When several such sites are scattered over the range of a group, some will more likely be encountered than others. Gradually, all members of the group will assemble at the one place, where other factors affecting movement make it more likely to be encountered. Here each individual can be assured of the greatest likelihood of encountering others, of fulfilling its acquired secondary drive of needing to be near others. In time, all other sites within the group's range will be ignored. Each individual may pass by one or more sites where food and water can be obtained in order to reach the one site where it most likely will find others of its species. It is as if food is no longer food merely because it has the correct visual and olfactory characteristics—there must also be other members of the respondent's own species standing nearby.

For the same reason that the ranges of individuals overlap, so do the ranges of neighboring groups. Thus, as the members of one group begin to spend an inordinate amount of time at one place, the several neighboring groups nearest to it may likewise be attracted to this one place. I have called this process the development of a behavioral sink. In a state of nature it may cause at least seven times the optimum number of animals to assemble at one place, with a resulting accompanying array of abnormal behaviors developing. Prominent among these are nearly total dissolution of all maternal behavior, predominance of homosexuality, and marked social withdrawal to the point where many individuals appear to be unaware of their associates despite their close proximity.

I have shown how this behavioral sink, with all its manifestations, can be induced to develop under experimental conditions with domesticated Norway rats. Such a behavioral sink also came to characterize Virginia deer, when after the mid-1930's large amounts of hay and grain were placed at widely separated points throughout the severe winter months.

The behavioral sink also has its time aspects. Where there is only a single site of a resource, or where attachment to one of several sites has developed through the process described above, it may happen that so many individuals aggregate at the site that each may interfere with the opportunity for his associates to obtain the resource available at that site. At least this will be so unless the individuals present spread their activities out over time.

For rats, just the opposite happens. In another of my experimental situations, one or two narrow parallel channels led to a source of water. In the one-channel situation, two rats could go in side by side. In the two-channel situation, a rat on one side would find water available only if another rat was at the opposite source of water. In both situations there was the opportunity for one rat to associate presence of another with his obtaining water. When 16, 24, or 36 rats were placed in a pen containing such a situation, the characteristic response became one where, when one rat went to get water, most of his associates would also rush over and attempt to crowd into the narrow channels. Under such circumstances most failed to secure any water. After awhile, all would go away and sleep for quite awhile even though most had received no water. This process would be repeated over and over again. Most rats lost considerable weight or died from lack of water, even though the source was vacant

from use most of the time, so that there was ample opportunity for drinking. Such is the time aspect of the behavioral sink.

Through the course of evolution, many species must have been subjected to the behavioral sink process often enough to threaten their survival as a species. Those which survived must have become genetically transformed into another species capable of maintaining the basic integrity of each individual despite the persisting crowding. On a theoretical basis this integrity is bought at the price of reduced social awareness. Each individual must be endowed with an heredity facilitating a diminution in the intensity, frequency, and complexity of responses to associates, and a reduction in the necessity for learned responses. The buffalo and the caribou of the American plains and tundra represent such forms. They have long since gone down a path of evolution forever barring them from the door to cultural evolution.

The physical environment has also fostered the evolution of other species which have followed along a quite different path but one that similarly precludes any future possibility of cultural evolution for them. In evolution it seems as though all possible paths, all possible opportunities, will be exploited. One of these is the abundant source of food under the surface of the earth—a mass of roots and rhizomes equal to that of plants above the surface, as well as the myriad invertebrates subsisting on the living and decaying underground plant material.

On every continent mammals have ducked under the surface and remained there. There is the marsupial mole in Australia. Mole-like Insectivora or gopher-like Rodentia occur across the other continents. Typically, each adult constructs its own subterranean network of tunnels without connections to those of its neighbors. There these troglodytes spend their lives, each alone, buffered from the sight, sounds, smells, and social stimuli churning in the world above. Contact among adults is restricted to the minimum required for copulation at the rare periods when the female is receptive. Shortly after weaning, the mother ejects her young from the home burrow to seek their own maze-like cell. Such is the culmination of evolution accompanying the stimulus deprivation associated with accommodating to the subterranean source of food. This whole process of accommodating to stimulus deprivation, including its end state, I wish now to designate as the "behavioral vacuum."

Research on the behavior of animals may provide insight into the human condition with regard to either its evolution or its present circumstances. The utility of such insights depends upon there being a relationship between the present human condition and its antecedents in simpler forms of mammals, or on the fact that comparable processes characterize both man and lower forms. Research on the behavior and sociology of animals other than man stems from two opposing perspectives. First, from the direct study of man insights develop which culminate in a paradigm amenable to exploration through the use of animal subjects. Second, on the basis of the knowledge of the evolution and natural history of a particular species one examines more rigorously the processes affecting the species in its natural setting or devises more controlled settings which will permit the process or phenomenon to be expressed in a more precise or exaggerated manner. This latter approach often produces insights not previously recognized on the human level, or which if seriously recognized may be seen in a different relationship to other processes. Those of us who are engaged in research on animals from this second point of view can only point out certain insights which we believe merit the consideration of those of our colleagues whose concern is directly with man.

For example, I have mentioned briefly here the explanation, developed in detail elsewhere, for the finding that so many species of mammals, up through the primates, live in compact groups of about twelve adults. By virtue of his biological heritage, *Homo sapiens* appears to have been long related, and presumably adjusted to, a way of life that was most harmonious when the population was fragmented into small social groups of about twelve adults. For this reason it behooves us to examine what restrictions upon culture such biological heritage may impose. From a theoretical point of view (Calhoun, 1964, 1967) a long heritage of a particular group size imposes the necessity for an intensity and frequency of interaction with associates commensurate with the stochastics of the relatively closed system of that size group. Furthermore, I have shown that, when we increase the group size of rats above that of about twelve, which does characterize the species in its native state, all members exhibit both physical and psychological withdrawal to greater degree than may be anticipated for individuals in a customary sized group. Thus we may suspect that if man does have a biological heritage most compatible with life in a relatively closed small social group, then a major function of culture may be to schedule contacts such that their frequency will approximate that which characterized life in the smaller, more closed social group of a much earlier stage of biological and cultural evolution.

These concepts relating to group size serve as background to others more directly related to the import of the physical environment. As noted above, the physical configuration of the environment, including the prevalence of stimuli which might elicit responses, can increase the likelihood either of an animal following a solitary way of life or, on the other hand, of it joining with its fellows in large massed groups even when much nearby similarly structured space remains relatively unused. These observations merely raise the question whether there are comparable situations on the human scene which may lead to either excessive isolation of excessive aggregations, either of which would alter the frequency of interaction. Judged by both mathematically derived formulations and observations on animals, such changes in frequency of interaction lead to types of social organization which I would judge to be completely incompatible with a cultural context of life such as characterizes man.

There is one final possible relevance of these studies on animals to the human situation. Merely increasing the number of relevant stimuli increased the number of excursions which rats made into their environment, where they engaged in responses appropriate to these stimuli. This raises a question, not yet answered even with animal experimentation, but still worth keeping in mind with regard to man's physical environment: Can responses to inanimate objects be equated with those to members of his own species with reference to an apparent need for a certain number of satisfactory social interactions per unit time? If there exists such an interchangeability between physical and social response eliciting objects, then the complexity of the physical environment must be evaluated against the existing social organization.

15. Human Territoriality
JULIAN J. EDNEY

Until a decade ago, psychologists had virtually ignored the effects of geographic location on human behavior. In fact, the effects of both location and of the molar physical environment are still given scant attention in current efforts to explain behavior; generally a person's physical surroundings are treated as a background variable, out of the main focus of interest.

From *Psychological Bulletin*, 81, No. 12, 1974, pp. 959–973. Copyright 1974 by the American Psychological Association. Reprinted by permission of the author and the publisher.
   [1] This article was written while the author was supported by U.S. National Institute of Mental Health Fellowship 1 F01 MH47570-03. It is based on a paper submitted in partial fulfillment of the requirements for the doctoral degree at Yale University.
   The author would like to thank J. Richard Hackman for his help and advice on an earlier draft of this paper; Nancy L. Jordan-Edney for her patience, moral support, and thoughtful advice; and P. E. Diebold, D. Feldman, and J. Rodin for their useful criticisms and suggestions.

But lately, attempts have been made to link behavior and molar environmental variables. The emerging discipline of environmental psychology and Barker's (1968) theory of behavior, ecological psychology (Barker, 1968), are evidence of this new direction. Territoriality is a phenomenon that links an organism's molar environment directly to his behavior, social or otherwise. Human territoriality can conveniently be characterized with a catchall description as a set of behaviors that a person (or persons) displays in relation to a physical environment that he terms "his," and that he (or he with others) uses more or less exclusively over time. Definitions of the phenomenon stress one or another of the behaviors in this set and therefore vary somewhat from this description and from one another. Having received the attention of ethologists and naturalists for many decades, the phenomenon has only lately attracted students of human behavior.

Unfortunately the available information on human territoriality is limited and unsystematic; ideas in the area are loose, definitional problems exist, and theories have never progressed beyond an elementary and informal stage. No particular paradigm characterizes research on the topic, and as yet there is no standard set of principles that can be reliably applied to problems in the area. Available research reports also reveal a diversity of assumptions and starting points. However, the topic holds the interest of workers in many fields, it is clearly relevant to environmental issues, and it lends itself to both pure and applied research. Elusive as the phenomenon may be, it has spurred considerable controversy in both professional and popular journals.

One of the purposes of this article is to highlight the features of territoriality that have drawn recent attention. Another is to provide a background for evaluating research. Since human territoriality traces its academic origins to animal territoriality, it is appropriate to introduce three seminal publications that involve the animal expression.

Territoriality in Animals

Appearing as a description of animal behavior as early as the eighteenth century, territoriality has been an established concept in ethological literature since the 1920s. Most of the research originally involved birds, although studies on fish, reptiles, rodents, ungulates, and primates are also reported. Carpenter (1958) noted that most of the research in his review was not experimental; a naturalistic method of observation predominated. (Influences of this kind of technique are later reflected in some studies of human territoriality.)

Territoriality seems to occur throughout the vertebrate phylum (Carpenter, 1958) but with wide variations that depend on species, habitat, season, climate, population pressures, social organization, food supply, and other factors. Territories may be held by single animals, by pairs,

or by groups, and they may be defended against all comers, or only against those of the same sex or species (Klopfer, 1968). Carpenter listed no less than 32 functions of territoriality that had been suggested before his review was published; these include insuring adequate space for individuals, regulating population, reinforcing dominance structures, reducing sexual fighting and killing, providing for security and defense, reducing the rate of spread of disease, regulating despotism, and localizing waste disposal. These functions stem largely from the fact that territoriality spreads individuals out in space. Carpenter pointed out that some of them may have important implications for evolutionary processes.

Wynne-Edwards (1962, 1965) suggested that territoriality is a link between social behavior (competition and dominance) and population control in many animals. Communities regulate their own numbers by the use of "conventionalized" competition, usually among males, for territory and the accompanying rights to food and (sometimes) mates. The winners are dominant animals and acquire social status, but since they are a fraction of the population, only a few community members get access to space, scarce resources, and females, thus limiting the size of the next generation. The next generation is also guaranteed food, because winners of territory spread themselves thinly over the terrain. Thus the habitat's food sources are not exploited beyond regenerative capacity, and a reasonable supply is ensured for the future.

The competition for territory is a central part of selection processes, because territory winners are often the only breeders in the community. Competition for real estate thus replaces Darwin's idea of biological selection through males competing for females.

Part of the appeal of Wynne-Edwards' theory is that it appears to apply to humans too (Wynne-Edwards himself cautioned against this application). There are attractive analogs to animal territorial relations in human society, including the relationship between territory ownership and social status, and territory size and social status. It certainly appears sometimes that humans also engage in conventionalized (i.e., symbolic, rather than tooth and claw) competition for possession of material goods including land; and it is clear that human territories also show a correlation between size and the status of their occupants (as in office sizes and the status of the occupants in a business building).

Lorenz (1969) and Ardrey (1966) are both writers who have helped place the concept of human territoriality into the public interest; in addition they both trade heavily on the appeal of animal analogs to human behavior. Lorenz (1969) referred to territory in his treatise on aggression in animals. He posited that intraspecific aggression is a crucial aspect of animal life and that it has important survival value for a community because it acts as a source of mutual repulsion among individuals of the same species (in opposition to the "herd instinct"), causing members of a group to space out over their biotope. This ensures that its sources of nutrition are not exhausted. Territoriality is, in essence, the spatial expression of this intraspecific repul-

sion.[2] Man, too, is subject to his aggressive instincts, and shows it in a history of bellicosity.

In Ardrey's (1966) view, man shares with other animals a specific drive to claim and defend territory, a drive that is genetic and ineradicable. However, territoriality is governed by an "open" instinct; its expression is shaped, but not determined, by experience; nevertheless, its effects cannot be suppressed without serious consequences. Territory provides three basic elements necessary to healthy life: security (strongest at the borders, where defense against outsiders is most likely to occur), and identity. Like Lorenz, Ardrey believed that aggression and animosity are natural states among vertebrates, including man. Friendliness and cooperation are secondary phenomena appearing only when outside threat unites individuals against a common enemy. Clearly this runs counter to the rational philosophy of Kant and that of Rousseau, philosophers who see man as a basically cooperative being. However, Lorenz seems to have drawn less spirited criticism for his propositions than Ardrey.

It is virtually undisputed that humans exhibit territoriality, at the national, family home, or temporary (my-seat-in-the-bus) level, but the question remains how meaningful the similarities are to animal territoriality. Ardrey's attempts to "beastopomorphize" man have been assailed for (a) oversimplifying in presenting animal territoriality as a unitary phenomenon; (b) basing his argument only on analogies (Klopfer, 1968); (c) failing to point out that human cultures vary in their territorial expression (some human groups are nomadic and display only transitory attachment to territory; some are strongly territorial; All-

---

[2] The Lorenz-Ardrey view is reflected by much of the animal literature that uses active defense as a defining characteristic of territoriality. In fact, territory occupants may not be in a continuous state of aggressive tension; some species work well with a system of mutual avoidance of other's territories, obviating aggressive defense. This view also lies behind the statement that one of the functions of territory is to reduce aggressive behavior. While it is true that aggressive individuals fight less when they are separated spatially, there are some indicators (especially in humans) that removing opportunities for territoriality produces more amicable relationships (e.g., Ehrlich & Freedman, 1971, stated that crowding women together in high-density conditions actually results in more cooperative feeling among

them). Territory may, in fact, promote aggressiveness. Eibl-Eibesfeldt (1970) pointed out that in some cases among animals, territory seems to be a prerequisite for aggressive behavior, as in stickleback fish (see also Lorenz, 1969, p. 152).

and, 1972); and (d) attempting to explain human behaviors simply by labeling them (Elms, 1972).

Despite Ardrey's arguments, it does not follow from the gross similarities between the territorial behavior of some animals and man that the underlying mechanisms are the same in both, nor that they are genetic. To assume so, incidentally, has an interesting political consequence: It relieves man of the moral responsibility for his territorially aggressive acts and invites the rationalization of human territorial warfare as simple fulfillment of man's genetic predispositions. A number of writers have at some point drawn on animal territoriality as a point of departure for discussing the human expression (e.g., Hall, 1966; Morris, 1969; Sommer, 1969), but a number of important differences can be noted, and based on points made by Sundstrom and Altman[3] we can summarize the arguments for distingushing between animal and human territoriality (especially as forwarded by Lorenz and Ardrey) as follows: (a) Human use of space is very variable and not like the stereotypic spatial expressions of animals. This suggests a learned, rather than a genetic, basis. (b) The association between territory and aggression, treated as fundamental by Lorenz and Ardrey, is not clear-cut in humans. (c) Territories serve primarily "biological" needs for animals (shelter, food sources), whereas humans use them also for secondary purposes (e.g., recreation). (d) Animals usually use only one territory and for continuous periods of time. Humans may maintain several territories (home, office, mountain cabin) in different locations. (e) Humans also "time share" temporary territories (e.g., tables at a restaurant), whereas this is rare among animals. To Sundstrom and Altman's

list we can add: (f) Total invasion of one group's territory by another is rare among nonhuman animals but occurs in human warfare. (g) By virtue of their weapons, humans are the only organisms that can engage in territorial warfare without trespassing. (h) Humans are also the only territorial organisms that routinely entertain conspecifics on home ground without antagonism (as in visiting). These differences indicate that animal territoriality serves best as a set of analogies for the human expression, not a source of direct explanations for it.

Human Territoriality

Definitions[4]

What is human territoriality? It may be premature to attempt a simplified, all-encompassing definitional statement at this point; Kaufmann (1971) suggested we may have to await a better empirical grasp of the phenomenon. Several definitions have been suggested, however, and they show a variety of meanings have been given to the phenomenon. Definitions can be grouped in three ways: First, those stressing active defense; second, those referring to defense plus other defining characteristics; and third, those excluding defense.

First, writers promoting the unity of animal and human territoriality stressed the role of active defense.

Lorenz (1969): "Territorial [behavior is] the defense of a given area [p. xiii]."

Ardrey (1966): "A territory is an area of space—water, earth, or air—that an animal or group defends as an exclusive preserve primarily against members of their own species [p. 3]."

Eibl-Eibesfeldt (1970): "I propose that any space-associated intolerance be called *territoriality*, where a 'territory owner'

---

[3] E. Sundstrom and I. Altman. Relationships between Dominance and Territorial Behavior: A Field Study in a Youth Rehabilitation Setting. (Tech. Rep.) Salt Lake City: University of Utah, January 1972.

[4] The format for this section is unabashedly and gratefully borrowed from Altman's (1970) study.

is that animal before which another con-specific must retreat [p. 309]."

Second, other writers recognized that there is more than simple defense of space in human territoriality.

Hall (1959): "The act of laying claim to and defending a territory is termed territoriality [p. 146]."

Brower (1965): "Territoriality [is] a tendency on the part of organisms to establish boundaries around their physical confines, to lay claim to the space or territory within these boundaries, and to defend it against outsiders [p. 9]."

Parr (1965): "Territory is the space which a person as an individual, or as a member of a close-knit group (e.g., family, gang), in joint tenancy, claims as his or their own, and will 'defend' [p. 14]."

Stea (1965): "Territorial behavior [reflects] the desire to possess and occupy portions of space [and, when necessary, to defend it against intrusion by others] [p. 13]."

Sommer (1966): "[Territory] is an area controlled by an individual, family, or other face-to-face collectivity. The emphasis is on physical possession, actual or potential, as well as defense [p. 61]."

Sommer (1969): "Territory is an area which is personalized (rendered distinctive by its owner in some way) and defended [p. 14]."

Pastalan (1970b): "A territory is a delimited space which an individual or group uses and defends as an exclusive preserve. It involves psychological identification with the place, symbolized by attitudes of possessiveness and arrangements of objects in the area [p. 4]."

Third, a few recent definitions avoid the term *defense*.

Proshansky, Ittleson, and Rivlin (1970a): "Territoriality in humans [is] defined as achieving and exerting control over a particular segment of space [p. 180]."

Sundstrom and Altman (1974): "Territorial behavior [is] habitual use of particular spatial locations [p. 115]."

Altman and Haythorn (1967): "Territoriality is defined in terms of the degree of consistent and mutually exclusive use of particular chairs, beds, or sides of the table [p. 172]."

Taken together, definitions of human territoriality include an interesting variety of concepts: space (fixed or moving), defense, possession, identity, markers, personalization, control, and exclusiveness of use. This indicates partly an initial confusion over a new concept and partly that the phenomenon is complex. Attempts have been made to delimit the phenomenon by broadening its definition until everything likely to be relevant is included.

Altman (1970): "Human territoriality encompasses temporarily durable preventive and reactive behaviors including perceptions, use and defense of places, people, objects, and ideas by means of verbal, self-marker, and environmental prop behaviors in response to the actual or implied presence of others and in response to properties of the environment, and is geared to satisfying certain primary and secondary motivational states of individuals and groups [p. 8]."

The last definition is clearly need- or motive-oriented. In this sense it offers "explanation," whereas most other definitions are descriptive. It also covers an enormous range of behaviors. Altman (1970) stated, in fact, that territoriality in humans covers possessiveness about ideas and objects as well as space. Finally, this last definition sets the most flexible tone for research directions.

Theoretical Work

Theory in human territoriality is at an elementary stage, consisting for the most part of limited conceptualizations. However, existing formulations can be organized on certain basic dimensions. One involves the amount of emphasis given to territoriality as a *physical* or *spatial* system, as opposed to a *behavioral* one.

Territoriality is a phenomenon that links behavior to geographic places, but writers vary in their emphasis on the environmental components (including the physical dimensions of a territory, its appearance, boundaries, and geographic relationship to others) and the behavioral components (e.g., related defense behavior, "enhancement of energy" [Ardrey, 1966], sense of possession, etc.). As an example of a physical approach, Roos (1968) described the concepts of home, core area, territory, and range as a series of concentric entities of increasing size. Stea (1965) distinguished topologically between territorial units, territorial clusters (groups of dwellings), and territorial complexes, which include several clusters. In a somewhat figural fashion, Lyman and Scott (1967) also conceived of territories in a "concentric" form: Humans make use of (a) inner (mental) space, (b) body territory, (c) free territory (any area where a social gathering occurs), and (d) public territory, the largest form. With regard to the physical accoutrements of territories, Goffman (1972) categorized territory markers as (a) central, (b) boundary, (c) ear markers, and Sommer (1966b) speculated that boundaries of various opacities will serve to delineate psychologically the territories in libraries; otherwise, theoretical work on the physical qualities of human territories qua territories is scant.

As a bridge to the behavioral side of the dimension, the links between territory size, on the one hand, and the occupant's status (a behavior variable) have been discussed by several writers (e.g., Ardrey, 1966; Sommer, 1969; Wynne-Edwards, 1962). It is clear that man, with many vertebrates, often displays a positive correlation between social status in a local community and the size of his territory there. The significance of this phenomenon is obscure; whether territory size serves to accentuate social distinctions and perpetuate them (Sommer, 1969) or whether social distinction functions as a means to better acquire large territories (cf. Wynne-

Edwards, 1962) is an open question. A confusing point is that large territories are not always associated with high status; members of the elite may trade a large country estate for a small city penthouse with no drop in status; clearly the desirability of the physical *location* of the territory is a mediating factor. The relationship between status and territory is further complicated by the finding that animals will sometimes substitute a pecking order (hierarchy) for a relatively democratic territorial order if crowded to the point that there is no room for individual territories (e.g., Davis', 1959, work with starlings). Thus, in some cases territorial space correlates positively with status, sometimes it is an alternative to it.

Leyhausen (1955) theorized that in many species a dynamic balance exists between "absolute hierarchy," a stable peck order, and "relative hierarchy," a democratic arrangement of individuals, each sovereign and outranking others on his own territory (see below); ecological factors like density affect which type predominates. Leyhausen suggested that the well-being of human communities depends on the balance between the two, that democracy has one of its indispensable biological roots in relative hierarchy and that territorial dominance (relative hierarchy) stands for the rights and liberties of the individual. Without elaborating the mechanisms involved, Leyhausen also suggested the balance between hierarchies is useful in balancing population numbers. Relative hierarchy is the important idea that the psychological phenomenon of dominance has geographic components: An individual dominates all others so long as he is on home ground; territory is thus a social equalizer for lower ranking organisms.

Leyhausen made two additional points: (a) territorality not only disperses individuals in space but also holds them together. Individuals are rarely dispersed as widely as possible, but to distances that reflect a balance between repulsive *and* attractive forces. Repellent forces among animals (leading to aggression) are easier to spot than attraction forces, but the latter operate, even among "solitary" animals. (b) The idea of a boundary around a home range (the area normally covered by a person on daily rounds) is spurious. The home range is a system of paths to points; the area enclosed by the paths is of little interest to the individual.

Territoriality is important as a behavior system that is woven into the social organization of communities. A number of writers (Ardrey, 1966; Esser, 1970; Lorenz, 1969; Sommer, 1969; Wynne-Edwards, 1962; and others) have noted that both dominance hierarchies and territoriality promote social order in the sense that both give structure to communities—one social, the other spatial. If one views territory as aggression reducing (cf. Lorenz), then both also reduce aggression; hierarchies because they put social distance between individuals, territories because they keep individuals separated spatially. This is the basis for much research interest in the relationships between dominance and territoriality in humans (see below). But there is also a more subtle mechanism through which territoriality maintains social order that applies to humans. This is the connection between territory and behavioral organization in terms of roles.

People learn through socialization that specific environmental contexts often accompany certain roles (enactment of shared expectations for behavior). Proshansky et al. (1970a) explained that prescriptions for social and occupational roles often include the exclusive use and the meaning of particular places (e.g., part of being a faculty member [role] is having access to the faculty lounge; the "meaning" of a room is endowed through its exclusive use as an office). Thus "territoriality is instrumental in the definition and organization of various relationships [Proshansky et al., 1970a, p. 180]" in a community. Although the idea that molar environments determine behavior is not new (cf. Barker, 1968;

Goffman, 1959) the idea that territories support social roles is an interesting contrast to the idea that behavior in territories is genetically determined.

Apart from role connections, territory sometimes has striking effects on the psychology of the individual that have yet to be explained. Ardrey (1966) stated that territory stimulates the individual, and gives a sense of security and identity, but he described this process as "mysterious." Lyman and Scott (1967) also stated that territory provides the individual with identity (is this more than simple spatial distinctiveness?) and allows personal idiosyncracy and freedom of action. A clear benefit provided by many, but not all, territories is *privacy* (the right of the individual to decide what information about himself should be communicated to others). Connections between territory and privacy have been mentioned by Pastalan (1970a), who stated "privacy may constitute a basic form of human territoriality [p. 88]" and who pointed out that privacy facilitates personal autonomy, vital to individuality. Privacy is basically an instrument for achieving goals of self-realization; by providing a context for emotional release, self-evaluation, and psychological protection, it also allows the individual a sense of control (Pastalan, 1970). To the extent that territory also provides these psychological benefits, its meaning is clarified.

Proshansky et al. (1970a) elaborated: "in any situational context, the individual attempts to organize his environment so that it *maximizes* his freedom of choice . . . In all cases psychological privacy serves to maximize freedom of choice [p. 175]." One way to achieve this desired freedom of choice is through the ability to control what goes on in defined areas of space. Since "territoriality [is] defined as achieving and exerting control over a particular segment of space [Proshansky et al, 1970a, p. 180]," it can be construed that "the inner determinant of territorial behavior is [the] desire to maintain or achieve privacy. Territoriality thus becomes one mechanism whereby [the individual] can increase the range of options open to him and maximize his freedom of choice [Proshansky et al., 1970a, p. 180]." Moreover, *crowding* is directly related to privacy and territoriality because crowding occurs when "the number of people an individual is in contact with is sufficient to prevent him from carrying out some specific behavior and thereby restricts his freedom of choice [Proshansky et al., 1970a, p. 182]." In sum, for Proshansky et al., "Freedom of choice . . . becomes a key concept in understanding privacy, territoriality and crowding [p. 182]."

Some territories (e.g., seats on a bus, places on a beach) do not offer much privacy, at least in a visual sense ("psychological" privacy may not be compromised by this); empirical work is clearly needed to determine if people are prepared to sacrifice territory for privacy, or vice versa. One further point not addressed by Proshansky et al. (1970a) is that freedom of choice may be *enhanced* in nonprivate, nonexclusive living arrangements (like communes) where people have relatively free access to other's spaces and possessions, broadening their spatial choices.

Apart from theoretical work that links two or more psychological concepts, the literature contains a conceptual analysis and two important taxonomic works. In the former, Altman (1970) suggested that the concept of human territoriality has a multifaceted meaning (see his definition above). Altman summarized research done to that date and suggested future research strategies should be multivariate, longitudinal, and situationally broad to encompass the variety of behaviors (cognitive, individual, social, motivational) that he saw subsumed by the phenomenon. He also proposed that the analysis of territorial phenomena should attend to internal mediating processes (cognitive-motivational), and that the phenomenon might profitably be studied in systems terms, serving both determinant and resultant

functions. To achieve the broadest understanding of territoriality, Altman stressed that a simultaneous appreciation is needed of four aspects of the phenomenon: (*a*) behavior forms—the various modes of territorial response, objects involved and functions involved; (*b*) situational contexts—physical-social determinants and settings; (*c*) antecedent factors—conditions producing and affecting territorial behavior; and (*d*) organismic factors—the needs, drives, and motivations of the organisms involved. Altman also suggested that humans exhibit such elaborate preventative measures in defending their territories that actual territorial invasion rarely occurs; full-scale aggressive territorial defense reactions are also atypical because there are numerous alternatives open to humans that suffice: verbal warnings, fine motor activity (e.g., frowning), etc.

Goffman (1972) offered a taxonomy of human territorial behavior. At the center of human social organization is the concept of the "claim," an entitlement of an individual to possess, control, use, and dispose of something: territory is one example of a claim. Territories are categorized as (*a*) fixed, (*b*) situational (usually temporary), and (*c*) egocentric (moving around with the claimant). Goffman listed eight forms of "territories of the self": personal space—the portable bubble of space sometimes seen as part of interpersonal distance[5]; stalls—well-bounded, temporary claims; use space—space near a

[5] Enough distinctions exist between personal space, in this sense, and true territory that the two are now usually regarded as different phenomena. Distinctions listed by Sommer (1959) are (*a*) personal space is carried around while territory is stationary; (*b*) territory boundaries are usually visible while personal space boundaries are not; (*c*) personal space always has the body at its center, territory does not; and (*d*) animals will fight to maintain dominion over their territory but will withdraw if others intrude into their personal space.

person with instrumental value (cf. Roos' jurisdictions); the turn—relational position, as in place in a queue; sheath—skin and clothes; possessional territory—personal objects arrayed around the body (markers); information preserves—private "cognitive" territories; conversational preserves—group "information" territories. Goffman also categorized markers: central markers—employed within territorial bounds; boundary markers—to designate the line between two adjacent territories; and ear markers—identification tags, signatures, etc. He also categorized six forms of territorial violation: invasion by a body, touching or defiling the sheath or possessions of another (e.g., sexual molestation), penetration of eyes (e.g., staring), intrusion of sound, inappropriate addressing through words (e.g., intruding into a conversation), and contamination by some form of bodily excreta. Under "territorial offenses" he listed encroachments (intrusion and obtrusion), self-violations (e.g., self-befoulment with excreta), and preclusiveness (maintaining inappropriate exclusive preserve).

Lyman and Scott (1967) also offered a taxonomy of four territorial forms: public territories, to which most individuals have freedom of access (but some groups may be discouraged, a form of discrimination); home territories, areas that allow freedom of behavior plus a sense of control and intimacy; interactional territories, an area where a social gathering may occur (e.g., a cluster of people at a party); and body territory, anatomical space and the immediate surrounds. Lyman and Scott identified three kinds of encroachment: violation (unwarranted use of a territory), invasion (uninvited crossing of a boundary), and contamination (rendering it impure). These can be reacted to in three ways: turf defense (aggressive defense), insulation (barrier erection, often anticipatory), and linguistic collusion (communal isolation via the use of special jargon or idiosyncratic communications).

Brower (1965) offered a minor taxonomy, classifying territorial occupancy as personal, as in homes, allowing privacy and control; community, as in private clubs; society, where all members of the public have access but behavior is somewhat restricted (e.g., public highway); and free, where there are minimal restrictions (e.g., a deserted beach).

Taxonomies are useful at this stage in the development of the topic: They demonstrate a variety of situations to which the concept can be applied, and illustrate that a number of perspectives can be organized on the topic. Nevertheless they do not really explain the phenomenon, and find their best use as foundations for further conceptualization.

A trend that may strengthen in the future is the systems approach to conceptualization (cf. Altman, 1970). Stea (1965), for instance, asserted that there is a mutual interdependence of behavior and physical environment; space and behavior are functionally related. Changing the defining characteristics of a territory (e.g., boundary size, shape, or differentiation) tends to change the behavior that occurs there. But conversely, a change in behavior may result in changes to the physical territory (e.g., in size, decoration, state of repair, etc.). Thus environments and contiguous behaviors serve each as determinants and effects. The assumptions of the systems approach are shared by many environmental and ecological psychologists; the approach has fundamental implications for future theory building because it plays down the role of determinism. Proshansky, Ittleson, and Rivlin (1970b) suggested, in fact, that environmental psychology will probably have to abandon the simple cause-and-effect paradigm; this may have an important impact on research in human territoriality.

Summary of theoretical points. In limited conceptualizations, human territoriality has been related to a variety of biological, social, and psychological concepts including population, resource distribution, dominance, status, aggression, control, freedom, privacy, possession, security, stimulation, and identity. As a concept it has been analyzed and taxonomized, but the phenomenon still awaits a full-fledged theory.

Empirical Evidence

Empirical studies on human territoriality have involved a variety of operational definitions and methodologies. As a result the research literature sometimes appears disjointed. This review treats the studies primarily by methodology on a "naturalistic observation-controlled experiment" dimension, giving meaningful order to the paradigms that have been employed. The studies are also grouped in sequence according to subject population.

For two reasons, many forms of territoriality are difficult to study in standard laboratory settings: (a) territoriality sometimes involves long periods of association between person and place, and (b) convincing feelings of personal attachment to artificial laboratory surroundings are difficult to elicit in subjects. Consequently, researchers are often required to use their ingenuity in adapting field methods to naturally occuring territories in order to test specific hypotheses. While the time problems partly account for the paucity of research in this area, the nature of the territorial phenomenon also brings special logistical problems into fieldwork, and this partly explains the slow accumulation of empirical work.

First, a number of studies have been concerned with people in institutions from which they are not free to leave. These studies often involve long-term observational techniques that parallel the naturalistic ethological techniques of early studies in animal territoriality. They generally assume, and demonstrate, that social interaction in groups is associated with spatial factors. These first studies all involve collections of people, and rarely consider the cognitive components of territorial behavior.

Roos (1968) described territoriality aboard a warship, where he observed crew members defending work spaces against one another. Roos made the distinction between jurisdiction (simple defense of space) and territory (ownership and defense of space), and recounted conflicts of territorial interest, especially where jurisdictional rights of some men clashed with the territorial rights of others (as when equipment repairmen invaded the habitual preserve of the radar operators). Territorial behavior, in Roos's scheme, is something that maximizes a person's control over space to enhance its positive value, and territory itself gives the potential for power, influence, comfort, and control; however, the writer saw definite limits to the usefulness of applying ethological concepts to human behavior.

A second field study described the arrangement of sleeping territories within cabin groups in a boys' camp. Blood and Livant (1957) showed that the members of a group (cabin) arranged their beds spatially to reflect the social structure of the group. Young boys placed their beds next to others according to friendship patterns and need for protection. Older boys (more than 10 years) manipulated these spatial relationships differently, however, to implement power structures within the group.

Neither Roos's (1968) nor Blood and Livant's (1957) studies reported quantified data. But like the following six psychiatric studies, they dealt with interactions within groups of people.

Lipman (1967) described the territorial qualities placed on everyday chairs in the day room of an old people's home. From his frequency-of-use data, it is clear that individual inmates became almost exclusively attached to specific chairs; they would keep to their personal seats despite considerable psychological costs and physical inconvenience in doing so. Inmates' seats obviously became more than something to sit in; as territories they had psychic and emotional significance to their occupants.

After noticing that some inmates were closely attached to specific spots on the ward floor, Esser, Chamberlain, Chapple, and Kline (1965) observed a ward of 22 mental hospital patients for 16 weeks. Since the inmates' group also had distinctive dominance patterns, the investigators attempted to relate these patterns to territorial behavior. Dominance was defined by a combination of factors: the number of personal contacts a patient made, whether he initiated these, and their duration. By dividing the ward space off into squares, and using time-sampled observations, observers noted the mobility of the patients. If a patient occupied a square or group of squares for more than 25% of the observation time, that location was defined as his territory simply by his occupation. Almost 50% of the patients were territorial by this criterion. Generally speaking, the top one third of the dominance hierarchy moved freely over the ward, and defended no personal territories. The bottom one third tended to claim spaces in remote areas of the ward. The middle third claimed larger territories and in central parts of the ward. Territorial patients also tended to avoid areas of the ward claimed by others—that is, their ranges were constricted. These distinctions were not statistically significant as the number of subjects involved was too small. Esser et al. claimed the relation between dominance and territoriality to be especially believable because the measures of dominance depend partly on the self-isolation habits of the patients. In fact the relationship is probably spuriously high precisely because these indexes are not independent. The study also included observation of overt aggressive behaviors. The authors claimed that territoriality was related to aggression, citing the fact that of all the territory-owning patients, only three did not show aggressive behavior. A close look at the data shows that this claim is unfounded since an equal proportion of nonholders show no aggression.

Esser (1968) later conducted a similar study in which he observed a group of hospitalized children for six weeks. A relationship between dominance (defined by social contact and by staff reports) and territoriality was discovered, which weakly resembles the previous finding. Again, since the definition of dominance was based indirectly on the self-isolation habits of the children, his finding is rather obvious. Here territoriality was defined either on a frequency of use *or* an active defense basis.

In a further study in the same paradigm, Esser (1970) recorded data for six weeks on 20 adult patients in another mental hospital ward. He defined territoriality as occupation of a space for more than 15% of the time-sampled observations and standing ground against a higher-ranking patient. Territoriality was exhibited by 7 out of the 20 inmates by these criteria; these individuals won 85% of all attempted physical acts of dominance on home territory, and 55% of those off home ground. Off home ground, simple status in the ward-dominance hierarchy was a fair predictor of winning acts of dominance, whereas on home ground, status position did not predict outcome. Analysis of the dominance behavior of the remaining 13 patients was not included, but from the limited data presented there is support for Leyhausen's (1965) notion of "relative hierarchy"—social dominance relative to home territory rather than to an absolute hierarchy.

In the same kind of setting, Paluck and Esser (1971b) observed the spatial behavior of three small groups of normally aggressive, retarded boys in a playroom over a three-week period, again using an exclusiveness-of-use criterion for territoriality. Normally the boys were verbally reprimanded for aggressive behavior, and while this proved effective in some cases, it did not reduce aggressive behavior related to defense of territory. Territories were interpreted by the investigators as basic and necessary reducers of psychological complexity in the boys' lives and enhancers of personal control for them, hence the difficulty in changing behavior linked to them. Twenty months after this study, Paluck and Esser (1971c) returned five boys from one of the original groups to the research setting. All immediately reclaimed or tried to reclaim their old territories; this was interpreted as "rigidity of spatial behavior" (it may simply have reflected fondness for the familiar).

The last two studies indicate territorial behavior can appear as early as five years of age. Since little is known about the development of territoriality in humans, studies are needed to explore its emergence and to link it to other developmental sequences.

A final study of Esser's (1973) was also intended to illustrate the significance of ethological concepts (territoriality and dominance) for understanding behavior in institutions. Observations were made of 17 institutionalized boys in a residential building over a period of 25 weeks. Territoriality (defined as a person spending more than 9% of the obsevation time in one place) was related to a person's dominance standing, as assessed by staff. In this study, territory holders generally held higher rank than nonholders. Interestingly, territorial fighting among the boys was associated with position in the pecking order, but was negatively associated with boys' standings on "general adjustment" (a measure that included behavior outside the building). It appeared that "territorial adaptation" was effective for raising status inside the building, but not for functioning on the outside.

Sundstrom and Altman (1974) pointed out that the relationship between territoriality and dominance has received mixed support. One of Esser's studies (Esser et al., 1965) showed patients were more territorial), whereas another observational study in the same paradigm (Esser, 1973) showed a positive relationship (high-dominant subjects were more territorial). A third study (Esser, 1968) showed no significant association.

In a study of their own, Sundstrom

and Altman (1974) investigated dominance-territory relationships over 10 weeks in a residential facility for 23 male juvenile offenders, using procedures similar to Esser's, and using two operational measures of territoriality: (a) "individual territorial behavior," or the degree to which a person limits his space usage to one or a few spaces; and (b) "area territorial behavior," or the extent to which an area's use is relatively exclusive to one user. The study is notable because it introduces a formula for quantifying territorial behavior. Dominance was defined as a relationship in which one person has the ability to influence another.

Results showed a variable relationship between dominance and territory: A positive association appeared during the first of three unequal time periods and a (nonsignificant) negative association for the final period. While dominance ranks within the group were stable over time, territory–dominance relationships were not, and it is not entirely clear what accounted for the changes.

It may be hazardous to generalize from institutionalized samples used in the studies reviewed this far since both subjects and settings are unusual. With reference to this point, Colman (1968) described striking changes in demeanor and behavior of a medical patient that occurred when the patient moved from a hospital setting to his own home. In the hospital he was typically defensive and agitated; at home he was at ease, in control and accommodating. Colman attributed the difference to the patient's territorial situation. A short note by Paluck and Esser (1971a) also indicated territorial behavior of retardates (used in two studies: Paluck and Esser, 1971b, 1971c) differs from normals in that retardates prefer filled territorial spaces (spaces with physical objects in), while normals prefer open spaces; normals were also less aggressive.

Two nonexperimental field studies follow that involve measurements of a variety of aspects of territoriality and everyday populations of normal humans. The findings were neither interpreted in the light of any ethological work, nor were they generalized to animals.

Edney and Jordan-Edney (1974) provided information on temporary group territories claimed in a public place. They measured the radii of territories claimed by groups of beach users, and related these to other data. Territories were defined as marked (personalized) spaces surrounding groups that groups saw as their own. Group territories were found not to expand regularly with number of people in the group; instead, space per person tended to decrease as group size increased. Measurements of local density were made around each group (distance to closest neighbors), and this was found to correlate only moderately with territory size. Territory size increased with time in same-sex groups, but mixed groups tended to deploy markers as time passed. Markers were hypothesized to serve a similar function to space as an expression of territorial consolidation.

A second nonexperimental field study was conducted in a suburban area (Edney, 1972b). It also involved group territories (family residences) but was primarily oriented to testing time–territorial relationships. It was hypothesized that human territoriality is primarily an extended association of a person or people with a given place. In this survey study, suburban homes defended with "no trespassing" signs and fences (forms of territorial defense) were compared with control properties with no defenses. Results showed that families living in defended homes had lived significantly longer on the property, but also *anticipated* a longer residence there in the future. Legal ownership of the property could not reliably account for this time–territorial relationship. An additional finding was that occupants of property with "no trespassing" signs answered the door significantly faster than controls (inter-

preted as heightened defensive vigilance).

College students have been used in a number of field studies. De Long (1970) observed a college seminar group for 16 weeks and found individuals' dominance ratings (based on "demonstrated leadership ability") correlated nonlinearly with their positions around the seminar table (participants' territories were determined according to three criteria reflecting predominant use of a particular position); the correlations also changed with leadership shifts in the group. As a study of spatial arrangements within seated groups, De Long's report falls under the "ecology of small groups" (developed primarily by Sommer, 1961), out of the main purview of this article; however, De Long specifically included criteria for territorial attachment to chairs. As a study of territoriality within groups, this study can be grouped with Esser's (1973) work, Cheyne and Efran (1972), Knowles (1973), Lipman (1967), and Altman's work (1970).

The following studies differ from those above in that they are all involve true experimental techniques. With the exception of Altman's studies they also all involve college student populations.

Interest developed early around temporary single territories in public settings. Sommer and Becker (1969) involved college students in a series of studies on the marking (personalization) and defense places in college libraries and cafeterias, where places at tables are typically claimed and identified with the claimer's belongings as "theirs" for the duration of the visit. First, Sommer and Becker conducted a paper-and-pencil study, showing that if students are asked to show where they would situate themselves to avoid others in the setting, they prefer territories in libraries that (a) face away from the main entrance, (b) are close to a wall, and (c) are toward the rear of the room. However, instructed to defend actively their claims, subjects locate their territories (a) facing the entrance and (b) more often in the middle of a table, or on an aisle. Small tables abutting the wall were also preferred for the defense.

Marking is explicitly included as a criterion of territoriality by some (e.g., Sommer, 1969) and has received some attention in the research. Testing the strength of various types of markers in a library, Sommer and Becker (1969) found their effectiveness as space reservers varied with surrounding population pressure. At moderate density, most objects (including library journals, books) were found to protect a single space claim totally, and to delay occupation of the rest of the table. Under heavy demand for space, more personal markers (personal jackets, sweaters) were more effective than impersonal ones. Invasion of marked spaces did occur (exclusively by males, incidentally), and the authors noted that claim jumpers often questioned neighbors about the status of marked space before settling. A study was therefore conducted to determine what factors effect protection of library spaces by neighbors; it was discovered that (a) neighbors would only support a marked claim if directly asked, and (b) the longer the original claimant was gone, the less the neighbor would support his claim against an invader (Sommer & Becker, 1969).

Sommer has been a major contributor to the human territoriality literature, and his work focuses primarily on individuals; like most other studies, there is little reference to cognitive aspects of the territorial process: The accent is on overt behaviors rather than on the *meaning* of the situation to subjects. Although Sommer included defense as a definitional component of human territoriality, it is never clear that active defense enters into his experiments.

Becker (1973) continued the work on spatial markers. Set in a college library, his experiments demonstrated that (a) given a choice, people prefer to settle at unmarked tables than at marked ones; (b) if they do settle at marked tables, people spend

less time there than at clear tables. Probing his subjects' understanding of inanimate markers, Becker found people interpret markers as representing the owner and as protectors of the owner's space. Interestingly, Becker suggested the effectiveness of a marker in reserving a space claim occurs not because it signifies an area is occupied, but because potential invaders space themselves from markers as they would from other people. Becker also noted the absence of active defense of personal spaces in libraries; he suggested that library places be termed "jurisdictions" (see Roos, 1968) since they are used temporarily and for specific purposes.[6]

The importance of active defense in human territoriality has become an open issue. While the majority of definitions include it as a criterion, none of the experimental research successfully uses active defense as a sole operational definition. Becker and Mayo (1971) argued that space claims in library and cafeteria settings are not real territories unless the claimants rebuff (i.e., defend against) invaders. Their experiment showed in fact that most occupants of criteria places (31 out of 33) flee when spatially invaded; and they concluded that marked claims at cafeteria tables are merely expressions of comfortable interpersonal distance. The problem

[6] It should be noted that the distinction between territory and jurisdiction was based initially on the factor of ownership (Roos, 1968). There is some confusion over the concept of jurisdiction, and in the long run it may obscure the concept of territoriality rather than clarify it. The problem lies in the fact that ownership of a territory can occur in several ways: legal ownership, possession through continued but not exclusive use of a place, exclusive use, joint ownership, etc. The opening description of territoriality in this article involves a claimant's feeling that a place is "his," and therefore recognizes that a given place may be claimed by more than one party. Research relating the concept of possession (itself poorly understood) to territoriality is needed.

is obviously definitional. If active defense is omitted as a definitional criterion and a standard of ownership used instead (in the sense that the regular occupant sees the space as "his"), cafeteria and library places still qualify as territories until the occupants leave.

Territories differ in the visibility and permeability of their boundaries. Many have fixed and impermeable perimeters (e.g., walls); however, Lyman and Scott (1967) suggested that temporary group territories (such as those enclosed by small conversing groups) are surrounded by invisible but psychological "social membranes" that function as barriers. A few experiments focus on factors affecting the permeability of these invisible boundaries. Deliberately stationing groups of people so as to interrupt pedestrian traffic in a university building hallway, Knowles (1973) varied both group size and the statuses (age) of the obstructing group members. He found that fewer passersby walked through stationary high-status groups than low-status groups, and fewer through a group of four than a group of two.

Efran and Cheyne (1973) conducted similar studies and discovered that the physical distance between a conversing pair of people in this kind of arrangement affects invasion of the space between them by passersby: Beyond four feet (the limit of Hall's, 1966, "personal distance") the boundary surrounding the stationary pair becomes ineffective, and passersby begin to walk between the conversationalists. Cheyne and Efran (1972) likewise showed that this kind of intrusion is less frequent when the stationary conversing pair is female, or a male–female combination, than when it is male. Control groups in the latter study also showed that people will walk between a nonconversing pair as much as they will between inanimate objects (waste barrels) placed at the same distances.

Efran and Cheyne (1974) focused more closely on the behaviors accompanying invasion into these temporary territories.

Requiring individual subjects to walk through stationary groups, they found that the moving invaders were emotionally affected by the experience, displaying subtle, agonistic facial expressions during the invasion, and giving negative mood ratings immediately afterwards.

Using an entirely different experimental approach to studying the territorial phenomenon, Edney (1973) used college dormitory rooms as natural territories. The experiment explored the relationships between territory possession and the psychological variable of control (intended to be broader than, and subsuming, the concept of dominance). Differences between the behaviors of normal tenants in the dormitory rooms and visitors were studied as they both occupied these rooms—thus subjects were run in resident–visitor pairs. Differences between residents, as a group, and visitors, emerged on a number of paper-and-pencil measures. Residents reported being more resistant to the control of others ("defensive control") than did visitors to the same room. Visitors saw the residents as being more "at home" than vice versa; and residents evaluated the physical territories more positively than did visitors. Asked on a separate question to attribute their behavior during the experiment to various causes, visitors attributed both subjects' behavior more to personality factors than did residents in the same rooms. The findings indicate that future investigations of cognitive factors behind territoriality will prove fruitful.

The following experiments are set in laboratory environments; they tend to involve analysis of variance methods and multiple dependent measures; results are often expressed as higher-order interactions between independent variables. Generally they provide ideas of what produces territoriality, as opposed to what effects existing territories produce.

Studying people's reactions to prolonged periods of social isolation, Altman and Haythorn (1967) observed the behavior of pairs of sailors confined in a small, 12-foot by 12-foot room, over periods of 10 days. Social withdrawal between the members of each pair or "cocooning" occurred as time progressed and territoriality (defined as the exclusive use of certain areas in the rooms or items of furniture). Territoriality was accelerated in pairs whose members were incompatible on certain traits (e.g., need dominance). As defined, territoriality actually occurred in significant amounts only with certain items of furniture; furthermore, there was a developmental sequence: fixed areas (beds) and highly personal things first, less fixed things (chairs) later. Active defense was not used as a criterion of territoriality. The authors suggested that personal space factors are important correlates of social–emotional states and that definition of one's own space is associated with emotional well being. The data clearly indicate that spatial adaptation to stressful conditions is partly a function of personality.

Altman, Taylor, and Wheeler (1971) reported complex data on a second social isolation study, showing that pairs of sailors able to complete a successful eight-day confinement period actually showed territorial behavior from the outset, and declined with time. By contrast, aborters of the mission started low, but rose in territorial behavior as their abort date approached (measures of stress, anxiety and social activity paralleled the territoriality data, suggesting a generally consistent behavioral pattern). Here it appears territoriality acted as an adaptive device in group functioning in that it set personal boundaries, established and facilitated bases of social interaction, and "smooths out functioning in a way analogous to social norms and conventions [Altman et al., 1971, p. 95]."

Completing the methodological continuum on which these studies have been ordered is Edney's (1972a) laboratory experiment that attempted to isolate the sufficient factors necessary to generate territorial feeling and behavior. Two factors were tested: (a) prior experience with a physical environment (a room), and (b) anticipated experience with it. Neither were confounded with social experience there. Results showed that (a) prior experience with the room reduced the distance subjects would stand from a stranger later introduced into the environment; (b) subjects claimed more floor space (in a model building task) when the stranger was present if they anticipated future return to the environment. Anticipation of return also produced higher levels of agitation (in a projective test) in the stranger's presence; in the same condition, the subjects also stood closer to the stranger. Together, these were interpreted as nascent territorial responses.

This review excludes research studies that deal metaphorically with the term *territory*, or that allude to the phenomenon without contributing to any understanding of it.

Besides an anecdotal note on the psychiatric benefits of individual enclosures for patients on hospital wards (Barton, 1966), it might be mentioned that the research in the area is generally not prescriptive in the sense that it does not indicate or recommend environmental changes. Applications may be generated from much of Sommer's, Altman's, and Esser's work, but are usually not specified in the reports. However, an exceptional example is a recent work that attempts to apply the concept of territory to human dwelling design. Newman (1972) pointed out specific architectural features in some apartment buildings that promote alienation among tenants (e.g., number of floors, arrangement of apartments along corridors); he made recommendations for future designs that will promote both cohesion among building occupants and defense of common territory in and around buildings, reducing antisocial behavior there.

Summary of empirical work. Variety in paradigm, operational definitions, and subject population characterize the empirical work on this topic. Human territoriality has been empirically related to marking, density, dominance, control, experience with the environment, personality, neighbors' behavior, sex, boundary strength and time, attribution, meaning of the environment, and other factors; studies have also involved both single-person and group spaces.

Conclusions

The literature on human territoriality reveals a variety of basic assumptions and approaches. Much of the research is fragmentary and as yet there are few organized progressions of investigation, making meaningful comparisons difficult. Human territoriality is a complex phenomenon, but empirical work is beginning to gather momentum. One point that will be important to keep in mind as this work progresses is that territoriality serves organisms at a number of levels: intraindividual, interindividual, and on the community level, and that each of these should be explored keeping an eye to the others for context and perspective.

Outstanding Issues

In addition to those problems raised elsewhere in this article, there are a number of problems clearly needing clarification in this topic. Outlining some of the most basic: (a) Does territorial expression operate "hydraulically" (expression in one mode reducing expression in another), as implied by Lyman and Scott (1967), or is it a "snowballing" phenomenon (the more one gets, the more one wants)? (b) Is territory necessary for health, happiness, and efficient functioning in humans? Despite Ardrey's (1966) statement that serious consequences occur if organisms are deprived of personal territory, individuals throughout history have chosen communal, space-sharing, aterritorial ways to live. An extension of this

question is (c) can fulfillment of related needs (e.g., for privacy, status, needs for ownership) satisfy the "territory drive"? (d) What are the determinants of territorial behavior? We are beginning to answer this question, but disputes over the role of genetics in territorial behavior still abound. (e) Can the concept of territoriality be applied meaningfully to cognitive domains? (e.g., defending ideas, opinions, creative products, etc.). How useful as analogies are "mental territories"? (f) Is territoriality always good? The literature almost uniformly touts personal territories as beneficial to the individual and group, but are there conditions under which it is detrimental (e.g., unfairly reinforcing social status distinctions, promoting patriotic chauvinism and warfare)? In addition to these issues, there are a number of interesting avenues of exploration as yet barely opened, for instance: (g) To what extent do legal decisions involving territory fit with our knowledge of the psychology of the phenomenon? (h) To what extent are there territorial "personalities" (cf. Altman & Haythorn, 1967)? Research is needed on both individual and group territoriality, on the relationships to mechanisms of social organization; sex differences, developmental aspects, and cultural differences have yet to be explored empirically. Studies that clarify the concept's relationship to adjacent concepts like privacy, interpersonal distance, and jurisdiction are also called for.

Human territoriality is particularly well placed as a "pure" research topic with relevance to current environmental problems. Future research will undoubtedly interest decision makers who create territories: architects, city planners, and other environmental designers. As a topic it is also located at the intersection of interests of a number of academic disciplines—ethology; social environmental, and clinical psychology; psychiatry; anthropology; sociology—and will likely draw supporting research from these areas in the future.

Some Analytic Dimensions of Privacy

ROBERT S. LAUFER, HAROLD M. PROSHANSKY,
AND MAXINE WOLFE

Introduction

Privacy is not one thing but many things. It can be described as a psychological phenomenon, a social phenomenon, a political phenomenon and, indirectly, even as an economic phenomenon. To further complicate the picture, the term as used by many theoreticians and practitioners within one field and in different fields may refer to some kind of need or drive state of the person, sometimes to forms of behavior, to affective or so-called inner experiences, or to some combination of these. Given this kind of complexity for a single term, it should be quite evident that it could be hazardous on our part or on the part of any theoretician to present *one* all-encompassing definition. By the same token we do not assume that the problem of definition is insignificant. However, too many scholars who have dealt with the issue have either assumed or attempted an encompassing definition of privacy and ignored the more serious problem of an adequate conceptualization of the phenomenon. *If* a definition of privacy is to emerge, we must begin by developing a conceptual framework which allows for the development of theory and research. Indeed, the problem of definition may be a specious issue since there may well be many terms which will emerge to deal with the multitude of experiences or behavior which are now subsumed under the one word. On the other hand, there is something interesting to observe in most definitions of privacy that exist. Even a cursory review of the literature indicates that they are simply operational or empir-

Adapted from a paper presented at the Third Annual International Architectural Research Conference, Lund, Sweden, June 1973, and at APA Meetings, Montreal, Canada, August 1, 1973.

ical definitions. By this we mean that they point to a behavior, situation, or event as an indication of what human privacy is. From a long range point of view, it is conceivable that out of the adequate and meaningful conceptualization we refer to above there will emerge a set of constructs which will provide an elaborate single statement that could encompass the many events now subsumed under the word "privacy".

The purpose of the present paper is to suggest a series of analytic dimensions along which the problem of privacy can be considered. These dimensions, which were developed through an interdisciplinary seminar, are by no means a final statement of a theoretical position but should be considered as working formulations. They deal with privacy as volitional and not as enforced (i.e. isolation).

Dimensions

Self-Ego Dimension

Privacy, as we understand it generally, is both the expression and the embodiment of the self and ego. Major developmental theorists agree that the development of the self is the process of the separation of the individual from the social and physical environment. This separation necessarily requires that the child experience aloneness and develop the ability to function in aloneness, in one form or another. Yet, at early ages aloneness is not volitional and can be a negative experience precisely because it is enforced and the child fears the inability to function alone. The developmental task of learning to function independently (self-autonomy) adds a critical aspect to the relationship between the self and privacy—volition: the ability to choose aloneness when capable of functioning in aloneness. The choice of aloneness, then, becomes a statement of the autonomy of the self. If the development of autonomy is the single most important expression of the evolution of a sense of self, then its expression in terms of privacy and privacy behavior can be described in terms of the volition of freedom of the individual to choose his movement across the boundary which distinguishes him as being alone vs. him as a separate individual interacting with others.

There is yet another sense in which the concept of self is critical in the understanding of privacy. Privacy, in various forms, can be seen as a way of both enhancing the self and protecting the self, even from itself (i.e., repression). If one examines any array of reasons given by individuals seeking and maintaining their privacy, then what is revealed, even in the purest sense of the word, are attempts to protect and nurture the self or the positive compliment of trying to extend and enhance the self.

Interaction Dimension

It is apparent that while privacy is often referred to as the individual's choice of aloneness, it is an *interactional* concept. By this we mean that however it is defined, it presupposes the existence of others, the possibility of interaction with them and the desire to minimize or control this interaction. Privacy in essense is a form of noninteraction with others in which, in a classic sense, both parties agree that one of them is to be alone. This implies a normative relationship in which failure of one party to agree either deliberately or unwillingly means that the other person's privacy is likely to be invaded. The management of social interaction, then, assumes a learned sensitivity to the importance of privacy.

At the simplest level we often see the exhaustion caused by unrelieved interaction. Thus, privacy can involve an active notion of withdrawal from others. The individual simply withdraws in order to go off and be alone, to relax, to collect himself,

to think things through. In effect, the person seeks to escape from the demands created by the presence of others. In addition, privacy functions as an opportunity to rehearse those aspects of behavior which may be included in social interactions. Especially for children, but also for adults, role playing and fantasy constitute an important aspect for such reality testing the nature of interactions and frequently, privacy is one of the necessary conditions for this pretesting.

In order for the individual to function effectively, over time, there must be a reasonable balance between interaction and privacy. The capacity to discern this balance is a function of the socialization experience of childhood wherein the opportunities for privacy are gradually expanded as the interactional patterns of the individual become more complex and demanding. This process provides incremental experiences with separate roles which demand the presentation of only certain information within certain relationships while keeping other material private or presenting it only in the context of other relationships. Thus, privacy also involves the need to control information about oneself in the process of interacting with others. There may be normative agreement as to what each actor will ask of the other and therefore reveal of oneself. Of course, individuals may differ in what they regard as private or public, but even where agreement occurs each actor may well still want to be private about information because it may get to others with whom he has quite a different relationship.

Privacy as interaction takes on still another form. It can be said that in groups and larger social systems, privacy, freedom of privacy, invasion of privacy, the consequences of invasion, etc., are all elements in the rights and privileges that define the role relationships between people. Thus, the boss can interrupt an assistant at will, but the reverse is unlikely to be true. Furthermore, the rights and obligations of boss and employee are learned in childhood through the rights of parents to have virtually total access to the lives of their children while keeping large portions of their own lives private.

Finally, privacy seems to be a necessary aspect of intimate relationships. Boundaries are taken down between the self and others and are put up between the intimates and the rest of the world. Privacy may be a necessary condition for certain types of intimate activities, i.e., sex, and growing intimacy necessarily means the decline of individual privacy and the growth of shared privacy. At the center of this process is the development and management of information exchange between the two people establishing the conditions of a shared privacy.

Life Cycle Dimension

An implication from the previous concept is that privacy as a phenomenon is by no means stable and must be viewed within a *time dimension*. Perhaps the key to understanding privacy is in its relation to the individual from birth to death. Yet, even the properties of the life cycle are not static. The periods of time devoted to specific activities (e.g., child bearing and child raising) will vary as a function of a changing technology, changing sociocultural patterns, and historical environment. Indeed, an analysis of the changing nature of privacy in human behavior and experience may be diagnostic of the shifting character of the properties of the life cycle. In the points that follow we will deal with the properties of the life cycle as they appear at the present time. The reader should focus on the way in which the concept of life cycle can aid in the understanding of the concept of privacy, rather than on the existing structure of the life cycle.

There are at least three elements in the notion of life cycle which are critical to an understanding of privacy. First, that at various stages and ages, individual needs, abilities, experiences, desires, and feelings

change and thus the concept and patterns of privacy should also change. At very early stages of the life cycle when children do not possess or own spaces, they can and do possess and own objects and privacy may at this age relate to the possession of things (Laufer & Wolfe, 1973). As children gain more independence from their families and have more freedom from supervision, privacy may function to allow opportunities for trying out new activities. The beginning of the search for intimacy with another person, the desire for sexual experimentation should necessarily make privacy more salient for certain behaviors (Laufer & Wolfe, 1973). At the other end of the age continuum, experiences with loneliness may make the need and times for privacy quite different than for earlier periods of life. It is interesting to find that older people who experience considerable loneliness are far more willing than many younger people to share aspects of their past private experiences.

Secondly, throughout the life cycle the individual takes on different roles and the society imposes different demands and requirements. In this respect we are first referring to the obvious social roles of youngster, adult, wife, husband, mother, etc. The woman with young children who is at home with them for major parts of her days is basically on call at any time. Finding time and space for privacy may be close to an impossibility. On the other hand, with changing roles for women, more women are entering "public life" and find that many of their previous concepts and patterns of privacy are no longer relevant to their new life style. Secondly, we are referring to the less obvious changes in roles and demands. An 18 year old who now has the right to vote has a new set of information which may have to be controlled—who he is going to vote for and where he stands on certain issues. As the individual grows older and becomes more susceptible to illness he takes on the role of patient more often and, with the changing character of medical technology, sees more doctors and is "exposed" more frequently and in many different ways.

As individuals move through the life cycle, their activities and environments change and hence, they have different experiences with privacy. As physical settings change, new problems may emerge. The child moves from the home to the school where more of the day is structured and there is less opportunity for physical privacy. The movement from home to college dormitory and from there to their own dwelling causes still other aspects of privacy to become salient. The movement into the occupational world and up the occupational ladder gives the individual more status and more privacy in the form of private offices, etc. Each of these environments, and the many more that we have not mentioned, places the individual in a different context and the opportunities, needs, and patterns for privacy will differ correspondingly.

Finally, as the individual progresses through the life cycle, the society is constantly changing and patterns of privacy and other behaviors learned at one point in time may conflict with emergent life styles, mores, and technologies, especially in the context of rapid social and technological change. The presence of TV cameras in lobbies, elevators, etc., means that behavior once considered private now becomes the subject of public scrutiny. Families could formerly depend on the thickness of walls to maintain their privacy, but newer housing does not provide that protection. For those who grew up in an environment forbidding casual intimacy, the emergence of the group process approach for dealing with intimate information (encounter groups) may be an intimidating or impossible experience.

Biography-History Dimension

An element that is embedded in all three of the previously mentioned dimensions is that of personal history and biography. One can specify the critical nature this element in so far as individuals manage information about themselves. Yet, the personal-history biography dimension is not simply the management of already available information. More critically, it is what can be aptly called the *calculus of behavior* aspect of information management. Simply stated, in many instances the individual has to ask himself, "If I am seen engaging in this behavior or that behavior or am seen with this person or that person, what are the consequences for me in the *future, in new situations,* etc?" Involved here are such matters as making friends with particular people, joining particular groups, frequenting a particular place, signing a petition, etc.

There are at least three aspects to the calculus of behavior. First, individuals may engage in various behaviors with the idea that they can manage the information in new and later situations and hence minimize the potential consequences.

Secondly, individuals may simply *not do* certain things because the risk of losing control over the information at some later, even distant point, is high or simply unpredictable or because, even at the present moment, the publicness or privateness of the act is ambiguously defined. This includes behavior which may have no immediate negative consequences. Individuals may not join political or social organizations which are presently acceptable because, as the McCarthy era showed, previous membership in the Communist Party became the basis for later reprisals. In a private transaction where individuals have the option of paying by cash or check, cash may be preferred, because checks constitute a permanent record.

In highly technologically complex societies, the calculus of behavior has a third and dynamic aspect to it at any moment in the individual's life. The person has to decide the probable consequences of behavior in terms of the type of recording and communication devices that exist—is it verbal, is it written, will it be seen and by how many others, etc. Information can now become available in environments and situations over which the individual has no control. The microfilming of bank checks provides a permanent record of transactions which are totally available to government inspection. The presence of computer equipment and the use of social security numbers as identifiers for all sorts of transactions means that at some point in time a mass of information about an individual can be compiled by unknown persons for unknown purposes. The experience with record keeping and communication technologies during the early stage of the life cycle seems to us to affect the calculus of behavior. If one grew up during periods of relatively primitive record keeping technologies, the ability to recognize the potential of the sophisticated techniques of today may be impaired. This would place older people at a disadvantage in gauging their behavior. It may also increase anger, hostility and anxiety as these individuals encounter the growing capacity of technology to create integrated, complex histories of their previous behavior. Furthermore, those individuals growing up during a period of sophisticated technology may develop adaptive and totally different concepts and patterns of privacy in which the potentials of recording and communication, i.e., new media, make information privacy an irrelevant aspect of daily life simply because it is uncontrollable.

The personal-history dimension of privacy may also be viewed differently in terms of life-cycle dimension. There are times in the individual's life when the possibility of the revelation of information about past behaviors is most salient, i.e., when applying for jobs, entering college, applying for professional licensing or union membership, or attempting to move up the career ladder. However, once the individual has retired or is past the work period, the revelation of past experiences may be irrele-

vant since the consequences for the future are minimal.

The crucial element of the personal-history dimension in terms of the calculus of behavior is that the *individual is often unable to predict the nature of that which has to be managed.* Changes in the socio-historical context and in technology are often unpredictable and, in fact, in advanced industrial societies there is a growing certainty about the unknowableness of the future.

Control Dimension

Implicit in all previous discussion is the issue of the control which the individual has over self, objects, information, and behavior. The need and ability to exert such control is a critical element in any conception of privacy. As we indicated earlier in our discussion, the development of autonomy is the single most important expression of the evolution of a sense of self. Autonomy encompasses both independence in functioning and the awareness of volition as a means of controlling the boundary between self and other. How does the child initially experience volition and control in relation to privacy? In early childhood, experiences with privacy may be as an "intruder" and as one intruded upon rather than as an individual entitled to or desirous of privacy. The young child is taught which rooms he may or may not enter, which conversations he may or may not hear. Yet frequently adults, and other children, act intrusively toward the child. Thus, one of the child's earliest experiences with volition and control is as it is exercised by others. At the early ages, when other people have control, the child has the concept that authority is omnipresent and omniscient. The notion that one can have thoughts and engage in behaviors that will not be known does not seem to be achieved for a number of years (Piaget, 1966; Freud, 1962). At some point, however, the child begins to experience his own ability to control. When the child has been successful in its first lie (Tausk, 1933) or in its first hidden behavior, there is the awareness, finally, that many things are not known unless they are *volitionally* revealed. Choice and control, then, are inextricably interwoven in the concept of privacy.

There are at least three aspects of control which are related to privacy: "control over choice", "control over access", and "control over stimulation". Privacy necessarily involves the control of choice or freedom of choice in that the individual chooses to be private, whether physically or psychologically. Once the individual has chosen privacy, as opposed to some other behavior, the question arises as to whether or not there is the freedom and ability within privacy to do what one wants. Freedom of choice is always a relative concept limited by the parameters of possible behavior in the society, community, and family.

The element of control over access evolves out of the need for limiting intrusion, interruption and observation of activities, thoughts, information. Control might take the form of a locked door, a private diary, or a secret. The important element in this situation is that the individual does not want others to know about or intrude upon behaviors, thoughts, or actions. Control over access may be a self-protective device, a self-enhancing device or simply a functional device, i.e., "I don't want anyone to come in when I'm working because other people distract me."

The third aspect of control relates in large measure to the ecological environment in which certain forms of privacy are achieved. There are a variety of stimuli which the individual seeks to control such as noise, people, visual stimulation, etc. Again, choice is an element here because the individual chooses the conditions which create privacy. Control does not necessarily mean the elimination of stimulation. In fact, it may involve the attempt to direct and choose the type and intensity of stimulation desired and consistent with other needs.

Control of stimulation is one way of setting the conditions which make up privacy or for determining the content of the private activity, i.e., being alone to listen to loud music.

The control dimension of privacy takes on added meaning when viewed in terms of the life cycle. In the early parent-child relationship children have little control of any sort, except in the area of fantasies, ideas and secrets once they become aware that they can control their revelations. In fact, except under the most extreme circumstances, access to thoughts is the one consistent area over which the individual has control and, hence, can experience privacy. Entering school and spending larger portions of time away from home gives children greater control over parents' access to information about behavior. From adolescence on, control generally increases in all areas (greater freedom from supervision, living on one's own), but at the same time there may be an increasing need for control (greater demands for interaction, more complex roles, information management). With the onset of old age, once again the need for constant care begins to erode control over the self and at the same time, the need for certain forms of control may be less important (the calculus of behavior). At each stage of the life cycle, then, the degree of control and the need for control will always be a function of the specific role the individual plays (child, student, husband, laborer, executive) and the goals he is seeking to achieve within these roles.

Control over privacy also varies depending on the level of interaction. Privacy as it involves the individual alone (monad) allows for as much control over all aspects of the situations as is possible in the human situation. If we introduce a second person (dyad), then a certain degree of sharing and/or withholding must occur. In this situation control involves setting up boundaries for intimacy while maintaining boundaries between the self and other based on intuitive understandings of the limits of giving out and holding in. If we then add a third person (triad), we have a group situation. In three or more person situations boundaries of the group become the focus of attention. We recognize the complexity of the relationships between individuals in a three person or larger group. Boundaries may be put up between one person and the other two or between each person and the other. However, control over information and behavior moves toward the concerns and purposes of the group and away from the interpersonal concerns characteristic of the dyad. Collective norms begin to govern control over information and behavior. The larger the group the more control becomes a function of the distinct characteristics and purposes of the group, i.e., control over party or state secrets. Also, when we move from the interpersonal to institutional level, control becomes a function of super and subordination. The rights and privileges attendant to status, class or position demand different levels of control over situations, behavior and information. The executive has access to areas of privacy unavailable to his subordinates. At the simplest level he has greater control over his working conditions and supportive services (private bathroom, dining room, bar, lounge, secretary). In addition, he has access to control over interaction with others, and information about others. The lower the individual is in the organization, the less his control or access to privacy. Furthermore, as the size of the group and the level of complexity increase, each individual's ability to control decreases or increases relative to their position in the structure. In the truly large organizations ability to control choice, access or stimulation is sharply limited for all but a very few at the very top.

Ecological-Cultural Dimension

Privacy as behavior and experience is rooted in spaces and places; i.e., privacy can be understood in terms of the structural, ecological, and meaning properties of the physical setting that circumscribe human behavior. Like Barker, we are suggesting that physical settings evoke and sustain behaviors and experiences that are "private" in character. The crucial question, then, is how does this happen? What are the underlying determinants that render spaces and places "privacy settings"?

First, we can assume safely that whatever the form of human privacy, some physical settings and their physical properties will be more congruent with this "form." If a physical setting "fits," it can evoke and will continue to evoke and support a related and relevant form of human privacy. Thus, the desire to hide a sustained form of behavior from others will do better in a bedroom with a door on it than an open sleeping setting. Yet structure alone can be deceiving. One must consider that the "fit" of spaces also depends on the ecology of groups. In other words, the presence or absence of a group may increase or decrease the "fit" of a physical setting. An isolated suburban home makes high hedges unnecessary for outdoor dining, or for loud family arguments.

Yet, space or place is more than a matter of structure or ecology of groups. By design, activity, and meaning, a physical space achieves its privacy character. Through socialization the person learns to accept, identify, and indeed act private in certain places and spaces over others. Thus, by definition, a "play room" wouldn't seem right—even with no one else present—to use for private matters, whereas a den and bathroom would. Indeed, the latter are institutionally designated as self-non-intrusion settings.

Third and not unrelated, but worthy of separate mention, is the socializing experience of the individual. Place identity is an aspect of self-identity; i.e., there are experiences in and with *places* that contribute to the development of a sense of self. Places have specific meanings for self—they may enhance, threaten, or simply define; and in this respect we internalize a lot of "privacy settings." The old family home is a place to escape from the outer public, as well as contributing in other ways to identity. One could argue that the clinging to memorabilia—graduation autograph book, private diary—are all environmental self-privacy or self-aloneness props.

Finally, we must turn to the physical environment as an instigator and maker of privacy in another way—in its unintended consequences. The design of physical settings may create needs, feelings, conditions for privacy, or its reduction because it leads to isolation. A noisy block pushes people to create their own more private world; but one that is too quiet may lead an "isolated individual" to attempt to break down its isolation aspects. If we consider cities, suburbs, and rural areas respectively, each facilitates and impedes privacy in ways relevant to the activities, interests and experiences of the people in them.

Furthermore, each of these settings, the urban, suburban, and rural, has a number of aspects which can facilitate or inhibit, create or eliminate, certain forms and patterns of privacy. For example, the relevance of personal history will be different within each of these settings. In rural areas the diffuse character of role, the containment of virtually all life activities within the local boundaries, and the low population density make privacy of personal history exceptionally difficult. The calculus of behavior in this environment must constantly account for the consequences of behavior which can rarely be kept private. The urban environment, on the other hand, is dominated by the segmentalization of roles, the separation of life's activities and a high density of population. In terms of the calculus of behavior, this means a great deal of behavior will remain private or at least be hidden from a large sector of the individual's circle of associations. The suburban environment differs from the urban primarily in terms of the density of its population. However, the symbiotic relationship of the middle class population of suburbia with the urban areas

and the high rate of geographic mobility of its population mean that urban patterns of the privacy of personal history will prevail. Personal history and biography are not the only aspects of privacy that differ in terms of location. The types of housing prevalent in these environments, the means of transportation, the level of stimulation from people and other things, also alter the essential means and conditions of privacy.

The crucial point we wish to emphasize in discussing this dimension is that when we speak of privacy behavior and the patterns of privacy we must ask "where," in its fullest sense.

Task Orientation Dimension

While we frequently probe for profound, underlying dimensions of privacy, it is clear that under some circumstances privacy has an *explicit functional* component. This may arise out of past experiences, it may be habitual, or it may simply be that the thing we are doing must be done alone. Only one person can drive a car and, under certain circumstances, he will be the only person in the vehicle. If one is writing a symphony, the presence of others, noise, etc., may simply be distracting. From this point of view, it is important to understand and accept the fact that it is possible to analyze the "privacy" behavior of individuals simply in neutral and, therefore, descriptive terms. On the other hand, the fact that someone is alone does not necessarily mean that he is experiencing a psychological or phenomenological state of privacy.

Ritual Privacy Dimension

The ritual dimension of privacy is somewhat similar to the task orientation aspect. There are certain rituals which societies try to get people to do in non-public places. Ritual activities such as sex, elimination, expressions of grief, visions, etc., are to be done in privacy and these exist in all societies. The existence of taboos (e.g., menstrual cycle) will also affect the ritual structure of privacy. Furthermore, not only are there norms governing the situational elements of ritual privacy, but the activities within the situation are also largely prescribed. Here again the reader should know that an analysis of privacy in terms of ritual procedures and the individuals involved would provide a comprehensive account, in its own right, of privacy behavior and experience in that society.

Phenomenological Dimension

Very early in this paper, we alluded to the fact that privacy is sometimes used to designate *behavior,* at other times the *experience* of the individual, and at still other times some combination of the two. What should be emphasized in this last dimension of our analysis is the fact that privacy is undoubtedly a unique psychological experience. To refer to it as phenomenological is simply to highlight the fact that, regardless of all other dimensions, there is a combination of affective and cognitive components that will forever elude the attempts at systematization by the behavioral scientist. We are not ashamed to say that the descriptions of the poet, the dramatist and the novelist about the yearnings to be alone undoubtedly get at the core of that human experience we call privacy.

Obviously, there is probably not a single, pure emotion involved since privacy, as we have already seen analytically, covers an array of purposes, functions and intentions that undoubtedly arouse not one kind, but many different kinds of feelings. To take but a few examples, privacy as a means of enhancing the self, e.g., to read a letter which praises us, has a vastly different affective consequence than privacy needed to defend and maintain the self.

There is yet another level of the phenomenological experience available to social science. The unmediated descriptions of the individual about the experiences with and of privacy constitute the richest source of evidence for the beginning of an analysis of the nature of privacy. The direct expression of the experience presents the issue of privacy in all its complexity and without analytic separation. Yet, if we are to begin to connect theory and research into an overview of privacy in human interaction, the direct unmediated experience of man in all his situations, feelings and longings must be examined. We must find out how man has used privacy to understand himself and to seek meaning in his species. However unique the phenomenology of privacy it is important to emphasize two significant factors: first, cultural and social settings undoubtedly contribute a group experience aspect to the nature of individual privacy; and secondly, keeping in mind our brief discussion of task and ritual privacy, there is no reason to assume that to behave "privately" necessarily means that the person experiences the human feelings of privacy as suggested by this last dimension.

The discussion above focuses on the conceptualization of privacy. We wish to emphasize, once more, that this is a working formulation which should be added to and changed as discussions and empirical research continue. Our own involvement in understanding privacy has taken both tacks: a year-long seminar discussion and the initiation and execution of a research project focusing on conceptions of privacy as a function of age and age-related experiences. It should now be clear why this became the focus of our first research endeavor. In each dimension we have considered as relevant to a conceptualization of privacy, we come back, again and again, to the importance of the experiences of childhood. Clearly, adults' understanding and consequent patterns of privacy will be related to childhood experiences, yet will have changed over time as a function of the ageing or maturational processes and of changes in the social-historical context within which the individual matured. It seemed reasonable to assume that during the process of development from childhood to adulthood the person defines and redefines the limits on other's rights to invade his privacy, and recognizes his own ability and choice in allowing or not allowing such invasion. The concept of privacy, as any other concept, should become more complex with age. The crucial question is: in what ways? The child's abilities, independence in functioning, demands he must meet, and daily life experiences change through the developmental process and should produce different concepts of privacy relevant to the life situation at specific ages. It was this thinking which led us to choose the focus that we did.

Preliminary Research

In order to obtain data on the concept of privacy at early stages in the life cycle, two of the authors (Laufer & Wolfe) initiated an interview study of 840 children between the tages of 4 and 19; 420 in New York City and 420 in Menominee Falls, Wisconsin (a suburban-rural district outside of Milwaukee).[1] These children were evenly divided by sex and socioeconomic background (lower, middle and upper middle class) and the New York sample was further subdivided by racial/ethnic background (white, black, Spanish). Each child was individually interviewed by a same sex, same race interviewer,[2] and for children who were predominantly Spanish-speaking the interview was conducted in Spanish.

[1] Supported by a research grant, #01802 from the Faculty Research Program at the City University of New York and by a research grant from the Society For The Psychological Study of Social Issues.

[2] We wish to thank Sue Fox, Rich Olsen, Jan Zyniewski, Carlos Hernandez, Cynthia Cook, and Josh Holahan (the City University Graduate Center) and John Krogman (University of Michigan) not only for their hours of interviewing (many of them unpaid) but, also, for their contributions, in our research meetings, to our thinking about privacy.

The interview consisted of a series of open-ended, fairly unstructured questions, including: 1) Would you please tell me all the things the word privacy means to you?; 2) Would you describe a time when you felt very private? How did it feel? (If the child replied that he was never private, we asked: What do you think it would be like? How do you think it would feel?; 3) Would you describe a time when you felt private and then somebody or something disturbed your feeling of being private? How did it feel? What did you do?; 4) We asked the children to describe what each of the following was like for them: a private place, a private thought, a private feeling, a private time, a private thing, a private thing to do and a private talk; and 5) We asked the children to tell us the ways other members of their family let them know when they were private or wanted to be private. In addition we asked the children for demographic data: age, area of residence, number of rooms in their house or apartment, number of people living with them, if they had their own room, etc.

One word about our own considerations of invasion of privacy in doing our research. We went into classrooms in various schools[3] and asked children to volunteer to be interviewed. Since we did not want to pre-expose the children to the nature of the topic, we said that we could not tell them what the interview was about but after the first question the topic would be clear and, if at that point or any other they decided not to continue, they could leave with no strings attached. In the younger grades, almost all of the children volunteered and as we went into adolescence, even though a large num-

[3] We would like to acknowledge our appreciation to the children, teachers and principals of the schools in which we have interviewed, especially The Woodward School (Gertrude Goldstein, Director), the Brooklyn Ethical Culture School, and the John Jay H.S. (Abe Venit, Principal) in Brooklyn, N.Y., and Dr. J. Magnuson, Superintendent of Schools in Menominee Falls, Wisconsin.

ber volunteered, there was a clear increase in the number of people who did not want to participate. This, we feel, is an unobtrusive measure of the growth, with age, in children's understanding of their control in choosing whether or not to reveal information about themselves. Also, in conducting our interviews, children had the clear and stated option not to answer any questions they did not want to. Again, the number of children exercising this option increased with age. We should also mention that it was rare for a child to terminate the interview.

Before we describe our preliminary results, we feel it is worth taking the time to discuss why we chose an interview with open-ended questions as opposed to scales, experimentation, or other techniques and methods. When we began planning our research, we attempted to develop a verbal, semi-projective device so that we might get at conceptions of privacy more subtly and, indeed, without using the word "privacy." We worked for quite a while devising incomplete stories representing "privacy" situations, intrusions, etc.,[4] with the idea that we would present them, verbally, to the child and ask: What is the child going to do in this situation? Why? What would you do?, etc. After a great deal of work, it became apparent to us that we had succumbed to the researcher's pitfall. We had created stories about privacy from an *adult* point of view, and a specific one at that (middle class, white, academicians). At that point it was clear to us that we had to have some very basic data on how children viewed, thought about, conceptualized, and described privacy, especially in relation to situations they had experienced. The individual, open-ended interview seemed the best way to achieve this end. Thus, the data we have to present will not be based on sophisticated quantitative research instruments or techniques, but we feel that we

have come to understand a great deal about the ways in which children think about, deal with and experience privacy.

We are presently in the process of analyzing the data from these interviews and will be completing the analysis within the next few months. From our initial analysis, we find the meaning of privacy *is* related to age and to age-related experiences:

1) Children as young as 5 years of age know what privacy is—in some fashion.

2) The number of different aspects of privacy included in a definition increases with age along with increased specificity of language allowing the respondent to pinpoint the desired conditions, i.e., from "being alone" to "seclusion".

3) Salient elements of the concept of privacy, i.e., being alone, appear at the earliest ages and remain critical over time.

4) The use of alone as a definition increases with age paralleling the theoretical notions of the development of the self. Controlling access to information is the most frequent definition at age 7, the time when children are first becoming aware of their ability to exercise control.

5) There are new elements of the definition which appear only at later ages (i.e., "my own sexual abilities are private" appears only among high school students), and privacy as an aspect of group situations and specific group reactions is more prevalent with older respondents, e.g., "alone with my girlfriend" (age 16), "alone with my friend" (age 10).

6) Possession of objects as an aspect of privacy is much more prevalent at the youngest ages (my toys), changes to possession of toys as a way of controlling who uses them, and drops out at older ages to be replaced with "having my own room" and "having my own apartment".

7) One of the constant but increasingly used (with age) definitions of privacy is the addition of conditional phrases which indicate the operative properties of the concept. The most significant operative conditions of privacy are control over intrusion, choice of

---

[4] Leanne G. Rivlin developed many of the stories.

privacy, and the ability to choose to be private. The meaning of privacy changes from "being alone" or "doing something by myself" to these aspects accompanied by "when I want to", "being able to", and "without being interrupted". These general conditional phrases appear infrequently among our youngest respondents and appear with increasing frequency as children grow older.

8) The saliency of certain aspects of privacy is related to whether or not a child shares or has his own bedroom. Children who have their own rooms define privacy in terms of the possibilities which physical aloneness allows, while children sharing a bedroom are much more likely to define privacy in terms of controlling access to information.

9) There are differences in definitions as a function of where a child lives. For instance, control of information is of minimal importance to New York children at age 7 but very important at age 15, while the reverse is true for the Wisconsin sample.

10) In regard to some of our other questions: our initial findings suggest that privacy is a mechanism for the management of social interaction and is closely tied to familial patterns of socialization. Frequently, the disrupters or invaders of privacy were family members (i.e., parents or siblings) and the child's feelings and response to invasion were a function of the invader. Young siblings could be reprimanded and removed if they did not share the room; parents had total access and generally overlooked any statement made by the child regarding intrusion. Descriptions of private situations frequently included mention of the family dwelling, especially among younger respondents. One strong indication of the importance of the family context at the earliest stages of development come from some of our youngest respondents (4 and 5 years of age) who were unable to define privacy for themselves, but were able to immediately describe how other members of their family use and acquire privacy, i.e., "daddy likes privacy in the bathroom," "my brother closes his door," and "my mother yells, 'damn it, I wish these kids were dead' ".

Conclusion

We end our analysis where we began with an emphasis upon the tentativeness of our formulation of the dimensions of privacy. We wish to draw your attention to the dynamic qualities of the dimensions of privacy in our analysis. Furthermore, the diverse elements of privacy and the need to recognize the changing quality of the content of the privacy phenomenon should make us leery of finding "an answer" to the meaning of privacy. The many disciplines with an interest in this area of investigation demand, and will continuously demand, an interdisciplinary approach to empirical or theoretical investigation. The first order of business, therefore, is to systematically develop interdisciplinary theoretical formulations susceptible to research. Our own project constitutes a modest first step in this direction. However, even as we embark in research either theoretical or empirical, we must remain constantly on guard against reifying our own constructs and remaining faithful to antiquated data. We live in a rapidly changing world. If, as we argued, the life cycle is subject to change as a result of technological, social, cultural and historical change, then surely even if we have evolved a useful working conceptual structure, the content is subject to change. Finally, even the framework itself may need modification as a result of time.

In social science research generally, but especially in this stage of investigation of the phenomenon of privacy, we must remain intellectually flexible, and guard against the development of vested interest in particular conceptual frameworks or data. We urge for ourselves and others interested in this field a permanent position of tentativeness towards our understanding of the phenomenon of privacy.

17. Stress-Inducing and Reducing Qualities of Environments
SUSAN SAEGERT

All organisms depend on the physical world around them to support life. Some environments do so with ease and an abundance of resources; others demand much of those who would live there. Extreme cold, shortage of food, the presence of disease-bearing insects and so on are clear threats to well-being. Less obvious environmental characteristics such as noise (Cohen, 1974; Glass & Singer, 1972; Carlstam, Karlsson & Levi, 1973) and crowding (Cohen, 1974; D'Atre, 1975) have also been found to interfere with the physical health and psychosocial functioning of human beings. This paper concerns these subtler types of harm in which human environments can not easily be divided into separate categories of inhabitant and physical threat.

Stress is essentially a systemic concept. Selye (1956) has used this term to describe increased wear and tear in the body as a result of attempts to cope with environmental influences. As a young researcher, Selye was struck by the similar reaction organisms had to a wide variety of different pathological agents ranging from specific bacterial infections to more general environmental factors. He characterized these responses as the "stress syndrome" or the "general adaptation syndrome". The G.A.S. is composed of three stages: (1) the alarm reaction in which the body shifts to a mobilized level of functioning, (2) the stage of resistance, in which the body's adaptive mechanisms attempt to counter the disturbing influence, and (3) the stage of exhaustion, in which the body's resources are depleted more rapidly than the strength of the stressor, and death results. The extensive theoretical and empirical research Selye has contributed to the development of this concept can not be done justice in so brief a summary. Yet his definition of the stress syndrome must be taken as a fore-most determinant of the way medical and psychological researchers think about this topic. Stress is seen as a constant part of daily life; it is the process by which an organism responds both defensively and creatively to environmental flux. The main defining property of a stressful situation is increased bodily activation, especially of the sympatho-adrenomedullary system. While such activation can lead to diseases of adaptation (Selye, 1964), it is also a component of most of the major joys and sorrows of life.

Stress has come to be seen as both a physical and a psychosocial syndrome (Appley & Trumbull, 1967; MacGrath, 1970; Kagan & Levi, 1974). Physical and social aspects of the environment, as well as individuals' physical states and personalities, may provoke stress reactions. Further the physical and psychological effects of these stressors have consequences for the individual and social behaviors of those involved. Certain kinds of task decrements as well as more aggressive or withdrawn social behavior are among the most common effects of stress. These, then, influence the way the physical environment is perceived and dealt with. Schorr's (1966) study of slum housing clearly develops some of these interrelationships. The exposure of the poor to physical hardship due to inadequate shelter from the elements, lack of facilities for hygiene, and lack of space for basic activities such as sleeping and childrearing are set in a general context of economic and social insecurity. These dilapidated physical environments sap the energy and health of their occupants, making it extremely difficult for them to act alone or in concert to improve their conditions. Further, these settings of danger and decay seem, quite probably, to create lower self-esteem and trust of others in those who inhabit them.

Stress-inducing Qualities of Environments

Certain qualities of the environment seem most likely to contribute to the stressfulness of any particular setting. Six of these will be discussed in some detail. While this list may not be exhaustive, it represents what seem to be the major concerns of current research on environmental stressors.

First, of course, environments can be physically threatening. Some physical stressors such as disease-bearing filth, extreme cold and heat, and exposure to wetness have been medically investigated. Yet the psychological and social consequences of these, for the most part, remain unknown. Limited studies of the relationship between heat and social affect have been attempted (Griffitt, 1970; Griffitt & Veitch, 1971), although the results are somewhat ambiguous. Even the medical effects of other physical irritants are just now being discovered. Although in some instances loud noise has been associated with increased incidence of somatic distress, hypertension and "nervous complaints", this is not always the case (Carlstam et al., 1973). Unpredictability of the noise is a more important determinant of task decrement (Cohen, 1974; Glass & Singer, 1972) but the medical effects of this factor do not seem to have been studied. Recent evidence suggests that various forms of heart disease are exacerbated by air pollution (Peacock, 1973). Although it has been shown that people behaviorally adjust to air pollution by remaining indoors and engaging in less active exercise (Peterson, 1975), the existence of psychosocial effects remains an open question. Overall, it appears that even these most obvious environmental stressors have not been extensively investigated, and never in the context of their full complexity.

A second stress-provoking quality of environments has been termed stimulus information overload. Since these two labels identify somewhat different phenomena perhaps attentional overload would be a more apt description. This can arise in three distinct ways. The first could properly be called stimulus overload, the second, information overload, and the third, decisional overload. Although some of the consequences of these are the same, each it will be argued also has unique antecedents and effects.

Sheer intensity and quantity of stimulation clearly have attention-getting properties. Self-reports of discomfort due to cold (Froberg et al., 1974), heat (Griffitt & Veitch, 1970), and noise (Glass & Singer, 1972) have been reported, as well as accompanying physiological arousal. Berlyn (1960) has shown that novel, intense, surprising or complex stimuli elicit attention. The pervasiveness of the orienting response to such stimuli as well as its rapid habituation have been amply documented (e.g. Sokolov, 1963). This sort of stimulation generally interferes with task performance only if it is unpredictable or uncontrollable, thus preventing habituation of the orienting response, or so intense as to cause pain (Carlstamm et al., 1973; Cohen, 1975; Glass & Singer, 1972). However, the cumulative effects of prolonged exposure to large quantities of intense stimulation have not been well-studied. On the positive side, highly stimulating, perhaps even stressfully so, environments seem to promote greater cognitive development especially if the organism is allowed to freely explore (Hunt, 1964).

In contrast to simple stimulation, information overload will be used to refer to a surfeit of cues in an environment that have adaptive significance for the inhabitant. These may be stimuli to which an organism innately responds, as Hamburg (1971) suggests humans do to encounters with strangers, or properties of the environment relevant to habitual or planned behaviors. For example, Milgram (1970), in his analysis of the experience of living in cities, elaborates the antecedents and consequences of overload occasioned by highly-populated environments.

Both types of overload so far described

evoke frequent orienting responses and arousal. However, there is some evidence suggesting that arousal caused by significant stimuli such as other people does not habituate, and indeed seems to increase over time (D'Atre, 1975; Epstein & Aiello, 1974; Saegert, 1974). Further, one would expect that the nature of the stimuli would determine the direction of the emotional response. Findings from various studies of emotional reactions to high densities support this hypothesis (e.g. Desor, 1973; Freedman et al., 1973; Saegert, Mackintosh & West, 1975). Constant, long-term exposure to more information about important social and physical aspects of an environment than can be processed would be expected to affect personality development as well as the form and quality of social relations. For example, children living in high-density dwelling units have been found to exert less control over what happens to them in an experimental situation (Rodin, 1975). In another study, college students living in such conditions have reacted less cooperatively and kept more distance from other subjects (Valins & Baum, 1974).

The third kind of overload, decisional overload, is rarely considered as a separate source of stress. Only in extreme cases can the environment be seen as its primary cause; rather, decisional overload is usually a quality of the person's relationship to the environment, greatly dependent on the personality, culturally-based expectations, tasks and goals of the individual involved. It arises from a set of plans for interacting with the environment that requires more decisions per units of time than the person is capable of making. The type-A personality or behavior pattern known to often be a precursor of heart disease (e.g. Freidman et al., 1968) is an example of this phenomenon. Very complex or hard to image environments might also create decisional overload, if they were the setting for the performance or cognitively complex tasks requiring use of the environment (Saegert et al., 1975). This combination of physical

environment and psychosocial orientation probably contributes to the dimension of experience in cities that Milgram has called the pace of life. The findings of Weiss and his colleagues (1973) on the causes of ulceration are also relevant: increased number of responses required and decreased amounts of relevant feedback, both factors increasing the number of decisions required, contribute to ulcer formation. One of the interesting points made in this research is that, while control over environmental stressors (as in the case of stimulus overload) may sometimes reduce stress, in other circumstances it may increase it. Research on human adaptation to change (Dohrenwend & Dohrenwend, 1974; Holmes & Rahe, 1967; Levi & Kagan, 1971) confirms the stressfulness of reorganization of social relations and life patterns. These various findings suggest that the probable results of decisional overload would include physiological stress and negative affect. Beyond that, it is difficult to speculate since little research exists specifically addressing this issue.

The third type of environmental stressor to be considered involves the suitability of an environment for the particular people and the activities that engage them. An environment can be stress-provoking when extraneous stimuli constantly interrupt ongoing activities or repeatedly interfere with task completion (Mandler & Watson, 1966; Weick, 1970). Frustration of goal-directed activity is taken to be the basic stress-provoking situation by many researchers (e.g. Arnold, 1967; Lazarus, 1967). The relationship between frustration and aggression is also well-established (Berkowitz, 1962). Certainly physical settings that interfere with desired activities can have the qualities most likely to provoke aggression along with frustration: (1) the frustration may seem arbitrary; (2) the environment can not retaliate against aggression; (3) the environment may be inflexible and unmodifiable. This kind of frustration may be experienced by children wanting to play in high-rise buildings prohibiting such activity, by commuters in a hurry to get home but tied up in traffic, by a museum-goer confronted with a lay-out so confusing that he can't find the exhibit he came to see.

Environments can bring different kinds of people together in ways that create stress and bring together people who might be compatible without providing the necessary props for successful interaction (Altman & Lett, 1970). Environmental frustration of activities that are important to one's self-image or social stataus can result in lowered self-esteem and/or anger and resentment of one's situation. In this way, the physical environment that places a person in the situation of constantly having to cross organizational boundaries, to produce innovative solutions to non-routine problems or to take on responsibility for the behavior of others in order to assure successful performance of activities would seem to create conflicts between the person and his role as well as between the person in his role and the environment, much like organizational environments with these properties (Kahn & French, 1970). One's relationship with physical settings may serve to heighten conflicts between personal needs and the requirements of a role as seems to be the case for a sizeable number of suburban housewives (Michelson, 1973; Saegert, 1975).

The fourth aspect of environments contributing to stress arises from the psychologically and socially meaningful messages associated with particular physical environments. Kahn and French (1970) emphasize the importance of self-evaluation in determining physical and mental well-being. They present convincing evidence that people experiencing increased status become healthier and those whose educational or class background exceed their current status are less healthy than others in the same circumstances. Further, it even appears that people subject to extreme stress of certain kinds may not be adversely affected by it if the status attached to the situation is high. For example, executives in one study had a lower incidence of peptic ulcer than did craftsmen even though the executives experienced decisional and information overload. The overload was reflected in a higher level of pepsinogen, generally associated with ulcers, but *not* in ulcer formation. Similarly, Radloff and Helmreich (1967) have reported that the difficulties experienced by submarine personnel do not generally contribute to debilitating long- or short-term effects because submarine duty within the U.S. Navy is considered very prestigious. Certainly environments differ in the status information they convey about inhabitants or users (e.g. Lansing & Marans, 1964; Niculescu, 1975); yet no research systematically relates such environmental messages to the well-being of those involved. Walter's (1972) impressionistic study of a Boston housing project does suggest that the stigma attached to the project may have contributed to the stressfulness of the environment, if not directly, then by creating mistrustful relations among inhabitants.

Aside from indications of status, environments convey other messages to the people in them about their personal and social worth, security and identity. Unfortunately, little research exists indicating what environments are saying to people about themselves and others and what the consequences of these messages might be. Researchers in environmental psychology (Ittelson et al., 1974) have speculated that a stable physical environment contributes to the cognitive and emotional development of children and that physical supports for territorial claims and privacy may be essential for feelings of security, autonomy and self-esteem. Those who study people's relationships to their environments are constantly confronted with statements about these messages from those whom they are studying: the residents of a "neighborhood in transition" say the situation indicates that the people who live there no longer care; students walking through the Times Square area of Manhattan see it as full of threats ranging from attack by muggers to the arousal of unacceptable sexual and violent feelings and reminders of human frailty embodied by the aging, incapacitated derelicts on the corners. These threats to peace of mind and self-esteem may be as stressful as threats to physical and mental functioning most often considered as environmental stressors.

So far, the environmental stressors described have concerned particular aspects of the person-environment relationship. The fifth quality related to stress has to do not so much with any particular aspect of the environment or the person's relation to it, but with the amount of attention, effort, energy and resources required in transactions with the environment. Researchers investigating differences in the experience of newcomers to urban and non-urban settings have lebelled this dimension "demandingness" (Franck, Unseld & Wentworth, 1975). The concept is similar to the idea of overload but it extends beyond the realm of cognition to include physical effort and expenditure of time and money. Its manifestations in the previously mentioned study include feelings of being stressed, extensive planning and reflection, a sense of challenge and fear, greater personal investment in social relations once achieved (and probably in other successfully completed activities), the evaluation that one's personality has been changed by the environment and an overall sense of personal growth. Although physiological responses were not measured, it would seem likely that experiences of environmental demandingness would be accompanied by physiological arousal. This concept could be extended to refer to the extent to which the environment is characterized by multiple environmental stressors. Carlstam and Levi (1971) employed such an approach in investigating urban conglomerates as psychosocial stressors. Since the term stress is used to describe a general systemic response, it seems important in understanding the stress-provoking aspects of environments to take into account the accumulation of discrete stressful experiences into a generally stressful, even if rewarding, environment.

The final environmental quality to be discussed, stimulus or information deprivation, should perhaps not be included in a paper on stress. Increased physiological activation rarely, and then only briefly, accompanies such experiences, nor are other common stress responses observed (Cohen, 1967; Prescott, 1967; Zubeck, 1969). However, normal behavior and experience does tend to be interrupted by lowered sensory input and decreased activity; hallucination and post-experimental loss of motivation are among the most dramatic results of such conditions. Various researchers have found that early sensory deprivation can give rise to hyperexcitability, susceptibility to convulsive disorders and localized motor impairment (Arnold, 1965; Butler, 1953, 1957; Riesen, 1961). Hunt (1961) has argued that stimulus and activity deprivation slows and perhaps permanently impairs human cognitive development. Although most studies of sensory deprivation have taken place in laboratory conditions that differ greatly from most naturally occurring environments, they may have applicability to some situations such as isolated environments or space and undersea exploration. However, the conditions considered by Hunt do include less unusual environments such as orphanages. Probably the major relevance of sensory deprivation studies to this paper is as a reminder that normal functioning and development require some experience of tension and challenge.

Stress-reducing Qualities of Environments

The issue for environmental planning is not to create environments in which stress is entirely absent, but rather to attempt to selectively limit the amount and types of stress the user of an environment must experience. The extent to which an environment possesses the six characteristics described should not exceed human ability to cope and adapt. Yet the simple absence of stress-inducing qualities in environments would be an unrealistic expectation. Obviously some of the very aspects of environments that can create stress also give places their unique characters and provide important opportunities. Reducing physical and psychosocial threats in a setting would probably be mainly beneficial for users whereas reducing stimulation or information in an environment might destroy many of the potential uses it has served. Suggestions have been made by other researchers of ways to ensure the liveability of cities (Ittelson et al., 1974, pp. 294–297) and to deal with the many complex functions and constraints of the built environment (Ittelson et al., 1974, pp. 341–391), while still providing challenges for the inhabitants and intellectual and aesthetic enrichment. A few considerations seem basic to such endeavors. The first is to keep in mind the human scale of an environment, to reflect in design and planning the range of needs, activities and capabilities users and potential users will bring to the setting. Secondly, the provision of alternative kinds of environments and flexible access to them is crucial. No one setting can maintain an integrity and fullness of purpose if it must serve all functions at once: a park that is also a shopping area, a transportation artery, an eating place and the surrounding area of a residential building might be vital and pleasant, but careful design is required so that the setting intended for multiple uses does not become a place fit for none of them. Some types of environments such as quiet retreats and busy challenging places must be provided as available options rather than alternative possibilities of a particular space. If these are to make the stresses people encounter manageable, the limited ability of stressed people to innovatively use and restructure environments must be remembered. Finally, environments must be understandable so that the options that exist and the modes of access to them can be used. Again, designers and planners of environments having stress-inducing qualities

or spaces intended as respites from these qualities should be aware of the lesser attentional capacity often resulting from stress (Cohen, 1974).

Speculations about the stress-reducing qualities of environments can be extended beyond methods for keeping environments from being overly stressful to consideration of the possible restorative potential of certain environments. Benson (1974) has presented evidence that meditation exercises can evoke what he calls the relaxation response which inhibits the bodily processes associated with stress. This procedure involves closing one's eyes in a quiet, comfortable environment and concentrating on repeating a one syllable word over and over again for a period of time approximately equivalent to a coffee-break. The lowered sensory input and decreased physical and mental activity of meditation have much in common with the sensory deprivation conditions created by researchers; indeed, the physiological effects as well as the presence of unusual mental imagery and subsequent reduction of motivation if the experience lasts an extended period of time are also very similar. Benson suggests that in most traditional societies religious rites, especially prayer and meditation, have provided valuable restorative experiences for people that may be missing in the active, secular, goal-directed lives of many moderns. It might be worthwhile to investigate the kinds of responses people have to environments for prayer and meditation, such as temples, cathedrals, oriental rock gardens, and the mountain retreats of many religious orders. In this vein, perhaps the aesthetic quality of environments deserves to be taken more seriously; as Langer (1967) has indicated in her speculations on the origin and function of aesthetic responses, we might begin to consider that appreciation of beauty like human intellectual and technical abilities plays an important biologically-based part in the selection and creation of environments in which human life can flourish.

18. Social Ritual and Architectural Space
DUNCAN JOINER

This paper explores what Stuart Wilson (1967) has described as the proto-linguistic properties of space organization. With specific reference to the office context, it examines the ways in which spaces and spatial relationships are used to supplement other methods of formal person-to-person communication, such as gesticulation, action and the spoken word.

There are many examples of formal situations where spatial relationships are used to reinforce social distinctions and to mould the kinds of social interaction to be expected within the spaces. The arrangements in the interior of a small Danish church, for example, reflect not only the formalities of the liturgy, but also the formal social structure of the villagers who use the building. A particular and clearly defined place is provided for each of the village's social groups. The priest conducting the service is provided with a richly carved pulpit, raised above the level of the congregation, so that he becomes the centre of attention both physically and symbolically. But slightly higher than the pulpit, and decorated with gilt panelling, a coat of arms and a canopy, is a box for the local lord and his family. The box juts out on the opposite side of the archway from the pulpit and the priest, standing in the pulpit, faces the box almost directly across the heads of the congregation below. Not only is the place for these important people set aside physically from the places for ordinary people, but the form and decoration of the box further emphasizes its difference from the other seating places in the room and the social

This paper reports on part of a postgraduate research study, under the direction of Professor Newton Watson, at the School of Environmental Studies, University College, London. It is an edited version of a paper given at the Architectural Psychology Conference at Kingston, in September 1970.

differences between its occupants and the occupants of the room generally. Along the nave of the church the box dominates the congregation's view quite as much as the symbols of religious significance—the font and the altar, which are secreted away behind the arched opening. Perhaps a distinction is also being made here between earthly wealth and majesty which can be seen but not touched, and religious mystery and sanctity which can be dimly seen as something glorious but which is also beyond the reach of common man.

In this example, there are three basic physical spatial qualities used to indicate the kind of social interaction to be expected in the space. They are position, distance and symbolic decoration, and these three work together to define a fourth quality—territory. The territories for the various social groups using the church are clearly defined—the raised box with its gates, the gallery, the pulpit and the nave. In the nave, the seating is also divided into territories for the smaller social groups of families, by gates at the ends of the pews. In some other churches in Denmark, the territories for various social groups are distinguished by the use of symbolic decoration alone—with ornate carving on the end boards of the front two rows of pews.

Courtrooms provide a further example of this kind of socio-spatial relationship. An empty courtroom conveys a great deal of information about the structure and underlying attitudes of British legal proceedings. However, court proceedings are by their nature a highly formalized kind of social interaction and it is to be expected that courtrooms, like churches, will be physically and symbolically formalized to accommodate formal rituals. This paper suggests that there is a highly structured or formal framework underlying nearly all kinds of social interaction, and that the ways in which people use spaces, or expect to be able to use them, in buildings of all kinds, and the ways in which they organize the moveable parts of the spaces, are as formalized as in the church example or in a British courtroom.

From the study of small office spaces—a very ordinary life situation—it appears that these spaces, like those in the previous examples, also convey at least two kinds of information. These are, information about the occupant, and information about how the occupant would like visitors to behave when in his room. The two are closely linked, in that if the visitor has some fore-knowledge of who the occupant is and what he does, he will expect to find certain cues about how he is to behave when he enters the occupant's room. The information about the occupant is also at least twofold and is related to expressions of himself and of his status and role in the organization.

The occupants of many single-person offices were interviewed and the rooms and their furniture layouts were measured and photographed. These sessions were gener-ally prearranged, half-hour appointments and the observer made notes about the pro-ceedings after each session, about what the occupant did and what the observer did during the half-hour. One of these notes is given, as an introduction to some of the more important social concepts related to the use of space.

Figure 18–1 is a plan of the office in which this session took place.

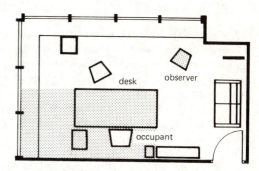

FIGURE 18–1a. Private and public zones in a director's office.

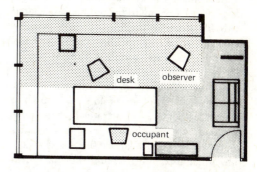

FIGURE 18–1b. Two sub-zones within the public zone.

'The receptionist in the ground floor en-trance lobby telephoned the occupant's secretary to say that I had arrived for my appointment and I was told to take the lift to the sixth floor. I was met in the sixth floor lift hall by the secretary who escorted me to the occupant's office, which is entered through her own office. As we went in, the secretary was leading, and she said, 'Come on in, Mr. Joiner', by way of introduction. The occupant was sitting at his desk smoking a cigar, but rose to his feet and stepped out to the door side of his desk to shake my hand as I entered. He then motioned me to sit in the chair nearest the door as he sat back in his own chair again, and our discussion (the interview) began. As I was recording the interview, I placed the microphone on the desk between us. The occupant sat forward in his chair and alert during the whole of the inter-view. After the interview, I started meas-uring the room, and the occupant read papers for a few minutes, and then went out before I had begun photographing. He entered again just as I had finished packing up my equipment, and the final farewell and hand-shake took place in the same position as the introduction—just inside the door.'

The first important point about the use of space in this office is illustrated by the introduction procedure. The occupant stepped out from behind his desk to greet the observer and then sat down again in his chair behind his desk. The location of the desk in the room divided it effectively into two zones—a private one, in which the occupant sat to work, and a public zone, in which the observer was received and seated. The differentiation of spaces to isolate specialized activities is of itself significant (Rapoport, 1969). But the phenomenon is also closely related to the social behavioural concepts of territoriality and interaction distance. Similar behaviour, associated with furniture arrangement in old people's homes and in mental hospitals, has also been related to territoriality (Lipman, 1970; Sommer, 1959).

The next stage in the interaction—the invitation to the observer to sit in the chair nearest to the door—illustrates that the public zone was subdivided into two smaller zones:– the space near to the door, where they greeted each other, and the space near the desk, which contained the visitors' chairs. The important physical factor here, between the two public zones, is their different distances from the occupant's private zone. In an experimental situation, Kenneth Little (1965) found that interaction distances between two people were markedly influenced by the degree of acquaintance of the two people, and by the setting. There appear to be commonly understood rules governing distances for interaction, which are determined by the degree of acquaintanceship, the content of the interaction and the setting (Ardrey, 1969; Goffman, 1969; Hall, 1969; Sommer, 1969). The arrangement of the visitors' chairs in this office could be construed as providing a range of occupant-visitor distances for various types

of interaction. So even within the inner subdivision of the public zone, there appears to be a further range of acceptable distances, with their physical markers—the chairs. Thus use of distance cues, which is apparently a fundamental and integral part of the communication process, has been called informal space—not because it lacks form or structure, but because it is unstated and universally recognized within a cultural group (Hall, 1969). As a complete stranger visiting on business unfamiliar to the occupant, the observer was invited to sit at the greatest distance within the inner subdivision of the public territory. Had the observer been well known to the occupant, and the nature of the business been familiar to him, the observer would probably have been invited to sit closer to him. And if the observer had been very well known to the occupant, then the observer would probably have been invited to sit on the boundary of the occupant's private zone, alongside him at his desk.

Hall (1969) has identified four distinct interactional distances—intimate, personal, social and public—all of which have a near and a far phase. Probably all of these except public distance are applicable at some time or another to the office context, and the distance between the observer and the occupant during the interview fits Hall's definition of social distance, close phase. Experimental work has shown that this complex relationship between distance and the nature of interaction is quite specific and predictable (Ardrey, 1969) and Gullahorn has shown that for clerical office workers, the interaction rate is largely determined by distance, and that business and friendship are secondary factors (Gullahorn, 1952). The use of distance as a social cue is also influenced by cultural background (Hall, 1959), personality and stigma, such as physical disability or deformity (Sommer, 1969).

Quite as important, and intimately connected with the use of zones in this interview situation, was the use of seating orientation and location within the room. In this particular case, the occupant had so arranged his room that he was facing the visitor across his desk. Not only did this mean that the desk was forming a distinct and physical barrier between the private and the public zones in his room, but also that he was directly facing the observer sitting in one of the visitors' chairs. So that, although during the interview it was the observer who was asking the questions, and leading the conversation, the occupant, because of his position, maintained his superiority and control over the situation. Physical proximity and position are important mainly in relation to intimacy and dominance, and their significance in this respect varies with the physical surroundings and the cultural setting. Bodily orientation is also used to convey meaning during interaction—change of orientation towards a person is used to start or terminate interaction with him, and people face those with whom they want to interact. People co-operating tend to sit side by side and those competing tend to sit facing each other (Argyle, 1967). Studies of social interaction in sitting rooms in geriatric homes have shown that seating distances and orientations not only influenced conversation patterns, but were also used to indicate the status of a person occupying a particular chair (Lipman, 1968). Similar findings—the influence of chair location and position on interaction patterns—have been found in studies of group interaction around tables (Sommer, 1959). This aspect of seat location and orientation for interaction was highlighted in a recent design analysis for doctors' surgeries, where the clients wanted to break down the feelings of nervousness and awe which patients experience while talking to doctors about personal and private matters. A solution to this problem, which was thought to give adequate dilution of the doctor-patient relationship, was that the surgeries were designed so that the patient approached the doctor from his side,

and sat by his side to talk to him (*Architects' Journal*, 1969). This arrangement is consistent with the seating positions adopted by co-operating groups in experimental situations (Argyle, 1967).

Another aspect of seating position and orientation which, it is suggested, is applicable to this office context is related to feelings of personal security. In the office described here, the occupant was seated with his back to a blank wall, in such a way that he could see all the visitors' chairs and the door with only minor head or body movements. Facing outwards from a wall location, one is able to see all that is going on in the room, and is able to face other people directly when they are entering the room, or are in the room. In this way, the occupant can be instantly ready for interaction with a visitor, the moment that the door handle turns, and he can maintain visual control over other people in his room. In observations of seating arrangements in old people's homes, Sommer found that the residents preferred to sit around the walls, looking into the room, even when seemingly more attractive arrangements were provided for them (Sommer, 1969).

The organization and use of the room to provide cues for interaction through territoriality, zoning, distance, and personal orientation, closely fits Goffman's (1969) theory of *performance*, where social distance is seen as the 'intersection of the structural and dramaturgical aspects of group behavior', and to which region and region behaviour are central concepts. Goffman says that the impression and understanding fostered by the performance will tend to saturate the region and the time span, so that any individual located in this situation will be in a position to observe the performance and be guided by the definition of the situation which the performance fosters. In the example of the interview situation, the whole of the occupant's room was the region in which the occupant was performing at the time of the interview, and in which he was creating impressions about himself, his organization and his role within the organization. It would have been difficult for him to convey these impressions had the interview taken place in another room, or in another building.

In Goffman's distinction between *front regions, back regions, and outside regions,* the important aspect seems to be the conceptual barriers between front regions and outside regions. These barriers are also used to foster impressions about the people and activities in the front region. In the office example here, the ground floor receptionist, the hallways, the lobbies and the secretary could all be considered as impression managing barriers between the outside and our occupant's front region. This use of objects and people for impression mangement has also been called presenting a *front* (Goffman, 1969) and in this example, both the occupant's personal front and the organization's corporate front are being presented by the use of expensive materials, spacious hallways and well-groomed receptionists and secretaries. Probably, the initial introductory ritual in this building, which involved interaction with a receptionist and a secretary, was not only to ensure privacy and freedom from interruption for the occupant, but was also a highly conventionalized piece of impression management provided by the organization.

The projection of a personal front, or self image is a necessary and unavoidable requirement for all social interaction (Argyle, 1967) and to be able to establish a personal front or self image, a person must engage in interaction and receive responses from others (Sprott, 1958). This need to establish an identity seems so fundamental to human existence that Ardrey has rated it even higher than people's needs for stimulation and security, and it can be shown from this office interview example that it is an important determinant of space organization and use.

Two components of self phenomena seem to be important in this context—self image and ego ideal (Argyle, 1967). When a person is engaging in interaction, and particularly when on his home range or territory, it becomes an extension of his physical person. When students move into dormitories, they immediately set about making changes to the furniture arrangements, and pinning up pictures (van der Ryn & Silverstein, 1967). This activity, which has been called *personalization* (Rapoport, 1967), can also be seen as using the room to extend the occupant's personal front. Similarly, the interviewee's room contained many symbols expressing his personal attitudes, his status, and his role in the organization, and the organization's objectives as well. These took the form of deep pile carpeting, expensive timber partitioning, comfortable chairs, a large desk, pictures on the walls, and the like. The layout of the furniture in the room is also used to sustain these impressions. Whether or not the occupant sits facing the door, for example, would tell us about his readiness for interaction. And whether or not his desk forms a barrier between himself and his visitors would tell us about the sort of interaction he expects, and hence how he considers himself in relation to his visitors—friendly, aloof, superior, etc.

The use of objects as symbols of status and rank is highly organized in most social institutions, not least in office cultures (Duffy, 1969; Lockwood, 1958). The civil service adheres to strict rules governing the size of room and the amount and quality of furnishing which an employee in each grade may use (Institution of Professional Civil Servants, 1968). The view held by Sommer that social and spatial orders serve similar functions seems directly applicable to the office situation (Sommer, 1969) and a quick glance at the civil service regulations of room size confirms this. Another significance attached to objects in a room, and one which has been seen to be very important in military barracks (Blake et al., 1956) and in student dormitories (van der Ryn & Silverstein, 1967), is their use to define personal space. Objects are used to express some aspect of the occupant's identity, and the place in which the objects are situated becomes associated with that person. In a recently completed school hostel building, this territorial significance of personal objects was exploited in the design of children's dormitories in an attempt to provide each child with a space recognizably his own (*Architect's Journal*, 1969). Although one might not have expected this to be important in single-person rooms, many of the objects, such as family photographs, paintings, vases, and the like seen in single-person offices during this study seem to be meaningful in this respect.

The last point to be made from the interview example concerns the occupant's behavior while his room was being measured and photographed. It may have been quite coincidental that he had a document to read and a brief visit to make during this time. However, both these acts could be construed as attempts by the occupant to act as a *non-person*, and to show *civil inattention* to the observer's activities (Goffman, 1963). While photographing and measuring his room, the observer was transgressing all the conventional and social interactional boundaries mentioned above, and by recording photographically his room from various positions, the observer was also seeing beyond the occupant's front region of impression management. The only way that the occupant could sustain this intrusion was to pretend to disassociate himself from it, by reading. But when his personal space bubble was in danger of being invaded, as it would have been when the cabinet behind his chair was being measured, his safest course of action was to leave the room. By returning to the room after the observer had finished, the occupant may have been attempting to restore in the observer the initial impressions that he and his room were fostering.

This example has suggested that office spaces are used and organized in a way which establishes interaction boundaries,

sets the pattern of interaction with which the occupant expects visitors to comply and fosters impressions about the role and status of the occupant in his organization. It has also suggested that the important components of the space organization in a single-person office by which these social interactional cues are achieved, involve the positioning of the desk in the room so that it divides it into two major zones and that the orientation of the desk and the occupant's seating position indicate the strength of the zone definition, and the expected interaction pattern. These are further supported by the location of the chairs for visitors, relative to the occupant's working position.

If, as suggested by this example, the ritualistic use of space associated with social interaction is an important influence on space organization, then we would expect to find the room layout qualities in the example given also existing in some degree in a large number of offices. Since the conduct of social interaction and its symbols are culturally based, we would also expect to find cultural differences in the layout of offices, as well as differences between the layouts of offices with occupants of different social standing. The important points for comparison here are, (a) in which direction occupants face when sitting: whether they look out of the windows, whether they look into their rooms, and whether or not they can see their doors. The facing direction could also be used as a measure of the importance of socio-cultural influences compared with some physical environmental ones. For example, it would be likely that an occupant who sat facing out of his window would consider that to be able to see the view is more important than to be able to see the door. (b) What strength of zone definition does the desk position and orientation provide?

In the study of offices, furniture arrangements were recorded in single-person rooms in seven commercial organizations, two government and one local government organization, and one academic institution.

The offices examined in the commercial and government organizations were occupied by clerical and administrative staff representing a wide range of status levels. The offices were all situated in central London, and the organizations were regarded as representing various cultural groups—commercial, government, and academic. A further cultural group was provided by a small sample of surveys made in single-person offices in a couple of Swedish commercial organizations. An exploratory study was also made of seating in bürolandschaft type offices in Sweden and in the United Kingdom, and in small multiple-occupant offices. The point here was to compare the spatial organization that an individual provides in a totally enclosed situation with what one of equivalent status and role provides in a virtually open situation, where the nearest objects for enclosure are often other people.

Although zone formation, personal distance, and body orientation are thought to be closely linked as cues for social interaction, for convenience, the analysis of the office layout plans was carried out in two sections—analysis of personal orientation within the room, and an analysis of the way in which the furniture divided the room into zones.

The main objective in the analysis of the occupants' seating orientations was to determine what parts of their rooms they could see or be aware of in a brief glance up from their work. The parts of the rooms considered in this analysis, were the windows and the doors, and for each room they were given a number according to which segment they fell into when the protractor (Figure 18–2) was placed over the occupant's chair on the plan. Parts of the room in segments 4 5 6 are outside of occupant's field of peripheral vision (assuming no head movement) and those within segments 7 8 1 2 3 are within his field of peripheral vision. Objects or parts of the room within segments 8 1 2 were considered to be within the occupant's direct facing direction, when he lifted his head from his

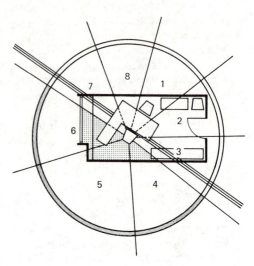

FIGURE 18–2.   Analysis of occupant seating orientation.

work. In this way the plans of the offices could be classified according to working position-window relationships, and working position-door relationships.

The description of zoning established for this study is related to the position and orientation of the desk in the room, which determines the degree of definition between the private and public zones, and the openness or closure of the spatial pattern, which possibly influences the degree of formality of expected interaction. The plans of all of the offices could be conveniently divided into six distinct groups. Figure 18–3 shows the characteristic desk arrangement in each group, and a definitive description of the furniture pattern to be expected in each. Group 1 arrangements have the highest degree of zone definition, and group 6 arrangements the least. Groups 1 to 4 provide for what are called *formal interaction*, where discussions are carried out over the desk top, with the occupant seated in his private zone, and the visitors seated in the public

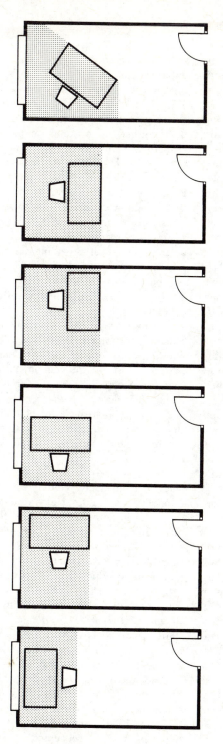

Group 1

Desk arranged as a diagonal barrier across the corner of the room opposite the door.

Group 2

Rectilinear arrangement-desk as a barrier open at both ends and opposite the door.

Group 3

Rectilinear arrangement-desk as a barrier open at one end and opposite the door.

Group 4

Desk arranged as a barrier within the room, but open on the door end.

Group 5

Desk against side wall, not as a barrier-occupant sits with one side to the door.

Group 6

Desk against wall or window at opposite end of the room from the door. Occupant has back to door.

FIGURE 18–3. Six zone formations.

zone. Groups 5 and 6 do not provide for this kind of formal interaction and although during interviews and discussions the occupant may still remain in his private zone, there is no clear physical barrier separating the two. In this way the personal orientation of the occupant, and the zoning pattern in each of the rooms could be tabulated. Some of these tabulations are shown in Tables 18–1 to 18–9. Differences in these comparisons have been considered to be significant when $p \leqslant 0.05$.

In most of the offices examined, furniture was arranged so that occupants could see their doors and their windows from their working positions at their desks (Table 18–1a). That more occupants sat facing their doors than their windows was shown to be less than marginally significant (Table 18–1b) but in view of the fact that in all of the rooms, the window was considerably wider than the door, the predominance of door-facing possibly becomes an important result. Being able to see the door from one's working position implies a readiness for interaction, and that a large proportion of the sample adopted this kind of seating position, suggests that to be able to see who is coming into the room, and to be instantly prepared for them—that is, to have one's *front* correctly displayed,—is possibly more important than to be able to glance out of the window.

Although furniture arrangements predominantly allowed occupants to see their doors easily from their working positions, there were significant cultural variations in this. Tables 18–2a to 18–2c compare occupants' seat-door relationships between academic, commercial, and government cultural groups. Nearly one third of the academic cultural group cannot see their doors, whereas all of the government group were sitting so that they could see their doors. Most of the commercial and government occupants were actually sitting facing their doors, but only one quarter of the academics had this arrangement. Over half of the academics sat sideways to their doors.

These cultural differences in desk orientation relative to the doors are also reflected in cultural differences in zone formation. Six distinct types of zone formation, showing various degrees of definition, were distinguished in the total sample of offices examined. Table 18–3, which compares the numbers with each of the zone formations in the five cultural groups, shows that the largest number of academics had arranged their rooms with group 5 and 6 zoning patterns, whilst the largest number of commercial occupants had group 1, 3, and 4, arrangements—all providing for formal interaction across the desk top. The greatest number of government and local authority occupants had group 1 zoning—the strongest definition.

These results show that the academics generally sat sideways to their doors, and adopted more open, and less defined zone patterns than did the commercial and government occupants who predominantly sat facing their doors. In other words, academic occupants who spend a lot of their time in their rooms talking with groups of students organize their rooms in such a way as to minimize their social distance and to play down their role in these discussions as leaders. Conversely, commercial and government occupants had arranged their rooms so that during discussions, their dominant role was sustained by maintaining social distance across their desk tops. Presumably this has been found to be important in the conduct of business negotiations.

Comparisons of seating orientation and zone formation by occupant status have shown that in the academic institution, status seems to have very little to do with how an occupant arranges his room. In the comparisons of seating orientation by status in academic offices, status groups were combined because of the small sample of high status occupancy offices examined. Tables 18–4a to 18–4c compare the seat-door relationships in rooms occupied by senior lecturers and staff of lower status, with those in the rooms occupied by departmental

TABLE 18–1a.   *Desk—Door and Desk—Window Relationships*
               General sample of 132 offices.

No. with door visible from working position (door in 78123)	110/132
No. with window visible from working position (window in 78123)	105/132

test of binomial proportions, z=0.81   p=0.2

TABLE 18–1b.   *Desk—Door and Desk—Window Relationships*
               General sample of 132 offices.

No. with door in general facing direction (door in 812)	67/132
No. with window in general facing direction (window in 812)	56/132

test of binomial proportions, z=1.3.   p=0.097

TABLE 18–2a.   *Desk—Door Relationships Compared by Cultural Groups*
               Numbers with all or part of door in arc of peripheral vision.

	Academic	Commercial	Government	Totals
No. with door visible from working position (door in 78123)	28	42	28	98
No. with door not visible from working position (door in 456 only)	16	5	0	21
TOTALS	44	47	28	119

$\chi^2=17.65$, df=2, p<0.001

TABLE 18–2b.   *Desk—Door Relationships Compared by Cultural Groups*
               Numbers with all or part of door in general facing direction.

	Academic	Commercial	Government	Totals
No. sitting facing door (door in 812)	12	30	22	64
No. not sitting facing door (door not in 812)	32	17	6	55
TOTALS	44	47	28	119

$\chi^2=21.21$, df=2, p<0.001

TABLE 18–2c. *Desk—Door Relationships Compared by Cultural Groups*
Numbers sitting sideways to doors

	Academic	Commercial	Government	Totals
No. sitting side to door (door in 67 or 34)	23	17	5	45
No. not sitting side to door (door not in 67, 34)	21	30	23	74
TOTALS	44	47	28	119

$x^2 = 9.16$, df$=2$, $0.02 > p > 0.01$

TABLE 18–3. *Zone Formation in Offices Compared by Cultural Groups*

Zone Formation	Academic	Commercial	Local Govt.	Government	Swedish Commercial	Totals
Group 1.	4	10	4	10	2	30
Group 2.	2	1	0	1	1	5
Group 3.	5	19	2	1	0	27
Group 4.	9	12	0	8	2	31
Group 5.	13	4	1	0	7	25
Group 6.	11	1	0	1	1	14
TOTALS	44	47	7	21	13	132

$x^2 = 66.6$, df$=20$, $p < 0.001$

TABLE 18–4a. *Academic Offices. Desk—Door Relationships Compared by Status*
Numbers with all or part of door in arc of peripheral vision.

	Lecturer Snr. Lecturer Status Levels 1 and 2	Tutor and Higher Status Levels 3, 4, 5	Totals
No. with door visible from work position. (door in 78123)	22	5	27
No. with door not visible from work position (door in 456 only)	11	5	16
TOTALS	33	10	43

$x^2 = 0.32$, df$=1$, $0.9 > p > 0.8$

TABLE 18–4b.   *Academic Offices. Desk—Door Relationships Compared by Status*
Numbers with all or part of door in general facing direction.

	Lecturer Snr. Lecturer Status Levels 1 and 2	Tutor and Higher Status Levels 3, 4, 5	Totals
No. facing door (door in 812)	8	3	11
No. not facing door (door not in 812)	25	7	32
TOTALS	33	10	43

$\chi^2 = 0.6$, df $= 1$, $0.5 > p > 0.3$

TABLE 18–4c.   *Academic Offices. Desk—Door Relationships Compared by Status*
Numbers with side to door seating arrangements.

	Lecturer Snr. Lecturer Status Levels 1 and 2	Tutor and Higher Status Levels 3, 4, 5	Totals
No. with side to door (door in 67 or 34)	19	4	23
No. not sitting side to door (door not in 67 or 34)	14	6	20
TOTALS	33	10	43

$\chi^2 = 0.377$, df $= 1$, $0.8 > p > 0.7$

TABLE 18–5.   *Academic Offices. Zone Formation Compared by Occupant Status*
Numbers in each of two composite zone groups.

	Lecturer Snr. Lecturer Status Levels 1 and 2	Tutor and Higher Status Levels 3, 4, 5	Totals
Groups 1,2,3,4	14	6	20
Groups 5 and 6	19	5	24
TOTALS	33	11	44

$\chi^2 = 1.1$, df $= 1$, $0.3 > p > 0.2$

TABLE 18–6a. *Commercial Offices. Desk—Door Relationships Compared by Status Numbers with all or part of door in arc of peripheral vision.*

	Clerical and Admin. Status Levels 1, 2, 3	Managers and Directors Status Levels 4 and 5	Totals
No. with door visible from work position (door in 78123)	18	22	40
No. with door not visible from work position (door in 456 only)	1	1	2
TOTALS	19	23	42

$\chi^2 = 0.81$, df $= 1$, $0.5 > p > 0.3$

TABLE 18–6b. *Commercial Offices. Desk—Door Relationships Compared by Status Numbers with all or part of door in general facing direction.*

	Clerical and Admin. Status Levels 1, 2, 3	Managers and Directors Status Levels 4 and 5	Totals
No. facing door (door in 812)	9	19	28
No. not facing door (door not in 812)	10	4	14
TOTALS	19	23	42

$\chi^2 = 7.5$, df $= 1$, $0.01 > p > 0.001$

TABLE 18–6c. *Commercial Offices. Desk—Door Relationships Compared by Status Numbers with side to door seating arrangements.*

	Clerical and Admin. Status Levels 1, 2, 3	Managers and Directors Status Levels 4 and 5	Totals
No. with side to door (door in 67 or 34)	10	4	14
No. not sitting side to door (door not in 67, 34)	9	19	28
TOTALS	19	23	42

$\chi^2 = 4.35$, df $= 1$, $0.05 > p > 0.02$

TABLE 18–7. *Commercial Offices. Zone Formation Compared by Occupant Status*
Numbers in each of four composite zone groups.

	Clerical and Admin. Status Levels 1, 2, 3	Managers and Directors Status Levels 4 and 5	Totals
Groups 1 and 2	4	7	11
Group 3	6	13	19
Group 4	5	7	12
Groups 5 and 6	5	0	5
TOTALS	20	27	47

$\chi^2 = 8.242$, df $= 3$, $0.05 > p > 0.02$

TABLE 18–8a. *Desk—Door Relationships Compared by Room Shape*
Numbers with all or part of door in arc of peripheral vision.

	Deep Rooms $d/w \geq 1.3$ $3.0 \geq w \geq 2.0$	Shallow Rooms $d/w < 1.3$	Totals
No. with door visible from work position (door in 78123)	41	30	71
No. with door not visible from work (door in 456 only)	7	6	13
TOTALS	48	36	84

$\chi^2 = 0.0019$, df $= 1$, $0.95 > p > 0.90$

TABLE 18–8b. *Desk—Door Relationships Compared by Room Shape*
Numbers with all or part of door in general facing direction.

	Deep Rooms $d/w \geq 1.3$ $3.0 \geq w \geq 2.0$	Shallow Rooms $d/w < 1.3$	Totals
No. facing door (door in 812)	14	24	38
No. not facing door (door not in 812)	34	12	46
TOTALS	48	36	84

$\chi^2 = 13.25$, df $= 1$, $p < 0.001$

TABLE 18–8c. *Desk—Door Relationships Compared by Room Shape Numbers sitting sideways to door.*

	Deep Rooms $d/w \geq 1.3$ $3.0 \geq w \geq 2.0$	Shallow Rooms $d/w < 1.3$	Totals
No. with side to door (door in 67 or 34)	32	9	41
No. not sitting side to door (door not in 67, 34)	16	27	43
TOTALS	48	36	84

$\chi^2 = 12.65$, df = 1, p < 0.001

TABLE 18–9. *Zone Formation in Offices Compared by Room Shape*

Zone Formation	Deep Rooms $d/w \geq 1.3$ $3.0 \geq w \geq 2.0$	Shallow Rooms $d/w < 1.3$	Totals
Group 1	14	13	27
Group 2	5	2	7
Group 3	7	18	25
Group 4	14	11	25
Group 5	24	1	25
Group 6	5	8	13
TOTALS	69	53	122

$\chi^2 = 26.75$, df = 5, p < 0.001

tutors and staff of higher status. The tables do not show any significant relationship between seat orientation and status in these two academic groups. Similarly, Table 18–5 which compares the zone formations found in the offices occupied by these two academic status groups, shows that there are only minimal differences between the ways in which academics of various statuses formed zones in their rooms. The small sample sizes in the status groups which has necessitated their combination in this analysis may be one cause of the insignificance of these results. That is, the status divisions analysed may be too coarse to yield any meaningful comparisons. In view of the very low levels of significances, however,

it would be best to accept, at least tentatively, that social status is not an important influence on room organization in academic offices.

In both the commercial and government organizations, however, the status level of an occupant was seen to have quite a considerable influence on the way in which he arranged his room. Tables 18–6a to 18–6c compare seat-door relationships found in commercial offices occupied by staff of managerial and higher status, with those found in commercial offices occupied by clerical and administrative staff grades. High proportions of both groups could see their doors peripherally, but significantly more of the high status group than of the lower one sat facing their doors directly. Side-to-door arrangements were more predominant among the lower status group. A comparison of zone formation by status in commercial offices suggests that the choices of zone formation were also very much contingent upon occupancy status. Table 18–7 compares four zone pattern groups in the two basic commercial status divisions. Two pairs of the six zone groups have been combined in this comparison to make the compared samples as equal as possible in size, but the combination still maintains the important division between the weak formations (5 and 6) and the stronger ones (1, 2, 3, and 4) which provide for formal discussion. The largest number of rooms for high status occupants had group 3 zoning, providing for formal discussion and a high degree of space definition. The zone formations in the rooms with lower status occupants are more evenly spread throughout the four zone groups. The indication of this result is that room layouts in commercial offices are very much contingent upon occupant status, with higher executives providing stronger territorial definition than executives of lower status.

The social and cultural groups of offices have also been compared on the basis of working position-window relationships, and the results of these comparisons broadly follow closely those for seat-door relationships. However, there was no clear relationship between status, and the extent to which occupants could see their windows in the academic offices or in the commercial offices. More academics than others sat sideways to their windows, but the generally large window width in most offices have made these comparisons insensitive.

The general comparisons of room arrangements in offices occupied by staff from different cultural groups, shown in Tables 18–2 and 18–3, indicate that seating orientations and zone formations follow cultural trends, and that the choice of room arrangement by an occupant is dependent upon his cultural background. The comparisons of seating orientation and zone formations between rooms of different occupancy status in the academic and commercial institutions, shown in Tables 18–4, 18–5, 18–6 and 18–7, support this assertion that room arrangement is culturally based. They have shown that status had little influence over an occupant's choice of room arrangement in academic offices, whereas in the commercial offices, seating orientation and zone formation appeared to be related to occupant status. So not only is the choice of room arrangement culturally based, but also whether or not occupant status will further influence the room arrangement seems also to be culturally based.

In commercial and government organizations, senior staff are often receiving visits from people from outside their organizations, and often have to interview people to whom they are not known personally, or may not want to be known personally. In the conduct of business agreements, and the organization and management of commercial or government concerns, it is therefore probably essential to be able to maintain dominance and control over discussions in one's office and to be ready for all kinds of interaction with a clear and well organized front, whether this be presentation of self, job or the organization. The junior commercial and government staff occupants were shown to have less clearly defined zoning in their offices. If social factors do influence room layout, then this would be a reasonable result, because junior staff tend to have few visits from outside their organizations, and close working relationships with their colleagues, neither of which depend upon the presentation of a clearly ordered front. Probably, academics of all status groups have similar attitudes towards their discussions with visitors, who are mainly students and other staff and colleagues. In this sort of institution where close working relationships are fostered, the presentation of a clearly defined working front, and the maintenance of social distance and barriers, through room arrangement and clearly defined zoning, would be irrelevant. In academic offices, the front adopted is a non-front. It is probable that academics do not rely very heavily upon physical appearance, their surroundings, or formalized social interaction for the presentation of status and prestige. Prestige is gained through academic achievement and is displayed through the formal expressions of this achievement such as the publishing of papers, and the widely used system of titles such as Dean, Professor, Reader, etc. For anyone about to engage in interaction with an academic, a knowledge of the work he has published, and the title 'Professor' on his door will provide a guide as to the interactional behaviour considered to be appropriate.

The comparisons of room arrangements so far described, have not taken into account any influence that the shapes of rooms may have upon the spatial arrangements within them. Although in all except perhaps two of the academic rooms examined, alternative furniture arrangements would have been possible, the only aspect of room shape which has been considered in the comparisons is the location of the windows and doors in relation to the occupants' seating positions. The comparisons shown in Tables 18–8a to 18–8c and in Table 18–9 suggest, however, that the plan-form shape of a room does have some influence upon the spatial arrangements within it. Table 18–8a, to 18–8c, which compare occupants' seat-door relationships in deep narrow rooms with those in shallow square ones, show that more people in the shallow offices than in the deep ones face their doors. There is also a significant influence of room shape upon whether or not people sit sideways to their doors. A greater proportion of the people in deep offices sit sideways than do those in the shallow ones. Room shape appears also to influence zone formation. Table 18–9 shows that whereas in deep offices, group 5 zoning is more predominant, in shallow rooms group 3 zoning is most predominant. In other words, the occupants of deep narrow rooms predominantly sat facing one side wall, and so had open zone formations, whilst the occupants of the wide square rooms predominantly sat facing their doors directly, and had closed and clearly defined zone patterns.

In the wide square rooms, the predominant zoning is in groups 1 and 3—the zone patterns that would be expected from senior staff in commercial and government organizations. Since many such senior staff do in fact have offices of this kind, this may explain the result. The difference may not be due entirely to room shape, but also to occupancy status.

The results presented in this paper have been interpreted as indicating, at least tentatively, that where the physical environment is physiologically adequate, sociocultural forces have a strong influence over the way that office spaces are organized, and that many of the physical room elements take on a significance related to the expected social interaction of the occupant. This study has attempted to show that the location and orientation of the desk in an office has interactional significance, and the study could probably be usefully extended to encompass many more aspects of the room. The responses to semi-structured interviews with many of the office occupants have provided the basis for some interesting speculation. For example, it seems possible that a window and a view may be important to an occupant not merely because it provides momentary relief from work and eyestrain; its real value for many executives may be its status value, and the way that it forms part of his display of status imagery. If this is the case, what better place to put the managing director's, or the permanent departmental secretary's office than on the 34th floor with a splendid view of London?

The introduction into offices by their occupants of personal elements of display might also provide the basis for worthwhile study. Even in the bürolandschaft-type offices visited, where the pinning up of pictures and postcards was officially forbidden, they were still appearing. It is likely that in a bürolandschaft office where there are no walls to mark out home ranges and territories, these small symbolic territorial markers may be of utmost importance. Position, distance and zoning are probably of special significance in these situations, and importance is attached to various parts of the space. For example, corner positions are of high status value and are generally occupied by senior staff. Figure 18–4 shows such a corner position in a Swedish example. All the symbols of display associated with a managing director are present. The locating of his secretary on the main circulation route provides an effective barrier to intrusion and a wall substitute.

The combination of spatial layout and the use of choice of objects of display contribute to an overall ambience in offices which varies from one culture to the next, and seems to be stereotyped within each. Equivalent single rooms in commercial, government, and academic organizations illustrate this cultural difference. The academic has an open seating arrangement, an an-

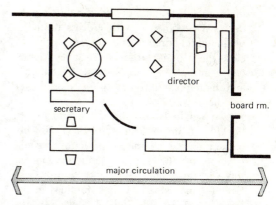

FIGURE 18–4.   High status position in a bürolandschaft type office.

tique book case and an antique and rather untidy desk—the stereotyped academic image. The government office has all the standard government allocation equipment for the occupant's grade, and could be used by any civil servant of the same grade. The commercial office has luxurious furnishings, a tidy desk, and pictures on the walls, and would live up to the expectations of any visitor from another company.

19.   *Privacy and Crowding in Poverty*
OSCAR LEWIS

As I grew older, I became aware of the restrictions one had to put up with when a whole family lived in a single room. In my case, because I lived in fantasy and liked to daydream, I was especially annoyed by having my dreams interrupted. My brothers would bring me back to reality with, "Hey, what's the matter with you! You look dopey." Or I'd hear my father's voice, "Wake up, you. Always in the clouds! Get moving, fast!"

Coming back to earth, I had to forget the pretty home I was imagining and I looked at our room with more critical eyes. The crude dark wardrobe, so narrow it reminded me of a coffin, was crowded with the clothing of five, seven or nine people, depending upon how many were living there at the time. The chiffonier, too, had to serve the entire family. Dressing and undressing without being seen was a problem. At night, we had to wait until the light was out or undress under the blanket or go to sleep in our clothing. Antonia cared least about being seen in her slip, but Paula, Marta and I were very modest. Roberto, too, would get up in the morning wrapped in his blanket and go into the kitchen to dress. We women wouldn't dress until the men and children went out so we could close the door. But there was always someone wanting to get in, impatiently banging and telling us to hurry. We could never dawdle.

It would have been a great luxury to be able to linger at the mirror to fix my hair or to put on make-up; I never could because of the sarcasm and ridicule of those in the room. My friends in the Casa Grande complained of their families in the same way. To this day, I look into the mirror hastily, as though I were doing something wrong. I also had to put up with remarks when I wanted to sing, or lie in a certain comfortable position or do anything that was not acceptable to my family.

Living in one room, one must go at the same rhythm as the others, willingly or unwillingly—there is no way except to follow the wishes of the strongest ones. After my father, Antonia had her way, then La Chata, then my brothers. The weaker ones could approve or disapprove, get angry or disgusted but could never express their opinions. For example, we all had to go to bed at the same time, when my father told us to. Even when we were grown up, he would say, "To bed! Tomorrow is a work day." This might be as early as eight or nine o'clock, when we weren't at all sleepy, but because my father had to get up early the next morning, the light had to be put out. Many times I wanted to draw or to read in the evening, but no sooner did I get started when, "To bed! Lights out!" and I was left with my drawing in my head or the story unfinished.

During the day it was Antonia who chose the radio programs we all had to listen to; in the evening it was my father. We especially hated the Quiz Kids (los niños Catedráticos) because my father would say, "A child of eight and he knows so much . . . and you donkeys, you don't want to study. Later you'll be sorry." When my father or Antonia were not at home, how we would fight over the radio!

If La Chata was in charge of the house, she lorded it over us in her own way. She made us wait in the courtyard until she finished cleaning and sometimes, due to the cold, I would have to go to the toilet. She would refuse to open the door and I would jump up and down yelling, for all the neighbors to hear, "Ay, La Chata, let me in. I have to go. I can't stand it any longer." Then she would get even by leaving the front door open so that the passers-by in the courtyard could see my feet under the door of the toilet. I would try to hide my feet and would beg her to please shut the front door. But she'd say, "Oh, who's going to notice a kid."

The toilet, with its half-door, gave us almost no privacy. It was so narrow that La Chata had to go in sidewise and leave the shutter ajar in order to sit down. Antonia would always crack some joke about the person using the toilet. If Manuel stayed in too long, as he usually did, she would say, "Cut it short or shall I bring you the scissors?" To me she'd say, "Are you still there? I thought you were already in San Lazaro." San Lazaro is the exit of the city sewage system and she meant that I had fallen into the drainpipe. Other times I was the one who gave trouble. I would tease Roberto when he was in the toilet by opening the front door, saying the smell was too strong. He would shout angrily, "Close that door or you'll see what happens." But I would escape into the courtyard before he came out. Or when someone was in the toilet I would begin dancing in front of the door and yelling that I had to go in. I remember Manuel coming out holding his magazine or comics between his teeth, pulling up his pants, looking daggers at me. Antonia never came out until she was ready, no matter how much of a scandal was made, and often were the times when I had to chase everyone out of the room so that I could use the chamber pot.

Sometimes the jokes were rude. Antonia was constipated and suffered very much from gas. She tried to hold it but often she just laughed and said, "Why should I hold it in if it gives me stomach aches." But if any of us went to the toilet for that reason she would joke about it, "How hoarse you are . . . you have a cough, pal." And we might say, "And when you go on like a machine gun at night we can even see your blanket rising." When we were little and someone made a noise my father would laugh and say, "Ay, who was that? It must have been a rat." But later he would scold harshly and send the guilty one to the toilet. When he was not present, Manuel and Roberto would carry on by calling each other names like "slob" or "pig" and making each other blush for shame. If no one commented, we usually passed over a slip and paid no attention to it.

But these annoyances were insignificant compared to that of being scolded in the presence of everyone else. I often thought that if my father had bereated me in private, I would not have minded so much. But everyone heard the awful things he said to me, even though they pretended not to, and it hurt and shamed me more. My sisters and brothers felt the same way. When one of us was scolded, the others felt equally punished. My father's words would build up little by little, until they covered us and made us fall in a crisis of tears. . . .

While I was going to school, I forgot my troubles. All I thought about was having work later, having clothes, continuing my studies, and fixing up my house nicely, as I had always dreamed about. "I would like our next-door neighbor to move," I thought, "and my father to take that room. I would help him have the wall between knocked down and that room would be used as a living room, with a fireplace, a nice day-bed suite, the floor waxed and the walls fixed up. Then we would have a place to entertain our friends. The same with the kitchen—the two in one, with a nice gas stove, knives and forks, curtains, and some big flower pots with green plants all the way to the front door. The bedroom would have its window on the street. And if thieves wanted to come in? Well, we would have bars put over the window. There would be a record player and nice lamps. I would help my *papá* pay for the labor and everything."

My ideal was to see my family united and happy. I dreamed of helping my brothers and sisters and of bringing them consolation so that they would not feel the way I did. Whenever my father made Roberto cry, everything within me rebelled and shouted: "No! It isn't fair." But I always remained silent. My heart ached seeing my brother in a corner of the kitchen with his head lowered, the tears rolling down his cheeks. Then I would say. "Don't mind *papá*, he's angry." Or I would motion to my brothers to go out into the courtyard so as not to hear my father any more.

My father's words were destructive to everyone, but Roberto was the one who felt them most deeply. Manuel preferred to become cynical. He remained silent while my father scolded him, but after a few minutes he would raise his head and go out into the courtyard, whistling. Finally, he began to turn his back on my father and leave immediately. Roberto remained rooted to the spot and cried.

I believe that this is what gave rise to my desire to help my brothers and my sister. I wanted to be (what a dreamer I was!) the one who guided and counseled them. For Manuel, I dreamed up the career of lawyer or teacher. For Roberto, I wanted the career of an architect or engineer. By that time my father would not work so much. I dreamed of winning the lottery so that I could buy him a farm and chickens and have nice upholstered furniture. At night he would sit in his easy chair in front of the fireplace, with his robe and slippers on, surrounded by all of his children (four) and he would think or say to us. "These are my children, my creation. I educated them!" I lived in hopes that all these things would come about some day.

20. *Neighbour on the Hearth*
LEO KUPER

The adage that an Englishman's home is his castle suggests a home fortified against neighbours and the world at large. Nothing could be less descriptive of much of contemporary English urban housing. In a very real sense, the general layout of the Braydon Road residential unit[1] and the design of its steel houses introduce an awareness of neighbours even within the inner sanctum.

Party Neighbours

The first involuntary link between neighbours is by ear, and this is a common feature of modern urban English housing. At evening, in place of the melodious notes recorded by the poets—"The curfew tolls the knell of parting day"—there is the quite unique and unforgettable noise of the neighbour's wife scratching at her grate with a poker, and the sudden rush of sound as the radio is tuned and quickly hushed. Dawn is heralded by the sound of wood being chopped, and the clatter of the neighbour's grate. Over week-ends other noises spell out the activities of the unseen neighbour. The husband is being handy; you follow his movements round the house; his daughter is picking out her favourite notes on the upper reaches of the piano, single

From Leo Kuper (Ed.), *Living in Towns.* London: The Cresset Press, 1953, Chapter 2. Reprinted by permission of the author and publisher.

[1] Braydon Road is a residential unit of ninety families in the urban area of Houghton, a neighbourhood unit on the outskirts of Coventry.

notes exuberantly sprinkled with random combinations. On rare party nights, or at Christmas, the virtuoso, your neighbour's wife, takes over the piano, and explores her memory of old tunes, largely with the right hand, but sometimes accompanied by a few belated chords with the left. Some sounds are difficult to place. Was that knocking at your front door or at your neighbour's front door? And it may be necessary to take a rapid inventory of all the members of your household—which is by no means difficult, since the even lower standards of insulation within the house have the effect of charting with most detailed intimacy all movements —and to analyse carefully the direction of the sound before deciding: "No, that was not our Jennie coughing; it must be Janice Carter." A sort of non-electrical radar process! Only one sound is quite unambiguous, and that is the water returning to the cisterns when the closet has been used. It fills the house with an avalanche of noise. No wonder, then, that many of our informants appreciate an outdoor closet, more especially if there are young children in the house.

In the Braydon Road residential unit, this close auditory linkage of neighbours is promoted by the design of the houses, which are semi-detached, and so arranged that most of the activities of the residents are carried out in the rooms immediately adjoining the dividing or party wall (see Figure 20-1).

The houses are described as nontraditional, but this refers to the material and methods of construction; they are permanent prefabricated steel houses. The interior

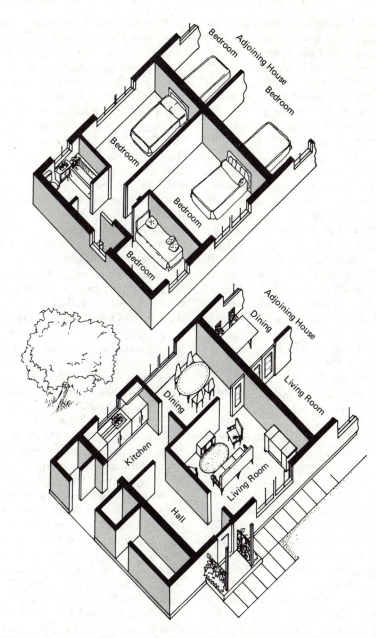

FIGURE 20–1. First floor plan (*top*) and ground floor plan (*bottom*).

arrangement of space, however, follows traditional lines and conforms to one of the models (the two-storey semi-detached, three-bedroomed house), provided in the Housing Manual issued by the Ministry of Health for the guidance of local authorities, and extensively reproduced throughout the country. At the outer ends of the house are the front doors, which give direct access to hallway and staircase. These, together with the kitchen, the bathroom and the small third bedroom, lie furthest away from the party wall, and therefore do not serve as insulating barriers between the two semi-detached units. The main living-rooms, on the other hand, the large lounge and dining recess downstairs, and the first and second bedrooms upstairs, are distributed along the party wall. In the first bedroom, a number of factors combine to fix the placing of the double bed. This is almost invariably with the head towards the middle of the party wall, an arrangement contemplated by the architect as indicated both in his sketches, which show the distribution of the main items of furniture, and also in the position of the electric light pull. Hence, of a winter's evening the party neighbours (as we shall describe the occupants of a pair of semi-detached houses), sit in their three-piece suites around the open grate, separated only by the narrow line of the party wall. And at night, the connubial heads lie, each on their own side of the partition.

Through the party wall, a variety of noises enter. We are not concerned with the problem of the standard of insulation of this wall. Our main interest is in the reactions of residents to these intimacies of noise, whatever the objective measure of the degree of insulation may be, since it is their reactions which are the basis of relations with neighbours. This introduces an element of variability, because of the different characteristics of the residents. Some are particularly sensitive to sounds, more especially those which they cannot control. "It's noises from *other* people that distress us." And they complain: "It's terrible, you can hear everything." Mrs. Hayes says of one such sensitive neighbour, that "when I clean my mirror, it bangs against the wall, and she knocks back. My husband says it's best to ignore people like that." Others enjoy noise associated with neighbours: "I don't feel so lonely when I know there's somebody about," and, "It's company in one way to hear noises." Again, the

party neighbours may be particularly quiet. They play the radio so low, that it is hard to believe they can hear the broadcasts; they speak quietly, quarrel in subdued tones, and their children are brought up in the tradition that children should be seen and not heard. In these circumstances, there is little neighbouring by ear. "You wouldn't know they had any children." "You wouldn't think anybody was living next door." This does not imply more effective insulation, but simply that the neighbouring unit houses one of the more muted patterns of the English way of life. And quite apart from this variability among residents, there is seasonal change, with greater vulnerability to sound in open-windowed summer.

Developing our picture of neighbour linkage by ear from the comments of the residents, we find that it is possible in these houses to entertain a neighbour's wife by playing her favourite records with the gramophone tuned to loud, or to mind her child or invite her to tea, all through the party wall. Residents are aware of many "vicinal" noises, extending from the unusual clamour of birthday celebrations to the sound of the daily routine. Informants mention the wireless, the baby crying at night, coughing, shoes dropped at bedtime, children running up and down the stairs or on the bedroom floors, strumming at the piano, and laughing or loud talk. In the connubial bedroom, the intimations from the neighbour may be shocking: "You can ever hear them use the pot; that's how bad it is. It's terrible"; or disturbing: "I heard them having a row in bed. One wanted to read, and the other one wanted to go to sleep. It's embarrassing to hear noises in bed, so I turned my bed the other way round" (that is, away from the architecturally preordained position). "I like to read in bed and I'm light of hearing, so it disturbs me to hear them talk"; or a little inhibiting: "You sometimes hear them say rather private things, as, for example, a man telling his wife that her feet are cold. It makes you feel that *you* must say private things in a whisper"; and, "It does make you feel a bit restrained, as if you ought to walk on tiptoe into your bedroom at night." Usually, however, only a murmur is conveyed, and that there may be some curiosity is indicated in the frequent comments: "You can't hear the actual words," or, "You can't distinguish what they say." These sounds do not always remain in their own natural element. Sometimes they materialise: "When they had the television at first, the noise used to rattle our ornaments"; and, in another case, the vibration shook a photograph off the sideboard. Or again, the party neighbours "nearly sent us crazy last week end. Their children played football upstairs and the whitewash came off our ceiling. They were reported for noise"—though not by our informant.

Yet many residents, while aware of vicinal noises, do not complain of them. This forbearance is not only an expression of British fortitude, of the "we can take it" spirit; there is also active adjustment between neighbours. This adjustment has two aspects—control over noise in the neighbour's house, and control over noise in one's own home. In the first case, the neighbour is approached, either indirectly by dropping a hint, knocking at the party wall, or directly, if the relationship is such as to allow of the discussion of difficulties without quarrelling; the real trouble arises when one of the neighbours is reserved, unapproachable, shy, or generally difficult. In the second case, there is a censoring of noises within the home by identification with the neighbours and their problems. It is in this sense more particularly that your neighbour sits on your own hearth. Thus, the arrangement of furniture may be influenced by neighbourly considerations; the radio or the piano is moved from the party wall. If the family is not already very quiet, it may be necessary to curb the children, to tone down the husband's games with them, to play the piano only in the daytime, to close doors softly, and generally to be as quiet as possible.

This consideration for neighbours, and identification with them, may be carried very far indeed. Mrs. Carroll tells us that her neighbour's vacuum interferes with her wireless, "so I suppose mine does with hers. I try to do my vacuuming quickly." And Mrs. Leek comments that when they know that Mr. Donnelly, the party neighbour, is in bed, "we keep quiet so as not to disturb him. He's on the opposite shift to my husband." The Loudens, similarly, hardly play their wireless at all, when their party neighbours are on night shift. Inability to control noises within the house, as for example, bronchial coughs, babies crying at night, or a Welsh husband who joins in with singing on the wireless, may give rise to uneasiness or even anxiety. Perhaps there is something in the comment made by one informant that she heard her neighbour's visitors, because they spoke much louder, due, she supposed, to the fact that "they may be used to brick houses." Her assumption that brick houses are better insulated than steel houses may not be correct; but the inference from her statement is that residents learn to adjust to the degree of insulation provided by their homes, and this is supported by our data. It raises the important question, with which we are not concerned in this study, of the effects of house design on personality. *What are the consequences of the particular standards of insulation against sound for the personality development of the residents and more especially of their children?*

Side Neighbours

The link with party neighbours is, to be sure, not entirely auditory. They are also seen, but only well out in the garden or coming into the house. And of the visual links, the most important is between side neighbours (see Figure 20–2).

The front doors of the houses have no handles (a deliberate omission in many English houses), and if the doors are prop-

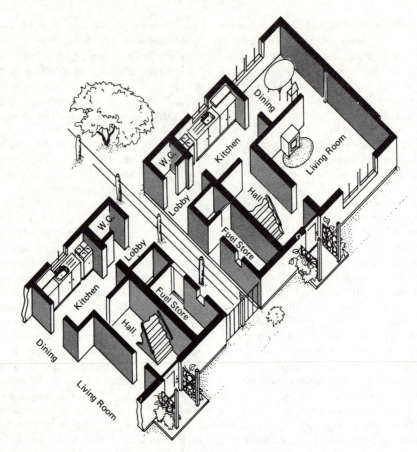

FIGURE 20–2.   Ground floor plan, adjacent houses.

erly closed, it is necessary to use a latchkey. Partly for this reason, but mainly to keep the front hall clean, most families walk round to the side of the house and into a narrow lane. This lane is divided into two by what is virtually a symbolic fence, made of strands of wire attached to artificial stone pillars. From each side of the lane, there is access to a semi-detached house through a corridor, which is part of the house structure. A water-closet and fuel shed flank the corridor, which leads into the kitchen. Beyond the kitchen is the dining recess, and if both kitchen doors are open, an unimpeded view is obtained from the lane

right through to the recess. The lanes are narrow, and the side neighbours (or occupants of the houses adjoining a common lane) are quite readily vulnerable by broomstick, as we had occasion to observe in a neighbouring unit with a similar house type. One morning, our attention was attracted by a great clamour of two women (side neighbours), and by the clash of shattering glass. Mrs. O'Grady's broomstick had that moment crashed through Mrs. Hemming's kitchen door. We joined the women in Mrs. O'Grady's house and took notes of the discussion, one of the few situations in which the investigator's notebook is quite irrelevant to rapport. Mrs. Hemming was in a state close to hysteria, and complained that Mrs. O'Grady's son had thrown dirt into her kitchen, and so she threw dirt back again. Mrs. O'Grady, calm, very much in the ascendant, said she had no intention of breaking the glass in the kitchen door, but "she's a misery to live by. Being childish, she throws dirt back in here and hits my baby. I never interfere with her. I don't notice her on the street. She says my kids wasn't brought up proper, just dragged up. When I was pally with her she wouldn't let the children fight it out, as I said they should." Mrs. Hemming confirms the former friendship, and asserts that she is not going to pay 22s. 8d. a week to live by Mrs. O'Grady; on the other hand, she has no intention of moving. Mr. O'Grady, on night shift and disturbed in his sleep, introduces his pyjama'd contribution, and finally, after many heated exchanges, the parties agree to put up a trellis between the side entries. Seven months later, this had not been done. A neighbour reports that "for about six months after the quarrel they did not speak to each other; they avoided each other at their back doors." (This is, incidentally, a considerable feat, involving reconnaissance every time the housewife plans an exit from her house.) "About six weeks ago they became friendly again. They talked, and then there was a little mutual visiting, but about three weeks ago they had a slight quarrel and dropped each other again."

This incident illustrates in somewhat dramatic fashion the intimate linking of houses by the side entry. The strength of this link varies with sitting arrangements. Only eight semi-detached houses have side entries directly opposite each other. For the most part, the houses are slightly staggered, with the result that side entries are taken out of the line which allows of visual contact from dining recess to dining recess. Nevertheless, the extreme intimacy of this siting aspect only disappears in the case of the corner houses, of the top houses which close off the cul-de-sac, and in a row of ten semi-detached houses in which the units are set back the full width of the house and separated by brick walls.

The close proximity of side neighbours may affect enjoyment of the amenities of the downstairs water-closet. A sex factor sometimes enters. Mr. Brown comments that: "It's embarrassing for women when men are in the next garden." One informant clearly wished to eliminate from her social personality any suggestion of natural functions: "I may only be going to clean it (the closet) or wash it, but it's all the same to them. For all they know, I may be going to the toilet."

The side entry not only gives access to the house, and to the fuel shed and closet. It is also the way out from the house into the garden. The kitchen doors lead into the dining recess or into the corridor; there is no back door to the garden. Hence it is through the side entry that men and children come and go, and the housewife is in and out with the carpet, laundry and ashes. As a result, it is impossible for residents not to be keenly aware of side neighbours:

"When one goes out the back way, one is immediately right on top of one's neighbours"; "as soon as she comes out of her door, we are face to face"; "being so near, people can see the sort of things you have and want to borrow them"; "we are putting up a partition. Every time you open the back door, you see your neighbour. Children quarrel, and with the unbroken view, it makes it difficult to keep the peace."

The second involuntary link is thus between side neighbours. But these links with side and party neighbours, are elements in a wider system of neighbour contacts, made possible or inevitable by the general layout of the residential unit.

Cul-de-sacs and Cloisters

The main components of the layout of Braydon Road are four cul-de-sacs (B, C, D, and E on Figure 20–3). Three have seven pairs of houses and one has eight. These cul-de-sacs are arranged on either side of a large plot of land which extends from an exit road, Barnett Avenue, to the lower end of the residential unit. They are widest where they abut on to this open piece of land, and narrow in staggered steps. On the plan they look a little like the open mouth of a crocodile. One cul-de-sac is closed off at its furthest end from the open land by two pair of houses, and the remainder each by one pair. Binding the residential area together and excluding access to the outside world except through the exit road, is a straight line of eight semi-detached houses (S on our sketch), which joins the lower cul-de-sacs, C and D. At the upper end, in Barnett Avenue, there is a certain irregularity. On one side of

the open strip are the five deeply staggered pairs, separated by brick walls, which we have already mentioned (J on the sketch); these are not in a cul-de-sac setting, and face a large undeveloped tract of land. The opposite side of Barnett Avenue consists of three groupings. L has four semi-detached units, arranged in a right angle at the corner of a grassed rectangle, with a large tree in the centre. A is quite irregular; four pairs of houses and a brick wall, which takes the place of the fifth pair in the original design, are distributed around three sides of something approximating a rectangular grassed court, which also features a tree. The final group, K, is one pair, and alone of all the houses shares with the J area direct access to the outside world.

The cul-de-sacs and the square give the impressions of a very intimate arrangement of houses. Density of development is not high by current standards—about eight houses to the acre. Yet the open spaces and

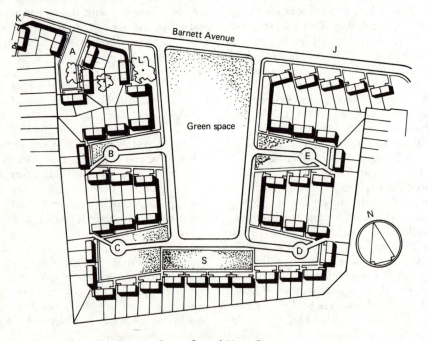

FIGURE 20–3. The Braydon Road Residential Unit, Coventry.

houses are so organised as to achieve the same result as a layout at high density. And a number of design elements contribute to make the residents accessible to each other visually at the fronts of their houses. The living-rooms have large glass windows directly overlooking the cul-de-sacs. These windows start at a low level from the ground, and at a convenient height for children to climb through from the inside or to peer into from the outside. Curtains are draped a little behind the windows, and back of them is the box-like shape of the living-room. The effect is not unlike that of a stage setting. Here, the family may seek to make its debut to the outside world by a display of possessions. And conversely through these windows neighbours gain some inside knowledge of the family's life. In fact, it is quite difficult for neighbours to avoid seeing into each other's homes, because no barriers are interposed. Separate front gardens were eliminated to enable the architect to handle the open spaces as a whole and to safeguard his design from the disturbing fences, privet hedges, trellises and other features of suburban gardens. In their place are narrow unfenced strips of ground, which run parallel to the house and may be cultivated by the tenants; large common forecourts; entry roads in the four cul-de-sacs, kept down to about twelve feet, ending in a large circle and so sited that the houses can be reached only on foot; and finally, narrow footpaths close beside the fronts of the houses and giving access to front doors and side entries. All these elements combine with the large front windows to link the houses into an involuntary community of the eye. Hence, it is possible to sit in the Canning's living-room and to tell the time by the clock in the house over the way. The Burtons' boy, aged 8, complains that he was seen in his pyjamas by the little girl across the road. One woman likes to watch people get off the bus some distance away and to follow their movements as they approach the steel houses; our own

field workers were under this same constant observation, and there is a feeling among residents that neighbours know when they receive callers. The inside space of these cul-de-sacs makes an ideal playground for children. The entry road, with its circle and lamp-post, is an effective cricket pitch, almost as if it were specially designed by the architect to train wicket keepers, because behind the lamp-post wicket loom the large windows of the living-rooms. And often of an afternoon, the women will sit at the front windows, watch their children at play, and observe the activities in the cul-de-sac. For a person sensitive to neighbours' reactions the effect may be rather like the telescreen described by Orwell in his novel *Nineteen Eighty-Four*. It is as if all actions and even thoughts are being observed. Thus, Mr. Dudley tells us: "There is no privacy. . . . You look across at the houses there—they must feel as though you are looking at them. You look out of the bedroom windows into their bedrooms. . . . You turn the corner coming home and everybody's eyes are on you in the cul-dec-sac. For the amount you pay it's degrading—especially to old residents of Coventry, who knew the town as it used to be." And Mrs. Dudley relates her embarrassment when she kissed her mother in the street: "Then I thought everybody would be making fun of me up here. They don't do that sort of thing here."

A community of the eye links not only the houses within the cul-de-sac, but also houses in adjoining areas through the back gardens. These, again, are divided from each other only symbolically, by strands of wire. To give a more pleasing impression of the area, brick walls were built parallel to the large central plot of land in such a manner as to prevent passers-by looking into the back gardens. The effect of this is to create a sort of cloister knitting together houses in adjacent areas (see Figure 20–4). This is the cloister of the wash line, of baby's napkins, and of men's and women's and children's clothes, and of household

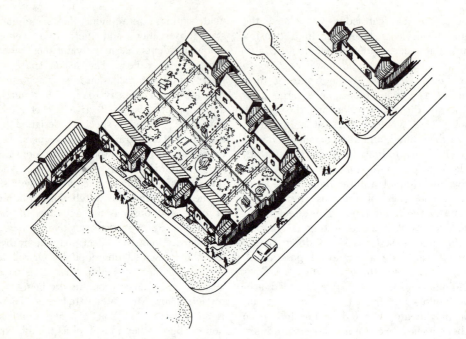

FIGURE 20–4. Layout providing for screened back gardens.

linen. It provides opportunities also for empirical research, as we found in a quarrel
between two women because one had dis-
closed how often her neighbour changed
her bed linen. Here too, is a field of activity
for the men: gardeners discuss their plans,
complain of the builders' rubble and clay
in the soil, exchange plants, give presents
of vegetables, and sometimes start hedges
and rustic fences for greater privacy. It
is an area of family recreation, and in some
sense of communal living, because there
are no effective physical barriers to keep
children and dogs, and for that matter,
adult residents, from wandering freely into
adjoining gardens.

Facing these back gardens are the
windows of the kitchen, the dining recess,
and an upstairs room. Hence it is not only
the area of backgarden living which is
drawn together, but also some aspects of
the inside domestic life. And so there are
complaints of lack of privacy in the dining
recess. "It's not very nice to be seen eat-

ing." Or a woman may be embarrassed
because neighbours might see her husband
wearing a vest in the dining recess, though
she herself has no objection to it. Or there
is general discomfort: "You don't really
feel free to walk about the house as you
like." And again, in the same way that a
person can be seen by neighbours it is
sometimes difficult to avoid looking at them.
When in the kitchen, "Every time you look
up, you're looking at the one across, and
you have to look somewhere."

Planned and Unplanned Consequences

Many of these consequences of the layout
were not intended by the architects. At
this stage it is difficult to get information
in detail as to the considerations which
were the basis of the decisions taken. A
general impression of these deciding factors
can, however, be gained from the resultant
layout. An architect town-planner described

to us what he regarded as its distinctive features, in the conventional phrases of his profession. He selects first the experiments in the third dimension (the building along the contours and the staggering of houses, giving an interesting skyline and play of shapes), and in the fourth dimension (that of movement, with constantly changing vistas and relationships between gable ends and façade as you walk). There is safety for the children in the segregation of foot and motor traffic, in the generous use of forecourts, and in the treatment of development roads. Urbanity and neighbourliness are suggested by the controlled architectural treatment. Asserting "the need for the perception of community in immediately recognisable terms," he finds the solution in *street* architecture and cites, as a good example, the Square A. Here, inspired (or accidental) use of existing hedgerow tree gives individuality to the group, and with its constant change of colour, foliage its attraction of bird life, secures an added awareness of natural processes within the urban setting: this too, in the grassed square, full of daisies. The effect of enclosure is simply achieved by linked walls and slightly rising ground. (Note the medieval village, with closely clustered cottages, and its friendly containing effect to the field worker returning home from the open country and limitless sky.) Colour wash can be used to suggest "our street—the one with red walls."

Some such considerations certainly entered into the layout of the area. Perhaps there is an occasional overstatement in this account of the architectural "mystique"; certainly, the large brick wall in Square A was a last-minute compromise and replaced a projected house. But there was clearly the intention to create a more intimate and secluded area of living, to provide safety for the children, and to pursue, in the third and fourth dimensions, some of the aesthetic satisfactions of contemporary architecture. These are the planned objectives which the architect realised in the Braydon Road residential unit. But flowing from these objectives are the unanticipated results, the unplanned consequences, which have the effect of drawing neighbours together in a great variety of linkages.

We may illustrate this by reference to some of the unplanned consequences of staggering the houses. The widened mouths of the main cul-de-sacs increase the distance between neighbours at the front, but bring the back windows more closely together; and tenants in these outer houses are more keenly aware of their proximity to back-garden neighbours. Conversely, the staggering of the houses, in the interior of the cul-de-sac, reduces the distance at the front while increasing the length of the back gardens; among these tenants of the inside houses there are frequent comments of overlooking at the front. Again the large irregular gardens of some of the top houses have the effect of insulating tenants from back-garden contacts, and similarly, in the deeply staggered houses of Area J, awareness of side neighbours is greatly diminished. There is a general tendency for the awareness of neighbours to be determined by siting factors, a result certainly not envisaged by the architect.

This relationship between siting factors and awareness of neighbours is influenced by a number of factors. Residents vary in their use of the house; it makes a difference to this awareness of neighbours if most activities are confined to the back of the house, and the front living-room is preserved as a sort of ceremonial parlour, or on the other hand, if there is no money to furnish the recess, and the front room is used as an all-purpose room, or again, if the tenants and their neighbours are keen or indifferent gardeners. Moreover, people vary in their requirements for privacy.

The attitude to privacy, in particular, throws much light on the different reactions of residents to the auditory and visual linkages. For those who like to hear and be heard, to see and be seen, the physical conditions of Braydon Road are no problem:

their difficulties lie in the "queer" behaviour and demands of residents, whose standards of privacy are high. For the "queer" residents, on the other hand, Braydon Road imposes the need of a variety of adjustments. The control of other people's noise is a somewhat intractable problem: if an approach cannot be made to neighbours, or does not produce the required results, the only solution may be to move from area to area in search of quiet neighbours. Some defence against being seen is provided by the use of window curtains, of lace or net, to supplement the inadequate draped curtains, and by hedges and rustic fences in the bark gardens. We have commented on the consideration shown by some residents in the control of noise within their own homes. This consideration extends also to seeing, so that residents will restrain the almost reflex action of looking into windows and doorways, and sometimes pretend not to notice their neighbours. But the control of one's own noise and visual impressions is not exclusively a recognition of social responsibilities: it serves the further function of securing for residents their standards of privacy, by keeping domestic activities from the public ear, and by demonstrating that more intimate contact is not desired.

The siting factors, with their planned and unplanned consequences, only provide a potential base for neighbour relations. There is no simple mechanical determination by the physical environment. The extent to which the awareness of neighbours will develop into active social relationships depends on the characteristics of the residents, their attitudes to neighbouring, their status,[2] aspirations, and their general compatibility. We will not be able to understand either the patterns of these social relationships nor the contribution of elements in the house design and the general siting arrangements, without an analysis of population characteristics, attitudes and status aspirations.

[2] I am using the word "status" in the everyday sense of "social standing," and not with the sociological or legal connotation of "institutionalized position."

Part IV

Individual Development and the Environment

A section of readings dealing with issues related to human development has been added to this edition of the book. Although the earlier edition had some four or five selections dealing with development, they were largely concerned with children. A special section on the life-span reflects the deliberate concern with developmental issues that has characterized much current work in environmental studies. A great deal of this work grows out of general discontent with settings, especially settings designed for particular age groups. This has stimulated planners and behavioral scientists alike to reflect upon the designs, a task that in turn has led to more basic tions concerning growth, development, and the fit between user characteristics and qualities of facilities.

This volume has selections concerning children as well as selections dealing with other stages in the life cycle running throughout. Much of the current work appears to fall into three major groupings. The first concentrates on the physical properties of individuals over the course of development, the variations in physical size and strength, that may affect use of and movement through settings. The second area of interest deals with the ways spatial properties and areas are cognized. Related to this are questions concerning spatial abilities, the growth of control over space. The third major area focuses on specific settings for particular groups, that is, places such as day care centers, hospitals, schools, dormitories, playgrounds, parks, facilities for the elderly. This work is predicated on the assumption that an understanding of particular age groups will facilitate the design process and improve the quality of the environment.

Many gaps in our knowledge exist. Most conspicuous is the fact that our understanding of human development often exists apart from an understanding of the settings in which this growth takes place. It has been common, in the past, to consider development in terms of physical growth, social influences, and social environments, but rarely was the physical context included. Even less common was an integrative approach to all aspects. Yet development obviously takes place within a particular milieu, or more accurately, within a variety of different milieus. It is really impossible to understand development without an accurate conception of settings and, conversely, it is difficult to understand how improved design and planning can proceed without understanding the importance of developmental factors. Yet this implies more than examining each of these components separately.

This section (Part IV) will approach development from a different perspective. What must be emphasized is that growth is a continuous process, extending over the entire life-span. Changes are occurring constantly. Some of these increase our size and/or powers; some have quite the opposite effect, but we are never at a fixed state in all our faculties. In trying to understand change, particular stages in development may be defined. These are really research artifacts and rough generalizations. It may appear to be a truism to say that we are each unique, but a close look at any group must reinforce this impression. We all may change, but the details and the rates are quite individual. This does not mean that we must abandon the concept of stages in our understanding of settings. It serves a useful function in generalizing about groups, but we must always appreciate its limits as well. Moreover, what becomes especially apparent is the fact that settings designed with specific age groups or stages in mind generally hold individual differences to be minimal.

The conception of development that we would like to communicate holds each aspect of growth, whether or not it is identified by a general name, intertwined with the setting. For example, the movement of a young child into the role of "student" means many things. One component is learning to deal with extrafamily members—neighbors, peers, and teachers. It also involves moving into a larger world, one that is less protected than home and composed of much greater variety. It means learning about places, a community, a school. Most important, all of this takes place as a series of unity experiences.

The continuous process of development begins with a unique individual born with specific attributes, a specific physical makeup, and sets of basic needs. Immediately, on birth, the satisfaction of these needs is dependent upon and mediated through social agents within specific settings. The extensive literature on the effects of social isolation, hospitalism, and stimulus deprivation provides clear evidence of the interdependence of nurturing, stimulation, and contact with the world and people in it. Survival for humans is thus a most complex phenomenon. In addition, other needs develop as a consequence of the child's social network, some far removed from physical survival. These are social needs or motives, a reflection of the individual moving through a social world. Thus a very basic need for food is overlaid with the effects of interaction with the people who provide nourishment, with specific types of food, and with particular settings in which eating takes place. What may appear as a very simple need emerges as a very complex phenomenon, with specific attributes of the setting very much tied in with its satisfaction.

As we look at this continuous process of development we are looking at more than basic needs and a specific culture. We are looking at a variety of internal and external influences that interact with each other to produce a particular individual. Development, from this perspective, involves the individual's biological makeup, a particular family in a specific culture, and all of these in continuous interaction with the environment. As the individual moves through the settings that define his/her life, they do more than act as the context for action. Each setting participates in the development of a sense of self in a very concrete way. For some, these settings will be rich and responsive, for others they will be impoverished, for others, resistant. For each person, the setting will contribute to the sense of worthiness, capability, and identity on some level. We are beginning to learn what it means to be environmentally disadvantaged. The consequences go beyond the health status of the individual to touch the core of what he/she can achieve in a variety of spheres of life. The definition of self may be fairly uniform over the life-span, or it may be discontinuous, but the setting always is a central component.

There is another aspect of settings to recognize as we try to understand their role in what we have described as the continuous process of growth. We are looking at development, recognizing at the very same time that many settings change less than the people within them. Most environments are built to a single level of use, some conception of average size and strength. At the same time they are inhabited by a wide range of users—some small, some large, some powerful, some physically or socially handicapped. Very few individuals are average in every sense. Yet the settings generally are geared to an average. Even facilities designed for specific groups, day care centers, schools, nursing homes, facilities for the aged, in fact, are occupied and used by an age and power mix. This does not diminish the value of focusing on development and spatial differences. Rather, it makes them even more important to understand. Too often problems that emerge from settings that do not support the goals and activities of the mixed groups of occupants within them can be overlooked, or responsibility may be shifted to the individuals or to the program. In the past there has been evidence of this, especially in institutional facilities. It is possible that future housing research may uncover the central role of setting in the development of family harmony, as well. What seems clear is the fact that settings, as components of social interaction, work, education, play and living, interact with the program within them and the various users (who differ in their physical attributes) and share responsibility for reaching goals.

Although the selections in Part IV are limited, pieces from other parts of the book can be added to round out an overview of development. In all, there are at least nine selections that are concerned with life cycle factors. To be sure, children and the elderly receive major emphasis, perhaps a reflection of what we have pointed to earlier, the limited tolerance of our settings for any but some mythical average person. They are also stages when the individual has limits on the power to control settings. However, by looking at these two ends of the life-span continuum against the backdrop of settings, we can begin to appreciate both the powerful effects of growth and change, and the specific physical and symbolic contributions of the physical world.

21. Extracts from *The Development of Spatial Cognition: A Review*

ROGER A. HART AND GARY T. MOORE

This paper is a review of current knowledge and a guide to the literature on the development of environmental cognition. We are interested in how people develop a knowledge of urban space. First, how do the fundamental concepts of space develop in the child? And, second, how do we come to know and represent in cognition the everyday large-scale physical environment?

In considering the child's conception of space, a number of questions arise. Is space given innately, is it built up empirically from sensations, or is it some interaction of the two? Is there an order of succession of sequence in the child's understanding of space? What is the role of experience in the understanding of space;

At the time of writing (1971–1972), the authors were graduate students respectively in Geography and Psychology at Clark University. Grateful acknowledgment is made for support in the preparation of this review by the Place Perception Project at Clark University, supported in part by the U.S. Office of Education (Grant #4493). The review covers all literature to May 1971 located in *Psychological Abstracts* (1927–1972) and *Current Geographical Publications* (1938–1972), as well as from other suggestions offered by our colleagues. The authors are now respectively members of the Environmental Psychology Program, CUNY, and School of Architecture and Urban Planning, University of Wisconsin-Milwaukee. Reprinted with permission of the authors and publisher from R. M. Downs and D. Stea (Eds.), *Image and Environment: Cognitive Mapping and Spatial Behavior*. Chicago: Aldine, 1973, pp. 246–288.

most particularly, what are the relative roles of action, perception, imagery, and language? Further questions arise in considering how the everyday physical environment is known. How do children and adults develop a knowledge of the spatial entities and relations of large-scale environments like neighborhoods and cities? What systems of reference do they use? These questions pose a set of issues sufficiently important to environmental design and planning and to environmental education to warrant special consideration.

Thus, this review is concerned with the development of cognitive representations of space, beginning with the child's first spatial concepts and advancing toward the adult's cognitive representations of large-scale environments. Our focus is on the major empirically-based theories and related findings on the structure or form of space as seen from a Wernerian-Piagetian structural-developmental point of view.

The review is in three sections. First, an attempt is made to provide some definitions and conceptual distinctions as a base for the field. The second section covers development of the fundamental concepts of space, starting with the epistemological problem of space and the resolutions of Déscartes, Berkeley, Kant, and Cassirer. Out of this tradition come Werner's and Piaget's empirically based theories of the development of the child's conception of space. The third section focuses on empirical research on the development of cognition of the larger physical environment. Following a discussion of the ontogenetic development of both geographic orientation and topographical representations and the systems of reference they utilize, we lead into the scant literature which deals with the microgenetic development of representations of new or unfamiliar environments. Parallels and discontinuities with the theories of Piaget and Werner are discussed throughout as a means both of providing coherence to otherwise unrelated studies and of suggesting avenues of theoretical explanation.

I. Definitions and Conceptual Distinctions

To provide a base for the field of spatial cognition, certain definitions and conceptual distinctions will be reviewed. First, we must clarify the terms *spatial cognition* and *cognitive representation* which, as used by the leading developmental psychologists, encompass the more specific terms *cognitive mapping* and *cognitive* or *mental maps* used both in the environmental behavior literature (Downs, 1968; Stea and Downs, 1970; Blaut, McCleary, and Blaut, 1970). For instance, the Russian psychologist Shemyakin (1962, p. 190) defines "spatial representation" as a "reflection of space in the minds of men . . . a reflex activity of the brain [which] creates for men a unified system of space." Piaget and Inhelder (1967, pp. vii, 454) define "spatial concept" as "the fundamental idea of space," and "spatial representation" as the symbolic and internalized mental reflection of spatial action. Werner (1948, p. 167) also refers to a "spatial concept" as the fundamental idea of space, and "representation" as an "intellectualized version [of] reflective thought." Similarly, Laurendeau and Pinard (1970, pp. 13–14) define "spatial representation" as "an implict action which is carried out in thought on the symbolized object . . . a mental reproduction [or] sketch of an object in thought."

Each of these theorists is referring to an internalized *cognitive* representation of

space, as opposed to external representations such as children's drawings (see Arnheim, 1967) and the maps of cartographic psychophysics (Williams, 1958; Ekman, Lindman, and William-Olsson, 1961; Robinson, 1967; M. Wood, 1968; Dent, 1970). It will be helpful, therefore, to distinguish between *external* representations and *internal* or *cognitive* representations. We can only *infer* internal representations from external representation (e.g., drawings, maps, verbal reports, models) or from overt spatial behavior. Thus external representations are only of interest in this review to the degree that they shed light on the development of the internal representation of space. In summary, *spatial cognition* is the knowledge and internal or cognitive representation of the structure, entities, and relations of space; in other words, the internalized reflection and reconstruction of space in thought.

The commonly used (and sometimes misused) terms *cognitive maps* and *cognitive mapping* imply map-like representations of geographic or other large-scale environments. As has been argued before (Blaut, 1969; Stea, 1969), it begs the question to suggest that spatial relations are necessarily represented in a cartographic form. Therefore, we prefer to use the more inclusive terms of development psychology —*spatial cognition* and *cognitive representation*. (It will be seen later that "cognitive mapping" is only one form of cognitive representation of large-scale environments). The terms *fundamental spatial cognition* and *macro-spatial cognition* are used, however to distinguish temporarily between two varieties of spatial cognition: the development of fundamental concepts of space, and the further differentiation and elaboration of these concepts into the development and representation of large-scale environments. This distinction, however, should not be taken to imply that these are necessarily different entities or follow different psychological processes and laws. The distinction is used in this review simply to distinguish between two bodies of literature, one primarily from developmental psychologists concerned with understanding the development of basic spatial concepts, and the other from a wide range of geographers, urban planners, psychologists, anthropologists, and educators concerned with large-scale environments, but who, for the most part it seems, have paid little attention to the work of developmental psychology. This review, then, is a first step toward bringing these two bodies of literature together.

The review focuses primarily on the *form* or *structure* of space. The fascinating questions of the development of the *experience* of space (environmental experience), of *mythical conceptions* of space, and the *content* of space (the *meaning* and *values* assigned to spaces at different times and by different cultures), has received attention largely in the phenomenological, anthropological, and psychoanalytic literature, and is not reviewed here (see Hallowell, 1942, 1955; Cassirer, 1944, 1955; Werner, 1948; Eliade, 1959; Rasmussen, 1959; A. Wallace, 1961; Scully, 1962; Erikson, 1963; Romney and D'Andrade, 1964; Straus, 1963, 1966; Beck, 1967; Hall, 1966; Bachelard, 1969; Buttimer, 1969; Rusch, 1970; Wisner, 1970; Tyler, 1971; see also the reviews by Lynch (1973), and Beck, 1964, pp. 3–33).

Another area of research closely related to the above is that of *environmental dispositions and preferences.* Unfortunately this latter area was entitled at one time "mental maps" (chap. 11) thus causing others to believe it a part of spatial cognition. This research deals with subjective or evaluative responses to environments, and only in some cases to maps or other external representations. Even in these latter cases, however, the external representations are constructed post-hoc by the experimenter and do not necessarily imply any parallel internal representation by the subject (see reviews by Craik, 1970a, 1970b).

An important distinction should be made between *spatial cognition* and *spatial perception.* Cognition, by lay definition held to include all the modes of knowing (perceiving, thinking, imagining, reasoning, judging, and remembering), would seem to include perception. Piaget and his followers (Piaget, 1963b, 1969; Laurendeau & Pinard, 1970) suggest that knowledge of the world includes two aspects: one of which is essentially *figurative,* related to the percepts or images of successive states or momentary configurations of the world by direct and immediate contact, and a second which is essentially *operative,* related to the operations which intervene between successive states and by which the subject transforms parts of the world into reconstructable patterns of schemas: Visual perception is only one form of figurative knowing, while cognition (or intelligence) is based on the operative mode. Another closely allied view, that of Werner and his followers (Werner, 1948; Wapner and Werner, 1957; Wapner, 1969), treats perception as a subsystem of cognition. In this view, knowledge about the world may be constructed by many means, perceptual judgments being only one. As development proceeds, perception becomes subordinated to higher mental processes. Cognitive structures available to the organism influence perceptual selectivity which leads to a reconstruction of the world through selected fields of attention. Perception is thus both a subsystem of cognition and a function of cognition (see Langer, 1969, pp. 148–156, for a review of these two positions.) Spatial perception and spatial cognition, therefore, are two separate but reciprocating processes; the precise relationship will be discussed later (see reviews of spatial perception by Wohlwill, 1960; Howard and Templeton, 1966).

An additional distinction should be made between *spatial cognition* and *spatial orientation.* Spatial orientation, or geographic orientation as used in this review, refers to the way an individual determines his location in the environment. It utilizes a topographical cognitive representation which is related by a reference system to the environment. Geographical orientation is discussed to the extent that it sheds light on the more general development of topographical representations (see reviews by Shemyakin, 1962, and Howard and Templeton, 1966).

The Concept of Development

Finally, we must distinguish between *development, learning,* and related concepts, and indicate the value as we see it of a structural-developmental approach to spatial cognition. Four concepts have been associated with transformations in an organism: growth, maturation, learning, and development (Harris, 1957). Briefly, *growth* is a nonspecific term generally implying any form of accretion, while *maturation* is more specific, implying physiological growth. It is more difficult to distinguish learning from development, a traditional controversy. *Learning* involves quantitative changes in the reception and retention of information or subject matter. It refers to the situation in which information is presented to the individual who changes through reacting to it and corrects initial attempts in response to indications about his prior successes (Ausubel, 1963; Hilgard and Bower, 1966; Deese and Hulse, 1967). On the other hand, *development* implies qualitative changes in the organization of behavior. Most often it refers to the situation where the individual changes as a function of interaction between current organization and discrepancy with the environment (see Werner, 1948; Piaget, 1963a,b,c; a similar distinction is made by Flavell and Wohlwill, 1969). The basic aims of the study of development are twofold: to describe the characteristic pattern of each level of organization, and to explain the relationship and transformation between these levels (Werner, 1948; Werner and Kaplan, 1963; Piaget, 1963b; Langer, 1969). Thus, theories of development are concerned with qualitative changes in

structural organization, whereas theories of learning are concerned with quantitative changes in the incorporation of specific information into structures (see White, 1970, for an excellent intellectual history of this issue).

Inherent in the structural-developmental point of view are some basic theoretical principles. White (1970) suggests that the broadest contemporary formulation of the position is the *comparative organismic-developmental theory* of Werner and his two principal colleagues at Clark University, Kaplan and Wapner (Werner, 1948, 1957; Wapner and Werner, 1957; Werner and Kaplan, 1963; Kaplan, 1966a, 1966b, 1967, in press; Wapner, 1969; Wapner, Cirillo, and Baker, 1971; see Langer, 1969, for a comparison with Piagetian theory).

One of the most important contributions of this group was to render the concept of development context-free so that it is not limited to processes unfolding over time or in relation to age, but is conceived as an *ideal* of *natural order* (Toulmin, 1961). In this way development becomes a manner of looking at and conceptualizing phenomena (Kaplan, 1966a, 1967). Implicit in the developmental point of view, and sometimes in tension with it, is the *organismic assumption* (Kaplan, in press). A human being is an organized unity in which the laws of the whole govern the functioning of the parts. Thus, human behavior is only understood in terms of, and in relation to, this underlying organization. The organismic focus on the description of structural organizations together with the developmental focus on the transformations between different levels of organization leads to the organismic-developmental perspective (see Moore, 1970, for a comparison of the assumptions of organismic-developmental and general systems theories).

Much of the richness of a developmental approach is contained in the *comparative analysis* of different forms of development. As well as *ontogenesis* (individual development over the life-span), other forms of development may be studied, including *microgenesis* (short-term individual change), *pathogenesis* (psychopathological change), *ethnogenesis* (cultural change), *historicogenesis* (historical change), and *phylogenesis* (evolution of species). The final step for a comparative organismic-developmental approach is to compare the results from each behavioral domain and to derive developmental laws applicable to mental life as a whole (Werner, 1948; Langer, 1970).

In summary, then, the values of the structural-developmental approach are twofold: first, only by understanding the development of a phenomenon can we fully understand and scientifically explain its mature form, or as Werner (1948, p. 5) has stated: "Complementary to [the discovery of the structural pattern] is the task of ordering the genetic relationship between particular levels." And Piaget (1970, p. 12): "Were it not for the idea of transformations, structures would lose all explanatory import, since they would collapse into static forms." Second, as any organism or system is always undergoing transformations, we might say that the only thing which is constant is change itself. Thus change or development becomes of prime scientific interest. (Similar arguments have been made in anthropology by Lévi-Strauss, 1949, and in geography by Blaut, 1961.)

II. The Development of Fundamental Spatial Cognition

Before we can ask the question of the development of knowledge of space in large-scale environments, we must ask the logically prior question of the genesis of the fundamental concepts of space in the child. The first question is whether space is ideal or real; that is, whether the concept of space is given innately to the child or is built up empirically from sensation. The

rationalist philosopher Descartes argued that the concept of space is given immediately as an innate idea before experience, whereas the empiricist Berkeley held that reality could only be contained in sensation. Kant (1902; Hendel, 1953) argued, however, that the *matter* of all phenomena (that which corresponds to sensation) is given in experience, but that their *form* is given a priori. Whereas both Descartes and Berkeley assumed that one could understand the ultimate nature of reality, Kant argued that since there is no way for us to apprehend the nature of "reality" except through man, it is impossible to completely separate the process of knowing from the resultant knowledge. There can be no complete understanding of truth in either sense or reason. Therefore, Kant argued, instead of naively assuming that knowledge can ever represent exactly what is real, we are led to the conclusion that what we take to be real is a product of the act of knowing (a *construction* of thought).

Cassirer's Theory of Symbolic Forms and Space

One of Kant's greatest followers was the philosopher Ernst Cassirer (1944, 1953, 1955, 1957) who attempted to understand the fundamental forms of human culture. Following Kant, Cassirer called space and time the principal modes of experience. He thus treated the problem of space extensively.

Cassirer (1944) was one of the first theorists to deal with space developmentally. He saw three fundamentally different types of spatial experience, as shown in Figure 21.1. The lowest order he termed *organic* or *active space*. The second order, *perceptual space*, a farther-reaching and more complex space, is characteristic of higher animals. The integration of different kinds of sense experience—visual, auditory, tactual, vestibular, and kinaesthetic—is not possible for animals lower on the phylogenetic scale. The highest order, *symbolic* or *abstract space*, is of greatest interest to Cassirer (1944, p. 43) because it is "the borderline between the human and animal worlds." Humans alone develop the ability to comprehend and represent the idea of abstract space—the space of "pure intuition," bereft of any necessary concrete referent.

Cassirer, like Werner who followed him, was a pioneer in the *comparative analysis of development*. Cassirer (1944, p. 46) suggested extensive parallels between ontogenesis, phylogenesis, ethnogenesis, historicogenesis, and pathogenesis, and on this basis made an important distinction between *concrete acquaintance* with, and *abstract knowledge* of, space and spatial relations. . . .

Werner's Organismic-Developmental Theory of Space

The first comprehensive theory of the development of space to be derived primarily from empirical findings was that of Werner (1948, 1957; Werner and Kaplan, 1963; see also Baldwin, 1967; Langer, 1969, 1970).

General Theory of Development. Werner wished to understand the development of mental life as a whole, whether in children, animals, psychotics, or peoples of different cultures. He argued that the essence of all forms of development is the differentiation and subordination of parts to the whole, formalized as the *orthogenetic principle: Insofar as development occurs in a process under consideration, there is a progression from a state of relative globality and lack of differentiation to states of increasing differentiation, articulation, and hierarchic integration* (Werner, 1948, 1957; Werner and Kaplan, 1963; Kaplan, 1966a).

Although the term "development" might seem at first glance only to be useful for the description of processes changing over time, the principle as used by Werner and by Piaget defines development in terms of the *degree of organization* and, thus, is

not *limited* to processes changing over time, but also may be used for the conceptual ordering of contemporaneous systems.

The more differentiated and hierarchically integrated a system is in the relations between its parts and between means and ends, the more highly developed it is said to be. If one system is more differentiated and hierarchically integrated than another, it is developmentally more advanced than the other. If a single system is increasing in differentiation and hierarchic integration, it is developing. . . . In this way, the orthogenetic principle is a formal definition of development and, as such, is applicable to the comparison of different systems and to the analysis of a single system in transition. (Wapner, Cirillo, and Baker, 1971)

Intimately connected to the orthogenetic principle are three developmental progressions: *progressive self-object differentiation, progressive constructivism* and *progressive perspectivism*. Werner and Kaplan (1963) show that development is marked by a shift in the organism-environment and means-ends relationships. In early stages of development, the infant cannot differentiate self from environment, nor means from ends. It reacts passively to stimuli. As the self becomes differentiated from the environment (usually before the age of 2), the child is capable of directing sensorimotor behavior toward goal objects, and, a little later, of differentiating means from ends so that behavior can be directed by alternate means to the same ends and new means-ends chains may be established. Nevertheless, the view of the young child is still egocentric. Subsequently (from about 2 to 8) the child becomes increasingly active in initiating and determining its own actions and perceptions, and begins construction of its own universe (the beginning of progressive constructivism). The child also becomes increasingly able to differentiate its own viewpoint from that of others (the beginnings of the shift from egocentrism to perspectivism). Finally (around 8 or 9) the child is actively able to construct knowledge about the universe, to clearly differentiate and integrate a wide range of means and ends, and to adopt the perspectives of others as well as his own. (The relative unimportance of these approximate age statements should be emphasized.)

Following a line of reasoning similar to other major developmental theorists, Werner (1948; see Langer, 1969, 1970) recognized three levels of development: *sensorimotor, perceptual,* and *contemplative,* progressing from concrete acquaintance with, to abstract knowledge of, the world. In addition, context-free and time-free *polarities of orthogenesis* were introduced to characterize developmental shifts (Werner, 1948; Kaplan, 1966a; Baldwin, 1967, pp. 497–504). These provide a methodological means by which to characterize varying levels of development (see Werner & Kaplan, 1963; Werner, 1948; Kaplan, 1966a; Baldwin, 1967, pp. 497–504).

Specific Theory of the Development of Notions of Space. The organismic-developmental theory treats the development of space from action-in-space to perception-of-space to conceptions-about-space as a function of increasing differentiation, distancing, and reintegration between the organism and its environment (Werner, 1948; Follini, 1966). Like Cassirer, Werner (1948, pp. 167–181, 382–390, 484–486) compares the two end-points of this development—the spaces of action and contemplation (see Wapner, Cirillo, and Baker, 1971, for the development of perceptual space) . . .

Piaget's Equilibration Theory of the Development of the Child's Conception of Space

The most extensive theory of the development of the child's knowledge of space is

that of the Swiss genetic epistemologist and psychologist Jean Piaget and his co-workers. Piaget's thought begins with the classical problem of epistemology—the nature of "reality" and whether there is any justification for assuming that one's impression of the world is "accurate." For Piaget (1963a, 1963b), the problem of knowledge is that of the relation between subject and object viewed biologically—how the subject comes to know (construct) the object. In this regard he has constructed a *genetic epistemology* (an epistemology studied empirically and developmentally rather than strictly philosophically). He began in the 1920's with the study of the origins of intelligence (1954a, 1962, 1963a, 1963b, 1968; Piaget and Inhelder, 1967, 1969; Piaget, Inhelder, and Szeminska, 1960) the work of developmental psychology for which he is best known.

General Theory of Development. Due to his complexity, thoroughness, and prolific output, it is almost impossible to summarize Piaget's theory and related findings. Fortunately, there are two excellent summaries by Piaget himself (1968; Piaget and Inhelder, 1969) and three other reasonably good summaries (Flavell, 1963, especially pp. 15–84; Baldwin, 1967; Langer, 1969, the last comparing Piaget's and Werner's theories).

Piaget (1963a) believes that the problem of the construction of knowledge reduces to an inherent *interaction* and *series* of *equilibrations* between the organism and its environment. He has empirically validated the Kantian contention that what constitutes the environment for a particular organism is an intellectual *construction* by the organism. Thus, all development is an interaction between maturation and socialization, between the organism and its environment. For Piaget, although development includes both maturation and learning, both are subordinated to the actual principle of *equilibrium,* which defines the subject-object (organism-environment) relation. The other crucial elements of his theory form a dialectic between *genesis* and *structure* (see Piaget, 1970).

Genesis: The Functional Invariants. Piaget (1963a, 1968) argues that the motivation for all biological and psychological development is *adaptation*. Adaptation is more than simply preservation and survival, it includes development from lower to higher orders of functioning. The process of development (as conceptualized by Piaget and by Werner) may be likened to a subtle mechanism which goes through gradual stages of adjustment in which the individual pieces become more *flexible* and *mobile* while the system as a whole becomes more *stable*. According to Piaget, intelligence is one form of adaptation. Although adaptation is obviously intrinsic to all living species, intelligence is not inherited; it is neither innate nor given simply through sensation, rather, it is formed through a complex interaction between the organism and its environment (Piaget, 1954a, 1963a, 1963b).

We do inherit, however *a mode of intellectual functioning* composed of *two functional invariants: assimilation* (the incorporation of the external world into already-structured schemas) and *accommodation* (the readjustment of schemas to the external world). Adaptation, then, is the equilibration of assimilation and accommodation. This ever-active functioning assures the construction of knowledge and the transition from any state of temporary equilibrium to a succeeding one (see Piaget, 1963a, pp. 6–7).

Essential to this theory is the notion of the *active organism* (Piaget, 1963a, 1963b). Piaget's findings strongly contradict the assumption of behavioristic "learning" theories that the child is a passive recipient of information from a "real" environment. On the contrary, his findings indicate that, in adapting to its environment, the organism actively initiates contacts and structures its experience. There-

fore, the impetus for moving toward higher levels of equilibration comes from this *intrinsic motivation* (Hunt, 1965).

Structure: The Major Periods of Development. Both Cassirer and Werner identified three forms of development—sensorimotor (or active), perceptual, and conceptual (or abstract-contemplative). Ontogenetically, three forms originate in an invariant sequence, yet overlap in time. Piaget's findings are consistent in these respects. But in addition he has paid careful attention to the description of the different stages (or periods) of conceptual development and the explanation of the transitions between stages.

To define and establish a stage, Piaget utilizes two general and four specific criteria (see Flavell, 1963; Laurendeau and Pinard, 1970). Generally, the notion of stages implies: (1) *hierarchization*—all stages are in a fixed order of succession, and (2) *equilibration*—each stage is a step in a developmental progression realized in successive degrees. Specifically, to distinguish one stage from another, the following criteria are invoked: (1) *qualitative differentiation*—each stage is qualitatively different from the one preceeding. (2) *integration*—each stage integrates the acquisitions or structures of all previous stages instead of simply substituting for them or adding to them, (3) *consolidation*—each stage involves aspects of the consolidation of achievements of earlier behavior and aspects of preparation for behavior at the following level, and (4) *coordination*—each stage is a coordinated whole by virtue of ties of implication, reciprocity, and reversibility: any behavior which can be done in one direction must be able to be systematically done in the opposite order.

On the basis of numerous experiments using these criteria, Piaget has identified four major periods in the development of intelligence: *sensorimotor*, *preoperational*, *concrete operational*, and *formal oper-*

ational. Each level is composed of an organized totality of mutually dependent and reversible behavior sequences known as *schemas* (or *schemata*).

The *sensorimotor period* extends from birth to the age of 2. In this stage, the human child changes from an organism capable only of reflex activity to an individual capable of coordinated actions and internalized thoughts (Piaget, 1954a, 1962, 1963a) . . .

Once the child is able to evoke mentally what has not actually been manipulated or perceived, he is able to "think," albeit at elementary levels. This defines the early childhood period of *intuitive* or *preoperational thought* (approximately 2 to 7). The child can now represent the external world in terms of symbols and can begin to operate on them mentally although these operations, far from being systematic, are at this level only intuitive and partially coordinated . . .

The stage of *concrete operations* (roughly 7 to 12) marks a decisive turning point in intelligence. Forms of mental organization develop which are highly stabilized equilibrations of constructions begun during the preoperational period. At this stage the child is capable of logical thought. As Piaget (1968, pp. 48–49) shows, the concept and explanation of *operations* are crucial to the understanding of intelligence.

Psychologically, an operation is, above all, some kind of action . . . rooted in the sensorimotor schemata. . . . Before becoming operational, they [actions] constitute the substance of sensorimotor intelligence, then of intuition. . . . Intuitions become transformed into operations . . . which are both *composable* and *reversible* . . . [i.e.] when two [mental] actions of the same kind can be composed into a third action of the same kind, and when these various actions can be compensated or annulled.

As a result of this formation of reversible operations, the child no longer fuses or confuses his own viewpoint with that of others; he is able to differentiate and coordinate different points of view independent of himself, such that the elements and relations are composable, associative, and reversible (Piaget and Inhelder, 1967). This progression from egocentrism to relational coordination directly parallels the progressive constructivism and progressive perspectivism of Werner's theory.

The final period of intelligence identified by Piaget is that of *formal operations* (from 11 to 14 or 15 and beyond). The logical operations of the earlier period begin to be transposed from the plane of concrete mental manipulation of "real" objects to the strictly ideational plane where they are expressed, Piaget (1968, p. 62) says, "in some kind of language (words, mathematical symbols, etc.), without the support of perception, experience or even faith." This stage marks the completion of the structural aspects of intellectual development, although much content is still to be attained.

Specific Theory of the Development of the Conception of Space. Piaget and his colleagues have devoted considerable attention to the problem of space (Piaget, 1954a, 1954b, 1962, 1963b; Piaget and Inhelder, 1967; Piaget, Inhelder, and Szeminska, 1960; Inhelder, 1965); the work includes over 1200 pages of experiments, findings, and tightly reasoned explanation. There are several partial summaries and reviews (Piaget, 1953; Piaget and Inhelder, 1969; Flavell, 1963, 1970; Holloway, 1967a, 1967b; Laurendeau and Pinard, 1970).

Four general conclusions arise from this research. First, Piaget has found *that the representation of space arises from the coordination and internalization of actions* (Piaget, 1954a; Piaget and Inhelder, 1967; Piaget, et al., 1960). Our adult understanding and representation of space results from extensive manipulations of objects and from movement in the physical environment, rather than from any immediate perceptual "copying" of this environment. Thus, it is primarily from acting-in-space, not perception-of-space, that the child builds up his knowledge-about-space. This conclusion is consistent with the distinction, discussed in Section I, between *figurative* and *operative* aspects of knowing. (Blaut, McCleary and Blaut, 1970; Lee, 1973; and Stea and Blaut, 1973 argue the importance of active experience in understanding large-scale spaces.)

A second general finding, which comes from Piaget's (1962) earlier work on the formation of symbols, and which was corroborated by Piaget and Inhelder (1967), is that *the genesis of the image arises from the internalization of deferred imitations.* Initially, the sensorimotor child copies or imitates other people's actions. Subsequently, as this imitation schema is internalized, and hence able to be deferred, the response becomes symbolic. The role of imagery will be discussed in more detail later in relation to other modes of spatial representation.

The third finding is that there are four levels or *structures* of spatial organization: sensorimotor, preoperational, concrete operational, and formal operational space (Piaget and Inhelder, 1967: Laurendau and Pinard, 1970).

Finally, many experiments (Piaget and Inhelder, 1967; Piaget et al., 1960) indicate that there are three classes of specific spatial relations which form the *content* of spatial cognition: topological, projective and euclidian or metric relations. Ontogenetically, the understanding of topological relations preceeds the understanding of projective and euclidian relations. The latter two develop in parallel, although the final equilibrium of euclidian relations is achieved slightly later than projective relations. These last two general conclusions, and some of the experiments which led to them, are elaborated below.

(We might note that the order of these ontogenetic developments are the exact reverse of the scientific discovery of space and of the order most often taught in elementary mathematics; Piaget, 1953).

Structure: Levels of Spatial Organization. As stated above, there are four major stages or periods of spatial organization: Stage I, sensorimotor space; Stage II, preoperational space; Stage III, concrete operational space; and Stage IV, formal operational space, the last three each having two substages. During the first stage (from birth to about 1½ or 2), *sensorimotor space* evolves and culminates in four important simultaneous developments (Piaget, 1954a; Flavell, 1963, pp. 129–162). The first one, the genesis of the *image*, has already been alluded to. The second involves the formation of *object permanence*, also the *object concept* (Piaget, 1954a, pp. 3–96). At birth and for the first year or so, when an object is removed from the immediate sight of an infant, he believes that it ceases to exist. Slowly, through playing with objects, the child comes to realize that an object still exists even if temporarily hidden. Thus the child develops a stable representation of objects in the world which transcends perceptual or tactual stimuli. Third, by the end of the sensorimotor period, the infant has developed from acting in a series of separate spaces centered on different personal needs and body parts (for example, postural space, buccal [mouth-related] space, tactile space, auditory space, and visual-perceptual space), to moving in a single coordinated space within which all objects are interrelated and begin to be represented (Piaget, 1954a, pp. 97–218). Because of this development, the child is able to move freely and confidently through a limited spatial terrain—for example, he can take shortcuts over routes (combination), return to a point of origin (reversibility), and detour around an object in order to get to another place (associativity)

(Piaget and Inhelder, 1969, pp. 15–17). This *sensorimotor group of spatial displacements* provides the base for all subsequent developments of spatial intelligence. Fourth, and signaling the transition to preoperational space, the sensorimotor schemas of the infant become sufficiently independent of immediate action to begin to be *internalized* into thought patterns (Piaget, 1962).

From these crucial beginnings, and with the advent of the symbolic function, representational space begins to develop in the child. The child must reconquer the obstacles overcome with the equilibrium of sensorimotor space, but this time on the level of symbolic representation. This internalization occurs in three additional stages ordered by degree of organization. Stage II, the formation of *intuitive* or *preoperational* space (from about age 2 to 7), has two substages: IIa, symbolic and preconceptual thought (from 2 to about 7), and IIb, intuitive partially regulated thought (from 4 to 7 or 8). Preoperational space, although representational, is still subject to the limiting conditions of sensorimotor and perceptual activity; that is, the first representations of space merely evoke successive states that have already been carried out on manipulated or perceived objects (Laurendeau and Pinard, 1970). Although certain rudimentary and isolated transformations can be performed, the representation of space is essentially static and not immediately coordinated into a reversible structure. As with preoperational thought in general, the preschool child can only return to a point of origin in thought by tracing a cyclical rather than symmetrical or truly reversible route. Furthermore, preoperational representations are egocentric; that is, the child's conception of space is still tied to his own point of view, although some beginning moves are made in the direction of decentering.

The child's conception of space gradually develops into the fully mobile, flexible, and reversible structures of Stage III, *concrete operational space* (from 7 to 12), also consisting of two substages: IIIa, the appearance of concrete operations (around 7 or 8); and IIIb, the organization of operations into logical structures (from about 9 to 11 or 12). During the early school years, spatial thought can finally disengage itself from images; it is transformed into operations which are, however, still concrete—that is, dependent on the presence of real or represented objects (Inhelder, 1965). The spatial structures, which by this time have achieved a considerable degree of abstraction, are formed through a logical coordination of space from multiple viewpoints (Piaget and Inhelder, 1967). Thus, the child is finally free of his egocentric orientation toward space.

Finally, in Stage IV, the *formal operational space* of adolescence and beyond, spatial operations can be completely removed from real action, objects, or space. The mathematical multiplication and coordination of space (Piaget, Inhelder, and Szeminska, 1960) allows the adolescent to survey the whole universe of spatial possibilities. In short, he has moved from the concrete spatial world to a new equilibrium, but this time in the realm of the possible, the hypothetical, and the infinite.

Content: Specific Spatial Relations to be Constructed. To know space as a geometric entity which has certain properties irrespective of transformations is the result of a series of developmental steps. On this problem alone Piaget and his colleagues have conducted over thirty experiments, summarized in two long volumes (Piaget and Inhelder, 1967; Piaget, Inhelder, and Szeminska, 1960). Following the organismic assumption introduced in Section I, the development of knowledge of spatial relations is inseparable from levels of structuring space, and from general cognitive development. Figure 21.1 illustrates some of these connections.

The three major types of relations or properties of space are defined as follows:

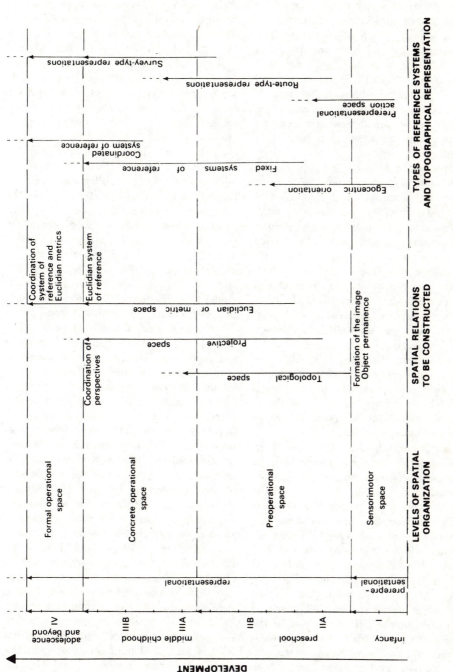

FIGURE 21-1.

269

Topological properties are simple qualitative relations like proximity and separation, open and closed, which remain invariant under continuous deformations excluding tears or overlaps. *Projective properties* are relations in terms of a particular perspective or point of view, such as a straight line, a triangle, or parallel lines which remain invariant under projective or perspective transformations. *Euclidian* or *metric properties* of space are relations in a system of axes or coordinates whose equivalence depends on mathematical-geometric equality; for example, an angle, an equal interval, or a distance . . .

Piaget and Inhelder (1967, pp. 17–79) devised a simple yet ingenious experiment to study the *sequence* of development of these fundamental spatial relations. Children ages 2 to 7 tactually explored a number of objects without being able to see them, and tried to match them with duplicates which could be seen but not touched. Thus the experiment was an excellent test of the development of the child's ability to internally *represent* different spatial relations. The findings indicated that, although infants can begin to form images near the end of the sensorimotor period, they are unable to differentiate topological shapes until they have entered the preoperational period. This is followed by a steady development in the ability to represent projective and euclidian shapes.

Piaget and Inhelder (1967, pp. 151–374) conducted seven experiments on the development of *projective space* broadly concerned with the development of the child's awareness of perspective and the interrelations between elements seen from different points of view. One intriguing experiment involved the coordination of perspectives of three mountains. A pasteboard model of three mountains was shown to children. A child is seated in front of the model and a small wooden doll is placed alternatively to the left, right, and to the rear of the model. After each placement, the child is shown a collection of ten pictures, each representing the mountains from different viewpoints, and is asked to select the picture which would correspond to the doll's view. Preoperational children (see figure) select the picture corresponding to their own view. With the appearance of concrete operations there is a progressive differentiation of points of view and certain projective relations are formed, but it is not until the final equilibrium of concrete operations that the two schemas are intercoordinated and children master a comprehensive coordination of viewpoints completely independent of their own point of view.

The final development in children's conception of spatial relations involves euclidian or metric space. Piaget and his colleagues have focused particularly on the systems of reference they use to organize space and conservations of length, distance, surface, and volume. Three interesting experiments were conducted to explore the coordination of systems of reference. In each case children were asked to make a plan or model of a large-scale environment, in a sense externalizing their "topographical schemas," or what we term "topographical representations" in Section III below. In one experiment, eight objects are placed on a blank cardboard base to form a model village. The child is given another piece of blank cardboard and a larger set of village pieces from which to choose and arrange a duplicate village. This experiment poses problems for the child because of the lack of other objects, lines, or angles to serve as reference markers. During the middle part of the preoperational period (see figure), the child picks out the correct number and type of pieces and tries to locate them in similar positions, but is able only to present topological relationships, and there is no coordination between the arrangement of objects and the external reference system provided by the card they lie on. Coincident with the onset of concrete operations, at about 7 to 8 years of age, a system of reference is constructed, but this does not become stabilized until concrete operations reach equilibrium, between 9 and 11 years of age. Not until the development of formal operations, at about 11 or 12, is the concept of a coordinated reference system attained which takes into account the additional projective and euclidian relations of proportional reduction to scale, accuracy of distance, and metric coordinates.

Finally, the conservation of the metric properties of length, distance, surfaces, and volume have been considered (Piaget et al., 1960, pp. 389–608). Generally, it has been found that the conservation of length and surface are not achieved until the concrete operational stage, when the child discovers through reversibility that a quantity has remained the same although a transformation has occurred. The conservation of volume is not achieved until the formal operational stage. These conservations are required for final equilibration of a fully coordinated and abstracted euclidian space.

In summary, the work of Piaget and his colleagues has demonstrated a number of important developments in the child's conception of space: the formation of object permanence; the genesis of the image; the sensorimotor group of displacements, representation through internalization of actions, the sequence of sensorimotor, pre-operational, concrete operational, and formal operational structurings of space, the sequence of topological, projective, and euclidian or metric contents of space, and the co-development of stages and specific relations of space into the coordination of perspectives and of euclidian systems of reference.

III. The Development of Spatial Cognition of Large-Scale Environments

Having reviewed research and theory on the general development of spatial cognition, we must now ask the more specific question of how representations of large-scale environments are constructed, and whether there is any difference in this construction from that of so-called "basic" spatial relations. Research on the develop-ment of representations of large-scale environments has been conducted since the turn of the century (see Gulliver, 1908; Stern, 1930; Trowbridge, 1913; Freeman, 1916). These representations have at least two functions: first, to facilitate location and movement within the larger physical environment, and second, to provide a general frame of reference for understanding and relating to this environment. Recognizing the importance of the first of these functions as part of orientation research, psychologists have implicitly been studying macro-spatial cognition for some time. The second function has been noted only recently but is equally important. For instance, Lynch (1960) suggests that "environmental images" help establish an emotionally safe relationship between men and their total environment by serving as organizers of activity and knowledge, as material for common memories which bind a group together, and as spatial referents for sense of familiarity. The importance of a spatial framework is evident from the writings of Lynch and those who have followed him (see Gulick, 1963; de Jonge, 1962; Stea and Downs, 1970; Appleyard, 1969a, 1970b; D. Wood, 1969, 1971).

The Ontogenetic Development of Geographical Orientation and Topographical Representations

Various terms have been given to an individual's cognitive representation of specifically large-scale environments: "imaginary map" (Trowbridge, 1913), "field map" or "cognitive map" (Tolman, 1973; Blaut, McCleary, and Blaut, 1970; Stea and Downs, 1970), "mental map" (Hallowell, 1955), "schema" (von Senden, 1960; Lee, 1973), "topographical schema" (Piaget, Inhelder, and Szeminska, 1960), and "topographical representation" (Shemyakin, 1962). We use the term *topographical representation* because it seems to be the most comprehensive and the least confusing: it implies neither a cartographic form (map) nor a habitual pattern (schema), but clearly refers to an internalized mental reflection of the physical environment. Shemyakin (1962, p. 193) has satisfactorily defined it as "a mental plan of some area which is a reflection in man's mind of the spatial placement of local objects in relation to each other and to himself." Thus it is still a cognitive representation but one explicitly pertaining to large-scale environments.

An essential element of topographical representations is a reference system which spatially orients the individual in some systematic manner to the environment. We use the terms *egocentric, fixed,* and *coordinated* to refer to three systems of orientation suggested by the literature. As there is evidence that these three systems of reference develop sequentially in ontogenesis, they are discussed in this order below (see Fig. 21.1).

Piaget, Inhelder, and Szeminska (1960, pp. 3–26) have provided the only complete account of the possible ontogenesis of topographical representations other than a nonempirical but insightful early paper by Freeman (1916) and the recent work of Stea and Blaut. Shemyakin (1962) has reviewed Russian research on geographical orientation and representation, but he offers no theoretical structure, and no detailed descriptions of research designs and statistical analyses. Nevertheless, his report is reviewed here because it summarizes a wealth of findings from largely inaccessible studies.

Egocentric Orientation. Ontogenetically, geographical orientation (like all development) is initially action-centered and egocentric. Numerous experiments have illustrated the effectiveness in man of a sensory system based primarily on proprioceptive input for the perception of body position; most do not concern us here because we are interested in the development of an individual's geographical or locational orientation rather than his "positional" orientation (see reviews of egocentric "positional" orientation by Witkin, Dyk, Faterson, Goodenough, and Karp, 1962;

Howard and Templeton, 1966, pp. 272–293; Wapner, Cirillo and Baker, 1971). Some of this literature, however, demonstrates how a child first orients to the physical environment using axes or planes defined entirely with respect to his own body. This may be referred to as an *egocentric orientation system.* There is much evidence that this system is based on a sense of localization through bodily movements (see reviews by Gregg, 1939; Shemyakin, 1962; and, most comprehensive, Howard and Templeton, 1966). Freeman (1916) believed that the direction to a place (actual or imagined; Ryan and Ryan, 1940) is "represented in the mind" in terms of movement of the body through turning the head or pointing, both of which bring us into alignment with the place. Through this method, Freeman (1916, p. 164) believed, a preschool child of 4 to 5 years of age builds up a "fairly definite notion of the direction of buildings or streets in the immediate vicinity of his home." This suggestion accords with Piaget's description of preoperational visual images as "internal imitations of actions, the objects being imagined and the actions internalized" (Piaget et al., 1960, p. 12). But this system serves only for representation while the child remains stationary. What of larger areas where the landscape must be traversed by the individual? It is not enough for the child to imagine movements, for he must link his movements to reference points.

As we have seen in Section II, Piaget has systematically studied the development of systems of reference. One part of this enquiry dealt specifically with the development of the child's reference system used to facilitate the representation of changes in his position in the larger environment (Piaget et al., 1960, pp. 3–26). Children aged between 4 and 10 were asked to build in a sand box a model of their school buildings and environs, using a variety of wooden pieces and ribbons representing such things as buildings, woods, and rivers; to draw in the sand or on a piece of paper the route from school to a well-known landmark; to make a drawing of the sand model; and finally, to make necessary changes to the plan after the school building was rotated through 180° by the experimenter. They found that an action-centered egocentric reference system was characteristic of pre-operational (Stage IIa) children: landmarks were not organized in terms of a spatial whole; routes were thought of in terms of the children's own actions first, the various landmarks being fixed in terms of them, instead of vice versa; and, the plan could not be rotated through 180°, nor could the routes be reversed in thought.

From this experiment, Piaget and his associates concluded that for preoperational children, representation occurs only when they think out a route. Landmarks are mentioned by these children, but are simply "tacked on" to recollections of their own actions (the routes traversed). That is, they can anticipate the spatial relations between one landmark and the next as they are walking, but are not able to build up a representation of the environment as an ordered whole. Only topological relations can be represented at the early preoperational level. While children can represent pairs of neighboring objects topologically, they cannot arrange three or more objects successfully into a coordinate system. This latter development involves reversibility and coordination, both characteristic of the later concrete operational period.

Having been interested in the genesis of representations specifically of large-scale environments, Stea and Blaut (Blaut and Stea, 1969; Blaut, McCleary, and Blaut, 1970; Stea and Blaut, 1973) have found what they consider a "primal" form of cognitive representation, namely the ability of first-graders and even some preschoolers to interpret and correctly identify objects from vertical aerial photographs. In addition, they have suggested that this early form of representation may in large part be due to a generalized cognitive model built up ini-

tially from post-infancy toy play as a surrogate for experience which the very young child lacks by not traversing routes in the larger environment (1969, pp. 22–26).

Based upon empirical findings, Shemyakin's (1962) account of the development of topographical representation largely accords with that of Piaget. He distinguishes two fundamentally different types of topographical representation: *route maps* and *survey maps*. Shemyakin (1962, p. 218) describes a route map as a representation constructed by mentally "tracing the route" of locomotion through an area. This seems to agree with Piaget's account of internalized actions in the form of known routes, as discussed above. By survey maps Shemyakin means representations of "the general configuration or schema of the mutual disposition of local objects." This seems equivalent to what Piaget describes as a true topographical representation utilizing a coordinate reference system (see Fig. 21.1).

From observations of orientation in blind persons, and of map drawing and orientation in sighted children, Shemyakin has suggested that route-map representations are a necessary prior development in the formation of survey-map representations. Observations of children (Shemyakin, 1940; Lyublinskaya, 1948, 1956; see Shemyakin, 1962) indicated the importance of route-mapping in the early development of topographical representations. Shemyakin argued that after a child learns to walk, a new stage in the understanding of space relations opens before him, citing Lyublinskaya's description of a 1½ year old child's early mastery of the "space of the route." From observations of movement in and immediately around the house, Lyublinskaya also suggested that "the child is not only able to orient herself in space among familiar objects, but retains also a pretty accurate representation of the position of individual familiar objects in space" (Shemyakin, 1962, p. 218). Even children of 6 to 8 years of age, when asked to draw a plan of some locality familiar to them, did so mainly by drawing the route. Shemyakin (1962, p. 219) assumed a correspondence between the construction of these external representations and the initial development of internal representations, observing that:

> Children usually began their work at the lower edge of the paper, and drew "away from themselves" (so) that the right and left turns coincided with the real position of their body in space. . . . [Asking them to draw] "toward themselves . . ." led to a sharp increase in the number of errors in the reproduction of [the] turns.

Furthermore, some children chose to sit at that side of the table that faced the required locality. These results are similar to those found by Piaget and his associates in the above experiment when children were asked to draw a familiar route: both clearly indicate an egocentric preoperational level of development. Unfortunately, there are many limitations in the use of children's drawings for inferring the nature of internal representations. Drawings cannot be a simple translation of an image representation, for only two of the three spatial dimensions can be represented in the picture plane (Arnheim, 1967, pp. 165–212). Also, Piaget and Inhelder (1967, pp. 45–46) point out that drawings lag behind image representation particularly when the child is dealing with complex wholes. Nevertheless, they believe that pictorial representations are valuable methodologically if limited to the spontaneous drawing of simple everyday shapes and checked with the use of other methods.

Route mapping is not unique to children. Appleyard (1969, 1970) found this same system was commonly used by adults in drawing maps of Ciudad Guayana. Rand (1969) found evidence of *both* a prior ontogenetic development of route-mapping in young children (see also Lee, 1973) and a prevalence of route-mapping in adult taxi-drivers' representations of a city (in contrast to the relationship- or survey-mapping of pilots). However, following Werner's orthogenetic principle discussed in Section II, even in the latter case, route-maps may be seen to be less integrated and hence less advanced developmentally than survey-maps (see Fig. 21.1).

Fixed Systems of Reference. For orientation in large-scale environments, Freeman (1916) noted the importance of the child's ability to free himself from the limitations of this early egocentric orientation system. Werner (1948) also noted the transition from egocentrism to perspectivism and its importance for organizing space. This development, according to Piaget (1963a), does not begin until the onset of reversible thought in the concrete operational period. At this stage, Piaget et al. (1960) have shown that the child's position and movements begin to be oriented in terms of fixed elements in the environment rather than the elements being oriented egocentrically to the child. The next stage in geographical orientation and topographic representations appears to be a transitional stage between early preoperational egocentric orientation and concrete operational coordinated systems of reference. We refer to this stage as that of *fixed systems of reference*.

Freeman (1916, p. 165) observed that children move from orientation with reference solely to themselves to orientation with reference to the position of some fixed object or of some fixed direction: the child thereby achieves a "detached view of a region as though it were seen from a distance." This accords with the second level in the development of topographical representations found by Piaget et al. (1960, pp. 14–21) in the model-the-school experiment described above. For early concrete operational children (IIIa), the spatial representation of the landscape is partially coordinated by the use of landmarks. The children are unable to coordinate the system as a whole, either in demonstrating with the wooden models the topographical relations between landmarks, or in describing a route. They can relate objects to each other in discrete local areas, but they cannot appreciate the totality of relations between landmarks which occur in the environment because the landmarks are fixed in partially coordinated *sub*groups, each based on an independent vantage point or on a particular journey.

W. Brown (1932, p. 126) also recognized a fixed reference system as a second stage in his human maze-learning experiment, and noted the particular importance of landmarks as reference points:

> Objects which can be perceived (a rough-spot or a tilting board) are able to serve as landmarks . . . objects which are recognized in this way assume a considerable effective value. The subject often expresses great satisfaction in finding them . . . the nucleus of any *locality* is an object.

As a means of representing areas larger than those lying within an individual's visual field, the hypothesis that features are organized in relation to a fixed reference point gains support from von Senden's (1960, p. 286) summary of clinical observations of orientation by the blind:

> The subject sets out from a perfectly definite central point, resembling the center of a spider's web, whence he gains acquaintance with the routes that matter to him, up to an outer periphery that can be more or less gradually extended. Wherever he may be, he always remains mentally in conscious relation to his fixed starting point.

Trowbridge (1913, p. 890) had earlier provided a convincing account of the efficacy of this system, suggesting the home as the necessary fixed object for children; in using this system "all changes of position . . . can be referred at any moment to definite distances and angles, forming a simple trigonometric figure which gives the direction to the home." Trowbridge (1913) suggested this *domicentric* system (which may be seen as a special case of fixed reference systems) is not only found in birds, beasts, fish, and insects, but also in uncivilized man" and young children. It was once thought to be an innate ability which remained as a vestigial sense in children (Warren, 1908; Hudson, 1922; W. F. Smith, 1933) but this has since been discounted (see Howard and Templeton, 1966).

Although domicentric orientation is not innate, children do seem to commonly orient themselves towards their home. In an aerial geography experiment, one of us (Hart, 1971) observed that children aged 8-9 years would not become involved in a geographical learning experience provided by flying and aerial photographs *until* they had first located their home or their school. Muchow and Muchow (1935), Lee (1973) and Rand (1969) offered similar conclusions on domicentricity based on observations of children's drawings and their behavior with regard to home and school.

Unfortunately there is still very little known about general fixed systems of reference. Most research on the development of orientation in children has been concerned with children's understanding of the cardinal directions, even though orientation to fixed familiar features would seem from the above analysis to be more likely for preoperational and concrete operational children. In fact, Lee doubts that even adults construct a rectilinear grid of coordinates to orient themselves in space; he suggests instead that in each of their "spatial schemata" they use a *polar* system consisting of a set of radiating lines from a fixed reference point.

Reference systems are but the framework for topographical representations. These can never be fully abstracted from those objects and space relations between them which form a given locality and distinguish it from any other locality (Shemyakin, 1960, p. 191). How the topographical representations themselves develop is a question which has been given little attention in the literature. Of course, we already know that the representation of space begins with the internalization of action on space; we might anticipate that walking or cycling would be most important to the child's formation of topographical representations and that more passive modes of travel would not serve the same purpose. This point is also argued convincingly by Lee (1973) and Stea and Blaut (1973a, b). As Lee says, walking is "intimate to the environment and therefore articulates the schema." Stea and Blaut suggest the importance of toy play as a surrogate for other forms of direct environmental experience. These hypotheses are supported by research findings on the role of kinaesthetic cues in geographical orientation (see Liebig, 1933; Howard and Templeton, 1966).

Given the importance of action and of domicentricity, it is not surprising that Rand (1969) found children's "trips and excursions to far-away places are remembered but not thought of as connected with, or of the same world, as their immediate habitat." Similarly, Lee found that the spatial world of primary school children in England was divided into various local "schemata" which bore a "detectable relationship to the physical world," but that "beyond this home area lay one total schema that might be called the 'elsewhere schema' in which physical dimensions were irrelevant" (1973). Rand (1969) claims that a deep sense of familiarity with the home area is necessary as a basis for further exploration and discusses the notion of home as "sacred space" from which the child can make "brief excursions into the profane world" (see Eliade, 1959). This seems sufficiently obvious to be a truism, but such statements are understandable: not only has there been little research into the development of topographical representation in children but there have been very few studies of children's environmental behavior. With an increasing awareness of the importance of early environmental experience in children's development into "rich and competent human beings" (Carr and Lynch, 1968), we can anticipate a growth of research in these fields (see Lukashok and Lynch, 1956; Cobb, 1959; Parr, 1967; Shelton, 1967; Bunge, 1969; Ladd, 1970; Anderson and Tindal, 1970; Colyard, 1971).

Coordinated System of Reference. The literature on the development of reference systems of a higher order than the fixed systems discussed above (with the exception of that of Piaget and his colleagues) has been totally concerned with children's understanding of cardinal directions. This sheds little light on the "spontaneous" development of reference systems in children. While knowledge of cardinal directions has pedagogical merit for the understanding of maps and for the communication of directions, it is not necessary in the formation of topographical representations of large-scale environments. For example, none of the 4- to 10-year old children in Piaget and associates' (1960) model-the-school experiment described earlier in this section were reported to have utilized the cardinal directions in the constructing of topographical representations. Nevertheless, this experiment confirmed the findings of Piaget's model landscape and model village experiments described in Section II: children who had achieved equilibration of concrete operations (Stage III*b*) can construct a topographical representation in line with a two-dimensional coordinate system. The coordinates, when drawn, do not necessarily run parallel with the margins of a piece of paper as with a cartographic grid. Rather they are based upon physical features in the experienced environment, but the end result for children of this level is always a coordinated whole (Piaget et al., 1960). In drawing the plan of the school area, children at this level use two complementary methods: either they group the elements of the plan in terms of relations between local areas, or they select one or more starting points and reconstruct routes which radiate from them. In this way any single part of the representation is related to all the other parts, for through associativity each point can be reached mentally by a variety of routes, and through reversibility each route can be represented in the reverse direction to that experienced. Thus, having progressed through egocentric nonrepresentational orientation and through a fixed system of reference wherein the first preoperational, partially-coordinated representations are developed, the child has advanced to the final stage of topographical representation, that of utilizing a *coordinated system of reference*.

The question now arises, how does the child coordinate the set of independent and fixed subgroups of space into a fully coordinated topographical representation? Piaget is the only researcher who has addressed this question (Piaget and Inhelder, 1967; Piaget, Inhelder, and Szeminska, 1960). What he seems to suggest is the following: the child decenters from each of the partially coordinated fixed systems of reference of the previous stage. Thereafter, through processes of reciprocal assimilation among the reference systems and reflective abstraction beyond them, he intercoordinates these structures and advances to a higher plane of thought, that of fully equilibrated concrete operations (III*b*).

Other writers have discussed what has been called *geocentric orientation* (Trowbridge, 1913: Freeman, 1916; Gregg, 1939; Lord, 1941), apparently equivalent to what we prefer to call a coordinated system of reference. A wealth of reports from anthropology reveals that neither is universally the final stage of development in ontogenesis (see reviews by Werner, 1948; Hallowell, 1955; Lynch, chap. 16). Werner (1948, p. 172) has suggested:

There must be a complete revolution in the history of the human mind in order to uproot the idea of space from its primitive, anthropomorphic, qualitative-dynamic ground and thereby elevate it to the free sphere of physical-geometric abstraction.

From the number of studies bemoaning children's ignorance of the western system of abstract cardinal directions and suggesting ways of teaching it (Gulliver, 1908; Trowbridge, 1913; Ridgley, 1922; Howe, 1931, 1932; Gregg, 1940; Lord, 1941; Kabanova-Meller, 1956), one can reasonably assume that ontogenesis demands a similar "revolution" in geographical orientation to that suggested by Werner. As we demonstrated in Section II, in the words of Shemyakin (1962, p. 190), "the crux of the general development of the understanding of space is the transition from a [fixed] point of reading to a system with a 'freely transferable' point of reading." Trowbridge (1913, p. 894) claimed that confusion results from poor teaching of cardinal directions leading to entirely erroneous "imaginary maps," and further suggested that:

Children should be seated in a special manner when studying geography, with the cardinal points of the compass marked in the room, and the maps in the books properly oriented . . . imaginary maps [should be] systematically corrected in childhood.

This suggestion and other similar ones (Kabanova-Meller, 1956; Ridgely, 1922: Howe, 1932) have been repeatedly reiterated by geography educators in the *Journal of Geography*. If all else fails, Gregg (1940) suggests, have the child think of places lying in specific directions and lean his trunk, incline his head, or turn his eye "vigorously" towards the place while calling out its name! None of these writers recognized the real problem: the most fundamental factor in the child's use of an abstract or coordinated system of reference is the prior development of his ability to recognize perspectives other than his own (see section II). Geographic education has only recently begun to take note of the crucial importance of considering development of the child's concept of space (e.g., Miller, 1967; Almy, 1967; Towler and Nelson, 1968; Towler, 1970; Blaut, 1969; Blaut and Stea, 1969, 1971; Blaut, McCleary, and Blaut, 1970; Hart, 1971).

In summary, there is considerable evidence that in developing topographical representations of the large-scale environment, the child utilizes a framework or system of reference for interrelating different positions, routes, patterns of movement, and himself in this environment, and that this system of reference is the most important component of spatial representation. Furthermore, the ontogenetic development of systems of reference proceeds through three stages: egocentric, fixed, and coordinated, the third stage being achieved in children with the equilibration of concrete operations. Furthermore, it appears that the topographical representations themselves, like all spatial representations, are formed initially on the basis of visual-motor connections. Though much of the evidence is anecdotal, the suggestion is that route-mapping ontogenetically precedes survey-mapping.

The Microgenetic Development of Topographical Representations

Following organismic-developmental theory, we would expect formal similiarities between the ontogenesis and microgenesis of macrospatial cognition (Werner, 1948; Follini, 1966). The *microgenetic* development of an individual's cognition of, and orientation in, a new and unfamiliar macrospace (e.g. when a child explores a new area or an adult moves to a new city) is an important yet relatively uncharted area of research.

Freeman (1916) claims that an individual visiting a new city constructs a system or orientation by unconsciously ap-plying the cardinal directions to various features; only if he makes a mistake does the person become conscious of the process. While this may be true for some, it is difficult to believe that cardinal directions are used as a reference system by all adults.

In summarizing the work of Khopreninova (1956) and Sverlov (1951), Shemyakin (1962, p. 230) emphasized the prior accumulation of a certain quantity of internally represented "route-maps" as the most crucial factor in the subsequent formation of "survey-maps." With these "route-maps," he claims, "a given locality is, as it were, presented as a system of roads leading 'there' and 'back'." This is similar to von Senden's description of the development of "schemas" in the blind. After a blind person has successfully represented a number of journeys, von Senden (1960, p. 287) says:

He then seeks to relate a number of such routes, all starting from the same point, by means of "lateral crossties," and so to create a network of relations, to encompass and knit together the parts of the region commanded in this way.

Von Senden points out that the blind use this method even for the exploration of rooms. Others have explored the question experimentally, simulating blindness by blindfolding their subjects (Brown, 1932; Liebig, 1933; Worchel, 1951; Follini, 1966).

Some different findings have come from recent studies of urban form. Lynch (1960) observed that the sequence in which subjects' sketch maps of cities were drawn develops in either of five ways: outward from familiar lines of movement; outward from a familiar dense kernel; inward from the construction of an enclosing boundary; from a gridiron pattern; or from an initial set of adjacent regions. Lynch's (1960, p. 86) suggestion that "this might have some relation to the way in which it [the image] first develops as individual becomes familiar with his environment" so far lacks empirical validation.

One of Lynch's colleagues, Appleyard (1969a) found that sketch maps drawn of the new city of Cuidad Guayana by 320 inhabitants were structured either *sequentially*, using roads and rivers as organizing principles, or *spatially*, using buildings and districts. His suggestion that sequential maps are of a lower developmental order than spatial maps accords with the findings of Shemyakin on route-maps and survey-maps reviewed above. Appleyard also noted that the maps ranged from primitive topological maps to positional maps. He argues that both of these are developmental distinctions, but provides no evidence of the transition between the two. It is interesting to note, however, that 75 percent of the maps were of the sequential type. If it is true that these are developmentally primitive, it could be that this large percentage resulted from the limited experience of most of the inhabitants with this new city (the survey was taken only three years after the start of construction). Therefore, it is possible that the development of a person's representations of a new environment proceeds from route-mapping (sequential) to survey-mapping (spatial).

Gittins (1969) conducted a thorough study of the development of representations of unfamiliar large-scale environments. In Section II we described his results as regards two different types of final *product* of the representation, but he was also interested in the *process* by which people form impressions. His methodology included asking his subjects (writers and scientists) at several points on a walking tour through an unfamiliar city to describe and draw the section of the city recently passed through and their current overall impression. At the end they were asked to describe in what way they approached the task of forming impressions.

He found that there were two different processes of cognitively structuring a city: *aesthetic-poetic* (characteristic of most of the writers), and *scientific* (characteristic of most of the scientists). The *aesthetic* process began with an initial intuition of the city which slowly but steadily became organized into a "comprehensive integrated conception" through the combining of a series of insights into a concrete, sensuous impression of the specific city traversed. The scientific process did not evidence intuition at the beginning, nor was there much organization for some time, until at mid-tour, a sudden reorganization occurred leaving a clear, articulate, abstract, "formula-like" structuring of the city, which applied to cities in general rather than to this particular city, and which was only slightly modified to incorporate aspects of the city experienced later.

IV. Conclusion

At the beginning of this review of work on spatial cognition, we saw that there were two quite separate bodies of literature, one emanating from developmental psychology, the other from behavioral geography and urban planning. Both address the same basic issue: How do we come to know the form of space? To the best of our knowledge, these two bodies of research have not previously been brought together. However, not only are the questions asked essentially the same, but, as we have tried to show, the findings are commensurate.

We have seen from Kant's contention and from the research of Werner and Piaget that the concept of space is neither innate nor learned; it is constructed by the child as a series of hierarchically integrated equilibrations through his adaptive interaction with the environment and by means of the reciprocating processes of assimilation and accommodation. From the internalization and reflective abstraction of actions arises the child's first intuitive understanding of space. However, Cassirer, Werner, and Piaget have made clear that the understanding of space is more than the learning or mere accumulation of facts which have some kind of real existence. Piaget (Piaget, Inhelder and Szeminska, 1960, pp. 23–24) light-heartedly noted that if it were simply a case of accumulation one might explain the development of topographical representations in the following manner: at four years of age, a child is brought to school by his mother, and is therefore aware only of the school, his home, and the local candy store; at seven, he knows a few roads, and can therefore describe fragmentary routes; and at nine or ten, he is allowed to roam free and consequently knows the topography intimately.

We have seen from Cassirer, Werner, and Piaget that there are several dimensions or polarities of the child's understanding of space. All three theorists have identified a progression from concrete to abstract space consisting of sensorimotor action in space, perception of space, and symbolic or abstract representation and thought about space. Werner expressed the same development as a progression from a fusion between the child and his environment to differentiation and, ultimately, reintegration. Both Werner and Piaget have shown a progression from egocentrism to perspectivism (or relational coordination) and that this progression is a dimension which seems to underlie many of the other developments in the child's understanding of space. Piaget has identified four levels of spatial intelligence: sensorimotor, intuitive or preoperational, concrete operational, and formal operational. We have used these levels as a framework for organizing findings on the spatial cognition of large-scale environments. Furthermore, we have used the progressions of general intellectual development identified by Werner and the stages and functional invariants identified by Piaget to begin to suggest explanations for the findings on macro-spatial cognition (see Fig. 21.1).

In the sensorimotor period of development, the infant moves in a space of action. His orientation to the larger environment is totally egocentric and he has no topographical representations.

As spatial actions become internalized through the dual process of assimilation of impressions from the environment into the sensorimotor schemas and accommodation of the schemas to the environment, the child's first images or iconic representations of space develop. This leads to a major new period, that of preoperational space, the beginning of representational space. During this period, most topological relations are formed, and projective and euclidian relations begin to be constructed. Egocentric orientation gives way to the onset of a fixed system of reference, centered first on the home (domicentricity) and later on a small number of uncoordinated routes, landmarks, and familiar places. The child no longer operates solely in a space of action for he begins to represent his routes (route-type representations). Generally, this is a period of gradual differentiation of the child from his environment, of the child's point of view from that of other people, and of elements and relationships from each other within the environment.

These differentiated but uncoordinated representations of discrete parts of a total space (e.g., routes, landmarks, barriers) begin to be coordinated with the onset of concrete operations during the early school years. Many other specific developments occur, such as the concept of the straight line, parallelity, proportional intervals, and angles. As we have shown, the child's understanding of these relations is a result of the grouping of partial structures into a coordinated whole through the equilibration of assimilation and accommodation. The child is now able to coordinate perspectives and construct a euclidian system of reference. Both of these are most important for his understanding of the large-scale environment. Furthermore, the child's individual route-type topographical representations become coordinated into a comprehensive survey-type representation.

Finally, with the onset during early adolescence of formal operations, which are a reflective abstraction from concrete operations, the individual is not only able to act in space and mentally coordinate his thoughts about concrete objects and spatial relations, but he is also able to reflect on these accomplishments and consider a theoretical space totally abstracted from any concrete particulars. The concepts of length, distance, area, and volume, all of which depend on the formal concept of infinity, are also able to be constructed and conserved. Thus, both a true metric space and a totally abstract space are possible for the adolescent.

It seems from the research literature on the ontogenetic development of spatial cognition that there are four domains of parallel development: levels of organization of spatial cognition (sensorimotor, preoperational, concrete operational, and formal operational); types of spatial relations (topological, projective, and euclidian): systems of reference (egocentric, fixed, and coordinated); and types of topographical representations (route and survey). Each of these developments in turn parallels the four periods of general intellectual development discovered by Piaget and the orthogenetic principle and developmental progressions elucidated by Werner. Furthermore, as we have tried to show, there seem to be certain direct correspondences and explanatory relations between the different domains of the development of spatial cognition.

22. Children's Play and Urban Playground Environments: A Comparison of Traditional, Contemporary and Adventure Playground Types

D. G. HAYWARD, M. ROTHENBERG, AND R. R. BEASLEY

A child's play is an important part of his or her cognitive, physical, social, and emotional development. Through play, a child learns about himself and his world. Further, the opportunity to play enhances one's ability to initiate independent activity—activity which is crucial to the exploration and construction of one's autonomy, identity and self-image as a constructive force.

The opportunities for play, therefore, are an important focus for investigation. Especially in cities, social and environ-

Adapted from *Environment and Behavior,* Vol. 6, No. 2 (June 1974), pp. 131–168, by permission of the publisher, Sage Publications, Inc., and the authors.

This research was partially supported by N. S. F. grant GZ-2562.

mental changes are influencing these opportunities. Specifically, social factors have diminished the freedom to use available opportunities. Apprehensive about crime, parents are more cautious about allowing their children to go out by themselves. Pedestrian density discourages children from using sidewalk space for their games, and heavy traffic precludes playing in the street. Moreover, the available opportunities have themselves diminished as higher-density development continues and is coupled with decreasing open space. As plans for development proceed, one may ask, "Where and when can the children play?" Unfortunately, this inquiry often meets with inadequate answers. Open space around high-rise buildings is planned more for security and maintenance than for use by children or adults. In addition, signs often proclaim no ball playing, no bike riding, or no playing on the sidewalks. The restrictions on opportunities for children's activity seem to emerge from all directions.

What happens to children as these opportunities diminish? As their choices and free play opportunities become more and more limited, how do they learn about themselves and their abilities, about their world and their relationship to it? What possibilities exist for children in the city to find places to meet others, to explore their environment, to aid in constructing an image of themselves and the world? One study (Bishop and Peterson, 1971) has systematically demonstrated that adults (designers, park officials) are quite insensitive to the play preferences of school-age children; therefore, play spaces planned by adults have a questionable relationship to the opportunities desired by children.

The paradox of this state of affairs is a serious one: at an age when a child would benefit from increasing independence and expansion of home range (Stea, 1970), he or she is faced with constraints in terms of range of travel, hour of outdoor activity, and time away from home. Many developmentally important freedoms are impinged upon, including peer group and interpersonal interaction, opportunities to develop physical prowess, and the freedoms to explore new places and new activities. The investigation of play spaces and the challenges and freedoms which they allow is therefore of central importance in planning facilities or programs for this age group in our cities.

In considering play spaces available to school-age children (six to thirteen years old), there emerged a variety of intentions and traditions of play. It appeared that all planned play spaces embodied untested assumptions about the users, the nature of the activity and the interaction of the physical environment and children's play. In essence, the planning of play areas was seen to be based on intuition about what a child needs and desires and how to pro-

vide for it. The recognition that many different needs and interests are served by play (e.g., physical release, peer group association, exploration, conversational and organizational skills, and so on) prompts a systematic consideration of children's play and its interrelationships with play spaces. What is needed is intensive observation of what is happening in a variety of different settings. The present study had this focus; the intent was to understand what influences operated in several different settings and to compare between settings when possible. This paper gives an overview of the methods employed and some of the major findings.

The three playgrounds which were studied are identified as the traditional playground, the contemporary playground, and the adventure playground. Recognizing that there may be differences in why any one of these three types had been planned in particular neighborhoods, we sought to choose play settings which were public, accessible, and in roughly the same neighborhood. Our interests in school-age children made it essential to select settings where this age group is normally present. In additon, it seemed important to select playgrounds that had the potential of being used by a variety of racial and ethnic groups.

Adventure or junk playgrounds were

FIGURE 22–1. View of the traditional playground.

FIGURE 22–2. View of the contemporary playground.

originally developed through European experimentation with materials for play. Adapted from the British Adventure Playgrounds, the concept of supplying play materials rather than conventional play equipment has recently been cited as a form which can expand the range of play opportunities available to children (Cooper, 1970; Nicholson, 1970). These playgrounds are often started on vacant, fenced-in lots, and children are encouraged to plan and replan the area as their interests evolve. Reactions to adventure playgrounds have been mixed: children are frequently enthusiastic and active, while often the community questions the undesigned and unattractive appearance (Spivak, 1969). The

FIGURE 22–3. View of the adventure playground.

adventure playground selected for this study is illustrated in Figure 22-3.

At each playground there was at least one hired play leader or supervisor whose job it was to work with children in their activities. The nature of the roles of these play leaders and the way in which they participated at each playground will be discussed in a later section.

Method

In deciding to undertake intensive observation of some playground settings, we sought to investigate many general and specific questions. Who uses playgrounds? What opportunities are available and usable for school-age children at playgrounds? Do playgrounds offer freedoms to a child—freedom in behavior, kinds of activities, interaction, and the like—beyond the use of equipment? What is the nature of the relationship between a child's play and the environment in which that play occurs? Specifically, what is the nature of children's play and the play/environment relationship at playgrounds which differ considerably in their design?

Underlying these specific questions about play and playgrounds were more general questions concerned with the relationship of child's behavior at playgrounds with a child's development. How can the behavior at playgrounds be interpreted in terms of developmental themes, challenges, and needs? What activities do school-age children choose to engage in? Do children primarily attend with and interact with peers, or are their playground experiences and decisions strongly mediated by adults? Further, how popular are playgrounds among school-age children? What do they think about the opportunities, challenges, and freedoms offered to them?

Three methods were selected to investigate many of these questions: behaviorial mapping, behavior settings' records, and interviews.

A description of each of the three methods follows in the order of their use during the study. Each new method chronologically overlapped the previous one.

Behavioral mapping

Behavioral mapping focuses on overt human behavior and provides a time sampling of behavior in relation to its physical locus (Ittelson et al., 1970). Specifically, a trained observer moves from place to place in the setting and records the location, age, sex, and number of participants in particular activities. Although this technique is best conceptualized as a time sampling of user behavior, it requires nearly continuous observation, since the sequence is initiated frequently.

The mapping technique focuses on overt behavior in a manner which approximates an instantaneous photograph; the activities recorded are directly observable, codified, and based on as little inference as possible. The list of activities was developed during pilot work and represented the range of activities likely to occur. The observer recorded the predominant activity of each person or group in a particular location. . . .

Each playground was divided into a number of physical areas in order to localize the specific activity (i.e., in relation to particular pieces of apparatus or topographic features).

Observations began at 10:00 a.m. and continued at twenty-minute intervals. The last round of the morning began at 12 noon, afternoon observations began at 1:20 p.m., and the last round of the day began at 3:40 p.m. Observers were randomly assigned to particular settings. Assignments were alternated periodically so that each setting was observed by different people. . . .

Young research assistants (i.e., late teens) were employed to collect these data. This practice was consistent with unobtrusive observation (Webb et al., 1966), and

the training of observers was not complicated by the use of young research assistants. During the training period, interrater reliabilities were computed for area, activity, age, size of group, and sex agreement. Reliability was computed by dividing agreed instances by one-half the total number of instances recorded by either observer. The overall realiability was 90%. The item reliability ranged from 85% (activities) to 96% (areas). The range of overall agreement between pairs of observers ranged from 87% to 95%.

Behavior Settings' Records

Behavior settings' records were collected to emphasize the flow, duration, and content of behavior for individual school-age children. This method consists of longitudinal observation to investigate what activities were engaged in and how these activities related to the child's interaction with the environment and with other children and adults. In addition to obtaining a description of activities, this method was selected because it allowed content analysis of the behavior at a detailed level.

Observers were instructed to focus on behavioral or conversational indicators of the child's goal in each activity, as well as the intensity of the child's involvement with the play. . . .

Observers were equipped with small tape recorders and arrived at each playground at or before 10:00 a.m. After allowing an arbitrary time lapse of five minutes, an observer selected the first school-age child who entered the playground. Remaining at a discreet distance from the child, the observer made a continuous detailed taped record of the child's ongoing activity, including the approximate age of the child, the activities undertaken by the child, the durations of those activities, the number of other children involved with the child. . . . The observer continued to record the sequence of the child's behavior for the entire time the child remained in the playground.

The behavior settings' records were analyzed as to ages of children, length of stay, the time spent in each kind of activity, and the total time within each playground. Further, a brief record of each child's style of play including specific conversations was made to supplement the quantitative measures.

Interviews

Interviews were conducted to sample children's preferences and satisfactions about their own play experiences and play settings. Specifically, this method sought to obtain the child's interpretation of his activity and its meaning. . . .

. . . The final interview schedule consisted of fourteen questions including why children came to a particular playground, how often they came, what they did there, and what they liked most about the place. Children were also asked, "Whose decision was it to come here?"; "What other playgrounds do you go to?"; and "How often do you go to them?"

An interviewer waited near the entrance of the playground, and after a fixed period of time he or she approached the first child to leave who appeared to be six years old or older. The interviewer would stop a child who was leaving the playground, introduce himself and ask if the child would mind being interviewed. If the child was accompanied by an adult, the interviewer also asked the adult's permission to interview the child. The interviews were conducted at the end of the data collection period so as not to influence any of the ongoing activity in the playgrounds.

Playground Users and Patterns of Use

One group of questions which this study sought to investigate focused on whether school-age children attended playgrounds and what part of the playground population those school-age children comprised. Since the behavioral mapping data collection enabled observation of all users, the relative proportions of each of four age groups were computed. (See Table 22–1.) The six to thirteen year old user group that was the focus of this study made up a greater part of the playground population at the adventure playground (44.58%), while this group was only a minor proportion of the total number of users at the traditional and the contemporary playground (20.84% and 22.21%, respectively).

TABLE 22–1. *Distribution of Playground Users According to Age Groups From the Mapping*

	Traditional Playground	Contemporary Playground	Adventure Playground
% Preschool	29.48	35.23	1.74
% School-Age	20.84	22.21	44.58
% Teenage	9.80	6.85	32.16
% Adult	39.78	35.71	21.52
Total %	100.00	100.00	100.00
Total Observations (n=)	(4,294)	(9,765)	(2,360)
Days of Behavioral Mapping	10.5	11	11

. . .

At the traditional playground and the contemporary playground, adults were the most predominant age group (39.78% and 35.71%, respectively), while preschool children were the second most predominant group (29.48% and 35.23%). In contrast, adults were the third most predominant age group at the adventure playground (21.52%), while there were practically no preschool children observed at this playground (1.74%). The adults at the adventure playground were primarily play leaders plus occasional day camp counselors, parents, or other neighborhood adults. The adults at the traditional playground were primarily nursemaids, parents, babysitters, and grandmothers, plus the play leader and day camp counselors. The adults at the contemporary playground were primarily parents and day camp counselors in addition to the two play leaders.

Teenagers at the traditional playground were day camp counselors and infrequent small groups who came by to swing or lie in the sun. For the most part, they were not active users, and there were few young teens observed. Teenagers at the contemporary playground were day camp counselors and occasional babysitters. There were very few young teens observed as participants at this playground. Teenagers at the adventure playground were predominantly young teens (i.e., thirteen to fourteen years old) plus occasional day camp counselors. Many children of this age group were part of the user group that was of interest in this study, and these young teens comprised the second most predominant age group at the adventure playground (32.16%).

This overall description of the users suggests that one might consider the sense of each playground in terms of which age groups are most prevalent. In other words, the presence and predominance of particular age groups undoubtedly has an effect on the behavior and ambiance of a playground. Adults, for instance, are a strong influence —perhaps the strongest influence. They usually create or enforce some set of rules about acceptable and desirable behavior, and children often look to adults for advice on how to do something, for suggestions of what to do, and for approval of their action. . . . The predominance of adults and preschool children at a playground, as at the traditional and contemporary playgrounds, may inhibit or even preclude the use of that playground by some school-age children and young teens. As suggested earlier, these older children are at a stage of development where they seek greater independence and autonomy. The change from mostly parallel play at preschool age to cooperative and competitive peer group interaction of an older age may be facilitated by some freedom from adult supervision. In this regard, the adventure playground offers a different kind of atmosphere from that usually found at playgrounds. Although there were always some adults present, it was primarily a place for school-age children and young teens. Discussion of the interview data demonstrates that the primacy of these older children and the relative easing of close adult supervision were important reasons why the children attended and why some of them regarded this playground as their favorite.

. . .

. . .The complete area and equipment use data for school-age children in all three playgrounds is presented in Table 22-2. In each playground there is an area which emerges as most used by school-age children, accounting for about one third of the total number of observations for that age group. At the traditional playground this primary feature was the swings. There were two sets of large swings with six swings on each set. At the contemporary playground, the sand areas were most used. The

TABLE 22–2. *Children's Use of Areas and Equipment From the Mapping (in percentages)*

Traditional Playground		Contemporary Playground		Adventure Playground	
Large swings	33.8	Sand areas	29.4	Clubhouse areas	33.8
Wading pool	28.5	Mounds and slides	23.3	Open areas	22.2
Bench areas	10.9	Bench areas	19.0	Tire and telephone	
Water fountain/		Sprinkler	10.7	structure	21.1
picnic tables	9.3	Concentric walls	6.8	Garden areas	14.9
Monkey bars	6.0	Monkey bars	6.5	Dirt hill	7.1
Seesaws	4.5	Water fountain	2.5	Water hole and	
Open areas	4.2	Tree house (broken)	1.8	junk pile	0.9
Slides	1.7				
Baby swings	1.1				
Total %	100.0		100.0		100.0

design of this playground is such that there are three sand areas which are central to the low walls, mounds, and climbing structures which make up the topography of the playground. The largest sand area included an arts and crafts table and a water trough. At the adventure playground, the clubhouse areas were the most used. Although the clubhouses in these areas did develop and change over time, the area definitions did not change much, since most of these structures depended on adjacent buildings for one wall of their construction.

From an understanding of the area usage data, one might speculate about some design considerations related to children's preferences and use of playgrounds. For example, one of the slides at the contemporary playground was built on a cobblestone "mountain" which had tunnels running through it. The slides were novel and interesting and were the most popular features of the playground. By contrast, the slides at the traditional playground were smaller, rarely used by school-age children (1.7%), and only slightly more used by preschool children (4.2%). Although the sliding experience at these two playgrounds cannot be strictly compared, the amount of

novelty and variety in the experience may make it more popular at one place than at another.

.   .   .

The differences in the use of sprinklers and wading pools are probably also related to design considerations. The wading pool at the traditional playground was very large, containing four separate sprinklers. It occupied the center of the playground, and, when people sat on the benches, they generally faced the pool. It was a good place for adults to keep an eye on the ongoing activity without being close enough to get wet themselves. At the contemporary playground, there was one sprinkler; it was not a wading pool as the drain could not be clogged and no water could build up, and only a few children could be directly in the sprinkler at one time. For many children, this sprinkler did provide a way to cool off, as well as encouraging some water play. At the adventure playground, there was no one area which served as a sprinkler or wading pool. Water was used in gardening, and a hose was occasionally hooked up to a nearby fire hydrant, allowing children to

TABLE 22–3. Activities of School-Age Children from Settings Records

Traditional Playground			Contemporary Playground			Adventure Playground		
Activity Description	n^a	TT^b	Activity Description	n^a	TT^b	Activity Description	n^a	TT^b
Swinging	44	359	Multiple equipment	44	489	Clubhouse	20	630
Water play	22	169	Water play	19	133	Building	13	162
Monkey bars	15	69	Sitting	15	75	Talking	10	126
Connective	13	93	Dressing	12	57	Passive activity	9	134
Seesawing	11	74	Sand play	11	102	Fixing up house	6	151
Playing	9	73	Arts and crafts	10	150	Multiple equipment	5	43
Enter/leave	8	18	Games	8	111	Watching	5	22
Sitting	7	26	Passive activity	7	71	Enter/leave	5	13
Passive activity	6	32	Watching	6	35	Digging	4	76
Sliding	6	30	Play fight	5	30	Painting	4	41
Multiple equipment	5	32	Eating/drinking	5	28	Resting	4	30
Eating/drinking	5	20	Exploratory	5	25	On tire house	3	41
Play with objects	4	15	Play with objects	4	59	Play with objects	3	18
Arts and crafts	3	123	Playing	3	53	Exploratory	3	13
Games	3	18	Connective	3	39	Gardening	2	62
Dressing	3	8	Pretend play	3	20	Arts and crafts	2	33
Exploratory	3	6	Enter/leave	3	14	Dirt play	2	23
Walking	3	6	Walking	3	8	Waiting	2	20
Talking	2	35	Sliding	2	29	Connective	2	9
Play with leaves	2	17	Baby sitting	2	14	Walking	2	3
Bathroom	2	15	Washing	2	11	Singing	1	50

TABLE 22–3. Activities of School-Age Children from Settings Records (Cont.)

Traditional Playground			Contemporary Playground			Adventure Playground		
Activity Description	n^a	TT^b	Activity Description	n^a	TT^b	Activity Description	n^a	TT^b
Bike riding	2	8	Buying ices	2	4	Eating/drinking	1	25
Watching	2	6	Talking	2	4	Trampoline	1	24
Climb tree	1	20	Sunning	1	27	Arguing	1	21
Baby sitting	1	7	Blow-up ball	1	24	Play fight	1	10
Feeding bird	1	7	Stalking bird	1	22	Climbing	1	7
Fighting	1	2	Acrobatics	1	13	Sitting	1	3
			Make seesaw	1	5	Water play	1	3
			Resting	1	3	Playing	1	2
			Standing	1	3	Play with rocks	1	2
			Break stick	1	1	Raking	1	1
Total minutes		1,288			1,659			1,798

[a] Number of instances observed.   [b] Total time observed for each activity in minutes.

cool off and play with water in the open area in front of the gardens. Evidence from the interview data indicates that the lack of shade trees and water fountain were a source of some complaints by the children.

.   .   .

Activities of Children and Adults

A second general group of questions related to what children did at playgrounds. Of the opportunities available, which were usable and engaged in by school-age children? All the methods employed in this study provided data for some of these questions, although it is primarily the behavior settings' records which are referred to here. These records emphasized the flow of a child's behavior and enabled examination of children's activities for the entire length of their playground stay.

The complete list of activities of school-age children compiled from individual records is presented in Table 22-3. In each playground, a modal activity accounted for at least one-quarter of the grand total of observation time at that playground. These modal activities were swinging at the traditional playground, play on multiple equipment at the contemporary playground, and clubhouse activity at the adventure playground. . . .

Short excerpts from the taped records of typical children are presented in Table 22-4. One excerpt from one child's record is presented for each playground and each is supplemented by the list of activities compiled from the observation of that particular child. The discussion of these excerpts is incorporated into the following discussion of typical activities.

At the traditional playground, activity was easily described according to the use of specific kinds of equipment. For example, descriptions such as swinging, water play, monkey bars, seesawing, sliding, and arts and crafts accurately characterized the kinds of activity that children engaged in. Even though a child swinging may have spoken to or observed others, the essence of these sequences focused on using the swings for distinct periods of time. The excerpt from Adrienne's transcript in Table 22-4 illustrates an unusually long sequence of swinging at the playground. . . . Although swinging was the most frequent activity here, the average duration was only 8.2 minutes.

The activity "multiple equipment" was the most frequently observed activity at the contemporary playground. This category is best explained as a continuous mode of activity which included varied equipment, each being used for a short time. The excerpt in Table 22-4 of a nine-year-old boy illustrates this kind of activity. He played on a slide, the monkey bars and the side of the wooden ("pyramid") structure during this sequence. In general, this type of activity focused on the flow of behavior taking place on the equipment, since the *essence* of the activity was not limited to one piece of equipment for extended periods of time. The close proximity of the features of this playground undoubtedly contributed to the nature of these play sequences. The features that held the longest-lasting appeal seemed to be the combination of big slide, monkey bars, and rope swing, with occasional balancing on tops of walls or quick visits to the sprinkler during these sequences. The average duration of play on multiple equipment at this playground was 11.1 minutes.

At the adventure playground, clubhouse-related activity was a central focus for the school-age children during the period of this resarch. The first phase of this activity involved makeshift building using loose materials to erect some kind of partial structure or enclosure. As illustrated by the excerpt of Jane's transcript in Table 22-4, children were typically intent on their activity and sometimes kept at it for long periods of time. Later, this building activity

Excerpt from traditional playground

The older girl (Adrienne, age 10) is pumping, she's swinging, she's very capable. Both girls are now yelling "I'm going higher." Adrienne just said "I want to do something fun," and she stopped swinging. She's speaking to the grandmother. Now she's off the swing and she's turning it completely around. And Adrienne is saying "This is going to be so much fun, and I'm going to go so high." Now she put the swing on her stomach, and she's just going 'round. And the swing was too low. She's trying to lift her feet but she keeps knocking them on the ground. Adrienne's swinging. She's going back and forth. She said she wants to stay here a while. She's still still going back and forth. She's still just swinging back and forth. Everytime she pumps she says "Oooh, oooh," as if it's a lot of effort.

List of activities:	swinging	15 min.[a]
	monkey bars	6 min.
	sitting	3 min.
	monkey bars	5 min.
Entered with:	grandmother and 8-year-old sister	

Excerpt from contemporary playground

The boy I'm watching is about nine. He came in with a day camp. The day camp had around 20 people in it. He's on the slide. The boy next to him said "Let's slide down together" and they did. They waited until they were both on the thing and they both slid down. Now he's climbing on the monkey bars. He jumped off. He just yelled, "This is fun," and is going back up the pyramid (slide is attached). The other boy went down and he was laughing. He doesn't just sit down. He carefully spreads his hands out. It's like a long process. Now the girl came down and she said, "Let's hold hands." And so the girl and boy are holding hands and a younger boy sat next to them and so the three of them are holding hands and they all slid down and they were all screaming "Aaah."

List of activities:	multiple equipment	9 min.[a]
	pretend play	9 min.
	sprinkler	2 min.
	buying ices	3 min.
	multiple equipment	20 min.
Entered with:	day camp	

Excerpt from adventure playground

(Jane, 10, was actively involved in assembling tires and boards, began building a structure.) It is now 5 minutes til 4, and Jane still hasn't completed her house. She's still looking for some more wood. Now the rain is coming down much heavier than it did before. Jane went back and picked up another tire; she's placing it to make another row for the wall. She's going back to area 8 for another one. Now she picked up a board. The rain is coming down pretty heavily now, but Jane is still continuously building her wall. Now she got a little help from the play leader Matt. Now Matt just left. The rain is coming down much heavier now. The little girl seems not to care about the rain. She's running back to get another piece of wood to make a roof on her house. The time is now 2 minutes til 4 and she is leaving the playground.

| List of activities: | building | 30 min.[a] |
| Entered with: | self | |

[a] Activity from which excerpt was taken.

tapered off as clubhouses became a little more stable; activity inside the clubhouses then became a focus for the children. Thus, the activity "clubhouse" was the modal activity at the adventure playground. This description of activity referred to a combination of talking, listening to music, eating and drinking, arts and crafts, and reading that went on inside the children's clubhouses. Building and clubhouse activity were coded separately; the average duration of building was 12.5 minutes, and the average duration of clubhouse activity was 31.5 minutes. . . .

.   .   .

It is interesting to speculate about the relationship between a child's activities and the environmental settings in which those activities occur. . . . The data from this study indicate that, for the age group studied, the opportunities and constraints of the physical environment may be seen to predict the majority of predominant activities. The traditional and contemporary playgrounds contained prebuilt features such as swings, slides, monkey bars, sprinklers, and seesaws, and these elements were dominant. They were often the reason for attending, according to the interviews, as well as being the focus of activities which children chose to engage in. Furthermore, instances of other kinds of play (fantasy, group games) were infrequently observed. It appeared that the kind of equipment available limited group interaction and promoted parallel and associative activity even when children attempted to go beyond the usual modes of equipment use. For example, adolescents using the swings did not speak to each other intimately—in fact, did not speak to each other at length. Rather, despite the apparent maturity of the children, the activity quickly assumed a side by side or parallel character, in which each participant concentrated on his own activity. . . .

This relationship is not simply an environmental determinism; rather, it is a combination of environmental features, social influences, the freedoms to make use of available opportunities, and other aspects of a setting that ultimately contribute to its atmosphere and to the behavior of its users. Not only did the equipment promote this style, but social factors influenced the use of equipment, operating to keep a child seated, moving straight, and so on. Both children and adults guided others' play by saying "It's against the law to stand up" (on the swings) and "Don't go sideways."

The atmosphere at the adventure playground is also attributable to a combination of the equipment, materials, roles, and interactions of age groups that were present. Consequently, a slightly different perspective emerges. The playground could change and evolve over time according to the children's interests, which contrasted with the sense of permanence at the other two playgrounds. Also, the interviews reveal a different set of reasons as to what attracted the children to this playground. Of the children who named this playground as their favorite, the most frequently cited reason was roughly that the setting allowed the freedom to do what you want. Although these children comprised a self-selected group, there is no reason to believe that they represented an essentially different population with respect to play. They reported that they used other playgrounds, too, but that the other playgrounds were used for specific-function activities, such as swinging, playing handball, using a sprinkler, playing knock-hockey, and so on.

One additional aspect of the atmosphere at each playground concerns the verbal interactions between children. The overwhelming majority of conversational excerpts and topics at the traditional and contemporary playgrounds focused on aspects of equipment use and mutual play activities. This focus on the very immediate environment was prevalent. Very few instances of older children's behavior or conversations were related to their experience in life beyond the playground. At the adventure playground, in contrast, children's conversations did not reflect a narrow focus on the immediate setting. Rather, the conversations dealt with building materials, mothers, dreams, marriage, seasons, fighting, spelling, clothing, house cleaning, and a host of other topics. Perhaps the opportunity for small groups of children to achieve some degree of privacy in their clubhouses led to some of this diversity. However, it is clear that children did bring their everyday life experiences with them into the playground, and this had the effect of supplementing the more conventional playground experience that went on there.

The Children's Choices

An additional set of questions investigated the children's opinions and choices relative to the opportunities, challenges, and freedoms offered to them by playgrounds. The questions of choice involve the people with whom a child attends playgrounds, the locus of the decision to attend and the frequency of attendance, the length of a child's playground stay, activities that children engaged in at other playgrounds, and children's choices of a favorite playground.

The mapping data provided information on the relative proportions of adults, teens, and school-age and preschool children in each setting. Supplementing that, the settings' records included data as to the people with whom each observed child entered each playground. These data, as enumerated in Table 22–5, offer another means of understanding the atmosphere within each playground, as well as the children's choices concerning attendance and behavior at the playgrounds. . . .

. . . The adventure playground was the only setting in which children entered by themselves or with peers (96.7%). These differential patterns of use serve as important indicators of the kinds of social interaction and the extent of adult control that occur in each setting. The traditional and contemporary playgrounds can be seen as places where children's interaction and play are mediated by caretaking adults. It is likely that adults viewed these two playgrounds as desirable places to visit for a number of reasons. In addition to offering a combination of sand, water, and equipment for the child, each place offered some conveniences—e.g., benches, shade, and water fountain, in an esthetic surrounding for adults' comfort and pleasure. Children presumably are also attracted to these environmental cues, by selecting these playgrounds when they are with adults. However, children alone and with peers visit in smaller numbers. . . .

TABLE 22–5. *Distribution of School-Age Children's Companions at Time of Entry, From the Settings Records*

Entered with:	Traditional Playground	Contemporary Playground	Adventure Playground
Caretaker	60.0	40.8	—
Day camp group	20.0	38.8	3.3
Peer or self	17.8	10.2	96.7
Younger child (the school-age child acted as babysitter)	2.2	10.2	—
Total %	100.0	100.0	100.0
Children observed (n)	(45)	(49)	(30)

The pattern of attendance at the adventure playground differs substantially. . . . This setting did not attract adults; it was dusty, dirty, there was no shade, no water, no benches, and perhaps they felt it was unsafe for preschool children. The adventure playground became a place with which children, including young teens, could identify; a place to be with, play with, and interact primarily with peers.

.   .   .

Each child was also asked how frequently he or she attended the playground they had just visited. . . . It is clear that neighborhood children came to these playgrounds more often than nonneighborhood children, and this frequency of attendance was directly related to the locus of the decision to attend. That is, children who lived in the general neighborhood reported that they had made the decision to come to the playground and also reported that they came frequently. This general conclusion was supported by the data at all three playgrounds. These data indicate that most of the children interviewed at the traditional and contemporary playgrounds attended infrequently (50% of the children at each of these playgrounds came once every week or less frequently than that). At the adventure playground, all children interviewed reported attendance at least as frequently as twice a week.

These differences in frequency of attendance apparently paralleled the differences in the length of a child's playground stay as compiled from the settings' records. The data indicating length of stay are presented in Table 22–6. Medians were chosen as the best measure of central tendency. The lengths of time that children stayed at a playground were ranked in a single series, and a Kruskal-Wallis one-way analysis of variance by ranks was conducted using the three independent samples. The differences between the lengths of stay at the three playgrounds were significant at the .001 level. Children stayed the shortest lengths of time at the traditional playground, the next longest at the contemporary playground, and the longest at the adventure playground.

In addition to the quantitative data about a child's frequency of attendance and the length of stay, we pursued the question of a child's preference for particular playgrounds or for the experience available at particular playgrounds. Of the 91 children interviewed, 87 reported visiting at least one other playground frequently; their activities at those other places indicated that similar playground experiences were available to many of these children. Children were asked if they had a favorite playground, considering all the playgrounds they knew and, if so, which playground it was. The responses to this question are presented in Table 22–7. Of the fifteen children at the traditional playground who had a favorite, four reported that particular playground as their favorite. When asked why, children reported that it was quiet, not crowded, and it had "things to do that I like." The remaining eleven preferred playgrounds with more things to play on, different equipment, or places where their friends were. Of the twenty-two children at the contemporary playground who had a favorite, sixteen reported that playground as their favorite. They liked it because it had lots of equipment, many things to do, and because "it's fun." Twenty-seven children at the adventure playground listed it as their favorite. Their reasons included: you can do what you want, you can have your own club, it's a good place to meet friends, and you can have fun here. Three others chose favorites according to specific features, such as a large field, a tennis court, and a swimming pool.

Considering these choices made and the preferences expressed by children at these playgrounds, there is a consistent relationship between preferences for particular playgrounds and the measures used as indicators of children's interest or pref-

TABLE 22–6. *Length of Playground Stay for School-Age Children From the Settings Records*

	Traditional Playground	Contemporary Playground	Adventure Playground
0–40 min.	35	32	8
41–80 min.	7	15	8
81–120 min.	2	2	8
121–160 min.	—	—	4
161–200 min.	1	—	—
201–240 min.	—	—	—
241–280 min.	—	—	2
Number of children	45	49	30
Median length of stay (min.)	21	32	75

H = 26.7   p < .001

TABLE 22–7. *Children's Reports of Favorite Playground From the Interviews*

	Traditional Playground	Contemporary Playground	Adventure Playground
Children interviewed (n)	(26)	(29)	(36)
Who had a favorite (%)	57.7	75.9	83.3
Who preferred the one they were using (%)	15.4	55.2	75.0

erence. Specifically, the settings' records indicate that children attend the traditional playground for only short periods of time; the interview data indicate that many children did not make the decision to be there, that the majority of the children who were there did not go there frequently, and that few children considered it their favorite playground. With slight variations, the data compiled at the contemporary playground show similar relationships, except that a greater proportion of children named this playground as their favorite. The settings' records indicate the longest length of stay at the adventure playground, while the interviews indicate that most children made the decision to be there, came almost every day, and named this playground as their favorite one.

Implications for Research and Planning

The data that have been presented combine to illustrate the nature of children's play at playgrounds and the play/environment relationship at these different playgrounds. The multimethod approach of this study was very useful in exploring these key questions since the data permitted examination of relationships from a number of viewpoints: children's activities over time, the overall activity profile of each playground, and self-reported preferences. For example, observations of behavior were supplemented by children's comments about their play experiences; the participation or intervention of adults was noted while focusing on a child's play sequences, and this was supplemented by data about the overt behavior of adults from the mapping. The multimethod approach was also useful in exploring differences and similarities across playgrounds. For example, strong indications emerged from each method supporting the modal activities in each playground. Most significantly, these methods allowed data to be collected in response to several different questions—questions about children's play, age group interaction, roles of participants within the physical context of the three playgrounds, as well as questions about the use of other playgrounds.

This study also raises questions which should be pursued beyond the available data. For example, the interactions between children's choices of activity and the constraints of particular settings is a fertile area for further study. An investigation is warranted regarding the role of playgrounds in the larger milieu of a child's life, at least as seen against the context of other, less formal places to play. Also, further study of qualities of behavior could contribute to a better understanding of the developmental significance of certain kinds of activity, especially as those qualities become more closely related to children's own expressions of desirable places and desirable opportunities.

Other aspects of the play/environment relationship should also be investigated. We have seen how the two prebuilt playgrounds provided for swinging, climbing, sliding, running, and other easily describable physical activities. However, those behaviors by themselves do not necessarily constitute play for school-age children. Many of the definitions of "play" suggest some freedom to explore, to act out life situations, and to invest oneself in the play experience, thus exploring one's own identity and one's relationship to the rest of the world. Yet these opportunities and freedoms may never be facilitated in playgrounds which are planned for physical activity only. It may also be a logical contradiction to expect an investing of self in a setting which is defined by immutable play equipment, which is designed and built by other people for

separate sequences of children's behavior.

Further, one should question whether a successful playground is one which attracts large numbers of people. Perhaps *heavy use* of a playground (many groups, large numbers of children) is counter to the needs of school-age children. The chance to see and recognize the same faces, make friends, and see some stability in neighborhood places is important, and speaks more for smaller, more intimate places than for well-used public facilities.

Children had fun and enjoyed themselves at each playground. They also devised challenges for themselves, whether that meant standing on a swing, doing somersaults on a slide, or planning and executing a clubhouse. However, the data lead one to speculate that older children might have found less challenge in the prebuilt playgrounds than did preschool children. Also, challenge per se is not always essential to children's choices of activity; they may spend a short time on a swing or slide relaxing or reliving previous play experiences. In general, though, children of this age group seek different levels of independence and challenge, and they seek more peer group interaction. It is important for these children to assess for themselves what they want as they seek to expand their horizons and interests. Perhaps it is the freedom, openness, and choice regarding their play and play settings which are crucial. If so, the atmosphere and opportunities at the traditional and contemporary playgrounds succeed only moderately well in offering older children the experiences they seek.

The frequent, lengthy, and self-chosen attendance by older children at the adventure playground may be attributable to the very lack of built equipment at the start of the summer, as this may have provided a sense of ambiguity, an openness in terms of any eventual activity. Bettelheim (1950), discussing his residential center, touches on this sense of children in the latency period wanting a between-activity space. He states that the more deterministic or functional the separate rooms became, the more the children used hallways and stairwells. He also considers the use of these spaces a means to find spaces other than those defined by infant or adult uses.

The ambiguity of the adventure playground offered the children a potential setting in which to define self as well as space. The playground was not totally open, yet it offered a selection of loose parts (e.g., tires, wood, tools, paint, plants, seeds, and the like) which supplied part of the potential for children to define their own activities (Nicholson, 1970). Thus, an important difference in the meaning of the environment to the users was that the built playgrounds were planned by others, they were permanent, and the potential for original combination was minimal; at the adventure playground, the form was created by the users and was only as permanent as they chose it to be. The fact that these activities took place on a vacant lot leased from the city had other consequences. After two years of life as a playground, construction eventually started, and the lot is now the site of a high-rise apartment building.

One particular interaction that emerges as being important focuses on the relationship between age groups. It was apparent that some freedom from adults was valued at the adventure playground. Also valued was the opportunity to establish smaller, more intimate groups of peers, as in clubhouses. If a playground focuses on providing challenges to young children (e.g., swings as at the traditional playground), then the opportunities desired by older children may very well be excluded. Segrated *use* may also occur naturally, as

at the adventure playground, where the place seemed to belong to school-age children and to young teens alternately, not simultaneously.

Each of the three playgrounds had predominant activities and patterns of use. The fact that different play settings develop into places where different activities take place is probably important to a child, as evidenced by the diversity of playground use reported. Certainly, in a city, a diversity of opportunity must be considered, including places with sand and water where children can go with day camp groups, and places where children can go with their parents. However, there should also be places which can fulfill the richer, more ongoing needs of children in this age group. School-age children are interested in more than mere physical activity, and opportunities for choice of play equipment, materials, and companions are crucial for their activity. Some freedom from adults, peer group interaction with more intimate groups of peers, opportunities for self-devised challenges, and a sense of ambiguity to allow the development of a vested interest in a neighborhood place are other qualities which should be considered in planning playgrounds for school-age children.

As the availability of open space in our urban areas decreases, it may be that the diversity of opportunity is as important as preference for specific activities. If so, the current availability of prebuilt playgrounds should prompt consideration of settings which can offer appropriately challenging and interesting activities for school-age children. The adventure playground examined by this study appears to be one such setting which can offer important opportunities for this age group.

23. Black Youths View Their Environment
FLORENCE C. LADD

How do people characterize urban neighborhoods? What do neighborhoods comprise in the poorer quarters of American cities? When they are depicted, which features are emphasized, and which ones obscured? How do adolescents regard their neighborhoods? These are a few of the initial questions which stimulated our inquiry into the character and quality of neighborhoods as represented by sixty urban adolescent black boys.

Aims of the Research

The major aims of this study are: (1) to develop an understanding of areas subjectively defined as neighborhoods by urban adolescent black boys through their graphic representations of their neighborhoods; (2) to discover the socially and psychologically significant aspects of the "contents" of their neighborhoods as reflected in their maps; and (3) to explore the potential informational value of map drawings to social scientists and planners who need varieties of data on the significance of urban living to persons of different age, ethnic, and socioeconomic groups.

While other techniques (for example, eliciting verbal descriptions of neighborhoods) were used in the research, this report is concerned with the neighborhood

Reprinted from *Environment and Behavior*, Vol. 2, No. 1 (June 1970), pp. 74–99, by permission of the Publisher, Sage Publications, Inc., and the author.
AUTHOR'S NOTE: The youths were subjects of the project "Pathways to Identity." The interview schedule, "Neighborhood, House and Travel," upon which this report is based, was one of several interviews used. I am indebted to Ulle Lewes for her assistance. "Pathways to Identity" was sponsored by the U.S. Office of Education, Contract OEG-0-8-000085-1810-010.

maps that subjects drew. There is evidence (Lynch, 1960) which suggests that the content of an individual's *graphic* and *verbal* descriptions of the same area differ. No doubt, each descriptive mode supplements the other. Since freehand maps or sketch maps are considerably more difficult to interpret from a social psychological viewpoint than are the contents of verbal descriptions of neighborhoods, it seems important to examine the maps first. Analyzing the maps prior to the analysis of verbal descriptions of neighborhoods reduces the likelihood of having interpretations of the map data influenced by our knowledge of subjects' verbal descriptions.

Overview of Relevant Research

Prominent among the antecedents of the present study is the seminal research of Lynch (1960) who introduced concepts and techniques for eliciting, organizing, and analyzing the elements of city images held by samples of adults in three urban areas (Boston, Jersey City, and Los Angeles). Subsequent studies of urban images, using modifications of Lynch's approach include the works of de Jonge (1962), Gulick (1963), Appleyard et al. (1964), Hassan (1965), Steinitz (1968), Carr and Schissler (1969) and Southworth (forthcoming). These studies are primarily concerned with defining shared images or "public images" of relatively large sections of cities and roadways.

Closer to the scope and concept of the present study is the research of the English psychologist Lee (1963–1964) who has reported findings on urban dwellers' delineations of their neighborhoods on an Ordnance Survey map and on sketch maps. First of all, Lee (1963–1964: 16) states that "except for the few upper-middle-class professional people who turn up in a random sample, neighbourhood was a really salient experience; not a vague, shifting one, but something that could be quickly and easily acknowledged, and fairly readily described." The neighborhoods of Lee's subjects showed considerable individual variation. For example, when the outlines of neighborhoods of eight persons living within one hundred yards of each other were superimposed, they showed almost *no* coincidence. Lee's comparison of measurements of the area of neighborhoods revealed that the average area in middle-class suburb and high density slum was "much the same," suggesting that "people do not delineate their neighbourhoods in terms of the population they contain, as planners do, or in terms of the number of houses—but only as space" (Lee, 1963–1964: 17).

Lee (1963–1964: 19) also found that three forms of behavior are associated with more "spatially extensive" neighborhoods: "These were the number of friends a subject had locally, the number of clubs and organizations to which she belonged locally, and her tendency to use local shops rather than town centre or nonlocal ones." According to Lee (1963–1964: 19).

This could be regarded as no more than a confirmation that the neighbourhood is a valid form of measurement, reflecting real differences in behaviour. But there was also a more ambitious hypothesis— that the intensity of these kinds of behaviour, which might be loosely grouped under the heading of "local involvement" or "community participation," are related to the *pattern* of the physical neighbourhood.

This formulation led Lee to create a measure called the *Neighbourhood Quotient*, the area an individual specified as his neighborhood as a ratio of an area of half a mile radius, surrounding his home. He reports fairly clear relationships between the *Neighbourhood Quotient* and social class,

length of residence, and subject's age.

Although our research was undertaken without knowledge of Lee's procedures and results, there are some similarities between them. More important, however, are the suggestions and questions raised by both studies which should provoke more precise research in the near future.

The appealing article by Tilly (1967) should be mentioned. Maps of Toronto sketched by three Tilly children serve to illustrate the necessity of conducting a developmental study of sketch maps to increase (A) our understanding of the cognitive processes involved in the development and representation of environmental spatial relations, and (B) the importance of comparing sketch maps of persons who share the same residence (apartment building or house). Finally, my (Shelton, 1967) research note, based on the maps of three adolescent boys living in the same Boston housing project, provides another example of the variations in the size and content of the neighborhoods of persons who share approximately the same physical space but whose psychological spaces obviously differ. While this phenomenon was not explored in the present study, two examples are included.

Subjects of the Study

The subjects of the study are sixty adolescent black boys from low-income backgrounds. The boys, who ranged in age from twelve to seventeen years, were attending P. T. Campbell Junior High School in Boston's Roxbury-North Dorchester when the study began (winter–spring 1967). Selected on the basis of socioeconomic indices from a larger (n = 98) group of black boys attending the same school, the subjects of this study represent the segment of that group with the *lowest* socioeconomic status in terms of (1) a specifiable criterion (e.g., family income below the federally defined poverty level of $4000 per annum) and (2) impressionistic reports of interviewers acquainted with signs of socioeconomic status among the population from which the subjects were selected.

Residential Setting

With the exception of five boys, the focal subjects live with their families in Boston's Roxbury-North Dorchester quarter within one-mile radius of the school they attended. The five subjects who do not live in the vicinity of the school come and go via public transportation, while the remainder of the subjects walk to and from school.

The area is largely residential. Much of the housing is old—built between 1890 and 1910. There are many detached frame duplexes; some single frame houses are occupied by a single family or have been "apartmentalized," accommodating several families. There are a few brick apartment buildings no more than three or four stories tall.

The condition of the housing varies considerably. Within a single block, there may be two or three attractive, well-maintained, recently painted houses and two or three extremely dilapidated houses with the condition of the other houses on the block ranging between these two extremes. There are frequent signs of urban renewal efforts —vacant buildings in various stages of demolition and deterioration await renewal and new tenants.

Throughout the area are several vacant lots littered with broken glass, rubbish, remnants of abandoned cars, and discarded household furnishings. These lots frequently serve as playgrounds for young children and improvised basketball courts for teenage boys.

The major commercial street in the area is a six-block section of Blue Hill Avenue, containing variety stores, repair shops, several store-front service organizations, restaurants, beauty parlors, barber shops, a pool room, a church, a drug store, a bar, a meat market, a grocery store, real estate offices, law firms, and so forth. Since the "rebellion" of June 2, 1967, the majority of the businesses remaining in the area are black-owned.

In 1964, 65% of the 70,000 residents of Roxbury-North Dorchester were "nonwhite" (that is, black). It is estimated that the area is 75 to 80% black. Many of the remaining whites are elderly; the number of white children enrolled in public schools in the area is negligible (that is, approximately 2%).

Procedure

The data used in this study are derived from the subjects' responses to the questions in an interview schedule called "Neighborhood, House and Travel." It was the last in a series of four or five interviews held with each subject. Interviews were tape recorded in individual sessions. There were no time restrictions on the performance of any of the tasks. These interviews were conducted by three black males trained to interview the subjects.

In the "Neighborhood, House and Travel" interview, subjects first were asked *to describe verbally their neighborhoods.* While a few subjects had difficulty with the language of the initial question, the concept "neighborhood" was immediately understood. Then each subject was given a sheet of white illustration cardboard (fourteen inches by twenty-two inches) on which he was asked *to draw a map of his neighborhood* with a black felt-tipped pen. He was instructed to indicate the location of his residence with an "X." There were no restrictions on making corrections. Approximately fifteen subjects crossed out lines or labels and then resketched them. Two subjects requested an additional sheet of cardboard each on which they extended their maps.

When the subject had completed the drawing, the interviewer proceeded to ask about his awareness of selected areas of the city, his housing and travels. Responses to the remainder of the interview will not be reported in this paper. This report is based on analyses and discussion of the neighborhood maps drawn by the subjects.

Data Analysis

One useful technique for organizing the data involved the development of *descriptive categories which would take into account form and content elements as criteria in the drawings.* Free sortings suggested several possible criteria. Finally, however, four categories or groups were decided upon. The groups are presented here with the descriptions used by the judges:

Group I
(n = 9)
: *Drawing is pictorial.* The subject represents houses, other buildings, and elements which might be part of a street scene. (Example given in Figure 21–1.)

Group 11
(n = 13)
: *Drawing is schematic.* It contains lines or areas which are not clearly connected to each other. It is poorly organized. (Example given in Figure 23–2.)

Group III
(n = 12)
: *Drawing resembles a map.* It seems well organized, that is, the connections between areas are clear. It could be used for orientation to the area. (Example given in Figure 23–3.)

Group IV
(n = 9)
: *Drawing resembles a map with other identifiable landmarks which would make the area recognizable.* Connections between areas are clear. Could be

used for orientation to the area. (Example given in Figure 23–4.)

Maps included in Group I are entirely pictorial. In these maps subjects have represented houses, other buildings, and objects such as lamp posts, trash barrels, mailboxes, trees, and so on in their neighborhoods as if they had been asked to draw a street scene. Typically, the subjects' residences were centrally situated on their maps. The drawings represent a single street or only part of a street.

While some of the maps in Groups II, 111 and IV also included a few pictorial features, there were other major distinguishing characteristics which set them apart. For example, Group II maps seemed "schematic" because there is little or no regard for the consistent use of a specifiable angle of orientation; scale and angle relationships may also have been disregarded. Maps in Group III resemble conventional street maps. Angles and continuity of streets correspond to the physical pattern. In addition to their correspondence to the physical plan of an area, Group IV maps include landmarks which give them the quality of some tourist maps; presumably, the landmarks in these maps have personal significances for the subjects.

Other aspects of maps which were assessed are:

(1) estimate of area of neighborhoods represented,
(2) number of streets included,
(3) number of landmarks,
(4) map organization,
(5) identification and position of subjects' residences, and
(6) accuracy of maps.

The various dimensions of the drawings which we have selected for analysis are considered in relation to subjects' ages, grade levels, and length of residence in a neighborhood.

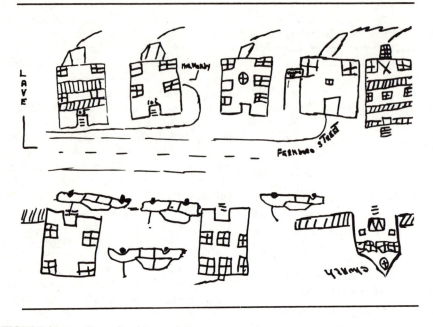

FIGURE 23–1.   Example of Group I Map.

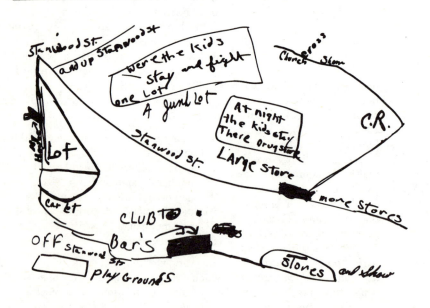

FIGURE 23–2.   Example of Group II Map.

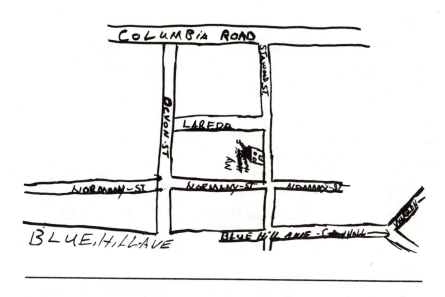

FIGURE 23–3.   Example of Group III Map.

Results and Discussion

Five judges, none of whom had had contact with the subjects or their neighborhoods, were asked to assign each of the maps to one of the four groups described above. Agreement among at least four of the judges was the criterion for inclusion in a category. There was agreement among at least four of the judges on forty-three (seven-two percent) of the sixty maps. Judgments of the remaining seventeen maps were divided among Groups II through IV.

What do these groupings reveal and how are they useful? Initially it seemed logical to separate those drawings that are predominantly pictorial from those that are schematic or resemble conventional maps. Three groups (Groups II, III, and IV) were formed to accommodate the latter set of drawings. This categorization implies neither that the subjects whose drawings are pictorial (Group I) do not apprehend the complexities of their neighborhoods nor that Group IV subjects apprehend their neighborhoods with all their details and complexities. We cannot infer that the subjects apprehend differently, only that their representations differ. This arrangement allows us simply to regard separately the products that resemble conventional maps and those that are pictorial.

That nine subjects drew pictures rather than more schematic, diagrammatic, or map-like configurations may reveal their levels of understanding of the task, their inexperience with maps, and/or their individual abilities to conceptualize and represent space and spatial arrangements. There is nothing to suggest that the nine subjects differed from the rest of the sample with regard to their previous experience with maps since all the subjects are from similar socioeconomic backgrounds and have attended schools that are similar in educa-

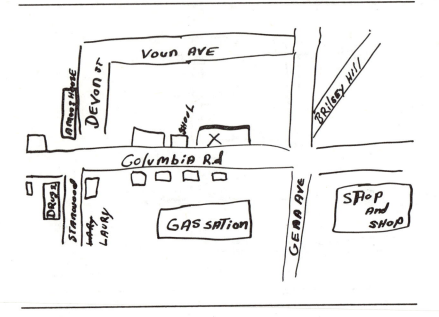

FIGURE 23–4.   Example of Group IV Map

tional quality. It seems probable, however, that their understanding of the task, and ability to conceptualize and represent spatial relations influenced their productions. In future studies we should attempt to estimate the influence of cognitive factors on the performance of mapping tasks.

It appears that age is unrelated to map groups. The Φ coefficient, .33, is not significant. Similarly, it was found that the relationships between subjects' grade level (7th or 9th grade) and the map groupings is not significant, ($\Phi = .16$). While there is no consistent relationship between length of time at a residence and map groups, ($\Phi = .27$) there are some indications of the influence of a recent move in individual maps. For example, in one case the subject appears to have attempted a synthesis of his old and new neighborhoods (Figure 23–5). In certain respects his map cor-

responds to the physical reality of the place; however, sections of his former neighborhood are inappropriately close to his present neighborhood. In reality they are separated by a distance of approximately 1.5 miles.

In another case, a subject who has lived for more than nine years at the same address rendered a sparsely marked, relatively undifferentiated map of his neighborhood; still another subject who moved three months prior to the mapping task drew a rather detailed differentiated map. It should be pointed out that residential choices for the subjects' families usually are restricted to the Roxbury-North Dorchester section. For a subject who had moved within the year, it is likely that his "new" neighborhood is one with which he was acquainted prior to the move. It may be near the neighborhood where he

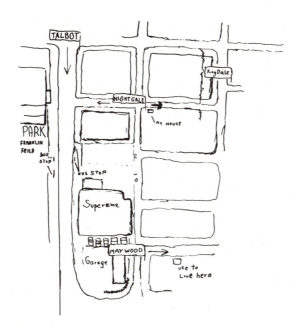

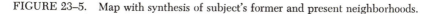

FIGURE 23–5.   Map with synthesis of subject's former and present neighborhoods.

was acquainted prior to the move. It may be near the neighborhood where he previously lived. This factor may obscure the influence of length of time at a residence on the contents of sketch maps of some neighborhoods.

Area of Neighborhoods

Because of the irregularities and distortions in the boundaries of the maps of several subjects, it is difficult to make comparisons with the corresponding area on base maps of Boston in order to estimate areas. Nonetheless, such comparisons were attempted. Our estimates range from approximately .008 square miles (a neighborhood of 1 block or less) to .750 square miles. To be sure, the map (Figure 23–6) of an area of approximately .750 square

miles is unusual in size. The map of this subject's neighborhood, extending far beyond the public housing project in which he lives, should be compared with the map (Figure 23–7) of another subject residing in the same housing project. While both subjects have a trip of the same distance between home and school, the subject who drew the larger map independently spends some of his time exploring various sections of Boston which may largely account for the atypical size of his neighborhood.

There is no clear relationship between neighborhood size and any of the factors we thought might influence it (e.g., length of time at a residence, distance between subject's residence and school). Perhaps other factors which were not considered in this aspect of the study, such as the range of sites of subjects' activities, might be related.

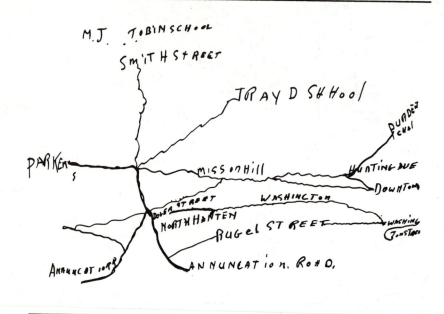

FIGURE 23–6.   Neighborhood map of subject residing in Mission Hill Housing Project.

TABLE 23–1.   *Subjects' Ages and Map Groups*

	Subjects' Ages		
	12-13 Years	*14 Years*	*15-16 Years[a]*
Group I	5	1	3
Group II	5	2	6
Group III	4	4	4
Group IV	2	4	3

[a] The single seventeen year old subject is not represented here; interjudge agreement on the most suitable group for his map was low.

TABLE 23–2.   *School Grade Level of Subjects and Map Groups*

	School Grade Level	
	7th Grade	*9th Grade*
Group I	7	2
Group II	9	4
Group III	7	5
Group IV	5	4

Number of Streets

With regard to number of streets represented, the variation ranges from part of a street to approximately twenty-five streets. A street might be represented by a single line, a set of parallel lines, or, in the pictorial maps, by depicting the set of buildings on one or both sides of the streets. Subjects identified most of the streets included in their maps, that is, street names are often printed along the lines representing the streets, or are indicated on the street signposts drawn by some subjects. Street names are often misspelled; usually a phonetic spelling is used. By inspection, there appears to be a slight relationship between correctly spelled street names and inaccurate street relations. The extent of this relationship will be determined precisely and reported in a future paper.

The subject whose map includes 25 or more streets named 24 of them (Figure 23–8). His planning the construction of the

TABLE 23–3.   *Length of Residence at Current Address and Map Group*

	Length of Residence	
	3 Years or Less	*4 Years or More*
Group I	4	5
Group II	10	3
Group III	6	6
Group IV	6	3

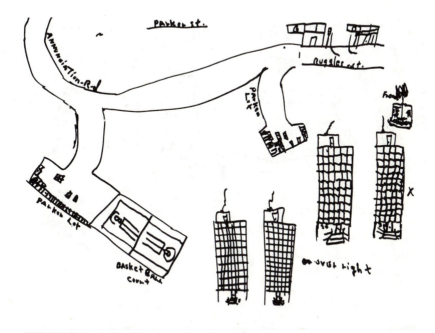

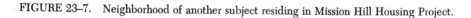

FIGURE 23–7.   Neighborhood of another subject residing in Mission Hill Housing Project.

map so as to be able to include many streets and his recall of street names is remarkable. His sketch map provokes question about his knowledge of other features in his environment and, more generally, about the cognitive abilities of the boy. It also raises questions about the stimulus value of the environment. Answers to these questions depend on knowledge of subjects' experiences, cognitive abilities, and other comparable data on subjects who have in common the same physical environment.

Landmarks

Several maps include landmarks, that is, identifying features which serve to distinguish one part of a subject's map from another. They also suggest the relative positions of places included in the map. Counted as landmarks are commercial buildings, churches, schools, railroad tracks, parks, playgrounds, vacant lots, and so on, represented pictorially and/or with labels. Houses and street names are not considered landmarks. According to Lynch (1960), the use of landmarks involves the singling out of one element from a host of possibilities. It involves the selection of some aspects that are "unique or memorable" in a particular context. What we have designated as landmarks in the maps of several subjects are what may be local "points of reference." Our interpretation of certain features as landmarks may be a spurious procedure; they may not have the value of landmarks for the subjects. Indeed, subjects should have been asked to include on their maps features they regard as landmarks.

There are, of course, a few subjects whose maps do not include landmarks. More often landmarks, however, are given; as many as seventeen were found on one subject's map. Generally speaking, ninth grade subjects' maps contain fewer land-

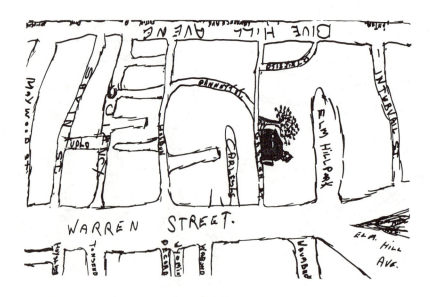

FIGURE 23–8.   Neighborhood map including 25 or more streets.

marks than do those of seventh graders. With regard to groups, the maps in Group IV, in part by definition, have more landmarks than those in other groups.

Organization

Organization in the maps refers to the overall relationships among the central features in each map and other elements in the map. In the pictorial (Group I) drawings, typically a single street is the primary organizing feature. In the other maps, organizing features are streets on which subjects live, commercial streets, and major intersections. Organization implies a framework or set of boundaries within which the area represented lies. Approximately half of the maps have definable boundaries. "Edges," the term used by Lynch (1960) may be more descriptively informative than the use of the term "boundaries." Most of our subjects' maps can be regarded as having edges although a few maps, of course, filled the sheet of cardboard, ending at points determined by the size of the cardboard rather than by the sense of a boundary or barrier. Nonetheless, edges or boundaries, as Lynch pointed out, are "for many people important organizing features, particularly in the role of holding together generalized areas." Our data offers additional support for this argument.

Identification and Position of Subjects' Residences

Recall that subjects were asked to indicate where they live on their neighborhood maps by marking an "X" at the site. Six subjects failed to indicate residential sites. (It is possible that interviewers failed to ask them to show where they live.) Twenty-three of the sixty subjects wrote "my house" (one wrote "my pad"; another wrote "I live here") to indicate the location; some of the subjects marked the location with an "X" as well. The residences of those who wrote "my house" are equally as often in the central portion of their drawings as they are on the periphery. In this regard they do not differ from those subjects who simply marked the sites with "X." We must examine the data more carefully in order to determine the significance of "my house" as an identifying label. It may be simply an expression of territoriality or it may bear some relationship to other aspects of personal identity.

Accuracy

Accuracy in this context refers both to labels and to the direction, elaboration, and condensation of streets and sites on the subjects' maps in comparison to their representation on a base map of Boston. Since we are primarily concerned with subjects' perceptions of their neighborhoods, accuracy is a dimension of minor interest here. By definition, Group III and IV maps are more "accurate" than are Group I and II maps. The meaning of the distortions, elaborations, and condensations in Group I and II maps should be examined in relation to intelligence, perceptual skills, and cognitive style. It has been suggested that the "inaccuracies" may have diagnostic significance.

Cases and Comparisons

It should be noted that although most of the subjects reside in the same section of Boston's Roxbury-North Dorchester area, variations in the physical aspects of their different environments render most of the drawings incomparable. Fortunately, however, there are a few sets of subjects who share the same physical environment. The maps of two brothers are presented for comparison (Figures 23–9 and 23–10).

Anthony, age twelve and his fifteen-year-old brother Jerome, have lived on Normandy Street with the rest of their family for almost four years. Both of their drawings were judged pictorial, that is, in Group I. Anthony's map (Figure 23–9) includes seven houses on one street. "My house" indicates his residence. Jerome's neighborhood map Figure (23–10) includes two streets but only four houses. An "X" marks his house. Only the signposts with the street name "Normandy" tell us that the subjects have approximately the same physical areas as a referent. Sizes, contours, and the arrangement of buildings show little or no similarity. Since they are pictures rather than maps and since accuracy was not suggested in our instructions, it is not surprising that there is little to compare in these maps.

The maps of two other subjects who live on the same street, Stanwood Street, provide more data for comparison. Twelve year old Reggie, and Garson, age 16, live several houses apart on the same side of the street. Reggie's map (Figure 23–11) includes Stanwood Terrace which does not appear on Garson's map (Figure 23–12) while the latter's map shows Blue Hill Avenue, not included in Reggie's map. Garson lives closer to Blue Hill Avenue than Reggie. Both subjects have included Devon and Normandy Streets. A base map (Figure 23–13) of the area is given for comparison. Although there is some overlap in the subjects' neighborhoods, neither lists the other among his friends. Their age difference, of course, may preclude the possibility of their friendship or acquaintance. Further comparisons of their descriptions of their neighborhoods are planned.

Summation

The results of this research are necessarily rudimentary and inconclusive; they do,

FIGURE 23–9.   Anthony's Map.

FIGURE 23–10.   Jerome's Map.

however, suggest some salient dimensions of neighborhoods as they are perceived and represented graphically.

First of all, there is a considerable degree of variety in the neighborhood maps of the Boston youths in this study. The variety reflects, in part, physical differences in the neighborhoods. Variations in the complexity, organization, and content of the maps also reflect individual differences among subjects. We need more information on subjects' cognitive syles, intellectual abilities, and neighborhood activities in order to develop better understanding of map features and variations.

Although the maps suggest the variety of streets and residences of neighborhoods, there is little or nothing which conveys their social and psychological significance. We may assume that some houses are represented because they are the residences of friends. We may infer that certain boundaries, such as streets with heavy traffic and railroad tracks, are psychological as well as physical boundaries. Only through interviews with subjects, however, can we begin to understand the personal meaning of boundaries, landmarks, and other features which are included or omitted. The social significances and functions of places can be ascertained best through interviews in which subjects discuss the maps they have drawn, or through a map drawing procedure more complex than we employed in this study. To develop a better understanding of the significance of neighborhoods, other data are needed to supplement the neighborhood maps.

With regard to their informational value to social scientists and urban planners, the maps suggest the area and structure of neighborhoods and their salient

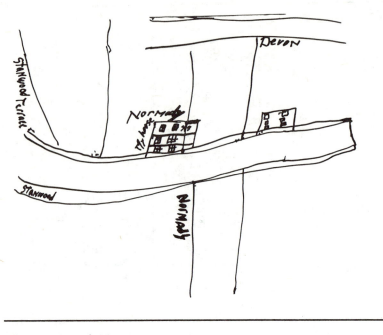

FIGURE 23–11.   Reggie's Map.

features as viewed by one group of urban adolescent youths. If we assume that the organization and complexity of maps to some extent reflect an individual's sense of coherence and complexity of his neighborhood, then planners and designers should study such maps and the neighborhoods they represent. Studies of this type may begin to suggest the features of urban neighborhoods that contribute to their social and psychological value to residents. Included in our data to be reported in a later paper are subjects' verbal descriptions of their neighborhoods. Comparisons of the verbal descriptions with aspects of their maps should reveal relationships between the significance and evaluation of neighborhood features and their graphic representation, a relationship of interest to social scientists as well as planners and designers.

Researchers interested in cognitive development may find in the maps included in this study and the maps of Southworth's (forthcoming) subjects (N equals twenty-eight, ages ten through twelve) evidence of the influence of age on graphic representations of space. Piaget and Inhelder (1967) have reported the developmental stages associated with levels of performance of a task in which they required their young subjects to draw objects (such as a church, houses, trees) included in a model. In an early stage (from four to six to seven years on the average) "the child picks out pieces which do correspond to those in the model and tries to locate them in similar positions. Nevertheless, he fails to locate a single position according to a system of reference, because he cannot "multiply" the relationships of distance and order along the three dimensions" (Piaget and Inhelder, 1967: 428). Not until a later stage, according to Piaget and Inhelder "is the concept of diagrammatic layout acquired in a broad and general way." While

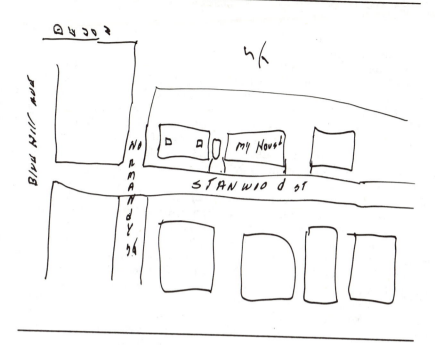

FIGURE 23–12. Garson's Map.

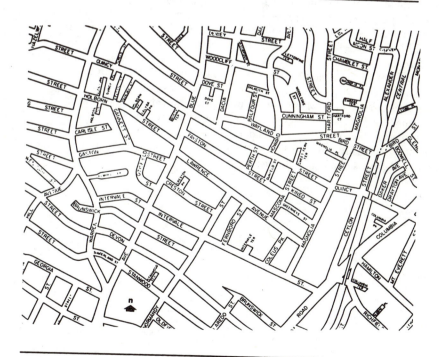

FIGURE 23–13. Base Map of Area Represented in Neighborhood Maps of Reggie and Garson

models, used in their demonstrations lack the complexity, mutability, and variability of an actual urban setting, Piaget and Inhelder (1967) offer a technique which could be used in conjunction with mapping neighborhoods and other districts. Studies with subjects of several age groups contribute further to our understanding of the development of the processes and skills involved in the representation of architectural and other objects in space.

Not only do we need more information about the ways in which children and adolescents perceive, organize, and represent urban areas, we should begin to examine the process of the development of psychological and social associations with neighborhoods and other places. Steinitz (1968) asserts that it is during the teenage years that the characteristics of meaningful places are "learned" by a native resident. The nature and stages of the "environmental learning" process and factors which influence the process should be studied.

The influence of residence in a neighborhood on perception and representation of that neighborhood should be analyzed systematically. While the relationship between residence time and organization and complexity of maps was negligible overall in this study, there are individual cases which suggest that length of residence influences the neighborhood perceptions of certain subjects. The influence of residential mobility specifically and, more generally, physical mobility should be studied for their effect on the content and quality of maps.

Except for street names in predominantly black residential areas, there is little or nothing in the maps of our subjects which seems related to race. Indeed, the maps drawn by Southworth's (forthcoming) young white subjects from Cambridge, Massachusetts bear a considerable number of similarities to the maps of our subjects. This suggests that the dominant culture, standard methods of teaching geography, and perhaps the physical similarities in the Boston-Cambridge area, contribute to the early formulation of map-making conventions even among young people. The phenomenon of the development of map-making conventions should be studied.

This report deals descriptively with only a few aspects of the drawing of neighborhood maps. In subsequent analyses of data on the same sample, we intend to explore, for example, relationships between types of neighborhood maps and verbal descriptions of neighborhoods, the influence of neighborhood use on map contents, and so forth. As Lynch (1960) has suggested, comparative studies of this kind with a wide range of environments and samples of subjects of various ethnic and social class backgrounds should be undertaken to contribute to our understanding of the interaction between individuals and their environments and their descriptions, graphic and verbal, of places they experience.

24. Toward an Ecological Theory of Adaptation and Aging
L. NAHEMOW AND P. LAWTON

The environmental docility hypothesis suggests that environmental stimuli ("press", in Murray's terms) have a greater demand quality as the competence of the individual decreases. The dynamics of ecological transactions are considered as a function of personal competence, strength of environmental press, the dual characteristics of the individual's response (affective quality and adapativeness of behavior), adaptation level, and the optimization function. Behavioral homeostasis is maintained by the individual as both respondent and initiator in interaction with his environment. Hypotheses are suggested to account for striving vs. relaxation and for changes in the individual's level of personel competence. Four transactional types discussed are environmental engineering, rehabilitation and therapy, individual growth, and active change of the environment.

Recent work in the psychology of stimulation (Wohlwill, 1975) has led to theoretical advances in the area of social ecology. We propose an elaboration in this area that is middle-range, in the sense of attempting to account for a limited aspect of human behavior. This contribution to the theory of man-environment relationships deals with the aspects of human responses that can be viewed in evaluative terms, that is, behavior that can be rated on the continuum of adaptiveness, and inner states that can be rated on the continuum of positive to negative. This is, perhaps, a limited view of the human response repertory, but it stems from the traditional concern of the psychologist with

From *Environmental Design Research*, Volume 1, edited by Wolfgang F. E. Preiser. Copyright © 1973 by Dowden, Hutchinson & Ross, Inc., Publishers, Stroudsburg, Pa.

mental health and mental illness. Similarly, our view of environment for this purpose is limited to the "demand quality" of the environment, an abstraction that represents only one of many ways of dimensionalizing the environment. We shall use our knowledge from the area of gerontology to provide content for the theoretical structure, but suggest that the constructs are more generally applicable to any area involving the understanding of mental or social pathology (see Lawton and Nahemow, 1973, for a more complete discussion).

One way to begin is to look at the old ecological equation

$$B = f (P, E)$$

to acknowledge its veracity and familiarity, but linger on a few of its implications:

1. All behavior is transactional, that is, not explainable solely on the basis of knowledge about either the person behaving or the environment in which it occurs.
2. Multiple antecedents may lead to the same behavior. Different personal qualities in different contexts may behave similarly, but the "meaning" of the behavior is not comprehensive unless both person and situation are analyzed.
3. The homeostatic principle is illustrated, in that the same behavior can be maintained in the face of a change in either the behaving individual or the environment, providing an appropriate change occurs in the second of the pair of determinants.
4. Behavior change may be instigated at either the personal or the environmental level.

If we add the evaluative element to behavior (adaptive vs. non-adaptive behavior or positive vs. negative affect), the equation also implies that

5. Even in the "best" environments, some individuals will be unable to behave in an adaptive manner.
6. Even the most capable individuals may not behave in an adaptive manner in the most malign environments.

The above implications are concerned with the prediction of the outcome of various person-environment transactions. Very early in our association with social gerontology it became plain that environmental solutions, as opposed to personality-change solutions, were prescribed for the problems of older people. It was clear that social planners, designers, and people in the helping professions were operating on the basis of the "environmental docility hypothesis". This hypothesis states: ". . . the more competent the organism—in terms of health, intelligence, ego strength, social role performance, or cultural evolution—the less will be the proportion of variance in behavior attributable to physical objects or conditions around him. . . . With high degrees of competence he will, in common parlance, rise above his environment. However, reduction of competence, or deprived status, heightens his behavioral dependence on external conditions" (Lawton & Simon, 1968).

This hypothesis was formulated on the basis of their finding that elderly apartment dwellers who were female, or foreign-born, or in poorer health, were more likely to choose physically proximate neighbors as friends than were males, native-born, or healthy tenants. Other research has provided findings consistent with this notion. Rosow (1967), for example, found that working-class (low status) elderly were more dependent upon their local neighborhoods for social interaction and help than were middle-class elderly. Mangum (1971) used multiple regression analysis to determine the relative contributions of environmental and personal factors in predicting adjustment to planned housing. For the low-income tenants, environmental factors were most predictive while for the higher-income tenants, personal factors were more predictive.

The model that we are proposing requires the following definitions:

1. *Individual competence* is the enduring ability that enables an individual to function—the analogue of "personality trait" as the inner aspect of behavior. Actually, competences are many, depending on the area, such as intelligence, motor and perceptual ability, social tact, and so on. The designation of degree of competence should specify the particular area of competence, and is meant to refer to intraindividual enduring characteristics that vary within minimum and maximum limits.

2. *Environmental press* are used in Murray's (1938) sense to refer to aspects of the environment that act in concert with a personal need to evoke behavior by the subject. At this level we refer to external aspects of the environment that are presumed to have some motivating force for the individual whether he is aware of them or not ("alpha press," in Murray's terms). Aspects of the environment defined as those that are *perceived* as important to the individual ("beta press") are not included here, nor are the infinite number of aspects of the environment that do not impinge on the subject in any way. "Demand character" is the index of the total magnitude of the environment's effect on the individual, whether he is aware of the effect or not. The demand character may sometimes be estimated statistically in terms of the proportion of variance accounted for by environmental factors. The demand quality in extreme form may be termed "stress", though by no means are all press stressful.

3. *Adaptive behavior* is the externally observable behavior of the individual evaluated either in terms of social norms or of an a priori value system based on

the assumption that pleasure to others, fulfillment of one's own potential, and the performance of complex tasks are separate but equally important bases for the establishment of norms.

4. *Affective response* is the self-evaluated quality of experience, ranging from positive through neutral to negative. Every person-environment transaction may be evaluated in terms of either and sometimes both the adaptive quality of the behavior involved and the quality of affect.

Further elaboration of the model requires the use of Helson's (1964) concept of adaptation level (AL) and Wohlwill's optimization function (1975).

5. *Adaptation level* is the perceiver's receptor status when the value of a stimulus is perceived as neutral, that is, as neither warm nor cool, loud nor soft, pleasant nor unpleasant. Much of the time we are at adaptation level with respect to our environment. A major

aspect of our capacity to cope with the tasks of living involves our being able to screen out awareness of our proximate visual, auditory, thermal, and other environments, in order to concentrate attention and effort on focal tasks.

6. The *"optimization function"* suggests that for moderate levels of stimulation positive affect is engendered by stimuli that depart in either direction from AL (McClelland, 1963: Wohlwill, 1975). As stimuli proceed further toward either higher or lower levels of intensity, they may begin to evoke a negative inner response.

The Model

The theoretical model, represented graphically in Figure 24-1, shows individual competence, which is represented on the ordinate, and environmental press, shown

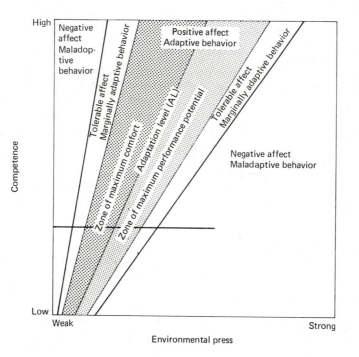

FIGURE 24-1. Graphic representation of an ecological theory of adaptation and aging.

on the abscissa. The diagonal line labeled AL represents a theoretical mean adaptation level for individuals of differing competence interacting with their environments. For an individual in a particular environment, the ebb and flow of environmental press remain within a constant range, resulting in the establishment of the adaptation level for that individual. Individuals of a given level of competence would be distributed normally to the right and left of the AL point for specific stimuli in accordance with the conditions elaborated by Helson (1964).

There is a range of environmental press adjacent to the individual's adaptation level where he experiences an inner sense of wellbeing vis-à-vis his environment and his behavior is adaptive (the shaded area of Figure 24-1). To either side of this positive outcome area is an area where higher and lower levels of press may test the limits of affective and behavioral adaptation. When the environmental press are either much greater or much less than those to which the individual has grown accustomed, he will experience a sense of discomfort and his behavior will become maladaptive. The region of positive affect and adaptive behavior is wider for persons of high competence. The dynamics of adaptation level are based upon homeostatic principles. Constant temporal variation occurs in both individual competence and environmental press. The beta component of environmental press (the perceived environment) will typically vary within what seems to be an objectively constant environment. Adaptation level is thus a theoretical point around which both personal competence and environmental press vary. For individuals who are both high and low in competence, the impact is vastly different for the competent and incompetent. For a highly competent person the zone of positive affect is sufficiently large so that normal oscillation in strength of environment press will very rarely throw the individual beyond the shaded central zone. As we travel down the

scale in competence, the central zone shrinks and the buffer zone, the area of tolerable affect, similarly shrinks. This means that for an individual of very low competence random variation in press will take him beyond the central zone where he has a sense of environmental mastery. This differential impact of environment press is stated by the environmental docility hypothesis.

The low point of environmental press might occur in sensory deprivation situations, the high point in many types of stressful or overloading situations. Individuals of high competence have a wide latitude of capacity to interact with the environment in ways that maximize positive affect. Note that as the individual's competence increases, the variability in environmental press which he can comfortably tolerate increases. Consequently, few high-competence individuals will show the breakdowns in behavior or affect that occur beyond adaptation range. Within that range, the following homeostatic reactions occur. When the environmental press are high, the person will become increasingly sensitized to his environment and try to make sense of it. When he is successful the perceived environmental complexity will be reduced. In Murray's terms, the beta component will be simplified. When occupying a region where environmental press are at a minimum, exploration and sensation-seeking will occur so as to increase the beta component of environmental press.

There are two different kinds of outcomes which concern us in the transaction between individual and environment: an affective and a behavioral response. Wohlwill's (1975) concept of optimization deals with the affective response to a stimulus as a function of its deviation from adaptation level. Slight variations from AL produce positive affect, but large variations produce negative affect. The gradient is the same for both positive and negative discrepancies from AL. The present theory incorporates this aspect of Wohlwill's theory. When we consider the variable of performance, however, we find that the zone of maximum performance is found to be at an environmental press level which is above adaptation level. For example, when environmental press increase slightly, the problems the individual faces are increased but still remain within the individual's capacity to solve. He is therefore put on his mettle. Frustrations may increase but the satisfactions derived from achievement increase as well and the person experiences positive affect. If the individual receives less challenge than usual from his environment, frustrations diminish and he relaxes. This comfort is more immediately rewarding, but there is less of the delayed gratification that comes from achievement, or increasing one's competence. Thus, the zone of positive affect includes levels of environmental press that are both higher and lower than AL. However, the subjective nature of the feelings is quite different in the two directions. We have therefore labeled one side the region of maximum performance, the other the region of maximum comfort.

This ecological theory of aging posits that the individual is operating at his best when the environmental press are moderately challenging. If the environment offers too little challenge, the individual adapts by becoming lethargic and thus operates below his capacity. On the other hand, it may be that the environment is too stressful and he has adapted by turning off. Actually, it is possible for both conditions to occur sequentially. Consider the example of a widower who had become used to having many services performed by his spouse. Overwhelmed by the unaccustomed demands of the new life, he retreats psychologically and as a consequence is placed in a nursing home. At first the simplified environment is appropriate to his psychologically weakened condition. Press level and personal competence are well matched. However, as the person gains confidence in coping with his simplified and benign environment, he gradually discovers that it is excessively simple. In fact, he is operating near the low-press borderline of his own positive adaptation area. Within his affective comfort zone he relaxes, but unchallenged he becomes dull.

When the environmental press are very strong the individual may panic and attempt to escape from the field either physically or psychologically. This escape-oriented behavior is not geared to dealing with the situation represented by the immediate environment, but it is adaptive in the sense that it may remove the person from an intolerable situation. In our model, this would mean a reduction in competence as well, which would result in his being diagnosed as "disturbed", but still might represent the best possible temporary solution to the stress situation.

The following illustration exemplifies a situation in which the dynamics of the system diminish an individual's competence. An eighty year-old woman who is showing signs of declining competence, but who is still able to function in accustomed surroundings is relocated. The environmental press increase beyond her tolerance level and her functioning is markedly impaired. A danger for the person of declining competence is that of being removed to a too-supportive environment. The person of moderate competence who, with some help, could continue to function in the community, might also adapt downward to the limited environment of an institution, that is, become too competent with functioning in the zone of comfort. In this case, she finds herself in a situation where it is difficult either to seek or to find stimulation. However, the environmental press are not so constantly low that she is really driven to the extremity of "maladaptive behavior." She seemingly adjusts very well to the home environment, but her powers decline markedly. What has happened is that in a situation with consistently low environmental press, the transactional balance adjusts with an adaptation level at lowered press, which leads to diminution of competence.

It is also possible for the dynamics of the system to improve the individual's level of functioning. Sivadon (1970) attempted to design a mental hospital in which the person was introduced to challenging environments in small doses so that he gradually built up a tolerance for greater environmental press, and ultimately changed his adaptation level. An increase in competence would theoretically follow.

An important element in the theory is the relationship of time to the dynamics of adaptation. Typically, environmental press diminish over time as a neutral consequence of the adaptation process. Thus, there tends to be a drift of AL from the right to the left in the diagram. The individual forms a cognitive map of his surrounds, develops concepts to reduce the environment to manipulable chunks, adjusts his coping mechanisms to the outer world and engages in other behaviors consistent with the process of adaptation. When entering a new environment, just the right amount of stimulation may be forthcoming for an individual *at that moment in time,* With increased familiarity, however, the environmental press gradually diminish. At first it was challenging, then comfortable, and finally dull.

The environment of many older people is reduced in complexity, in terms of lowered role demands, less economic freedom, dwindling inter-personal worlds, and in some cases deprived physical surroundings—a weakening of environmental press. Concomitantly, their competence may be reduced by comparison to younger people. It is our thesis that reduced press extended over a long time may lead to adaptation levels for sensory and affective experience that are significantly lower than those of younger people and ultimately lead to reduced personal competence.

For every individual there is an area in which changing environmental press are associated with positive outcome and an area in which self-initiated or externally initiated action may have a considerable impact upon the level of environmental demand in his behavioral world. As individual competence decreases, the area where maladaptive behavior and negative affect are risked becomes enlarged. Small changes in level of environmental press in people of low competence may evoke gross changes in quality of affect or behavior. Consequently, environmental intervention for therapeutic goals may be most fruitfully applied to this population.

Applications of these concepts to intervention schemes may be illustrated by the ecological change model implied by the basis ecological equation. Intervention may be applied either to the environment or to the individual. The individual's role may be as initiator or as a respondent to an external change. This transaction may be represented by the following dichotomies which suggest the fourfold prescriptive model for change shown in Figure 24–2.

The traditional concerns of the helping professions are represented in change attempts applied to the individual by trained therapists (cell C). While one may argue that effective change requires much active initiatory behavior from the subject, his independence is much more complete in the processes of growth and self-actualization (cell D). Our large body of design professionals operates primarily in cell A, where we presumably take into account not only the needs of individuals of low competence but the fact that life is made easy for most of us by programming a substantial amount of our everyday behavior. That is, we are at AL most of the time for very good reasons, and it is therefore appropriate to attempt to design in such a way as to free our attention for what really counts. Presumably in cell B the individual is initiating environmental change which may be either rewarding in itself (stimulus-seeking, tension creation) or in its outcome, whether that be ultimately an outcome that raises his competence, re-establishes an

Point of Application	The individual's role	
	Respondent	*Initiator*
The environment	A Social & environmental engineering	B The individual redesigns his environment
The individual	C Rehabilitation, psycho-therapy	D Growth, self-therapy

FIGURE 24–2. Ecological change model.

adaptation level that is within the bounds of positive affective experience, or enables him to shift his AL toward the "comfort" side.

Thus change may be approached from four points of view, any of which may, given the right person and the right situation, optimize the functioning level of the individual. It is clear that for any given level of supportive service, there will be some people who are too well and some who are too sick to enable a positive outcome. Our institutionalized widower may find that his socially engineered environment has made too many pre-digested decisions for him, and that there is practically no way for him to construct actively any part of his environment. Another institu-tional resident of lower competence may attempt more environmental change than he can handle (e.g., hoarding, fecal decoration, or occupation of another's territory) and downward environmental programming—e.g., increased support or institutional con-trol—may be necessary. Other areas of application of these principles may be found in housing, the operation of neighborhood services, or the design of parks and recrea-tion areas. In any of these pursuits, the important principles are (a) that support and demand are equally important in main-taining behavior and (b) that both tension reduction and tension creation are per-sonally satisfying, depending on the person and the situation.

Part

V

Research Methods in Environmental Psychology

To date there is no research methodology that is characteristically environmental psychology. Given the newness of the field and the status of its "Theoretical Conceptions and Approaches" as described in the Introduction to this earlier section of our volume, this is to be expected. It is clearly symptomatic of a field of scientific inquiry that in its response to the continuing demands for solution to significant human problems it is unable to draw upon theoretically and conceptually organized systems of knowledge which, if available, would provide the basis for formulating these problems. Where such bodies of knowledge exist, empirical methodologies that are theoretically consistent with them also exist, and both in turn provide a basis for defining new problems and the methods for their investigation. This is not the case for research into person/environment problems at the present time, nor is the situation likely to change in the near or even distant future.

What we find, then, is a variety of measurement techniques and research methods being employed which have been borrowed from the other behavioral sciences or research problem areas. Apart from the nature or problem to be studied, there is little to distinguish the use of these research techniques and methods in environmental psychology from their use in other fields of research. A review of the relevant research literature—and to some degree even the small number of selections on research methods presented here—suggests three kinds of concerns in the study of environmental psychology, each of which fosters a particular research emphasis or strategy. Thus the concern of the architect with user needs, the general influence of the cognitive approach in the fields of social and personal psychology, as well as a growing interest in the meaning and value of physical settings for the individual, have all fostered a considerable emphasis on verbal methods and techniques of data collection, for example, interviews, questionnaires, self-report, semantic differential. Of course all of the limitations and problems that are involved in the use of these research methods and techniques in other fields of behavioral sciences are carried over with their use in studying person/environment relationships. In effect, problems in the internal consistency, reliability, and validity of these measurement procedures are by no means diminished when they are used by the environmental psychologist.

The use of verbal techniques or methods of measurement is based upon the assumption—among others—that the individual is aware of his or her physical setting or some aspect of it and thus can make appropriate verbal responses to questions about it. Although this assumption is often valid, it is by no means always valid. In fact, individuals most often respond to their physical settings without being conscious or aware of the setting or their responses to it. Considering the "constant" presence of physical settings as a vehicle for human responses, and the fact that such settings have designed purposes that lead to repetitive, stereotyped expressions of behavior, it is small wonder the people to a large extent are unaware of this physical setting and their behavior and experience in relation to it. It is for this reason that environmental psychologists have turned to the use of observational techniques and methods as a means of measuring such behavior and experience; not only must these techniques be developed for each set of specific research purposes, but observers must be trained to use them in ways that ensure the reliability and validity of the particular measurement techniques.

Finally, there are those environmental psychologists who have formulated questions of how individuals relate to their physical settings in much the same way they have formulated questions with respect to other areas of research interests. For these researchers, environmental problems, no less than others, can be attacked by means of experimental laboratory approaches, simulation techniques, contrived situations, or any other methods and techniques that have traditionally been employed by the behavioral sciences. If the social psychologist can establish small groups in the laboratory, then the environmental psychologist can certainly "create" crowds and study them in this setting in much the same way. And if confederates can be used to create "social incidents" in real-life social contexts, for example, studies of helping behavior, there is no reason to believe that similar "incidents" cannot be employed to investigate territoriality, privacy, crowding, and other environmental problems.

It should be emphasized that some investigators may use all three of these research methods depending, of course, on the physical setting problem they are investigating. Indeed, problems in person/environment relations can be formulated in terms that would require all three methods in order to answer the questions raised. As we have already suggested, methodological diversity of this kind among researchers in the same specific problem area reflects the newness of the field of inquiry as well as its lack of a guiding coherent theoretical system. On the other hand, it cannot be emphasized too strongly that every measurement technique and research method used in environmental research—whether stated or not—has inherent in its use a host of assumptions about people and the underlying processes that relate them to their physical settings. To the extent that these assumptions are of doubtful validity, to that degree can we expect to generate masses of "data" that fail to cumulate into a body of scientific knowledge.

The precariousness of the use of the various research methods and techniques we noted above takes on even more serious proportions when viewed in the light of the essential nature of person/environment relationships. To ignore the inherent form and quality of these relationships is to risk the serious outcome that has beset some of the other behavioral sciences; namely, the accumulation of trivial data that have little if any consequence either for the development of theory or for solving significant human problems.

What is the essential character of the relationships between the people and their physical settings? Simply stated, it can be described as a complex, ongoing integrated process in which the person is acted upon by the physical setting and in turn modifies it by reactions to it, thereby eliciting new responses, and so on. This process is continuous and inexorable and as a consequence establishes a fundamental integrity in the phenomena designated as person/environment relationships that must be preserved in the study of these relationships.

If this is indeed the case, then one must seriously question the use of the traditional research paradigm of varying a number of physical environment dimensions (while all others are held constant) in order to measure their effects on the behavior and experiences of the person (or vice versa). And in this same vein, one must also ask whether the laboratory or other contrived research strategies can be the basis for accumulating knowledge about the relationships between people and their physical settings. The critical assumption that there are basic principles underlying the complex social behavior of the individual that have continuity regardless of how the reality of events is stripped by experimenter ingenuity has to be carefully reconsidered. It has been seriously challenged by the failure to accumulate meaningful knowledge by this approach over a fifty-year period in a number of fields; for example, small group research, attitude measurement in college settings, and so on. Not unrelated to the questions of isolated cause-and-effect relationships and the validity of laboratory research is the question of whether quantification of the complex process we call person/environment relationships is possible. Perhaps we have been unable to measure "quality of life" in physical settings small or large because it simply cannot be quantified. The argument against quantification in this respect grows even stronger if one considers that attempts to quantify most human psychological processes, whether attitudes, values, or other characteristics, provide little convincing indication that individual behavior and experience can be conceptualized by means of linear or curvilinear scales.

Of course there are other environmental psychologists who would not treat the methodological issues we have raised here in the same way. Indeed for some they may not be issues at all, for they would take the view that the "complexity of interaction process" we have ascribed to person/environment relations is not unique to these events; furthermore one can extract particular dimensions for study without being concerned about the process as a totality, or the fact that the investigation and its methods involves "stripping" the problem down into manageable and manipulable form. Which approach is correct or viable remains to be seen. Furthermore, for those environmental psychologists who subscribe to the view that the integrity of person/environmental events must be preserved in the study of these events as they unfold in real life settings, there are a host of "other" methodological difficulties that present themselves. These difficulties extend from the rather patent fact that the research process itself is alien to the integrity of these events, to matters of what constitutes the unit of analysis in the study of such events, and finally to questions of how to study physical settings over extended periods of time.

To some degree it may well be that contrary to the general scientific maxim that the scientist must be objective by remaining scrupulously separate from the events studied, the environmental psychologist must be an inherent part of or intimately related to the events studied. Only by such "total involvement" can a methodology for study and analysis that preserves the integrity of the events themselves and makes the research process itself an inherent but neutral part of the events themselves be achieved.

As we have said before, whether this approach or more traditional approaches will meet the challenge of understanding people and their relationship to physical settings, only time can tell. Our purpose in this introduction was *not* to establish the polemic of methodological orientations in the field of environmental psychology but rather to highlight differences in research techniques, methods, and of course, in general approaches or points of view.

25. The Comprehension of the Everyday Physical Environment
KENNETH H. CRAIK

In 1965, Studer and Stea were able to compile a preliminary directory listing over 170 persons who are professionally interested in the relation of behavior to the physical environment. The directory is only one of several signs of the increasing attention being paid to the possible implications and significance of behaviorial science research for the environmental planning and design professions. The source and potential of this awareness is broadly interdisciplinary in scope as is evidenced by the inclusion in the directory of persons in the fields of

Reprinted by permission of the *Journal of the American Institute of Planners*, Vol. 34, No. 1, January 1968, and the author.

anthropology, architecture, city and regional planning, engineering, design, geography, landscape architecture, psychiatry, psychology, sociology, and zoology.

Psychologists, after an unduly tardy entry, seem now ready to review the directions they might take in advancing knowledge in this area. The recent year-long faculty seminar series devoted to the topic, "Psychology and the Form of the Environment," held in 1965 and 1966 at the M.I.T. Department of City and Regional Planning, and the second National Research Conference on Architectural Psychology, held at the University of Utah in May 1966, document the growing commitment among psychologists to explore, to foster, and even to undertake research approaches in environmental psychology.

Surprisingly, the initiative in the development of research in environmental psychology has been with the disciplines of environmental design and planning. A full understanding of the tardiness of psychology in attempting to study the behaviorial implications of what have become constant, extensive, and often massive transformations in the structure of the everyday physical environment will require an enterprising and scholarly investigation into the history of ideas and the history of a science. In the meantime, it can be suggested that scientific psychology, since its beginnings in the 1870's, often has been willing to forfeit immediate attacks upon a whole range of significant and compelling aspects of human behavior (Sanford, 1965). It has tended to concentrate its energies upon the study of basic, if apparently simple and inconsequential, processes and, perhaps more importantly, upon the development of a repertory of quantitative methods and techniques appropriate to the phenomena it ultimately seeks to investigate and to understand. However, in recent years, particularly since World War II, scientific psychology has been emerging from its seclusion in the laboratory and more eagerly seeking problems in the "real" world upon which to test and to expand the usefulness of its methods and concepts.

During these same decades of psychological seclusion, man's physical environment has increasingly become man-made, man-influenced, and urban. The planning and design professions have occupied the best vantage points from which to observe this tendency and from which to absorb and gauge the dramatic implications it may have for human experience and behavior. Thus, as the psychologists somewhat timidly emerge from their laboratory retreats in search of phenomena of real human significance to study, the environmental planners and designers, with a sense of urgency—and perhaps a tinge of guilt— have attempted to attract their attention and efforts to the momentous trends and deeds that the planners and designers have witnessed—and sometimes wrought.

The selection of problems for study, and the sequence and timing of attack upon them, move according to quite different criteria in research and in practice. In research, strategy tends to be guided by the conceptual framework and techniques already at hand, by the relative likelihood that solutions to the problems will be attained, and by the general theoretical interest and feedback provided by the research project itself. In professional practice, the structure of problems is seen in the context of social purposes, of the relative desirability that solutions be attained, and of the urgent necessity that judgments be rendered, decisions reached, and actions taken. Nevertheless, it might be valuable to select a simple yet central problem in environmental psychology and to sketch out the form and pathways that research directed to it would likely take. In doing so, some basis might be laid for an appraisal of the sort of contributions the environmental planning and design professions can reasonably expect environmental psychology, as well as related branches of the behavioral sciences, to make to their own endeavors.

The Exploration of a Problem

How do people come to grasp cognitively the everyday physical world in which they live and move? What terms and categories do they employ in talking and thinking about it? What aspects and qualities of it do they distinguish and attend to? What assumptions and expectations do they bring to it? What are the factors that influence the particular way a specific person comprehends his physical surroundings? These are surely some of the questions to which the environmental psychologist would be expected to turn his attention. How would he proceed in exploring the structure and ramifications of this problem from the point of view or research strategy and design?

In tracing the course of an environmental psychologist's exploration of a problem, it will be seen that the research strategy follows in a rather straightforward way from the necessary process of defining the terms of discourse, identifying the elements of the problem, and studying their interrelationships. Out of this basically commonsensical procedure, terminology is introduced, methods are developed, research projects are conceived, and some by-products of practical interest to the design and planning professions emerge. Often, as the exploration of the main problem is pursued, subsidiary topics of investigation unexpectedly spin off, which also lead to scientific and practical gains.

I. A Unit of Discourse: "The Environmental Display"

In the long run, psychological research should yield an understanding of the manner in which any entity of the everyday physical environment is comprehended. The term "environmental display" will be adopted to signify generally "that which is comprehended"—that is, those units of the everyday physical environment, of which buildings, urban scenes, and forest glades are instances. Environmental displays may be considered to vary along at least two important dimensions: scale, and natural to man-influenced. As Figure 25–1 suggests, a flower would be small scale, natural; a tool, small scale, man-influenced; the Grand

Canyon viewed from the air, large scale, natural; and Manhattan Island viewed from the air, large scale, man-influenced. A field of tulips growing upon reclaimed land in Holland would be intermediate on both dimensions. The term "display" has been chosen because of its flexible application along these continua and because of its connotation of something that is to be reacted to in preceptual-cognitive-affective modalities.

II. The Elements of the Problem: A Model for the Comprehension of Environmental Displays

The next step in the process is to consider the essential components of the problem. These structural elements are quickly revealed when the environmental psychologist attempts to design a simple study of the comprehension of a single environmental display. He is immediately forced to make decisions about these issues: Whose comprehension am I to study (Observers)? By what means am I to present the environmental display to the observer (Presentation of Environmental Displays)? What behavioral reactions of the observer am I to elicit and record (Nature and Format of Judgments)? By what standards might I evaluate the observer's comprehension (Validational Criteria)? A review of the possibilities inherent in each of these issues serves to enrich our conception of the problem. They are presented in summary form in Table 25–1, and a brief discussion of them follows.

A. Characteristics of the Observers. At first glance, it would appear to be most appropriate to study the comprehensions of a representative sample of the general public. For some purposes, this approach would be the best method for selecting the observers. However, for other purposes, the observations of specific subgroups of the general population would warrant investiga-

Natural to man-inflenced

	small	a flower	a tool
Scale			
	large	Grand Canyon	Manhattan Island

FIGURE 25–1.

TABLE 25–1. *A Process Model for the Comprehension of Environmental Displays*

Observers 1	Presentation of Environmental Displays 2	Nature and Format of Judgments 3	Validational Criteria 4
Special competence groups: architects planners real estate appraisers stage designers "space" managers, i.e., hotel, theatre, resort managers, building superintendents, etc. Special user-client groups: elderly persons migrant workers college students Groups formed on the basis of relevant personality measures Everyman, general public	Direct experience: looking at walking around and through driving around and through aerial views living in Simulative exploration Cinematic and photographic studies Sketches and drawings Models and replicas Tachistoscopic views Laser beam presentations No presentation	Free descriptions Adjective checklists Activity and mood checklists Q-sort descriptions Ratings Thematic potential analysis Symbolic equivalents Multisensory equivalents Empathic interpretations: "role" enactments "role" improvisations Social stereotypic cues Beliefs about human consequences Viewing time "Motational" systems	Measures of objective characteristics of environmental displays Judgments by experts Any judgment-form in Column 3 based upon more extensive acquaintance with the environmental display

tion. Several groups come readily to mind, including:

1. Groups whose members are thought to possess special competence in the comprehension and description of environmental displays, such as architects, planners, real estate appraisers, stage designers, and "space managers"—persons who have practical knowledge of the ways people behave in and use space, for example, hotel and resort managers.

2. Groups whose modes of comprehension of the nonhuman environment are of particular interest to architects and planners. Elderly persons, migrant workers, physically disabled persons, psychiatric patients, and college students would constitute groups belonging to this category.

3. Groups formed according to personality dimensions that are thought to be theoretically relevant to individual variations in the comprehension of the nonhuman environment. The theory of C. G. Jung, for example, would lead to such hypotheses. Extravert sensing types, as an instance, would be predicted to react to

the nonhuman environment in a manner characteristically different from that of introvert intuitive types. A subclass of this category would be the formation of groups of observers on the basis of especially developed personality scales assessing persons according to their more enduring dispositions, attitudes, and beliefs concerning the nonhuman environment.

B. Presentation of Environmental Displays.

Once a group of observers has been selected, the next step is to present to them the environmental display to be comprehended. The practical problem is this: how to present the environmental display to the group of observers within a reasonable and efficient time span, but in such a way that the full and complex character of the display is conveyed to them. A wide range of possible media of presentation is available. The appropriateness of the individual media to specific research purposes, of course, will vary. Some of the media of presentation of environmental displays may be briefly appraised as follows:

1. *Direct experience.* The direct experience of looking at environment displays, walking or driving around and through them, and taking in aerial views of them has a certain epistemological priority. The site visit also has the advantage of conveying the environmental display through all the sense modalities it might be capable of stimulating. However, there are also limitations to the use of the site visit, in addition to the obvious one of costliness. For example, anyone who has watched architectural students on a house tour will realize the striking differences in exploratory and observational strategies that they employ compared with other groups. Thus the free exploration and observation of the site visit leaves indeterminate the precise nature of the environmental display which in fact has been presented to the observers, as well as the degree of equivalence of presentation which exists among the observers. More-

over, if one is willing to accept these limitations, it might be noted that an even more thorough presentation of the environmental display would consist in having the observer use or reside in it, in whatever sense that might be appropriate to the specific nature of a given environmental display.

2. *Simulative exploration.* Attempts are being made to approximate the free exploration of an environmental display while maintaining fairly precise recordings of the specific explorations of each observer (see Weiss and Boutourline, 1962; Winkel and Sasanoff, 1966). Either through sequential presentations of photographic slides, with choice points that move the observer directionally through the display, or through observer-guided remote-controlled mobile television cameras at the environmental display, the observer is presented with a considerable amount of freedom to visually roam and explore the display, yet the sequence of his explorations is recorded, allowing a determination of what, in fact, has been presented to him. The limitation of this method, and of many of the following methods, is the degradation of the full nature and richness of the original environmental display. In this case, visual aspects of the display alone are being simulated. However, considerations are being made of the possibilities of simulating auditory and olfactory experiences within the context of this method (Stea, 1966).

3. *Cinematic and photographic studies.* Although again at some loss of the full richness of the original environmental display and of full monitoring of the observational sequences of the viewers, cinematic and photographic studies nevertheless can convey a great deal of information about an environmental display, with a high degree of verisimilitude. In addition, recent studies of cinematic presentations of environmental displays that have employed the eye-movement camera suggest that some monitoring of the attentional pat-

terns of the observers can be achieved (Carr & Kurilko, 1964).

4. *Sketches and drawings; models and replicas.* Sketches, drawings, and models take on a certain importance as media of presentation due to their traditional use in architecture and planning. In addition, the development of miniaturized television cameras will soon allow the simulative exploration of models and replicas of environmental displays.

5. *Tachistoscopic views.* The very brief exposure of photographic presentations of environmental displays afforded by the tachistoscope may be useful in investigating the salience of certain elements of such environmental displays as urban scenes (Vigier, 1965), as well as in establishing affective qualities of features of displays.

6. *Laser beam presentations.* The possible development of full dimensional presentations of objects through the use of Laser beam holograms (Leith & Upatnieks, 1965) may offer opportunities in the future for much more extensive and realistic presentation of environmental displays within the laboratory setting than is now feasible.

7. *No presentation.* In studies of enduring images of familiar environmental displays, it will be of interest to study the different descriptions given when the environmental display is identified only by name, and when it actually is presented.

C. The Nature and Format of Judgments.

The kinds of descriptive judgments and other behaviorial reactions requested of observers of environmental displays and the format provided for guiding and assisting them in making their responses are of central importance, for they are the signs by which the nature of the observer's comprehensions is made known to us.

Column 3 of Table 25–1 lists several possible kinds of response eliciting and recording procedures. Some of the methods stress the ease of recording the impressions and judgments in everyday language and

highlight the advantage of obtaining standardized and comparable responses from observers. Other procedures listed in Column 3 are suggested in the light of an assumption that many reactions to the nonhuman enviror ment are subtle and are neither customarily nor easily talked about in everyday discourse. These procedures, therefore, entail unusual modes of responding to environmental displays. If the subtlety of reactions to the everyday physical surroundings has been one factor in hampering the development of behavioral science research in this area, as it indeed appears to have been, then the psychologist, if anyone, should be able to make a contribution. Responses are, after all, the business of the psychologist.

Table 25–2 presents a brief description of each response format. This assortment of response formats that might be employed in studying the comprehension of environmental displays, while far from complete, does serve to illustrate the impressive variety of responses to the nonhuman environment that are potentially contained in the human repertory.

D. Validational Criteria.

If a specific investigation were directed toward assessing the accuracy or quality of the observers' comprehensions of environmental displays, then some well-founded description and assessment of the displays would be required to serve as criterion. There is no simple basis upon which to select validational criteria. In some cases, objective measures of physical attributes of the environmental displays may be appropriate, especially if the original descriptive responses made by the observers were in those terms (such as the relative size of components of the environmental displays). In other investigations, the judgment of experts, that is, of observers with special competence or experience, would do. In some instances, responses of the same sort as those made by the observers whose ac-

TABLE 25–2. *Response Formats for the Descriptive Assessment of Environmental Displays*

Free descriptions: Free descriptions of environmental displays made by the observers in either spoken or written form have the advantage of placing minimal constraints upon the natural, spontaneous manner of response, but the disadvantage of not easily allowing quantitative comparisons among responses.

Adjective checklists: Adjective checklists have been successfully used in the recording of staff impressions in personality assessment programs (see Gough & Heilbrun, 1965). An ACL may consist of 300 adjectives drawn from everyday usage, which the observer checks as applicable or not applicable to the person, object, or concept described. Special adjective checklists can be developed for use in environmental psychology. The advantages of the adjective checklist method are its use of everyday language, the brevity and ease with which judgments are made and recorded, and its wide and flexible application and forms of analysis.

Activity and mood checklists: Like the adjective checklist, mood checklists are simple, standard, and brief means of recording impressions (see Nowlis, 1965; Clyde, 1960). A special mood checklist for the assessment of environmental displays can be developed, with a special effort being made to embody in it "atmospheric" mood referents. In addition, an activity checklist, consisting of perhaps 300 verbs expressing a wide range of discrete human activities might be developed. The latter checklist would be useful in describing an environmental display in terms of both its observed and its potential capacity for human activity.

Q-sort descriptions: The Q-sort method is another procedure that is widely used in the field of personality assessment for the purpose of obtaining standardized, comparable, and quantifiable observer description of persons and person-relevant concepts (see Block, 1961). A Q-sort deck typically consists of 50 or 100 statements, each on a separate card and each expressing an important characteristic, which are sorted by the observer into piles of specified number along a dimension ranging from "most characteristic" to "least characteristic" of the entity being described. Special Q-decks can be developed that would be appropriate to the description of environmental displays.

Ratings: Ratings are another standard and flexible technique for obtaining observer judgments. An especially sensitive form of the rating scale, the Semantic Differential, can be fruitfully employed in the descriptive assessment of environmental displays (see Osgood, Suci, Tannenbaum, 1957; Carroll, 1959; Lamm, 1965).

Thematic potential analysis: One subtle and relatively implicit reaction to environmental displays such as buildings, rooms, rural and urban scenes, and so forth, is likely to be an automatically functioning scanning response designed to answer the question, "What might go on here; what might occur here?" A method for assessing this response-characteristic of environmental displays is the thematic potential analysis. In this procedure, a series of environmental displays would be presented to a large number of observers. The observers would be requested to write a story about each display, with instructions to this effect: "Create a brief story that might fittingly take place here." Techniques for thematic analysis have been carefully developed in psychology, under the impetus of the Thematic Apperception Test (TAT), which could readily be adapted to the task of sensitively analyzing the protocols

TABLE 25–2.   *Response Formats for the Descriptive Assessment of Environmental Displays (Continued)*

obtained from the suggested procedure (see Henry, 1956; Saarinen, 1966; Michelson, 1966). Individual differences among observers in the thematic potentials they ascribed to environmental displays would be studied. In addition, a method would be available for assessing the thematic potential of environmental displays such as urban scenes and for grouping them according to the results of the thematic analysis, for further study.

Symbolic equivalents: The study of metaphorical expression, either in terms of the production of metaphors or the preference for metaphors, has been profitably employed in personality research (see Barron, 1958; Knapp, 1960). An appropriate adaptation of these techniques would require of the observer the production of metaphorical expressions as the mode of reacting to environmental displays. The produced metaphors can be analyzed in terms of the individual styles of sensitivity of given observers and in terms of the typical metaphorical expressions elicited by given environmental displays. It would be possible, when sufficient research has been conducted, to establish multiple-choice preference procedures for metaphorical reactions to environmental displays which might assess meaningful individual consistencies among observers.

Multisensory equivalents: Another equivalence procedure that would be more exploratory in nature involves the presentation of a series of musical sequences, color sequences (perhaps projected upon a full-wall screen), and other sensory projections. The observer's task would be to select those phases of each such series that in some way represent some aspect of the experience of a given complex display (such as walking up Market Street in San Francisco on a Saturday afternoon). This expressive preference or equivalence procedure would help to elaborate the full response-characteristics of given environmental displays.

Empathic interpretations: Two methods for establishing empathic sets in observers are available. In the "role enactment" procedure, an anecdote would be recounted which illustrates the vivid enactment by a person of a physical object, in this particular case, a bathtub. After telling this story to the observers, the experimenter would then instruct them: "In the same way in which that person 'was' the bathtub, you 'be' the ———— (environmental display which is being comprehended) and 'being it' describe yourself." Using this procedure, it would be possible, for example, to compare descriptions of given environmental displays made by means of an adjective checklist under standard conditions with those made under "role enactment" conditions. Furthermore, if over a variety of environmental displays described by a variety of observer groups, certain adjectives are checked consistently more frequently under the empathic set, those adjectives could be constituted into a scale that would be scored for descriptions made under standard conditions. The resulting Empathic Set scale would provide useful information about both observers and environmental displays.

The "role" improvisations technique would also be exploratory in nature. The general method has been found to be valuable in personality assessment (see Moreno, 1934; Harris, 1955; Sarbin, 1954). Under these usages, the two assessees are assigned roles, such as doctor and patient, and instructed to improvise an interaction between themselves. As an appropriate adaptation, the two observers would be

TABLE 25–2. *Response Formats for the Descriptive Assessment of Environmental Displays (Continued)*

instructed to "be" two given environmental displays, such as the Eiffel Tower and the Statue of Liberty, and to personify them in an interaction. Many clues to the more subtle reactions to specific environmental displays and to the nonhuman environment in general might be gained by this exploratory procedure.

The two methods for obtaining empathic interpretations of environmental displays are somewhat akin to the techniques employed by the Synectics group (see Gordon, 1961).

Social stereotypic cues: In their comprehension of the everyday physical environment, persons make inferences about the kinds of people who will be associated with kinds of environmental displays. The Gough Adjective Check List would be an appropriate device for investigating the social stereotypic cues provided by environmental displays. In this procedure, the observers are presented with the environmental display and asked to record their judgments about the kinds of people who would probably live in, work in, or in general be found in and around the environmental display.

Beliefs about human consequences: Another class of inferences commonly made about environmental displays relates to their human consequences. For example, the observers might be asked to record their judgment of what the effect would be upon them if they were to live in, work in, or in some other way be associated with a given environmental display for two years (five years, ten years, and so forth). The format employed here could be a description of themselves on the Gough Adjective Check List conveying these effects upon themselves, which would be compared with their present self-description, or the format could be adapted from that employed by the Guilford Consequences Test (see Christensen, Merrifield & Guilford, 1958), in which the observer simply lists as many such consequences as he can.

Viewing time: A gross indication of the course of attentional processes during the observation of environmental displays would be the amount of time the display, or elements of it, are held in view. Tracking the course of such fluctuating deployments of attention is a difficult task. Three methods are available. The portable eye-movement camera achieves noteworthy fullness of coverage but entails the use of a somewhat cumbersome and unnatural apparatus (see Carr & Kurilko, 1964). Methods for the simulated exploration of environmental displays would provide relevant data. Another, simpler method would be the serial presentation of environmental displays by means of photographic slides, in which the viewing time is under the option and control of the observer. Each of these methods has potential value in research on the deployment of attention, both as characterological or stylistic modes of observation or as response characteristics of the environmental displays.

Motational systems: Motational systems have been developed as standardized methods, akin to choreographic notational systems, whereby trained observers may note the sequence of principal elements and features in the experience of moving through environmental displays, as in the movement along highways and pedestrian pathways (See Thiel, 1961; Appleyard, Lynch & Myer, 1964; Halprin, 1965; Abernathy & Noe, 1966; Casey, 1966; Rose, n.d.).

curacy is being assessed might serve as criteria, if the descriptive judgments made by the criterion observers were founded upon more extensive acquaintance with and surveillance of the environmental displays.

III. Directions in which Research Would Proceed

Commonsensical analysis of the problem has revealed four elements that must be considered in research on the comprehension of environmental displays (Figure 25–2).

By focusing upon each of these elements in turn, four domains of research are generated, each with distinctive methodological demands and conceptual and practical implications. It would be burdensome to treat the total structure of each domain here. Instead, research on the media of presentation will be traced in some detail, and the nature of the remaining research domains will be sketched in broader strokes.

A. Study of the Media of Presentation. Establishing the effects of differences in the media of presentation upon the comprehension of the environmental displays has practical priority in research in environmental psychology. Consider a study of the comprehension of a sample of town squares and plazas by nursemaids. The experimenter would be faced with the decision to employ direct or indirect media of presentation—to send the nursemaids to the sites or to use some presentations such as photographs or models.

It is clear that knowledge of the degree of comparability of comprehensions of environmental displays evoked by the different media of presentation is fundamental to the planning of other research in this field. The paradigm for studies that would yield this kind of knowledge is straightforward. A series of existing environmental displays would be selected. Presentations of each display would be developed in a standard form, using, for example, these media:

1. Direct exploration (complete freedom to roam about the actual displays)
2. Viewing a model of the environmental displays
3. A photographic slide series
4. A complete set of architectural elevations, plans, and perspectives

Observers would be assigned to a given medium of presentation and instructed to describe the environmental displays as they are presented, by the use of the several developed response formats, such as the Environmental Display Adjective Checklist. (It should be noted that a major preliminary effort would be required to develop standardized and technically sound versions of the response formats suggested in Table 25–2, such as Environmental Display Adjective Checklists and Q-Decks, Mood and Activity Checklists, Thematic Potential Analysis procedures and so forth.) Observers of media 2, 3, and 4 would try to describe the display as it would appear if it had been directly presented to them. The findings would be analyzed primarily in terms of the similarity of the descriptions based upon indirect media to those based upon direct exploration.

A research program that developed such empirical estimates of the comparability among media would be useful in determining the degree to which substantive research findings gained on the basis of one medium would be applicable to other media, especially to direct exploration. Such research would also provide in-

Observers

Environmental Displays

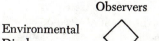

Media of presentation

Response formats

FIGURE 25–2.

teresting general information on the be-havorial reactions to the different media. The research requirements in this area would be extensive, for it would be necessary to sample widely from classes of media, observers, response formats, and displays, before stable and reliable generalizations could be established.

Although this research endeavor follows directly from the nature of the problem and the requirements of research strategy, it would also have practical implications for the disciplines of environmental design and planning. A considerable amount of anecdotal evidence and folklore wisdom surrounds the issue of how best to convey a proposed project solution to clients, planning commissions, citizen groups, and others, through professional presentations. The research on the media of presentation would provide systematic baseline evidence concerning the relative equivalence of the various indirect-media to direct-media presentations. This consideration leads to another research tactic altogether: the possibility of experimenting with basic innovations and alterations in the nature of each indirect medium, using as a target for improvement the degree of equivalence of the resulting descriptions to direct-media descriptions. Finally, it would be fitting to take heed of the traditional use of a *combination* of indirect media in professional presentations (for example, plans, sketches, elevations, and so forth) and to search systematically for optimal combinations of indirect media, again using as the target of improvement the approximation to direct-media descriptions. An assumption implicit in these considerations is that the chief purpose of professional presentations is to convey an accurate, veridical notion of the proposed design or planning solution to the audience. Of course, to the extent that the overriding purpose is persuasive rather than descriptive, the importance of achieving direct-media equivalence may be lessened.

Another direction of research will be briefly noted to further illustrate the close interplay between systematic research and practical by-products. A personality psychologist viewing this domain of research would immediately become interested in possible stable differences among individual observers in the ability to make direct-media descriptions upon the basis of indirect-media presentations. Even in the use of indirect media that evoke comprehensions that on the whole poorly approximate direct-media descriptions, it would probably be found that some individuals are consistently better than others in making this approximation. The personality psychologist would be interested in what other abilities, skills, traits, and dispositions are correlated with the ability to make this descriptive and comprehensive leap from the indirect-media presentation to a direct-media grasp of the nature of the environmental displays. That is, he would ask: what are individuals like, in terms of their personality as a whole, who perform this trick especially well or especially poorly? He would wonder whether the same personality syndrome appears with regard to all indirect media or whether there are further refinements in this constellation of abilities, skills, traits, and dispositions, depending upon which indirect medium is involved. He would be interested in whether certain groups display more of this capacity than others. He would attempt to determine which indirect media are most suitable for particular groups. There would be practical implications here for the choice of indirect media for professional presentations to varying audiences. Also at the practical level, it would be important to determine to what degree the capacity to make direct-media descriptions upon the basis of indirect-media presentations is possessed by students in the environmental design and planning disciplines and how essential this capacity is to effective performance in these fields. If the capacity were found to be either essential or especially helpful, quick, standard methods for assessing candidates on the degree to which they display this ability might be developed; and, taking an ameliorative approach, methods for training and improving performance in this skill might be explored.

B. Study of the Observers: Individual and Group Differences in the Comprehension of the Everyday Physical Environment. Individual and group differences can be observed in the comprehension of the non-human environment if the research design holds constant the media of presentation, the response formats, and the environmental displays, but varies systematically the criteria for selection of observers. For example, if the medium is photography, if the response format is the Environmental Display Adjective Checklist descriptions, and if the environmental display is a typical subway station under Manhattan Island, then, in what way would architects, corporate presidents, janitors, Sierra Club members, and opera singers differ in their comprehensions of the subway station? Would Democrats differ from Republicans in their descriptions? Or children from adults? Or males from females? If the contrasting observer groups were selected upon the basis of personality traits and dispositions, rather than upon the basis of membership in socially differentiated groups, then a different set of questions must be asked: Would extraverts differ from introverts? Dominant persons from submissive persons? Would groups who differ in their motivation for achievement, or their cognitive flexibility, or their level of anxiety also differ in their description of the subway station?

If differences among groups defined socially or according to social variables or personality traits did emerge, then interest would turn to the generality of the differences: would the differences hold up if the media of presentation were systematically varied? Over what range of response formats

and of environmental displays would these differences among groups in the comprehension of the everyday physical environment be discovered?

The impetus for research in this domain comes from both scientific and practical sources. The full sociopsychological understanding of a subgroup of the human population, whether it be defined sociologically or in terms of personality, will remain strikingly incomplete if that group's distinctive style of comprehending the everyday physical environment remains unexplored and unknown. At the practical level, the need for systematic understanding of specific client groups for whom the increasingly total environmental transformations are being made is perhaps even more urgent. With the advent of massive urban renewal programs and the creation of entire new communities, the relationship between the planners and designers, on the one hand, and the user-clients and inhabitant-clients, on the other, has become increasingly attenuated and indirect. Some new, reliable, empirical means of providing the necessary information and understanding of client groups has become necessary.

C. Study of Human Responsiveness to Environmental Displays. The third domain of research arises out of an interest in the list of possible response formats presented in Table 25–2. As this already extensive list, which nevertheless is presently only suggestive and incomplete, becomes increasingly expanded, the following question will arise: Do these response formats, each and every one, elicit totally different, independent, and unrelated dimensions of responsiveness to given environmental displays? Or is there rather some structural ordering and overlapping among them? Let us explore how such structure in human responsiveness might show itself. Take the research design in which a constant group of observers, using the same medium of presentation, respond to a variety of environmental displays by means of a wide range of response formats. In the analysis of the data, it might be noticed that whenever a cluster of adjectives was checked as descriptive of an environmental display, a certain metaphorical image was also applied to that display. Or perhaps it is revealed that whenever a certain theme appeared in the Thematic Potential Analysis of an environmental display, a combination of items from the mood checklist and the verb checklist was also designated as descriptive of it. This kind of comprehensive overlap or semantic correlation among response forms would demonstrate order among them. The structure of responsiveness to environmental displays may be fairly constant or it may vary with the nature of the observers, the environmental displays, or certain observer-display combinations.

D. Study of Environmental Displays: The Assessment and Appraisal of the Everyday Physical Environment. If the research design holds constant the observer groups, the media of presentation, and the response formats, but varies the environmental displays, then a domain of research focused upon the behaviorial characteristics of environmental displays is generated, which might take three forms:

1. *Descriptive assessments.* On some sensible basis, a team of observers is selected. A class of environmental displays is defined and chosen for assessment study, such as, for example, the class of shopping centers, movie theaters, nursery schools, or vestpocket parks. A sample of actual, existing environmental displays is randomly drawn from this class for assessment. The team of observers is presented with the sample of environmental displays, perhaps forty of them, by means of all possible and useful media of presentation; and the members of the assessment team respond to each environmental display independently by means of a wide variety of response formats. From this data would emerge an empirical, wide-ranging psychological description of this class or type of environmental display. Psychologically defined subgroups within the sample of environmental displays might also be identified on the basis of the relative similarity of the descriptive assessments they evoke. It would also be possible to explore the degree of association of individual response variables with variations in objective, physical characteristics among the sample of displays.

2. *Evaluative assessments.* Evaluative assessments combine a full-range descriptive assessment of a sample drawn from a class of environmental displays with an appraisal of the relative success or goodness of the individual environmental displays. If a descriptive assessment were made of a sample of forty vestpocket parks, drawn randomly from the total nationwide class of vestpocket parks, it would also be possible to identify the degree to which each park had been successful in its function and purpose. It is quite likely that a group of persons with expert understanding of the requirements and functioning of vestpocket parks would show high agreement in their ratings of the relative success of the parks, if they were given an opportunity to observe and study them. Other evaluative indices might also be employed, such as a measure of the relative use of the parks by their neighborhood population, the injury rate, and so forth. Any of these measures, which express an appraisal of the environmental displays in terms of the success in which they are considered to have met their purposes, can be employed as *criterion indices*. By correlating the *criterion indices* with the findings of the full-scale *descriptive assessment,* it would be possible to determine the psychological characteristics of successful and unsuccessful parks. A differentiated picture would emerge of the ways in which the excellent and the inadequate environmental displays are comprehended and systematically described by human observers.

3. *Preconstruction predictive assessments.* The practical, social limitation of evaluative assessments is that inadequate environmental displays have already been constructed or otherwise brought into being. Would it be feasible to attempt to predict the ultimate evaluative criterion indices of environmental displays before they are constructed or otherwise developed into actual form? In order to make diagnostic predictions of useful accuracy in the preconstruction stage, several prerequisites would have to be met. First, a fund of systematic empirical knowledge concerning stable relationships between descriptive characteristics of environmental displays and evaluative criterion indices would have to become available. Secondly, since at the preconstruction stage, only indirect media presentations are possible, the kind of research discussed earlier concerning improvement in the ability to make direct-media descriptive assessments upon the basis of indirect media presentations would have to have moved ahead. Given these two prerequisites, however, it might well become possible to predict at the preconstruction stage both how human observers, and even specific subgroups of observers, will most likely comprehend the environmental display and how the environmental display will be evaluated in terms of its success in fulfilling its function. The ability of environmental psychology to develop predictive power in this area can be expected to have important effects upon the development and selection of protypical designs and plans for man-influenced environmental transformations and to place the process of design and planning more directly under rational guidance.

Conclusion

If any lessons are contained in this case study of research strategy in environmental psychology, they are perhaps these:

Appropriate Time Perspectives Must Be Developed

When the intricacy and scope of the research possibilities uncovered by analysis of the present problem are considered, and when it is recognized that this problem is only one selected from the domain of environmental psychology, which in turn is only one field of environmental behavioral science, then it is evident that any expectation of immediate cognitive gratification must be destined to frustration. Even with the most generously financed, large-scale, crash program of research imaginable, the magnitude of the methodological and empirical groundwork that must be established as the basis for a mature branch of research makes it imperative to think in terms of decades rather than months or years, and makes it incumbent upon behavioral scientists in this field to be humble in their advice and proclamations as well as incumbent upon environmental planners and designers to be patient in their expectations.

The Claims of Science and the Claims of Practice Must Be Kept in Balance

There is a danger that environmental behavioral science will be mistakenly considered applied research, because of the valuable encouragement the field has been receiving in its beginning period from the environmental planning and design professions. However, what is true of the problem treated here—the comprehension of the everyday physical environment—will be true of the problems environmental behavioral science will be encountering generally: they will be basic, fundamental problems concerning human behavior and experience. While it will be greatly beneficial to the research enterprise if the professions exert strong and steady pressure upon environmental behavioral scientists to speak to professional needs, and to carry on research appropriate to their needs, it will often be necessary and wise for the scientists to move in other directions. In the fullness of time, of course, all issues will be dealt with, but there will necessarily be sequential constraints upon the timing and ordering of the development of the field.

Scientists and Practitioners Should Share a Commonsensical Grasp of the Nature of the Problem

The review of possible directions of research on the comprehension of environmental displays has demonstrated the often overlapping but essentially tangential relationship between the inherent conceptual structure of a problem and the context of professional practice. Since the points of contact will inevitably be intermittent rather than constant, it will promote understanding on the part of the professional disciplines if they are aware of the more abstract and socially indifferent perspective scientists bring to bear upon the conceptual structure of problems. On the other hand, if the scientists are to be alert to the social significance of their research and to practical implications of their methods and findings, then they will always need to be familiar with developments within the environmental planning and design disciplines.

26. The Use of Behavioral Maps in Environmental Psychology

WILLIAM H. ITTELSON, LEANNE G. RIVLIN, AND HAROLD M. PROSHANSKY

Behavior always occurs someplace, within the limits of some physical surroundings. Recent recognition of the importance of this self-evident fact has led to a growing number of studies relating various aspects of behavior to the physical spaces in which they are observed. Any data of this kind can be thought of as constituting a *behavioral map*. The necessary features of such a map are descriptions of behavior and of participants and statements relating the behavior to its physical locus. Behavioral mapping as thus defined is a very general technique for studying environmental influences on behavior. As might be expected in any new field of inquiry, this technique has so far not been widely used, but those who have used it have found it extremely fruitful. We wish here to describe procedures for producing and using behavorial maps in the study of environmental psychology.

General Characteristics of Behavioral Maps

The familiar architect's floor plan provides the prototype of all behavioral maps—a scale drawing of a physical space with each area labeled according to the kinds of behavior expected to occur there. It presents, in capsule form, the salient features encountered in any attempt at behavioral mapping: categories of behavior, physical locations, and a technique for relating one to the other. "Living room," "bedroom," "kitchen"; these labels represent, at the same time, physical areas and rather gross behavioral categories. Both aspects can on occasion be made more precise. An architect can, for example, divide a living room into separate areas for "TV viewing," "reading," and "conversation."

The same information can be conveyed in other ways than labels on a floor plan. For the purpose of relating behavior to its physical locus, it may be more useful to use a table in which rows represent physical locations and columns represent behavior. An index mark at the intersection of a row and column then indicates whether that behavior occurs at that location. Other possible ways of presentation include graphs, pictures, and combinations in which, for example, tables may be superimposed on plans or graphs or pictures. The optimum presentation varies with the nature of the specific problem and the audience being addressed.

The behavioral maps discussed in this paper will be tabular in form for the most part, but it should be clear that in our terminology the floor plan, the table, and any other methods of data presentation are all equivalent behavioral maps that differ only in the manner in which they visually present the same information.

The information needed to use a behavioral map as a research tool differs in two significant ways from that provided by the prototypical architect's floor plan. First and most obvious is the nature of the behavior categories. The floor plan implies very broad groupings of behavior. For research purposes, however, the behavior categories must be explicit, precise, and relatively narrow, and in addition, relevant to the particular problem under consideration. Let us consider, for example, a room conventionally labeled "bathroom" on the plan. The behaviors implicitly associated with this label are bodily functions, washing, and grooming, and these are what the room presumably is designed for. Kira's study (1966) of the bathroom, however, clearly reveals that these are only a small sample of the total range of behaviors that characteristically go on in that area. The bathroom, according to Kira, also functions as a private telephone booth and as a refuge from family quarrels, among other things. These categories of behavior not only explicitly extend the types of behaviors expected to occur in the "bathroom"

beyond those implied by the label, they also are more relevant to an understanding of the problems related to the structure of family life than are the behaviors more conventionally associated with that area. Behavioral maps, therefore, require a detailed analysis of behavior into relevant categories.

The same study of the bathroom suggests the second characteristic of behavioral maps which sets them apart from the architect's floor plan. The behaviors ascribed to the bathroom were learned about empirically; they were not postulated on theoretical or a priori grounds. The bathroom is not intended to be a telephone booth; and there is no reason to believe that anyone would assume that it would be used as a telephone booth, except for the very simple fact that it can be observed to function in that way. Behavioral maps, then, are empirical; they describe observed behavior. Since any complete description of observed behavior must be quantitative, it follows that behavioral maps also are quantitative; they deal with amounts of behavior in addition to qualitative descriptions. For example, to say that the bathroom may be used as a telephone booth is interesting but tells us relatively little about the actual functioning of the bathroom until we also have information such as how often it serves this purpose compared to its other functions and how much telephoning occurs there compared to other more conventional places in the home.

Mapping the Psychiatric Ward: An Illustrative Example

The two characteristics of behavioral maps —the analysis of behavior into relevant categories and the empiricial observation of these behavior categories—constitute the two major technical problems of behavioral mapping. They will be discussed here in the context of specific procedures developed for the mapping of two psychiatric wards of a large, private, urban general hospital. The wards have a patient population of approximately 22 patients each, and are devoted to an active treatment program. A patient's stay rarely exceeds three months. During that time a variety of therapeutic techniques may be used, including drugs, electric shock, psychotherapy, and several activity therapies. The wards will not be described in any more detail here since the interest of this paper is in behavioral mapping techniques rather than in behavior on the psychiatric ward. Fuller descriptions of the wards and analysis of behavior on them have been presented elsewhere in this volume.

Categories of Behavior

Presumably, any category or set of categories of behavior could be used in constructing a behavioral map. Before empirical work can be carried out, however, decisions have to be made as to what kinds of behavior are relevant to the problem being studied. A basic decision, even before the types of behaviors are considered, is whether the focus is to be the behavior of individuals or the behavior of groups. All behavioral maps reported here concentrate on individuals, but we are also developing approaches to the mapping of group activity.

In dealing with the psychiatric ward, it seemed desirable to look at behaviors that most nearly describe the daily round of activities of the patients. These would also presumably be most likely to be related to the physical surroundings in which they take place. Eating, sleeping, reading, talking, watching television—these are what the patients actually do. At the same time, they involve direct commerce with the environment. For these reasons, attention was focused on common-sense descriptive categories of the gross, overt, observative behaviors that, taken together, actually make up the daily routine of the patients.

Once the basic decision as to the kinds of behaviors to be studied is made, the development of the actual behavioral categories is a straightforward process applicable to any setting. It involves three steps: cataloguing observed behaviors, generalizing the behaviors into categories for observation, and combining observational categories into analytic categories.

Cataloguing the behavior on the psychiatric ward was carried out by having observers on the ward record, over extended periods of time, all specific examples of a particular behavior that they observed. This, of course, resulted in a very large list of detailed units of behavior. After observations had been conducted for a sufficiently extended period of time, so that major examples of behavior presumably had not been missed, the list was examined, and duplicate, trivial, or obviously totally idiosyncratic observations were eliminated. The resulting inventory was a list of some 300 descriptions of behavior, samples of which are listed in Table 26–1.

Clearly such a list is too long and too specific to be useful in the collection of data. Summary observational categories were therefore derived from this list. Trained judges sorted the list of behaviors into groups that were judged to be more or less homogeneous within themselves and distinct from the others in terms of some observational characteristic; that is, they represented sets of behaviors that could be readily described for the observers and in turn identified by them. Table 26–1 also indicates the list of observational categories and sample behaviors under each.

For the purpose of analysis, the observational categories were still further combined into analytic categories that were appropriate for the particular problems being studied. Analytic categories may vary from problem to problem. In the behavioral maps described below, six summary analytic categories are used: isolated-passive, isolated-active, social, mixed-active, miscellaneous, and traffic behavior. The observational categories are indicated in Table 26–1.

It should be noted that the way in which behaviors are grouped into observational and analytic categories is crucial to interpreting the data. Clearly, different combinations could produce different results. The procedures for the categorization are of great importance. The use of trained judges is a well-accepted technique, although it is not the only one. We are presently investigating the use of multivariate techniques for determining whether there is an underlying dimensional structure to the inventory of behaviors. The results of this approach are not available at the present time, but they may ultimately lead to a better technique for categorizing the inventoried behaviors.

Observational Techniques

The general methodological and technical problems involved in the use of observational procedures in the social sciences have been fully discussed in volumes devoted to those problems and need not be presented here. In any social-science study, alternative approaches are available to the investigator; in this section we will briefly indicate the specific procedures used.

All the data were collected through the use of well-trained observers who spent considerable time on the ward becoming thoroughly familiar with the functioning of the ward and well known to the ward occupants. They were introduced to and accepted by all as students of "ward architecture." They were instructed to be friendly with ward personnel and patients, but to avoid direct involvement in ward activities. Whether the presence of the observers affected behavior on the ward cannot be directly answered. Ward personnel, however, reported no differences between periods with the observers present and periods without them.

The location and timing of observations typically involved complete coverage of all physical spaces of the ward on an instantaneous time-sampling basis. What this meant in practice was that all areas of the ward were observed every 15 minutes by enough observers so that the total observation time, while not actually instantaneous, did not exceed three or four minutes. This general procedure, which was used for all the maps reported in this paper, was varied in a number of ways for specific problems. On occasion, only a single area in the ward was observed, if that area was of particular relevance to a question raised. Similarly, the instantaneous time-sampling procedure occasionally was modified to include continuous observations over longer periods of time. This made it possible to record the duration of activities and patterns of flow of activities, which can be of more interest for certain problems than the instantaneous recording of behavior. The choice between instantaneous or continuous observation must be made in terms of the particular problems studied. It can be noted, however, that in this context time and space vary reciprocally; that is, if a complete coverage of spaces is required, a time-sampling procedure becomes necessary. On the other hand, if complete coverage over time is needed, spaces must be sampled or selected. The only alternative in either case is to flood the ward with so many observers that behavior must inevitably be altered.

Observations were recorded on data sheets designed for quick and easy use by the observers. The sheets permitted direct punching of the data. A sample sheet is given in Table 26–2. It will be noted that the observer recorded, in addition to data such as the location and time of observation, the number of participants engaged in each category of behavior described in the previous section. The participants themselves are identified in only the broadest terms—for example, male or female patient, staff, or visitor. Even so broad an identifi-

TABLE 26–1. *Classifying Behavior into Categories*

Behavior	Observational Categories	Analytic Category
Patient reclines on bench, hand over face, but not asleep Patient lies in bed awake	lie awake	
Patient sleeps on easy chair One patient sleeps while others are lined up for lunch	sleeping	Isolated Passive
Patient sits, smiling to self Patient sits, smoking and spitting	sitting alone	
Patient writes letter on bench Patient takes notes from a book	write	
Patient sets own hair Patient sits, waiting to get into shower	personal hygiene	
Patient reads newspaper and paces Patient reads a book	read	Isolated Active
Patient and nurse's aid stand next to alcove Patient stands in doorway smoking	stand	
Patient paces between room and corridor Patient paces from room to room saying hello to other patients	pacing	
Upon receiving lunch some patients take it to bedroom Patient sits at table and eats by self	eating	
Patient cleans tables with sponge Patient makes bed	housekeeping	
Two patients listen to record player Patient turns down volume on radio	phonograph-radio	Mixed Active
Patient knits, sitting down Patient paints (oils), sitting down	arts and crafts	
Patient and registered nurses watch TV together Patient watches TV, goes to get towel, returns	TV	
Patient stands and watches a card game Patient sits on cans in hall watching people go by	watching an activity	
Patients play soccer in corridor Patient and doctor play chess	games	
One patient talks to another in reassuring tones Four patients sit facing corridor, talk sporadically Patient fails to respond to doctor's questions	talk	Social
Patient introduces visitors to other patient Patient stands near room with visitors	talk (visitor)	Visit
Patient comes in to flick cigarette ashes Patients go to solarium	traffic	Traffic

TABLE 26–2. *Ward Observation Form*

Date 7/15 Ward 10 Observer 3 Time M _____ Census M 4
  A _____ F 24
  E 8:15 T 28

Day / Room	Talk M F S V	Games M F S V	Watching an Activity M F S V	Writing M F S V	Read M F S V	Stand M F S V	Pace M F S V
Ind						1	
Group 1	1 1						
Group 2	1 1						
Group 3							
Group 4							
Group 5							

	Personal Hygiene M F S V	Lie Awake M F S V	Sleep M F S V	Sitting Alone M F S V	Arts & Crafts M F S V	TV M F S V	House-keeping M F S V
Ind				1 1			
Group 1						2	
Group 2							
Group 3							
Group 4							
Group 5							

	Phono-Radio M F S V	Eating M F S V	Hospital Routine M F S V	Traffic M F S V	M F S V	M F S V	M F S V
Ind							
Group 1							
Group 2							
Group 3							
Group 4							
Group 5							

cation required considerable training and familiarity on the part of the observers since, in the hospitals studied, patients, staff, and visitors alike wore street clothes. Specific identification of individual patients is obviously desirable for certain purposes, but it can be done only at the sacrifice of other forms of data.

In summary, then the behavioral maps of the psychiatric ward described here were obtained from reports of observers, who recorded, on a time-sampling basis for every area of the ward, the number of patients, staff, and visitors engaged in each of a predetermined set of behavior categories.

The maps discussed below report only the data on the behavior of the patients. The behavioral map is presented as a table, the rows of which represent physical areas of the ward and the columns, behavior categories. The numbers at the intersections of rows and columns are the numbers or the percentages of patients engaged in the particular behavior at the particular place. A map presenting the actual number of individuals observed (in our terminology, an "observed map") is necessary and useful for a description of the actual uses to which the various locations on the ward are being put. For all practical questions of design, assignment of staff, requirements for facilities, and so on, the important determinant is the actual number of users. For most nonapplied research problems, however, the observed map is of limited value because it does not permit comparison of different situations involving different absolute numbers of individuals. For this purpose, a map showing percentages based on the observed number divided by the potential number of users (in our terminology an "adjusted map") is preferable. All of the maps discussed below are adjusted maps.

Reliability and Validity of Behavioral Maps

Table 26–3 represents a typical sample map of a hypothetical average psychiatric

ward. It is hypothetical in the sense that the data represent average figures for a number of different wards observed on many different occasions. The columns represent the analytic behavior categories described earlier, that is, social, isolated-passive, isolated-active, mixed (mostly television watching), miscellaneous (mostly visiting), and traffic. The rows represent the entire ward divided into major areas, bedrooms, and public rooms. For present purposes, no finer discrimination of spatial locations is necessary. For other purposes, however, it is valuable to differentiate among bedrooms of different sizes and number of occupants, and also among public rooms of varying functions, such as the dayroom, the hallway, the dining room, and so on. The numbers in the table represent the percentage of patients assigned to the ward who were actually observed to be engaged in the particular behavior at the particular location indicated.

The data in Table 26–3 were obtained from a number of different locations at many different times. Clearly, this table is of use only if the data on which it is based are reliable. Since a number of different observers must necessarily be used in order to cover the times and spaces involved, a special check of interobserver reliability was conducted by having two observers independently report the same ward at the same times. Interobserver agreement was high. Of 693 physical areas observed, 583 or 84 percent were reported identically by the two observers; that is, the observers identified all participants and categorized all behaviors in each area in exactly the same way. Of 797 individuals observed, 83 percent were reported identically. When behavioral maps were constructed from the data for each observer, they were almost identical. The mean difference in the percentage of patients reported for each of the six analytic categories was less than 1 percent, and the range was from 0 to 2.2 percent.

The reliability of the instrument itself is more directly revealed by a split-half

TABLE 26–3.　*Behavior on an Average Ward[a]*

	Traffic	Visiting	Social	Mixed Active	Isolated Active	Isolated Passive	Total
Bedrooms	0.1	3.2	3.9	0.8	5.7	10.4	24.1
Public rooms	2.7	6.5	14.3	9.4	4.6	2.6	40.1
Total	2.8	9.7	18.2	10.2	10.3	13.0	64.2

[a] Unless otherwise indicated in this and subsequent tables, the numbers represent the percent of the patients assigned to the ward engaged in each activity, and the times of observations were 9:30 A.M.–12:30 P.M.; 1:30–4:30 P.M.; 6–9 P.M.

check, in which the data obtained from 50 percent of the observations were compared with that obtained from the remaining 50 percent. In one such check, the percentage of patients assigned to each of the observational categories in one-half of the observations differed from that obtained from the other half by a mean of 0.55 percent, with a range from 0 to 2.7 percent. Behavioral maps constructed from these data differed by even smaller amounts.

Repeated observations represent another way of assessing the reliability of a measurement technique. Table 26–4 represents a comparison of the data obtained on three separate days of the week, and we find that repeated observations yield almost identical behavioral maps of the wards. Similarly, Table 26–5 presents data obtained on two separate wards in the same hospital. The wards are virtually identical in physical construction and very similar in patient and staff characteristics. They are, of course, both operated under the same general set of hospital administrative procedures. Clearly, the behavior on the two wards as reflected in the behavioral maps is virtually identical.

In summary then, interobserver reliability is high, split-half reliability is high, and reliability is high for repeated observations of the same situation at different times and also for repeated observations of different but similar situations. We feel relatively secure in concluding from these diverse observations that the behavioral maps produced by the techniques described

above are indeed reliable within the limits of accepted scientific practice.

The question of assessing the validity of the behavioral mapping technique is much more complex. Indeed, the very meaning of validity in this context is not clear. The observational categories were designed to be directly and easily observed and identified. It has been argued that in dealing with this type of overt, easily observed behavior, high reliability is tantamount to high validity. This is probably the closest we can come to a rigorous assessment of the validity of the behavioral maps.

While the fact may not be directly related to the question of validity, however, it is interesting that the pictures of the wards derived from the behavioral maps agree quite well with descriptions obtained in other ways. For example, Table 26–6 compares estimates of the way patients distribute time spent in their bedrooms derived from their responses to items in an interview with the actually observed distribution of activities in the bedrooms. While such estimates should be evaluated with caution, it is remarkable to note an almost exact duplication between the observed distribution and the estimated one. Similarly, although they are not reducible to quantitative form, qualitative descriptions of the uses of various parts of the ward obtained from staff members agree in almost every detail with corresponding pictures drawn from the behavioral maps. In short, the description of behavior on the

TABLE 26–4. *Comparison of Behavior on Three Different Days: Average Ward*

	Traffic	Visiting	Social	Mixed Active	Isolated Active	Isolated Passive	Total
Monday	3.2	3.4	20.6	11.2	10.1	14.0	62.5
Wednesday	3.2	7.8	21.6	11.2	10.4	14.4	68.6
Friday	3.4	8.0	20.2	9.8	14.0	12.0	67.4

TABLE 26–5. *Comparison of Behavior on Two Wards*

	Traffic	Visiting	Social	Mixed Active	Isolated Active	Isolated Passive	Total
Bedrooms							
Ward 1	0.0	3.3	3.4	1.0	6.5	10.3	24.5
Ward 2	0.2	3.1	4.4	0.6	4.9	10.4	23.6
Public rooms							
Ward 1	2.5	4.7	14.5	10.0	4.1	2.3	38.1
Ward 2	2.9	8.3	14.1	8.8	5.1	3.0	42.2

ward given by the behavioral map is in very close agreement with the picture reported by those most intimately familiar with the ward.

A number of objective conditions are readily translatable into expected behavioral differences that can be verified by examining the behavioral maps. For example, a fairly large amount of visiting would be expected on visiting days and a correspondingly small amount on nonvisiting days. Table 26–7 compares the distribution of activities on visiting and nonvisiting days and indeed reflects the expected differences. Other evidences of consistency with objective expectations can be found by examining almost any behavioral map. Table 26–3, for example, shows that traffic takes place primarily in the public rooms; in this case, halls are subsumed in the public rooms category. The same table shows that television viewing occurs exclusively in the public rooms, which indeed is where the television set is located. Less obvious but still internally consistent is the distribution of social and isolated-passive behavior; the public rooms

are chosen primarily for social activities, while isolated-passive activities take place primarily in the bedrooms. In short, wherever fairly certain predictions can be made on the basis of objective differences in the situation, these differences are reflected in the behavior as recorded in the behavioral maps.

It seems fairly justifiable to conclude, therefore, that the behavioral mapping technique produces reasonably reliable and accurate descriptions of the quantitative distribution of behaviors in the various parts of the psychiatric wards studied.

TABLE 26–6. *Comparison Between Observed Distribution of Activities in Bedrooms and Patients' Estimates of Their Activities*

	Social (%)	Isolated Active (%)	Isolated Passive (%)
Observed	29	28	43
Estimated	29	31	40

TABLE 26–7. *Comparison of Behavior on Visiting Day and Nonvisiting Day*

	Traffic	Visiting	Social	Mixed Active	Isolated Active	Isolated Passive	Total
Bedrooms							
Nonvisiting	1.1	0.6	1.8	0.1	5.5	13.8	22.9
Visiting	0.9	6.7	2.1	0.0	5.0	11.3	26.0
Public rooms							
Nonvisiting	3.4	1.3	13.0	18.0	6.9	7.1	49.7
Visiting	3.5	6.0	8.6	14.0	7.7	5.4	45.2
Total							
Nonvisiting	4.5	1.9	14.8	18.1	12.4	30.9	72.6
Visiting	4.4	12.7	10.7	14.0	12.7	16.7	71.2

Some Uses of Behavioral Maps

Behavioral maps were developed as a technique for studying the relationships between behavior and the physical space in which it occurs. Four general examples of ways in which they can be used for this purpose will be illustrated here from the studies of psychiatric wards. These types of uses are not limited to the psychiatric wards, however, but can be of value in studying any setting.

1. Description. Any of the behavioral maps already described provides a shorthand description of the distribution of behaviors throughout the ward. These descriptions, in terms of percentages, are the basic data on which most other uses of behavioral maps are based. However, for some purposes, distribution of actual numbers of patients, rather than percentages, are necessary. The designer of a specific facility, for example, needs to know the number of individuals for whom he is designing. Also for the student of ward behavior it is useful to bear in mind at all times the meaning of the percentages in terms of actual numbers of patients. Table 26–8, an "observed" map, shows such a picture, at a particular moment in time, of the 24 patients assigned to one ward. Eight patients were off the ward; of the sixteen remaining, six were in the bedrooms and ten in the public rooms. In

the bedrooms, three patients were lying in their beds, probably asleep, one was probably engaged in personal hygiene, one was entertaining a visitor, and one was talking to a staff member. In the public rooms, four patients were engaged in social conversation among themselves and with staff members. Two were entertaining visitors, two were watching television, and one was probably working on a craft project.

2. Comparison. For purposes of comparing two different situations or conditions, "adjusted" maps showing percentages rather than actual numbers must be used. As an example, Table 26–9 compares the use of spaces on the ward by male and female patients. Some interesting differences clearly emerge. The women tend to use their bedrooms more than the men, and this difference is reflected in all categories of behavior except social. Here the overall trend toward much greater social activity by the males produces the only category in which male use of bedrooms exceeds female. The total use of the public rooms by men and women is approximately equal, but the distribution of activity is markedly different; the men devote almost half of their time in the public rooms to social activity, while the women spend less than one-third of the time there socializing. In contrast, the single most popular activity

TABLE 26–8. *Distribution of Actual Numbers of Patients*[a]

	Traffic	Visiting	Social	Mixed Active	Isolated Active	Isolated Passive	Total
Bedrooms	0	1	1	0	1	3	6
Public rooms	1	2	4	2	1	0	10

[a] Total N = 24.

for the women in the public room is television watching which, together with visiting, accounts for 50 percent of their activity. These and similar examples illustrate the kinds of comparisons that can fruitfully be made with the use of behavioral maps.

3. General Principles in the Use of Space

The major value of behavioral maps, as a research tool, lies in the possibility of developing general principles regarding the use of space that apply in a variety of settings. It is premature to attempt such generalizations at this time, but two examples will illustrate the way they may ultimately emerge.

Peaking is a descriptive generalization used to indicate the fact that certain areas consistently show a predominance of a single type of activity. In Table 26–9, for example, the bedrooms show a characteristic peaking at isolated-passive behavior.

In some cases, peaking is a product of an interaction effect between space and occupants, as shown again in Table 26–9 by the marked peaking in the public rooms of social behavior for male patients only.

Constancy and reciprocity of behavior refer to two related observations. First, certain kinds of behavior tend to remain virtually constant over wide varieties of conditions, and second, spaces are used reciprocally for this behavior. When the behavior increases in one area, it decreases in another. Table 26–10 shows data derived from behavioral maps made at three different times of the day. Here all behavior (except traffic) is combined into two major analytic categories: nonsocial and social. Social behavior in this case is defined as all behavior that primarily involves interaction between two or more individuals, while nonsocial behavior is primarily not concerned with interactions among individuals. From Table 26–10, clearly nonsocial be-

TABLE 26–9. *Comparison Between Male and Female Patients on One Ward*

	Traffic	Visiting	Social	Mixed Active	Isolated Active	Isolated Passive	Total
Bedrooms							
Male	0.0	3.0	4.1	0.6	5.2	9.0	21.9
Female	0.4	3.7	2.9	1.2	7.6	10.7	26.5
Public rooms							
Male	3.2	3.4	18.8	6.3	4.3	3.1	39.1
Female	2.0	5.8	11.2	13.0	4.0	1.7	37.7
Total							
Male	3.2	6.4	22.9	6.9	9.5	12.1	61.0
Female	2.4	9.5	14.1	14.2	11.6	12.4	64.2

TABLE 26–10.   *Distribution of Behavior in Afternoon Compared to Morning and Evening*

	Combined Nonsocial Behavior			Combined Social Behavior		
	Bedrooms	Public Rooms	Total	Bedrooms	Public Rooms	Total
Afternoon	18.9	13.2	32.1	6.5	13.9	20.4
Morning	15.3	19.2	34.5	6.1	23.1	29.2
Evening	13.6	19.8	33.4	10.9	23.6	34.5

havior remains virtually constant at one-third of the total ward activity over the entire day. The bedrooms and public rooms function reciprocally for this behavior, which is higher in the bedrooms and lower in the public rooms in the afternoon and the opposite during morning and evening. In contrast, social behavior shows no such constancy or reciprocity. Once again it should be emphasized that this is offered as an illustration of the kinds of generalizations that may emerge through the use of behavioral maps and not as an established conclusion regarding social and nonsocial behavior on the ward.

4. Prediction.   Behavioral maps showing quantitatively the predicted or expected distributions of behavior in a new facility can be prepared in advance of construction or occupancy. To the best of our knowledge, this application of behavioral maps has not yet been made, but it potentially offers a useful tool for quantitatively checking the validity of assumptions behind the design of spaces and facilities.

27. An Approach to an Objective Analysis of Behavior in Architectural Space[1]

GARY H. WINKEL AND ROBERT SASANOFF

Introduction

The design profession has long lacked a method for the objective analysis of behavior in architectural spaces. Architects continue to rely upon intuitive design concepts evolved from individual experiences even though increasing environmental complexity and rapid technological change place severe restrictions upon the human

This article is condensed from *An Approach to an Objective Analysis of Behavior in Architectural Space.* Architecture/Development Series No. 5, Seattle, Wash.: University of Washington, College of Architecture and Urban Planning, August, 1966. Presented by permission of the authors and publisher. The authors acknowledge the support of the United States Steel Institute in carrying out this project.

[1] The authors are greatly indebted to the United States Steel Institute, part of whose grants made reproduction of this study possible. The authors also wish to acknowledge their indebtedness to Serge Boutourline, Jr. and Robert Weiss, who laid the theoretical and experimental foundation for this work; to Professor Robert Dietz, Dean of the College of Architecture and Urban Planning of the University of Washington, and Elizabeth Sutton Gustison, Director of the Museum of History and Industry in Seattle, Washington, for their support and cooperation.

being's ability to encode this complexity and utilize it in a rational manner. There are a few architects, however, who have raised serious questions concerning continued reliance upon the "cult of the individual" (Alexander, 1964, and Van der Ryn, 1965). It is their feeling that architects must make a change toward the evolution of methods which will allow the decision-maker to approach environmental problems more rationally. This report concerns one step in a continuing series of related studies seeking to provide a laboratory tool for the *experimental* study of behavior in architectural environments.

The initial purpose of this project is to assess the feasibility of bringing a real world environment into the laboratory via what is termed "simulation." The ultimate objective is to develop a tool, here called the simulation booth, for the study of proposed, as yet unbuilt architectural, urban, or designed landscape environments, for use as a means of predicting certain aspects of user behavior in these environments before they are built.

Photographic representation was used to simulate a real world system. The real world system was the interior of a museum, and the user behavior studied in this environment was movement through the museum; as well as patterns of exhibit viewing. Color photographs of the interior of the museum were used to allow observers to report on how they would move through the museum and which exhibits they would view.

Observed patterns of user movement in the real world system were compared with patterns of user movement obtained in the simulated space.

Although this study involves a museum it is not concerned with museums *per se*. It is only concerned with how well a specific space in a specific museum could be simulated within a laboratory setting, using pedestrian traffic and patterns of exhibit viewing as the dependent variables to be cross-compared. A museum was selected as the setting for this study for reasons to be discussed later, but a supermarket, a shopping center, or a public park could have served just as well. The reader is therefore cautioned against using this report as a basis for decisions concerning the operation or design of museums.

The Real World and the Tracking Study

The real world system selected for simulation was the Museum of History and Industry in Seattle, Washington. This setting was chosen because the occasional change in exhibits would allow even regular visitors to find themselves in the position of a "tourist" rather than that of an "habitué" (Thiel, 1964), thus increasing the tendency of their behavior to reflect the influences of the perceived environment rather than that of habit. Other reasons for the selection of the museum included the opportunities it provided for a variety of experiences (due to the physical configuration of the building), the apparent heterogeneity of its visiting population in terms of socio-economic background, age, and education, and finally, for the shelter it provided from inclement weather.

Movement through the museum was selected as the user-behavior of interest because it was possible to obtain highly reliable estimates of movement patterns; because movement was one variable which appeared to be more easily amenable to study in a simulation setting; because movement is one variable which may be influenced by the form and content of any kind of space; and because movement in the museum situation represents an exceedingly crucial aspect of user behavior operating to define a complete "museum experience."

It should be noted that movement is not a single-dimensioned variable. In addition to specification of path, movement patterns will reveal the number of exhibits visited, the particular points on the floor which the visitor passes over, the elapsed time spent in motion or at rest, head movements and body orientation, etc. Thus movement can serve as a potentially rich user behavior.

Because the focus of this study is architectural, movement through space was chosen as the user behavior which seemed best suited to understanding how visitors utilize the Museum of History and Industry. Had the focus been upon the educational features of the museum, a greater amount of time might have been spent concentrating upon devices which measured the amount of information the visitor retained from his experience of the museum. It is important to note, however, that movement through the space can define the kinds of information available to the viewer and hence data on movement is fundamental to an understanding of the types of experiences assimilated by the visitor.

The space consists of the main exhibit hall, a rectangular room 60 feet by 88 feet with a ceiling height of 13 feet. There are four doors on three sides leading into either auxiliary exhibition spaces or passageways to other points in the museum. A floor plan of the space is shown in Figure 27–1. This hall is lined with illuminated glass cases on all sides, in which permanent displays are presented. In addition, the main hall was furnished with four temporary "island" displays, free-standing in the center of the space, composed of four different trucks or wagons.

A brief description of the auxiliary rooms is necessary. The space on the plan labeled "animal wing" is a small rectangular room containing the stuffed heads and bodies of animals from various parts of the world. The heads are mounted on vertical panels arranged around the room so that the visitor must move around the entire room to view them. There are also cases with animals arranged against naturalistic backgrounds.

The space on the plan labeled "mari-time wing" contains exhibits representative of oceanographic research and industry.

The space labeled "ramp" leads down from the main exhibition hall to exhibitions of various modes of transportation.

The space labeled "main entrance" is a wide corridor fitted with an information and souvenir counter and a variety of permanent exhibits. Most visitors to the museum enter through this hall.

The Tracking Method

The method of data-gathering employed is called "tracking" (Weiss & Boutourline, 1962). Plans of the main gallery of the museum were furnished each of the investigators along with a stopwatch. Using these plans the investigators could track and record the movement of subjects through the space by drawing a line on the plan corresponding to the movement of the subject in the actual space.

Movement was indicated by lines on the maps, with arrows interspersed to show direction of movement. If the subject moved to an exhibit, the line was drawn up to the exhibit and the time spent at that point recorded. If for some reason the subject stopped in the middle of the floor, not at an exhibit, the time spent at that point was also recorded (a stop being defined as an actual physical cessation of movement). Time spent in the ancillary galleries was also recorded, although the observer did not follow the subject into these spaces. Also noted was the amount of time elapsed between the time the subject entered and left the main gallery.

In addition to this information the observer recorded other user behavior in the space, such as "trouble with children," "family conference," "crowding about exhibits," "lack of access to auxiliary galleries" and "indecision as to where to go next."

After the subject left the main gallery for an "exit" (defined for our purposes as

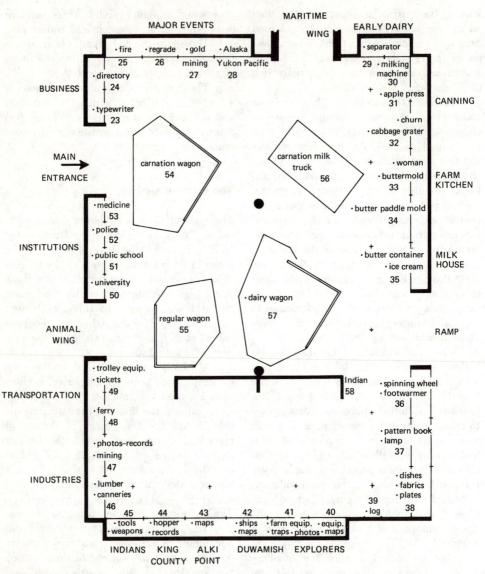

MARITIME

MAJOR EVENTS   WING   EARLY DAIRY

·fire ·regrade ·gold ·Alaska   ·separator

25   26   mining Yukon Pacific   29 ·milking
·directory   27   28   machine
BUSINESS | 24   30
                                                +   ·apple press   CANNING
·typewriter   31 ↑
| 23   ·churn
                                              ·cabbage grater
                                                    32
                        carnation milk |
MAIN →   carnation wagon   truck   +   ·woman   FARM
ENTRANCE   54   56   ·buttermold   KITCHEN
                                                    33 |
                                              ·butter paddle mold
·medicine   34
| 53
·police   +   MILK
INSTITUTIONS | 52   ·butter container   HOUSE
·public school   ·ice cream
| 51   35
·university
| 50

ANIMAL   regular wagon   dairy wagon   +   RAMP
WING   55   57

·trolley equip.
·tickets   Indian ·spinning wheel
TRANSPORTATION | 49   58   ·footwarmer
                                                    36
·ferry   +
| 48
·photos–records   ·pattern book
·mining   ·lamp
| 47   37
INDUSTRIES ·lumber +   +   +   +   ·dishes
·canneries   + ·fabrics
46   ·plates
    45   44   43   42   41   40   39   38
·tools ·hopper ·maps ·ships ·farm equip. ·equip. ·log
·weapons ·records   ·maps ·traps ·photos ·maps

INDIANS KING   ALKI DUWAMISH EXPLORERS
COUNTY POINT

FIGURE 27–1. Floor plan of museum.

down the ramp, or out the entrance corridor) the observer interviewed him briefly
to obtain information on his museum-visit
patterns and significant memories of his
visit, if any. The subject's sex, estimated
age, and whether he visited the museum
alone or with a group was also noted on a
form provided for this purpose.

At all times the tracker attempted to
remain inconspicuous. It was found that
observation at an appropriate distance allowed the preservation of an anonymity
consistent with careful data collecting.

Subjects were selected by the following
procedure, designed to produce a random
sample: the hand of the stopwatch was

allowed to pass an arbitrary time point, and the first person thereafter passing an arbitrarily-selected mark at the entrance became the subject to be tracked.

Most of the tracking data was collected by five graduate students of the Department of Architecture of the College of Architecture and Urban Planning, of the University of Washington.

The Simulated World and the Tracking Study

Having established patterns of user behavior from an analysis of the data collected in the real world, attention was next turned to the creation of a laboratory reconstruction of this real world, in which we could observe user behavior for comparison with that of the real world.

One of the most pervasive difficulties which a research worker encounters in environmental study is the sheer enormity of the systems under consideration. One solution to this difficulty involves abstracting parts of the system so that they may be more easily brought into the laboratory for controlled study. The process of abstracting elements of a system sometimes involves the danger that patterns which may exist among the elements of the fully intact system become lost or minimized as a consequence of the abstraction. Rather than ignore such patterns, it seems apparent that research must proceed with an appreciation of system characteristics and attempt to incorporate them into the research designs ultimately selected.

It is only recently that methodologies have been devised which take pattern relationships between or among elements of the system into account. Current work in the area of large-scale systems has led to the development of techniques which have been given the generic term "simulations." The most reasonable definition of this term is given by Thomas and Deemer (1957). They suggest that "to simulate is to attain

the essence of, without the reality." Inherent in this definition is the realization that complete realism is not necessary for successful simulation. Successful simulation requires only that one be able to reproduce the system under study as accurately as possible without actually employing the system itself. Such a specification tends to make simulation broader in scope than most of the "conventional" methods of experimentation. As a matter of fact, experimentation represents one facet of simulation [see Harman (1961) and Larsen (1963) for discussions of types of simulation].

The approach taken in the present study does not fit in any clearly delineated classifications. It is of course a "laboratory" simulation, in Harman's sense, but this term seems uncomfortably broad. The present method is *not* static and is *not* a dynamic process frozen in time. The advantage (assumed at the present time) of the simulation booth is that it provides a technique for allowing the subject to make his experience dynamic (within the limits of the bulky slide mechanisms used). Also, in its being a three-dimensional space which can be programmed by the subject to change in time (the present authors' restricted definition of a "dynamic" system) the analogue used in the simulation booth represents a less abstracted transformation than a detailed architectural plan. It seems to the authors that the abstraction involved in such a plan leads to an ambiguity which the simulation booth attempts to overcome.

One other advantage is present in the use of the present kind of simulation technique. *It provides a method for checking the results of the simulation booth against behavior in the "real" space.* This advantage should not be underestimated. At whatever level of abstraction at which the simulation booth operates, it is not so far removed from a working system that it ceases to be devoid of any "real world" meaning. Thus, the technique itself makes for a relatively easy transformation from one set of behavioral data (obtained from those operating in the "real world") to another set of behavioral data (obtained from the subjects who experienced and used the simulation booth). The choice of type of simulation must always make provision for an evaluation of the simulation data compared to data obtained from the working system. Without such a provision, the simulation effort might occupy the status of an interesting intellectual exercise, but not much more.

The Simulation Method

The real world was simulated by means of the projection of photographs on screens within a "simulation booth." With a suitable "vocabulary" of photographs of the real world the attempt was made to recreate this real world in the laboratory, in terms of the user behavior of interest. The vocabulary of photographs of the real world presumably was such that it would be possible to enable a subject in the simulation booth to "move" through the simulated world as fully and spontaneously as he could in the real world.

The equipment used for this part of the study was as follows:

1 Nikon 35 mm. camera and f 1.4, 35 mm. lens (lens angular coverage ± 50 degrees horizontally)
1 Majestic tripod
1 Weston Master III exposure meter
2 50-foot tapes
2 wooden "t's"
2 levels
1 metal shim, ³⁄₃₂″ thick
1 plumb bob
 Ektachrome high speed film (daylight) ASA 125

The floor of the main gallery of the museum was divided up on a 5-foot-square grid. This grid was set up by laying off 5-foot intervals along the base of walls of the main gallery. One of the two "t's" was placed at one of these 5-foot points. The other "t" was placed on a grid interval at a 90-degree angle to the first "t" on an adjacent wall. The 50-foot tapes were attached to the "t's" at the wall, and points on the floor were marked where the tapes crossed.

After all grid points had been marked on the floor, the camera was mounted on the tripod. The platform of the tripod was divided into 8 equal angular parts (at 45 degrees each). The plumb bob was attached to the tripod itself so that it hung from the center of the tripod platform. The tripod was then centered over each grid-point on the floor by means of the plumb bob.

The camera was attached to the tripod platform, with the ³⁄₃₂″ metal shim placed between the bottom of the camera and the tripod platform, so that the camera was tilted about 3 degrees down from the horizontal. This was done so that more of the floor and less of the ceiling would be seen in the slides.

The tripod was positioned vertically so that the lens was at about eye height (5'-7"). Eight exposures at 45 degree increments (as marked on the tripod platform) were at each grid-point on the floor, with the first shot always taken in a specified direction. In the museum the first shot was perpendicular to the ramp side wall. All photographs were taken when there were no people in the gallery.

Close-ups were also taken of the exhibition cases along the side walls. In each case one photograph was taken in an "up" position and one in a "down" position, in such a way that the entire vertical dimension of the objects in the case was covered.

The exposures varied according to the local light conditions. The light was a mixture of yellow (tungsten), blue (fluorescent), and natural daylighting. Besides the variety of color there were intensity variations. The aperture of the lens was held constant at f.8 or f.16 (in order to attain a greater depth of field), and the shutter speed varied between 1 and 3 seconds, depending upon the light conditions.

The apparatus used for equipping the simulation booth was as follows:

3 Bell and Howell 2″×2″ manual projectors, with 4″ lenses
3 Screens each 30″×40″, of white illustration board
3 Adjustable stands for the screens
2 Compartmented slide trays
3 Blank slides
  Boxes of end tags
  Platform, desks, chairs, pencils, papers, tacks, etc.

The simulation booth was initially established in a building on the campus of the University of Washington and, later, at the museum. Figure 27–2 shows the disposition of the equipment in the simulation booth. The platform (36″ high) was located in one corner, and positioned on it was a 30″ high desk. The three projectors were arranged on this desk, with their lenses about 6″ above the top of the desk so that the total height of the lenses was thus 6 feet above the floor.

A second sloping platform was arranged 18″ over the projectors for the sectioned slide trays. These trays were compartmented so that there were pigeon holes for each set of 8 slides taken in the museum. The placement of the sections in the slide trays was analogous to that of the points on the museum floor. Each slide was tagged with a flag showing its point on the museum floor and the direction of the photograph.

The screens were diagonally opposite the projector platform at a distance of 8′-6″. Each of the three screens were placed together with their edges touching. The width of the projected image was 36″. The projectors were adjusted so that the rays of the two outer projectors crossed, and so that the axis of each projector was perpendicular (90 degrees) to its screen. The images did not overlap.

The subjects were seated about 3′-6″ from the screen. The distance from the ground to the top of the subject's head was about 4′6″. The subjects were invited into the booth and seated in front of the screens. They were told to adjust the position of the chair so that they could see the screens well. After they were seated they were given the following instructions:

We have taken some photographs of the main gallery at the Museum of History and Industry. We have arranged these photographs in such a way that you may go anywhere you wish in the Museum merely by telling us which way you wish to go. (At this time the experimenter pointed to each of the three screens and said to the subject that he could go "left," "straight," or "right" in the room.) It is important that you try to tell us as much as possible how you would act in the museum if you were actually there. If, for example, you would stop at some exhibits please tell us that. It is, however, important to realize that there are *no right or wrong answers* in this experiment. What is most important is that you do what you think you would do in the museum if you were there. The photographs will help you make your decisions.

We have the slides arranged so that the first photograph you will see will be the view of the museum as you walk into the main entrance. The next set of photographs will put you in the main hallway leading into the main gallery. We will walk you up to the gallery, put you inside the door, and from that point you tell us where you wish to go. If you want to stop at any time and look around the main gallery you may do so.

At this time the first photographs were shown to the observer. He was told that he was being walked up the hallway to the main gallery by the experimenter. After he was inside the door, the observer was

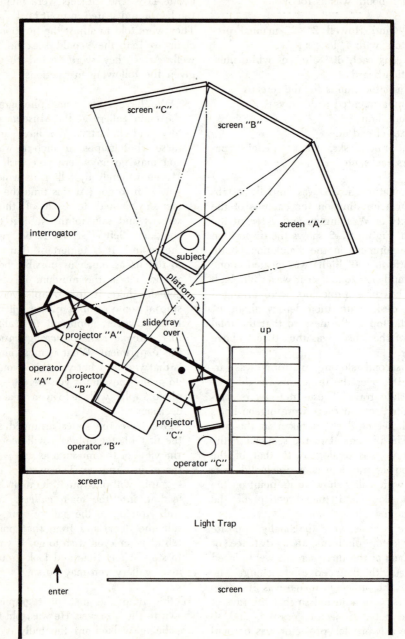

FIGURE 27–2. Floor plan, simulation booth.

shown the full view of the main gallery from the door. The first set of three photographs shown to him revealed the view from 90 degrees to his right and left and the next set showed the views from 45 degrees to his right and to his left. The order of presentation was randomized over the subjects. From that point on, the observer told the experimenter in which direction he wished to go, as well as what he wished to see.

During the time that the observer was in the simulation booth, the experimenter followed the course of the observer's "trip" in the gallery by marking it on a floor plan of the gallery along with a note on the particular exhibits "seen" by the observer.

At the end of the "trip" through the museum (that is, at the point at which the observer indicated that he wished to leave the main gallery and not return) the observer was given a blank map of the floor plan and was asked to mark on it his trip through the museum, and also to label, in a non-detailed manner, the things he remembered seeing. After this was completed, the observer was interviewed about his reactions to the simulation booth and the museum.

Two groups of subjects were used for the simulation study. One volunteer group consisted of 14 male and 14 female students at the University of Washington, 18–20 years old, most of whom were either architecture or interior design majors. The other group consisted of 43 actual museum visitors, randomly selected just before they entered the museum. Their mean age was 35, and 75 percent of the sample were males.

Since the observers used in the first simulation booth analysis were not entirely representative of the usual visitors to the museum, it seemed advisable to repeat the simulation using a second group of observers drawn from the population of individuals who actually visited the museum. In this phase of the study, the simulation booth was relocated at the Museum of History and Industry, and was arranged there according to the same specifications previously used at the University.

The subjects who were selected for participation in the museum study were chosen by the same randomizing procedure as those subjects who provided the original real-world data. The major difference was that these subjects were chosen *before* they entered the museum.[2]

Methods of Data Analysis

A number of analytic procedures suggested themselves for use with the data. There are advantages and disadvantages to each of these methods, but if used in combination they can provide a reasonable picture of the results.

The first analysis made consisted of collations of the separate tracking maps into composite maps, which give an overview of the paths which the subjects followed in their museum experience. Each of the individual tracking maps was combined into a single map, representing the path behavior of the sample. The method of presentation which was utilized involved the breakdown of the composite maps in such a way that the path behavior of the sample becomes clearer. Thus separate maps were made for Saturday and Sunday. The justification for doing this was simply the assumption that possibly a different sample visited the museum on each of those two days. There may be more subtle differences between the groups than this, however, but in the absence of any information to the contrary, it was decided to make separate maps for those days. A second breakdown involved whether the person tracked turned right or left at the main

[2] A brief description of the methods of data analysis follows. For a more complete analysis and discussion of the results, the reader is referred to the original study.

entrance. This was done so that the visual presentation might be clearer on the maps.

One of the most immediately apparent advantages of composite maps is that they summarize a good deal of information which can be quickly grasped by inspection. The size of the sample taking a particular path can be assessed and the direction or the sequences of movement can be relatively easily evaluated.

For the purposes of this study, however, the composites do not provide complete information about the paths and in some cases obscure the relationships which actually exist between movement patterns and sequential experiences, for example, the diversity of paths taken by some of the samples who were tracked in the museum. Visual inspection of the composite maps alone does not provide any criteria for assessing the significance of path diversity when it is encountered. For the purposes of simulation it is necessary to provide the criteria which the composites lack.

More important, perhaps, is the fact that the composite maps do not possess any means for inducing the set of experiences enjoyed by those visitors who take a particular path through the main gallery. Unfortunately, it is not possible to assume that if the same path was taken by two different visitors that they then enjoyed the same set of experiences. Reflection on the point for a moment will easily suggest why this is so. The first visitor may have used a path to get from one point in the gallery to another, while the second visitor may have used the path to experience the set of exhibits which are available to him. Composite map path indicators obscure this kind of information.

To compensate for some of these disadvantages of the composite maps a more objective procedure was adopted. Factor analytic techniques were utilized with the data. The results of the factor analysis were studied to see if they would provide information on the relationships between particular paths taken and sets of exhibits which

were visited by the sample. It was possible to subdivide the paths taken from each of the adjunct galleries (maritime, animal, and ramp area) as well as the main entrance, and relate the direction taken from each of these points (either right, straight, or left) with the set of exhibits seen by each visitor. Such information provided a more quantitative estimate of the behavior of our visitors to the museum. This estimate could be used later when comparisons were made between the behavior of our "vicarious visitors" to the museum and those who actually visited the museum.

Conclusions and Implications

One of the goals of the present study was to evaluate an experimental technique for the simulation of selected environments. Ultimately, it is expected that the simulation technique can be developed into a practical design tool which will allow predictions of user behavior in certain kinds of architectural spaces.

The justification of any experimental tool lies in its ability to predict, with a minimum amount of error, phenomena observed in the "real" world. The results indicated that there are similarities between the real and the simulated world. It is not overly surprising that the similarity was not closer since any new technique usually contains unanticipated error components. The problem is simply to identify and remove those elements in the technique which are contributing to errors.

An initial identification of possible errors in the simulation probably can be traced to the "unreal" aspects of the simulation as currently used. Objective consideration of the simulation device indicates that in many ways it is a very arbitrary method for extracting and reproducing the essence of a space. For the present, attention must be directed toward the refinement of the experimental techniques so that they will bring the simulated data into closer congruence with the real world data.

Briefly, there appear to be two sets of variables which should be more closely examined in any future simulation effort: (1) the freedom which the booth gives to the observer and (2) the clarity of the visual information presented to the simulation booth observer.

Attempts to account for the overestimation of path behavior shown by some of the simulation booth groups led to a suggestion that the booth cannot replicate some of the negative aspects of museum visiting. For example, walking a few steps cannot be considered to be an overly fatiguing experience, but there can be no doubt that the comfort entailed in "viewing" the museum while seated in a chair may increase the propensity of the observer to seek a broader range of experiences than might be the case in the real world experience. Combining the relative ease of movement with experimental instructions that there can be complete freedom of behavior while in the museum may contribute to the increased number of paths taken by the simulation booth observers. Alterations in either the instructions (e.g. a de-emphasis upon freedom of movement) or the manner in which the museum is visited (e.g. having the observer stand while he is shown the slides) may bring the simulation booth data into closer congruence with the observed real world.

A second factor which potentially might account for the observed path overestimation offers much greater possibilities for future study. This factor is concerned with the degree to which a comprehensive "image" of a space can be attained if it is experienced as an abstraction, as it is in the simulation booth.

As the observer "moves" about the main gallery the slides restrict his ability to visually scan his environment extensively. If the observer wishes to "get his bearings" (or clarify his "image" of the space) he must ask the experimenter to let him look around the museum. Although

this option was available to the observers very few of them requested it. Two hypotheses suggest an explanation for this finding: (1) it does not "look good" if the observer becomes lost in the main gallery and must constantly ask for information concerning his present location, and (2) the waiting time required to simply turn an observer around in the space may convince him that the resulting information is not worth the effort. The net effect of inability to orient and establish the relationship between the "self" and the external space denies to the simulation booth observer an experience which is readily accessible to the actual museum visitor. Thus, it is quite likely that the actual museum visitor can form a better integrated visual image or picture of the main gallery than his simulation booth counterpart. If the actual museum visitor does possess a superior information base about the space there will be a corresponding decrease in any ambiguity or uncertainty about his environment. It is well known from information theory (Garner, 1960) that there is an inverse relationship between uncertainty and redundancy in information. One of the consequences of redundancy is that the rate of responsiveness decreases since no new information is forthcoming. Translating such an information processing model into the museum experience, it seems reasonable to suppose that the actual museum visitor moves about the main gallery less because his visual scanning of the environment quickly establishes the redundancy in the gallery. The simulation booth observer can do this visual scanning only if he is willing to pay the price of his time while slides are laboriously changed. Since most of the observers do not take the time, their uncertainty can only be reduced by actually "moving" through the main gallery.

Some evidence obtained from comments spontaneously made by the museum simulation booth sample indicated that some of the observers were uncertain about which parts of the gallery they had visited.

Often a partitioned area appeared to be another room. The observers would then move into the partitioned area and seem disappointed that they had simply entered another section of the main gallery. Once committed to the area, however, the natural tendency was to continue in the path selected.

A more searching test of the hypothesis that the simulation booth observer had greater difficulty orienting himself could be obtained if he were given a blank piece of paper and requested to draw the gallery as well as the path he took through it. Such information was available from the student simulation sample, and it confirmed that most of them did have a reasonably good idea of where they were and where they had been. It is possible that being architecture majors, their ability to orient themselves spatially was more developed than the observers from the museum simulation sample. It might be added that the data from the student simulation sample was closer to the real world data than the data from the museum simulation sample. Unfortunately, due to time considerations it was impossible to give the same test to our museum sample. Unsolicited comments, however, did suggest that some of the visitors were just a little confused about their various locations in the simulated museum.

A testing device which might allow the simulation booth observer greater opportunities to scan his environment with a minimum of difficulty is television. Preliminary work in our laboratory has demonstrated the feasibility of utilizing closed-circuit television equipment in conjunction with a scale model environment. Currently this work is being extended to include study of a model of the main gallery of the museum which was used in the present study. Televised "visiting" might reveal patterns of movement which are in closer congruence with actual path behavior.

One of the ultimate goals of the simulation technique would be to allow both researchers and designers an opportunity to test alternate designs which have been proposed as solutions to architectural problems. The utilization of the technique for such a purpose will necessitate adaptations in the equipment depending upon the type of information the designer hopes to obtain. For example, in the present study our primary dependent variable was movement, inferred from patterns of exhibit viewing. If the designer were interested in those elements which the observer looked at as he moved about the gallery different equipment would be required (e.g. an eye movement camera). If he were concerned about the effects of other people in the space a device would have to be included which would allow the superimposition of crowds in the space.

The addition or deletion of equipment is an advantage to the simulation technique because it increases its generalizability. It should not be assumed, however, that the present simulation device will answer all kinds of questions of concern to the architect. But if the device can increase the information base even in limited areas its utility is apparent.

At a level of analysis other than movement the simulation method might be very useful in understanding those components of design which are related to potentially "rich" user behaviors, such as aesthetic preferences, attitudes, and affective responses to design, the relationship of design elements to the formation of coherent or incoherent mental images of the external world, and possibly an initial understanding of the role which the physical environment plays in human behavior.

From an educational point of view, the use of the simulation booth as an "experience generator" should not be overlooked. In the long run, the tendency of the simulation booth to overestimate the amount of movement on the part of observers may be one of its chief assets rather than liabilities. If the simulation booth can control the rate of information input (by restricting the amount of visual scanning which can be done) it may force the observer to look at things that otherwise might have been ignored. Hence, the use of the simulation technique as a "controlled information output device" might be closely connected to the development of *enriched* mental images which have many branches and cross connections. In many ways, this possibility is the most exciting of the many directions that research in this area might lead.

Any final evaluations of the simulation technique will depend upon the limits of those who use it. Hopefully the method will be useful enough so that it may be included in the architect's basic "tool kit."

28.   *A Walk Around the Block*
KEVIN LYNCH AND MALCOLM RIVKIN

What does the ordinary individual perceive in his landscape? What makes the strongest impression on him and how does he react to it? In recent research at the Massachusetts Institute of Technology we have recorded the impressions of persons as they walked through the city streets. Other studies of urban perception have been made, but we believe this to be the first where responses have been recorded while actually moving through the city itself.

In this sample there were interesting agreements about what parts of the scene were most remarkable, and how these parts could be fitted together to make a whole. Spatial form seemed to be a fundamental impression. Spatially dominant buildings, of dominant use or association, also appear in the front rank. Of next importance was the quality of the city "floor," or pavement; and the contents and details of the various storefronts.

The Search for Order in the Environment

Most of these people felt strongly about their visual world, even if they found difficulty in being articulate about it. Emotions were associated with the spatial characteristics, in particular, and with the apparent coherence (or lack of it) in the whole

From *Landscape*, 1959, *8*, 24–34. Reprinted by permission of the publisher and authors.

scene. They seemed to search for, or try to create, a sense of order and continuity in what they saw. The look of the world about them did indeed make a difference in their lives.

The trip began at the corner of Berkeley and Boylston Streets in Boston, and each time the interviewer told his companion: "We are about to take a short walk. Don't look for anything in particular, but tell me about the things you see, hear, or smell; everything and anything you notice." A tiny microphone was attached to the subject's lapel, and the interviewer recorded his comments as they went around the block, through the alley, and into the park. (See Figure 28–1.)

The block itself is not an extraordinary one. It has many typical features of an American shopping street, but with some touches of Boston tradition, and much physical contrast in small compass. Boylston Street, on one side, has a wide range of offices and middle-income specialty stores, while Newbury Street, on the opposite side, caters to a wealthier class, with its elegant dress shops, decorators, beauticians and haberdashers. These shops occupy the ground floors of old, narrow-footed, business buildings which vary markedly in height. Traffic on both streets is one-way, and that on Boylston is quite heavy.

Between the streets is a narrow alley, neither meaner nor dirtier than most. At the eastern end, across Arlington Street, lie

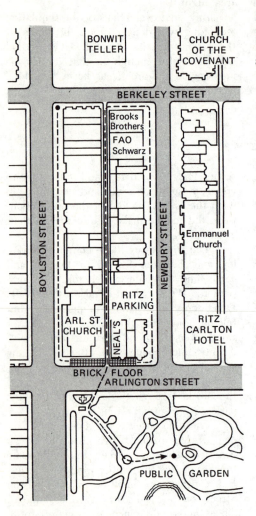

FIGURE 28–1. The Block itself: The dotted line shows the course of the walk, starting at the corner of Boylston and Berkeley Streets.

the Public Gardens, planted in the romantic style. At the corner of Arlington and Boylston stands the old brownstone Arlington Street Church, completed in 1861, and one of the first buildings to occupy the newly-filled Back Bay lands. At the western

end of our block facing Berkeley Street is Bonwit Teller's, occupying the building built in 1864 for the Museum of Natural History. During the interviews the weather was cold, sometimes sunny. The trees were bare, and there were a few patches of old snow on the ground.

Twenty-seven subjects made this tour, which was an outgrowth of earlier tests along Copley Square, in Boston, and Brattle Street, in Cambridge. After the walk, the subjects were tested for their memories of the event, both verbally and through photographic recognition. Some of the subjects were very familiar with the area, and for others it was their first visit. They varied in age, sex, occupation and national background, but the group was too small to be truly representative of American city-dwellers.

Since the process of perception is so rapid and complex, often so difficult to verbalize, the findings must be regarded only as the perceptions which were "at the top of the heap" in the whole conscious-unconscious sensing of the environment. Furthermore, a recorded tour in itself is sufficiently abnormal as to intensify, and possibly distort, the usual day-by-day perception of the city.

Yet with all these qualifications, the results are a first clue as to how our cities affect us. Even aside from its value as a research tool, the method used has potential value in the training of designers, and as a device to make the layman more directly aware of the environment in which he lives.

The Walk Itself

The walk proceeded first along the wide Bolyston Street sidewalk. Two-thirds remarked almost immediately on the spatial quality of the street—its breadth, the width of the sidewalk, the height of the flanking buildings and the open vista at the Garden end.

I like the openness, I like the width of the sidewalks, I like the feeling of uncrowded space. You can never feel at the bottom of a well on this spot.

One or two referred to the heights of the buildings along the street, with the remark that they were not so high as to be uncomfortable. This same sense of scale is implied in the word "house" which several people used, even though few of these business buildings could have been residences in the past. Some subjects were conscious of the general architectural disunity:

Each individual building is almost ugly, and they don't seem to fit together at all.

A woman recalled after the walk:

There were all different styles of houses, they didn't seem to match, especially the heights of the houses varied so much, with some houses you could see the sides and you could see that they were not really meant to be exposed.

One walker summed it up briefly:

I think it is the hodge-podgeness of our streets, like down ahead of us, that is so sort of discouraging.

The majority of our walkers commented at one time or another on some sign they saw. However, there was little consensus of recognition of any particular one. Out of the vast number of signs strewn along the path, only a small minority were noticed at all, and some subjects referred to this welter of communication with irritation:

The first thing I notice are the signs along the street, a confusion of signs.

They sort of reach out and grab you by the throat.

A large clock on a standard in the center of the wide sidewalk excited the comment of a third of the subjects, as did a sidewalk book stall, both because of their intrinsic interest as well as their position in space. But a mid-sidewalk sign farther down the street was blissfully ignored. Alongside the Arlington Street Church a number of newly-painted trash cans caught everyone's eye, no doubt because of their bright yellow and black colors, contrasting with the gray of the sidewalk and the brown of the façades.

All but one of the walkers commented at one time or another upon the stores themselves, and the contents of their windows. Window-shopping is undoubtedly a pleasant and absorbing occupation for many of them. Like the signs, the consensus of selection seemed weak, but the interest was real, and not marked by irritation.

At least half spoke of the parked cars along the sidewalk edge, most often in reference to the problem of parking itself. Almost as many remarked upon the moving traffic, although with little emotional connotation at this stage. But up to this point, of the multitude of other details to be seen or discussed, almost all were passed by in silence or with only scattered comment: street furniture, people, colors, smells, sounds, weather.

At the Arlington Street Church the subjects' animation once again matched that with which they first greeted Boylston Street. Only three failed to comment upon this church which, by its associations, position, material, form and landscaping, contrasts strongly with the remainder of the block. Their remarks conveyed pleasure as well as interest:

Seems to be the most exciting thing on the street, the church.

Every time I look up, I tend to look at our church steeple.

Being of sandstone, it has a much

richer character, really, than most stone buildings.

As they approached this corner and remarked upon the church, they were struck even more forcibly by the space of the Public Gardens opening up across the street. Only one walker was so stubborn as not to mention it at all. The comments were precise and emphatic in their pleasure:

Well, the nicest part of this section is definitely the Public Gardens.

And the comments are often well-considered:

I often envy the people who are able to stay . . . [where] they can look out onto the Public Gardens, across the Common. . . . People don't realize what a beautiful thing, not only in the daytime, but at night. . . . Here you get the feeling of spaciousness and at the same time you don't feel lost.

Distant objects could now be appreciated:

Look at that dome on the State House. That certainly shines.

The space of the Public Gardens was one of the strongest experiences of the entire journey. It also called attention to details within itself: one-third of the subjects noticed the statue of Channing which faces the church, and several pointed out the old iron fence which encloses the Garden.

Around the corner on Arlington, the subway entrance, a low masonry box in the middle of the sidewalk, elicited diverse comments. To one women it was:

These ugly subway entrances—low, squat and dirty, black and cold-looking holes in the ground.

But to a little girl it held promise of adventure:

Why don't we go down there, and go out to another town?

Here the sidewalk material changed from patched cement slabs to brick. This drew a surprising amount of attention, mixing pleasure with the uneasiness of high-heeled women:

Brick sidewalks, hazardous, but very pleasant just to have a different texture for a sidewalk.

Over one-half spontaneously recalled the floor material in the post-walk interview:

I recall here the sidewalks seemed to be the major point of interest or the things that struck one most. It was a sidewalk which was in rather poor condition, extended for a great distance before the eye.

The mouth of the alley did not escape attention. Some were struck by its narrowness alone, others by a happy accident of the city—the view that opens up at the far end of the slot:

The spire of the New England Mutual Hall at the end of the alley—certainly dramatic—I've never noticed that before.

Particularly striking at night as you come along, to see the tower lighted as you glance up the alley.

Past the Arlington Church and across the mouth of the alley is one of the few stores in which there was common interest. "Neal's of California," with its gaudy display of women's apparel, stands in sharp feminine contrast to the church on one side and a dignified antique store on the other. Since the stores abut directly on the sidewalk, while the church is well set back, Neal's is also spatially prominent. Half of the observers seem impelled to pick it out.

A woman's shoe store with the whimsical address of "Zero Newbury" leads around the corner and into Newbury Street itself. Only one-third of the subjects referred to the Newbury space in comparison with the two-thirds who spoke up about Boylston Street, but among these there seemed to be a new enjoyment of the total composition:

> I think looking down the street here, where the sun hits the buildings two blocks or so down, is a sort of unified loveliness. At least, all are approximately the same height, all built at approximately the same time, all have certain characteristics very definitely in common. . . . And I like the punctuation marks of church steeples here and there.

While another puts the feeling of harmony in a more prosaic way:

> There aren't any old signs sticking out.

Three separate buildings draw comments from one-half to two-thirds of the walkers on Newbury: the Ritz Carlton Hotel on the corner, with its connotations of luxury, its sheer cubical mass standing in contrast to the space of the Gardens; the Church of the Covenant at the Berkeley Street corner, whose tall spire is silhouetted against the sky; and the Emmanuel Church, which is also in architectural contrast to its surroundings, but which gets less mention, due probably to its more subordinate mid-block position. It is interesting to note that this is the only building in the entire walk to sustain any significant comment which is not spatially exposed on at least two sides.

One feature on Newbury Street roused more comment than any building: the Ritz-Carlton parking lot, which separates the corner stores from those further up the street, and whose cars project forward over the sidewalk itself. The spontaneous remarks expressed annoyance:

> An ugly little spot where they've cut out some buildings and provided parking . . . a gaping hole.

This parking lot here has always annoyed me. It separates the shopping. I always hate to walk across the lot from one store to the next.

Newbury Street was impressive particularly for its social connotations and personal associations. The non-familiar subjects immediately picked up its class character:

> This seems to be the more fashionable sector. Seems to be more exclusive, since they don't have too much show and pomp in the windows, and no big signs.

The habitués found pleasure and many memories:

> Dear old Newbury Street . . . it's just the epitome of the top aristocratic Boston.

> I can walk in this area and never get tired of it. When I'm away, this is the only—not really the only place—but the place I think of most.

But some of the comments were uncomfortable:

> In an area like this, I've always felt sort of like a stranger . . . sort of like this wasn't particularly your street . . . where the stores sell expensive things not particularly useful to myself.

The small, select stores with their carefully chosen, unpriced displays all came in for comment. But only two, F. A. O. Schwarz and Brooks Bros., caught nearly as much attention as Neal's of California. Schwarz has windows full of attractive toys and Brooks Bros. is remarkable for its corner position, and for its social standing. It might be noted here that throughout the walk only three stores drew the attention of more than half the observers, and all of these had spatial position in which at least two sides of the store were exposed.

At this point another of the strong impressions of the walk appears—the Bonwit Teller store across Berkeley Street, occupying the entire narrow end of the block from Boylston to Newbury. Spatially isolated on three sides, set among trees and grass in a stony environment, it is an obvious period piece of warm red brick and carved stone trim set against the massive smooth backdrop of the New England Mutual building. It is particularly remarkable for its contrast of contemporary commercial use in a building symbolizing institutional values of another time, and for its mannered additions of awnings and show windows. More people chose to comment on this single structure than any other in the total walk, except for the Arlington Street Church.

And I do like Mr. Bonwit. I like it largely because of space, the effect of non-crowding. I know it was an old M.I.T. building at one time [it wasn't]. It's very distinguished, it's done with taste, and mainly it's space, I think, that makes it largely attractive. If the front steps were level with the sidewalk, and there was a new building on each side, it would just be something else, another rather homely spot.

The attention may be captured just as handily, even if the feelings are quite different:

I hate that monstrous awning coming out, it's so affected . . . like a worm coming out of a hole. . . . I've never heard anything so silly as converting a museum into a women's dress store and then showing it from the outside.

Two spontaneous post-walk memories of this building are interesting:

Bonwit's . . . was the dominant thing. It filled your eyes . . . set the mood for the whole place.

I have never realised that it was a museum until the other day [i.e., during the walk], when I looked at it from across the street at Brooks Bros. and noticed that these columns went up the front of it and gave it this museum or post office-like, type of atmosphere. Suddenly I saw the building as a whole though I had passed by it a million times. I had noticed its very obvious distinctive qualities but not the whole building.

Half of the walkers looked up along Berkeley long enough to catch a glimpse of the towering silhouette of the John Hancock building, two blocks away. The majority opinion was unfavorable:

You are suddenly faced with a very ugly mass, the John Hancock, which rises much too high, much too out of shape.

Just as the tour seemed about to end, we turned abruptly down into the alley, which, though not spotless, was reasonably neat by alley standards. In emotional vigor, the comments on this alley and on the Public Gardens stand alone. Three-quarters of the subjects reacted strongly, particularly to the spatial constriction of the alley and to its real or imagined dirt. The tone of voice, the facial expression conveyed the impact as well as the actual words:

Do we have to walk down here? There is no place to walk. Oh, this is awful . . . if they did have a fire people would come down here and land on the garbage, and they'd be killed for sure. . . . I'll bet its stinky in the summer.

Heaven knows what we're going to get into, in the way of rats and trash . . . it's back alleys and they should all be done away with . . . they're horrible eyesores.

Seems like the alley wants to make you

look down not up. Seems as the walls are closing in.

As they proceeded down the alley they were preoccupied with the confinement of space, the lack of light, the dirt and water on the ground, the trash barrels which line the way. In this constricted volume their eyes no longer moved freely about but were turned downwards to the floor, or were fixed on the spot of light at the alley's end. Yards, breaks in the side-walls or lighted windows caused them to turn their heads automatically. Smells were mentioned for the first time, not because the alley was actually very odorous, but because alleys are supposed to smell, and the subjects noticed the lack of them.

Little contrasts caught their attention, such as a small window with shelves of china displayed, or a "poor little weed tree" fighting for life in a storage yard. Their eyes went up to see such things as the tops of fire escapes, outlined against the sky.

But the principal impression, along with the space and the dirt, was the contrast between the backs of the shops lining the alley, and the memory of their fashionable façades on Newbury Street. To the strong physical impression was added the dramatic and human one—of the wealthy shoppers in front and the poor workers behind. Almost half of the tourists were moved to speak when they passed the windows of a basement workroom:

Isn't it amazing—you walk down one street with ladies in furs, and you go down the alley . . . tailor shops down there. Miserable place to work. . . . You forget how many people there are working out of sight.

Ah, this is the true life of the city with the false façade!

Yet despite the sense of drama many of them felt, they were glad to get out again:

The one thing that really saves this alley is the fact that you look out and see that very broad space which gives relief to it. Pigeons flying there, and the sun silhouetted by the buildings.

The spatial release at the end of the alley was correspondingly strong. The Ritz-Carlton parking lot, which had been an irritation on Newbury Street, now became a window from the alley prison.

What a relief! This parking lot with the open space. . . . It feels so good coming out of that dark alley!

And when they came to the end of the alley itself, with the space of the Gardens before them, they were full of joy. These moments of relief were vividly remembered later:

When we finally came out into the Ritz parking lot, it was open, open space and the sunshine came in . . . everything looked so sunny and so clean and nice.

Crossing that street into the park was like . . . a sense of freedom, really.

In all of these reactions to space, it is notable how closely interwoven was the perception with the sense of potential movement on the one hand, and the sense of light or sun on the other.

Before reaching the Gardens, however, they had one more trial; they must cross the traffic of Arlington Street. Until this spot their reaction to traffic and parked cars had been mild, primarily sympathetic with the problems of the driver. There had been little consciousness of traffic noise, and some even managed to call a street a "quiet" one, in the midst of sounds of auto horns. But at this crossing they were faced with the problem of fording the traffic stream, and each one betrayed the anxiety and tense care that this required:

Cars keep coming around here. These cars keep coming around and I can't get by. They never stop—yes, here they come! Exactly what I'm talking about; they never stop going down the street!

During the crossing, there was no mention of any other feature of the environment.

It was with a sense of marked relaxation and pleasure that all entered the Public Gardens. The spatial liberation again came in for almost universal comment. For a second time a significant number of comments were made about other people in the scene: the moving, brightly dressed skaters, enjoying the last ice of the season. Half the walkers specifically mentioned the trees.

It seems like a very good idea to have a park in the middle of the city, if only for cars to go around as well as a place for a quiet walk in between the trees. . . . This is a place I'd like to explore more and look at in more detail. . . . The very idea of trees is pleasant, and there haven't been many on surrounding streets, if any at all.

Several people seemed to enjoy being able to see and hear the city from a little distance while in the park. They were particularly taken by the contrast of park and the city which visibly encloses it. Here they enjoyed two worlds simultaneously.

One man voiced his underlying anxiety that this open space may be one day swallowed up:

Tremendous real estate value this area must be! I wonder if and when Boston will do away with it?

While another looked at it in terms of personal associations:

A park has always been for me a sort of quiet ground from the battle of the city. As you walk along any of the avenues that lead to Central Park, this one

also, the battle crowds on, and when you finally get to the park, all of a sudden things are quiet and it's a different world.

The Walk Analyzed

After the trip, in some cases within a few hours and in others in two or three days, the subjects were interviewed again. First they were asked:

Try to put yourself back at the beginning of the walk, and describe to me in detail the sequences of things and events you noticed.

When they had completed this description they were then asked various questions; whether they remembered any particular buildings, features of buildings, people, sounds, smell, traffic signs or pavements. They were asked how many definite areas they had passed by; if they felt the areas had any order or continuity and why; and whether this part of the city seemed to fit into their pictures of Boston. Some were asked to describe their feelings on the walk, and to say what made the greatest impression on them. All subjects were given a set of photographs of buildings, street views, pavements, details, etc. They were asked to say which objects they had seen on the journey. In general the items noted in the walk interview and in the spontaneous recall of the post-walk interview coincided very well, and a lapse of two or three days versus a lapse of one or two hours made surprisingly little difference in what was mentioned.

The fundamental impressions for almost all our observers came from certain individual buildings and open spaces. Moreover, there is agreement on particular buildings or spaces, and this is consistent between walk and recall. The buildings noticed are remarkable for singularities of style, material, use or association, but particularly for their spatial quality. Only a few structures received significant mention which were not somehow prominent in space.

We might assert that open space is the most impressive feature of all in the city-scape. We might buttress this assertion by speculation that "building" is an expected element of city description, culturally what one "should" discuss; while space relations are seemingly more esoteric and more difficult to verbalize. Thus their frequency is all the more striking.

The spaces remembered afterwards seemed to be either those which were clearly defined in form, or which made evident breaks in the general continuity. In certain earlier (and less systematic) interviews for instance, the space of entering cross streets was ignored, except where heavy on-coming traffic forced recognition of the street as a break in continuity. There was a unanimous reaction of dislike to what was described as the "huge and formless" space of a railroad yard.

Somewhat less strong than spaces or structures, but still a dominant impression, was that of the city floor, the sidewalk pavement. Particularly evocative were the material and the state of repair. There was interest in variations of texture or color, but some irritation at rough surfaces, especially from women in high heels. As a footnote, it is surprising to find that 16 out of 27 people commented on the width of the Boylston Street sidewalk in their spontaneous recall. Four described it in their first sentence, four more in the second, and six in the next few sentences.

Next in interest was the impact of storefronts and their window contents. For most of our subjects these were a pleasant and absorbing feature of the stroll. But there was little unanimity as to which particular stores were singled out for comment. Much depended on the particular interests of the observer.

Signs were also important during the walk itself, but we found only one sign which drew common remark. Some sense of this scatter of attention may be gleaned from the fact that 78 different signs were noted by some one of the walkers; yet only six signs received the attention of more than two people, and only three the attention of more than three. Of these latter three signs, two were associated with buildings or stores which had received overwhelming attention for other reasons, the third was the clock in the Boylston Street sidewalk. Ninety-five percent of the people commented on signs while walking, but only 25 percent later recalled them. The subjects seemed highly conscious of the visual clamor, and often irritated by it, but particular signs seemed to make only a scattered and transitory impression.

Succeeding in frequency of mention were the two categories of street detail and people. The former includes such a miscellany of smaller objects as street furniture, fences, fire escapes, waste containers, subway entrances and statues, and this makes generalization difficult. Specific reasons may usually be attached to the choice of specific items, such as the relation to the Gardens of the Channing statue and the iron fence; the spatial prominence of the book-stall, or the subway entrance; the association with dirt of the alley barrels and the Boylston waste paper container (although the latter was undoubtedly also characterized by its bright color); the spatial constriction of the alley which forced an upward view and thus the silhouetting of the fire escapes. It is interesting to note that one type of detail which has been the subject of some recent design discussion—the street furniture (parking meters, light poles, etc.)—was only rarely mentioned.

There was somewhat greater unanimity in regard to the people selected for comment, and usually the remark seemed to involve a class or group: the dramatic contrast of the seamstresses in the alley basement; the well-dressed women on Newbury who symbolized the street; the skaters in the Gardens, bright moving objects in a peaceful setting. Some of the subjects indicated that during a more normal walk they would be much more observant of others than they seemed to be in these experiments. It may be that there was something in the test situation which implied that their attention should be upon the inanimate environment, and that the rest was not "the city."

Traffic came in for some comment, with somewhat more focus on the parked cars than on the moving ones, until the street had to be crossed. Up to this point, the emotional reaction was low, except where the parked car protruded onto the sidewalk. Feelings were intense and anxious while crossing, however, and all other perceptions were momentarily shut out. These pedestrians seem to accept, or at least to be hardened to, the car, until it threatens their safety, view, or freedom of movement.

Vegetation also played a role of some significance; not only its presence but its absence was expressed. Comments ran toward wishful replantings of street trees, or sadness at "pathetic" grass islands in the vortex of traffic. In fact, there was not much vegetation to notice, but where it occurred, as in the Public Gardens, there was a universal, and very positive, reaction of pleasure. Curiously enough, as with the signs, the recall of this part of the environment seemed to be quite low, in contrast to its relatively high mention during the walk. Why it should be forgotten so easily is a puzzle.

Few people talked about the weather, although there was perhaps a significant unconscious impression which was not verbalized. Sounds and smells were both equally low in conscious awareness. Some sounds were recalled after direct questioning, but even then smells could not be remembered. In both cases, we are probably dealing with a level of habituation, so that the signal rarely receives attention unless it varies significantly from the normal level. Thus, many of the "mentions" of sound or smell were actually the lack of it, i.e., a "quiet" street or an "odorless" alley.

Several obvious elements drew almost no comment at all: color for example (which may nevertheless be important in making another object noticeable), or the sky; wall materials and textures, overhead wires, upper floor façades or doorways.

The recognition of photographs also agreed with the interview results, since people tended to recognize easily photographs of items which were mentioned frequently, and vice versa. Unfortunately, since the photographs did not always cover what later proved to be some of the key visual features of the environment, this particular test was not so useful as it might have been.

The Need for Order

But how were these perceptions fitted together? This was a fundamental point. Take the way in which our particular block was mentally organized. It is interesting to note that interviewees did not hesitate to try to discover whether the area possessed any sense of order for them. Some broke it down into many sub-areas, and others felt it was all one thing. In the "average" case, it was organized somewhat as follows: the three fundamental parts were Boylston Street, Newbury Street and the Public Gardens. Arlington and Berkeley Streets were considered as parts of one or the other of these. The alley was a puzzle, since it didn't "fit" well; usually it was considered either as a separate area or as something which occupied the "backs" of Boylston and Newbury and thus either sewed them together or belonged ambiguously to one or the other. In some cases it was simply forgotten; in one case even explicitly ignored as a part that was rarely seen and thus in a sense didn't exist. Here is a typical example from a foreign viewer:

I could make out three distinct, different impressions. There was the semigaudiness of Boylston Street and the sounds associated with that. There was the relative quiet, possibly even quaintness of the Gardens. Newbury Street was very distinctly on a different level than Boylston. . . . Then there was the alley, of course. . . . These areas stand off from each other, they don't go together. . . . Let's say, with any one of two impressions, Newbury or Boylston, the alley must be along with it; it's just necessary. So perhaps: the alley and Boylston; the alley and Newbury; and the Gardens.

This same agreement as to the organization of certain parts of the environment, coupled with indecision and disagreement as to other parts, could be detected in earlier exploratory studies. For example, the upper end of a certain street, with its large colonial houses, was easily organized as a distinct entity. This was contrasted to the lower end, a busy shopping district, by all observers. Between these two regions, lies another piece of the street which corresponds neither in use nor in physical form to either end. On the other hand, it has no sharp character of its own, being a mixture of apartments, offices, houses and irregular spaces. The observers found this to be a section that they could not easily attach to either the upper or the lower end, yet they were unwilling to give it a life of its own. Feeling compelled to organize their walk, and unable to leave their organization incomplete or to "forget" this section (as some were able to do with the Boylston alley), they responded by attaching it, half-heartedly, to one or the other of the strong "ends." The result was agreement on two classes into which the walk fell, separated by a weak, oscillating boundary.

Thus we have organizational consensus at one point, due to suggestions inherent in the physical form itself, coupled with disagreement in regard to the rest, where the unit into which a part is put depends primarily on past experience. Where this organizational indecision was strongest we found hints of feelings, not only of puzzlement, but of discomfort.

There was apparently a drive to organize the environmental impressions into meaningful patterns, which could be handled with economy. Since the city environment is complex and fluid, this is a difficult operation. Since the present environment so often does not suggest links by its physical shape, the process becomes all the more difficult. Yet it persists, and the resulting mental organization, while apparently quite loose, ambiguous and even contradictory at points, is nevertheless clung to firmly. Certain elements seem particularly important in furnishing distinctions for area classifications in the city, such as people and activity; land use; and general physical form, spatial form in particular.

Native and newcomer agree surprisingly well as to *what* is worth their notice, but significant differences appear between them in the way they organize these things (see Figures 28–2 and 28–3). The more familiar observer tends to establish more connections, and not to break his environment down into as many isolated parts. Thus a stranger might divide the walk into six parts: the four sides of the block, the alley, and the Gardens. For an old hand, however:

Brooks Bros. rounds the corner and Charles Antell rounds the other corner, and the Arlington Street Church rounds the third corner, and well, the fourth corner is a little bit broken up; there's two places there, but you sort of get this feeling like you never come to the end of the street and then make a sharp corner, you just sort of make a round corner there. This whole block therefore seems to be a very complete continuous compact tightly set-in block, and the stores such as Bonwit's, Peck and Peck, Schraffts, and so forth, which are on the outer

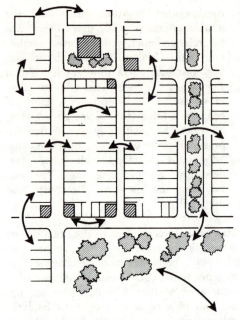

FIGURE 28–3. The native organizes his environment: Familiarity with the area enables him to see similarities (often imaginary) between streets, blocks, buildings and open spaces.

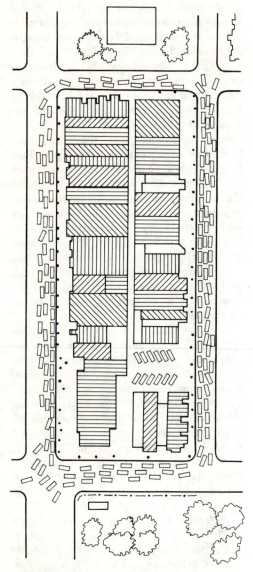

FIGURE 28–2. The stranger organizes his environment: He sees no overall uniformity in the buildings or the types of business; signs and street furniture break the block up into small confused areas; heavy traffic isolates him from the other side of streets.

periphery of this square belong to the square, definitely.

Not only is the block considered as one,

but the façades facing the block are also drawn into the unit. Even the rectangular shape with its sharp corners cannot be allowed, and the form is distorted towards the seamless circle. (Compare the previous quotation from a stranger: "these areas stand off from each other, they don't go together.") Note also in this quotation that the corner of Boylston and Berkeley is resistant to the neat organization, which puts a key use to mark each corner from both directions; but that the resistant material is forced into place anyhow.

No, this is definitely all a piece of one material as far as I am concerned. There is a distinction between Boylston and Newbury. . . . But the whole area has always been very much one grouping, one place.

It is also true that there were the people

who were less able to distinguish this block from its context in the larger Back Bay district. The streets are not boundaries for them. For the unfamiliar, however, this block seems to have no particular relation to the rest of the city.

These findings might be generalized in the following hypothesis: the individual must perceive his environment as an ordered pattern, and is constantly trying to inject order into his surroundings, so that all the relevant perceptions are jointed one to the other. Certain physical complexes facilitate this process through their own form, and are seen as ordered wholes by native and newcomer alike. Subsequent use and association simply strengthen this structure. Other complexes, however, do not encourage this fitting together, and they are seen as fundamentally disordered by the newcomer. For the native, this "disordered" complex may also seem to be an organized one, since habitual use and perception have allowed him to put the collection together by means of associated meanings, or by selection, simplification, distortion or even suppression of his perception. This progressive imputation of order is often alluded to, implicitly or explicitly:

I don't feel any sense of real order and yet I didn't feel that everything was jumbled and I suppose that is because I am familiar with the area. To me it didn't seem confused, it seemed right.

I've always liked this section, ever since I first became familiar with it about fourteen years ago. Although it has undergone some change, I feel the change has been a progressive one toward blending and uniformity of buildings rather than of strange contrasts and conflicts of colors, sizes and shapes.

Thus this sense of order can finally be achieved by familiarity despite physical chaos. Yet there is evidence that this organization is achieved only by real effort and by distortion of the pattern of reality, and that even after it is accomplished it is attended by emotions of insecurity where the required organization is particularly ruthless. Certainly it lacks the conviction and depth of a relationship which is backed up by physical pattern.

An "old hand" may recognize a shopping district as an organized entity where strangers say it is chaotic. Intensive use and association have satisfactorily overcome physical confusion, even if the satisfaction would be deeper were the spatial form more continuous. At least the physical continuities of land use and activity are there to back up the mental category.

But, even for the native, there is no satisfaction in the "fringe" of that shopping district. He can tell that it is more commercial than residential, and thus ought to go with the shopping, and he can hold it there in his mind when it is necessary for practical purposes, but the reality keeps wandering off, keeps contradicting him. It is like a restless animal which one must constantly correct. For the newcomer, moreover, the fringe makes no particular sense at all, and he is likely to recognize the fact, with some discomfort.

Some newcomers may ask for a very sweeping and rigid kind of physical organization:

I had no idea that the town would be built up as it is, just on cow paths and up little hills. . . . I just supposed that the city would be beautiful, quite modern, that the stores would be in order, the dress shops together and the bridal shop with it and not off in a corner all by itself; the antiques would be together and the big business areas would be business areas.

Very possibly this observer might change her mind about such a "neat" city were she to live in it long, but the wish is indicative of the troubles she is facing. The native may be able to handle, and indeed find more pleasure in, a more intricate and complexly organized environment, but organized it must be, whether by city dwellers or by the sweat of his own brow.

Our study suggests one further remark. The method used may not only be useful for research purposes, but may be an educational tool as well. Such a recorded walk in itself tends to heighten the perception of the city. When combined with a discussion in the field of general interview results, along with the critique of the surrounding forms, it might prove to be an excellent way of awakening the citizen's interest in the form of his city, sharpening his critical abilities, and heightening his ultimate pleasure in a well-shaped environment.

Part VI

The Natural Environment

This section on the natural environment is new to the second edition, and most of the material presented here was not even touched upon in the earlier edition. However, before discussing the reasons for the introduction of this new topic area, a word of caution in approaching it seems to be in order. The distinction followed here between the natural environment and the built environment (which is the topic of the following section) is frequently made and seems intuitively fairly obvious and innocuous. What could be more obvious to common sense and observation than that the tree is a product of nature and the automobile parked beneath it a human artifact? The air we breathe and the sun shining on us seem obviously natural phenomena, while the noxious odor is another human artifact, in this case a by-product of the same automobile. But it is also equally obvious that these distinctions are tenuous and difficult to define. The tree would not be there had it not been planted by some person and nurtured by artificial fertilizer. And the car, of course, would not be there were it not for the use and manipulation of a wide variety of natural products and resources. Following this line of thought one might be tempted to suggest that the distinction between the natural and the built environment should rather be considered as a continuum, a matter of degree, rather than a dichotomy or a matter of absolute distinction. However, even this approach, although it is undoubtedly useful in a descriptive way, falls down on closer analysis. Any distinction between the natural and the artificial implies in one sense or another that humanity stands outside or separate from nature. This view, of course, is deeply ingrained in all of us who have been touched by Western culture and tradition, but we know that as a scientific statement it is both false and misleading. We do not and cannot stand outside of nature. Humanity and all human works are as much a part of the natural ecological system as is any other part of the system. In this larger sense all environments are natural, and any statement that suggests that it is possible for anyone to encounter anything that is not a natural product is immediately suspect from a scientific point of view.

If the distinction between the natural and the built is theoretically not valid and useless as defining a set of analytic categories for scientific study, when then do we make it at all? The answer, of course, has already been suggested. Phenomenologically, we make the distinction all the time; it is ever present in the experiences of each of us. We seem to have no difficulty in distinguishing the natural from the artificial and in attributing specific and different sets of properties to each. We may be able to convince ourselves logically that the city with its automobiles and its noise and its smells is just as much a natural phenomenon as are the rolling fields and distant mountains. But at the same time we know that they mean vastly different things to us, that they are associated with quite different types of feelings, perceptions, and experiences. One represents nature to us, and the other, people, and this distinction is a psychologically important one. In short, there is a clear and salient phenomenological difference between environments that we label natural and those that we label built. In this sense the experience of the natural environment is an important part of the totality of human experiences and a significant area for psychological study.

The readings in this section do not exhaust all possible aspects of this topic, but they do touch upon some of the most important facets of the human experience of the natural environment. Historically, the oldest view of nature, and one that is still very much a part of contemporary experience, is the instrumental approach that sees nature as either a resource to be used for human purposes or an obstacle to be overcome in achieving these purposes. The theoretical and practical limitations and dangers of this view have been discussed so extensively and so eloquently in recent years that it hardly seems necessary to elaborate on them in this context. However, it would be a mistake for any of us to assume that the exploitative view of nature has disappeared from human thinking. Quite the contrary. It remains, according to all evidence, a basic constituent of the approach to nature of large segments of the population, in spite of the fact that it is predicated on the primitive beliefs that nature is unlimited and that humanity can somehow stand outside nature and use it. How to replace these beliefs, so deeply ingrained in the fabric of our cultural heritage, with others more consistent with our best current understanding represents perhaps the most significant challenge in the area of environmental education today.

The direction in which this educational process is moving can be described as an attempt to replace an exploitative view of nature with one that can be called an ecological view, that is, a view of people and their work as part of the total natural process. In this view human purposes are equally salient, but the ways in which those purposes can be achieved, and indeed the very nature of the purposes themselves, become subjects for critical investigation. This venture necessarily encompasses the whole range of human activity, and only a few selected examples are represented here. For instance, the use of natural resources to achieve particular goals is tied in with the concept of the preservation of environmental quality so that the satisfaction of one purpose does not lead to the denial or rejection of another. Similarly, large-scale natural disasters are not seen in this view as outside obstacles to be overcome, but rather as part of the total process within which human activity occurs. At still another level the goal of ever-increasing abundance for all is seen to be in need of reevaluation in the light of the finite character of the system within which we all operate. These and many other examples illustrate the gradual shifting of an experience of nature as something to be used, to an understanding of ourselves as part of the natural system itself.

But there is another important aspect of the human experience of the natural environment which is quite different from approaching the environment in terms of the attainment of tangible goals. The natural world has always had an important symbolic significance which is reflected both in the early origins of religion as well as in the most current folklore. One of the major aspects of the contemporary upsurge of interest in the recreational use of natural areas is undoubtedly to be found in the combination of the physical characteristics of the area with their symbolic meanings. These meanings range from the aesthetic, a search for the experience of beauty, to the spiritual, a search for the deeper meanings of life within the context of the natural setting. These symbolic significances of the natural world are rapidly taking their place as important and perhaps even vital aspects of complete human experience.

The combination of the symbolic meanings of the natural environment, together with an ecological approach, has led to the awareness of the need for what has come to be called an environmental ethic. All societies are constantly acting on the environment and making choices as to alternative actions. These choices require some sort of evaluative system that as yet does not exist. Choices, therefore, are made either in a vacuum or on the basis of irrelevant criteria. The development of such a system of evaluation or an environmental ethic remains perhaps one of the most important pieces of unfinished business facing us today, and in this effort the experience of the natural environment will play an important and perhaps determining role.

29. The Tragedy of the Commons
GARRETT HARDIN

At the end of a thoughtful article on the future of nuclear war, Wiesner and York (1964) concluded that: "Both sides in the

From *Science*, Vol. 162, December 13, 1968, pp. 1243–1248. Copyright 1968 by the American Association for the Advancement of Science.

arms race are . . . confronted by the dilemma of steadily increasing military power and steadily decreasing national security. *It is our considered professional judgment that this dilemma has no technical solution.* If the great powers continue to look for solutions in the area of science and technology only, the result will be to worsen the situation."

I would like to focus your attention not on the subject of the article (national security in a nuclear world) but on the kind of conclusion they reached, namely that there is no technical solution to the problem. An implicit and almost universal assumption of discussions published in professional and semipopular scientific journals is that the problem under discussion has a technical solution. A technical solution may be defined as one that requires a change only in the techniques of the natural sciences, demanding little or nothing in the way of change in human values or ideas of morality.

In our day (though not in earlier times) technical solutions are always welcome. Because of previous failures in prophecy, it takes courage to assert that a desired technical solution is not possible. Wiesner and York exhibited this courage; publishing in a science journal, they insisted that the solution to the problem was not to be found in the natural sciences. They cautiously qualified their statement with the phrase, "It is our considered professional judgment. . . ." Whether they were right or not is not the concern of the present article. Rather, the concern here is with the important concept of a class of human problems which can be called "no technical solution problems," and more specifically, with the identification and discussion of one of these.

It is easy to show that the class is not a null class. Recall the game of tick-tack-toe. Consider the problem, "How can I win the game of tick-tack-toe?" It is well known that I cannot, if I assume (in keeping with the conventions of game theory) that my opponent understands the game perfectly. Put another way, there is no "technical solution" to the problem. I can win only by giving a radical meaning to the word "win." I can hit my opponent over the head; or I can falsify the records. Every way in which I "win" involves, in some

sense, an abandonment of the game, as we intuitively understand it. (I can also, of course, openly abandon the game—refuse to play it. This is what most adults do.)

The class of "no technical solution problems" has members. My thesis is that the "population problem," as conventionally conceived, is a member of this class. How it is conventionally conceived needs some comment. It is fair to say that most people who anguish over the population problem are trying to find a way to avoid the evils of overpopulation without relinquishing any of the privileges they now enjoy. They think that farming the seas or developing new strains of wheat will solve the problem—technologically. I try to show here that the solution they seek cannot be found. The population problem cannot be solved in a technical way, any more than can the problem of winning the game of tick-tack-toe.

What Shall We Maximize?

Population, as Malthus said, naturally tends to grow "geometrically," or, as we would now say, exponentially. In a finite world this means that the per-capita share of the world's goods must decrease. Is ours a finite world?

A fair defense can be put forward for the view that the world is infinite; or that we do not know that it is not. But, in terms of the practical problems that we must face in the next few generations with the foreseeable technology, it is clear that we will greatly increase human misery if we do not, during the immediate future, assume that the world available to the terrestrial human population is finite. "Space" is no escape (Hardin, 1962).

A finite world can support only a finite population; therefore, population growth must eventually equal zero. (The case of perpetual wide fluctuations above and below zero is a trivial variant that need not be discussed.) When this condition is met, what will be the situation of mankind? Specifically, can Bentham's goal of "the greatest good for the greatest number" be realized?

No—for two reasons, each sufficient by itself. The first is a theoretical one. It is not mathematically possible to maximize for two (or more) variables at the same time. This was clearly stated by von Neumann and Morgenstern (1947, p. 11), but the principle is implicit in the theory of partial differential equations, dating back at least to D'Alembert (1717–1783).

The second reason springs directly from biological facts. To live, any organism must have a source of energy (for example, food). This energy is utilized for two purposes: mere maintenance and work. For man, maintenance of life requires about 1600 kilocalories a day ("maintenance calories"). Anything that he does over and above merely staying alive will be defined as work, and is supported by "work calories" which he takes in. Work calories are used not only for what we call work in common speech; they are also required for all forms of enjoyment, from swimming and automobile racing to playing music and writing poetry. If our goal is to maximize population it is obvious what we must do: We must make the work calories per person approach as close to zero as possible. No gourmet meals, no vacations, no sports, no music, no literature, no art. . . . I think that everyone will grant, without argument or proof, that maximizing population does not maximize goods. Bentham's goal is impossible.

In reaching this conclusion I have made the usual assumption that it is the acquisition of energy that is the problem. The appearance of atomic energy has led some to question this assumption. However, given an infinite source of energy, population growth still produces an inescapable problem. The problem of the acquisition of energy is replaced by the problem of its dissipation, as J. H. Fremlin has so wittily shown (1964). The arithmetic signs in the

analysis are, as it were, reversed; but Bentham's goal is unobtainable.

The optimum population is, then, less than the maximum. The difficulty of defining the optimum is enormous; so far as I know, no one has seriously tackled this problem. Reaching an acceptable and stable solution will surely require more than one generation of hard analytical work—and much persuasion.

We want the maximum good per person; but what is good? To one person it is wilderness, to another it is ski lodges for thousands. To one it is estuaries to nourish ducks for hunters to shoot; to another it is factory land. Comparing one good with another is, we usually say, impossible because goods are incommensurable. Incommensurables cannot be compared.

Theoretically this may be true; but in real life incommensurables *are* commensurable. Only a criterion of judgment and a system of weighting are needed. In nature the criterion is survival. Is it better for a species to be small and hideable, or large and powerful? Natural selection commensurates the incommensurables. The compromise achieved depends on a natural weighting of the values of the variables.

Man must imitate this process. There is no doubt that in fact he already does, but unconsciously. It is when the hidden decisions are made explicit that the arguments begin. The problem for the years ahead is to work out an acceptable theory of weighting. Synergistic effects, nonlinear variation, and difficulties in discounting the future make the intellectual problem difficult, but not (in principle) insoluble.

Has any cultural group solved this practical problem at the present time, even on an intuitive level? One simple fact proves that none has: there is no prosperous population in the world today that has, and has had for some time, a growth rate of zero. Any people that has intuitively identified its optimum point will soon reach it, after which its growth rate becomes and remains zero.

Of course, a positive growth rate might be taken as evidence that a population is below its optimum. However, by any reasonable standards, the most rapidly growing populations on earth today are (in general) the most miserable. This association (which need not be invariable) casts doubt on the optimistic assumption that the positive growth rate of a population is evidence that it has yet to reach its optimum.

We can make little progress in working toward optimum population size until we explicitly exorcise the spirit of Adam Smith in the field of practical demography. In economic affairs, *The Wealth of Nations* (1776) popularized the "invisible hand," the idea that an individual who "intends only his own gain," is, as it were, "led by an invisible hand to promote . . . the public interest" (1776/1937, p. 423). Adam Smith did not assert that this was invariably true, and perhaps neither did any of his followers. But he contributed to a dominant tendency of thought that has ever since interfered with positive action based on rational analysis, namely, the tendency to assume that decisions reached individually will, in fact, be the best decisions for an entire society. If this assumption is correct it justifies the continuance of our present policy of *laissez-faire* in reproduction. If it is correct we can assume that men will control their individual fecundity so as to produce the optimum population. If the assumption is not correct, we need to re-examine our indivdual freedoms to see which ones are defensible.

Tragedy of Freedom in a Commons

The rebuttal to the invisible hand in population control is to be found in a scenario first sketched in a little-known pamphlet in 1833 by a mathematical amateur named William Forster Lloyd (1794–1852). We may well call it "the tragedy of the commons," using the word "tragedy" as the philosopher Whitehead used it (1948, p.

17): "The essence of dramatic tragedy is not unhappiness. It resides in the solemnity of the remorseless working of things." He then goes on to say, "This inevitableness of destiny can only be illustrated in terms of human life by incidents which in fact involve unhappiness. For it is only by them that the futility of escape can be made evident in the drama."

The tragedy of the commons develops in this way. Picture a pasture open to all. It is to be expected that each herdsman will try to keep as many cattle as possible on the commons. Such an arrangement may work reasonably satisfactorily for centuries because tribal wars, poaching, and disease keep the numbers of both man and beast well below the carrying capacity of the land. Finally, however, comes the day of reckoning, that is, the day when the long-desired goal of social stability becomes a reality. At this point, the inherent logic of the commons remorselessly generates tragedy.

As a rational being, each herdsman seeks to maximize his gain. Explicitly or implicitly, more or less consciously, he asks, "What is the utility *to me* of adding one more animal to my herd?" This utility has one negative and one positive component.

1) The positive component is a function of the increment of one animal. Since the herdsman receives all the proceeds from the sale of the additional animal, the positive utility is nearly +1.

2) The negative component is a function of the additional overgrazing created by one more animal. Since, however, the effects of overgrazing are shared by all the herdsmen, the negative utility for any particular decision-making herdsman is only a fraction of −1.

Adding together the component partial utilities, the rational herdsman concludes that the only sensible course for him to pursue is to add another animal to his herd. And another. . . . But this is the conclusion reached by each and every rational herdsman sharing a commons. Therein is the tragedy. Each man is locked into a system that compels him to increase his herd without limit—in a world that is limited. Ruin is the destination toward which all men rush, each pursuing his own best interest in a society that believes in the freedom of the commons. Freedom in a commons brings ruin to all.

Some would say that this is a platitude. Would that it were! In a sense, it was learned thousands of years ago, but natural selection favors the forces of psychological denial (Hardin, 1964), p. 56). The individual benefits as an individual from his ability to deny the truth even though society as a whole, of which he is part, suffers. Education can counteract the natural tendency to do the wrong thing, but the inexorable succession of generations requires that the basis for this knowledge be constantly refreshed.

A simple incident that occurred a few years ago in Leominster, Massachusetts, shows how perishable the knowledge is. During the Christmas shopping season the parking meters downtown were covered with plastic bags that bore tags reading: "Do not open until after Christmas. Free parking courtesy of the mayor and city council." In other words, facing the prospect of an increased demand for already scarce space, the city fathers reinstituted the system of the commons. (Cynically, we suspect that they gained more votes than they lost by this retrogressive act).

In an approximate way, the logic of the commons has been understood for a long time, perhaps since the discovery of agriculture or the invention of private property in real estate. But it is understood mostly only in special cases which are not sufficiently generalized. Even at this late date, cattlemen leasing national land on the Western ranges demonstrate no more than an ambivalent understanding, in constantly pressuring federal authorities to increase the head count to the point where overgrazing produces erosion and weed-dominance. Likewise, the oceans of the world continue to suffer from the survival of the philosophy of the commons. Maritime nations still respond automatically to the shibboleth of the "freedom of the seas." Professing to believe in the "inexhaustible resources of the oceans," they bring species after species of fish and whales closer to extinction (McVay, 1966).

The National Parks present another instance of the working out of the tragedy of the commons. At present, they are open to all, without limit. The parks themselves are limited in extent—there is only one Yosemite Valley—whereas population seems to grow without limit. The values that visitors seek in the parks are steadily eroded. Plainly, we must soon cease to treat the parks as commons or they will be of no value to anyone.

What shall we do? We have several options. We might sell them off as private property. We might keep them as public property, but allocate the right to enter them. The allocation might be on the basis of wealth, by the use of an auction system. It might be on the basis of merit, as defined by some agreed-upon standards. It might be by lottery. Or it might be on a first-come, first-served basis, administered to long queues. These, I think are all objectionable. But we must choose—or acquiesce in the destruction of the commons that we call our National Parks.

Pollution

In a reverse way, the tragedy of the commons reappears in problems of pollution. Here it is not a question of taking something out of the commons, but of putting something in—sewage, or chemical, radioactive, and heat wastes into water; noxious and dangerous fumes into the air; and distracting and unpleasant advertising signs into the line of sight. The calculations of utility are much the same as before. The rational man finds that his share of the cost of the wastes he discharges into the commons is less than the cost of purifying his wastes before releasing them. Since this is true for everyone, we are locked into a system of "fouling our own nest," so long as we behave only as independent, rational, free-enterprisers.

The tragedy of the commons as a food basket is averted by private property, or something formally like it. But the air and waters surrounding us cannot readily be fenced, and so the tragedy of the commons as a cesspool must be prevented by different means, by coercive laws or taxing devices that make it cheaper for the polluter to treat his pollutants than to discharge them untreated. We have not progressed as far with the solution of this problem as we have with the first. Indeed, our particular concept of private property, which deters us from exhausting the positive resources of the earth, favors pollution. The owner of a factory on the bank of a stream—whose property extends to the middle of the stream—often has difficulty seeing why it is not his natural right to muddy the waters flowing past his door. The law, always behind the times, requires elaborate stitching and fitting to adapt it to this newly perceived aspect of the commons.

The pollution problem is a consequence of population. It did not much matter how a lonely American frontiersman disposed of his waste. "Flowing water purifies itself every ten miles," my grandfather used to say, and the myth was near enough to the truth when he was a boy, for there were not too many people. But as population became denser, the natural chemical and biological recycling processes became overloaded, calling for a redefinition of property rights.

How to Legislate Temperance?

Analysis of the pollution problem as a function of population density uncovers a not generally recognized principle of morality, namely: *the morality of an act is a function of the state of the system at the time it is performed* (Fletcher, 1966). Using the commons as a cesspool does not harm the general public under frontier conditions, because there is no public; the same behavior in a metropolis is unbearable. A hundred and fifty years ago a plainsman could kill an American bison, cut out only the tongue for his dinner, and discard the rest of the animal. He was not in any important sense being wasteful. Today, with only a few thousand bison left, we would be appalled at such behavior.

In passing, it is worth noting that the morality of an act cannot be determined from a photograph. One does not know whether a man killing an elephant or setting fire to the grassland is harming others until one knows the total system in which his act appears. "One picture is worth a thousand words," said an ancient Chinese; but it may take ten thousand words to validate it. It is as tempting to ecologists as it is to reformers in general to try to persuade others by way of the photographic shortcut. But the essence of an argument cannot be photographed: it must be presented rationally—in words.

That morality is system-sensitive escaped the attention of most codifiers of ethics in the past. "Thou shalt not . . ." is the form of traditional ethical directives which make no allowance for particular circumstances. The laws of our society follow the pattern of ancient ethics, and therefore are poorly suited to governing a complex, crowded, changeable world. Our epicyclic solution is to augment statutory law with administrative law. Since it is practically impossible to spell out all the conditions under which it is safe to burn trash in the back yard or to run an automobile without smog-control, by law we delegate the details to bureaus. The result is administrative law, which is rightly feared for an ancient reason—*Quis custodiet ipsos custodes?*—"Who shall watch the watchers themselves?" John Adams said we must have "a government of laws and not men." Bureau administrators, trying to evaluate the morality of acts in the total system, are singularly liable to corruption, producing a government by men, not laws.

Prohibition is easy to legislate (though not necessarily to enforce); but how do we legislate temperance? Experience indicates that it can be accomplished best through the mediation of administrative law. We limit possibilities unnecessarily if we suppose that the sentiment of *Quis custodiet* denies us the use of administrative law. We should rather retain the phrase as a perpetual reminder of fearful dangers we cannot avoid. The great challenge facing us now is to invent the corrective feedbacks that are needed to keep custodians honest. We must find ways to legitimate the needed authority of both the custodians and the corrective feedbacks.

Freedom to Breed Is Intolerable

The tragedy of the commons is involved in population problems in another way. In a world governed solely by the principle of "dog eat dog"—if indeed there ever was such a world—how many children a family had would not be a matter of public concern. Parents who bred too exuberantly would leave fewer descendants, not more, because they would be unable to care adequately for their children. David Lack and others have found that such a negative feedback demonstrably controls the fecundity of birds (Lack, 1954). But men are not birds, and have not acted like them for millenniums, at least.

If each human family were dependent only on its own resources; *if* the children of improvident parents starved to death; *if,* thus, overbreeding brought its own "punishment" to the germ line—*then* there would be no public interest in controlling the breeding of families. But our society is confronted with another aspect of the tragedy of the commons.

In a welfare state, how shall we deal with the family, the religion, the race, or the class (or indeed any distinguishable and cohesive group) that adopts overbreeding as a policy to secure its own aggrandizement (Hardin, 1963)? To couple the concept of freedom to breed with the belief that everyone born has an equal right to the commons is to lock the world into a tragic course of action.

Unfortunately this is just the course of action that is being pursued by the United Nations. In late 1967, some thirty nations agreed to the following (U Thant, 1968, p. 3):

"The Universal Declaration of Human Rights describes the family as the natural and fundamental unit of society. It follows that any choice and decision with regard to the size of the family must irrevocably rest with the family itself, and cannot be made by anyone else."

It is painful to have to deny categorically the validity of this right; denying it, one feels as uncomfortable as a resident of Salem, Massachusetts, who denied the reality of witches in the seventeenth century. At the present time, in liberal quarters, something like a taboo acts to inhibit criticism of the United Nations. There is a feeling that the United Nations is "our last and best hope," that we shouldn't find fault with it; we shouldn't play into the hands of the archconservatives. However, let us not forget what Robert Louis Stevenson said: "The truth that is suppressed by friends is the readiest weapon of the enemy." If we love the truth we must openly deny the validity of the Universal Declaration of Human Rights, even though it is promoted by the United Nations. We should also join with Kingsley Davis (1967) in attempting to get Planned Parenthood—World Population to see the error of its ways in embracing the same tragic ideal.

Conscience Is Self-Eliminating

It is a mistake to think that we can control the breeding of mankind in the long run by an appeal to conscience. Charles Galton Darwin made this point when he spoke on the centennial of the publication of his grandfather's great book. The argument is straightforward and Darwinian.

People vary. Confronted with appeals to limit breeding, some people will undoubtedly respond to the plea more than others. Those who have more children will produce a larger fraction of the next generation than those with more susceptible consciences. The differences will be accentuated, generation by generation.

In C. G. Darwin's words: "It may well be that it would take hundreds of generations for the progenitive instinct to develop in this way, but if it should do so, nature would have taken her revenge, and the variety *Homo contracipiens* would become extinct and would be replaced by the variety *Homo progenitivus*" (Tax, 1960, p. 469).

The argument assumes that conscience or the desire for children (no matter which) is hereditary—but hereditary only in the most general formal sense. The result will be the same whether the attitude is transmitted through germ cells, or exosomatically, to use A. J. Lotka's term. (If one denies the latter possibility as well as the former, then what's the point of education?) The argument has here been stated in the context of the population problem, but it applies equally well to any instance in which society appeals to an individual exploiting a commons to restrain himself for the general good—by means of his conscience. To make such an appeal is to set up a selective system that works toward the elimination of conscience from the race.

Pathogenic Effects of Conscience

The long-term disadvantage of an appeal to conscience should be enough to condemn it; but it has serious short-term disadvantages as well. If we ask a man who is exploiting a commons to desist "in the name of conscience," what are we saying to him? What does he hear?—not only at the moment but also in the wee small hours of the night when, half asleep, he remembers not merely the words we used but also the nonverbal communication cues we gave him unawares? Sooner or later, consciously or subsconsciously, he senses that he has received two communications, and that they are contradictory: (i) (intended communication) "If you don't do as we ask, we will openly condemn you for not acting like a responsible citizen"; (ii) (the unintended communication) "If you *do* behave as we ask, we will secretly condemn you for a simpleton who can be shamed into standing aside while the rest of us exploit the commons."

Everyman then is caught in what Bateson has called a "double bind." Bateson and his co-workers have made a plausible case for viewing the double bind as an important causative factor in the genesis of schizophrenia (1956). The double bind may not always be so damaging, but it always endangers the mental health of anyone to whom it is applied. "A bad conscience," said Nietzsche, "is a kind of illness."

To conjure up a conscience in others is tempting to anyone who wishes to extend his control beyond the legal limits. Leaders at the highest level succumb to this temptation. Has any President during the past generation failed to call on labor unions to moderate voluntarily their demands for higher wages, or to steel companies to honor voluntary guidelines on prices? I can recall none. The rhetoric used on such occasions is designed to produce feelings of guilt in noncooperators.

For centuries it was assumed without proof that guilt was a valuable, perhaps even an indispensable, ingredient of the civilized life. Now, in this post-Freudian world, we doubt it.

Paul Goodman speaks from the modern point of view when he says: "No good has ever come from feeling guilty, neither intelligence, policy, nor compassion. The guilty do not pay attention to the object but only to themselves, and not even to their own interests, which might make sense, but to their anxieties" (1968).

One does not have to be a professional psychiatrist to see the consequences of anxiety. We in the Western world are just emerging from a dreadful two-centuries-long Dark Ages of Eros that was sustained partly by prohibition laws, but perhaps more effectively by the anxiety-generating mechanisms of education. Alex Comfort has told the story well in *The Anxiety Makers* (1967); it is not a pretty one.

Since proof is difficult, we may even concede that the results of anxiety may sometimes, from certain points of view, be desirable. The larger question we should ask is whether, as a matter of policy, we should ever encourage the use of a technique the tendency (if not the intention) of which is psychologically pathogenic. We hear much talk these days of responsible parenthood; the coupled words are incorporated into the titles of some organizations devoted to birth control. Some people have proposed massive propaganda campaigns to instill responsibility into the nation's (or the world's) breeders. But what is the meaning of the word responsibility in this context? It is not merely a synonym for the word conscience? When we use the word responsibility in the absence of substantial sanctions are we not trying to browbeat a free man in a commons into acting against his own interest? Responsibility is a verbal counterfeit for a substantial *quid pro quo*. It is an attempt to get something for nothing.

If the word responsibility is to be used at all, I suggest that it be in the sense Charles Frankel uses it (1955). "Responsibility," says this philosopher, "is the product of definite social arrangements." Notice that Frankel calls for social arrangements—not propaganda.

Mutual Coercion Mutually Agreed Upon

The social arrangements that produce responsibility are arrangements that create coercion, of some sort. Consider bank-robbing. The man who takes money from a bank acts as if the bank were a commons. How do we prevent such action? Certainly not by trying to control his behavior solely by a verbal appeal to his sense of responsibility. Rather than rely on propaganda we follow Frankel's lead and insist that a bank is not a commons; we seek the definite social arrangements that will keep it from becoming a commons. That we thereby infringe on the freedom of would-be robbers we neither deny nor regret.

The morality of bank-robbing is particularly easy to understand because we accept complete prohibition of this activity. We are willing to say "Thou shalt not rob banks," without providing for exceptions. But temperance also can be created by coercion. Taxing is a good coercive device. To keep downtown shoppers temperate in their use of parking space we introduce parking meters for short periods, and traffic fines for longer ones. We need not actually forbid a citizen to park as long as he wants to; we need merely make it increasingly expensive for him to do so. Not prohibition, but carefully biased options are what we offer him. A Madison Avenue man might call this persuasion; I prefer the greater candor of the word coercion.

Coercion is a dirty word to most liberals now, but it need not forever be so. As with the four-letter words, its dirtiness can be cleansed away by exposure to the light, by saying it over and over without apology or embarrassment. To many, the word coercion implies arbitrary decisions of distant and irresponsible bureaucrats; but this is not a necessary part of its meaning. The only kind of coercion I recommend is mutual coercion, mutually agreed upon by the majority of the people affected.

To say that we mutually agree to coercion is not to say that we are required to enjoy it, or even to pretend we enjoy it. Who enjoys taxes? We all grumble about them. But we accept compulsory taxes because we recognize that voluntary taxes would favor the conscienceless. We institute and (grumblingly) support taxes and other coercive devices to escape the horror of the commons.

An alternative to the commons need not be perfectly just to be preferable. With real estate and other material goods, the alternative we have chosen is the institution of private property coupled with legal inheritance. Is this system perfectly just? As a genetically trained biologist I deny that it is. It seems to me that, if there are to be differences in individual inheritance, legal possession should be perfectly correlated with biological inheritance—that those who are biologically more fit to be the custodians of property and power should legally inherit more. But genetic recombination continually makes a mockery of the doctrine of "like father, like son" implicit in our laws of legal inheritance. An idiot can inherit millions, and a trust fund can keep his estate intact. We must admit that our legal system of private property plus inheritance is unjust—but we put up with it because we are not convinced, at the moment, that anyone has invented a better system. The alternative of the commons is too horrifying to contemplate. Injustice is preferable to total ruin.

It is one of the peculiarities of the warfare between reform and the status quo that it is thoughtlessly governed by a double standard. Whenever a reform measure is proposed it is often defeated when its op-

ponents triumphantly discover a flaw in it. As Kingsley Davis has pointed out (Roslansky, 1966, p. 177), worshipers of the status quo sometimes imply that no reform is possible without unanimous agreement, an implication contrary to historical fact. As nearly as I can make out, automatic rejection of proposed reforms is based on one of two unconscious assumptions: (i) that the status quo is perfect; or (ii) that the choice we face is between reform and no action; if the proposed reform is imperfect, we presumably should take no action at all, while we wait for a perfect proposal.

But we can never do nothing. That which we have done for thousands of years is also action. It also produces evils. Once we are aware that the status quo is action, we can then compare its discoverable advantages and disadvantages with the predicted advantages and disadvantages of the proposed reform, discounting as best we can for our lack of experience. On the basis of such a comparison, we can make a rational decision which will not involve the unworkable assumption that only perfect systems are tolerable.

Recognition of Necessity

Perhaps the simplest summary of this analysis of man's population problems is this: the commons, if justifiable at all, is justifiable only under conditions of low-population density. As the human population has increased, the commons has had to be abandoned in one aspect after another.

First we abandoned the commons in food gathering, enclosing farm land and restricting pastures and hunting and fishing areas. These restrictions are still not complete throughout the world.

Somewhat later we saw that the commons as a place for waste disposal would also have to be abandoned. Restrictions on the disposal of domestic sewage are widely accepted in the Western world; we are still struggling to close the commons to pollution by automobiles, factories, insecticide sprayers, fertilizing operations, and atomic energy installations.

In a still more embryonic state is our recognition of the evils of the commons in matters of pleasure. There is almost no restriction on the propagation of sound waves in the public medium. The shopping public is assaulted with mindless music, without its consent. Our government is paying out billions of dollars to create a supersonic transport which will disturb 50,000 people for every one person who is whisked from coast to coast 3 hours faster. Advertisers muddy the airwaves of radio and television and pollute the view of travelers. We are a long way from outlawing the commons in matters of pleasure. Is this because our Puritan inheritance makes us view pleasure as something of a sin, and pain (that is, the pollution of advertising) as the sign of virtue?

Every new enclosure of the commons involves the infringement of somebody's personal liberty. Infringements made in the distant past are accepted because no contemporary complains of a loss. It is the newly proposed infringements that we vigorously oppose; cries of "rights" and "freedom" fill the air. But what does "freedom" mean? When men mutually agreed to pass laws against robbing, mankind became more free, not less so. Individuals locked into the logic of the commons are free only to bring on universal ruin; once they see the necessity of mutual coercion, they became free to pursue other goals. I believe it was Hegel who said, "Freedom is the recognition of necessity."

The most important aspect of necessity that we must now recognize, is the necessity of abandoning the commons in breeding. No technical solution can rescue us from the misery of overpopulation. Freedom to breed will bring ruin to all. At the moment, to avoid hard decisions many of us are tempted to propagandize for conscience and responsible parenthood. The temptation must be resisted, because an appeal to independently acting consciences selects for the disappearance of all conscience in the long run, and an increase in anxiety in the short.

The only way we can preserve and nurture other and more precious freedoms is by relinquishing the freedom to breed, and that very soon. "Freedom is the recognition of necessity"—and it is the role of education to reveal to all the necessity of abandoning the freedom to breed. Only so, can we put an end to this aspect of the tragedy of the commons.

30. *The American Scene*[1]
DAVID LOWENTHAL

Face to face with the look of his own country, the well-traveled American is characteristically dismayed. Henry James, more than most others, viewed the American scene at the turn of the century with outright distaste. After his twenty-five years abroad, America seemed bleak and raw, except at Harvard College, where the mellow tones of the older buildings allowed

From the *Geographical Review*, 1968, 58, 61–88. Copyrighted by the American Geographical Society of New York. Reprinted by permission of the author and publisher.

[1] This paper is condensed and revised from a lecture delivered at the Graduate School of Design, Harvard University, in November, 1966. It is part of a longer work in preparation. The author acknowledges with gratitude the assistance of the John Simon Guggenheim Memorial Foundation, for a fellowship in 1965–1966, and his indebtedness for the title to Henry James's book (1907).

him to hope that "we are getting almost ripe, . . . beginning to begin, and we have that best sign of it, . . . that we make the vulgar, the very vulgar, think we are beginning to end" (James, 1907, p. 61). If the American scene was elsewhere deplorable, it was because American society was unformed, American taste untutored. James attributed the sordid shabbiness of New Hampshire's wayside farms and people to "the suppression of the two great factors of the familiar English landscape, the squire and the parson" (James, 1907, p. 23). That America seemed such "an ugly . . . wintering, waiting, world" was a consequence, he believed, of "the vast general unconsciousness and indifference" (James, 1946, pp. 461 and 464) about its appearance; things looked as they did because almost no one cared.

A pioneer conservationist decided a century ago that although others "think that the earth made man, man in fact made the earth" (Lowenthal, 1958, p. 248). This insight was ecological, but the statement is as true esthetically. Landscapes are formed by landscape tastes. People see their surroundings through preferred and accustomed glasses and tend to make the world over as they see it. Such preferences long outlast geographical reality. Thus the English, although now mainly "town-birds through and through," still think of rural England as their true home; for them, Browning's chaffinch still sings on an orchard bough (Lowenthal & Prince, 1965).

Images and Stereotypes

The American scene, as much as any other, mirrors a long succession of idealized images and visual stereotypes. Let us examine a few historic responses to that scene and see how they are reflected in contemporary landscape and townscape.

A literary historian has categorized typical Eastern reactions to Western landscapes in terms of *vastness, astonishment,* *plentitude* (owing to the apparent inexhaustibility of wildlife), *incongruity* (the contrast between landscapes fit for the gods and their mean and petty human inhabitants), and *melancholy* (owing to the absence or transience of man and his works; Jones, 1964, pp. 379–386). But such responses were not new, nor were they confined to the West. They were equally appropriate in early settlements in the East, in forest as in prairie, in the salt marshes of Massachusetts as in the Sierras. America has usually struck visitors as vast, wild, and empty, formless and unfinished, and subject to violent extremes. A few examples will illustrate each trait.

Size

No aspect of the American scene is more notorious than the scale of the landscape and the size of objects in it. Eyes accustomed to European vistas and artifacts may take years to adjust, as one visitor put it, to "the unnerving bigness of everything" in America (Shepheard, 1963). " 'Too big,' said one of our Frenchmen, peering a mile down into the Grand Canyon; but he was wrong. In England something of that size would be absurd, but there it is in scale (although the American woman who wrote in the visitors' book before us 'Very pretty' was probably cutting it down to size too far)" (Seddon, 1962). The initial shock is the same in every kind of landscape; "the streets remain streets, the mountains mountains, and the rivers rivers—and yet one feels at a loss before them, simply because their scale is such that the normal adjustment of man-to-environment becomes impossible" (Lévi-Strauss, 1961, p. 83).

So it has seemed from the start. Weary weeks on the Atlantic, eyes strained between sky and ocean, did not habituate travelers to the continental scale of America. They expected monotony from the sea, but not from the land. West Indian landforms contrasted pleasantly with the solitude of the voyage. But the continent itself dismayed them; instead of circumnavigable islands, America proved to be an intractable hunk of land, more and more alien, interminable, and unrewarding the farther they moved into it. And it conformed less and less with European preconceptions about promised lands, visions chiefly Arcadian, insular, and small-scale. The long search for the Northwest Passage was more than a yearning for the fabled East; it was also an expression of active distaste for the American impediment. Only the trapper, the lumberman, the religious fanatic, and the most optimistic imperialist waxed enthusiastic over the endless forest and swamps, the prairies and deserts, of North America.

Limitless frontiers did attract a few. Jefferson (1955, p. 19) thought the "smooth blue horizon" seen where the Potomac clove the Blue Ridge was a view "worth a voyage across the Atlantic." Eighteenth-century fashion admired panoramic views and primitive nature; many paid homage to America on both counts. But they enjoyed landscapes more as set pieces than as real places. The botanist Bartram dutifully gazed "with rapture and astonishment . . . [at the] amazing prospect of grandeur" in the southern Appalachians yet confided he felt as lonely as Nebuchadnezzar, "constrained to roam in the mountains and wilderness" (Van Doren, n.d., pp. 292–293).

America has continued to affect folk as "huge, vague, breeding as much fear as hope" (Dangerfield, 1965, p. 26). The hero alone in space has been a central theme in American literature since Cooper's "Leather-stocking Tales." And spaciousness is also a cardinal quality of American landscape paintings. The people in those landscapes are dwarfed by nature, seldom an integral part of the scene. Even the genre figures of Bingham, Eakins, and Mount seem dominated by their environments.

The classic reaction to American space is that of Rölvaag's poneer wife, who dreaded the "endless plain . . . [that] stretched far into the Canadian north, God alone

knows how far from the Mississippi River to the western Rockies. . . . Endless . . . beginningless. A grey waste . . . an empty silence . . . a boundless cold [where] snow fell; . . . a universe of nothing but dead whiteness" (1927, p. 241). Today's resident is apt to feel the same way. As a native of Bismarck put it, "We look out over all the space and figure, hell, it's too big for us, it's too wide, there's too much of it, and we get gloomy. Your North Dakota man can get good and gloomy" (Hamburger, 1965, p. 8).

"The American imitates nature, with whose great works he is in constant communication," said an observer a century ago. "Only an appreciation of the grandeur of such a fall as that of Niagara, could fit a man to construct the bridge that spans its river" (Miller, 1965, p. 304). Eighteenth-century European scientists had earlier asserted that nature and man in the New World were more puny than in the Old. "In America, there is not an animal that can be compared to the elephant," asserted Buffon (in Chinard, 1947, pp. 30–31), and "all the animals which have been transported from Europe . . . the horse, the ass, the sheep, the goat, the hog, etc., have become smaller. . . . [All species] shrink and diminish under a niggardly sky and an unprolific land, thinly peopled with wandering savages." Jefferson and others took great pains to refute these taunts, citing the elk and the moose, and mammoth bones discovered in Ohio.

Pride thus paved the way for a cult of bigness. The dinosaur became emblematic. Americans soon boasted that they had the largest animals, the longest rivers, the highest mountains, the tallest trees. And they created gargantuan structures to match. New York skyscrappers and the Golden Gate and Verrazano bridges reflect ambitions of the same order as that of the medieval cathedral builders who aimed at record heights. The best-known American structures are monumental. Boulder Dam, Fort Knox, the Mormon Temple, the Empire State Building are admired less for their efficiency or beauty than for their size. Size is preferred even in things that might be better small. But local planners can hardly be blamed for thinking big when the biggest projects get the largest federal allocations. They "want to see big, really important open spaces," as one planner put it, lest their funds be "wasted and frittered away on a bunch of little playgrounds and parks" (Whyte, n.d., p. 26).

The mania for bigness reached its peak at the turn of the century. "Make no little plans," Daniel Burnham (1955, p. 201) urged his fellow architects, "make big plans." That they did so is evident in Newport's "cottages," Roosevelt's Sagamore Hill, with foundations twenty feet thick, and the Flatiron Building in New York, deliberately designed "to dwarf the 'ordinary' buildings around " it (Gowans, 1964, p. 308). But the later progressive architects liked plenty of room too. And Americans still build as though bigger were always better.

The prevailing gridiron pattern, with straight streets at right angles, also accentuates size and space. In New York, Sartre's (1957, pp. 119 and 122) "glance met nothing but space. It slid over blocks of identical houses . . . to lose itself in empty space, at the horizon. . . . The moment you set foot on " a Manhattan avenue "you understand that it has to go on to Boston or Chicago." In smaller towns the grid emphasizes every aspect of the terrain and draws the eye away from the houses out to the lonely horizon.

Wildness

The nature of America, like its scale, leaves the spectator alone in an alien world—alien both in what it contains and in what it lacks. America is still full of unfamiliar, undomesticated, unclassifiable things, "a waste and howling wilderness," as Michael Wigglesworth (1871–1873, p. 83; see Heimert, 1953) described it in the seventeenth century, "where none inhabited but hellish fiends, and brutish men."

Even more than these strange shapes and species, the virtual absence of man's artifacts appalled viewers. Indians were few, nomadic, ephemeral; their works scarcely detracted from the powerful impression of emptiness. Melancholy amid "dreary wastes and awful solitude," two eighteenth-century poets conjured up future kingdoms to people the forlorn continent (Freneau & Brackenridge, 1957, p. 9). But even in southern New England, the longest settled, most densely populated and socially domesticated corner of the country, the sense of wilderness still endures. An English bird watcher in a nature reserve near Groton, Massachusetts, suddenly became conscious that he was "on a vast continent —exotic, tropical, rich in the possibility of surprises undreamed of in Shropshire." By English standards the woods and undergrowth seemed chaotic and impenetrable. The very absence of dreaded snakes, groundhogs, and wolves struck him as sinister, the silence foreboding. He moved along more rapidly, stumbled against a stump, fell, could not get up for fright. "What kind of a fool are you?" he asked himself. "Do you really imagine you are in any danger, here within five miles of America's most exclusive school?" But the answer was yes (Ellis, 1960, p. 24). After all, even a resident like John Hersey (1953, p. 50) has characterized summertime Connecticut as an "equatorial jungle."

Perhaps the most cogent summary of American wildness is Gertrude Stein's (1936, pp. 17–18): "In the United States there is more space where nobody is than where anybody is. That is what makes America what it is." To be sure, other countries have uninhabited wilderness; those of Tibet, of Chile, of Algeria, for example, may be more extensive. What gives American emptiness its special poignance is its pervasiveness in ordinary landscapes. In a night train on the outskirts of a Kansas town, the traveler realizes that "beyond is America . . . and no one there. . . . It's only ten, fifteen minutes since you've left a thriving town but life has already been swallowed up in that ocean of matter which is and will remain as wild as it was made" (Barzun, 1954, p. 3).

Over much of the country, man and his structures seem to be insignificant or temporary features of the landscape. Even the sturdy New England farmhouse looks to many Europeans "like a temporary wooden structure hastily erected against the elements and marauding savages" (Alsop, 1962, p. 10). But it is in the metropolis that impermanence is most sharply felt. An English essayist recalls "lonely moments in some American city at night when you are on the edge of nightmare" and begin to fear that the place is "no more than a huddle of people . . . round a camp fire who will have packed up and moved on . . . in the morning" (Pritchett, 1965, p. 155).

Formlessness

Compared with Old World landscapes, those of America appear generally ragged, indefinite, and confused; parts stand out at the expense of a unified whole. Over much of the country topographic features are large, vague, and indefinitely structured, and vegetation tends to cloak patterns of terrain. The quality of American light is also partly responsible for the absence of clearly defined structure. Frequently bright, hard, undiminished by moisture, it seems to separate and isolate features rather than to join and compose them.

Man's structurers mirror nature. Boundaries between city and country are blurred and smudged. Localities neither begin nor end, and little seems fixed. Unfenced, "the little houses sit lightly, barely engaged with the ground and the landscape," as Banham (1961, p. 305) has put it: Le Corbusier (1964) felt that the absence of framing walls and fences gave the American landscape a pleasing amplitude. But most ob-

servers tend, with Henry James (1907, pp. 161–162), to inveigh against "this diffused vagueness of separation . . . between the . . . [place] you are in and the . . . [place] you are not in," and to deplore "the indefinite extension of all spaces . . . ; the enlargement of every opening, . . . the substitution of . . . far perspectives and resounding voids for enclosing walls."

Visual flux, with continual rebuilding, is the rule in the skyscraper city. As Kouwenhoven (1961) argues, "the logic of cage construction" is that of something "always complete but never finished." He concludes that America "is not an artifact; . . . America is process."

But the process produces artifacts, even if they are not rooted in place. They create America's most distinctive look— casual chaos. A French anthropologist (Lévi-Strauss, 1961, p. 99) provides a classic account of the genesis of the vacant lot: "Patches of dead ground . . . were once owned, and once briefly worked, by Man, Then he went off somewhere else and left behind him a battleground strewn with the relics of his brief tenure. . . . [On it] there has arisen a new, disorderly, and monotonous vegetation." From railroad cutting to riverbank, from city park to town dump, this landscape engulfs the country. More ragged than the primeval wilderness, it divides and subverts any ordered scene. Hence Dickens' (1957, p. 116) description of an open space in Washington as "a melancholy piece of waste ground with frowzy grass, which looks like a small piece of country that has taken to drinking, and has quite lost itself."

Extremes

America also strikes observers as subject to terrifying—or exhilarating—extremes. Nature here is not only on a larger scale but more violent than the early settlers had ever experienced. They endured torrid summers and bitter winters and despairingly noted savage vagaries of climate. Within this framework of excess, tornado, flood, and drought often wreaked havoc. And extremes are not confined to climate and weather; a modern visitor remarks that "the whole of American life is tempered by the threats of . . . overwhelming natural excesses. . . . In almost every State there are turbulences of scenery, grotesque formations or things of feverishly exaggerated size" (Morris, 1962, p. 41).

Sounds as well as sights tend toward excess. Early travelers mistook the roaring rush of passenger pigeons for tornadoes. They described rivers as angry, violent, fierce, reckless, headstrong, flowing with deafening turmoil. Beyond was silence; wide grasslands swallowed sounds as if they had never been uttered. On the Arkansas prairies Thomas Nuttall (1905, p. 205) remarked that "no echo answers the voice, and its tones die away in boundless and enfeebled undulations." Silence made the scene inhumanly lonely. On a wide plain near Pittsburgh a German novelist a century ago found "absolutely nothing. . . . Far and wide there was not a bird, not a butterfly, not the cry of an animal, not the hum of an insect" (Kürnberger, 1926, p. 301).

Such extremes stimulated some folk as they depressed others. But all felt that nature was of a different order in the New World than in the Old. The physical fundament seemed not only larger but less malleable.

To the excesses of nature have been added those of man. In their buildings, as in their behavior, Americans resemble the landscape they inhabit—exaggerated, vehement, powerful, unpredictable.

Insiders and Outsiders

Vast and wild, teeming yet lonely, formless, violent, and extreme—no wonder America seemed to the first Europeans like the original Creation, now chaos, now garden. "In the beginning all the world was America," John Locke said (1924, p. 140); the phrase conveys the threat as well as the promise of the New World. This was a land that simultaneously attracted and repelled, but in the end had to be brought to terms. Empty, it must be filled; unfinished, it must be completed; wild, it must be tamed.

To the Elizabethans, America was simply a vision; to the settlers that vision was a challenge requiring action. Action became so strong a component of the American character that landscapes were often hardly seen at all; they were only acted on. Immediate necessity made a mockery of mere contemplation. To wrest a living from the soil, to secure frontiers against hostile forces, seemed to demand full attention. Appreciation of the landscape itself, apart from its practical uses, was disdained as pointless and effete.

The irrelevance of "science values" to real life is dramatized by Mark Twain (1929). After a typical tourist blurb about majestic panoramas, Twain turns around and derides the tourist view as artificial, self-conscious, above all ignorant. The tourist only enjoys the view because he is an outsider and doesn't understand it. Before he becomes familiar with the Mississippi, Twain's pilot enjoys the stock responses to a glowing sunset on the silvery water. But after he learns the river, he looks at the same scene "without rapture" and comments, "This sun means that we are going to have wind tomorrow; . . . that slanting mark on the water refers to a bluff reef which is going to kill somebody's steamboat one of these nights; . . . that silver streak in the shadow of the forest is the 'break' from a new snag" (pp. 79–80).

Perception of *scenery* is open only to those who have no real part to play in the landscape. Those who know it and work in it have to concentrate on the humdrum realities; "the choice is between the mawkish sentiments of the passengers and the bleak matter-of-factness of the pilot" (Marx, 1964, p. 324). Asked to be pilot or passenger, what red-blooded American would hesitate? We are all pilots, happy only when we are steering some ship, whether it is plow or airplane. We disdain the mere onlooker and dismiss his opinion of the landscape. What right has a passive spectator to impose his judgment? However drab a hotel or ugly a junkyard may seem to the passerby, if it fulfills its function there is no ground for complaint. A dealer may arrange his layout to attract customers, but not for beauty alone. We do not prettify the rugged face of workaday America in order to enjoy its looks.

In short, the landscape is worthy of its hire. Its ultimate critics are its residents, not its visitors. Such is the lesson of William James's "On a Certain Blindness in Human Beings" (1958).

Journeying in the mountains of North Carolina, I passed by a large number of "coves" . . . which had been newly cleared and planted. The impression of my mind was one of unmitigated squalor. The settler had . . . cut down the more manageable trees, and left their charred stumps. . . . The larger trees he had girdled and killed . . . and had set up a tall zigzag rail fence around the scene of his havoc. . . . Finally, he had irregularly planted the intervals between the stumps and trees with Indian corn. . . . The forest had been destroyed; and what has "improved" it out of existence was hideous, a sort of ulcer, without a single element of artificial grace to make up for the loss of Nature's beauty.

Then a mountaineer told James, "Why, we ain't happy here, unless we are getting one of these coves under cultivation."

I instantly felt that I had been losing the whole inward significance of the situation. . . . To me the clearings [were] . . . naught but . . . a mere ugly picture on the retina. . . . But, when *they* looked on the hideous stumps, what they thought of was personal victory. The

chips, the girdled trees, and the vile split rails spoke of honest sweat, persistent toil and final reward.

And he points his moral: "The spectator's judgment is sure to miss the root of the matter, and to possess no truth" (pp. 149–169; see also Lowenthal, 1962–1963).

Many Americans would still agree. The editor of *Landscape* derides "beautification" as empty and idle. Abandon "the spectator stance," he urges, and ask instead what chances the landscape offers "for making a living . . . for freedom of choice of action . . . for meaningful relationships" —all emphatically *non*visual standards. And he concludes that "we should never tinker with the landscape without thinking of those who live in the midst of it. . . . What the spectator wants or does not want is of small account" (Jackson, 1963–1964).

The epitome of functionalism in landscape, perhaps, is the state capitol grounds of Oklahoma City: no trees, gardens, fountains, or other humdrum frivolities adorn the mall, but "a maze of oil derricks, . . . all pumping away." It has been proposed that the capitol itself should sport a derrick set in the rotunda with its top jutting up through the nonexistent dome, "so that everybody could see who was boss in Oklahoma City" (Hamburger, 1965, pp. 194–195).

A rare protest against the purely monetary view of landscape appears in a utopian novel of a generation ago. Americans, the author notes, "ruined lovely views by unsightly structures. It never occurred to anyone that an ordinary view was worth saving when put into competition with a commercial interest." In the writer's utopia, by contrast, "no farmer merely farms but is an artist in landscape architecture as well. . . . [They] consider how the field will look when [plants] first come up through the earth, and when they are full grown . . . and when they are dead and when they are stubble. . . . What interested them was the effect upon a certain view.

. . . They looked upon their whole farm as a great living canvas" (Wright, 1958, pp. 297–298).

Ideal Versus Reality

Most Americans reserve such esthetic considerations for select landscapes only. Thus the comment of a visitor from the Great Plains on first seeing the Hudson River Highlands: "It looks like scenery should look!" (Kahn, 1966). The gulf between ideal and reality, between "how things *ought* to look" and the easy acceptance of surroundings not remotely resembling that ideal—this cleavage takes many forms. Each illumines a facet of national behavior of value for environmental design and planning. (I do not mean to imply that any of these is unique to this country, only that they are recognizable as American attitudes.) Let us look briefly a few of them.

The Present Sacrificed to the Glorious Future

Americans build for tomorrow, not for today. They *"love* their country, not, indeed, *as it is,* but *as it will be,"* a traveler noted in the 1830's; "they do not love the land of their fathers; but they are sincerely attached to that which their children are destined to inherit" (Grund, 1837). A New York State settler challenged an eighteenth-century visitor to "return in ten years and you will not recognize this . . . wild and savage [district]. Our humble log houses will be replaced by fine dwellings. Our fields will be fenced in, and the stumps will have disappeared" (Crèvecoeur, 1964, p. 493). In similar fashion I was taken in 1966 to see the view from the roof of a new building at the University of California, Los Angeles, where my hosts ignored the actual campus as it looks today and instead described how it *would* look in 1980.

The current American scene is not a finished landscape, but an embryo of future greatness. Meanwhile we endure protracted labor pains. Vast areas of our cities are

occupied by wrecking crews and bulldozers, sand and gravel, rubble and structural elements—semipermanent wastelands dedicated to Tomorrow. A large proportion of the cityscape is in painful gestation at any time. The vaguest tidings of Urban Renewal, if sufficiently sweetened and signposted, persuade the citizen to suffer the laying waste of his city for years on end. At the Manhattan end of the Brooklyn Bridge, fifteen acres have been scheduled for total demolition since 1956, but new buildings are not to be finished until 1970 —that is, half a generation. This aspect of urban progress long ago caught Tocqueville's attention (1956–1957, p. 56). He was dismayed that those clearing ground for the city of Washington "have already rooted up trees for ten miles around lest they should interfere with the future citizens of this imaginary metropolis."

Living in the future, Americans are predisposed to accept present structures that are makeshift, flimsy, and transient, obsolete from the start. "Downtowns and suburbs still bear the imprint of frontier-camp design," Pushkarev (1966, p. 111) points out. Elevated transit lines, overhead wiring, exterior fire escapes, are among the fixtures that stem from that spirit. We live in throw-away stage sets.

But the habit of discarding buildings almost as soon as they are put up has its compensations. "If something is built wrong," writes an observer of Los Angeles, "it doesn't matter much. Everyone expects it to come down in a decade or two" (Rand, 1966, p. 56). Because we invest so lightly in our buildings, we can—and do— experiment easily. Innovations embellish the whole countryside.

The Present Dimished by Contrast with an Idealized Past[2]

Old Sturbridge Village, the Minute Man National Historic Monument, the Trustees

[2] See David Lowenthal, 1966.

of Reservations, the Society for the Preservation of New England Antiquities—such Massachusetts-based institutions all testify to our wish to preserve, and if necessary to manufacture, an idealized Historyland as a sanctuary from the awful present. That past includes not only historic buildings and places but also a pastoral countryside and a sublime wilderness.

These romantic tastes are by no means unique to America. What is striking is how fast they took root here, after our initial rejection of whatever was old or natural. As early as 1844 the American Art Union promoted the sale of Hudson River School paintings as an antidote to the abysmal environment of city folk: "a painted landscape is almost essential to preserve a healthy tone to the spirits, lest they forget in the wilderness of bricks . . . the pure delights of nature and a country life" (Ward, 1966, p. 64). And this at a time when the countryside was half an hour's walk from New York City!

Hudson River paintings still inspire moral exhortation. The village of Garrison-on-Hudson recently exhibited dozens of colorful paintings by Cole, Kensett, Durand, and Church in its picturesque railroad station. In another room, labeled "Chamber of Horrors," a revolving spotlight flickered over black-and-white photographs of the bleak contemporary scene—litter in and along the river, abandoned shacks and piers, garbage dumps, decaying industries. A recorded commentary urged visitors to remake the river as it used to be. No one questioned whether the nineteenth-century Hudson really conformed to the painters' views of it; no one seemed to doubt that the present scene was one of unmitigated blight. Funds raised by the exhibit will be used, appropriately, for reconstructing a Hudson River sloop—not a replica of any specific ship, but an ideal nautical composite.

The preferred past is history expurgated and sanitized. When Walt Disney unveiled his new model of nineteenth-cen-

tury New Orleans at Disneyland in 1966, he was not entirely satisfied with the mayor of New Orleans' remark that it looked "just like home." "Well," Disney replied, "it's a lot cleaner" (New York Times, 1966).

The visitor to historic sites seldom cares whether he is looking at a real relic or a fake. A Charleston resident contends that "if you point to an alley and say 'Catfish Row,' visitors are perfectly satisfied and return North happy" (Hamburger, 1965, p. 32). As a promoter of Lincoln's supposed birthplace remarked in the 1890's, "Lincoln was born in a log cabin, weren't he? Well, one cabin is as good as another" (Hosmer, 1965, p. 141). Even a replica of Uncle Tom's fictional cabin meets the demand for historic atmosphere.

As treasured heritages, History and Nature are not only altered to fit "a dream-image of an immutable past" (Whitehill, 1966, p. 44); they have also become objects of isolated pleasure and reverence, fenced off and enshrined in historical museums and wilderness preserves, out of touch with the rest of the landscape. By contrast with the idealized past, the present workaday environment is considered not worth looking at.

Nature is likewise thought preferable to artifice. The favored landscapes are wild; landscapes altered or disturbed or built on by man are considered beneath attention or beyond repair. Adoration of the wilderness, like idealization of the past, focuses attention on the remote and the special to the neglect of the nearby and the familiar (Lowenthal, 1964).

Conservationist organizations contrast sordid scenes dominated by man with lovely landscapes devoid of human activity—telegraph poles versus trees, a mass of people versus a mass of sand. The implication is clear: man is dreadful, nature is sublime. Yet Americans do not take so dim a view of human activities as the English, whose feelings are epitomized in Cowper's sanctimonious—and mistaken—apothegm that "God made the country, and man made the town" (Cowper, 1814, p. 40). From the start Americans have considered themselves chosen people—not mere servants in the great task of transforming nature, but junior partners to the Deity, and sometimes more than that. Watching the conversion of an old farm into a luxurious estate an onlooker remarked, "It just goes to show you what God could have done if He'd had money" (Morris, 1946, p. 40).

Individual Features Emphasized at the Expense of Aggregates

"Featurism," as defined by an Australian architect, is "the subordination of the essential whole and the accentuation of selected separate features. . . . A featurist city has little or no consistency of atmospheric quality and plenty of numbers on the guide map directing the visitor to features of interest. . . . Each new building is determined to be arresting" (Boyd, 1960, pp. 9–11).

Accentuation of features is perhaps less deliberate in America than in Australia. But it has been pervasive since the first settlements. Weak relationships mark even the old New England clustered villages. The houses may be homogeneous in style, but they are fragmented by distance and by the absence of any binding framework. As an English observer put it, they stand out around their central greens "like plucked chickens." Other places are only collections of heterogeneous buildings marooned in wastelands. It is the same in cities. No office structure in New York lines up its cornice or parapet with another. New York's Lever and Seagram buildings are "each elegantly and humanely designed within its boundaries," but they are separated, the visitor notes, by "a rush of cars, browbeaten shrubs, dumb pavements. . . . The art of making a pattern in the environment is entirely neglected" (Nairn, 1965, pp. 13 and 3).

Features of interest often lack all connectivity. Americans glory in the most arcane juxtapositions, as is suggested by a sightseeing advertisement for the "Only Tour in Key West That Will Take You to the Following Points of Interest: Monument of Cesar Romero's Grandfather—Gold Star Mothers' Monument—Home of Tennessee Williams—May Sands Elementary School—The Tree That Bears the Fruit on Its Trunk—The Oddest House—Or the Most Artistic House in Key West—The Unique Cigar Makers Home—The Miracle Tree—A Visit to the City Cemetery—Maine Monument—The Gun Turret of the Maine" (*New Yorker*, 1965).

Hunger and impatience help to account for disconnectedness. In America, as Henry James (1907) explained, a place "has had to have something for everybody, since everybody arrives famished; it has had to . . . produce on the spot the particular romantic object demanded. . . . It has had to have feature at any price . . . which accounts . . . for the general rather eruptive and agitated effect."

Noting the contrast between our new buildings and the subtopia around them, an English architect asked his American colleagues "how it was that they could see their splendid, shining buildings put up in surroundings that would make a Balkan sanitary inspector blench." They replied that "it was surprising what you could get used to, and anyway they were so busy doing architecture they had not yet had the time to worry about the spaces between" (Casson, 1957, p. 36). But the condition has other roots: our fluid social structure, our disposable dwellings, the absence of strong local ties.

The tendency to concentrate on features is promoted, too, by the American sky, which tends to highlight specific objects and to stretch distances. In American paintings space is not a palpable atmosphere, but an empty, shapeless void. Instead of clouds framing a landscape, "a cloudless sky descends to lengthen the reaches of river, field, or pavement" (McCoubrey, 1963, pp. 115–116). In Andrew Wyeth's canvases, for example, things and people are seen alone; he invests both the animate and the inanimate "with an air of detachment, by cutting the objects off from the whole" (Schroeder, 1965, p. 562). The industrial landscapes of Hopper and Sheeler have the same isolating quality, their structures seeming to inhabit a void.

But American structures sometimes fit together in an unselfconscious manner. House types in a small town, neon signs along a highway, the skyscrapers of Manhattan, relate to one another in a fashion celebrated in the paintings of Charles Demuth, Stuart Davis, and Robert Rauschenberg (Jellicoe, 1966), which organize a large number of seemingly unrelated things in a single comprehensive design.

The Nearby and the Typical Neglected for the Remote and the Spectacular

The National Parks were orginally set up to enshrine the freaks and wonders of nature, and park literature still touts the Grand Canyon, the Grand Tetons, Yellowstone, and Yosemite as unique. If they were typical, who would bother to go and see them? And so with the works of man. If they are not unique, they are valueless, quickly passed by and soon forgotten. Litchfield, in the western Connecticut highlands, is heralded as the ne plus ultra of Federalist gracious living, while a score of nearby villages of almost equal grace go nearly unnoticed. Their counterparts in neighboring New York State, crossroad and railroad villages with massive, high-gabled roofs, remain unappreciated as visual entities because no architectural accolade has come to the individual houses.

In the West, neglect of the general in favor of a single focus of merit goes further still. Half a century ago Puget Sound boasted several attractive cities and many livable towns. Seattle alone is still alive. Up and down the coast the moribund harbors and decayed buildings of Bellingham and Port Angeles, Everett and La Conner, speak not only of the passing of

enterprise, but of the feebleness of local spirit. The sense of neglect and abandonment is keenest in Tacoma, the region's second city, which used to be thought of as a Boston to Seattle's New York. The Tacoman sense of identity is now about on a par with that of Yonkers or Hoboken. Once the most glamorous city in the Pacific Northwest, Tacoma today appeals to one refugee from the East mainly "because it's such a nothing town. This gives it a real charm" (Michener, 1966, p. 46; see also Wolfe, 1963).

Where urban visual qualities are a matter of pride, Americans are apt to allude to the general setting rather than to anything near at hand. Seattleites daily admire Mount Rainier, fifty miles away, while ignoring the tawdriness under their noses. Above the smog in the Berkeley Hills people enjoy the lights of San Francisco, fifteen miles across the Bay. The greatest feature of Jersey City is the New York skyline. And New Yorkers themselves appreciate Gotham mainly when they desert the squalid streets to circumnavigate Manhattan at fifty miles an hour on an elevated parkway.

Long ago Tocqueville (1956–1957) noted that Americans built "some monuments on the largest scale" and also "a vast number of inconsiderable productions," but that "between these two extremes there is a blank." The long-run effect of the cult of uniqueness is the same as that of museumizing history and nature. The features most admired are set apart and deluged with attention; the rest of the country is consigned to the rubbish heap.

Scenic Appreciation—Serious and Self-Conscious

For many people "seeing" is an activity of specific purpose and fixed duration, as in the cartoon of the maid, about to draw curtains across the window, who turns to ask, "Is Madam through with the moon?" We dichotomize experience as we zone places: certain intervals are set aside for looking at things; the rest of the time we are blind.

From these habits of mind and sight scenic views inevitably take their character. Americans enhance preferred views by landscaping, and highlight them with identifying markers. But scenic promoters do not merely inform the traveler that he is now crossing Chipmunk Creek or ascending Hogback Hill; they give him a thumbnail sketch of the geology and natural history of the area, a disquisition on the domestic economy of the Indians, and an arrow on a trunk pointing out the route of Washington's retreat or Grant's advance. The signs along Virginia's Skyline Drive are so numerous, prominent, artful and information-laden that the conscientious traveler is not so much seeing a landscape as reading a book or viewing a museum diorama.

Like exits from a modern highway, the scenic experience is not only signposted but numbered; to get the most out of a landscape, one is supposed to see a prearranged sequence, as along Boston's Freedom Trail. But the art of ordering experience is most fully developed for views of nature. "A trail should have a definite purpose," the Forest Service (1965, p. 51) notes. "Upon reaching his goal, the traveler should have a feeling of accomplishment . . . of having 'found' most of the interest points along the way, of having struggled to the top of the overlook where he can rest and enjoy his prize—the scenic view spread out before him."

Where nature lacks such stimuli, man must provide them. Thus a well-known landscape architect "improved" a New Hampshire hill which hotel guests used to saunter up for the view. Blocking off the easy path with hemlocks, he located a new trail "steeply up the roughest, wildest part of the hillside. . . . Pulling themselves from rock to rock, they [the guests] carefully pick their way until they finally break out at the very top. They have made it! Nothing, they may think, as they rest enjoying

the view, is more exhilarating than mountain climbing" (Simonds, 1961, pp. 30–31). Climbing has become an end in itself, tending less to enhance than to supersede looking.

The well-blazed trail, the obstacle-course mentality, and the segregation of scenery within quotation marks tend ultimately to make any scenic view appear contrived. In such circumstances, to "beautify" is merely to plug in replicas of esthetic treasures, like the giant-size billboard copy of Gainsborough's "Blue Boy" along a New Jersey highway. We destroy by overemphasis as surely as by neglect and vandalism.

Comments on the American scene are often doctrinaire and imprecatory. City and country, suburb and slum, whatever critics see appalls them. The loss of natural and historic treasures; the ubiquity of litter, both the used-up old and the shoddy new; the absence of vital or well-integrated human landscapes—these are defects on which designers have moralized at length. Many of the remedies they recommend would require wholesale reform of American character and behavior. But values are no easier to alter than habitats. The present vogue for beautification is skin-deep; a few petunias along Pennsylvania Avenue are hardly harbingers of a design renaissance. People are not suddenly going to wake up and demand a better environment.

It used to be said that "the views of nature held by any people determine all their institutions" (Emerson, 1950, p. 548). But it may make more sense to stand this statement on its head: our whole way of life determines our views of nature. To be effective, therefore, planning and design should be grounded on intimate knowledge of the ways people think and feel about environment; this calls for a substantial familiarity with social and intellectual history, with psychology and philosophy, with art and anthropology. All these fields contribute to our knowledge of how we see the world we live in, how vision and value affect action, and how action alters institutions.

Beyond such knowledge still other unknowns confront us. To what extent are people aware of their surroundings at all, and when and where? How much do we really see at home, on vacation, on the way to or from work, in field or factory, office or classroom? Let us try to look around wherever we are—not necessarily with close attention to form or detail, but fleetingly, musingly, dreamily, provocatively, *any* way, just as long as we see *something*. For "without vision the people perish."

31.   *Experiencing the Environment as Hazard*[1]
ROBERT W. KATES

Environment is that which surrounds us, the ambience of individuals, of social groups, of our species. So all pervasive is environment, that it escapes, in its totality, our comprehension, at least in this mode of consciousness. Inevitably we fraction it and destroy it, to reconstruct it in more narrow comprehensible slices. How we choose to emphasize the environment: as nurture, haven or home—as deprivation or stimulation to the senses—as myth or symbol—or as threat and hazard—is partly the essence of the conference. Our topic, the emphasis of the environment as threat or hazard, is no more or less pure than other emphases; indeed it is inevitable that each environmental plane we slice intersects with others. Thus the environment as hazard is integral to the environment as nurture or resource—men encounter hazard in the search for the useful. And the environment as hazard serves as a source of stimulation, and is rich in the mythical and the symbolic.

This choice of emphasis arises not out of some conceptual insight but out of the accident of research thrust and the concern with applied human and social problems of man-environment interaction. Nevertheless, the study of *homo in extremis* is a useful focus for insights beyond the problems at hand. Reasoning from the extremes, be they of environmental stress or any other set of data, is an ancient and honorable practice of scientific and philosophical inquiry. In this paper, we consider each of the five major conference approaches to experiencing the environment, emphasizing what we know of each from our studies of the environment as hazard. We begin by describing these studies and our current concept of their underlying structure.

[1] Paper prepared for the Clark University Conference, "Experiencing the Environment," Hopkinton, Massachusetts, January 7–8, 1975. This paper, while written by the author, draws heavily on his shared work with Ian Burton and Gilbert F. White, and their forthcoming volume entitled *The Environment as Hazard* to be published by Oxford University Press; ideas and words of close colleagues Martyn Bowden and Anna Kirby; the research and fellowship of the many members of the Commission on Man and the Environment of the International Geographical Union. The author gratefully acknowledges the financial support of the National Science Foundation.

Studies of the Environment as Hazard

The environment as hazard has been under intensive study for some twenty years. Most attention has been given to the study of hazards of the natural environment, more recently to that of the made environment and little to that of the social environment. Participants in these studies have expanded from a small group of teachers and students at a single university (Chicago, 1955–61) to groups at several universities

(Chicago, Toronto, Clark and Colorado, 1962–68), to collaboration through the interested organizations of a single discipline (International Geographical Union, 1969–72), to international collaboration through many disciplines (Scientific Committee on Problems of the Environment, 1973–). And while geographers have been prominent in the leadership of these studies, economists, engineers, psychologists and sociologists have been active as well.

In specific terms, much of the early effort concentrated on flood studies in the United States and as recently as six years ago, we had available substantial studies of other hazards only for North America and Britain. In these studies, we had followed a simple research paradigm, which sought to: 1) assess the extent of human occupance in hazard zones; 2) identify the full range of possible human adjustment to the hazard; 3) study how men perceive and estimate the occurrence of the hazard; 4) describe the process of adoption of damage reducing adjustments in their social context; and 5) estimate the optimal set of adjustments in terms of anticipated social consequences.

In general, these studies provided evidence for a pattern of declining death rates and increasing damage, despite substantial investment in technical means for coping with hazard. In so doing, they raised serious questions as to the efficacy of the prevailing approach to natural hazard loss reduction. But six years ago we knew little as to the prevalence of this pattern in the nonindustrialized world and were at a loss for ways of systematically comparing hazards of varied origins and impact. Thus we sought to organize, with the collaboration of many colleagues, a series of field studies, which when concluded told us in some detail about the ways in which people adjust to different hazards. They raised more questions than they answered, but they did outline some of the patterns of hazards and adjustments in roughly comparable form.

Specifically, we compared findings from local studies of: tropical cyclones in Bangladesh, the United States, Puerto Rico, and the Virgin Islands; droughts in Australia, Brazil, Kenya, Mexico, Nigeria, and Tanzania; floods in India, Malawi, Sri Lanka, the United Kingdom, and the United States; volcanoes in Costa Rica and the United States; and coastal erosion, frost, urban snow, volcanoes, and high winds in the United States. Comprising 28 studies at 73 sites and interviews with approximately 4,800 households, these studies revealed the diversity of adjustments for coping with natural hazard.

Although five of the studies involved habitats where the vulnerability to extreme events is uniform, the others embraced a wide range of risk. The frequency of damaging events was high in some places and rare in others: in contrast to San Francisco and its decades without serious earthquakes, residents of Boulder reported high winds on an average of three times per year, and farmers in the Ganga flood plain noted floods once in five years on the average.

By design, the people interviewed were mostly men who were heads of their households, between the ages of 37 and 54 with families. They varied in education from almost wholly illiterate pastoralists in Northern Nigeria to sites in the United States where almost all those interviewed were at least high school graduates; in income from Shrewsbury, England with perhaps $2,000 U.S. per capita yearly, and from Sri Lanka where the annual income is less than $200 U.S.; in occupation the studies included sedentary farmers, shifting cultivators, fishermen, city laborers, artisans, small businessmen, manufacturers, teachers, and government workers.

In no sense, however, was the set of study areas representative of the world's population at risk. Nor was it intended to be a statistically valid sample. Rather, it was a selection from different cultures and hazard situations, drawn partly by intent and partly by the fortuitous cooperation of investigators. The results permitted initial probing of the immense variety of the environment.

Seven sets of these studies were of sufficient breadth as to constitute studies of the national experience for a single hazard where the research paradigm was aplied in a reasonably consistent and comprehensive manner. The comparative research design called for at least one comprehensive study in both a developing and industrial nation for each of several natural hazards, and for at least one hazard of substantial human origin. To compete the set of studies, we had to draw upon United States experience in two cases, floods and hurricanes. And we were not able to develop a comprehensive study of air pollution (the hazard of substantial human origin) in a developing country. Instead we drew on some limited findings and reports from Mexico to provide some measure of comparative experience. The seven studies that emerged from the collaborative effort were studies of drought in Australia and Tanzania, floods in Sri Lanka and the United States, hurricanes in Bangladesh and the United States, and air pollution in the United Kingdom with supplementary data from Mexico. Detailed anlysis for 21 sites has been published (White, ed., 1974), and an overall synthesis will be published this year (Burton, Kates and White, forthcoming).

In addition to the studies of air pollution, which were consciously chosen to bridge hazards arising from the natural and made environment, a growing body of data dealing with the made environment or interaction between the natural and made environment has been collected in roughly the same tradition. These include studies of water quality (Baumann, 1969; White, Bradley and White, 1972), water quality technology (Baumann and Kasperson, 1974), weather modification (Sewell, 1966, 1968), and work currently underway into the hazards of nuclear power production.

Formal study of the hazards of the social environment have been limited to a few comparisons (Golant and Burton, 1969, 1970), reading the work of others, and some preliminary collection of statistics of hazard risk and oc urrence. All of the foregoing can be integrated into a simple conception of the environment as hazard emphasizing the approaches of our conference.

The Environment as Hazard: A Conceptual Model

In the terminology of this conference, the environment becomes hazard in the course of being acted upon by society, such interaction leads to the generation of hazard events, and consequences of those events, which in turn are reacted upon by individuals and societies seeking to cope with the threatening consequences. This process is shown schematically in Figure 31–1 and is elaborated upon by drawing primarily from the natural hazard findings supported by insights from studies of the hazards of technology and the made environment.

In describing the environment as hazard in these categories, caution should be exercised in interpreting these. Acting upon, experiencing, reacting to—are categories of convenience—they try and relate to the approaches of the conference organizers, and serve to order the presentation of finding and insight. But they are not a sequence of human behavior, neither in the world of life, or of hazard; the schema of such behavior escapes the dimensionality of graphics or words and at our best we only approximate it, in inner understanding.

Acting Upon Environment: An Interactive View of Hazard

The earth suddenly shakes, houses collapse, people are buried in the ruins, fires start, disease spreads, the rescue teams move in.

ACTING UPON   —   EXPERIENCING   —   REACTING TO

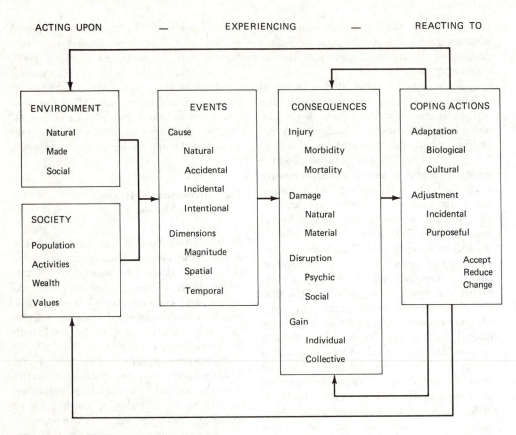

FIGURE 31–1.   The environment as a hazard.

The world knows that an earthquake has occurred. The rains do not come, the crops (planted in expectation of rain) wither and die, the water holes dry up and the cattle fall ill, there is less food, the people perish. The world knows there is a drought. In the conventional wisdom, these events are ascribed to nature, to the environment, or to God.

Much of the content of natural hazard research, the way it is structured and written, and the information incorporated in it, arise from a set of ideas and definitions about the nature of natural hazard. The first idea views nature as neutral; catastrophic events are seen as human events, a product of man. If man is absent from an area in which an extreme natural event

occurs, then he is not usually affected by it. Insofar as man is present, the density and distribution of population, the style and level of economy, the shape and size character of his buildings, patterns of production, consumption and leisure all affect in significant and powerful ways the consequences of the event. The most important idea, therefore, is that natural events are indeed natural and that hazards—the threat potential for man and his works—are by definition human phenomena. If we extend Bishop Berkeley's dictum, it can be said that not only is there no sound when the tree falls unwitnessed in the forest, but there is also no danger from falling trees.

A second fundamental idea is that

interaction between man and nature involves many transactions, some of which are beneficial to man, others harmful. It is the harmful that we call hazards. Many elements in nature cannot be easily allocated either to beneficial or to harmful categories. They may be both simultaneously. But it is the human search for the beneficial that often results in the harmful. Invariably the events that cause harm can only be quantitatively, not qualitatively, distinguished from the normal circumstances of nature—the flood from the rains that water the plants, the storm from the winds that bring the moisture.

The idea that the search for utilization of natural resources creates hazard can be extended to both the made environment and the social environment that surrounds us. In making and using things, we create threat as well—buildings can burn, cars can hit, and drugs can poison. Similarly, in joining with others in complex social relationships, we become vulnerable to violence from war and crime, to illness from propinquity and social mixing, or to deprivation from unemployment and inflation.

Experiencing the Environment as Hazard: Events

The environments—natural, made and social—are the sources of events that only necessarily become hazardous as they intersect human populations—carrying on activities, possessing material wealth, and having values. Using the national studies of natural hazards, estimates of the population at risk from some of the major hazards considered are between 5% and 15% of the national population with two exceptions: drought in the peasant society of Tanzania (90%) and air pollution in the urbanized society of the United Kingdom (50%). These exceptions can be generalized: hazard events of natural origin affect the greatest number in rural societies; hazard events

of the made and social environments affect the greatest number in urbanized societies.

The distinctions between events originating in natural, made or social environments are constructs of the author; how is the cause or source actually experienced? Embedded in our language and our law is the distinction between the Act of God (or nature?) and the Act of Man. The Acts of Man, in turn, can be seen as either intentional acts (with good or bad intentions) or accidents (with or without imputed negligence). We can also try to distinguish the accidental—a chance failure or unintended happening—from the incidental, what we might do without failure or intention in the course of the pursuit of other ends.

Historically, yesterday's Act of God frequently becomes today's Act of Man as more and more control and responsibility for environment is achieved or assumed. And for many, the Act of God is not accidental, more intentional than Acts of Man. Thus while the distinction may hold meaning in any given society, universal meaning for these categories appears unlikely.

Events not only have cause, but they have generalized dimensions independent of their interaction with society. These dimensions describe the size and the spatial and temporal distributions of events with hazard potential. In turn, these dimensions seem to collapse into the continuum between the pervasive or chronic and the intensive or acute. *Intensive* hazard events are characteristically small in areal extent, intense in impact, of brief duration, sudden onset, and poor predictability. *Pervasive* hazards are widespread in extent, have a diffuse impact, a long duration, gradual onset, and can be predicted more accurately.

The sets of natural hazard events which fall most easily into the intensive class are: earthquakes, tornadoes, landslides, hail, volcanoes and avalanches; and into the pervasive class: drought, fog, heat waves, excessive moisture, air pollution and snow. Other hazards are less susceptible to grouping, and examples can be found at both ends of the spectrum as in the case of floods, for example. These might be described as *compound* hazards, displaying mixed characteristics. Some flash floods are close to intensive events, while others—the great riverine and deltaic floods—are very close to pervasive events. Other events such as tropical cyclones, while less variable as between upstream and downstream flooding, have some characteristics of both and are intermediary between the polar events. We would further include among compound hazards: extreme winds, blizzards, tsunamis, and sand and dust storms. The pervasive-intensive continuum provides a way in which we can make comparisons between hazards and seems to influence the resulting pattern of adjustment and choice.

A typology of the events of the made and social environments is yet to be developed, but it seems possible that similar characteristics will be found. The distinction between acute and chronic disease in medicine, between rapid onset, short duration and slow onset, long duration (Wingate, 1972) suggests such similarity.

Experiencing the Environment as Hazard: Consequences

The consequences of events involve threats to person: morbidity and mortality, damage to activities and wealth both natural and man-made, disruption to psychic and social activities and well-being, and as often forgotten, the antithesis of the foregoing, instances of individual and collective gain.

The ultimate experience with consequences of hazard is death, but fortunately, such experience is limited. In developed countries, the natural environment contributes little to what is primarily the burden of age and disease. Out of slightly less than two million Americans who died in each of recent years, perhaps 500 died as a consequence of natural hazard, 50,000 from the violence of others (war and crime) and of self (suicide), 100,000 in accidents

with the made, built, and machine environment. More difficult to give quantitative expression to is the effect of environmental events on disease rates: natural and man-made radiation on birth abnormalities and malignancies; the pollutants of the made environment on respiratory diseases and cancer; the hazards of poverty and poor housing on childhood mortality; or the pace of society on cardio-vascular disease. In developing countries, these proportions may be reversed, as many have died from natural hazard in Bangladesh as from heart trouble in the U.S. A graph of global disaster (Figure 31–2) suggests that disaster of the made environment is more frequent and less costly than natural disaster.

The monetary value of damage is considerable as well. Damage and preventive measures for natural hazard cost an estimated $10 billion per year in the U.S.; air and water pollution $30 billion; accident, wage and health costs $25 billion; and fire losses $2.5 billion.

Psychic and social disruption are poorly documented, although in an out-of-court settlement, the Pittston Coal Company paid the survivors of the Buffalo Creek disaster $6 million over and above direct losses for community disruption—the first case so recorded. Individual and collective gains range from the grocer who temporarily profits from his competitor's flood or fire to the sense of well-being and solidarity some communities and nations evidence when performing well in the face of a disaster.

To experience events does not imply experiencing consequences, although in common language, the events and consequences of many hazards are confused. Floods can mean high water flowing over the bank of a stream or high water that drowns people, destroys buildings, washes away soil. All of us employ the familiar phrase "it was only an accident, no harm done."

But, in many ways, it is important in understanding hazard experience to separate events from their consequences. For ex-

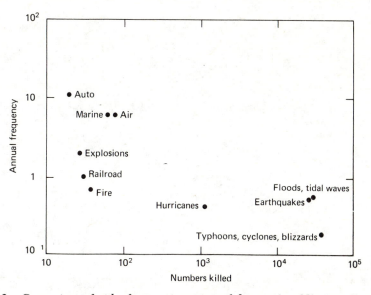

FIGURE 31–2. Comparison of risks from various types of disaster (world). (Based on Sinclair *et al.*, 1972.)

ample, a puzzling problem of early hazard research was why experience of a recurring hazard event was not more strongly linked to the future expectation of such an event. The lack of such expectations seemed to become more rational on further analysis. It was discovered that, while there are many who felt that hazard events may recur, they also felt that they may not experience them, and even if experienced, they may not personally suffer the potential consequences (Kates, 1962). Similarly, a point of contention among highly skilled analysts of nuclear power hazard is whether the probability of accidental event sequences is independent of consequences and therefore multiplicative or whether there are chains of closely linked events (common made failure) and consequences.

Reacting to the Environment as Hazard: Coping

People survive and indeed prosper in the face of environmental hazard because they cope with the hazard by adaptations and adjustments. Adaptations are long-run responses that are deeply engrained as part of human biology or culture. Adjustments are short-run responses purposefully or incidentally adopted. Together they work to reduce the hazard consequences to some level of general tolerability.

Starr suggests that for developed countries there are two general levels of tolerance. One is related to voluntary exposure to death hazards at risks of 10^{-3} to 10^{-6} fatalities per hour of exposure and a thousandfold more stringent standard for involuntary exposure (Starr, 1972). Both levels of risk are related to the curve of potential benefits (see Figure 31–3).

An example he cites is aviation safety. In the 1920's, risk from commercial aviation was about the same as general (private, pleasure) aviation today. But over that period, adjustments were developed to reduce such risk to the present level, which while maintained in the face of new aircraft, routes, etc., will probably not be diminished. Commercial aviation in its infancy, he implies was a voluntary risk, as is general aviation today. Over time it be-

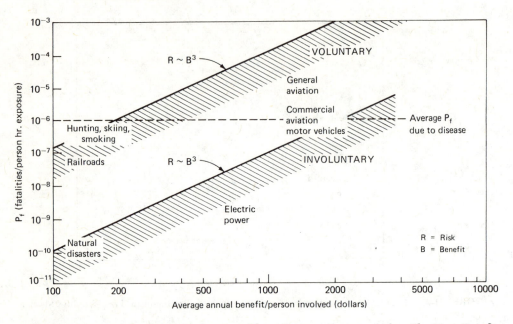

FIGURE 31–3.   Risk vs. benefit; voluntary and involuntary exposure. (After Ch. Starr, Benefit-Cost Studies in Socio-Technical Systems, April 1971.)

comes necessity with stringent control until a balance is reached of societal risk and effort. Similarly the low death rates from natural hazards in the U.S. may be close to the reasonably preventable annual minimum, and the focus is on reducing property damage losses and preventing catastrophic deaths, rather than further prevention of isolated deaths.

Adjustments take three major forms: measures to accept losses by hearing, sharing or distributing losses; measures to modify events or reduce the vulnerability of society to loss; and on rare occasion, changes in basic location or livelihood systems. These purposeful adjustments vary tremendously by hazard and society, but nevertheless are universally found. And almost all individuals and societies have more than one such adjustment at hand, though seldom is any individual or collective group aware of the entire range of adjustments. In the comparative study of natural hazards, separate adjustments enumerated

range from a low of seven for drought in Yucatan to 263 for floods in Sri Lanka.

Over most of the globe, and for most of mankind throughout human history, there have been little or no external assistance. If drought or flood threatened, those directly affected were left to cope as best they could; the national government, if it existed at all, had at its command neither the resources nor the technical capacity to respond. Under such circumstances, individual and community adjustments flourish. Studies of folk or pre-industrial societies reveal the enormous ingenuity that is employed to develop and adapt adjustments to natural hazards.

On the Ganges delta lands in Bangladesh, farmers have developed many ways of protecting themselves against the hazard of cyclonic storms and the accompanying tidal floods (Islam, 1971, 1974). Small protective levies or bunds are constructed to keep out the sea water. Tanks are excavated for water supply, and the material removed is used to construct elevated platforms of refuge where people and livestock may find safety above the level of the surrounding flood waters. Shelter belts of trees are planted. Houses built of dried mud, wood and grass are designed to withstand strong winds and some flooding. Special anchoring devices and supports are constructed. These adjustments are effective in saving property and preventing loss of life in the smaller cyclonic storms. When disaster strikes in the form of an extreme magnitude event, however, these adjustments are of no avail, and high loss of life results. Damage to property and livelihood may also be total, although the actual value of the losses in cash terms may be small as measured by international standards. Similar patterns, with less tragic consequences, are seen in the studies from Tanzania and Sri Lanka.

The pattern of folk or pre-industrial response to natural hazards may be characterized in general terms. The number of adjustments is large, and often a high rate of adoptions is found among individuals and communities. They often involve modifications of behavior or of agricultural practices more in harmony with nature than in attempts to control or manipulate environment. The adjustments are low cost and may often be added to in small increments. To this extent, they are flexible, easily increased or reduced in scale. While in use, they may be closely related to social customs and supported by norms of behavior and community sanctions. Technological and capital requirements are commonly low. The adjustment pattern may require cooperative action by community or local groups but not depend at all on outside assistance either in the form of technical knowledge, financial assistance or legal approval. The pattern of adjustments adopted is in this sense flexible and may vary quite drastically over short distances according to local variations in hazard severity or cultural practice.

Although effective in preventing property losses and loss of life from low magni-

tude hazard events, the folk or pre-industrial pattern is ineffective in the prevention of major disasters. When such events occur, a high level of government or social organization may be needed to intervene. At such time, national governments in pre-industrial societies commonly respond by offering relief, emergency food supplies and assistance. The scale of this help may very well be small in relation to the losses suffered. It may be sufficient, however, to permit a population to recover slowly and become reestablished in the same hazard area. Theoretically, the available adjustments at individual and community levels continue to include any folk or pre-industrial choices, even in highly complex industrial societies. Commonly, however, these choices have ceased to be adopted and have been replaced by adjustments at the community and national levels.

In the modern industrial state, a different pattern has emerged as technological capacity to manipulate and manage the environment has grown and theoretical alternatives have developed at the national level. Governments have been drawn steadily into activities designed to protect citizens from natural hazards. The expanded role for national governments in modern states arises largely from the opportunities provided by new technology. The construction of dams, major irrigation projects, sea walls, the design of monitoring forecasting and warning systems with complex equipment, is clearly beyond the scope of individual action. And the large indivisible capital requirements also place many such adjustments beyond the reach of community or regional resources.

What emerges, therefore, is a picture of great complexity in the many ways individuals and societies can react to hazard, but the range of purposeful adjustments does not account for the entire set of mechanisms which enable human beings to survive and even prosper in the face of extreme environmental variation. These include: 1) adjustments, the choice for which is never made because they are part and parcel of the habitual activity of daily and seasonal life and work; 2) activities whose purposes are varied and remote from hazard adjustment but whose net functional effect is to diminish the burden of hazard; and 3) unconscious shifts in individual cognition and affect in the direction of reducing the perceived or felt sense of threat and loss. These habitual, incidental and unconscious adjustments may rival and even prove more significant than the outcomes of more conscious choice.

Perceiving and Cognizing the Environment as Hazard

Events, consequences, adaptations and adjustments—these are the categories of a set of scientific observers. How are these perceived and cognized by those who live and work in areas of recurrent hazard? Again, we draw heavily on comparative studies of natural hazard, touching lightly on hazards of the made environment, even more lightly, on the social environment.

In a rough and ready way, the interaction we hypothesize between the environment and society is widely recognized. Most people can cite clear advantages related to life, livelihood and location for their site. Some, not all, will list the hazard as the principal disadvantage, and these are mainly in rural areas and areas of high vulnerability. Most also recognize that others in similar settings have similar problems with hazards, and some, mostly at rural sites, believe that there are sites somewhat less exposed than theirs, where they might earn as good a living.

It is uncommon to find people who are totally unaware or ignorant of risk from natural hazards prevalent in their location. At the same time, the knowledge of events is often less than the best scientific record. Events more recent are better known than those further removed in time. Events more frequent are better appraised

than those that are not. Events with greater impact on everyday life and livelihood are more accurately assessed than those with trivial outcomes. All of this, up to a point; most people cannot extend their imagination beyond the commonly experienced; many see order in random events; some are blissfully ignorant.

Yet in contrasts between the best scientific estimates of the magnitude and probability of events there is less of a gap between trained observers and residents of hazardous areas than most surmise, and greater limitations on both the formally and informally trained than most realize. For example, we held an early hypothesis that one significant distinction between scientific and lay perceptions was the concept of probability and randomness (Burton and Kates, 1964). Our recent work, however, shows that, world-wide, 74% of our respondents choose the random explanation in a story format for the recurrence of events—hazards can occur at any time. And Slovick, Tversky and Kahneman (Slovick, Kunreuther and White, 1964; Tversky and Kahneman, 1974), in their studies of cognitive bias, show subtle and significant biases in the appraisal of probability even by skilled and experienced scientists. Overall, in the hazard literature, the distinction between trained and untrained assessors has given way to varying, sometimes contradictory, interpretation—some choosing to focus on the relatively widespread knowledge.

The most careful comparison comes from the London, Ontario, study (Hewitt and Burton, 1971; Moon, 1971):

In the study of the hazardousness of London, Ontario, an effort was made to compare for the first time in a systematic way "lay" appraisals with more "objective" assessments across a range of hazards. Expectations of frequency of hazard events were investigated by asking respondents how often a given event could be expected to occur in the next fifty years. Responses are plotted in Figure 31–4 together with the objective estimates.

Events were described as more likely to occur 5, 10, 15, or 20 times in 50 years rather than the old values of 4, 7, 9, or 11, 14, or 16 and so on. A preference for round numbers is to be expected. The distributions of responses for tornadoes, hurricanes and floods, all show a pattern highly sheered to the left. This coincides well with observed frequencies.

While all three hazards are thought of as rare events, tornadoes appear to pose the greatest threat in the minds of London residents. This may be because of the dramatic effects of tornadoes that are frequently reported in the mid-west of the United States including areas in southern Michigan continuous to southern Ontario. That 140 people consider that no floods will occur in the next 50 years is very likely due to the high degree of confidence placed in the Fanshawe Dam which does reduce flood peaks. Most significant about tornadoes, hurricanes and floods, however, is the fact that the subjective estimates of frequency coincide so closely with objective assessments.

The expectations of frequency of ice storms and blizzards are quite clearly in a different category. Both have a bimodal distribution with marked peaks towards each extreme. Ice storms are expected to occur between 1 and 5 times in 50 years by 86 people and between 46 and 50 times by 62 people. Similarly blizzards are expected to occur 5 times or less in 50 years by 148 people while 59 others expect blizzards to occur 46 times or more in 50 years. This suggests a major discrepancy in definition of ice-storms and blizzards. Most dramatically in the case of blizzards, people tend to see them as common events occurring almost every year or as rare events occur-

ring only a few times in 50 years. In neither case do the peaks of subjective frequency coincide with objective estimates based on the observed record. In fact the reverse is true, and the objective frequency tends to fall in an area of very low subjective expectation (Moon, 1971). The significance of these observations is that they strongly shape the propensity of individuals or households to adopt adjustments to specific hazards where the perceived frequency is low. Differing concepts of what a hazard signifies may also affect the receptivity of populations to warnings or other advice about adjustments.

(Burton, Kates, and White, forthcoming)

Despite the large number of available actions for coping, many, but not most, know of one or more actions that can be taken to reduce damage from the hazard. Many take some positive action to reduce losses, but few take preventive action much in advance of the hazard event, and few choose a large number of adjustments. In general, more people bear losses than share losses, more accept losses than reduce damages. Of those that reduce damages, more seem to try to modify events than to prevent effects, and many more seek to reduce damages than change their livelihood or land use. Fewer still move their residence even when the hazard is severe, and those that do move are likely to be low income farmers fleeing drought, dwellers in the path of lava flows or residents of eroding coastlines. Our overall impression of human effort expended in coping is shown in Figure 31–5.

Consequences, like the events, are widely recognized. Some people, especially at rural sites or places of high vulnerability, regard resultant damages as substantial. But everywhere, as with events, consequences are not easily seen to exceed experience, and collective experience does not necessarily portend individual fate. As with events, the gap between perceived

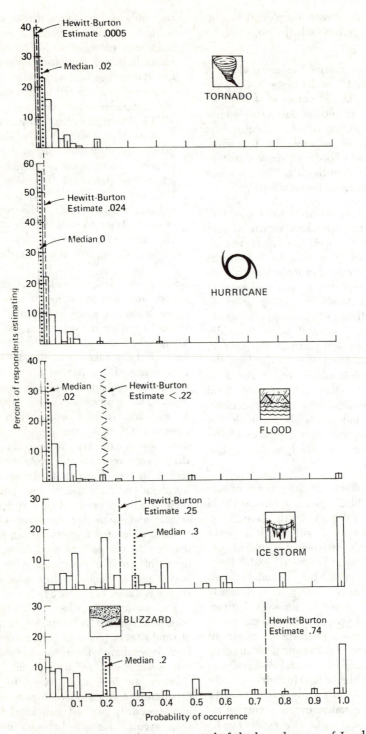

FIGURE 31-4. Experts and laypeople: an appraisal of the hazardousness of London, Ontario.

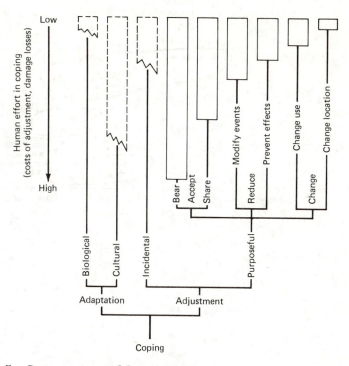

FIGURE 31–5. Coping actions and human effort.

consequences, between scientist and lay-person may be less than assumed. A list of 126 diseases has been scaled by both patients and doctors as to the seriousness of the disease with a rank correlation of .95 between both groups (Wyler, Masuda and Holmes, 11968, 1970). Yet if compared with the actual risk of death, the perceived seriousness of both patients and doctors is poor. Leukemia, cancer, multiple sclerosis, etc. are all perceived as more serious than the more frequent strokes and heart attacks.

These same researchers have tried to measure the seriousness of social readjustments, all of which may have some stress, but not all of which might be called hazards. While values may have changed somewhat in the seven years since the study was done, it is still sobering that divorce is viewed as more stressful than a term in jail, which in turn is viewed as more serious than a death in the family (Holmes and Rahe, 1967).

We know little of how the events and consequences from each domain of nature, urb and society are comparatively appraised. Golant and Burton found that 58 Torontonians using semantic differential ratings discriminated between natural hazards, man-made hazards and quasi-natural hazards of air and water pollution along factorial clusters of concepts related to disruptiveness, cause of source, and magnitude (see Figure 31–6).

In a related study, they analyzed the risk avoidance of 206 respondents of 12 hazards classified as natural, physical (direct injury to person), and social (psychic-social distress). Hazard experience is compared with perceived seriousness (preferred risk avoidance) in Table 31–1. With the exception of auto accidents, the least

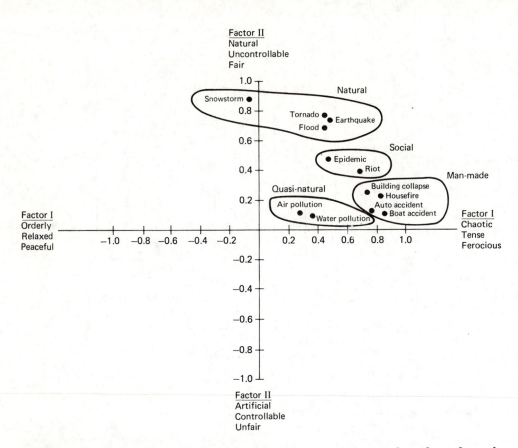

FIGURE 31–6. Some evidence for the causal distinction between natural, made, and social environmental hazard events is found in the groupings of the factor analysis of semantic scales of concepts and hazards. (Adapted from Golant and Burton.)

TABLE 31–1. *Ranking of Hazards Based on Respondents (Total Sample) Greatest Avoidance Measures and Experience*

Avoidance Rank	Hazard	Avoidance No.	%	Experience No.	%	Experience Rank
1	Auto Accident	160	77.7	127	61.7	4
2	Attacked and Robbed	127	61.6	11	5.3	12
3	Tornado	110	53.4	19	9.2	11
4	Forest Fire	107	51.9	29	14.8	8
5	Earthquake	106	51.5	27	13.1	9
6	Failing in School or Job	105	50.9	68	33.0	7
7	Illness	95	46.1	166	80.6	1
8	Loneliness	79	38.4	152	73.8	2
9	Flood	74	35.9	27	13.1	10
10	Public Embarassment	73	35.4	108	52.4	5
11	Being Disliked by Someone You Admire	72	35.0	90	43.7	6
12	Thirst	55	26.7	128	62.1	3

experienced are the most feared. A similar study is now being done in Austria.

The environment as hazard is perceived, cognized, acted upon and reacted to in varied ways. But on a global level, there is some limited order and structure. The varied environments of hazard provide significantly different sets of events characterized as pervasive/chronic or intensive/acute. The perceived events reflect this intrinsic difference. Coping actions and resultant consequences vary with the flexibility of livelihood systems, and the available resources, knowledge and efficacy of adjustments. These are structured by the nature of societal development.

Contained within the structure of environment and society is the "prison of experience" accounting for much of the variation in human behavior. Twelve years ago, I described the prison of experience in relation to flood hazard:

A major limitation to human ability to use improved flood hazard information is the basic reliance on experience. Men on flood plains appear to be very much prisoners of their experience, and the effect of such experience is not consistently in the direction of taking individual action to reduce flood damage.

Improved flood hazard information would include data on floods greater than those flood plain managers have experienced. The observations in LaFollette and elsewhere suggest that managers have a great deal of difficulty conceptualizing and acting upon this information.

Floods need to be experienced, not only in magnitude, but in frequency as well. Without repeated experiences, the process whereby managers evolve emergency measures of coping with floods does not take place. Without frequent experience, learned adjustments wither and atrophy with time.

Conversely, limited experience encour-

ages some managers to feel that floods are not so bad after all, and they lose their motivation to seek further for alternatives. With limited experience, other managers appear to decide that they have received the flood that nature has had in store for them and that they will not have another flood for some time.

Recently experienced floods appear to set an upper bound to the size of loss with which managers believe they ought to be concerned. Since much flood damage is caused by floods greater than have recently been experienced, this experience serves to negate the effect of improved information that seeks to expand the expectation of the flood plain manager.

(Kates, 1962)

Today, the prison of experience still seems central to perception and cognition but less rectangular and more trapezoidal in shape, being lesser and greater at the same time than the reality it could contain. The perceived experience of hazard is lesser than the reality—human memory being biased to the recent and impressionable, cognition biased to the ordered and determinate. It is also greater than the reality—we can share in the memory of others close to us, experience by empathy, myth and symbol. But the distortions, whether they narrow or enlarge our perspective of experience, do not really provide in meaningful ways substitutes for experience. The bars, be they steel or rubber, contain us, and in that we face some peril. For environmental hazard for which we have little or no relevant experience is increasing.

Experiencing the Unexperienced

For most people everywhere, on balance, the everyday is more secure, the exceptional may be less so. The life expectancy of people rises, rapidly in poor nations through increased survival of the young, slowly in rich nations pressing on a ceiling of medical, life, and environmental understanding. We live longer in America today than fifty years ago, die less of infectious disease, and more of stress, diet and malignancy. Cars kill us more frequently than in the past, but other accidents less; the balance is in our favor. Least of all, we die from natural hazards. In this, we are fortunate. Deaths have climbed from nature elsewhere in the world, despite the relative constancy of thirty global disasters per year over the past twenty-five years (Dworkin, 1974).

In places of rapid social change, the social environment may be less secure but not necessarily less satisfying. Our own society appears somewhat more perilous in recent times; crime rates, while dropping, are higher than we have been accustomed to, business failures and unemployment are up, while inflation is frightening. Global peace is obtained at the price of great peril, and the price of more restrained warfare continues to be high.

The hazards of the made environment seem to offer much recent concern, both to scientists and the public alike (see Figure 31–7). Scientific reports of man-made environmental hazard have climbed more or less steadily until some 5% of all reports in *Science* concern them (Halverson and Pijawka, 1974). Public concern evidences similar trends—40% of forty-five major public alarms over technology peaked over the last four years (Lawless, forthcoming). By and large, these newly created or recognized environmental hazards are too new to assess or measure their consequences; we

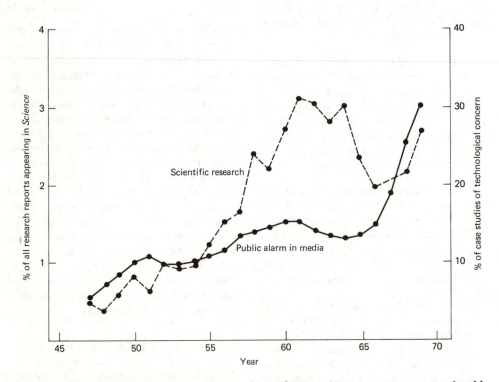

FIGURE 31–7. The graph of public alarm in the media is a 5-year running average of public alarm as based on 45 case studies of alarm as evidenced by major newspapers and periodicals (Lawless, forthcoming). The graph of scientific research is based on analysis of research reports appearing in the interdisciplinary journal *Science* (Halverson and Pijawka, 1974).

have yet to experience their peril. Can we?

The central role of experience as social learning in coping with the hazards of the natural environment is a missing ingredient with newly created or recognized hazards of technology. Such risk appears removed from everyday experience; we are buffered by special assessors of hazards or guardians of the environment, both self- and societal-appointed. It is not clear from what we know that we can simply tell others about hazards, even when we are relatively sure about them. Experience with smoking and seat belts does not auger well for the prevention of less common risks through informational or educational activity. And with such less common risks, the events and consequences are much more uncertain. Nor will the uncertainty be easily resolved; the hazards are too new and too many, they may affect many before we detect them, act upon us for a long time before we control them.

There are, of course, ways of substituting for experience. Science and poetry try to do so by analogue, metaphor, or simulation. We are asked to transfer experience in one realm to another. But we are indeed constrained by what we know, and there is question if we can know beyond the experiential.

We might ask how well we might fare by reflecting on how others fared in unknown lands. Martyn Bowden has reflected on this:

Coping with risks of unknown magnitude is the challenge of the explorer (and to a lesser extent of the frontiersman). The former faces unknown regions peopled by fantasies, the latter is a heroic figure who leaves the comfortable and the known for a period of adaptation during a self-imposed disaster. The experiences of both tell us much about contemporary man's conceptions of unknown risks. Both were essentially uniformitarian through and through. The maps showed terrae incognitae in the regions traversed first by explorers; sailors crossed seas where serpents swam (on maps) to lands where dragons and gorgons dwelt; settlers of the west moved into regions labelled "desert"—the unknown lands, serpentine seas, and irreclaimable deserts were not parts of their adventurous imagery. Rather they projected into these regions what they wanted to find (usually a world familiar to them, and idealization, a simplification of the familiar world they had left). Terrae incognitae were really known by projection from the familiar, by principles of symmetry, latitudinal analog, projection and extension of the known to the unknown. At the most, the unknown lands were simplifications, exaggerations of the known brought together perhaps in unfamiliar combinations.

(Bowden, personal communication, 1974)

More sophisticated analyses seemingly recognize the limitations of the known but cannot escape it. The Rasmussen report on reactor safety is an assessment of accident risks in U.S. commercial nuclear plants (U.S. Atomic Energy Commission, 1974). It attempts to estimate the likelihood of accidents that release large amounts of radioactivity to the environment and to assess the consequences of such releases. It deals with an event that begins with an accident the likelihood of which is estimated at 1 in 17,500 per reactor year. It draws upon the experience of perhaps 40 reactors for a total of 200 reactor years. To bridge the gap, it reconstructs all conceivable (to the assessor) sequences that could lead to the accident, working back from the unknown to the known; reducing the unknown accident rate to the known failure rates of small parts, bits of metal, pipes, and people. The logic is known as fault-tree analysis, and it cost $3,000,000. It is more rigorous and searching than sailors and frontiersmen; nonetheless it is still constrained by experience. To reduce the unknown into knowable parts, or to extend the known into the unknown appears structurally alike.

It may be that the limits of experience are adaptive, for if we knew more of the perils, we would be less venturesome and deny ourselves the blessings of new lands

or new power. But we become each day more clever at creating, recognizing and disseminating threat; we lag in our ability to attend to and cope with threat. In the absence of experience, we may never know what happened.

32.   Recreation as Social Action
SAMUEL Z. KLAUSNER

An operational definition of outdoor recreation begins with the observation of human action set in a natural environment. Some outdoor recreation engages the natural environment. A site called a *recreational facility* is a natural environmental feature that has been socially transformed. Skis and guns are not simply physical objects but are culturally developed tools for coping with problems set by the natural environment. Implements are defined in terms of the social action in which they participate. Skis and guns may be used in a variety of social acts, only some of which are recreational. When they are part of recreational activity, they assume a special meaning. What is *recreational activity?* Does it, as Joffre Dumazedier (1967) says of leisure, have the force of an "independent fact," to be considered on its own terms, with its own dynamic?

To define recreation as leisure time activity begs the question. What is leisure or how does one "do" leisure? In everyday affairs, leisure is contrasted with work. Intuitively, this distinction is not difficult to grasp. Individuals have little difficulty in telling an interviewer whether they are working. It is more difficult to articulate the criterion by which a layman or a researcher makes this distinction. It is not possible to

From Samuel Z. Klausner, *On Man in His Environment* (San Francisco: Jossey-Bass, 1971), pp. 140–166. Reprinted by permission of Jossey-Bass.

arrive at a viable distinction in terms of the intrinsic nature of the activities, in terms of the experience of the actor, or in terms of the productivity or rationality of the activity.

A difference in the intrinsic nature of work and of leisure activities is not a good guide. The same intrinsic activities appear under both headings. Fishing is work for one person and sport for another. Driving is work on Monday and recreation on Sunday.

The pleasure-displeasure distinction does not help. Some people find more pleasure in work than in leisure. There are certainly times when people prefer work to leisure. The contrast between effort and relaxation does not distinguish work from leisure. A girl may think of her relaxed function as a receptionist as work and of her vigorous activity in a swimming pool as recreation. A classification of acts according to their immediate productivity also will not clearly separate work from other activities. Playing golf with a client, a leisure activity, may be as income-relevant as signing a sales contract with him, a work activity. The rationality with which means are related to goals does not characterize one sphere to the exclusion of the other. Football tactics, called play, are more rationally planned than the work of a graphic artist.

Why are none of these criteria satisfactory for distinguishing between work and leisure? The reason is that the distinction between the meanings of these activities is not given on the level of individual behavior. The distinction rests on social criteria. Work and leisure are distinguished by the goals of the systems, usually social, in which they are integrated. Work is an attribute of a role in a social system. The sociology of work, as understood, for instance, by Theodore Caplow (1954), is the study of the way work roles emerge and are structured relative to one another, the way role occupants are recruited, and the influence of occupying particular work roles on the individual's performance in other roles. Work is a role in a social system; one goal of that social system involves a production-consumption function. A tangible, usually marketable, product is the conscious goal of work. Leisure might produce such a product but only tangentially.

In addition, work is supported by societal sanctions. Some broader group, of which the work group is a part, rewards and punishes the worker for occupying or failing to occupy a work role and for the manner in which work is performed. These sanctions, or rewards and punishments, may take the form of money but are also at times rendered as prestige or social acceptance. The demand that one shall work is considered legitimate in most of society and is supported by moral sanctions (the virtue of work and the immorality of nonworking) and by coercion (the giving or withholding of the means of physical sustenance). Both criteria, production-consumption-relevance and social sanctions, are necessary to define the character of work. Work is the name given to all activities performed as a member of a group which is oriented to production-consumption and sanctioned by the broader society. Organized sports, for example, carry performance-contingent sanctions, but the participants are not oriented to production-consumption goals. Sports which are so oriented become professional, and participation in them defined as work.

In defining work, leisure has been defined negatively as an activity not involved in a system of production-consumption and lacking performance-dependent sanctions. Leisure then appears as part of a residual category of all activities not defined as work or not accomplished as part of one's occupation. This residual category must be further partitioned to arrive at a definition of recreation.

Nonwork activities are not all, by their very nature, recreation. The deacon of a church or the mother of a family is neither working nor playing. (In labor force statistics and economic analyses, they may be classed as working but not as gainfully employed.) Religious groups may have working leaders—who receive performance-contingent rewards—and nonworking communicants. Recreation may play a part in religious group life (the church picnic) or in family life (family camping). It may even be an adjunct to work (the company bowling team). Religious and family groups exist alongside occupational groups. They are neither work nor recreational groups.

Recreation in its pristine form may, like work, be defined in terms of a social context. This context seems to engage a group which, on the one hand, is wider than the primary group of a particular family but which, on the other hand, is narrower than the community of common economic interest, the network of occupational groups. Recreational activities take place in groups that are often culturally more homogeneous than occupational work groups and often culturally more heterogeneous than family groups. Recreational activities may follow family lines, as they do in traditional societies, or ethnic, ethnoreligious or racial lines. In a small, culturally homogeneous town, the recreation group and the community could be coterminous. In a large urban setting, recreation may be a neighborhood affair, especially where neighborhoods are also culturally homogeneous. Among those emancipated from residential constraints in establishing friendships, recreational time is shared with members of a *social circle*—a delimited community sharing some particular style of life (the country club, the Bohemians, the professional circle). The style of life may be determined by ideology or some composite of income level and ways of allocating income among consumption items.

A group assembled around a recreational activity may be called a recreational group. Recreation, however, does not generally form the sole basis of relations within such a group. Rather, recreation is one among many functional activities in such groups, just as work is one among many functional activities contributing to the goal of an occupational organization. (Some sporting or playing associations, formed specifically around the development of a particular game, exemplify a limiting case in which interest in the game provides the principal reason for the existence of the group.)

In the United States, the principal prestige ranking system, the system of authority, and the distribution of incomes are all based on work. This is a peculiar feature of certain Western societies. In Bedouin society, for example, rank, authority, and income are more closely tied to lineage than to work. The Soviet Union illustrates an extreme form of the American orientation. Recreational activities there tend to be viewed as adjuncts to occupational relations. The work group and the recreational group are often identical.

Recreational activities, like the larger class of leisure activities to which they belong, have been defined as not oriented to the goal of production-consumption and not subject to an obligation to participate. More precisely, however, recreation activities do not appear obligatory in the eyes of the broader society. No economic penalties are imposed for nonparticipation. In a society in which the occupational system is dominant, recreation may appear peripheral or even unimportant. While recreation is not geared directly to occupational goals, it does contribute to the life of certain nonoccupational social groupings. The importance of recreation rests on its contribution to such groupings and the part they play in the broader society.

Recreation meets certain of the functional requirements of these groupings and is indeed subject to obligatory norms. The affirmation of group solidarity and culture is one such functional requirement. It is a talent function rather than a manifest goal. Unlike the goals of production, solidarity is not attained by manifestly pursuing it. Group solidarity, like love, rests upon trust and commitment. Manifest pursuit vitiates it. Recreation that appears purposeless when judged in terms of the instrumental goal-oriented action of the occupational group is far from purposeless when viewed within the context of the subgroups of which it is a part.

Further, while the broader society does not impose sanctions for recreational participation, recreational groups do require participation on the part of their members. One's office mates may not really care if one takes a vacation, but one's family may press the requirement. People in certain social positions must give dinner parties which people in related social situations must attend. In a traditional society, violation of these recreational mores could lead to economic sanctions. In our society such nonparticipation may lead to ostracism from the offended group, but would provoke economic sanctions only insofar as the recreational groups are articulated with occupational groups. (Once entering a recreational situation, one is subject to many rigid rules—the rules of play—but this is another problem.)

Our earlier definition of work may now be modified. Work is an activity within an occupational social system. Concretely, it is usually accomplished within an organization. It contributes to the attainment of a goal of that organization and to a goal of the society to which it belongs—specifically, to the goal of production. The broad society rewards this performance with goods and services. The norms of obligation are legitimated and compliance enforced by the broader society which, because of the economic interdependence of individuals and groups, has a stake in work performance.

Recreation, on the other hand, tends to take place within more culturally homogeneous subsocieties—principally, within family, ethnic, religious, and ideological groupings, including social circles composed of individuals sharing a common life style. Roger Caillois (1961), the French sociologist, defines play as an activity in which "property is exchanged but no goods are produced." It contributes, among other things, to the integration of such subsocieties. They, in turn, impose an obligation to participate in recreation. This obligation is not necessarily supported by the broader society.

Recreational activity is not apparent in societies at earlier stages of cultural development. While there is a prejudice in our society about the lazy and lackadaisical primitive who knows no work discipline, to term his nonworking activities recreational may be an improper borrowing of concepts from our own culture. A culture must have rationalized the concept of time to have the notion of recreation. A rational concept of time is one in which events are ordered discursively and perceived as occurring discretely in sequence. In cultures with a prerational concept of time, the continuous present is predominant. A discursive time order of activities, such as work on the one hand and recreation on the other, is difficult to imagine in these situations. Lacking the temporal distinction, work and recreation blend.

While recreation requires a temporal separation of activities, it is not necessarily spatially separated from work. Both may occur on the same precincts but not at the same time. Even outdoor recreation may not be spatially separated from work. Hunters and loggers may use the same territory. Spatial separation arises secondarily in the effort to separate recreational from production-consumption activities and from the

social relationships organized around those activities.

The Dutch historian Johan Huizinga (1955) finds a play element in such serious work-like activities as law, war, and philosophy—as long as the actor is not striving for direct material profit. In effect, any absolute distinction between work and play is analytical. In actuality, work and recreation overlap to a greater or lesser degree. Perhaps the earliest distinction between work and play, more precisely between work groups and recreational groups, arose in religious contexts. In a polytheistic age, religious holy days were set aside for the worship of special deities. The sabbath was a consecrated tithe of time. It was called a time of surcease from labor but was, in effect, a shift from the usual to special labors related to worship. Religious holy days might involve communal celebrations or pilgrimages to a central shrine. Greek games formalized certain aspects of these celebrations—separating audience and participant, stressing competitiveness and excellence in performance. These were no longer worshipful activities but activities under the protection of deities. Games were modeled on myths of the activities of the gods.

In early modern Europe, sports and games were disengaged from religious life and, in fact, became a competing focus of social organization. The Reformation church opposed certain sports and leisure amusement as wasteful or even sinful. James I promoted sports as part of his fight against Puritanism. The ambivalent attitude toward fun, as opposed to productive activity, reflected in the Reformation position is still with us. Today, recreational and devotional activities compete for time on the Saturday or Sunday sabbath.

Recreational activity can be thought of as a symbolic drama played by a group. In recreation, a group may be experimenting dramatically with solutions to group problems. The experiment may flow into real situations in which those solutions are applied. This is the sense in which the playing fields of Eton were related to the battle at Waterloo. Literary criticism, the sociology of literature, and the sociology and psychology of play have evolved methods for analyzing the symbolic meanings of such activities (Burke, 1941; Lowenthal, 1957). Recreation may also be a ritual drama of reaffirmation or rededication to the existence of a particular group. Models established in the sociology of religion suggest this function (Durkheim, 1954).

The dramatic meaning, the function of the drama for the group, is given by the content of recreational activity. A classification of dramatic themes could generate a typology of recreation. Such a formidable task will be deferred at this time. However, some correspondence exists between the *form* recreation takes and the *content of* the drama played through that form. A classification of forms of recreation is a fundamental requirement for research. One classification is suggested here.

Recreational form may be classified along three dimensions—one regarding the ecological relation of man to nature, a second regarding the social relation of man and man, and a third regarding the psychological relation of man to himself. All of these relations rest upon a symbolic interpretation by man of his situation. In this sense, they are all mediated by culture. The following illustration is developed for the case of relatively extended vacations. With some modifications, it could be applicable to other types of recreation.

Extended vacations contain elements of a drama about residential, occupational and social mobility. They may be dry run experiments in mobility. Vacations specifically designed to keep the vacationer within a single social circle, such as the gathering at a spa of the old European elite, may be dry runs for residential mobility. Such vacations are also occasions for political sparring, matchmaking and reaffirming the integrity of one class as contrasted with other classes.

Spatial location and movement—the ecological dimension—seem to be crucial in the definition of a vacation. All vacations (with the exception of the limiting case of the homebound vacation of television watching or digging in the garden) involves some geographic and social movement. The individual or group abandons the physical and social environment of the residential community and selects a spatial and a social setting appropriate for the vacation. This appropriateness is dependent upon the dramatic content to be expressed. Spatial movement may be classified in terms of a physical characteristic of the territory toward which it is oriented. Movement may either be to *open spaces* such as the desert or the seashore, or to enclosed *inner spaces* such as forests. This defines two polar types of vacation classified in relation to topography. Dramas associated with gaiety and sexuality may tend to seek out the seaside setting, while those associated with solemnity and labor may have more affinity for the forest glen. These associations between form and content may be presumed to be culturally influenced and individually learned. The physical symbol vehicle, open or inner space, must be appropriate for the symbolic meaning which it carries. Conceivably the inner spaces offer more resistance to life and so become associated with work, while the open spaces involve the explosively created meanings associated with water and expanse and so are associated with these activities.

The point is that, at base, the classification is of two types of social action. The classification may be constituted in terms of the topographic features because of some widespread cultural evaluation of these features. The topographic features seem to have similar meanings, often similarly understood stage settings, for large numbers of people. The general relation between agorophobia (open space) and eroticism has been documented in psychoanalytic practice (Abraham, 1927) and that between claustrophobia (inner space) and the struggle to free oneself, archtypically, to be reborn, has been described by Bertram Lewin (1935).

Some vacation movement vacillates first to inner and then to open spaces. People travel, sometimes emerging at open land and sometimes penetrating into the woods. The process of movement itself, rather than the destination, is then the primary setting. This type may be called *nomadism*. Movement to inner and to open spaces, as opposed to nomadism, involves a sedentary relation to topography during the vacation. Movement to open space and a sedentary settling in open space is one extreme pole of the dimension and a sedentary settling in enclosed inner space is the other pole. Nomadism is an intermediate form between the two poles.

A second distinction rests upon a change in social relations—in effect, a matter of the direction of social movement. In leaving the occupationally determined community of residence, the vacationing group, or single person, may seek isolation from all other groups or persons. Such movement, from a social center outward, may, by physical analogy, be called *centrifugal*. Alternatively, the group or person may leave to join another group—go to a resort, a religious community or a summer colony of a particular political shade or to visit other members of the family. Movement that assembles vacationing persons or groups into another group may be called *centripetal*.

The South Sea island paradise, the centrifugal vacation utopia, is atypical in our culture. Literature on outdoor recreation suggests that centripetal vacations are the more popular. Margaret Mead (1962), commenting on the centrality of centripetal movement, has noted that 51 per cent of those who traveled on vacation did so to visit kin. Many outdoor activities, such as camping along the way, were secondary to this primary purpose. Gurin and Mueller also found that centripetal vacationers in America outnumber centrifugal. They say that for a minority the appeal of the outdoors is associated with getting away from people, but that for the majority it is a chance to share activity—to be gregarious.

Centripetal vacations are an occasion for reaffirming belongingness to groups not ordinarily integrated through the occupational and income stratified residential pattern of American society. These centripetally formed groups tend to be more homogeneous than the community of residence with respect to ethnic background or political ideologies, particularly minority ideologies. Most frequently, as Mead noted, they are kin groups. Perhaps for the first time in history, in America members of extended kin groups are geographically separated while still belonging to the same territorial and national society. The vacation is a way of compensating for the occupationally induced mobility and consequent separation of like-minded or otherwise related people.

Max Kaplan (1960) notes that sometimes centripetal vacationers are from different backgrounds but share leisure interests. Grouping around specialized leisure time interests, such as sports events or the intercommunity meetings of fraternal orders, may be part of the process of forming new social groups. These are affirmations of what Charles Kadushin (1968) has called "social circles, informal networks of individuals who share a common interest."

Centripetal vacations, while contributing to the integration of special groupings, have total societal functions. In strengthening the family units of which the society is composed, the centripetal vacation contributes to broad societal maintenance (a pattern maintenance-tension management function). Because families in mobile American society cut across class lines and because ideological or interest gatherings bring people together from different occupational strata, the centripetal movement may dampen a tendency for the society to polarize along social class lines (an integrative function).

Certain broad social functions are subserved by both centripetal and centrifugal vacations. Integration of local polities is encouraged as travelers resident in one jurisdiction submit themselves to another jurisdiction. The requirement of reciprocity in the treatment of these citizens and the accompanying diffusion of ideas restrain tendencies to localism.

Vacations have been classified topographically with respect to whether open or secluded sites are sought, and then they were classified social relationally with respect to the temporary dissolution or reformation of groupings. A third general dimension for classifying outdoor vacations rests upon the allocation of individual psychological energies. A vacation may offer an opportunity to "give out" in some new setting—to expend energy, to relate actively to the environment. A vacation may, contrariwise, offer an opportunity to "take in," to relax and become reenergized, or to submit, to be soothed or passively encounter the environment. The active and the passive orientations are two forms of psychological encounter between the vacationer and his environment. The classification is based on manifest activity or passivity. In a deeper sense, of course, manifest activity toward the outer environment may cloak an attitude of "taking in," gobbling it up, while the outwardly contemplative individual may be in inner struggle.

Conceived in terms of activity/passivity, vacations may subserve a personality function. The problem of allocating energies (a tension management function with reference to the internal functioning of the personality and a goal attainment function with reference to the relation of the personality to its situation) is central to any personality. Activities induce new tension which displace old ones. The passive vacation involves a disengagement from the sources of tension. The way tensions are related to objects has implications for a sense of ego competence. The active vacation involves a mastering orientation through which the ego develops an image of itself as more competent. It is associated with a frontier atmosphere, with ruggedly individualistic people. Ego competence is not usually at stake in the passive vacation. The passive vacationer's sense of ego competence, of control, rests on submission of the self to the environment, a mystical merging with the environment to absorb its strength.

Of course, all of these meanings, whether based on a response to a physical feature or on social and psychological action, have the status of hypotheses. It remains to be determined empirically whether open space does provide a setting for more expressive behavior or whether an active camping vacation involves testing of one's sense of competence. Joseph Sonnenfeld (1969) has tested the meanings of various landscape and climatic features such as rain, fog, and sunshine for Eskimo groups by applying Osgood's semantic differential. He has begun to trace some cross-cultural differences in environmental meanings but, principally, has illustrated the need for such empirical verification of hypotheses such as those suggested here. Together, the moves to inner/outer land, centripetality/centrifugality and activity/passivity, define a three dimensional conceptual space. Values along each of the three dimensions are continuous. A recreational occasion may be located by its triplet of values, its location on these three coordinates. Thinking of the dimensions, only as a trichotomy and two dichotomies, however, twelve (2 x 2 x 3) distinct formal settings for recreation are defined. Each setting is a stage for a relatively distinct type of recreational drama.

For simplicity, here are some examples based on two of these dimensions: the psychological dimension of activity/passivity and the social dimension of centripetality/centrifugality. A cross-classification of these two dichotomies defines four *ideal typical* vacations: centripetal-passive, centrifugal-passive, centrifugal-active, and centripetal-active.

A vacation may involve centripetal social movement and place the vacationers in a passive relation to the environment. The individual or group may join another group for the purpose of relaxing together. A religious retreat exemplifies a centripetal-passive vacation. The individual may contemplate, seeking the gift of the spirit, while in a community in a quiet wooded spot. The religious centripetal-passive form is infrequent in the United States but common in Thailand where men may enter and leave a monastery by arrangement. The assembly of a regular clientele at a country hotel provides an American example.

A centrifugal-passive vacation is exemplified by a family or individual seeking to relax in isolation from others. The esthetic motif may be prominent as vacationers stroll through beautiful scenery with minimal exertion. The centrifugal-active vacation of an individual or group involves exertion in circumstances of isolation from other individuals or groups. Hunting, fishing, and hiking—involving the development and testing of skills, exemplify this type of vacation. Family members, lodging in a country cabin, may assume ordinary tasks under unusual conditions and be welded more closely together in their accomplishment. A centripetal-active vacation is exemplified by individuals gathering from all over the country for an annual sport parachuting competition. Of course, the participants rather than the observers are the active ones.

The table presents these illustrations, schematically cross-classifying the three topographic, two social and two psychological relations. Twelve basic forms of vacations are defined.

Several other attributes of vacations are subsumed by these primary dimensions. Calvin Stillman (*Black Rock Forest Papers*, No. 28, 1966) distinguishes between hunters who want a touchable environment and those who are satisfied to observe it. Touching is, manifestly, an active orientation to the environment; observing is a way of passively taking it in. Thus Stillman's distinction overlaps that between activity and passivity. Burch (1965) emphasizes the dimensions of self-sufficiency in the case of the family camping group. This is another way of stating the choice of centrifugal rather than centripetal form. The group that goes away centrifugally, to be alone, is seeking to be self-sufficient.

Elwood Shafer et al. (1969) use landscape categories in assessing preference ranks assigned by campers to scenic photographs. They classify landscapes into zones of water, sky, vegetation, and nonvegetation. Water and sky seem to be special cases of the inner-open space dimension. The matter of vegetation, degree of aridity, seems to be an additional significant dimension not considered in our scheme. So much of human life has been organized with respect to verdant and arid conditions that these features must carry a heavy symbolic loading.

A vacation may also be described in terms of its esthetic character. Esthetic experience of nature may be associated with the psychological dimension of passivity. Franklin Thomas (1925) quotes Wilhelm von Humboldt's characterization of the appreciative vacation (from Humboldt's *Cosmos*, p. 3): "Mere communion with nature, mere contact with the free air, exercises a soothing yet strengthening influence on the wearied spirit, calms the storm of passion, and softens the heart when shaken by sorrow to its inmost depths." Stillman (*Black Rock Forest Papers*, No. 27, 1966) offers his own expression of this mood: "Any great natural phenomenon has a special meaning for persons who behold it. For many of us this meaning is positive and personal, beyond articulate expression. It is something we treasure, something dear to us; something whose preservation is important to us" (p. 4). This imagery of esthetic appreciation is inconsistent with an active manipulatory orientation. Hunting, for instance, exemplifies the active orientation. Tony Peterle

Topology of Vacation Forms

Topographic Relation	Direction of Social Movement	Psychological Orientation		Illustration
Sedentary, Open Land	Centripetal	Active	1	Beach surfers
		Passive	2	Beach front hotel guests
	Centrifugal	Active	3	Family camping on beach
		Passive	4	Stereotyped South Sea island paradise
Nomadic	Centripetal	Active	5	Teen-age western summer tour
		Passive	6	Cruise ship
	Centrifugal	Active	7	Hiking
		Passive	8	Sightseeing
Sedentary, Inner Land	Centripetal	Active	9	Boy scout summer camp in mountains
		Passive	10	Country hotel guests
	Centrifugal	Active	11	Lone cabin in woods
		Passive	12	Private serviced lodge in mountains

(1967), studying hunters in Ohio, found that those who enjoyed the esthetics of the natural environment hunted less. This may, of course, be a special case of the inverse correlation between hunting—known to be culture-group related—and level of income. Logically, though, active exertion of effect upon environment would tend to be associated with an aggressive attitude toward that environment, a desire to change or exploit it in use rather than contemplatively enjoy it.

Three other important dimensions have not been included in our recreation typology: the length of time allocated to the recreation, its location in social time, and the size or type of the recreational group. Each of these dimensions refers to a level of analysis different from that from which our three dimensions are drawn.

Differences that follow from various lengths of time do not seem, in themselves,

to involve qualitative distinctions of meaning (except, of course, insofar as they allow the selection of different options). A family picnic in the local park and an overnight family stay at a camp ground are both characterized by inner space location, centripetal social movement, and an active psychological orientation. The overnight outing would, however, provide for a more intense drama, placing both a greater strain on family relations and holding the possibility of greater integration. Length of time may affect the intensity of a particular type of vacation. It is a significant variable for economic analysis which is less concerned with the social psychological meaning of a commodity than with the demand for it. Time allocated in traveling to a site and at the site is crucial for an operations analysis of travel flow on site usage (Cesario, 1969). Abbot Ferriss (1962) also classifies activities according to the time spent in them or the money required to engage in them. He did this to measure the intensity of interest or demand for particular types of vacation. The priorities established in scarce time may be indicators of meaning. Time budgets, a well established social research tool (Sorokin and Berger, 1939), have been used to demonstrate changes in the relation of work and leisure, although they are costly to collect in a reliable way (Converse, 1968).

A classification according to the location of the vacation in social time—whether over Labor Day or midwinter—places it in a broad cultural context, and is likely to have consequences for its meaning. Weekend recreation, summer vacations, and holiday outings are all tied to cosmic changes and to changes in the types and rates of general social interaction. The special meanings of these occasions are linked more to the content than to the form of recreation. Location in social time controls the articulation of recreation with other activities. The yearly gathering around the Christmas tree unites recreation to religious institutions; a visit to Gettysburg on Memorial Day binds it to political institutions. These cultural-content distinctions are important for analysis of the place of recreation in the broader social setting.

The cultural character of the vacationing family or club—like location in social time—defines the relation between recreation and these other social institutions. Some vacations are planned to coincide with meetings of political organizations while others are vital events in the yearly calendars of churches and families.

The size of the vacationing group is yet another important distinction. Size may simply reflect the type of group or it may be relevant in its own right. A vacation may be solitary, a small group or a mass activity. Each of the twelve settings defined above may accommodate groups of varying sizes. For the single vacationer, the proposed dimension may be used to assess the meaning of the vacation for the individual personality. For a group of vacationers, these dimensions may be used with reference to social system analysis. Recreation may be integrative for an individual personality (helping to articulate the values or energies of a person) or for a social system (helping to articulate relations among a plurality of persons).

A typology is a first step in planning research. It defines the variables. However, a typology alone tends to have a static ring. Vacations may be conceptualized in more process-oriented terms. The moment that one's focus is shifted from the forms to the content, from topography, social movement and energy economics to the dramas being played in these settings, it is difficult to resist a sense of social process. One common vacation theme seems to be that of "rebirth." Such colloquialisms as refreshment and recharging batteries suggest this imagery. A vacationing family pulls away from its usual surroundings, isolates itself for a time in an environment with a different set of physical and social challenges and then returns to its original setting. A vacation of this type is judged successful when some relationships among family members are fortified. Max Kaplan (1960), using this rebirth imagery, writes that leisure either renews or develops personal identity.

A vacation promotes rebirth by encouraging a regressive social or personality process, a return to a simpler mode of social or personality organization. It is facilitated by withdrawal from usual role obligations, particularly the occupational, and the assumption of new, more earthy, roles. A forest is a particularly apt setting for a play around the theme of regression and rebirth. The forest has served as a secluded hideout, or a place to hide in, from time immemorial. Merriman and Ammons (1965) describe the advantage of the isolation of the forest, the charm of treading where no sign of human intrusion is found. Complex cultures have failed to develop in the depths of the forest. For Thomas

(1925), it is an environment which imprisons and prevents growth of large social groups because its inhabitants must struggle for the essentials of survival. William Goode (1962) has pointed out that in such a situation individuals avoid their usual class position, with its privileges and burdens. Status in the forest depends on camping skills. There is an unmasking of the individual. This unmasking may be a prelude to social regression. The division of labor, which civilization has carried to a high degree, may be reversed with each family member taking on a wider set of tasks. The norms which, outside the forest, supported all the highly specialized statuses slip away. In a socially regressed state, with some social norms in abeyance, a reorganization of the relations of authority among members of the family is possible.

In the family camping situation, one type of reorganization is around leadership. In American society, the types of labors and skills necessary for forest survival are more likely to be possessed by males. The matriarchate, which has come to characterize the American urban family, is rejected in the wooded camp. The woman pursuing household type chores is somewhat more dependent on male assistance in the successful accomplishment of her tasks. The rebirth through camping is characterized by reassertion of patriarchal control.

Regression and rebirth under the best circumstances are not smooth processes. Families held together by routine may be strained by the travail of a vacation. With the usual authority structure disrupted, some adult campers—particularly in the absence of children—may become licentious, engaging in excessive drinking and even brawling and destroying of property. Delinquents in the camp setting, like delinquents in the city, are only a minority. Vacation delinquents are probably not the psychological and social siblings of urban delinquents. Model citizens at home may become delinquent when the authority structure and the usual role relations are

placed in abeyance. Social disorganization, even in its simple, nondelinquent forms, may be needed to clear the way for a new reintegrative process. A family may emerge better integrated after working through a chaotic period to new norms. The reassertion of patriarchal authority is one resolution. If the normative disorganization is not resolved, the family may emerge weakened and the vacation considered unsuccessful—even when the weather and mosquitoes have been kind.

The paradigm presented above rests on two proposals and a suggestion about their connectedness. It is proposed that the content of recreation may be analyzed in terms of a drama in which the players symbolically deal with a life problem. This concept could be validated by establishing a classification scheme for the dramas—much as the scheme for interpreting stories in the Thematic Appreciation Test has been developed. Then, dramas of groups with different life problems might be compared in terms of some criteria of meaningful coherence between dramas and life situations. The proposal would not, however, fall on some particular classification of dramatic themes. If no themes associated with social or personal characteristics of a population could be discovered, the proposed approach would not be useful for empirical research—although it might still retain some descriptive interest.

The second proposal, for a formal typology of settings (the one elaborated in this paper), could also be tested. Coordinates might be assigned to particular vacation activities through an empirical investigation. The assumption is that the different formal settings are associated with some nearly universal symbolic significances—that entering a forest, for instance, indeed means—or is significant because it means—isolating oneself from the usual social environment or placing oneself in a situation in which one is compelled to struggle against environmental resistance. These meanings could be tested on an individual level with attitude measuring scales and on a group level by a content analysis of social communication.

These two proposals are independent. The validity of the proposal about the dramatic themes does not depend on the validity of the proposal about the formal characteristics of settings. Conceivably one proposal might prove useful and the other not. However, the third proposal that individuals seeking particular dramas are drawn to particular settings depends on the joint validity of the first two proposals. This relation could be tested by observing the statistical likelihood of certain dramatic content being played in one formal setting or another.

A few suggestions for studies in outdoor recreation that might be implemented at an early date are appropriate here. The gathering of original data is the most expensive part of social research. This fact places a premium on secondary analysis of data already available. Data gathered in the course of national sample studies, such as the National Recreation Survey (Ferriss, 1962), have not been fully exploited. Despite the misfortune that some socially relevant questions were not asked in the survey, a theoretically oriented treatment of the measured demographic factors to outdoor activity is possible. Few organizations have the resources to obtain national population samples of the quality which the Bureau of the Census provided for this survey. A secondary analysis of those data might encourage the Bureau to include more sociologically relevant indicators in future surveys. What follows are some specific leads for applied—rather than theoretical—research in outdoor recreation.

A prime research question is one of population parameters. What are the relevant recreational groups within the broad national population? As noted above, the recreational community is wider than the family and narrower than the occupational-residential community. Inner city populations consist of a multitude of recreational communities, ethnic, ethno-religious, political-ideological, and racial among others. Each community differs in the way its members distribute themselves among the types of recreation. Italo-American and Polish-American communities each congregate at different locales and engage in different activities. Both differ from the Negro community in their concepts of recreation. The Negro community itself is not homogeneous. The recent migrant from the rural South and the second or third generation city dweller are struggling with different problems which they may dramatize through the recreational medium. It would be worthwhile to explore, in depth, the meanings of outdoor recreation for each of these recreational circles.

The example of vacations away from home, one among many forms of recreation, was selected for elaboration in this paper. A conceptual scheme might begin with this broad classification of vacations and then proceed to a more specific typology of meanings of particular sites, times, and activities. What are the life problems people express in their recreational play? Through what manifest activities and in what settings do they enact these dramas? What proportion of the population selects each type of vacation? What are the social, cultural, and psychological characteristics of those choosing one rather than another type?

Questions of meaning may be answered with the help of two techniques: drawing upon the tradition of clinical psychology, depth interviews could be conducted with some small samples; drawing upon the tradition of anthropology, participant-observation of people engaged in recreation could go far towards clarifying the meaning of that activity.

To extrapolate to the future, it is necessary to learn something of the laws of development of recreation patterns of individuals. This might be done in two ways. A less exacting but also less expensive way would be to collect recreational life histories and subject these to sociological and psychological analysis. A preferable approach, and a more time-consuming one, would be to repeatedly interview the same panels (a selected group or sample) of vacationers over several years. Both these approaches could produce developmental data on the recreation life of a population.

The life dramas of low-income Negroes are different from those of the white middle class. Their recreational preferences may also differ. The association between recreation and sexuality differs across class lines. Sex-homogeneous recreational activities, such as hunting by males and card playing by females, are common in the white middle class. Among low-income Negroes, sex-heterogeneous recreation is relatively more frequent. Family picnicking may also be assuming greater importance in the urban Negro than in the urban white populations. Some recreational activities even take their name from the type of food consumed—beer parties, weiner roasts.

Among youth using recreational facilities one observes a good deal of aggressive (not necessarily hostile) behavior. This drama may have to do, in part, with the establishment of dominance-submission relations—at least micro-orders of dominance or submission. (The macro-order is set in the larger social system.) Youths also seem to enjoy testing themselves against some natural barrier—the seeking of stress (Klausner, 1968): Stress seeking is not classbound but is probably differentially distributed among classes. Facilities might make provision for such activities. The functional equivalent of the mountain for the mountain climber may be needed—at a lower cost than access to the mountain entails—in the more congested city environment.

A conceptual distinction has been drawn between work and recreation. What, however, is the relationship between these two worlds, the world of work and the world of recreation. One might think that the unemployed, having more leisure time, would participate more in available free recreation in the park or playground than would their employed brethren. This would lead one to expect a positive correlation between use of local facilities and unemployment. More likely, unemployment and recreational participation are negatively correlated. In the American situation, where status and rank—even in primary groups such as the family—are contingent upon position in the occupational structure, it is likely that alienation from one's occupation would imply alienation from the social relations of the recreational community. Such a study could elucidate some links between recreational and vocational rehabilitation. It might throw light, not only on the case of the unemployed but also on the problem of the role of recreation in the rehabilitation of socially, culturally, or physically handicapped persons in general.

The typology of vacations presented above deals with meanings sought by vacationers. Vacationing could be examined as a system in its own right. The community of vacationers and the community of suppliers of vacation facilities are bound together in a broader system of vacationing. A study of this sort, in tandem with studies of vacationers, would be necessary background for rational planning of the social-organizational and physical facilities of vacationing.

Each type of vacation makes its own demands on facilities. Behavior of the suppliers is not independent of the behavior of the vacationers. Facilities are required for the meeting and mingling of groups of people and for opportunities for isolated living. Suppliers provide the raw material for people to act upon, such as wilderness or lakes, and equipment for engaging in the activities, such as skis and canoes. They also provide amenities which minimize the vacationer's need to look after his own comforts. Knowledge of the interaction of suppliers and consumers of recreational services and goods is an initial requirement for predicting future recreational demand.

The classification of vacation spots into inner and open space was based on some general meanings which such places might assume. A playground or a park becomes endowed with certain more specific social meanings by virtue of the social activity that takes place on it. Various locales become associated with specific groups. Davis (1967) hypothesizes "that one chooses the campground where he will take up more than transient residence with the same social considerations (and possibly with a higher degree of realization) that guide his choice of neighborhood, club, and other associations." In some cases the social criteria applied might, of course, differ for home and for camp.

The relations among the groups associated with various locales may not be peaceable. Locations, say within a park, become territories for which social groups may compete. When the group controlling the facility commands overwhelming social power and uses this power to exclude another group, the question becomes one of discrimination in the use of public and quasi-public facilities. The less powerful—excluded—group may appeal for admission to outside forces such as the constitution or the judiciary.

When the groups are more nearly matched in power, an outright conflict over the facility may erupt. Such conflicts are extensions of broader social conflict. The facility is merely one battleground. The current struggle over public accommodations is a case in point. Gang fights in public parks are another. Under what conditions does violence erupt in a recreational facility and how can it be managed? An answer may be approached by collecting and analyzing a series of case studies of violent incidents in such facilities.

Sometimes facilities shift "ownership." A kind of Gresham's law, not necessarily related to the relative power of the groups involved, seems to operate. The arrival of one social group may lead to peaceable evacuation of the territory by another social group. The shifting of the population of users of a recreational facility may be a miniature example of the invasion and succession rule of urban residential shifts.

The type of activity in an area may change. At one time a forest may be a locale for isolated backwoods camping and at another time for social campgrounds. The direction of change is probably from isolated to social use. At one time, a site may serve people interested in active vacations; and at another time, it may serve people interested in passive relaxation. Commercial development would induce or reflect a change in that direction.

The same physical facility may serve more than one type of vacationer without conflict when their needs are complementary. Davis (1967) found that the Maine woods serve hunters at one season and family campers at another. All of this suggests the importance of studies of the natural history of recreational facilities.

The inner city has a special problem with facilities, resulting from the mobility of its population. The demand for given facilities in given locals may change over time. One population may want rocks to romp over. City parks across the country attest to this demand. City Negroes are less likely than their white fellow citizens to attend the carefully developed zoos and art museums of the cities. Facilities must be constantly reassessed with respect to current client populations.

In sum, outdoor recreation invites historical, methodological and substantive studies. Vacation, as a meaningful man-environment relation, may be studied in terms of the types of meaning the vacation has for individuals and groups, the structure of the relations between vacationers and suppliers of vacation facilities, and the natural history of the vacation sites. These studies can draw on the theoretical insights of a variety of sociological fields. We have not discussed all of the relevant sociological fields that seem pertinent to such an enterprise. Considering the history of neglect, however, this attempt to plot a set of directions will, it is hoped, serve as a new beginning in the study of human action in the nonhuman environment.

Let us assume that a variety of recreational possibilities for a population is visible above its cultural horizon. Then if, as has been argued, recreation expresses a life drama, and if various subgroups—differently situated in society—have their own interest-determined dramatic problems, then each subgroup might seek different types of recreation. Each group might even seek different formal settings for their recreation.

This seems to be the case. Urban Negroes (even with income held constant) are rarely found among backwoods campers. Bowling attracts more of the working class than of the social elite. Sports participation is related to class and ethnic position. Games, for cultural-historical reasons, are associated with certain social groups—tennis with the English and baseball with the Americans. Some games are associated with regional cultures—sport flying with the western United States and scuba diving with the Florida Coast.

This fact of class and regional recreational bias has a consequence for governmental interest in recreation in the United States. Typically individuals project the recreational culture of their own social circle, or social class, on the larger society. Members of each class or circle either believe that others share their recreational interests or that it would be good for them if they did. The absurdity is now apparent. Each social group uses recreation, in part, to work through different problems.

Outdoor recreation planners and officials in the United States come from a narrow band within the middle class. The policy making, operating, and research personnel are almost entirely white, of English or Western European descent, disproportionately from rural backgrounds and devoted to a physically active life style. They have tended to project an image of outdoor recreation—created in their own milieu—upon the whole of the society. Thus, prominence is given to activities in the woods, such as hunting and fishing, or water-related activities, such as boating and swimming (Bureau of Outdoor Recreation, 1967).

The wealthy among inner-city residents create their own, nongovernmentally dependent, recreational facilities. The demands of the inner-city impoverished population for allocation of funds and facilities will be increasingly visible as they learn to exercise the vote and other means of political influence. At present their pressure is most directly felt at the municipal level. Some municipalities are projecting the demands of these groups to Washington and attracting federal funds to urban recreational projects.

Recreational requirements of the impoverished sector of inner-city populations are not easily communicated to decision makers. One reason is the inability of this population to formulate and articulate its preferences. A second reason has to do with the clogging of the channels—through which such information should flow—because of the lack of research or of other mechanisms for gathering information. And, finally, the natural limitations to appreciation by one class of the message of another affects the reception of the message. Research is one way to open the flow of information at all three points—by articulating demand, opening communications channels, and interpreting the demand to the policy maker.

Part VII

The Built Environment

In contrast to the preceding section (Part VI), on the natural environment, the built environment represents an area well covered in the previous edition and one that is usually the focal point of much discussion in any book on environmental issues. However, we have already pointed out that the built environment, like the natural environment, is not a useful, definable, analytic category for scientific study. Any environment that is touched by man is already influenced by him. The environments encountered by all but a few humans living today are the products of a long period of planning and intervention. We have seen that this applies to the so-called natural as well to the built environment. Why, then, do we persist in referring to a category of the built environment? The answer remains the same. It represents an important aspect of people's everyday experience. Just as we know intuitively what we mean by a natural setting, so also we know what we mean by a built setting. The built environment in this section, then, stands in contrast to the natural environment of the preceding section, not in terms of objective definition, but rather in terms of commonsense experience. What people in general consider to be the built environment is the subject of this particular section.

Of course, the built environment encompasses far more types of settings than could possibly be included in the space allowed. In selecting from the vast literature available for inclusion in this section, we did not attempt to make any systematic sampling of the kinds of built settings that have been studied, nor to be representative or inclusive of all the important researchers who have devoted themselves to this topic. Rather, we have attempted to offer some indication of the range and types of studies which are being and can be carried out in the built environment. The particular settings represented in this section are those which for most people are probably considered the most extreme cases of the totally built environment, that is, large-scale institutional settings, such as hospitals, schools, prisons, and large housing developments. Although these settings may, however, represent extreme cases of the built environment, they are by no means the only settings that have been studied. The literature on each of them is indeed extensive, but the same can be said for a number of other settings that are not represented in the readings in this book. The interested reader is urged to follow up the selections here with more intensive reading in the particular setting that occupies his interest. For example, in the category of specific building types, dormitories have been studied quite extensively as have offices, whereas many other settings, day care centers to choose an example, are only beginning to come into the fore as focal points for investigation. But specific building types are not the only settings in which the built environment can be studied. The city as a whole is dealt with in the next section (Part VIII), but many subparts of the city are appropriately studied under the general category of the built environment. The vast network of transportation systems within and between cities is perhaps the most important and interesting topic that is not included in this particular section. Subways, for example, have been studied in great detail, the most notable efforts being those going into the Bay Area and the Washington subways. Stations and terminals were included in these studies, but the more general investigation goes beyond the subway and includes both railroad and bus terminals about which a considerable body of literature is developing. Some of this work is closely related to the general problem of pedestrian movement in the built environment, both within buildings and in pedestrian malls and sidewalks. Another element within the city of particular interest to students of the built environment are urban parks, playgrounds, and other types of open spaces.

This list could be expanded considerably, but already serves to demonstrate not only that a large number of settings have been studied, but more generally it illustrates a particular characteristic of studies of the built environment, that they tend to be setting rather than problem oriented. There are, of course, many problems that stretch across different settings. We have already seen mention of such issues as crowding, stress, territoriality, and environmental quality, to mention but a few. However, these tend to be discussed in other contexts, and studies specifically aimed at the built environment continue to be organized around a particular setting or a particular building type. This setting orientation of studies of the built environment is related to a second characteristic of most such studies. The research on the built environment in almost all cases grows out of the immediate design problems involved in the particular building or setting. The studies do not deal with the totality of all questions that might be raised in such a setting, but more typically are aimed at those questions that are directly related to issues of interest designer. Thus the investigator of the built environment most frequently asks questions related to how the particular setting does or might facilitate particular kinds of behavior which are hopefully or necessarily to be carried out in that setting. Does the setting support certain kinds of behavior? Does it interfere with or obstruct desired activities? Does it encourage unwanted behaviors? How can the design be changed in order to influence what goes on in the setting in a desired direction? In general, then, the particular problems studied in the built setting tend to be those that are directly and uniquely relevant to that setting. This emphasis on the setting and setting-related problems provided one of the strongest points for such research, that it tends to have immediate and useful practical applications. Designers tend to be impatient with theoretical generalizations and want to know what they can do now for the particular setting they are designing today. The challenge to the students of these settings is to provide this immediately usable information while at the same time embedding it in a context that allows for generalizations that go beyond the immediate setting and that hopefully will help shed light on the more general problems of human activities in relation to the environment.

33. *The House as Symbol of the Self*
CLARE COOPER

My work of the last few years has comprised sociological surveys of people's responses to the designs of their houses and communication of the resultant guidelines to architects. But I have experienced a nagging doubt that I was merely scratching the surface of the true meaning of "the house." There seemed to be something far deeper and more subliminal that I was not admitting, or that my surveys and investigations were not revealing. The exciting personal discovery of the work of the psychologist Carl Jung has opened a door into another level of my own consciousness which has prompted me to consider the house from a wholly different viewpoint. This paper is a tentative initial exploration into the subject.

The reader must expect no startling,

A slightly abbreviated version of a paper with the same title that appeared in Jon Lang et al. (Eds.), *Designing for Human Behavior.* Stroudsberg, Pa.: Dowden, Hutchinson & Ross, 1974.

all-embracing conclusion; there is none. This is a speculative think piece and is deliberately left open-ended in the hope that it will motivate the reader, and the author, to think further and more deeply in this area.

Jung's Concepts of the Collective Unconscious, the Archetype, and the Symbol

Three of the most significant contributions of Carl Jung to the understanding of the human psyche are the concepts of the *collective* unconscious, the archetype, and the symbol. . . .

Initially embracing Freud's theories, Jung became increasingly dissatisfied as his studies of persistent motifs in his patients' dreams and fantasies, and in primitive mythology and folk tales, revealed what seemed to be *universal* patterns which could not be accounted for solely by the theory of an *individual* unconscious. He began to postulate the theory of an individual unconscious plus a universal or collective unconscious linking man to his primitive past, and in which are deposited certain basic and timeless nodes of psychic energy, which he termed *archetypes*.

. . . The archetype can only provide a potential or possibility of representation in the conscious mind, for as soon as we encounter it through dreams, fantasies, or rational thought, the archetype becomes clothed in images of the concrete world and is no longer an archetype: it is an *archetypal image or symbol*. . . . If we can think of the archetype as a node of psychic energy within the unconscious, then the symbol is the medium by which it becomes manifest in the here and now of space and time. Thus a symbol, although it has objective visible reality, always has behind it a hidden, profound, and only partly intelligible meaning which represents its roots in the archetype.

Although impossible for most of us to define or describe, we are all aware of the existence of something we call "self": the inner heart of our being, our soul, our uniqueness—however we want to describe it. It is in the nature of man that he constantly seeks a rational explanation of the inexplicable, and so he struggles with the questions: What is self? Why here? Why now? In trying to comprehend this most basic of archetypes—self—to give it concrete substance, man grasps at physical forms or symbols which are close and meaningful to him, and which are visible and definable. The first and most consciously selected form to represent self is the body, for it appears to be both the outward manifestation, and the encloser, of self. On a less conscious level, I believe, man also frequently selects the house, that basic protector of his internal environment (beyond skin and clothing) to represent or symbolize what is tantalizingly unrepresentable.

The French philosopher Gaston Bachelard has suggested that just as the house and the nonhouse are the basic divi-

sions of geographic space, so the self and the nonself represent the basic divisions of psychic space (Bachelard, 1969). The house both encloses space (the house interior) and excludes space (everything outside it). Thus it has two very important and different components; its interior and its façade. The house therefore nicely reflects how man sees himself, with both an intimate interior, or self as viewed from within and revealed only to those intimates who are invited inside, and a public exterior (the *persona* or *mask,* in Jungian terms) or the self that we choose to display to others.[1]

Most of us have had the experience of moving from one house to another, and of finding the new abode initially strange, unwelcoming, perhaps even hostile. But with time, we get used to the new house and its quirks, and it seems almost as though it gets used to us; we can relax when we return to it, put our feet up, become ourselves. But why in this particular box should we be ourselves more than in any other? It seems as though the personal space bubble which we carry with us and which is an almost tangible extension of our self expands to embrace the house we have designated as ours. As we become accustomed to, and lay claim to, this little niche in the world, we project something of ourselves onto its physical fabric. The furniture we install, the way we arrange it, the pictures we hang, the plants we buy and tend, all are expressions of our image of ourselves, all are messages about ourselves that we

[1] For the purposes of this paper, we will accept the Jungian view of "self," which he saw as both the core of the unconscious *and* the totality of the conscious and the unconscious. To illustrate with a diagram:

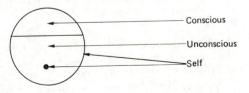

want to convey back to ourselves, and to the few intimates that we invite into this, our house. Thus, the house might be viewed as both an avowal of the self—that is, the psychic messages are moving from self to the objective symbol of self—and as a revelation of the nature of self; that is, the messages are moving from objective symbol back to the self. It is almost as if the house–self continuum could be thought of as both the negative and positive of a film, simultaneously.

The House as Symbol-of-Self: Examples from Contemporary Architecture

Man was a symbol-making animal long before he was a toolmaker: he reached high degrees of specialization in song, dance, ritual, religion, and myth before he did in the material aspects of culture. Describing the rich symbolism of the man-made environment in part of Africa, Amos Rapoport notes:

> Among the Dogon and Bambara of Mali every object and social event has a symbolic as well as a utilitarian function. Houses, household objects, and chairs have all this symbolic quality, and the Dogon civilization, otherwise relatively poor, has several thousand symbolic elements. The farm plots and the whole landscape of the Dogon reflect this cosmic order. The villages are built in pairs to represent heaven and earth, and fields are cleared in spirals because the world has been created spirally. The villages are laid out in the way the parts of the body lie with respect to each other, while the house of the Dogon, or paramount chief, is a model of the universe at a smaller scale (1969, p. 50).

Rapoport concludes significantly that "man's achievements have been due more to his need to utilize his internal resources than to his needs for control of the physical environment or more food."

It would seem that there is an inverse relationship between technological advances and the cultivation of symbol and ritual. For so-called civilized man, the conscious recognition of the symbolism of what we do, how we live, and the houses we live in, has been all but lost. But if we start to delve beneath the surface, the symbolism is still there.

In a recent study of how contemporary California suburbanites chose their homes, Berkeley sociologist Carl Werthman (1968) concluded that many people bought houses to bolster their image of self—both as an individual and as a person in a certain status position in society. In one large suburban development near San Francisco, for example, he noted that extroverted self-made businessmen tended to choose somewhat ostentatious, mock-colonial display homes, while people in the helping professions, whose goals revolved around personal satisfaction rather than financial success, tended to opt for the quieter, inward-looking architect-designed styles conforming to current standards of "good design."

In the contemporary English-speaking world, a premium is put on originality, on having a house that is unique and somewhat different from the others on the street, for the inhabitants who identify with these houses are themselves struggling to maintain some sense of personal uniqueness in an increasingly conformist world. On the other hand, one's house must not be too way-out, for that would label the inhabitant as a nonconformist, and that, for many Americans, is a label to be avoided.

The house as symbol-of-self is deeply engrained in the American ethos (albeit unconsciously for many), and this may partly explain the inability of society to come to grips with the housing problem—a problem which is quite within its technological and financial capabilities to solve and which it persistently delegates to a low level in the hierarchy of budgetary values. America is the home of the self-made man, and if the house is seen (even unconsciously) as the symbol of self, then it is small wonder that there is a resistance to subsidized housing or to the State's providing houses *for* people. The frontier image of the man clearing the land and building a cabin for himself and his family is not far behind us. To a culture inbred with this image, the house—self identity is particularly strong. In some barely conscious way, society has decided to penalize those who, through no fault of their own cannot build, buy, or rent their own housing. They are not self-made men.

Numbers of studies in England, Australia, and the United States have indicated that when asked to describe their ideal house, people of all incomes and backgrounds will tend to describe a free-standing, square, detached, single-family house and yard. For example, in a recent survey of 748 men and women in thirty-two metropolitan areas in the U.S. 85 percent said they preferred living in a single-family house rather than in an apartment (Michelson, 1968). It is difficult to say whether the attachment to this form is the form itself, or the fact that it subsumes territorial rights over a small portion of the earth, or the fact that apartments can rarely be owned. But we do know that almost universally the image of the high-rise building for family living is rejected. An apartment is rarely seen as home, for a house can only be seen as a free-standing house-on-the-ground.

One could argue that people have been conditioned to want this through advertising, model homes salesmanship, and the image of the good life portrayed on television. To a certain extent this must be true, but these media are in turn only reflecting what seems to be a universal need for a house form in which the self and family unit can be seen as separate, unique, private, and protected.

The high-rise apartment building is rejected by most Americans as a family home because, I would suggest, it gives one no territory on the ground, violates the archaic image of what a house is, and is perceived unconsciously as a threat to one's self-image as a separate and unique personality. The house form in which people are being asked to live is not a symbol-of-self, but the symbol of a stereotyped, anonymous filing-cabinet collection of selves, which people fear they are becoming. Even though we may make apartments larger, with many of the appurtenances of a house, as well as opportunities for modification and ownership, it may still be a long time before the majority of lower- and middle-income American families will accept this as a valid image of a permanent home.[2] It is too great a threat to their self-image. It is possible that the vandalism inflicted on high-rise housing projects is, in part, an angry reaction of the inhabitants to this blatant violation of self-image.

Even the edge-of-town mobile home park occupied by the young retireds and the transient lower middle class is somehow looked down upon by the average American home owner as violating the true image of home and neighborhood. A person who lives in a house that moves must somehow be as unstable as the structure he inhabits. Very much the same view is held by house owners in Marin County, California, about the houseboat dwellers in Sausalito. They are "different," "Bohemian," "nonconformists," and their extraordinary choice of dwelling reflects these values.

The contrasting views which people

[2] The urban rich accept apartments because they generally have a house somewhere else; the elderly seem to adapt well to apartments because they offer privacy with the possibility of many nearby neighbors, minimum upkeep problems, security, communal facilities, etc.; and for mobile young singles or childless couples the limited spatial and temporal commitment of an apartment is generally the ideal living environment.

of different socioeconomic classes in the U.S. have of their houses reflects again the house as a symbol-of-self in a self–world relationship. The greater are people's feelings of living in a dangerous and hostile world with constant threats to the self, the greater is the likelihood that they will regard their house as a shell, a fortress into which to retreat. The sociologist Lee Rainwater (1970) has shown that this image of the self, and of the house, is true for low-income blacks (particularly women) in the ghettoes and housing projects of this country. With increasing economic and psychic stability (and in some cases, these are linked), a person may no longer regard his house as a fortress-to-be-defended, but as an attractive, individual expression of self-and-family with picture windows so that neighbors can admire the inside. Thus, for many in the middle-income bracket, the house is an expression of self, rather than a defender of self. The self-and-environment are seen in a state of mutual regard instead of in a state of combat.

The fact that the decoration of the house interior often symbolizes the inhabitants' feelings about self is one that has long been recognized. It has even been suggested that the rise in popularity of the profession of interior decorating is in some way related to people's inability to make these decisions for themselves since they're not sure what their self really is. The phenomenon of people, particularly women, rearranging the furniture in their house at times of psychic turmoil or changes-in-self, is a further suggestion that the house is very intimately entwined with the psyche.

The pregnant woman—in a very special psychological and physiological state of change—is especially likely to identify with the house, both in dreams and in reality:

Sudden compulsive urges to do thorough house cleaning seem common among pregnant women. They are, on the one level, practical attempts to prepare for the coming baby; but when the house is already amply clean and delivery is impending, there may be a second, more significant level. The woman may be acting out her unconscious identification of the house with her own body. She may feel that if she cleans out the house and puts everything in order, she is in some way doing something about that other living space, the "house" of her unborn child. For her, it is an object rather than a word, which has taken on secret meanings (Colman and Colman, 1971).

An interesting contemporary development is the interior decoration of the urban commune. In a number of examples in the Berkeley–Oakland area visited by the author, it was very noticeable that the bedrooms, the only private spaces of residents, were decorated in an attractive and highly personal way symbolic of the self whose space it was. The living rooms, the communal territory of six or eight or more different personalities, however, were only sparsely decorated, since; presumably, the problem of getting agreement on taste from a number of disparate and highly individual selves was too great to overcome. Interestingly, the more normal family house may display an opposite arrangement, with bedrooms functionally but uninterestingly decorated, and the living room, where guests and relatives are entertained, containing the best furniture, family mementos, art purchases, photos, and so on, and representing the collective family self. The only exception to this pattern may be the teenager's room—highly personalized as a reflection of his struggle to become an individual with a personality separate from his parents.

In a recently published study of living rooms, Edward Laumann and James House (1972) have found that the presence or absence of certain objects are good if not perfect clues to status and attitudes. It is the living room rather than any other room in the house which provides these clues because

The living room is the area where "performances" for guests are most often given, and hence the "setting" of it must be appropriate to the performance. Thus we expect that more than any other part of the home, the living room reflects the individual's conscious and unconscious attempts to express a social identity.

For example, they looked at a random sample of 41 homes from among 186 respondents (all of which were one-and-two-family home dwellers in Detroit) who had annual incomes over $15,000 and presumably had enough money to decorate any way they wanted. They found that those with a traditional decor—French or Early American furniture, wall mirrors, small potted plants and/or artificial flowers, paintings of people or still lifes, clocks—tended to be the white Anglo-Saxon establishment, occupying occupations and status positions similar to their fathers. Those with a more modern decor, characterized by modern furniture, wood walls, abstract paintings, solid carpets, and abstract designed curtains, tended to be upwardly mobile, non Anglo-Saxon Catholics whose families had migrated to the United States from southern and eastern Europe after 1900.

The findings of this study of decorative styles of living rooms seem to tie in well with the result of Werthman's study of choices of house styles, for in both cases there appears to be a strong correlation between the style selected and the self-image of the consumer. . . .

These are just a few examples of how the house-as-self linkage becomes manifest in individual and societal behavior and attitudes; no doubt the reader can add many more instances from his personal experience. The thesis is not a new one: but it seems that the Jungian notions of the collective unconscious, the archetype and the symbol, may offer a useful conceptual structure to tie these examples together. Since the house–self symbolism seems to arise again and again, in many disparate settings, and since there appears to be little conscious sharing of this phenomenon, it seems reasonable to suggest that it is through the medium of the collective unconscious that people are in touch with an archaic and basically similar archetype (the self) and with a symbol for that archetype that has changed little through space and time (the house). Perhaps we can comprehend the essence of the house–self analogy more easily by looking at evidence from literature, poetry, and dreams—forms of expression that may get closer to true unconscious meanings than sociological surveys or similar empirical investigations.

The House-as-self as Manifested in Literature, Poetry, and Dreams

In her introspective autobiography, written in the form of a diary. Anaïs Nin saw quite clearly both the security and sustenance that can ensue from living in a house that reflects one's own self-image, and the phenomenon of projecting onto the home one's inner fears and anxieties:

When I look at the large green iron gate from my window it takes on the air of a prison gate. An unjust feeling, since I know I can leave the place whenever I want to, and since I know that human beings place upon an object, or a person, this responsibility of being the obstacle when the obstacle lies always within one's self.

In spite of this knowledge, I often stand at the window staring at the large closed iron gate, as if hoping to obtain from this contemplation a reflection of my inner obstacles to a full, open life. . . . But the little gate, with its overhanging ivy like disordered hair over a running child's forehead, has a sleepy and sly air, an air of being always half open.

I chose the house for many reasons. Because it seemed to have sprouted out of the earth like a tree, so deeply grooved it was within the old garden. It had no cellar and the rooms rested right on the ground. Below the rug, I felt, was the earth. I could take root here, feel at one with house and garden, take nourishment from them like the plants (1966, p. 4).

The notion of house as symbol of mother or the womb is one fairly common in literature, and indeed has been the inspiration of a number of organic architects who have tried to re-create this safe, enclosed, encircling feeling in their designs. In the following fictional account, we see how the house takes on a symbolic maternal function in response to the fear of the man within and the storm outside:

The house was fighting gallantly. At first it gave voice to its complaints; the most awful gusts were attacking it from every side at once, with evident hatred and such howls of rage that, at times, I trembled with fear. But it stood firm. . . . The already human being in whom I had sought shelter for my body yielded nothing to the storm. The house clung to me, like a shewolf, and at times I could smell her odor penetrating maternally to my very heart. That night she was really my mother. She was all I had to keep and sustain me. We were alone (Bosco, 1964).

Here, in the unusual circumstances of a storm, one can see how this human, protective symbol of the house might well be conceived. But what of ordinary circumstances? How does the house-as-self symbol first begin to take root? Undoubtedly, one must look for the roots in infancy. At first, the mother is its whole environment. Gradually, as the range of senses expands, the baby begins to perceive the people and physical environment around it. The house becomes its world, its very cosmos. From

being a shadowy shell glimpsed out of half-closed eyes, the house becomes familiar, recognizable, a place of security and love.

The child's world then becomes divided into the house, that microspace within the greater world that he knows through personal discovery, and everything that lies beyond it, which is unknown and perhaps frightening. In a sense, the child's experience reflects the assessment of known space as made by preliterate societies. As Mircea Eliade has written:

One of the outstanding characteristics of traditional societies is the opposition that they assume between their inhabited territory and the unknown and indeterminate space that surrounds it. The former is world (more precisely, our world), the cosmos; everything outside it is no longer a cosmos but a sort of "other world," foreign, chaotic space, peopled by ghosts, demons, foreigners. . . . (1959, p. 29).

As the child matures, he ventures into the house's outer space, the yard, the garden, then gradually into the neighborhood, the city, the region, the world. As space becomes known and experienced, it becomes a part of his world. But all the time, the house is home, the place of first conscious thoughts, of security and roots. It is no longer an inert box; it has been experienced, has become a symbol for self, family, mother, security. As Bachelard has written, "geometry is transcended."

As we become more ourselves—more self-actualized, in Maslow's terms—it seems that the house-as-symbol becomes even less tied to its geometry. A writer quoted by Bachelard (Spyridaki, 1964) describes his house thus:

My house is diaphanous but it is not of glass. It is more of the nature of vapor. Its walls contract and expand as I desire. At times, I draw them close about me like protective armor. . . . But at others,

I let the walls of my house blossom out in their own space, which is infinitely extensible.

The symbol has become flexible, expandable according to psychic needs. For most people, the house is not actually changeable, except by such measures as opening and closing drapes and rearranging furniture to suit our moods. For one French poet (Bachelard, 1964 p. 65) these alternate needs of expansion and contraction, extroversion and introspection, openness and withdrawal were made physical realities in the design of his dream home—a Breton fisherman's cottage around which he constructed a magnificent manor house.

In the body of the winged manor, which dominates both town and sea, man and the universe, he retained a cottage chrysalis in order to be able to hide alone in complete repose. . . . The two extreme realities of cottage and manor . . . take into account our need for retreat and expansion, for simplicity and magnificence.

Perhaps the suburban home buyers' yen for both an opulent facade with picture-window view and colonial porch and for a private secluded den is a modern manifestation of this need.

If we start to consider the messages from the unconscious made manifest through dreams, we have even more striking evidence of the house-as-self symbol. Carl Jung (1969, pp. 182–183) in his autobiography describes quite vividly a dream of himself as house, and his explorations within it.

His own interpretation of the dream was as follows:

It was plain to me that the house represented a kind of image of the psyche—that is to say, of my then state of consciousness, with hitherto unconscious additions. Consciousness was represented by the salon. It had an inhabited atmosphere, in spite of its antiquated style.

The ground floor for the first level of the unconscious. The deeper I went, the more alien and the darker the scene became. In the cave, I discovered remains of a primitive culture, that is the world of the primitive man within myself —a world which can scarcely be reached or illuminated by consciousness. The primitive psyche of man borders on the life of the animal soul, just as the caves of prehistoric times were usually inhabited by animals before man laid claim to them (p. 184).

Jung describes here the house with many levels seen as the symbol-of-self with its many levels of consciousness; the descent downward into lesser known realms of the unconscious is represented by the ground floor, cellar, and vault beneath it. A final descent leads to a cave cut into bedrock, a part of the house rooted in the very earth itself. This seems very clearly to be a symbol of the collective unconscious, part of the self-house and yet, too, part of the universal bedrock of humanity.

Jung, unlike Freud, also saw the dream as a possible prognosticator of the future; the unconscious not only holds individual and collective memories but also the seeds of future action. At one period of his life Jung was searching for some historical basis or precedent for the ideas he was developing about the unconscious. He didn't know where to start the search. At this point he started having a series of dreams which all dealt with the same theme:

Beside my house stood another, that is to say, another wing or annex, which was strange to me. Each time I would wonder in my dream why I did not know this house, although it had apparently always been there. Finally came a dream in which I reached the other wing. I discovered there a wonderful library, dating largely from the sixteenth and seventeenth centuries. Large, fat folio volumes bound in pigskin stood along the walls.

Among them were a large number of books embellished with copper engravings of a strange character, and illustrations containing curious symbols such as I had never seen before. At that time I did not know to what they referred; only much later did I recognize them as alchemical symbols. In the dream I was conscious only of the fascination exerted by them and by the entire library. It was a collection of incunabula and sixteenth-century prints.

The unknown wing of the house was a part of my personality, an aspect of myself; it represented something that belonged to me but of which I was not yet conscious. It, and especially the library, referred to alchemy of which I was ignorant, but which I was soon to study. Some fifteen years later I had assembled a library very like the one in the dream.

Thus here in another dream Jung sees an unexplored wing of the house as an unkown part of himself and a symbol of an area of study with which he would become very absorbed in the future, and which permitted him to expand his concepts of the transformation of the self.

From many house dreams I have collected, two will suffice here to further emphasize the point. In the first one, the dreamer had, in reality, just lost a close friend in an auto accident. She reports the dream thus:

I was being led through a ruined house by a tall, calm man, dressed all in white. The house was alone in a field, its walls of rubble, the layout and doorways no longer visible. The man guide led me slowly through the house pointing out how it used to be, where rooms were connected, where doorways lead to the outside world.

My interpretation of this dream is that, the tall man is a part of me, maybe my masculine, strong, calm side, and he is pointing out that despite the fact that my self-life-house appear to be in ruins right now, due to my shock and grief at A's death, there is part of me that calmly and clearly will know how to find my way way through the chaos. It was a very comforting dream at a time of great stress.

In another dream, the dreamer was in reality under much pressure from students and colleagues in his academic job. He described his dream thus:

There was a house, a large English stately home, open to the public to look at and traipse through. But on this day, it was temporarily closed, and visitors were disappointedly reading the notices and turning away. I was in the basement of the house, sorting through some oil paintings, to see if there was anything there of value.

With the aid of a therapist, skilled in the interpretation of dreams, he saw the following message within the dream:

I need to 'close up shop,' take a vacation from all the pressures and human input I'm experiencing right now, and have time to sort through some ideas in my unconscious (the basement of the house) to see if any are of value in guiding my future direction.

Returning to Jung's autobiography, he describes how, later in his life, he made manifest in stone the symbol which had at times stood for self in his dreams. He describes how he yearned to put his knowledge of the contents of the unconscious into solid form, rather than just describe them in words. In the building of his house—the tower at Bollinger on Lake Zurich—he was to make "a confession of faith in stone"

At first I did not plan a proper house, but merely a kind of primitive one-story dwelling. It was to be a round structure with a hearth in the center and bunks along the walls. I more or less had in mind an African hut where the fire, ringed with stone, burns in the middle, and the whole life of the family revolves around this centre. Primitive huts concretise an idea of wholeness, a familial wholeness in which all sorts of domestic animals likewise participate. But I altered the plans even during the first stages of building, for I felt it was too primitive. I realized it would have to be a regular two-story house, not a mere hut crouched on the ground. So in 1923 the first round house was built, and when it was over I saw that it had become a suitable dwelling tower.

> The feeling of repose and renewal that I had in this tower was intense from the start. It represented for me the maternal hearth (p. 250).

Feeling that something more needed to be said, four years later Jung added another building with a tower-like annex. Again, after an interval of four years, he felt the need to add more and built onto the tower a retiring room for meditation and seclusion where no one else could enter; it became his retreat for spiritual concentration. After another interval of four years he felt the need for another area, open to nature and the sky, and so added a courtyard and an adjoining loggia. The resultant quanternity pleased him, no doubt because his own studies in mythology and symbolism had provided much evidence of the completeness and wholeness represented by the figure four. Finally, after his wife's death, he felt an inner obligation to "become what I myself am," and recognized that the small central section of the house

> which crouched so low and hidden was myself! I could no longer hide myself behind the "maternal" and "spiritual" towers. So in the same year, I added an upper storey to this section, which represents myself or my ego-personality. Ear-

lier, I would not have been able to do this; I would have regarded it as presumptuous self-emphasis. Now it signified an extension of consciousness achieved in old age. With that the building was complete (p. 252).

Jung had thus built his house over time as a representation in stone of his own evolving and maturing psyche; it was the place, he said, where "I am in the midst of my true life, I am most deeply myself." He describes how

> From the beginning I felt the Tower as in some way a place of maturation—a maternal womb or a maternal figure in which I could become what I was, what I am and will be. It gave me a feeling as if I were being reborn in stone. It is thus a concretisation of the individuation process. . . . During the building work of course, I never considered these matters. . . . Only afterwards did I see how all the parts fitted together and that a meaningful form had resulted: a symbol of psychic wholeness (p. 253).

In examining at some length Jung's own reflections on the house as dream-symbol, and the building of his own house as a manifestation of the self, we are not just examining one man's inner life; hopefully, there is something here of the inner symbolism of all men. . . .

We must return again to Jung's concept of the collective unconscious. It should be possible if his notion of an unconscious stretching through space and time beyond the individual is correct to find comparable indications of the house-self linkage in places and times far removed from contemporary Western civilization. . . .

Making Space Sacred

In the opening chapter of his book *The Sacred and the Profane: The Nature of*

Religion entitled "Sacred Space and Making the World Sacred," the noted historian of religion, Mircea Eliade (1959) describes how for many preliterate societies, space was not homogenous; inhabited parts were seen as sacred while all other space around was a formless, foreign expanse. In settling a new territory, man was faced with both a horizontal expanse of unknown land, and a complete lack of vertical connections to other cosmic levels, such as the heavens and the underworld. In defining and consecrating a spot as sacred, be it shrine, a temple, a ceremonial house, man gave himself a fixed point, a point of reference from which to structure the world about him. In doing so, he consciously emulated the gods who, many believed, created the world by starting at a fixed point—for example, an egg, or the navel of a slain monster—then moving out to the surrounding territory. . . . Through finding a sacred space, generally with the aid of signs or the revelations of animals, man began to transform the shapeless, homogeneous chaos of space into his world.

Once located, the sacred space had to be consecrated, and this very often took the form of a construction which had at its center a pillar, pole, or tree. This was seen as a symbol for the cosmic axis and the means by which communication was made possible from one cosmic level to another. Whether seen as a ladder, as in Jacob's dream, or as a sacred pillar, as worshipped by the Celts and Germans before their conversion to Christianity, the vertical upright was an almost universal symbol for passage to the worlds of the gods above and below the earth.

Having created a sacred place in the homogeneity of space, man erected a symbol for the cosmic axis and thus centered this place at the Center of the World. But, Eliade maintains, there could be many Centers of the World, and indeed the Achilpa people of the Arunta tribe of Australian aborigines always carried the sacred pole with them so as not to be far from the Center or its link with other worlds. The religious man of fixed settlements, although he knew that his country and village and temple all constituted the navel of the universe

also wanted his own house to be at the Center and to be an "imago mundi". . . . (He) could only live in a space opening upward, where the break in plane was symbolically assured and hence communication with the "other world," the transcendental world, was ritually possible. Of course the sanctuary—the Center par excellence—was there, close to him . . . but he felt the need to live at the Center always. . . . (p. 43).

Thus it was that the house, like the temple and the city, became a symbol of the universe with man, like God, as its center and in charge of its creation. The house, like the temple or shrine, was sanctified by ritual.

Just as the entrance to the temple was, and still is, regarded as the dividing line between the sacred and the profane worlds and is suitably embellished to ward off evil spirits which might attempt to enter the inner sanctum, so the threshold of the house is regarded as one of the most important dividing lines between inner private space and the other public world. . . .

The location of the threshold varies in different cultures (see Rapoport, 1969, p. 80), and it may well be that this location vis-à-vis the outside world is symbolic of how the people as individuals relate to the rest of society. In the American house, the front yard is generally unfenced and part of the streetscape, and may be viewed as semipublic territory; the real threshold to the house is the front door itself. This may reflect an American interpersonal trait of openness to strangers and of (initial at least) friendliness to people they hardly know. In England, however, the fenced front garden with a gate puts the initial threshold at some distance from the house itself, and is probably symbolic of the greater English reserve at inviting strangers into their houses and at opening up to people before they know them very well. The compound of a Moslem house puts the threshold even more forcibly and deliberately at some distance from the house, and reflects the extreme privacy required by individuals, particularly women, from strangers and neighbors.

. . . Lord Raglan (1964) in his study of the origins of the house suggests that . . . since one of the most widespread primitive beliefs about the creation of the world was that it originated from an egg, so many of the first cosmic manifestations in temples and houses were round or spherical in shape. . . . An original belief in the world as circular began to be replaced by a belief in the world as square, and starting in Mesopotamia and Egypt, and spreading later to China, India, Rome, North America, and Africa, the temple and the house as cosmic manifestations, began to be built on a square or rectangular plan, instead of a circular one.

In most parts of the world, the rectangular house predominates today, but the circular shape has often been retained in the form of the dome for religious or important secular buildings (e.g. city hall, the state capitol, the opera house), recalling much earlier times when the circle had specific cosmic significance.

To summarize Lord Raglan's thesis he suggests that house forms were derived from the forms of temples (the houses of the gods), and symbolize man's early beliefs concerning the form and shape of the universe. Drawing conclusions from his studies of myth and folklore, rather than buildings, Elaide comes to similar conclusions

By assuming the responsibility of creating the world that he has chosen to inhabit, he not only cosmicizes chaos but also sanctifies his little cosmos by making it like the world of the gods. . . . That is why settling somewhere—the building a village or merely a house—represents a serious decision, for the very existence of man is involved; he must, in short, create his own world and assume the responsibility of maintaining and renewing it. Habitations are not lightly changed, for it is not easy to abandon one's world. The house is not an object, a "machine to live in"; it is a universe that man constructs for himself by imitating the paradigmatic creation of the gods, the cosmogony (Eliade, 1959, pp. 56–57).

The Self-House/Self-Universe Analogy

It seems that consciously or unconsciously, then, many men in many parts of the world have built their cities, temples, and houses as images of the universe. My contention is that somewhere, through the collective unconscious, man is still in touch with this symbolism. Our house is seen, however unconsciously, as the center of *our* universe and symbolic of *the* universe. But how does this connect with my earlier arguments regarding the house-as-symbol-of-self? Primitive man sees his dwelling as symbolic of the universe, with himself, like God, at its center. Modern man apparently sees his dwelling as symbolic of the self, but has lost touch with this archaic connection between house–self–universe.

The phenomenon of dreaming or imagining the self as a house—that package outside our own skin which encloses us and in which we feel most secure—is perhaps the first glimmering of the unconscious that the "I" and the "non-I" are indeed one and the same. As Alan Watts has so eloquently written in the *The Book; On the Taboo Against Knowing Who You Are* (1966, p. 43), the notion that each individual ego is separate (in space) and finite (in time) and is something different from the universe around him is one of the grand hoaxes of

Western thought. Although virtually impossible for most of us nonmystics to grasp in more than a superficial way, this knowledge of our indivisibility from the environment is buried deep within the collective unconscious and becomes manifest symbolically (often without our recognizing it) in fantasies, flashes of intuition, dreams, poems, paintings, and literature.

The so-called mentally ill may in fact be more closely in touch with these lost connections between self and environment than any of us realize. After a long career working with schizophrenics, Harold Searles (1960) noted:

It seems to me that, in our culture, a conscious ignoring of the psychological importance of the nonhuman environment exists simultaneously with a (largely unconscious) overdependence upon that environment. I believe that the actual importance of that environment to the individual is so great that he dare not regonize it. Unconsciously it is felt, I believe, to be not only an intensely important conglomeration of things outside the self, but also a large and integral part of the self. . . . (p. 395)

The concreteness of the child's thinking suggests for him, as for the member of the so-called primitive culture and for the schizophrenic adult, the wealth of nonhuman objects about him are constituents of his psychological being in a more intimate sense than they are for the adult in our culture, the adult whose ego is, as Hartman and Werner emphasize, relatively clearly differentiated from the surrounding world, and whose development of the capacity for abstract thinking helps free him . . . from his original oneness with the nonhuman world (p. 42).

Perhaps it is the so-called normal adult who, having been socialized to regard self and environment as separate and totally different, is most out of touch with the essential reality of oneness with the environment which small children, schizophrenics, preliterate people, and adherents of certain Eastern religions understand completely. There are certain religions, for example Buddhism, that regard the apparent separation of the individual and the universe as a delusion. My contention is that in thinking, dreaming, or fantasying about self and house as somehow being inextricably intertwined, as being at some level one and the same thing, man may be taking the first step on the path towards what Zen adherents would term enlightenment. He is ridding himself of the delusion of the separation of man from his environment.

Conclusion

If there is some validity to the notion of house-as-self it goes part of the way to explain why for most people their house is so sacred and why they so strongly resist a change in the basic form which they and their fathers and their fathers' fathers have lived in since the dawn of time. Jung recognized that the more archaic and universal the archetype made manifest in the symbol, the more universal and unchanging the symbol itself. Since self must be an archetype as universal and almost as archaic as man himself, this may explain the universality of its symbolic form, the house, and the extreme resistance of most people to any change in its basic form.

For most people the self is a fragile and vulnerable entity; we wish therefore to envelop ourselves in a symbol-for-self which is familiar, solid, inviolate, unchanging. Small wonder, then, that in Anglo-Saxon law it is permissible, if necessary, to kill anyone who breaks and enters your house. A violation of the self (house) is perhaps one of man's most deep-seated and universal fears. Similarly, the thought of living in a round house or a houseboat or a mobile home is, to most people, as threatening as is the suggestion that they might change their basic self-concept. A conventional house and a rigidly static concept of self are mutually supporting. Perhaps with the coming of age of Reich's Consciousness III generation, and the social movements (civil rights, women's liberation, human potential movement, etc.) which are causing many to question the inviolate nature of old self-concepts, we can expect an increased openness to new housing forms and living arrangements, the beginning of which are already apparent in the proliferation of communes and drop-out communities.

This long statement on house-as-symbol-of-the-self brings me back to my original problem: how to advise architects on the design of houses for clients who are often poor, whom they will never know, let alone delve into their psychic lives or concepts of self. I have no pat answer, but if there is some validity to the concept of house-as-self, we must learn ways—through group encounters, resident-meetings, participant observation, interviews—of empathizing with the users' concepts of self, and we must devise means of complementing and enhancing that image through dwelling design. If in new housing forms we violate this image, we may have produced an objective reality which pleases the politicians and designers, but at the same time produced a symbolic reality which leaves the residents bewildered and resentful.

Certainly, one area that every architect involved with house design can and should investigate is his or her own biases based on images of self. Bachelard, in his very thought provoking study *The Poetics of Space*, suggests somewhat fancifully that along with psychoanlysis, every patient should be assisted in making a topoanalysis, or an analysis of the spaces and places which have been settings for his past emotional development. I would go further and say this exercise should be required of every designer. He or she should begin to understand how present self-images are being unconsciously concretized in design, and how scenes of earlier development (particularly childhood between the ages of about 5 and 12) are often unconsciously reproduced in designs in an effort, presumably, to recall that earlier often happier phase of life.

In the past few years, as a teacher in the College of Environmental Design at Berkeley, I have had students draw, in as much detail as they can remember, their childhood environments. After an interval of a few weeks, they have then drawn what for each of them would be an ideal environment. The similarities are often striking, as also are the similarities they begin to observe between these two drawings, and what they produce in the design studio. The purpose of the exercise is not to say that there is anything wrong with such influences from the past, but just to point out that they are there, and it may well be to his advantage as a designer to recognize the biases they may introduce into his work.

In the field of man's relationship with his environment, the type of approach which might be termed intuitive speculation seems to have been lost in a world devoted to the supposedly more scientific approach of objective analysis. As Alan Watts has speculated, this emphasis on the so-called objective may indeed be a sickness of Western man, for it enables him to retain his belief in the separateness of the ego from all that surrounds it. Although certain objective facts have been presented in this paper, it is hoped by the author that its overall message is clear: allow yourself to be open to the consideration of relationships other than those that can be proved or disproved by scientific method, for it may well be in these that a deeper truth lies. . . .

34. Architecture, Interaction, and Social Control: The Case of a Large-Scale Public Housing Project
W. L. YANCEY

In this paper we will argue that the architectural design of the Pruitt-Igoe Housing Project, located in St. Louis, Missouri, has had an atomizing effect on the informal social networks frequently found in lower- and working-class neighborhoods. Without the provision of semi-public space and facilities around which informal networks might develop, families living in Pruitt-Igoe have retreated into the internal structures of their apartments and do not have the social support, protection, and informal social control found in other lower- and working-class neighborhoods.

It is clear that social and economic factors, particularly the level and stability of incomes and occupations, are major determinants of the life styles of the poor. Yet there is also evidence which indicates that the physical environment in which families live, in particular the design and condition of dwelling units, has an effect on the manner in which they live (Schorr, 1963; Wilner et al., 1962).

Among the effects of architectural design which have been identified by previous research is that of the physical proximity of

Reprinted from *Environment and Behavior*, Vol. 3, No. 1 (March 1971), pp. 3–18, by permission of the Publisher, Sage Publications, Inc., and the author.

Author's Note: This paper is based in part on research supported by grants from the National Institute of Mental Health, Grant MH-09189, "Social and Community Problems in Public Housing Areas," and from the Urban and Regional Development Center, Vanderbilt University. Many of the ideas presented stem from discussions I have had with the directors of the Pruitt-Igoe research—Alvin Gouldner and Lee Rainwater. This paper was presented at a Symposium on Environmental Perception at the meetings of the American Psychological Association at Miami Beach, Florida, on September 5, 1970.

dwelling units on the development of informal of informal relationships between families. Gans (1963) has pointed out that the effects of proximity on informal relationships is somewhat contingent on differences in life styles exhibited by various groups. Gans' research indicates that it cannot be assumed that a particular architectural design will have the same effect on all social groups. The presence or absence of a particular design should have a variant effect on the total social life of a particular group, depending on the interdependence of the architecturally related behavior to other dimensions of the group's life. More specifically we should find that the architectural relationships between dwellings and the effects of such spatial relationships on the social relationships that develop between families will have varying degrees of significance, depending on the importance of informal neighboring relationships in a particular social group.

In this paper, we will argue that informal networks among neighbors are an important means by which the urban lower and working classes cope with poverty and deprivation and that these networks are at least in part dependent on the semi-public space and facilities that are present in many working- and lower-class neighborhoods. Finally, we will review results of an ethnographic study of the Pruitt-Igoe Housing Project which indicate the nature of the consequences stemming, in part, from the absence of such space and facilities and the networks that might otherwise have developed.

Social Class and Informal Networks

There is some ambiguity in the sociological literature concerning the importance of informal networks among different social classes. On the one hand, there are authors who argue that the frequency of neighboring and sociability is particularly prevalent in upper- and middle-class suburbs (Whyte, 1956; Bell and Boat, 1957; Fava, 1957). On the other hand, studies of the urban working and lower classes have shown rather strong interpersonal networks of neighbors and strong attachment to neighborhoods (Bott, 1957; Young and Wilmott, 1957; Gans, 1962; Fried and Gleicher, 1961; Fried, 1963; Suttles, 1968).

Careful reviews of these studies indicate that there is a difference in the character of social relationships with neighbors found in the middle class as compared to the working and lower classes. While neighboring is found to be frequent in both areas, "the intensity of social interaction tends to decrease as one moves from working class areas to upper income bracket residential suburbs" (Herberle, 1960: 279).

Illustrative of this debate are the results of a survey directed by John McCarthy and myself in Nashville and Philadelphia. The survey was taken in what were principally lower- and working-class neighborhoods in the two cities, with a smaller proportion of what might be considered lower-middle-class respondents. A total of 1,178 interviews were completed, 712 in Nashville, and 466 in Philadelphia. Approximately equal numbers of these were with black households (576) and white households (602). Samples were systematic, rather than random, and were not designed so as to be representative of either city.

Using a scale developed by Wallin (1953), we found no relationship between casual neighboring relationships and social status.[1] In contrast to these results were those obtained when we asked our respondents to tell us how far away their closest friends lived. In this case, lower-status respondents were more likely to have

friends living nearby than were those of higher status.[2]

These results conform to statements by Alan Blum (1964) and Rudolf Herberle (1960), suggesting that once the distinction is made between casual acquaintances and relatively high levels of interdependence, lower-class respondents are more closely tied to their neighbors. Among the lower class, friends are more likely to be neighbors. While, among the middle class, one might be friendly with his neighbors, friendships are more likely to be based on common interests, rather than upon physical proximity[3] (see Gans, 1961).

There is also considerable literature suggestive of the functions of informal networks for the lower and working class. Marc Fried's (1963) research on the depressing effects of urban renewal and relocation, particularly for families who had strong personal ties to the Boston West End, is illustrative. Gerald Suttles' recent research in Chicago's Adams area documents the manner in which the development of neighborhood networks based on physical proximity, age, sex, and ethnicity provided social and moral norms, as well as a means of integration into the larger groups. He writes

> Within each small, localized peer group, continuing face-to-face relations can eventually provide a personalistic order. Once these groups are established, a single personal relation between them can extend the range of such an order. With the acceptance of age grading and territorial usufruct, it becomes possible for slum neighborhoods to work out a moral order that includes most of their residents [Suttles, 1968: 8].

A recent study of an all-white slum neighborhood in St. Louis found similar informal networks. Of particular interest here, and complementing the work of Suttles (1968), is the finding that the level of personal integration into networks was strongly related to the perception of human dangers in the environment. Persons who were not integrated into such networks were more likely to express concern over allowing their children out of the house, felt that they were vulnerable to strangers entering the neighborhood, felt unsafe on the street at night, and felt that children in the neighborhood were out of control (Wolfe et al., 1968).

There are also some indications that the presence of ecologically local networks is more important to lower- and working-class urban dwellers than to their middle-class counterparts. Herbert Gans has noted that the move to suburban areas by middle-class families results in part in having more privacy from neighbors than they had in inner-city apartments. Gans' research suggests that, for the middle class, the move to suburban areas results in few changes in life style that were not intended. He writes: "They are affects, not of suburban life, but of the larger cultural milieu in which people form their aspirations" (Gans, 1963: 192).

The limited consequences of moving to suburbs by middle-class families stand in sharp contrast to those reported by Marris (1962) and Young and Wilmott (1957). These studies of the relocation of lower- and working-class communities indicate that the move to suburbia resulted in significant and unintended changes in their life styles. No longer available in the suburban housing estates were the amenities of the slum—the close proximity to work, the pub, and to friends and relatives. They changed their way of life and began focusing energies more sharply on their homes and jointly pursued family lives, and much less or separate activities by husband and wife participating in sex-segregated peer groups.

In addition to the ethnographic evidence on the relative importance of ecologically local informal networks, there is considerable research indicating that, much

to the dismay of urban renewers, lower- and working-class populations are as satisfied with their neighborhoods as are members of the middle class (Foote et al., 1960; Fried, 1963). Our recent survey in Nashville and Philadelphia indicated that there was no relationship between social status and neighborhood satisfaction. Over sixty percent of our respondents were satisfied with their neighborhoods, no matter what their social and economic status.

The works of Fried (1963), Gans (1962), and Foote et al. (1960) also indicate that among the lower and working classes, neighborhood satisfaction is rather closely tied to the presence of informal networks of friends and relatives. Results from our survey support this proposition. Without social class controls, we found no relationship between the proximity of friends and neighborhood satisfaction. When we controlled on the social class, we found that neighborhood satisfaction was related to the proximity of friends in the lower socioeconomic group, while there was no relationship in the higher-status respondents.[4]

These survey data suggest that, not only are the existence and integration into ecologically local informal social networks significant for the lower and working classes, but our results go slightly beyond the earlier studies in that they are suggestive of the relative importance of such networks for different social and economic levels. While social and economic factors are the principal variables that determine the life styles of the poor, they have developed ways of coping with and adapting to poverty, thus making the condition less oppressive. We have argued that among these adaptations is the development of ecologically local informal neighborhood relationships. When these are disrupted, or a community is designed which makes their development almost impossible, we should expect to see their importance made manifest by other differences that emerge in the life styles of a particular group. The Pruitt-

Igoe Housing Project community is illustrative of one such group.

The Case of Pruitt-Igoe

The Pruitt-Igoe Housing Project consists of 43 11-story buildings near downtown St. Louis, Missouri. The project was opened in 1954, had 2,762 apartments (many of which are currently vacant), and has as tenants a high proportion of female-headed households, on one form or another of public assistance. Though originally containing a large population of white families, the project has been all-Negro for the past several years. The project community is plagued by petty crimes, vandalism, much destruction to the physical plant, and has a rather widespread reputation as being an extreme example of the pathologies associated with lower-class life (Demerath, 1962; Rainwater, 1966a, 1966b).

Pruitt-Igoe represents, in its architectural design, an extreme example of a national housing policy whose single goal is the provision of housing for individual families, with little knowledge about or concern for the development of a community and neighborhood. Unlike normal slums, with their cluttered streets and alleys, Pruitt-Igoe provides no semi-private space and facilities aound which neighboring relationships might develop. There is a minimum of what is often considered "wasted space"—space within buildings that is outside of individual family dwelling units. An early review of the project's design (*Architectural Forum*, 1951) praised the designers for their individualistic design and the absence of such wasted space between dwelling units.

Walking into the project, one is struck by the mosaic of glass that covers what were grassy areas and playgrounds. The barren dirt, or mud when it rains, is constantly tracked into the apartments. Windows, particularly those on the lower

floors, are broken out. The cost of replacing glass in vacant apartments led the Housing Authority to cover many with plywood. Streets and parking lots are littered with trash, bottles, and tin cans. Derelict cars provide an attractive source of entertainment for children. Fences around "tot lots" are torn; swings, sliding boards, and merry-go-rounds are noticeably unpainted, rusted, and broken.

Within the buildings themselves, the neglect is more apparent. Entering the buildings via one of the three stairwells, one is struck with the stale air and the stench of urine, trash, and garbage on the floors. One is also struck by the unfinished construction—the unpainted cinderblocks and cement. These unfinished walls in the stairwells are decorated with colorful graffiti.

The alternative route into the building is the single elevator. The elevator is used as a public restroom, as well as a means of transportation up into the buildings. Even though it is mopped every morning, the smell of urine is noticeable throughout the day. Many individual building elevators are without handrails and in need of painting; all have the reputation of breaking down between floors.

On the fourth, seventh, and tenth floors, there is an open gallery, or hall, the only level public space within the building, one side of which is lined with broken windows and steel gratings. Next to the incinerator, open garbage is often found on the floor. The laundry rooms, located off the gallery, are sometimes used as lavatories. We observed residents and officials urinating in them.

The physical danger and deterioration of Pruitt-Igoe is but a reflection of the more pressing human dangers. Residents of Pruitt-Igoe continually expressed concern with being assaulted, beaten or raped. We were frequently warned of such dangers and told that we should never enter buildings alone and should stay out of the

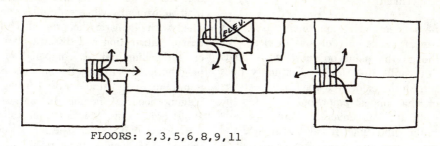

FLOORS: 2,3,5,6,8,9,11

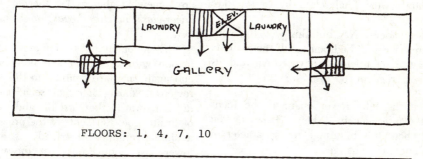

FLOORS: 1, 4, 7, 10

PRUITT-IGOE TYPICAL FLOOR PLAN

elevators, especially after dark. We were told stories of people being cut by bottles thrown from the buildings and warned never to stand immediately outside of a building. In addition to the physical violence, there was also the danger to one's self—the verbal hostility, the shaming and exploitation from children, neighbors, and outsiders (see Rainwater, 1966a).

One of the first things pointed out by the residents of Pruitt-Igoe was the distinction between "private" space within apartments and the "public" space and facilities. In our early interviews with families, we asked what they liked about living in the housing project. Almost without exception, what they liked was limited to the physical space and amenities within the family unit. Characteristic of these interviews is the following exchange:

Interviewer: How do you like living here in Pruitt-Igoe?

Respondent: I like living here better than I like living on O'Fallon Street [in a private housing slum] where we had a first floor, but did not have heat provided in the winter and windows were broken out. We did have an inside toilet, but no modern plumbing—we had no water. I like living here because it's convenient.

Interviewer: What do you mean by "convenient?"

Respondent: The apartment itself—it's easier to take care of and to clean. Although the paint on these walls holds dirt badly, the Housing Authority does furnish the paint. We don't have a choice of what kind of paint, but I painted the walls. It's real convenient here, especially in the wintertime. It's always so nice and warm here, and I only have one rent to pay. I don't have to pay for gas and electricity and all that. I just pay once. I like that. I like this apartment, it's good for the kids. Here we have separate rooms.

Interviewer: Each child has a separate room?

Respondent: No, but this way the children have a bedroom and the parents have a bedroom. It gives them and us more freedom.

When the interviewer changed the focus of the interview by asking, "How do you feel about this building?" the character of the interview changed.

Respondent: "Well, I don't like being upstairs like this. The problem is that I can't see the kids. They're just too far away. If one of them gets hurt, needs to go to the bathroom, or anything, it's just too far away. And you can't get outside. We don't have any porches.

And there are too many different kids around here. Some of them have parents, some do not. There are just a variety of families. Some have husbands, some not.

If it weren't for the project police, the teen-agers would take over. I've got some children that are teen-agers, but I still think they are the most dangerous group.

This pattern of responses repeats itself throughout our research. The results of a survey taken in the housing project indicate that 78% of the residents were satisfied with their apartments, while only 49% were satisfied with living in the project. This pattern of satisfaction and dissatisfaction with one's dwelling unit as compared to one's neighborhood is exactly the opposite of that found in most studies of housing and neighborhood satisfaction. In contrast with Pruitt-Igoe, slum dwellers generally are dissatisfied with their specific dwellings, while satisfied with their neighborhoods.[5] In Pruitt-Igoe, the familiar aspects of slum living, such as fires and burning, freezing and cold, poor plumbing, dangerous electrical wiring, thin walls, and overcrowding of children and parents into single rooms are somewhat abated. *Yet the amenities of lower-class neighborhoods are apparently lost.*

Complementing the pattern of satisfaction with apartment and neighborhood, and again in sharp contrast to the research reviewed above, informal social networks did not form in the corridors and stairwells of Pruitt-Igoe. Residents of the projects had a similar number of friends as in other lower-class populations, yet these friendships bore little or no relationship to the physical proximity of families to each other.

In Pruitt-Igoe, relationships with neighbors ranged from occasional friendship and helping patterns to (more frequently found) open hostility or isolation. As one woman explained when we asked about troubles in the project:

I think people bring trouble on themselves, but like the kids—see, the kids get fighting and the parents they get into it too. Now us, we mind our own business. I say little to the people across the hall. We don't have any friends in the building. Most of our friends are from work. Some of them we have known for a long time.

Still another replied, when asked about her neighbors:

They are selfish. I've got no friends here. There's none of this door-to-door coffee business of being friends here or anything like that. Down here, if you are sick you just go to the hospital. There are no friends to help you. I don't think my neighbors would help me and I wouldn't ask them anyway. I don't have trouble with my neighbors because I never visit them. The rule of the game down here is *go for yourself*.

The Consequences of Atomization

Gerald Suttles notes that in the Adams area in Chicago, conflict between residents in the area results in the reinforcement of the small informal group. He writes (1968: 228):

Individuals in the Adams area achieve a positive association with co-residents of the same age, sex and ethnicity primarily because conflict with other persons forces them together into small face-to-face groupings. Otherwise, people might remain almost wholly isolated, associate indiscriminately, and be dependent on such dyadic relations as they could form.

Of particular interest here is his discussion of the sequence through which such groups develop. New residents of the area restrict their children's movement to the areas immediately around or close by their homes. As a result, small and continuous face-to-face associations develop around the immediate proximity of the home. They provide means of controlling children and provide "assurances that relieve their apprehension." Conflict with persons outside these small groups forces the residents to "throw their lot in with a definite group of people" (Suttles, 1968: 228).

In a similar manner, mothers in Pruitt-Igoe attempt to keep their children in close proximity to their apartments. Yet in contrast to the slum, the architectural design of the project is such that as soon as a child leaves an apartment he is out of his mother's sight and direct control. There are no areas within buildings, except the galleries (which cannot be seen from the apartments and which are shared by some twenty families) in which children can play. As one mother explained:

I find that I can't keep up with the children when they leave the house to play. When they go out they play with just anybody; there are some people in the project who raise their children and some who don't. I want to have control over who they play with and when so many people live in one place you just can't choose your kid's playmates. If we were in a house I could keep them in a yard and see who they play with.

Mothers fear the early introduction and socialization of their children into sex and other troubles. They also see the adults in the housing project as being irresponsible, deviant, and beyond control. Said one:

They tell their children one thing and go out and do the very opposite. They see kids in a fight and rather than break it up, will get into it themselves.

Yet attempts to control children who are members of unknown families frequently resulted in conflict between adults. Thus one woman reported:

I used to watch the kids in this building. In the beginning I tried to discipline them. I'd tell them every time I found them doing something mischievous what was wrong and what was right. But kids don't like that; their parents don't like it. They don't want somebody else to discipline their children. They put the blame on you. Watching children is dangerous.

Another explained that after she had "made one of the neighbor's boys do right," his mother came and said she was going to bring a gun.

The conflict is further escalated when one of the two adults calls the police. As one woman explained, after she was told the police had been called because her son had gotten into a fight:

Well, I'm not going to get shook because the police are coming. They always come to this house and tell me how bad my children are. It's too bad the parents had to call the police and could never take the time to come up and talk to me first.

Apparently without the informal networks, informal social control that might otherwise be based on the small social group is not strong enough to resolve such conflicts. Thus, as a means of resolving what might otherwise have been a relatively small complaint, a more powerful authority—the policeman—is called upon. This, in turn, further exacerbates the atomization that exists.

Our interviews and observations with families in the housing project contain many references to the police. A sample survey of the Pruitt-Igoe Housing Project showed that over 90% of the residents of the project indicated that there should be more policemen patrolling the area. As one lady explained:

In other projects they have enough policemen, but not here. You put lights in and they take them out, or the police never turn them on. They have policemen but they don't do any good. They are not here long enough. They used to have auxiliary policemen down here. But as soon as they took them away there was all kinds of raping and stealing all over the project. It has turned into a jungle.

Other features of the architecture, apart from the lack of semi-public space and facilities, have contributed to the fears that characterize the community. The design of the stairwells is such that they represent almost completely uncontrolled space. They are public in the sense that anyone can enter them without being challenged, yet they are private in that no one is likely to be held accountable for his behavior in the stairwell. This lack of accountability is particularly prevalent in the center stairwell, where a small anteroom separates the individual apartments from the stairwell. This room creates a buffer zone between the totally private apartment and the stairwell. Pruitt-Igoes fear this stairwell more than others, and it is said to be used by teenagers as a relatively private place in which they can engage in sexual intercourse. As one teen-ager explained, "All you have to do is knock out the light on the landings above and below you. Then when someone comes, if they are not afraid of the dark, they stumble around and you can hear them in time to get out."

The isolation, the lack of accountability for entry into the stairwells, and the fears that are centered around them are somewhat interdependent with the lack of informal networks. Given the number of families who have rights to this space, it should not be surprising that strangers can enter it without being challenged. While interviewing in lower- and working-class neighborhoods, one often encounters persons on the street who question you as to where you are going. After an introduction, such persons often give interviewers instructions as to where a family can be found, when they will return home, or how to get through an alley to an apartment. Later, when such an interviewer returns and introduces himself, he often gets a response such as "Oh yes, you were here earlier." During our three years of intensive research in Pruitt-Igoe, such an experience never occurred. The presence of outsiders was noticed by the residents, but they were never challenged.

Absent from the architectural design of Pruitt-Igoe is what has sometimes been referred to as wasted space. We choose to call it "defensible space." In lower- and working-class slums, the littered and often trash-filled alleys, streets, and backyards provide the ecological basis around which informal networks of friends and relatives may develop. Without such semi-public space and facilities, the development of such networks is retarded; the resulting atomization of the community can be seen in the frequent and escalating conflict between neighbors, fears of and vulnerability to the human dangers in the environment, and, finally, withdrawal to the last time of defense—into the single-family dwelling unit. The sense of security and control that is found in other working- and lower-class neighborhoods is not present.

There are at least two alternative hypotheses which might be used to explain the atomized nature of the Pruitt-Igoe community. The first of these stems from the research and literature on social stratification, which rather clearly show that the level of interpersonal trust is lower in the lower class than in any other segment of the population. Thus it is argued that Pruitt-Igoe, being representative of the lowest class, is therefore a community of people none of whom trust one another. A comparison of Pruitt-Igoe's residents' responses to questionnaire items measuring the level of trust indicates that, while they are less trustful than are persons of higher status, they are not different from other lower-class populations (see Rainwater and Schwartz, 1965).

Perhaps a more credible hypothesis, one which might be termed the "police state" theory, stems from the public nature of life in public housing. Over fifty percent of the residents are on some form of welfare assistance. Welfare workers and housing authority officials maintain a rather close scrutiny of their clients who might otherwise break one of the many rules governing residence in the project. Under such a "police state," residents of the project may fear that becoming friendly with neighbors will result in their being turned in to the authorities. We observed neighbors calling the police about one another, as discussed above, and some families complained that neighbors had reported them to the housing authority or welfare office for an infraction of one of their rules.

Without a comparative study of Pruitt-Igoe with another housing project with a similar population, similar reputation, and similar administration by caretakers, it is difficult to adequately judge the effects of architecture per se. David Wilner's study of public housing in Baltimore shows, in contrast with Pruitt-Igoe, that with an architectural design which facilitated interpersonal interaction by the provision of common space and facilities, an increased amount of neighboring, visiting, and mutual aid was found among persons moving from a slum into a public housing project (Wilner et al., 1962: 161).

We obviously believe that architecture does have an effect on the manner in which the poor cope with poverty. And we further suggest that designers of housing for the poor, rather than viewing the space between dwelling units as something to be avoided or reduced as far as possible, should provide semi-public space and facilities around which smaller identifiable units of residence can organize their sense of "turf." Designers should minimize space that belongs to no one and maximize the informal control over the space required to get from one dwelling to another. In a word, if housing must be designed for the ghetto—if we must reconcile ourselves to not being able to change the social forces which produce the world of danger that lower-class families experience—the architect can make some small contribution by facilitating the constructive adaptations that have emerged as a means of defense against the world of the lower class.

Notes

1. When status was measured by education, we found a positive, although weak, relationship. When status was measured by income, we obtained the opposite results.

Neighboring and Social Status. Percentage of each status group scoring "high" on neighboring items:

Education Completed			Weekly Income		
0-7 yrs	25.2	(306)	00-$59	41.2	(240)
8-11 yrs	33.8	(409)	60-129	29.9	(421)
12 yrs	33.8	(225)	$130+	28.6	(318)
College	30.7	(192)			

2. *Friends' Distance and Social Status.* Percentage with first friend living on same block:

Education Completed			Weekly Income		
0.7 yrs	43.7	(300)	00-$59	40.7	(231)
8-11 yrs	31.6	(415)	60-129	29.3	(413)
12 yrs	26.8	(220)	$130+	19.9	(311)
College	14.5	(186)			
Probability		.0074	.0027		

Similar results were obtained with each of three friends.

3. We also found that higher-status persons are more likely to have friends whose occupations are similar to their own, in level of prestige, than are members of the lower and working classes.

4. *Neighborhood Satisfaction and Proximity of First Friend by Social Status:* Percentage satisfied with neighborhood:

		T-1 Distance in Blocks		
		0-4	5-25	26+
TOTAL SAMPLE		72.9(541)	69.4(264)	70.0(240)
Education completed				
0-8 yrs	LO	74.8(262)	76.0(71)	71.0(60)
9-12 yrs	MD	70.0(203)	61.9(126)	63.2(87)
College	HI	77.3(66)	67.3(61)	78.2(78)

As these data reveal, without social and economic controls there is little or no relationship between friends' distance and neighborhood satisfaction. Yet when we control on the level of education, we find that there is a relationship in the lower class, but not in the middle class.

Similar results were obtained with the second- and third-friend responses and when social status was measured by income and occupation. The levels of significance, beyond the .05 level, are not always achieved, but in every case the pattern of a stronger relationship between the proximity of friends and satisfaction with neighborhood is found in the lower-status groups.

5. A survey taken in the private slum neighborhood directly adjacent to Pruitt-Igoe found the more usual pattern of satisfaction with housing and neighborhood. The results of this and a survey taken in Pruitt-Igoe are presented below.

	Percentage Satisfied	
	Pruitt-Igoe	adjacent slum
with apartment	78	55
with project living	49	
with neighborhood	53	74
	(n = 154)	(n = 69)

In more recent years, vandalism and lack of maintenance have resulted in the deterioration of the plumbing and heating of the building. Thus these data, if gathered more recently, would probably not be found to be as striking as they were when this study was done in 1965.

35. The Early History of a Psychiatric Hospital for Children: Expectations and Reality
LEANNE G. RIVLIN AND MAXINE WOLFE

When a new building is completed and occupants begin to move in, there occurs, in a very real sense, a test of the planning process. Yet in the excitement of the premiere, seldom do occupants or designers consider this rare moment, and when they do, they generally concentrate on mechanical or convenience problems.

Our own work over the years, mainly in adult psychiatric hospitals (Ittelson et al., 1970a), has pointed out how essential it is to look at details of what actually takes place within the built environment. Even more important is the task of examining these data against the background of the architect's intentions and the philosophy or philosophies of the occupants. Success or failure, or more realistically, a position somewhere in between, can only be evaluated from the vantage point of a set of goals. The complex question, when looking at the completed building, is *whose goals*—the designers, the administrators, the staff, the persons served within the building? Unhappily, these are rarely identical and less often are they explicit. Yet we are convinced that considering each set of goals and attempting to understand them from the very first moment of a building's life history can be vital to any evaluation process.

The description of the early life history of a new children's psychiatric hospital, reported in this paper, presents some evidence for the value of a longitudinal approach to the study of a building. Although the details of this research are unique to the total institution, and, more particularly, to the special problems of providing psychiatric care for children, the general prin-

Reprinted from *Environment and Behavior*, Vol. 4, No. 1 (March 1972), pp. 31–71, by permission of the Publisher, Sage Publications, Inc.

Authors' Note: This research was supported in part by U.S. Public Health Service grant MH 18010. Data collection and analysis were assisted by Miriam Liebman, Robert Beasley, Michael Cryor, Ronald Goodrich, Verena Hirsch, Richard Olsen, Emilie O'Mara, Alan Wakelam, and Polly Ware.

ciples that emerge are appropriate for a variety of building types.

Most psychiatric philosophies today, including behavior modification approaches and milieu therapy (Colman, 1971; Stanton and Schwartz, 1954) consider the physical setting of the hospital as an integral part of the treatment. In reality, the physical structure, the hospital itself, is rarely designed with a specific philosophy in mind. The design and construction phases generally precede the selection of a hospital administration, and seldom does an explicit treatment policy act as a planning guide.[1] Buildings are more often constructed to be either adaptable to changing philosophies over the years or to act as neutral backgrounds for the philosophy that is currently in mode. Yet examining the history of psychiatric care, one can find a very close relationship between the philosophy of treatment (with emphasis on either punishment, isolation, education, or rest) and the facilities provided for the mentally ill. The very location and form of the structure often communicate this message.

Today it is not unusual to find architects and administrators deeply concerned with the use of space appropriate to the goals of an institution, but details of how this can be accomplished more often grow out of intuition than on concrete information (Bayes, 1967; Bayes and Francklin, 1971; Nellist, 1970). A psychiatric facility for children has certain special considerations, a result of planning a total environment appropriate to the needs of its young patients. For a child, the physical environ-

[1] A notable exception is L'Institut Marcele Rivière in France, which was built directly out of a treatment philosophy and incorporates aspects of the physical structure in the therapeutic program.

ment is likely to assume a more prominent and quite different role than in the case of adults (Piaget and Inhelder, 1969). This is particularly true for children with psychiatric problems severe enough to require hospitalization. For these children with an incomplete sense of themselves as unique and separate from the outside, conceptions of the physical world are more direct expressions of their level of ego development than would be true for adults (Searles, 1960). For the disturbed child, there is an exaggeration in the process of differentiating himself from the world. Spaces and objects in space frequently take on the qualities of significant people in that setting (e.g., Goldfarb and Mintz, 1961; Rubin, 1962). Often objects assume affective qualities that the child is unable to express toward people.

There is growing research documenting the specific qualities of space to which children are most sensitive. Hutt and Hutt (1970) and Hutt and Vaizey (1966), for example, have considered density and social behavior. They have observed the increase in aggressive and destructive behavior in normal and brain-damaged children as the number in a room increases. Autistic children did not reveal this pattern of aggression, but rather responded to increases in density by seeking supportive interaction with adults, and retreating to the periphery of the room.

There is a common conception of psychiatric patients that their behavior is a reflection of their pathologies alone. It is now becoming clearer that this is only partly true—that the building they are in, the objects that surround them, and the numbers of persons with whom they live, all act to produce the patterns of behavior that we see. The answer to the complex question of space use thus rests on an understanding of the specific qualities of occupants, but always in the context of their setting.

The study of the children's hospital not only provides information on how the patients and staff use a new building, interesting in itself, but uncovers the history of the interaction of a building and its occupants, never a static or predictable story. It reveals the complex interaction of a design, rules for use set down by the authorities, and the dynamic qualities of the occupants who sometimes comply, but often exert their individuality on the patterns of the use of space. Planners are rarely kept informed of the extensive remodelling their buildings undergo from the very moment they are opened—and even before. All this acts as a kind of prologue to the drama of the life history of a building, setting the tone that will linger until the building is no longer used.

Our longitudinal approach centers on three major areas:

(a) the relationship between the predictions of designers and administrators and the use of a building over time;
(b) the patterns of use over time;
(c) physical and functional changes made made by the occupants over time.

These three dimensions were studied through several sources of data: a study of the program of the building; an analysis of interviews; informal observations over time; and a series of time sample observations of the facility. The program of the hospital was obtained in addition to correspondence with those responsible for planning. Interviews with the architect of the hospital and its director provided data on intentions and expectations. Three formal observation (mapping) studies, undertaken during the first two weeks of occupancy, two months and four months later, yielded quantitative information regarding the actual use of space. Informal observations of changes over time have

continued up to the present time. All combine to form the study of this facility, during its first year-and-one-half of use.

Description of the Children's Psychiatric Hospital

The children's psychiatric hospital, where the present research was conducted, is a state psychiatric facility designed to provide in-patient care for 192 children ranging in age from 5 to 15. Combining residence facilities, a school, and areas of occupational therapy, recreation, diagnosis, and treatment, it is located on an extensive tract of land which also contains a large state psychiatric facility for adults. A visitor to the children's hospital must pass through a rather long, winding road leading to a number of high-rise buildings, belonging to the adult hospital. The irregular roofs of the children's hospital provide a marked contrast to other structures in the setting.

The building (Figure 35–1) is organized around a central open space (A) accessible through glass doors. The primary circulation route rings the court and the various functions of the building radiate from it. There are four major areas: (1) living; (2) recreational and community; (3) school; and (4) administrative. The building is two stories high and, other than the infirmary, no area is more than a half-level from the main floor.

There are eight "houses" or ward units, each designed for 24 children, arranged in four sets of two "houses" each, one above the other (one-half floor above and one-half floor below the main level.) The 48 children from each set of houses share a common dining room on the main floor. There are no facilities for food preparation; meals are prepared in the adult psychiatric hospital and transported, via a tunnel, to the children's hospital building.

Six of the eight houses are identical in design (Houses 2, 3, 4, 5, 6, 8) and contain a total of 24 defined rooms. There

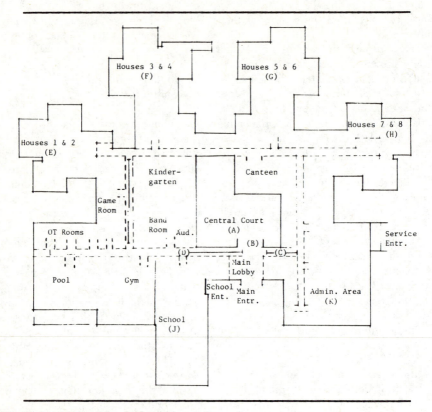

FIGURE 35–1.   Floor plan: children's hospital.

is a center corridor leading to three eight-person living units or apartments, a communal day room with kitchenette, a nurse's station, a laundry room, an office, and various storage facilities. Each eight-person living unit has a small entry foyer with a bathroom, a living room, and four bedooms located around the living room. There are two single-bed rooms, one two-bed room, and a four-bed room. None of the bedrooms has doors.

Two houses (1 and 7) were originally designed for autistic children. These houses have the same amount of floor space and the same basic design as the other six houses. However, only two rooms within each eight-person living unit were defined by walls, a large room designed to serve as sleeping quarters for six children as well as the living room for all eight children, and one two-bed room.

The furniture for the living units was either designed or selected by the architect. The beds have a storage unit which can be attached at the head or used separately. These beds have no casters, but are light enough to be moved easily. The living room furniture includes multi-use ottomans and benches. The floors are covered with indoor-outdoor carpet.

There is liberal use of glass throughout the hospital. Each bedroom has windows, and the living room of each unit has a picture window and a door which take up a large section of one wall overlooking the grounds.

There are 23 rooms used by all the children for their daily activities. With the exception of the canteen, all of these "community areas" are situated along two major corridors (Figure 35–1, D and I). These include a game room, a kindergarten, a music room, four occupational therapy rooms, the pool, gym, library, and auditorium. The canteen is on the rear corridor directly opposite two of the houses.

Additional indoor areas of the hospital include the school, administrative offices, and an infirmary. The school area (Figure 35–1, J) is separate from the living and recreational areas and has an entrance from outside the building as well as one from the main corridor.

The offices for all administrative functions and staff members (psychiatrists, psychologists, social workers, and so on) are in a wing of the building which is separate from all other facilities (K). A fully equipped hospital unit is on the second floor of the building.

There are three outdoor play areas (two with playground equipment) and an outdoor basketball court and baseball field. Outside the hospital are barbecue grills, benches, and water fountains.

In order to evaluate our findings dealing with the use of the hospital in relation to what was intended, it is necessary to have an adequate understanding of the variety of views affecting its design and use. We feel this can best be achieved by examining the *program* requirements, the *architect's intentions,* and the *director's* point of view, as well as the actual general functioning of the hospital.

The Program

The space program for the state-run children's hospital was completed in 1964, with slight revisions made in 1966. It did not provide any information about the therapeutic bases for program decisions or the treatment philosophy. Furthermore, the program arose at a time when such facilities were viewed primarily as hospitals under a medical model. Treatment was essentially viewed as medical or physical treatment to be administered by a staff whose contacts with patients would be limited to their professional duties.

The program in its final form called for a *residential* facility for 192 children, ranging in age from 5 to 15. Except for the description of some of the children as "autistic," no definite information was available as to their disorders. The program required a total of 80,885 square feet of space. This was to be a facility with all services the children would need.

There were, of course, many restrictions placed on the design. Some of these are critical in understanding problem areas that developed after completion. The "total community" concept was one of these features. The hospital or infirmary unit had to be included. The program prohibited the use of separate cottages for living space. Each living unit was designed for 24 children. Neither the bedroom nor the bathroom stalls could have doors. Two separate wards were to be designed for autistic children, and it was specified that the bedroom space be undivided. No rationale was given for this decision.

As indicated earlier, the hospital shares an extensive tract of land with a large adult psychiatric institution. A number of the program requirements were based on the use of as many facilities as possible in the larger hospital. Therefore, food preparation facilities were not part of the program. Also, certain administrative functions were to be carried out at the larger hospital—records, personnel, and the like, so that space was not provided in the children's hospital for these functions.

The Architect's Intentions

From interviews with the architect, we were able to reconstruct information about the bases for various design decisions and, most importantly, the aims and expectations he had for the eventual use of the facilities. With little or no relevant literature available and with minimal information from the department (except for the space program), he had to work out his own guidelines. He contacted professionals involved in residential treatment of children and tried to incorporate their views into his design.

The architect believed that in order to provide opportunities for personal contact and to avoid making the institution overwhelming, the patient population should not exceed 80 to 90 children. Faced with the program requirement for 192 children, he attempted to give the institution a character which would enable an individual child or groups of children to find their "own places." Since the program prohibited the use of separate cottages, the architect tried to reach his goal by (1) using the series of houses in different wings, and (2) organizing the building into its four separate but interconnected areas (house, community, school, and administrative).

The architect divided the houses into three living units with the intention of making each unit a small apartment, providing for both private and small-group activities much as in a family situation. The houses, made up of the three living units and communal space (the day room, kitchenette, and the corridor) could also be used for larger group activities in which all 24 children could participate.

He included the kitchenette with the hope that this alternative might offset the deficiencies caused by the children's meals being the same as those in the adult facility.

Originally, the architect had intended to eliminate permanent bedroom divisions within each apartment or living unit. He preferred a module setup, where the furniture would be used to partition the areas and establish personal bed-spaces. He felt this would provide maximum flexibility in the use of space. Each child would have a personal place within view of the activity center. Since the use of furniture for partitions was unacceptable under the state program, his alternative plan was to use a form of the office partition—with a soft, rather than porcelain finish. He was most anxious to see potential for adaptation, but this plan was also unacceptable. The final design utilizes block walls to separate the rooms, but they have none of the flexibility the architect originally sought.

The decision to give each living unit or apartment one four-bed, one two-bed and two single-bed rooms was also set by the departmental requirements. No rationale was given for this specification. The architect's own feeling was that since no permanent decision about the age or sex of children to be housed in different wards was made prior to the construction of the building, the resulting distribution represented an attempt at maintaining some flexibility for the future. It was also his impression that this compromise might not be optimal for any age group. He suggested that older children might prefer private rooms, and that he woud have preferred to have all single rooms.

In designing the living quarters, the architect's intention was to eliminate the institutional feeling through the use of carpeting, draperies, glass, and more personalized furniture. Each child has a bed and wardrobe combination with shelves, storage space, and mirror. He felt that the design and interior decor represented a compromise between making the living unit *indestructible* without having it look like a jungle or a jail. The architect, however, also believed that it would be impossible to separate the quality of the environment from the effects of those who used and maintained it. If staffing in the hospital were ample and good, the attempt at a "deinstitutionalized" atmosphere would work. On the other hand, if the maintenance were poor, the design and interior decor of the hospital could prove to be worse than that in the average institution.

Several areas of the building were intended to provide communal space for all patients. These included the center court, the canteen, and the auditorium (with a seating capacity of 250). The main corridor was also intended as communal space. The original design specified a twelve-foot-wide corridor that was to be furnished as a lounge space in a number of areas. Due to budget restrictions, the width was reduced to eight feet. The architect felt that the narrower corridor gave the feeling of a labyrinth and would not serve his original intentions of encouraging social interaction and casual contacts.

The program called for the use of the central facility of the larger state hospital for food preparation. The architect could not alter this aspect of the program, although he considered it a mistake.

In general, the architect designed the building with the idea that children would be spread throughout the hospital and the variety of different spaces (both in size and function), would offer the greatest options for use.

The Director's Philosophy and Predictions about Use of Space

Soon after his appointment in the spring of 1969 the director issued a statement of the therapeutic philosophy for the facility. The emphasis was community-oriented and stated: "Inherent in this view is the notion that re-establishment of at least tolerable child-community relationship depends upon 'treatment' of both the child and the community. And this perforce necessitates continuing interaction between the child and the community even at the height of their discontent with each other." One aspect of this view included provision for out-patient care (day-care and after-care) to reach two and one-half times the number of in-patients.

In terms of specific aspects of the design, the use of six identical houses was sharply criticized by the director. He felt

that mirror-image houses would create difficulties for children with orientation problems. He was also unhappy with the long and numerous corridors on the same basis.

The director disagreed with the architect's original plans for the elimination of permanent dividers in the apartments or living units. The use of separate bedrooms was viewed as important in giving the children a homelike atmosphere. In fact, from the director's point of view, there was no sound therapeutic basis for the lack of definition of rooms in the two houses designed for "autistic" children. He believed this concept emanated from a viewpoint stressing supervision and control rather than therapy. He felt that the same erroneous concept led to the exclusion of doors on the bedrooms: "Many people believe that if you can't see a child, he is going to do bad things."

The director also would have preferred all single bedrooms. He believed that children, regardless of age, need privacy, which is best achieved in their own room. He predicted that four-bed rooms would create the greatest problem because, after the placement of furniture, there would be little available floor space.

Based on his community-oriented philosophy, the director saw the pool and other recreational areas as excessive. He believed that the children should use the facilities available in the surrounding community so that they are not isolated during treatment. Also, in line with the community-oriented philosophy was the director's criticism of the infirmary or hospital unit. He believed that if a child had a minor ailment (e.g., a cold or virus), he should remain in his house much as he would with his family. If the child had an illness requiring hospitalization, then he should be sent to a regular hospital—again, as would occur at home.

Finally, he criticized the lack of food preparation facilities and stressed the psychological importance of having food-making close to home and the value of adult-child interactions that take place in connection with food preparation. He agreed with the architect in anticipating that the kitchenette could be used in this way. The use of central facilities located in the adult hospital was seen by the director as a mistaken notion about the relationship between the two institutions. He viewed them as autonomous institutions while the state program characterized them as interdependent.

These views really represent part of our data in that we will be comparing the actual use of space (from our systematic observations) with the expectations of those involved in the planning and administrative processes.

Functioning of the Children's Psychiatric Hospital

The children's hospital was programmed and subsequently designed as a traditional *in-patient* facility. Ready for occupancy in December 1968, it remained unoccupied (due to inadequate funds for staffing) until December 1969, when it opened on a *day-care* basis with twelve children. It provided day-care services for two months, officially opening as a combination day-care and residential facility in March 1970.

Even at the time of its official opening,

staff funds for personnel were far below what was required. As a result, the hospital has always functioned with a census far below the original plan (see Table 35-1).

By May 1971, 14 months after the opening, the census had reached 22 full-care and 30 day-care patients. In June 1971, severe budget cuts forced the closing of several older state children's psychiatric facilities, and the children's hospital was forced to admit more children despite a concurrent freeze on staff hiring. Between June and August 1971, one day-care and 10 full-care children were admitted, bringing the census up to 32 full-care and 31 day-care patients. Since the opening of the hospital, only two children have been discharged. Therefore, even with these new admissions and the small discharge rate, the hospital—17 months after opening—is operating far below its orginally programmed capacity of 192. It is interesting to point out, however, that recently the director was able to have the capacity of the building officially reduced to 125 beds.

Due to the small number of children during our three studies, only one of the eight houses (House 2) was used. Even this was only partially occupied since there were only four full-care children at the beginning of the first study and five at the end. During study 1, all the children were

TABLE 35-1.   *Age,[a] Sex and Resident Status of Patients for the Three Mapping Studies[b]*

	Full Care						Day Care					
	Males			Females			Males			Females		
Ages	A	B	C	A	B	C	A	B	C	A	B	C
Study 1	0	3	1	–	–	–	0	2	5	0	5	0
Study 2	0	6	4	0	0	1	1	2	4	0	6	1
Study 3	0	8	3	0	0	2	1	4	4	0	6	0

[a] Age group A=under 7; Age group B=7–11; Age group C=12–15.

[b] Study 1 took place the first two weeks of occupancy; study 2 took place two months later, and study 3, six months after the hospital opened.

in one living unit. The other two living units were vacant. Very little furniture had been placed in the house because there were not enough staff members to assemble it. The dining room was not furnished, and meals were served in the day room.

During study 1, the canteen was unfurnished and generally unused. The game room contained a pool table and a tennis table. Both the band room and gymnasium were in use, as were two of the four OT rooms. However, the library was completely empty, the pool unfilled; supplies were limited. Despite the confusion of the initial phase of occupancy and the shortage of equipment, the morale of staff and patients seemed quite high. The children had considerable freedom, and although the director had been concerned that the building's design would cause confusion, they appeared to navigate about the hospital with ease. Rooms were unlocked and available for use at will, and there was fairly unlimited choice of activities, to the point of permitting roller skating in the corridors. Even school attendance was not mandatory. When a crisis situation developed, if a child started acting out, several staff members would go to the area and an on-the-spot therapy session would occur.

By study 2, several changes had occurred. All the rooms in living unit 1 were occupied, as well as 2 bedrooms in living unit 2 and 1 bedroom in living unit 3 (assigned to a female patient). The dining room had opened for use. One of the four OT areas was made into an animal room while the remaining OT room became a woodwork shop. However, the OT rooms were no longer being used as much. The therapists complained that with a total census of only 23 children, the rooms were not large enough for any more than 4 or 5 patients at one time. For larger groups, they began using the OT rooms in the school building and reserved the other rooms for use with individual patients or groups of 4 or less. Toward the middle of the second study, a jukebox was set up in

the canteen, but there was still little other furniture. The houses appeared rather sparsely furnished, and there was obvious wear on the carpeting. Several windows had been broken and were boarded up, awaiting repair.

Changes had also occurred in the administrative policies of the hospital. Children were divided into groups for activities with one or two child development workers responsible for each group. There was still some freedom of choice, in that a room could be unlocked upon request. At the same time the doors were being locked, sheets of paper were placed over glass panels in the doors—apparently to prevent the children inside from being distracted and to prevent the children outside from being disruptive.

Overall, the changes reflected a growing structuring of the child's day. Measures were being taken to aid in supervisory control of the children, in part due to problems that had been encountered (children climbing up to the roof; finding the access to the upstairs infirmary as a place to hide, and the like). By study 3, all glass door panels had been covered by paper. The house still had minimal furniture, and it was evident that housekeeping and maintenance were inadequate, as reflected in torn areas of carpeting and several broken windows. House 7 had been transformed into administrative office space. The game room was rarely used. Candy and ice cream machines had been moved into the canteen as were a few tables. The library had been furnished and was functioning, and the pool was also in use.

In terms of administrative organization, children were now assigned to groups with whom they went to almost all activities. Each child had a program card listing where he was to be at each time period. The child had the alternative of going to the defined activity or remaining in the house. Freedom of choice had disappeared almost entirely. Almost all doors to activity rooms and to the house area were kept locked, whether or not they were occupied.

Thus, several major trends can be seen to have evolved in the first six months of the hospital's life history. The census had increased, although at a low rate. The number of rooms that were available for use had also increased. However, this was offset by the increasing restrictions placed upon the children by the locking of doors and the structuring of the child's day, by programming all of his activities.

Although our mapping studies thus far cover the first six months of occupancy, we have continued interim observations on a weekly basis. A number of physical and functional changes occurred between October 1970 and October 1971. In March 1971, a decision was made to divide the children into two houses according to age; one for adolescents, and one for younger children. All the children were moved out of House 2 and into Houses 3 and 4. Day-care children were assigned to house activity groups according to age, although they were not assigned to a specific living unit or bedroom. House 2 was utilized as a depository for their coats. The offices in the two new houses were converted into "quiet rooms"—a way of dealing with children who were acting out.

The second major change was the conversion of House 1 (one of the "autistic" houses) into an occupational therapy and kindergarten area. This move required that some renovations be made, including putting doors on the day room. The art therapists seemed much more satisfied with the new arrangements even though there were inconveniences, because the area was not designed for crafts and lacked a sink in the painting room. Two of the four rooms originally designed for OT are unused, one has remained a woodwork shop, and the fourth is used as a club room. The specially designed kindergarten room, located on one of the main corridors, now is a staff library. The nursery children were moved into one of the living units in House 1, again requiring renovations. Part of the large window in the combined living/sleeping room was made into a door providing direct access to the play area, stairs were built from the door down to ground level, and a fence was installed around the play area to enclose it. Smaller-sized swings also had to be installed.

The game or recreation room was used from the opening of the hospital until the winter of 1970. At this time, the table tennis and some furniture were moved into the canteen, and the game room remains locked and unused.

The infirmary floor is now being used for a half-day day-care program for adolescents who have been expelled from schools. There are now 7 patients with an eventual goal of 11 patients for each half-day session. Clearly, the qualitative data reveal that there have been changes in the use of space, as well as in administrative policies regarding the use of space.

Mapping Studies

Three studies were conducted in order to follow the use of space as it developed over time. The initial study (study 1) began the first day the hospital opened as a residential facility and continued for two weeks. Study 2 was conducted for a one-week period two months later, and the third study was done four months after that. Thus, weeks 1, 2, 10, and 31 in the life history of the hospital were the major focus. In the time between studies, weekly observations were made in order to keep abreast of all changes and developments.

The basic approach used in quantifying and describing behavior patterns and use of space was the *behavioral mapping technique*, an observational method developed in our earlier studies of adult psychiatric wards (Ittelson et al., 1970b). The major adaptation necessary in using this technique in the children's psychiatric setting was the development of a list of behaviors evidenced by children in such a setting. They were derived from a pilot study in the children's psychiatric ward of the hospital that serves as a referral source for the children's psychiatric hospital. The resulting 69 activities were incorporated into the observation procedure, which involved coding each behavior observed into one of these activities. For the purposes of data analysis, the coded activities were combined into 19 analytic categories which we felt appropriate to the present study. Table 35–2 presents a list of the 19 categories and the activities contained within them.

For observation purposes, the children's hospital was divided into two areas. Only one of the eight houses (24 rooms) was in use during these studies, and it constituted the *living* area. The 23 rooms used by all children for daily activities (game room, occupational therapy, gym, and so on) constituted the *community area*. For the studies cited here, no formal observations were made in the school, administrative wing, dining rooms, or outdoor areas.

TABLE 35–2. *Description of Categories of Behavior*

Category	Description of Behaviors Included
1. Aggression	Aggression toward objects, people, self and undirected; arguing; disturbing an activity; restraining a child
2. High-energy physical release	Chasing; climbing; jumping off things; roughhousing; running
3. High energy organized	Dancing, marching, rhythmicizing; exercising; active games, sports
4. High energy unorganized	Play; fantasy play; roller skating; bike riding
5. Low-energy organized	Arts and crafts; sitting games; teaching; playing with or caring for animals
6. Isolated active	Looking out window at an activity; personal hygiene; reading; wandering; watching an activity; writing
7. Isolated passive	Crying alone; hiding; lying awake; sitting alone; sleeping; standing alone; looking out window
8. Domestic	Eating and drinking; housekeeping: food preparation
9. Media	Phonograph, radio, television
10. Music	Play instrument; singing
11. Orientation	Looking for a person; looking for a place
12. Meeting	Group meetings; patient-staff conference
13. Exploration	Explore objects; explore places
14. Cuddling/holding a child	Self-explanatory
15. Idiosyncratic behavior	Pathological behavior which is specific to the person. Including head banging, hallucinations, etc.
16. Talking	Self-explanatory
17. Telephoning	Self-explanatory
18. Traffic	Walking through, to or from an area with no other concomitant behavior
19. Miscellaneous	Arriving; leaving; hospital routine; preparing for activity; transporting objects; waiting

One observer was assigned to each of the areas (living and community). Every fifteen minutes they made a predetermined tour of the locations, recording all ongoing activities, the number, resident status (full- or day-care), and sex of the patients involved in each activity, the number of staff and visitors present, and whether the room was locked or unlocked. Observations were made throughout the active periods of the day: the *morning* hours following the arrival of day-care patients, and before lunch (10 a.m.–12 p.m.); the *afternoon* hours following lunch and until the day-care children left (1 p.m.–4 p.m.); the *evening* hours following dinner and before bedtime (6 p.m.–9 p.m.). There was a total of eight hours of observation per day on Monday through Thursday and five hours on Friday, since most children went home for the weekend at 5 p.m. Study 1 observations took place for two weeks, making a total of 296 separate observations for each room or area. Studies 2 and 3 covered one week each, with a total in each study of 148 separate observations of each room or area.

Two reliability studies were conducted, one prior to study 1 and a second prior to study 3. A reliability study for study 2 seemed unnecessary since the same observers were used in studies 1 and 2, and the studies were only eight weeks apart, although practice time was provided. Before each reliability study, the observers were familiarized with the hospital and the patients and were thoroughly trained in the use of the observation instrument. Following training, pairs of observers simultaneously collected a complete set of observational data. Two types of reliability scores were obtained: overall interobserver agreement and interobserver reliability for each variable recorded (i.e., specific activity, number of participants, and the like). The overall interobserver reliability in study 1 ranged from 81% to 96%. In study 3, the range was 84% to 100%. The reliability of the observations in the two areas of

the hospital (living and community) were essentially similar. Reliabilities for each specific variable were high, averaging 87% in the first study and 91% in study 3. With a total of 69 activities, the average reliability of the coding of observed activity was 78% in the first study and 85% in the third study. Thus, the reliabilities for specific variables were sufficiently high to justify the use of the instrument.

Mapping Results

The data represent the *number* of children involved in each activity, providing a profile of the distribution of children engaging in different types of activities. By examining this distribution for the two separate areas of the hospital (house and community), we can obtain a picture of the extent to which these areas were used and thus investigate the patterns of use over time.

These data were analyzed in two ways. First, we compared the number of children engaged in each activity in each area of the hospital with the total number of children engaged in any activity in all areas of the hospital. This total is dependent on two factors: the number of observation periods within the study and the number of patients in the hospital. During study 1, we observed for two weeks, while observations for studies 2 and 3 cover only one week of time. Therefore, the total number of children observed in activities in studies 2 and 3 is roughly one-half of the number in study 1. Study 3 figures are somewhat higher than those of study 2 and reflect an increase in the number of patients (see Table 35–3). Second, we compared the number of children engaged in each activity in each area of the hospital with the total number of children involved in activity within that area only.

The first comparisons made were the percentage of patients engaged in each activity in the entire hospital during studies

TABLE 35–3.   *Frequency and Percentage of Patients Engaged in Activities[a]: Studies 1, 2, and 3[b]*

| | Entire Hospital | | | | | | | | |
| | Study 1 | | | Study 2 | | | Study 3 | | |
	f	%[c]	Rank	f	%[c]	Rank	f	%[c]	Rank
High-energy organized	414	17.47	1	201	12.48	2	186	7.77	7
Talk	382	16.13	2	207	12.85	1	208	10.93	4
High-energy unorganized	261	11.02	3	132	8.19	6	155	8.14	6
Low-energy organized	241	10.18	4	188	11.67	3	216	11.35	2
Traffic	203	8.57	5	147	9.12	5	210	11.04	3
Isolated active	178	7.52	6	124	7.70	7	207	10.88	5
Isolated passive	120	5.06	7	166	10.30	4	230	12.09	1
Total number of patients observed in an activity in the entire hospital	2,366	100%		1,611	100%		1,903	100%	
Total number of patients	16			26			28		

[a] The activity categories will differ in subsequent tables because their frequency of occurrence differs over the various comparisons.

[b] For this and subsequent tables, it must be noted that study 1 covered two weeks of observations, while studies 2 and 3 each covered a single week.

[c] Based on all patients observed engaged in an activity in the hospital for this study.

1, 2, and 3. Table 35–3 presents these data in terms of the activities in which the largest percentage of children were observed. (In all, 19 categories of behavior were used. For a complete listing, see Table 35–2.)

An examination of Table 35–3 reveals a definite change over time in the types of activities in which the children engaged.

By study 2 a pattern of activity types had been established, crystallizing by study 3, in which the activities children engaged in became less social, more passive or withdrawing, and less likely to involve high energy.

When the hospital opened, talking and high-energy organized behaviors involved about 34% of the children. By study 2, this decreased to 25% and by study 3, to 19%. The changing pattern of children engaged in other prevalent activities (increases and decreases) resulted in a fairly even distribution across all activities. While our previous studies in adult hospitals suggested that this flattening out represents greater freedom of choice by occupants, an examination of the distribution of activities by location in the children's hospital (to be discussed later), will reveal the extent to which other factors operated to influence the pattern here.

By examining the percentage of children engaged in different activities, broken down by specific locations in the hospital (see Table 35–4), we can see how patterns of use evolved for each area. In all three studies, there was almost no change in the percentage of children observed in each area. Thus, at any given moment in time, an average of 29% of the children would be

TABLE 35–4.   *Distribution of Patients in House and Community: Areas Studies 1, 2, and 3*

	House		Community		Total	
	f	%	f	%	f	%
Study 1	673	28.36	1,693	71.46	2,366	100
Study 2	494	30.66	1,117	69.34	1,611	100
Study 3	526	27.64	1,377	72.36	1,903	100

located in the house, and 71% in community areas. The changes in the patterns of activity can be viewed as real changes in the patterns of use within each area. They were *not* a function overall changes in the distribution of children between the two areas of the hospital.

Before describing the changes that occurred, it is useful to examine the activities characterizing each area over all three studies (see Table 35–5). Children more frequently engaged in talking in community areas than in the house. Similarly, traffic, high-energy behavior, low-energy behavior, and isolated active behavior consistently involved more children in community areas than in house areas. There were very few activities in which the children engaged more often in the house than in the community areas. Essentially, in study 1, the house had little distinctive character of its own. Only media (TV, phonograph) and meetings involved more children in the house than in community areas. The only behavior that finally did appear to characterize the house was isolated passive behavior. This activity involved few children in either house or community areas in study 1, but doubled in the house by study 2 and tripled by study 3.

To pinpoint the changes within an area, we compared the number of children engaged in each activity in each area to the total number of children engaged in any

TABLE 35–5.   *Percentage of Patients Engaged in Activities: Studies 1, 2, and 3*

	House versus Community Areas[a]					
	Study 1		Study 2		Study 3	
	House	Community	House	Community	House	Community
Talk	6.29	9.84	4.34	8.50	3.36	7.57
Traffic	1.68	6.88	1.61	7.51	1.47	9.56
High-energy organized	.50	16.98	1.24	11.23	.42	9.35
High-energy unorganized	1.56	9.46	.99	7.20	1.31	6.83
Low-energy organized	1.60	8.57	1.24	10.42	.32	11.03
Isolated active	2.23	5.28	3.23	4.47	2.89	7.99
Isolated passive	2.74	2.28	7.39	2.92	9.62	2.47
Media	2.02	.80	2.23	1.74	3.41	.47
Meetings	3.12	.04	2.23	—	.79	—

[a] As a function of all children engaged in any activity in the entire hospital.

activity within that area. As Table 35–6 indicates, there were substantial changes over time in the use of the house. During study 1, talking reflected a peaking or predominance, with the reminder of the children distributed over a rather wide variety of activities perhaps reflecting a degree of freedom to do what one wanted, there. Only one-tenth of the children spent their time in the house engaged in isolated passive behavior. By study 2, two months later, a dramatic reversal had occurred, with 24% of the children involved in isolated passive behaviors and only 14% observed talking. By study 3, over one-third of children observed in the house were withdrawing, while only 12% were observed in conversations. By study 2, patterns of use of the house as a place for passive and withdrawal behaviors had been established, and these were strengthened by study 3. The decrease in the percentage of children involved in domestic behavior can be explained by the use of the dining room (outside the house) by study 2. Prior to that, when meals were served in the day room, children were involved in preparation and cleaning up. The concurrent increases in behavior of a less social type during these time periods (e.g., isolated active increased from study 1 to 2, media increased by study 3) substantiates the changes in the milieu of the house.

The use of the community areas, summarized in Table 35–7, also revealed changes over time. During study 1, high-energy organized behaviors involved about 24% of the children at any one time, almost double the percentage of children engaged in any other activity. This organized high-energy behavior reflected the free choice available to the children in the early days of the hospital. During study 1, both the gym and game room were open and available and children seemed to take advantage of these opportunities. By study 2, children had access to these rooms only during limited time periods, and by study 3, only specific children could go to these rooms during a given time period. Similarly, the decrease in high-energy unorganized behaviors (play, skating, bike-riding) re-

TABLE 35–6. *Frequency and Percentage of Patients Engaged in Activities: Studies 1, 2, and 3*

| | House versus House | | | | | | | | |
| | Study 1 | | | Study 2 | | | Study 3 | | |
	f	%	Rank	f	%	Rank	f	%	Rank
Talk	149	22.13	1	70	14.17	2	64	12.16	3
Meetings	74	10.99	2	36	7.28	5	15	2.85	7
Isolated passive	65	9.65	3	119	24.08	1	183	34.79	1
Domestic	58	8.61	4	26	5.26	7	21	3.99	—
Isolated active	53	7.87	5	52	10.52	3	55	10.45	4
Media	48	7.13	6	36	7.28	4	65	12.35	2
Traffic	40	5.94	7	26	5.26	6	28	5.32	5
High-energy unorganized	—	— —		—	— —		25	4.75	6
Total number of children observed in any activity in the house	673	100%		494	100%		526	100%	

TABLE 35–7. *Percentage of Patients Engaged in Activities Studies 1, 2, and 3*

| | Community versus Community | | | | | | | | |
| | Study 1 | | | Study 2 | | | Study 3 | | |
	f	%	Rank	f	%	Rank	f	%	Rank
High-energy organized	402	23.74	1	181	16.18	1	178	12.93	3
Talk	233	13.76	2	137	12.24	3	144	10.46	5
High-energy unorganized	224	13.23	3	116	10.37	5	130	9.44	6
Low-energy organized	203	11.99	4	168	15.01	2	210	15.25	1
Traffic	163	9.63	5	121	10.81	4	182	13.29	2
Isolated active	125	7.38	6	72	6.43	6	152	11.04	4
Isolated passive	54	3.19	7	47	4.20	7	47	3.41	7
Total number of children observed in any activity in the community areas	1,693	100%		1,119	100%		1,377	100%	

flected increased scheduling of the children's time and their assigned places within the hospital. By study 2, low-energy organized activity had increased, and, by study 3, it was the activity involving the greatest number of children. By study 3, isolated active behavior (basically, watching an activity) and traffic had increased. These changes reveal a flattening out of the distribution of children across activity groupings within the community areas. This flattening out appeared to be a function of the increasing structuring of the children's time, rather than a result of freedom of choice on the part of the child.

It is of particular interest to look more closely at the four locations within the community areas which were specifically designed to serve as communal space for all patients. The center court was one of these areas. Over the year and one-half that the hospital has been occupied, this court has hardly been used. Of the 6,140 activities observed in community areas, in all three studies combined, only 36 took place in the court. The auditorium has also

rarely been used. The canteen was unused for the major part of our studies. The amount of activity in the corridors remained fairly stable over the studies, accounting for approximately 44% of the activity in community areas and 31% of activity in the hospital as a whole. However, the pattern of use changed over time, with decreasing evidence of social behaviors such as talking and increasing traffic. Isolated passive behavior, never high in the corridors, practically disappeared by study 3, further supporting the decreasing choice available to patients as to where they could withdraw.

Part of the analysis of the mapping data focused on the locked conditions of the various rooms of the hospital. Specifically, for each room that could be locked, observers recorded one of four conditions: (1) locked and occupied, (2) locked and unoccupied, (3) unlocked and occupied, and (4) unlocked and occupied. The most interesting way to look at these data is to consider locked and unlocked conditions in terms of whether the room was occupied.

These results, summarized in Table 35–8, reveal that in study 1, 92.92% of the occupied rooms were unlocked. By study 3, only 66.77% of the occupied rooms were unlocked. Clearly, there was an increasing tendency to contain children in the rooms, over the studies. Conversely, looking at unoccupied rooms, the probability that these rooms would be locked also increased over the three studies. The picture which emerges suggests that the locking of doors served a dual function: keeping children in and also keeping outsiders out.

Discussion

Examining patterns of use over time, against the context of the building form, the planners' expectations, and therapeutic and administrative policies, one sees the complex factors that finally led to the deveopment of a personality for an institution. Playing no small role in the process are the myriad of unexpected events that occur during the early stages, all acting upon the occupants—patients and staff alike.

The original program for the children's hospital clearly was based on a medical model. In marked contrast with the self-contained design and the physical isolation was the community-oriented philosophy of the director. The community model philosophy translated into two policies that clashed with the medical model of the design: (a) the inclusion of day-care services, and (b) the maximal use of community facilities.

Although the number of day-care children will eventually be two and one-half times the size of the residential population, no provisions for day-care exist within the hospital. While the architect designed the building and furniture to give each child his own place, in fact, for the majority of patients, this will not be possible. At present, with a small census, the day-care children do have a place to hang their hats —in an unoccupied house, but this is likely to continue only until that space is needed for other purposes. An additional aspect of treatment philosophy, the integration of day-care patients with full-time residents, has meant assigning day-patients to the same house groups as in-patients of their own age. Since each house contains bedroom and locker facilities for only 24 children, day-care children do not have their own place in any real or personal sense. When the full-care census increases to capacity, the problem will probably intensify.

The use of community facilities has meant that the recreation areas within the

TABLE 35–8. *Frequency and Percentage of Rooms Locked[a] as a Function of Occupancy*

	Occupied				
	Locked		Unlocked		Total Number of Rooms
	f	%	f	%	
Study 1	68	7.08	892	92.92	960
Study 2	137	26.00	390	74.00	527
Study 3	216	33.23	434	66.77	650
	Unoccupied				
Study 1	2,855	81.92	630	17.58	3,485
Study 2	1,527	84.18	287	15.82	1,814
Study 3	1,522	89.37	181	10.63	1,703

[a] Based only on rooms that can be locked.

hospital are vastly underused. In an attempt to stimulate use of the hospital's own facilities, and as a way of involving the surrounding community, the director has offered the community use of the gym, auditorium, pool, and small meeting rooms. But, largely due to location, this becomes a difficult and often unsuccessful undertaking.

A further departure from the medical model resulted in the conversion of the fully equipped hospital unit (infirmary) into a half-day treatment center for adolescents. The hospital was never used, and given the philosophy of treatment, it probably never will function as designed. The provision of rooms and services alien to the basic treatment philosophy not only represents a waste of space, but also creates underused and vacant areas, resulting in supervision problems for the staff.

The director, who initially was enthusiastic about the interiors, has felt the need to replace the carpeting with tile and the broken glass windows with plexiglass. The effort to provide more homelike fixtures has led to the closing of the game room, a result of damage to the attractive, low-hanging globe lights. As the director predicted, they became targets for hurling objects. There is a self-perpetuating quality about destruction—especially damage that is not easily or quickly repaired. Children who have difficulty in controlling their aggression are further stimulated to destructiveness by the sight of destruction that goes unheeded (see Sorosky et al., 1969). For these children, awareness that repairs are being made, and even participation in the process, are important experiences in developing self-control and responsibility. What our findings suggest is not that indestructible materials must be used, but rather materials that can be replaced quickly, perhaps even with the help of the children.

The hospital up to this point has never functioned in the overall manner anticipated by the architect. His distribution of public, semi-public, and private space was predicated on the assumption that there would be 192 children and sufficient staff to supervise them in the building. With the building fully occupied, both patients and staff would be spread throughout, and there would be few areas into which a child could go where staff would not also be present. This acts to provide a subtle sense of supervision, a covert form of observing the children without actually following them around. This intention would have been quite consistent with the director's therapeutic philosophy of an unstructured program, on-the-spot therapy when needed, and a deemphasis on control, although the present use of quiet rooms runs counter to early expectations. The small number of children and staff resulted in large unoccupied, unpopulated sectors of the hospital. As our data indicated, communal areas were rarely used, only one house was occupied, and children did easily slip away from supervision. Although a variety of possible ways of dealing with the problems might have been offered at this point, it is important to recognize that the solution selected was administrative rather than architectural, the locking of rooms, scheduling of activities, and ultimately programming the children's time. One possibility that could have been tried was consultation with the architect in an effort to use the building in a more effective manner. In this case, as in so many others, this kind of option was not even considered. Rather, an administrative solution was decided upon resulting in changes in therapeutic policy and the general functioning of the hospital. Both community and house areas were affected by this characterization of spaces. The general milieu of the hospital became more subdued. The physical location of the house reinforced its role as a place for total withdrawal. Withdrawal in itself is not necessarily undesirable. It is a right anyone has. But there are many ways a child can withdraw—by remaining in a group but uninvolved, by standing at the periphery of activities, and the like. When the area in which withdrawal is acceptable is also physically isolated from all other ongoing activities, withdrawal means total removal and lack of involvement at any level. In fact, the nature of the withdrawal in the house was of the most total form—sleep. Although the children did receive medications, the withdrawal does not seem specifically a response to drugs. There is evidence that some forms of withdrawal where the patient is in the presence of others although not involved with them are critical stages in the therapeutic process, a nonthreatening way for patients to test out their role in social interactions, without actually committing themselves to deep involvement. Where this is discouraged by limitations on the patient's freedom of choice, one important dimension of learning and change may be undermined. Presentation of transitions is especially critical for the institutionalized child—whether these are physical or social stimuli (Stroh and Buick, 1964).

A number of details incorporated into the building under assumptions inherent in the architectural program later proved to be areas of inflexibility that, in turn, created problems. One such area was the two undefined houses designed for autistic children. These houses proved to be a definite obstacle when the decision was made to divide the children by age and assign them to two separate houses. It would have been much easier to move some children from the already occupied House 2 to House 1, directly beneath. This was not possible because House 1 lacked defined bedrooms. The final decision involved a complete move of all children to two different houses (3 and 4) because they had divisions between rooms. It was essential that the occupied houses be located near each other—the small staff made it important to use a single dining room and single corridor area.

This move to different houses in turn set up a series of subsequent changes. The new houses were located in the center of the rear corridor rather far from community spaces. It was decided to move the occupational therapy rooms (already too small, according to the staff) closer to the new living area. Since House 1 was not regarded as a good living space, it was converted into an OT area. The therapists rather liked the cozy atmosphere of the house, and the larger, sunny rooms outweighed the inconvenience of lacking built-in equipment and sinks. The old OT suite is now unused. To the credit of the architect and staff, there was sufficient physical and administrative flexibility to permit this drastic alteration, but it reflects the chain of events that a weakness in program can precipitate. At the base is the inadequate conception of what autistic children require. Interestingly the few autistic children in the hospital, all young day-patients, initially were placed in the kindergarten area, a self-contained suite of indoor and outdoor facilities. When House 1 was renovated, one living unit was converted into a new kindergarten area, a move that required changes in order to provide some of the amenities available in the original rooms. This move, too, tended to concentrate patients in one general area, again facilitating supervision. Clearly, this need would not have arisen had the hospital been fully populated, for the kindergarten area would have been reasonably close to occupied houses. This need to keep patients and services together not only facilitates control of children, but also may help to stimulate the development of a psychological center of the building An understanding of these centers provides a useful way to understand the character of a building, whether that setting is a school (see Myrick and Marx, 1968) or another form of institution. It might be suggested that the children's hospital still is searching for its psychological center, for that area where people congregate and socialize. The social areas of the house, which might have served that function, really had no identity in the early stages. Their later flavor seems colored by the role of the house as a place to withdraw. Recent changes in the hospital may well stimulate the development of a heart center, if it is not too late for this to occur.

The question of the specific functions of particular areas (for example, the role of various parts of the house) raises the entire issue of the balance of public to private, individual to group spaces all necessary aspects of daily life. Their importance to design has been clearly articulated by Chermayeff and Alexander (1963) in terms of residential space. It very likely is even more critical in the case of the total institution. For children, whose lives are structured by adult rules, the balance of private to communal spaces, and their freedom to move in them will really explain the array of observed behaviors. In the children's psychiatric hospital, several aspects of the building design were intended to provide private to public or communal spaces. In the case of the house, we have described the character of use, with private activities basically taking over, but for the most restrictive and withdrawn activity, namely sleeping. But other areas of the hospital had explicit communal functions associated with them that never materialized. The center court is one such area. Despite good weather, our observations revealed very limited use. Most of the time the doors leading to the court were locked, suggesting that children were being kept out as a control measure. Although access to the court would have provided alternative routes for the children, its use was actively discouraged. Both the architects and our own research team had expected the court to be a central core of the building, a point of reference, a gathering spot, perhaps a psychological center for the building. Our observation forms were designed to pick up subtle differences in the use of various parts of the court, uses, of course, that never materialized. The need to control certainly explains much of why activity in the court was so limited, as does

the fact that rooms running off the court were minimally used. Perhaps, too, this kind of inner space is not the kind of area that functions with ease in our culture and climate. It is a strange sort of space, neither indoor nor outdoor, protected from the outside but still not private, a form most appropriate to warm areas or areas where the boundaries between a family's communal inside and communal outside space can be blurred. In the children's hospital, the court was a place to look out at from within. But even the sight lost its aesthetic appeal as lack of maintenance led to a steady deterioration, testimony to its limited role in the lives of the children.

Communal space for children is probably the hardest to provide. A balance must be struck between large and cold spaces (such as the auditorium, which was rarely used) and smaller, more intimate spaces. The dining room (an area we did not observe) probably is the most natural communal space (with the possible exception of corridors), although it was not open between meals. Corridors, originally conceived of as natural avenues for contacts, lost that potential in the need to decrease their width and the subsequent structuring of the children's day. They have been the site of decreased social interaction over time. The canteen was unused for six months and now has become an activity center for sitting games, table tennis, model-building—that is, more organized activity.

As indicated earlier, the design of the children's hospital was predicated on interdependence with the adult facilities, located nearby. Many service areas were eliminated on the assumption that they would be provided more economically by the larger institution. Since opening, there has been a clear movement for autonomy in every possible direction. With the exception of food services, still provided by the adult kitchens, the children's hospital is self-sufficient and the need for additional administrative space has led to the conversion of one house for these functions. Here again, a program requirement obstructed fulfillment of the use of space as intended by the architect.

In reviewing the past year and one half of the life history of the children's psychiatric hospital there is both evolution of space utilization patterns and changes in treatment philosophy. Our analysis has suggested that these changes in philosophy were products of the attempts of the administration to meet realities, many of them unexpected. All grew out of the best intentions, by the most dedicated of staffs, yet often the consequences were diametrically opposed to the working philosophy that opened the building. What does this say? That a staff must stick to original intentions, despite problems with their facility whatever the realities? This is most unrealistic Rather, our observations raise other possibilities. First, the unexpected will always occur especially in a new building, and constant review of ongoing events in terms of long-range goals seems essential. More

particularly, in terms of the physical form, the use of the potential of the building is limited if it and perhaps the designer are not given an opportunity to continuously participate in the program. It is regrettable that the architect's role ends just at the point when it is most crucial to have his active participation. It would seem that on-going contact between designer and occupants is essential, to use a facility to its maximum, to meet new crises and changes, and to effect modifications where events suggest that they are needed. If administrative rules replace details of design, if hasty renovation substitutes for a consideration of alternative uses of a building, the end product may well be a policy by default.

Space utilization patterns, much like personalities, grow and change in response to events. But there is durable, long-lasting quality, too, where early characteristics affect later patterns of use. It is this long-range factor that makes skillful use of the infancy period so essential.

36. The Use of Space in Open Classrooms
LEANNE G. RIVLIN AND MARILYN ROTHENBERG

The popularity of open-plan arrangements in offices, homes, and schools raises some critical questions regarding the meaning and consequences of this way of organizing available space. Clearly, the motives behind the decision to open up spaces are varied. Some grow from specific philosophic orientations or esthetic preferences; some aim toward achieving a particular

This research was supported by a U.S. Public Health Service Grant MH23709. Instrumental to the design and conduct of studies were the efforts of Fred Wheeler, Fran Justa, Sheree West, and Bill Hilton. Sue Fox, Geoffrey Weiland, Alan Sommerman, Alan Wallis, and Ron Erickson have all participated in data collection and analysis at various stages of our work.

look or image, others toward improving supervision, surveillance, or even safety, and still others hope to magnify the impression of spatiousness. A benefit commonly cited is the flexibility yielded by open arrangements, and in some cases, reduced construction costs. Striving for a sense of openness whatever the setting may also be a reflection of the increasing scarcity of space as a shared resource and a sense of the world as closing in. However, the meaning of *open* as applied to *space* cannot be considered to be singular.

Increasing numbers of school systems in this country and elswhere have embraced the idea of open-classroom and open-space approaches as a solution to a variety of educational problems, and perhaps some economic problems, as well. Although open-classroom procedures vary considerably, they generally involve a program incorporating children's interests and a flexible use of space and learning materials. The different aims that underlie these programs make partialling out the design component from the educational one a very difficult task. Since goals are an integral part of what happens in settings, it is essential to try to understand what they are before considering whether the physical context supports, facilitates, or obstructs the educational process. Studying the use of space from this perspective is a two-stage process of evolving a conception of the goal—or more accurately, the goals—of the users, and then examining empirical data against these goals. In the case of the school, users can be the administrators, teachers, children, and parents. In other circumstances, the aims of planners, interior designers, and architects' views can also provide a backdrop for the analysis.

Since open classrooms embody both an educational policy and a setting that departs from traditional forms, they provide especially good opportunities for environmental studies. The number of studies of open classes is growing (see, for example, Durlak, 1972; Brunetti, 1972). Understanding the way environment and program operate demands an intimate understanding of specific settings. We have found that a research strategy that summarizes an array of details on specific classes, where it is possible to take a long and close look at these classes over time, provides the most satisfying approach to studying these complex, large-scale environments. Relevant data include descriptions of what the room is like, the users and where they are located, what they are doing and with whom, and all of this over the natural course of time—in the case of a classroom over the academic year. Each piece of information can then be viewed in the context of a

long-range and detailed backlog of data essential for meaningful generalizations.

Our work took place in two public elementary schools using open-classroom approaches. Both schools were located in a large urban area. Both occupied old, traditional-design buildings and had student bodies from varied backgrounds. School A was an experimental school with 400 children, offered to parents as an educational alternative to existing local schools. School B was a larger facility of about 1250 students contained in a single building with an attached annex. The approaches to open-classroom techniques in both schools were fairly similar. Although the rooms were structurally intact, each had physical arrangements and furniture and equipment that broke up the space, creating special areas and providing a variety of working sectors (see Figs. 36-1 and 36-2 for typical rooms). The rooms were made up of many elements, none specifically mandated by the administration. Within rough limits of fire regulations and safety codes, teachers were free to reorganize space, build or acquire furnishings, and change them at any time. In fact, each of the rooms was different, reflecting the teacher's conceptions of what the setting should be.

In order to provide the detailed information necessary for understanding how space was used, eight classes, four in each school, were selected for intensive study. Class size was about 30 students. In the first school (School A) efforts were concentrated in one mini-school consisting of four classes located on one floor. The classes were interaged and contained groupings covering a kindergarten–first grade, a second–third grade, a second–third–fourth grade and a third–fourth grade. Rooms varied in size from 594 to 1035 square feet. In the second school (School B) four classes in one wing were selected for study. These consisted of three second-grade classes and one first-grade class, with rooms ranging from 864 to 900 square feet. In both

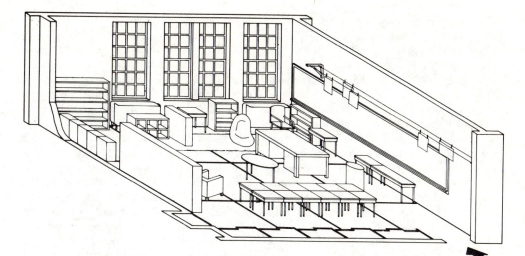

FIGURE 36–1.   School A, Room 3.

FIGURE 36–2.   School B, Room 7.

schools the classes were drawn from a group of teachers who had expressed a desire to work with us. Our criteria essentially were to choose cooperative teachers in proximal rooms in order to facilitate work in a functional section of the school. A cluster of classes made frequent observations and informal visits easier and less disruptive. All the teachers in the group were women.

Gathering Relevant Data

The specific techniques that were used included repeated observations of classrooms, repeated tracking (following the complete days of individual children), interviews with teachers, children, and parents, and the use of a model of the classroom in conjunction with an interview with students. In addition, after the first observations were completed, a series of environmental workshops were held with the teachers and a group of children. The observation results will be the main emphasis of this paper.

The observations of classrooms took two different forms. One set, *furniture mapping*, traced the location of furniture and equipment in each classroom throughout the school year. Directed to the question of what these potentially changeable rooms were like when viewed over time, the observer recorded the type, magnitude, and location of physical changes within the rooms. Using a floor plan of the rooms divided by a grid into twelve equal sectors, the physical elements were observed and coded biweekly. The specific location of the furniture and the functional areas (for example, reading, math, science) were recorded so that changes could be determined. The grids were analyzed to identify functional areas, addition and removal of pieces, new combinations and transpositions, and shifting and rotation of pieces both within and between functional areas.

The second set of observations concentrated on people within the room. The specific method was *behavioral mapping*, a naturalistic time-sample technique for describing patterns of activities and use of physical space. For each school a detailed floor plan was made of the study sites (classrooms, corridors, ancillary rooms). The twelve-sector grid used for the furniture mapping provided the divisions for locating behavior within the rooms. Since each classroom was divided in such a way that sector number 1 was the far corner and sector number 12 near the area of the door, it was possible to compare portions of each of the rooms. Preparation of the observation instrument involved compilation of an exhaustive list of coded classroom activities and materials.

Prior to mapping an observer handbook with complete instructions was pre-

pared. Three observers were trained in the mapping procedure until adequate reliabilities were obtained. The specific procedures had trained observers make a regular tour of the research site every 30 minutes using a predetermined sequence. They identified the activity in each sector of the room, including number of participants, teachers, visitors, male or female students, specific sector (1 through 12), location within sector (center, edge, corner), and materials and equipment in use. In cases where an activity and its participants bridged more than one area, the predominant site and range were recorded. The form had room for comments for each activity observed. Observations took place at three points during the school year, in October, January, and May of 1973–1974, with another set completed for the 1974–1975 academic year. Four full days of observations (9:00 A.M. to 3:00 P.M.) were done for each time period. This paper deals with results of the first year's work.

An essential component of behavioral mapping, and in fact all our observations, is that the observers get sufficiently close to ongoing activity to pick up necessary detail wihout disturbing the flow of activity. It is very important, therefore, that members of the research staff become familiar visitors to the sites involved in the study. In fact, preparation of the observation forms and training of observers provided much of that opportunity. By the time data were recorded, there was considerable assurance that the presence of the observer did not intrude on class routine to a noticeable extent.

Results on Furniture Arrangement

The physical layout of the classroom remained quite stable over the academic year. Changes were infrequent, generally involving pieces of furniture that were easiest to move, such as small tables. Desk and chair arrangements remained intact, as did particular interest areas (math, science, library). The essential stability of the rooms was reflected in minimal changes to the position of the teacher's desk and the set place of the major seating areas in each room. Seven of the teachers had desks, and six of these desks remained in the same grid sector for the entire year. The one exception was a single change made when a loft was moved into one room. The patterns of use in these rooms over the school year must be considered against the stable physical arrangements.

Results on Patterns of Use

In order to get some sense of what is happening within the classroom it is possible to look at the distribution of children across the 12 sectors of each room. It is necessary to do this without a prior conception of ideal distribution because this is really impossible to define. Over the school year, none of the rooms had what might be considered to be an even distribution of occupants. In the most extreme cases (two classes in School A and one class in School B), half the total number of persons observed were in two sectors of the room—that is, in one sixth of the total area (see Figs. 36–3 and 36–4). In many cases this resulted from group meetings, but its frequency represents a concentration of children beyond what might be expected in light of the choices offered by the educational philosophy of open classrooms. In some rooms the uneven use reached rather dramatic levels. In one case, 45 percent of all the persons were in one sector, with 9 percent or less found in each of the remaining sectors. All classes had at least one sector with double the expected number of persons, that is, 16 percent or more. Only one room, on its second mapping, revealed less than 16 percent in each sector. However, this instance illustrates the value of bringing additional information to a specific comparison. Although children in this par-

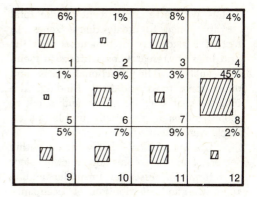

FIGURE 36–3. Percent of observations of children by location: School A, Room 1, Mapping 3.

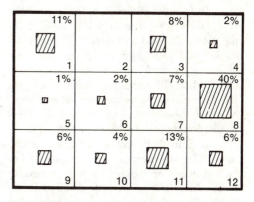

FIGURE 36–4. Percent of observations of children by location: School B, Room 7, Mapping 1.

ticular class were not concentrated in one single area, they were often involved in a group lesson wherever they happened to be. Children kept stable seats in which they did their assigned work and from which they listened to lessons, a pattern reminiscent of so-called "traditional" rooms and programs. In the other rooms the heavily used sectors were areas free of furniture in which group meetings were held.

It is possible to note a kind of linking effect, that is, the tendency for an area in which density peaked to be adjacent to other heavily used areas. Frequently, the sectors with over 10 percent of the total activity joined to create dense zones. In fact, it is necessary to remember that the grid lines are researcher's artifacts to facilitate analysis. The functional areas and dense zones cross grid lines. Findings also indicate that corridor space and ancillary rooms, although potentially usable spaces, rarely were occupied.

The question of what went on within sectors of the classrooms adds another piece of information essential to understanding room use and distribution of occupants. When we consider activities observed in the two schools, there were interesting similarities and differences (see Table 36.1). For School B, writing was consistently the most frequently observed activity over the year, accounting for at least one-fifth of the total. Talking and arts and crafts occupied the next two ranks. In the case of school A, writing was most frequently observed at the beginning, with talking in the first place the remainder of the term. None of these, however, reached the level of the predominant activity in School B.

In School B, three activities constituted 47 to 50 percent of all observed behavior, while in School A it is necessary to consider four or even five different activities (in the case of the second mapping) to reach that level. This apparently reflects a different program emphasis, with greater variety revealed in School A, the alternative school. While there was a tendency for writing to decrease over the year for School A, it remained fairly stable for School B. Talking took a different pattern, rising in rank between first and second observations. For School B this rise was followed by a leveling off in the final mapping, where it remained second in rank but represented a smaller percentage of the total activities observed. For School A, talking rose from second place to first by midyear but the total percentage increased somewhat in the final mapping. There is a very real question whether the relatively stable room arrange-

ments supported the activities and their more changeable patterns over time.

Most interesting is the finding that the over-all patterns of activities in the two schools paralleled each other to a considerable degree. This occurred despite the fact that the schools were quite different in organization and seemed, at least on the surface, to have somewhat different conceptions of open settings. School B had a more structured approach to education, while School A, offered to parents as an educational alternative for their children, made a conscious effort to be innovative. In fact, although there was a greater variety in School A, much of the same activity took place in both places. Neither school had much "working," that is, use of and handling of materials, mainly math or science. Yet manipulation of tangible objects is frequently viewed as desirable in open-education settings since it involves a type of learning that suppports the more abstract form. This behavior rarely reached much more than 6 percent of the total activity observed in either school.

It is useful to examine individual class patterns against the background of data for schools. In some classes activities were more evenly distributed than in others. Where a single activity dominated, apparently the teacher emphasized a particular topic or skill. This was especially true of two classes, one in each school where writing reached over 30 percent of total observed activity in the first mapping. Later, this leveled off, with other activities increasing, suggesting less directed activity as the school year progressed. Interestingly, the change in activity emphasis was not reflected in supportive room changes.

The distribution of *size of group* involved in activities for all rooms over three mappings indicates that individual work was the predominant mode. Over one-half of the activities observed had a single child involved in them. The two-person group was the second most commonly observed

TABLE 36–1. *Ranks and Percents of Activities Observed in the Two Schools over Three Mappings*

Rank	School A			School B		
	Mapping I	*Mapping II*	*Mapping III*	*Mapping I*	*Mapping II*	*Mapping III*
1	Writing (19.9)	Talking (16.5)	Talking (19.5)	Writing (26.1)	Writing (20.7)	Writing (22.7)
2	Talking (13.3)	Writing (13.9)	Reading (10.4)	Arts & Crafts (11.8)	Talking (16.4)	Talking (13.8)
3	Arts & Crafts (12.3)	Traffic (7.8)	Writing (10.4)	Talking (11.3)	Working (13.4)	Arts & Crafts (10.9)
4	Watch act (8.4)	Reading (7.6)	Arts & Crafts (8.9)	Reading (6.3)	Reading (7.5)	Reading (8.0)
5	Traffic (6.3)	Watch act (5.6)	Working (6.5)	Working (5.7)	Arts & Crafts (6.5)	Traffic (8.0)
6	Games-Sit (4.8)	Working (5.5)	Traffic (5.5)	Teaching (5.1)	Traffic (6.4)	Working (6.0)
7	Play (4.8)	Arts & Crafts (5.0)	Watch act (5.3)	Traffic (4.3)	Watch act (4.5)	Look at obj (4.1)

activity unit. These patterns were found in both schools for the three mappings, although specific classes demonstrated more variety than others. Groups of eight or more were least frequently observed, occurring between 1 and 9 percent of the totals.

Another dimension of the patterns of use within classrooms concerns the specific location of teachers. Although teachers differed in over-all styles and use of the room there was an overwhelming tendency to concentrate their time in limited locations. When areas were ranked according to the percentage of time teachers were observed within them, the first ranked sector revealed a range of 21 to 72 percent. Combining the first three ranks, which accounts for one-quarter of the total area of the room, a range of 47 to 89 percent was revealed.

Again, looking at specific classrooms illustrates the meaning of the predominant location of the teacher. In one classroom where teacher location was an extreme in the range, that is 72 percent of time seen in one area, the teacher was never observed in fully one-half of the room's sectors. The teacher's prime location was an area that traditionally constituted the center-front of the room, that is, the space between the door and window in front of the blackboard. Yet the work involved was *not* predominantly board work. In this place, the teacher led group meetings, group sings, and story time. Afterward, she remained there to work with individual children who came up to her. The other end of the range was a teacher seen in a single location a maximum of only 21 percent of the observations. In this classroom the teacher was observed in each grid location at least 3 percent of the time. Scanning the teacher locations reveals another interesting pattern. Seven of the eight classrooms were structurally similar, that is, doorways, blackboards, windows, and closets were in pretty much the same place in each room although arrangements of furniture and equipment differed. In all of these rooms, the teacher's

prime location has been identified as the front sectors, especially areas near the windows and blackboard. Moreover, as we move away from this sector, we find decreasing teacher use.

Paralleling the view of over-all activity is a picture of the activities of teachers (see Table 36.2). Over all mappings, talking and teaching combined to account for between 39 and 55 percent of the teacher's time in both schools. Obviously, the fine line between these two types of activities would sometimes be difficult for an observer to distinguish, since all activity involving a teacher could be perceived to have an educational component. However, observers were trained to consider the teacher's behavior as concretely as possible, that is, to code for teaching only where obvious instruction was in evidence. Each instance of teacher/child interaction was to be viewed as closely as possible in terms of content instead of fitting it into stereotyped roles.

For School A talking and teaching were almost equally balanced. In School B teaching averaged about 27.6 percent of the observations over the year, with talking at 19 percent. In addition, 15.6 percent of the time the teacher was observed checking work, a behavior seen only an average of 7.5 percent in School A. Group meetings and large group lessons involved at least 26 percent of the teacher's observations in both schools, and administrative duties about 6 percent.

Summary of Interview Results

The activity patterns in the rooms and ancillary areas (which, it must be emphasized, received minimal use) can be viewed against a brief summary of interview results. These were undertaken to provide the picture of goals essential for an understanding of observations. Children in both schools were asked to consider the setting and what they liked and disliked. A com-

TABLE 36–2. *Percent of Teacher Activity over First Three Ranks for Both Schools over Three Mappings*

	School A			School B		
	Mapping I	Mapping II	Mapping III	Mapping I	Mapping II	Mapping III
Talk	25.0	19.7	28.2	21.6	19.7	15.7
Teach	23.2	22.7	20.9	23.5	35.7	23.6
Check Work	—	9.8	—	10.5	19.7	16.5
Group Meet	9.8		11.8			

mon criticism was the lack of a place to go for privacy. This was especially strong in School A, as was the expressed need for quiet places. In both schools, the request for ways of improving the setting elicited ideas for shifting movable objects, mainly furniture. Inadequate space and storage were complaints of parents and teachers in both schools. In addition, teachers added to the list of environmental criticisms the problems of crowding and lack of privacy. These interviews combine with observations to suggest that distribution of people across spaces was at the heart of some of the environmental difficulties encountered.

General Implications

There is a basic question as to how we can apply the varied information on the classrooms we have studied to understand the way settings support, facilitate, or obstruct the educational process. The schools in which we have worked consider the setting to be an integral part of open education, but all of us, teachers, administrators, researchers, and perhaps the children as well, may question what this really means. We have found relative stability of furnishings in the rooms although there was freedom offered to shift many elements. There was a preponderance of individual work, mainly writing, despite a value expressed for group projects and use of materials.

There was uneven use of the room and concentration of teacher's presence in a limited set of sectors, despite the freedom offered to work with a variety of group sizes in a variety of places. We have worked with individual teachers and students on environmental projects and have found awareness of many problems, although there was sometimes a question as to whether this sensitivity was reflected in their day-by-day use and arrangement of the classroom space. All of this raises serious questions regarding the meaning of "open" to the teachers and their students, the degree to which awareness of the potential of a setting leads to its use. There was some understanding of goals, however partially articulated, and these appeared to head in the direction of informal classes and flexible use of space. Yet there were a series of unanticipated problems because the departure from traditional procedures had many different and often conflicting meanings.

In some classes the arrangement formed a display, the exposed materials offered to the class perhaps as an invitation, perhaps facilitating access. In other classes decentralized work surfaces were the theme—decentralized in two possible senses, with students decentered from the traditional desk assignments, given varying degrees of freedom to select their work places, or, in other cases, specialty areas such as math, science, and reading decentralized and arranged over the room. Other rooms were open for what might be an esthetic or symbolic reason, the arrangement satisfying some ideal conception of what a classroom should look like, and this could relate little or much to what would take place there. Other classes had more informal arrangements of chairs and tables in a plan that moved away from the rigid order of a traditional room although allowing for the total class lessons that took place. The consequence for the children was to liberate them in varying degrees from set places and open up choices, but apparently within a limited range. And this in turn created some serious difficulties.

Observation of the rooms pointed to the convergence of children about a portion of the total available space. This concentration of people and activity was often counter to the general goals of open classrooms, including flexible use of space, variety of individualized activity, group work, and emphasis on manipulation of materials.

In their interviews, teachers and children expressed the need for more space, private areas, and quiet. To the teacher, the desire for additional space (a comment of those in rooms of varied dimensions) in part may be a response to the concentration of children. In fact, teachers were in the thick of activity, perhaps acting as a magnet, perhaps encouraging close proximity as a means of surveillance and control. The result was congestion around a set of points anchored by the teacher's presence at the front of the room. Within these rooms *front* can mean many things, a reflection of past classroom experiences, the opportunity to control access to the door, the proximity of the blackboard to name a few possibilities. Yet a prominent feature of open classrooms is the freedom of mobility offered to teachers. The blackboard does not have to function as the primary teaching mode, nor does the teacher's desk have to be his/her home base. Rather, the individualized and informal use of space is offered to teachers much as to pupils. Despite this, a narrow "home range" characterized all the teachers studied. Apparently, powerful holdovers in the form and perception of the room continued to shape use of the space by the teachers, and in turn by the children as well.

There were unintended consequences of using space in this way. The teacher was on "center stage" much of the day, available for questions and comments and mediating conflicts that occurred in the surrounding cluster of children. For the children there seemed to be constraints on the process of matching what they wanted to do with the most appropriate sites. In part, this could have been a function of the inadequacy of other areas. A review of the rooms suggests that although there were work surfaces in or near the teacher's zones, other tables were available in other areas. The desire for private places, despite many sectors that, in fact, were sparsely used, suggests that there were limits on the freedom to use space. It is necessary to question the meaning of the convergence against functioning of the rooms over time, the aspirations of the teachers and the available literature on density effects.

Convergence can be viewed on a number of levels. On one level it is merely concentration of persons and activities that can coexist without interference. On another level it implies congestion, that is, limits on shared spaces and resources, but minimal accommodation to coordinate individual and group efforts. The third level is the phenomenological experience of limits on personal freedom, commonly identified as crowding. Although it is not possible to separate each of these levels in the data gathered, there is a clear impression that each existed within the classrooms studied, and that at any moment in time, more than one level could be operating.

It was often possible to see concurrent activities, some involving individuals, some involving groups, accompanied by an overlay of interaction where children and teacher apparently could accomplish what they set out to do enhanced or unaffected by social contacts. Similarly, there were instances of interference, where the sounds, movement, and variety of tasks went beyond what could be easily accommodated by individual children. Longitudinal data reveal a wide range of working styles. What might be a stimulating setting for one child could be overload and disturbance for another. There were individual children who were distracted by small things, while others would be absorbed in the midst of considerable activity. However, evidence that crowding was experienced at times emerges from interview comments regarding noise, lack of privacy, and insufficient room.

We are only beginning to understand the complex consequences of crowding on social interaction and cognitive tasks. The results of studies are almost as varied as the research strategies. Most studies deal with very young children, generally examining the impact of crowding on free play. The day-by-day effects of crowding are rarely if ever analyzed, so that making direct application to a real-life classroom setting must be approached with caution.

Although a number of studies with children suggest stressful reactions to the presence of many others and/or limited space, reactions vary with the age, composition, and size of the groups involved (see, for example, Hutt & Vaizey, 1966; McGrew, 1972; Loo, 1972; Rohe & Patterson, 1974). There is some experimental evidence that for young children concentration about the teacher decreases visual attention to him/her (Krantz & Risley, 1972).

A multimethod analysis of open classrooms reveals a complex relationship between physical structure and arrangement, teacher and student working styles, and distribution over space. Use of the setting cannot be understood without considering each component of the system. The *open* as applied to classrooms is not a specific interior design or a type of program. Rather, it emerges as a process of increased choices and degrees of environmental awareness. These choices may vary as we look at different open classrooms, but the alternatives are much more numerous than the set working spaces and highly routinized work in traditional schools and programs. In the open classrooms we studied, each teacher articulated the choices along different dimensions. The convergence described in the profile of classroom activities suggest some mixed motives and unintended consequences that, in turn, limited freedom within the room. Immersed as they were in ongoing activities, it was difficult for occupants to stand apart and evaluate what was taking place. Yet contacts with teachers clearly pointed to growing awareness of the many elements within the room that participated in the open classroom process. Research results point up the particular need for a deliberate planning process in which each of the elements—teacher, children, activities, group size, time, and physical arrangements—can be considered in the context of immediate and long-range goals.

Part VIII

The City and Urban Design

The conceptual and empirical nexus for understanding human existence in a complex industrialized society is the "city." And in this respect cities are not just social, political, economic, and cultural systems, but geographical and physical systems as well. Although not all built environments are necessarily the modern urban setting we call the city, it is difficult not to think of this setting when reference is made to the individual's built environment. Furthermore, with each passing decade, it becomes patent that the city or urban setting is not *a* way of life but *the* way of life. Supported by a continuing output of an inexorable advancing technology, urbanism is increasing at an accelerated rate, and with such growth there continues to emerge a host of environmental problems that in turn cast considerable doubt on the viability and efficacy of this way of life.

The concern with and study of human behavior and experience in relation to the urban setting is by no means a new scientific endeavor. Ever since their emergence

491

as scientific fields of inquiry, anthropology, sociology, political science, economics, and other behavioral sciences have been interested in the dynamics of urban life as the analytic locus for defining and understanding the particular problems that identify their domains of interest. Yet the city, conceived analytically and studied empirically in each of these disciplines, is always viewed as a sociocultural system "aided and abetted" by a system of technology. Interest in the city as a physical system, as a world of sights, sounds, smells, and other forms of stimulation in relation to a variety of objects and places—for example, buildings, streets, hospitals, theaters, schools, and so on—was frequently ignored. To some degree sociologists who in time become identified as social ecologists and demographers gave considerable attention to residential location and particularly the quality of the urban neighborhood as a determinant of social pathology. But here too, as in many other subsequent theoretical and research endeavors focused on the effects of urban life, what was investigated was one social variable in relation to others, for example, neighborhood—and therefore social class and other social variables—in relation to crime rate. The problem of the direct influence of the physical setting itself on behavior and experience was virtually never considered.

Over the last three decades, all that appears to be changing. There has been an increasing interest on the part of behavioral scientists in the influence of the city—as a space and place—on the behavior and experiences of people. To some extent these researchers were both lured and "pushed" into this problem area by the increasing demand of architects, designers, and planners to know more about what their clients needed, wanted, and expected in the succession of "built environments" that characterized living in a city; but perhaps more important, by the environmental crisis of the 1960s and the increasing evidence of serious health problems resulting from the pressure and pace of modern city life.

From the point of view of the environmental psychologist this shift in emphasis from the city as a social system to the city as a physical system is an important and necessary step for understanding and solving many of the problems we identify with life in the city. The fact is that crowding, noise, tall buildings, air pollution, housing decay, and any number of other physical setting factors do have consequences, not just for how individuals behave, but how they feel. The mere size and numbers of people in a large city—its alleged impersonal character—has long been recognized as a significant influence in these respects. As the English poet Charles Colton pointed out:

If you would be known, and not know, vegetate in a village;
If you would know, and not be known, live in a city. (Lacon, Vol. 1, No. 334)

For all the more recent concern with the city as a pattern of interlocking and interrelated physical settings that shape and define to some degree what individuals do, think, and feel, the actual output of empirical research has been relatively small. Furthermore, where research or theoretical formulations have been undertaken and reported—including those presented in this section of the present volume—they still tend in many instances to use the physical setting as a backdrop against which social and cultural variables are related to each other; or they emphasize the behavior or experiences of the inhabitants, rather than the physical setting and its significant design characteristics. What kinds of research are sorely needed?

First and perhaps foremost is research on what for want of a better phrase can be described as "physical style of life." In the understandably great concern of researchers and practitioners with the problems of urban stress, they have turned their attention to the conspicuous threats to human life and human dignity. Without denying the significance of noise, urban blight, crowding, and air pollution in understanding the behavior and experience of a city's residents, the fact is that from an analytic point of view they do not by themselves reveal the basic processes that underlie person/environmental relationships in an urban setting. In fact, even if all of these urban problems disappeared, one would still not know whether urban life was good for its inhabitants, without examining these basic processes. To reveal them requires systematic investigations of behavior and experience as it occurs in the mundane experiences of the person. This means, then, that all physical settings require study: transportation facilities, work settings, recreational facilities, outpatient clinics, public eating facilities, apartment dwellings, and so on.

The need to study and integrate the findings based on the study of all of these settings cannot be stressed too strongly. For in fact it is in their unique properties and in the interrelationships among these properties that the nature and meaning of the urban style of life in its physical sense will be revealed. The essential point is that the "city dweller" is socialized not just by people, personalities, and social groups, but by spaces and places; by physical systems that are internalized as conceptions of time, movement, distance, familiarity, safety, beauty, and purpose that provide structure for that individual (and his existence) we call the "urban dweller."

The work of Lofland, part of which is presented in this section, is an important breakthrough in terms of understanding how in spite of the diversity and complexity of physical style of life in urban settings, individual experience and behavior are functional. How does the individual become identified and in turn identify others in order to establish meaningful patterns of social interaction in a setting where the number of people, activities, functions, and "living requirements" are well beyond the physical and social capacities of the single person? But there are still other questions to be answered. These involve considerations of expressive behavior, movement, and awareness among the "passersby" of a city. In many urban settings, the rule rather than the exception is large numbers of individuals either stationary or in movement in a variety of physical settings pursuing similar but independent purposes. Whether the term "crowds" or "crowding" is used, what seems to occur is a nonovert strategic social interaction that serves to maintain the integrity and functional character of these nonpersonal "interpersonal" relationships. Oddly enough, urban dwellers are highly skilled in these forms of behaviors, yet we know little about how they are learned, what happens when they are disrupted, and the limits they impose or allow in the design of a variety of public spaces and places in large urban settings. Ostensibly the "dynamics" of the behavior and experience of the individual that has been conceptualized as "personal space" must be considered in relation to these settings as well as in relation to those of a more personal and functional nature.

There is still another set of problems that barely have had their surface scratched by systematic research. It is rather paradoxical that poets, playwrights, novelists, and even social practitioners, have given more attention to the problem of "identity" with cities than behavioral scientists. Although there are many factors that undoubtedly contribute to the desire of individuals to be part of and identified with large urban settings, there can be no question that the design and physical characteristics of cities play an important role in this aspect of self-identity. *Place identity* or the sense that individuals have that who and what they are depends on their being in the appropriate places or behavior settings is necessarily rooted in the properties of a city as a physical setting.

If urbanism is not merely today's way of life but tomorrow's as well, then the study of the city as the physical setting for human life must assume the highest research priority for environmental psychologists and other behavioral scientists. Given the inexorable advancing technology of the past which produced its unintended as well as its expected consequences, we can expect such consequences even more so in the future. The failure to know what is coming reflects not so much a lack of planning as a lack of understanding. To the extent that environmental psychologists can reveal both the structure and process that defines person/environmental interactions in the complex urban setting we call the city, to that degree will a society be able both to plan and to understand the consequences of changes it introduces into the day-to-day physical style of life of the individual.

37. The Experience of Living in Cities
STANLEY MILGRAM

"When I first came to New York it seemed like a nightmare. As soon as I got off the train at Grand Central I was caught up in pushing, shoving crowds on 42nd Street. Sometimes people bumped into me without apology; what really frightened me was to see two people literally engaged in combat for possession of a cab. Why were they so rushed? Even drunks on the street were bypassed without a glance. People didn't seem to care about each other at all."

This statement represents a common reaction to a great city, but it does not tell the whole story. Obviously cities have great appeal because of their variety, eventfulness, possibility of choice, and the stimulation of an intense atmosphere that many individuals find a desirable background to their lives. Where face-to-face contacts are important, the city offers unparalleled possibilities. It has been calculated by the Regional Plan Association (New York Times, June 15, 1969) that in Nassau County, a suburb of New York City, an individual

Barbara Bergen worked closely with me in preparing the present version of this article. I wish to thank Dr. Gary Winkel, editor of *Environment and Behavior*, for useful suggestions and advice.

From *Science*, Vol. 167, March 13, 1970, 1461–1468. Copyright 1970 by the American Association for the Advancement of Science.

can meet 11,000 others within a 10-minute radius of his office by foot or car. In Newark, a moderate-sized city, he can meet more than 20,000 persons within this radius. But in midtown Manhattan he can meet fully 220,000. So there is an order-of-magnitude increment in the communication possibilities offered by a great city. That is one of the bases of its appeal and, indeed, of its functional necessity. The city provides options that no other social arrangement permits. But there is a negative side also, as we shall see.

Granted that cities are indispensable in complex society, we may still ask what contribution psychology can make to understanding the experience of living in them. What theories are relevant? How can we extend our knowledge of the psychological aspects of life in cities through empirical inquiry? If empirical inquiry is possible, along what lines should it proceed? In short, where do we start in constructing urban theory and in laying out lines of research?

Observation is the indispensable starting point. Any observer in the streets of midtown Manhattan will see (i) large numbers of people, (ii) a high population density, and (iii) heterogeneity of population. These three factors need to be at the root of any sociopsychological theory of city life, for they condition all aspects of our experience in the metropolis. Louis Wirth (1938)[1], if not the first to point to these factors, is nonetheless the sociologist who relied most heavily on them in his analysis of the city. Yet, for a psychologist, there is something unsatisfactory about Wirth's theoretical variables. Numbers, density, and heterogeneity are demographic facts but they are not yet psychological facts. They are external to the individual. Psychology needs an idea that links the individual's *experience* to the demographic circumstances of urban life.

One link is provided by the concept of overload. This term, drawn from systems analysis, refers to a system's inability to process inputs from the environment because there are too many inputs for the system to cope with, or because successive inputs come so fast that input A cannot be processed when input B is presented. When overload is present, adaptations occur. The system must set priorities and make choices. A may be processed first while B is kept in abeyance, or one input may be sacrificed altogether. City life, as we experience it, constitutes a continuous set of encounters with overload, and of resultant adaptations. Overload characteristically deforms daily life on several levels, inpinging on role performance, the evolution of social norms, cog-

nitive functioning, and the use of facilities.

The concept has been implicit in several theories of urban experience. In 1903 George Simmel (1950) pointed out that, since urban dwellers come into contact with vast numbers of people each day, they conserve psychic energy by becoming acquainted with a far smaller proportion of people than their rural counterparts do, and by maintaining more superficial relationships even with these acquaintances. Wirth (1938) points specifically to "the superficiality, the anonymity, and the transitory character of urban social relations."

One adaptive response to overload, therefore, is the allocation of less time to each input. A second adaptive mechanism is disregard of low-priority inputs. Principles of selectivity are formulated such that investment of time and energy are reserved for carefully defined inputs (the urbanite disregards the drunk sick on the street as he purposefully navigates through the crowd). Third, boundaries are redrawn in certain social transactions so that the overloaded system can shift the burden to the other party in the exchange; thus, harried New York bus drivers once made change for customers, but now this responsibility has been shifted to the client, who must have the exact fare ready. Fourth, reception is blocked off prior to entrance into a system; city dwellers increasingly use unlisted telephone numbers to prevent individuals from calling them, and a small but growing number resort to keeping the telephone off the hook to prevent incoming calls. More subtly, a city dweller blocks inputs by assuming an unfriendly countenance, which discourages others from initiating contact. Additionally, social screening devices are interposed between the individual and environmental inputs (in a town of 5000 anyone can drop in to chat with the mayor, but in the metropolis organizational screening devices deflect inputs to other destinations). Fifth, the intensity of inputs is diminished by filtering devices, so that only weak and relatively superficial forms of involvement with others are allowed. Sixth,

[1] Wirth's ideas have come under heavy criticism by contemporary city planners, who point out that the city is broken down into neighborhoods, which fulfill many of the functions of small towns. See, for example, H. J. Gans, 1968; J. Jacobs, 1961; G. D. Suttles, 1968.

specialized institutions are created to absorb inputs that would otherwise swamp the individual (welfare departments handle the financial needs of a million individuals in New York City, who would otherwise create an army of mendicants continuously importuning the pedestrian). The interposition of institutions between the individual and the social world, a characteristic of all modern society, and most notably of the large metropolis, has its negative side. It deprives the individual of a sense of direct contact and spontaneous integration in the life around him. It simultaneously protects and estranges the individual from his social environment.

Many of these adaptive mechanisms apply not only to individuals but to institutional systems as well, as Meier (1962) has so brilliantly shown in connection with the library and the stock exchange.

In sum, the observed behavior of the urbanite in a wide range of situations appears to be determined largely by a variety of adaptations to overload. I now deal with several specific consequences of responses to overload, which make for differences in the tone of city and town.

Social Responsibility

The principal point of interest for a social psychology of the city is that moral and social involvement with individuals is necessarily restricted. This is a direct and necessary function of excess of input over capacity to process. Such restriction of involvement runs a broad spectrum from refusal to become involved in the needs of another person, even when the person desperately needs assistance, through refusal to do favors, to the simple withdrawal of courtesies (such as offering a lady a seat, or saying "sorry" when a pedestrian collision occurs). In any transaction more and more details need to be dropped as the total number of units to be processed increases

and assaults an instrument of limited processing capacity.

The ultimate adaptation to an overloaded social environment is to totally disregard the needs, interests, and demands of those whom one does not define as relevant to the satisfaction of personal needs, and to develop highly efficient perceptual means of determining whether an individual falls into the category of friend or stranger. The disparity in the treatment of friends and strangers ought to be greater in cities than in towns; the time allotment and willingness to become involved with those who have no personal claim on one's time is likely to be less in cities than in towns.

Bystander intervention in crises. The most striking deficiencies in social responsibility in cities occur in crisis situations, such as the Genovese murder in Queens. In 1964, Catherine Genovese, coming home from a night job in the early hours of an April morning, was stabbed repeatedly, over an extended period of time. Thirty-eight residents of a respectable New York City neighborhood admit to having witnessed at least a part of the attack, but none went to her aid or called the police until after she was dead. Milgram and Hollander, writing in *The Nation* (1964), analyzed the event in these terms:

Urban friendships and associations are not primarily formed on the basis of physical proximity. A person with numerous close friends in different parts of the city may not know the occupant of an adjacent apartment. This does not mean that a city dweller has fewer friends than does a villager, or knows fewer persons who will come to his aid; however, it does mean that his allies are not constantly at hand. Miss Genovese required immediate aid from those physically present. There is no evidence that the city had deprived Miss Genovese of human associations, but the friends who might have rushed to her side were miles from the scene of her tragedy.

Further, it is known that her cries for help were not directed to a specific person; they were general. But only individuals can act, and as the cries were not specifically directed, no particular person felt a special responsibility. The crime and the failure of community response seem absurd to us. At the time, it may well have seemed equally absurd to the Kew Gardens residents that not one of of the neighbors would have called the police. A collective paralysis may have developed from the belief of each of the witnesses that someone else must surely have taken that obvious step.

Latané and Darley (1969) have reported laboratory approaches to the study of bystander intervention and have established experimentally the following principle, the larger the number of bystanders, the less the likelihood that any one of them will intervene in an emergency. Gaertner and Bickman (unpublished) of The City University of New York have extended the bystander studies to an examination of help across ethnic lines. Blacks and whites, with clearly identifiable accents, called strangers (through what the caller represented as an error in telephone dialing), gave them a plausible story of being stranded on an outlying highway without more dimes, and asked the stranger to call a garage. The experimenters found that the white callers had a significantly better chance of obtaining assistance than the black callers. This suggests that ethnic allegiance may well be another means of coping with overload: the city dweller can reduce excessive demands and screen out urban heterogeneity by responding along ethnic lines; overload is made more manageable by limiting the "span of sympathy."

In any quantitative characterization of the social texture of city life, a necessary first step is the application of such experimental methods as these to field situations in large cities and small towns. Theorists argue that the indifference shown in the Genovese case would not be found in a small town, but in the absence of solid experimental evidence the question remains an open one.

More than just callousness prevents bystanders from participating in altercations between people. A rule of urban life is respect for other people's emotional and social privacy, perhaps because physical privacy is so hard to achieve. And in situations for which the standards are heterogeneous, it is much harder to know whether taking an active role is unwarranted meddling or an appropriate response to a critical situation. If a husband and wife are quarreling in public at what point should a bystander step in? On the one hand, the heterogeneity of the city produces substantially greater tolerance about behavior, dress, and codes of ethics than is generally found in the small town, but this diversity also encourages people to withhold aid for fear of antagonizing the participants or crossing an inappropriate and difficult-to-define line.

Moreover, the frequency of demands present in the city gives rise to norms of noninvolvement. There are practical limitations to the Samaritan impulse in a major city. If a citizen attended to every needy person, if he were sensitive to and acted on every altruistic impulse that was evoked in the city, he could scarely keep his own affairs in order.

Willingness to trust and assist strangers. We now move away from crisis situations to less urgent examples of social responsibility. For it is not only in situations of dramatic need but in the ordinary, everyday willingness to lend a hand that the city dweller is said to be deficient relative to his small-town cousin. The comparative method must be used in any empirical examination of this question. A commonplace social situation is staged in an urban setting and in a small town—a situation to which a subject can respond by either extending help or withholding it. The responses in town and city are compared.

One factor in the purported unwillingness of urbanites to be helpful to strangers may well be their heightened sense of physical (and emotional) vulnerability—a feeling that is supported by urban crime statistics. A key test for distinguishing between city and town behavior, therefore, is determining how city dwellers compare with town dwellers in offering aid' that increases their personal vulnerability and requires some trust of strangers. Altman, Levine, Nadien, and Villena (unpublished) of The City University of New York devised a study to compare the behaviors of city and town dwellers in this respect. The criterion used in this study was the willingness of householders to allow strangers to enter their home to use the telephone. The student investigators individually rang doorbells, explained that they had misplaced the address of a friend nearby, and asked to use the phone. The investigators (two males and two females) made 100 requests for entry into homes in the city and 60 requests in the small towns. The results for middle-income housing developments in Manhattan were compared with data for several small towns (Stony Point, Spring Valley, Ramapo, Nyack, New City, and West Clarkstown) in Rockland County, outside of New York City. As Table 37–1 shows, in all cases there was a sharp increase in the proportion of entries achieved by an experimenter when he moved from the city to a small town. In the most extreme case the experimenter was five times as likely to gain admission to homes in a small town as to homes in Manhattan. Although the female experimenters had notably greater success both in cities and in towns than the male experimenters had, each of the four students did at least twice as well in towns as in cities. This suggests that the city-town distinction overrides even the predictably greater fear of male strangers than of female ones.

The lower level of helpfulness by city

TABLE 37–1. *Percentage of entries achieved by investigators for city and town dwellings (see text).*

Experimenter	Entries achieved (%)	
	City*	Small town†
Male		
No. 1	16	40
No. 2	12	60
Female		
No. 3	40	87
No. 4	40	100

* Number of requests for entry, 100.
† Number of requests for entry, 60.

dwellers seems due in part to recognition of the dangers of living in Manhattan, rather than to mere indifference or coldness. It is significant that 75 percent of all the city respondents received and answered messages by shouting through closed doors and by peering out through peepholes; in the towns, by contrast, about 75 percent of the respondents opened the door.

Supporting the experimenters' quantitative results was their general observation that the town dwellers were noticeably more friendly and less suspicious than the city dwellers. In seeking to explain the reasons for the greater sense of psychological vulnerability city dwellers feel, above and beyond the differences in crime statistics, Villena (unpublished) points out that, if a crime is committed in a village, a resident of a neighboring village may not perceive the crime as personally relevant, though the geographic distance may be small, whereas a criminal act committed anywhere in the city, though miles from the city-dwellers' home is still verbally located within the city; thus, Villena says, "the inhabitant of the city possesses a larger vulnerable space."

Civilities. Even at the most superficial level of involvement—the exercise of everyday civilities—urbanites are reputedly deficient. People bump into each other and often do not apologize. They knock over another person's packages and, as often as not, proceed on their way with a grumpy exclamation instead of an offer of assistance. Such behavior, which many visitors to great cities find distasteful, is less common, we are told, in smaller communities, where traditional courtesies are more likely to be observed.

In some instances it is not simply that, in the city, traditional courtesies are violated; rather, the cities develop new norms of noninvolvement. These are so well defined and so deeply a part of city life that *they* constitute the norms people are reluctant to violate. Men are actually embarrassed to give up a seat on the subway to an old woman; they mumble "I was getting off anyway," instead of making the gesture in a straightforward and gracious way. These norms develop because everyone realizes that, in situations of high population density, people cannot implicate themselves in each others' affairs, for to do so would create conditions of continual distraction which would frustrate purposeful action.

In discussing the effects of overload I do not imply that at every instant the city dweller is bombarded with an unmanageable number of inputs, and that his responses are determined by the excess of input at any given instant. Rather, adaptation occurs in the form of gradual evolution of norms of behavior. Norms are evolved in response to frequent discrete experiences of overload; they persist and become generalized modes of responding.

Overload on cognitive capacities: anonymity. That we respond differently toward those whom we know and those who are strangers to us is a truism. An eager patron aggressively cuts in front of someone in a long movie line to save time only to confront a friend; he then behaves sheepishly. A man is involved in an automobile ac-

cident caused by another driver, emerges from his car shouting in rage, then moderates his behavior on discovering a friend driving the other car. The city dweller, when walking through the midtown streets, is in a state of continual anonymity vis-à-vis the other pedestrians.

Anonymity is part of a continuous spectrum ranging from total anonymity to full acquaintance, and it may well be that measurement of the precise degrees of anonymity in cities and towns would help to explain important distinctions between the quality of life in each. Conditions of full acquaintance, for example, offer security and familiarity, but they may also be stifling, because the individual is caught in a web of established relationships. Conditions of complete anonymity, by contrast, provide freedom from routinized social ties, but they may also create feelings of alienation and detachment.

Empirically one could investigate the proportion of activities in which the city dweller or the town dweller is known by others at given times in his daily life, and the proportion of activities in the course of which he interacts with individuals who know him. At his job, for instance, the city dweller may be known to as many people as his rural counterpart. However, when he is not fulfilling his occupational role—say, when merely traveling about the city—the urbanite is doubtless more anonymous than his rural counterpart.

Limited empirical work on anonymity has begun. Zimbardo (1969) has tested whether the social anonymity and impersonality of the big city encourage greater vandalism than do small towns. Zimbardo arranged for one automobile to be left for 64 hours near the Bronx campus of New York University and for a counterpart to be left for the same number of hours near Stanford University in Palo Alto. The license plates on the two cars were removed and the hoods were opened, to provide "releaser cues" for potential vandals. The New York car was stripped of all movable parts within the first 24 hours, and by the end of 3 days was only a hunk of metal .rubble. Unexpectedly, however, most of the destruction occurred during daylight hours, usually under the scrutiny of observers, and the leaders in the vandalism were well-dressed, white adults. The Palo Alto car was left untouched.

Zimbardo attributes the difference in the treatment accorded the two cars to the "acquired feelings of social anonymity provided by life in a city like New York," and he supports his conclusions with several other anecdotes illustrating casual, wanton vandalism in the city. In any comparative study of the effects of anonymity in city and town, however, there must be satisfactory control for other confounding factors: the large number of drug addicts in a city like New York; the higher proportion of slum-dwellers in the city; and so on.

Another direction for empirical study is investigation of the beneficial effects of anonymity. The impersonality of city life breeds its own tolerance for the private lives of the inhabitants. Individuality and even eccentricity, we may assume, can flourish more readily in the metropolis than in the small town. Stigmatized persons may find it easier to lead comfortable lives in the city, free of the constant scrutiny of neighbors. To what degree can this assumed difference between city and town be shown empirically? Judith Waters (unpublished), at The City University of New York, hypothesized that avowed homosexuals would be more likely to be accepted as tenants in a large city than in small towns, and she dispatched letters from homosexuals and from normal individuals to real estate agents in cities and towns across the country. The results of her study were inconclusive. But the general idea of examining the protective benefits of city life to the stigmatized ought to be pursued.

Role behavior in cities and towns. Another product of urban overload is the adjustment in roles made by urbanites in daily inter-actions. As Wirth has said (1938): "Urbanites meet one another in highly segmental roles. . . . They are less dependent upon particular persons, and their dependence upon others is confined to a highly fractionalized aspect of the other's round of activity." This tendency is particularly noticeable in transactions between customers and individuals offering professional or sales services. The owner of a country store has time to become well acquainted with his dozen-or-so daily customers, but the girl at the checkout counter of a busy A&P, serving hundreds of customers a day, barely has time to toss the green stamps into one customer's shopping bag before the next customer confronts her with his pile of groceries.

Meier, in his stimulating analysis of the city (1962), discusses several adaptations a system may make when confronted by inputs that exceed its capacity to process them. Meier argues that, according to the principle of competition for scarce resources, the scope and time of the transaction shrink as customer volume and daily turnover rise. This, in fact, is what is meant by the "brusque" quality of city life. New standards have developed in cities concerning what levels of services are appropriate in business transactions (see Figure 37-1).

McKenna and Morgenthau (unpublished), in a seminar at The City University of New York, devised a study (i) to compare the willingness of city dwellers and small-town dwellers to do favors for strangers that entailed expenditure of a small amount of time and slight inconvenience but no personal vulnerability, and (ii) to determine whether the more compartmentalized, transitory relationships of the city would make urban salesgirls less likely than small-town salesgirls to carry out, for strangers, tasks not related to their customary roles.

To test for differences between city dwellers and small-town dwellers, a simple experiment was devised in which persons

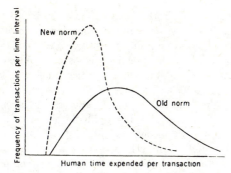

FIGURE 37-1. Changes in the demand for time for a given task when the overall transaction frequency increases in a social system. [Reprinted with permission from R. L. Meier, *A Communications Theory of Urban Growth*, 1962. Copyrighted by M.I.T. Press, 1962].

from both settings were asked (by telephone) to perform increasingly onerous favors for anonymous strangers.

Within the cities (Chicago, New York, and Philadelphia), half the calls were to housewives and the other half to salesgirls in women's apparel shops; the division was the same for the 37 small towns of the study, which were in the same states as the cites. Each experimenter represented herself as a long-distance caller who had, through error, been connected with the respondent by the operator. The experimenter began by asking for simple information about the weather for purposes of travel. Next the experimenter excused herself on some pretext (asking the respondent to "please hold on"), put the phone down for almost a full minute, and then picked it up again and asked the respondent to provide the phone number of a hotel or motel in her vicinity at which the experimenter might stay during a forthcoming visit. Scores were assigned the subjects on the basis of how helpful they had been. McKenna summarizes her results in this manner:

People in the city, whether they are engaged in a specific job or not, are less helpful and informative than people in small towns; . . . People at home, regardless of where they live, are less helpful and informative than people working in shops.

However, the absolute level of cooperativeness for urban subjects was found to be quite high, and does not accord with the stereotype of the urbanite as aloof, self-centered, and unwilling to help strangers. The quantitative differences obtained by McKenna and Morgenthau are less great than one might have expected. This again points up the need for extensive empirical research in rural-urban differences, research that goes far beyond that provided in the few illustrative pilot studies presented here. At this point we have very limited objective evidence on differences in the quality of social encounters in city and small town.

But the research needs to be guided by unifying theoretical concepts. As I have tried to demonstrate, the concept of overload helps to explain a wide variety of contrasts between city behavior and town behavior: (i) the diffences in role enactment (the tendency of urban dwellers to deal with one another in highly segmented, functional terms and of urban sales personnel to devote limited time and attention to their customers); (ii) the evolution of urban norms quite different from traditional town values (such as the acceptance of noninvolvement, impersonality, and aloofness in urban life); (iii) the adaptation of the urban dweller's cognitive processes (his inability to identify most of the people he sees daily, his screening of sensory stimuli, his development of blasé attitudes toward deviant or bizarre behavior, and his selectivity in responding to human demands); and (iv) the competition for scarce facilities in the city (the subway rush; the fight for taxis; traffic jams; standing in line to await services). I suggest that contrasts between city and rural behavior probably reflect the responses of similar people to very different situations, rather than intrinsic differences in the personalities of rural and city dwellers. The city is a situation to which individuals respond adaptively.

Further Aspects of Urban Experience

Some features of urban experience do not fit neatly into the system of analysis presented thus far. They are no less important for that reason. The issues raised next are difficult to treat in quantitative fashion. Yet I prefer discussing them in a loose way to excluding them because appropriate language and data have not yet been developed. My aim is to suggest how phenomena such as "urban atmosphere" can be pinned down through techniques of measurement.

The "atmosphere" of great cities.   The contrast in the behavior of city and town dwellers has been a natural starting point for urban social scientists. But even among great cities there are marked differences in "atmosphere." The tone, pacing, and texture of social encounters are different in London and New York, and many persons willingly make financial sacrifices for the privilege of living within a specific urban atmosphere which they find pleasing or stimulating. A second perspective in the study of cities, therefore, is to define exactly what is meant by the atmosphere of a city and to pinpoint the factors that give rise to it. It may seem that urban atmosphere is too evanescent a quality to be reduced to a set of measurable variables, but I do not believe the matter can be judged before substantial effort has been made in this direction. It is obvious that any such approach must be comparative. It makes no sense at all to say that New York is "vibrant" and "frenetic" unless one has some specific city in mind as a basis of comparison.

In an undergraduate tutorial that I conducted at Harvard University some years ago, New York, London, and Paris were selected as reference points for attempts to measure urban atmosphere. We began with a simple question: Does any consensus exist about the qualities that typify given cities? To answer this question one could undertake a content analysis of travelbook, literary, and journalistic accounts of cities. A second approach, which we adopted, is to ask people to characterize (with descriptive terms and accounts of typical experiences) cities they have lived in or visited. In advertisements placed in the *New York Times* and the *Harvard Crimson* we asked people to give us accounts of specific incidents in London, Paris, or New York that best illuminated the character of that particular city. Questionnaires were then developed, and administered to persons who were familiar with at least two of the three cities.

Some distinctive patterns emerged (Abuza, unpublished). The distinguishing themes concerning New York, for example, dealt with its diversity, its great size, its pace and level of activity, its cultural and entertainment opportunities, and the heterogeneity and segmentation ("ghettoization") of its population. New York elicited more descriptions in terms of physical qualities, pace, and emotional impact than Paris or London did, a fact which suggests that these are particularly important aspects of New York's ambiance.

A contrasting profile emerges for London: in this case respondents placed far greater emphasis on their interactions with the inhabitants than on physical surroundings. There was near unanimity on certain themes: those dealing with the tolerance and courtesy of London's inhabitants. One respondent said:

When I was 12, my grandfather took me to the British Museum . . . one day by tube and recited the *Aeneid* in Latin for my benefit. . . . He is rather deaf, speaks very loudly and it embarrassed the hell out of me, until I realized that nobody was paying any attention. Londoners are extremely worldly and tolerant.

In contrast, respondents who described New Yorkers as aloof, cold, and rude referred to such incidents as the following:

I saw a boy of 19 passing out anti-war leaflets to passersby. When he stopped at a corner, a man dressed in a business suit walked by him at a brisk pace, hit the boy's arm, and scattered the leaflets all over the street. The man kept walking at the same pace down the block.

We need to obtain many more such descriptions of incidents, using careful methods of sampling. By the application of factor-analytic techniques, relevant dimensions for each city can be discerned.

The responses for Paris were about equally divided between responses concerning its inhabitants and those regarding its physical and sensory attributes. Cafés and parks were often mentioned as contributing to the sense that Paris is a city of amenities, but many respondents complained that Parisians were inhospitable, nasty, and cold.

We cannot be certain, of course, to what degree these statements reflect actual characteristics of the cities in question and to what degree they simply tap the respondents' knowledge of widely held preconceptions. Indeed, one may point to three factors, apart from the actual atmospheres of the cities, that determine the subjects' responses.

1) A person's impression of a given city depends on his implicit standard of comparison. A New Yorker who visits Paris may well describe that city as "leisurely," whereas a compatriot from Richmond, Virginia, may consider Paris too "hectic." Obtaining reciprocal judgment, in which New Yorkers judge Londoners, and Londoners judge New Yorkers, seems a useful way to take into account not only the city being judged but also the home city that serves as the visitor's base line.

2) Perceptions of a city are also affected by whether the observer is a tourist, a newcomer, or a longer-term resident. First, a tourist will be exposed to features of the city different from those familiar to a long-time resident. Second, a prerequisite for adapting to continuing life in a given city seems to be the filtering out of many observations about the city that the newcomer or tourist finds particularly arresting; this selective process seems to be part of the long-term resident's mechanisms for coping with overload. In the interest of psychic economy, the resident simply learns to tune out many aspects of daily life. One method for studying the specific impact of adaptation on perception of the city is to ask several pairs of newcomers and old-timers (one newcomer and one old-timer to a pair) to walk down certain city blocks and then report separately what each has observed.

Additionally, many persons have noted that when travelers return to New York from an extended sojourn abroad they often feel themselves confronted with "brutal ugliness" (Abelson, 1969) and a distinctive, frenetic atmosphere whose contributing details are, for a few hours or days, remarkably sharp and clear. This period of fresh perception should receive special attention in the study of city atmosphere. For, in a few days, details which are initially arresting become less easy to specify. They are assimilated into an increasingly familiar background atmosphere which, though important in setting the tone of things, is difficult to analyze. There is no better point at which to begin the study of city atmosphere than at the moment when a traveler returns from abroad.

3) The popular myths and expectations each visitor brings to the city will also affect the way in which he perceives it (see Strauss, 1968). Sometimes a person's

preconceptions about a city are relatively accurate distillations of its character, but preconceptions may also reinforce myths by filtering the visitor's perceptions to conform with his expectations. Preconceptions affect not only a person's perceptions of a city but what he reports about it.

The influence of a person's urban base line on his perceptions of a given city, the differences between the observations of the long-time inhabitant and those of the newcomer, and the filtering effect of personal expectations and stereotypes raise serious questions about the validity of travelers' reports. Moreover, no social psychologist wants to rely exclusively on verbal accounts if he is attempting to obtain an accurate and objective description of the cities' social texture, pace, and general atmosphere. What he needs to do is to devise means of imbedding objective experimental measures in the daily flux of city life, measures that can accurately index the qualities of a given urban atmosphere.

Experimental Comparisons of Behavior

Roy Feldman (1968) incorporated these principles in a comparative study of behavior toward compatriots and foreigners in Paris, Athens, and Boston. Feldman wanted to see (i) whether absolute levels and patterns of helpfulness varied significantly from city to city, and (ii) whether inhabitants in each city tended to treat compatriots differently from foreigners. He examined five concrete behaviorial episodes, each carried out by a team of native experimenters and a team of American experimenters in the three cities. The episodes involved (i) asking natives of the city for street directions; (ii) asking natives to mail a letter for the experimenter; (iii) asking natives if they had just dropped a dollar bill (or the Greek or French equivalent) when the money actually belonged to the experimenter himself; (iv) deliberately overpaying for goods in a store to see if the

cashier would correct the mistake and return the excess money; and (v) determining whether taxicab drivers overcharged strangers and whether they took the most direct route available.

Feldman's results suggest some interesting contrasts in the profiles of the three cities. In Paris, for instance, certain stereotypes were borne out. Parisian cab drivers overcharged foreigners significantly more often than they overcharged compatriots. But other aspects of the Parisians' behavior were not in accord with American preconceptions: in mailing a letter for a stranger, Parisians treated foreigners significantly better than Athenians or Bostonians did, and, when asked to mail letters that were already stamped, Parisians actually treated foreigners better than they treated compatriots. Similarly, Parisians were significantly more honest than Athenians or Bostonians in resisting the temptation to claim money that was not theirs, and Parisians were the only citizens who were more honest with foreigners than with compatriots in this experiment.

Feldman's studies not only begin to quantify some of the variables that give a city its distinctive texture but they also provide a methodological model for other comparative research. His most important contribution is his successful application of objective, experimental measures to everyday situations, a mode of study which provides conclusions about urban life that are more pertinent than those achieved through laboratory experiments.

Tempo and Pace

Another important component of a city's atmosphere is its tempo or pace, an attribute frequently remarked on but less often studied. Does a city have a frenetic, hectic quality, or is it easygoing and leisurely? In any empirical treatment of this question, it is best to start in a very simple way. Walking speeds of pedestrians in different cities and in cities and towns should be measured and compared. William Berkowitz (personal communication) of Lafayette College has undertaken an extensive series of studies of walking speeds in Philadelphia, New York, and Boston, as well as in small and moderate-sized towns. Berkowitz writes that "there does appear to be a significant linear relation between walking speed and size of municipality, but the absolute size of the difference varies by less than ten percent."

Perhaps the feeling of rapid tempo is due not so much to absolute pedestrian speeds as to the constant need to dodge others in a large city to avoid collisions with other pedestrians. (One basis for computing the adjustments needed to avoid collisions is to hypothesize a set of mechanical manikins sent walking along a city street and to calculate the number of collisions when no adjustments are made. Clearly, the higher the density of manikins the greater the number of collisions per unit of time, or, conversely, the greater the frequency of adjustments needed in higher population densities to avoid collisions.)

Patterns of automobile traffic contribute to a city's tempo. Driving an automobile provides a direct means of translating feelings about tempo into measurable acceleration, and a city's pace should be particularly evident in vehicular velocities, patterns of acceleration, and latency of response to traffic signals. The inexorable tempo of New York is expressed, further, in the manner in which pedestrians stand at busy intersections, impatiently awaiting a change in traffic light, making tentative excursions into the intersection, and frequently surging into the street even before the green light appears.

Visual Components

Hall has remarked (1966) that the physical layout of the city also affects its atmosphere. A gridiron pattern of streets gives the visitor a feeling of rationality, orderliness, and predictability but is sometimes monotonous. Winding lanes or streets branching off at strange angles, with many forks (as in Paris or Greenwich Village), create feelings of surprise and esthetic pleasure, while forcing greater decision-making in plotting one's course. Some would argue that the visual component is all-important—that the "look" of Paris or New York can almost be equated with its atmosphere. To investigate this hypothesis, we might conduct studies in which only blind, or at least blindfolded, respondents were used. We would no doubt discover that each city has a distinctive texture even when the visual component is eliminated.

Sources of Ambiance

Thus far we have tried to pinpoint and measure some of the factors that contribute to the distinctive atmosphere of a great city. But we may also ask, Why do differences in urban atmosphere exist? How did they come about, and are they in any way related to the factors of density, large numbers, and heterogeneity discussed above?

First, there is the obvious factor that, even among great cities, populations and densities differ. The metropolitan areas of New York, London, and Paris, for example, contain 15 million, 12 million, and 8 million persons, respectively. London has average densities of 43 persons per acre, while Paris is more congested, with average densities of 114 persons per acre (P. Hall, 1966). Whatever characteristics are specifically attributable to density are more likely to be pronounced in Paris than in London.

At second factor affecting the atmosphere of cities is the source from which the populations are drawn (Park, Burgess, & McKenzie, 1967). It is a characteristic of great cities that they do not reproduce their own populations, but that their numbers are constantly maintained and augmented by the influx of residents from other parts of the country. This can have a determining effect on the city's atmosphere. For example, Oslo is a city in which almost all of the residents are only one or two generations removed from a purely rural existence, and this contributes to its almost agricultural norms.

A third source of atmosphere is the general national culture. Paris combines adaptations to the demography of cities *and* certain values specific to French culture. New York is a mixture of American values and values that arise as a result of extraordinarily high density and large population.

Finally, one could speculate that the atmosphere of a great city is traceable to the specific historical conditions under which adaptations to urban overload occurred. For example, a city which acquired its mass and density during a period of commercial expansion will respond to new demographic conditions by adaptations designed to serve purely commercial needs. Thus, Chicago, which grew and became a great city under a purely commercial stimulus, adapted in a manner that emphasizes business needs. European capitals, on the other hand, incorporate many of the adaptations which were appropriate to the period of their increasing numbers and density. Because aristocratic values were prevalent at the time of the growth of these cities, the mechanisms developed for coping with overload were based on considerations other than pure efficiency. Thus, the manners, norms, and facilities of Paris and Vienna continue to reflect esthetic values and the idealization of leisure.

Cognitive Maps of Cities

When we speak of "behavioral comparisons" among cities, we must specify which parts of the city are most relevant for sampling purposes. In a sampling of "New Yorkers," should we include residents of Bay Ridge or Flatbush as well as inhabitants of Manhattan? And, if so, how should we weight our sample distribution? One approach to defining relevant boundaries in sampling is to determine which areas form the psychological or cognitive core of the city. We weight our samples most heavily in the areas considered by most people to represent the "essence" of the city.

The psychologist is less interested in the geographic layout of a city or in its political boundaries than in the cognitive representation of the city. Hans Blumenfeld (1969) points out that the perceptual structure of a modern city can be expressed by the "silhouette" of the group of skyscrapers at its center and that of smaller groups of office buildings at its "subcenters" but that urban areas can no longer, because of their vast extent, be experienced as fully articulated sets of streets, squares and space.

In *The Image of the City* (1960), Kevin Lynch created a cognitive map of Boston by interviewing Bostonians. Perhaps his most significant finding was that, while certain landmarks, such as Paul Revere's house and the Boston Common, as well as the paths linking them, are known to almost all Bostonians, vast areas of the city are simply unknown to its inhabitants.

Using Lynch's technique, Donald Hooper (unpublished) created a psychological map of New York from the answers to the study questionnaire on Paris, London, and New York. Hooper's results were similar to those of Lynch: New York appears to have a dense core of well-known landmarks in midtown Manhattan, surrounded by the vast unknown reaches of Queens, Brooklyn, and the Bronx. Times Square, Rockefeller Center, and the Fifth Avenue department stores alone comprise half the places specifically cited by respondents as the haunts in which they spent most of their time. However, outside the midtown area, only scattered landmarks were recognized. Another interesting pattern is evident: even the best-known symbols of New York are relatively self-contained, and the pathways joining them appear to be insignificant on the map.

The psychological map can be used for more than just sampling techniques. Lynch (1960) argues, for instance, that a good city is highly "imageable," having many known symbols joined by widely known pathways, whereas dull cities are gray and nondescript. We might test the relative "imagibility" of several cities by determining the proportion of residents who recognize sampled geographic points and their accompanying pathways.

If we wanted to be even more precise we could construct a cognitive map that would not only show the symbols of the city but would measure the precise degree of cognitive significance of any given point in the city relative to any other. By applying a pattern of points to a map of New York City, for example, and taking photographs from each point, we could determine what proportion of a sample of the city's inhabitants could identity the locale specified by each point (see Figure 37–2). We might even take the subjects blindfolded to a point represented on the map, then remove the blindfold and ask them to identify their location from the view around them.

One might also use psychological maps to gain insight into the differing perceptions of a given city that are held by members of its cultural subgroups, and into the manner in which their perceptions may change. In the earlier stages of life, whites and Negroes alike probably have only a limited view of the city, centering on the immediate neighborhood in which they are raised. In adolescence, however, the field of knowledge of the white teen-ager probably undergoes rapid enlargement; he learns of opportunities in midtown and outlying sections and comes to see himself as functioning in a larger urban field. But the process of ghettoization, to which the black teen-ager is subjected, may well hamper the expansion of his sense of the city. These are speculative notions, but they are readily subject to precise test.

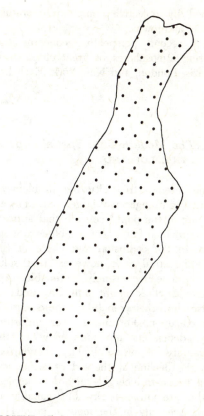

FIGURE 37–2. To create a psychological map of Manhattan, geographic points are sampled, and, from photographs, the subjects attempted to identify the location of each point. To each point a numerical index is assigned indicating the proportion of persons able to identify its location.

Conclusion

I have tried to indicate some organizing theory that starts with the basic facts of city life: large numbers, density, and heterogeneity. These are external to the individual. He experiences these factors as overloads at the level of roles, norms, cognitive functions, and facilities. These overloads lead to adaptive mechanisms which create the distinctive tone and behaviors of city life. These notions, of course, need to be examined by objective comparative studies of cities and towns.

A second perspective concerns the differing atmospheres of great cities, such as Paris, London, and New York. Each has a distinctive flavor, offering a differentiable quality of experience. More precise knowledge of urban atmosphere seems attainable through application of the tools of experimental inquiry.

38. *The Modern City: Spatial Ordering*
LYN H. LOFLAND

In the preindustrial city the problem of identifying strangers was largely solved by an ordering of the populace such that appearances provided fairly accurate clues to identities. In the confusion and chaos of the early industrial city, however, that solution became increasingly untenable. Appearential clues might still be used, of course, but their reliability could not be counted upon. Fortunately (or unfortunately, depending on one's view of the desirability of urban living), concurrent with the decline of the old order, a new order began to emerge—an order incipient in the preindustrial city but capable of dominance only in the modern city. That order . . . is spatial. In great sprawling cities of the twentieth century, location, not appearance, becomes the major key to identification.

Characteristics of the Modern City

The "modern city" like the "preindustrial city" is an intellectual construct. Some contemporary urban settlements—Los Angeles and Detroit (together with their surrounding suburbs),[1] for example—probably are better exemplars of the type than others. And while throughout the world, modern cities are in the process of becoming,[2] it is in the most highly industrialized and technologically developed countries that they have attained their most advanced form. Not surprisingly, then, it is the cities of the United States which will be receiving the major share of our attention in the following pages.

Two of the modern city's many characteristics are of central interest: its tendency toward specialized public-space use and the tendency of its populace to mask their heterogeneity. Again, I ask the reader to bear in mind that any actual city may exhibit one or the other of these characteristics to a greater or lesser degree. My concern here, as throughout, is not with reproducing "reality," but with abstracting from it.

Specialized Public Space Use

In many respects, the ideal of the modern city is like the ideal of a well-ordered

Chapter Four from *A World of Strangers: Order and Action in Urban Public Space*, by Lyn H. Lofland, © 1973 by Basic Books, Inc., Publishers, New York.

[1] The preindustrial city could, more easily than can the modern, be located within its political boundaries. The twentieth-century phenomenon of "massive metropolitanization" pushes the meaningful limits of a city far beyond those which are legally designated. The concept of the "modern city," then, as it is used herein, includes not only the actual "political" entity, but its surrounding satellites and semisatellites as well. The exact end points of the modern city, of course, remain indeterminant.

[2] See, for example, Schwab, 1965, on African cities.

home: a place for everything and everything in its place.[3] And, as in the well-ordered home, the spatial distribution of activities and persons in the city is more complex than it might at first appear. Consider, for example, that in the home, the "place" for an item, person, or activity may be a wing, a floor, a room, a section of a room, a section of a section of a room, and so on. Additionally, certain areas may be designated as appropriate for a multiplicity of purposes and persons (for example, the recreation room). Others may be quite limited (children and dogs stay out of mother's bedroom; don't play in the living room). And, what may be appropriate at one time may not be at another (don't go into the study while brother is working; keep off the kitchen floor—it's just been waxed). In discussing the spatial segregation of the modern city, then, I am not merely making reference to such well-known phenomena as homogeneous neighborhoods or suburbs. I am referring more importantly to the designation of certain smaller locales (a bar, for example) as being appropriate for certain persons and activities; to the designation of different appropriate activities and persons at different times in the same locale (during the New Orleans' Mardi Gras, or New Year's Eve, or Halloween or in the morning rather than evening). I am referring also to the fact that within any given space—say a block-long street—a multiplicity of activities and per-

sons designated as appropriate may exist side by side; that is, who and what are okay here may not be the same as who and what are appropriate next door. In sum, then, I ask the reader to bear in mind that spatial segregation may be in terms of large areas or neighborhoods, in terms of sections within larger areas, in terms of locales or places within sections, in terms of small spaces within locales, in terms of time within any area, section, locale, or small space, and so forth.

The Spatial Segregation of Activities. A good deal of what went on in the public space of the preindustrial city has simply disappeared from the public space of the modern city. It has moved into private or semiprivate quarters. Educating the young is now thought to be an activity requiring isolation and relative quiet and is largely relegated to buildings in which no other doings are permitted. And those few occasions when the young are brought "out in the world" are not always greeted with enthusiasm by the surrounding community. I recall being present at Greenfield Village in Dearborn, Michigan, during an invasion of grade-school age children on a "field trip." From the harried expressions on the faces of the accompanying teachers, the museum's personnel, and the adult visitors, I had the distinct impression that a law outlawing such youthful excursions would have received overwhelming support.

So, too, the elimination of body wastes is no longer tolerated as a public activity. In fact, in the United States there seems to be some tendency to confine it entirely to the home. As Edward T. Hall has noted:

The distribution of public toilets in America reflects our tendency to deny the existence of urgency even with normal physiological needs. I know of no other place in the world where anyone leaving home or office is put to periodic torture because great pains have been taken to hide the location of rest rooms. Yet

---

[3] It should come as no surprise that sociologists "discovered" the spatially segregated city at the same time and in the same place that the spatially segregated city was coming into its own: early twentieth century America. For some peculiar reason, however, sociologists came to believe that spatial segregation was an inevitable "given" in urban development. They even produced a special subarea to handle one of nature's social "constants"; they called it ecology. For a brief history of this development, see R. E. L. Faris, 1967, especially Chapter 4, "Research on the Ecological Structure of the City."

Americans are the people who judge the advancement of others by their plumbing. (Hall, 1959:138).

The exception to this, of course, is the gas station where rest rooms are prominently located and often advertised. Apparently the designers of public facilities are of the opinion that the only Americans who ever have to "go" are those in automobiles. At present, the public elimination activity of the few remaining nonhuman animals in the city—mostly dogs and cats—is still grudgingly tolerated. But the controversies that have emerged in the 1970s in a number of cities over how to handle the "dog mess" problem suggest that even that may eventually be banished.[4]

Nor are the public areas of the city enlivened any longer by punishments and executions. Gone are the whipping post, the gibbet, the stake, the pillory, and the stocks—those artifacts of urban life in "the good old days." The "humanitarian movements" that accompanied industrialization in both England and the United States apparently operated on the motto "out of sight, out of mind," and through their efforts a whole spectrum of man's inhumanities to man moved indoors, behind walls and out of sight.[5]

[4] Along Rio de Janeiro's Copacabana beach, the problem has been solved in a typically modern way by setting aside specialized space for specialized activity. The first "pipi-dog" or dog toilet is under construction ("A Place for the Dogs to Go," *San Francisco Chronicle*, June 30, 1972).

[5] I am here, and throughout this chapter, perhaps overly cynical regarding the humanitarian and reform movements of the nineteenth and twentieth centuries. Many sincere and honestly dedicated individuals were unquestionably involved in them. Nevertheless, a purview of continued injustices and inhumanities in modern industrial nation states suggests to me that such movements succeeded more in hiding cruelty than they did in alleviating it. Relevant works on these movements include

Other activities which added to the hubbub of the public space of the pre-industrial city have simply been rendered unnecessary by modern technology: water collection, garbage and waste disposal, and, in large measure, the distribution and collection of news. The struggle over the use of certain public space for advertising purposes continues, however, as when conservationists and "city beautiful" groups battle mightily with business interests over outdoor billboards and signs.

This is not to suggest that nothing is supposed to go on in the modern city's public space. A great many things are deemed appropriate. There is, however, a tendency to assign certain activities to certain spaces, thus avoiding the "pile up" that was characteristic of the preindustrial city. Some of the more interesting struggles that go on in the contemporary urban settlement have their basis in this tendency toward the avoidance of pile-up. In many cities, for example, the populace has been unable to decide whether streets (as distinct from sidewalks) should be reserved exclusively for pedestrians or exclusively for transportation vehicles. The utopian visions of city planners—with their overground malls and underground streets, or their underground malls and overground streets, or their overground streets and above-ground malls—illustrate clearly this preference for separation.

So, too, soliciting by prostitutes in many cities is tolerated only so long as it can be contained. Having set aside certain public areas for certain activities, city fathers and populace alike look askance at any spill-over. One can be certain that the following newspaper item did not go unattended in city hall:

Hookers are now soliciting on Muni-

Lane, 1967; Schlesinger, 1968; Gusfield, 1963; Flexner, 1970; Gursslin, Hunt, and Roach, 1959–1960; and Adrian, 1961: chap. 3.

[cipal] buses! Explained one to Lenore Cautrelle: "Well, you see, I can't afford a car." (Herb Caen, *San Francisco Chronicle*, April 22, 1970)

But if city hall fails to take the initiative, citizens groups may feel compelled to do so:

A group of actors and actresses, including Joan Hackett, Lee Grant and Peter Falk, yesterday asked Mayor John V. Lindsay to establish a "Red Light" district outside the Times Square area [of New York City] to rid it of *prostitutes and other undesirables.*

In a letter to the Mayor signed by Miss Hackett, the group said, "Quite simply stated, we propose cleaning up the Broadway area now, and when legislation permits, establishing a 'Red Light' district in New York *out of any business area,* but especially [out of] the most exciting theater area in the world." (" 'Red Light' District Requested," *San Francisco Chronicle,* June 20, 1972, p. 54; emphasis added)

Frequently, activity pile-up is controlled by means of licenses and permits. While retail buying and selling remains very much a public activity, it has largely been moved indoors, off the streets and walkways. Certainly much of this movement is due to technological innovations, economic pressures, and the general rationalization of business, but the practice of licensing, and thereby controlling the numbers of street vendors, was undoubtedly of some import as well.[6]

In many cities, entertainment, ceremonials and pageants, religious expressions, and political meetings and debates are thought to be most appropriately undertaken in the

[6] On the development of this practice in nineteenth century Boston, see Lane, 1967:54. See also Anderson, 1961:42 and throughout.

public areas set aside specifically for such purposes: nightclubs, auditoriums, arenas, churches, meeting halls, and so forth. The spilling-over of these activities into streets, parks, playgrounds, and squares is allowed, but controlled by permit. The situation in Detroit, described below, is typical of most modern cities:

You had a story about a bongo drummer getting arrested at Belle Isle beach for playing a musical instrument in a public park. Does that mean I could get ticketed for playing my harmonica in Palmer Park?

D. N.

Yep, also for preaching or speechmaking without a permit. You get pinched if you draw large crowds, disturb others using the park. Penalty is up to $100 fine or 30 days in jail. You will be safe with your harmonica playing if you keep it to yourself. The bongo player didn't. Some 35,000 people were near the beach; hundreds gathered around him. Then gawking motorists created a traffic hazard. As for speechmaking, five parks allow it if you have a permit. If you can't get one, take your soapbox to the front of the Old County Building. You need no permit there, mostly because passerby seldom stop to listen (Action Line, *Detroit Free Press,* July 2, 1966)

Much additional activity that cluttered the public areas of the preindustrial city has, in the modern city, been "controlled" by the simple expedient of making it completely illegal (Stinchcombe, 1963). In one medium-sized American community, for example, among the many acts that are prohibited in public places are the following:

Beg in any public place;
Utter vile, profane or obscene language in any public place;
Engage in any indecent, insulting, im-

moral or obscene conduct in any public place;

Make any immoral exhibition or indecent exposure of his or her person;

Improperly, lewdly or wrongfully accost, ogle, insult, annoy, follow, pursue, lay hands on, or by any gesture, movement of body or otherwise wrongfully molest any person in any public place or public vehicle;

Engage in any disturbance, fight or quarrel in a public place:

Collect or stand in crowds, or arrange, encourage or abet the collection of persons in crowds for illegal or mischievous purposes in any public place;

Jostle or roughly crowd persons in any street, alley, park or public building;

Loiter on any street or sidewalk or in any park or public building or conduct himself in any public place so as to obstruct the free and uninterrupted passage of the public;

Disturb the public peace and quiet by loud, boisterous, or vulgar conduct. (Ann Arbor, Michigan Ordinance Code, Ann Arbor: Municipal Codification Service, Inc., 1957, chap. 108, paragraph 9:62)

Ordinances like these, of course, with their usefully vague wordings can be and are enforced quite selectively. In many instances they probably only legalize practices of spatial segregation which developed independently of the law and which subsequently came to be seen as proper. Thus the fact that these ordinances (and others like them) can be used to control such preindustrial city pastimes as hanging about, begging, or socializing and playing in the street, does not gainsay the fact that the original reduction of these activities was undoubtedly the consequence of forces having nothing at all to do with law.

One of the characteristics of an industrially developed and technologically advanced society is that it tends to keep a rather large proportion of its population tied up in organizationally controlled work and play. The old floating populations, so characteristic of preindustrial and early industrial cities, are, in the modern city, largely eliminated. When enough people are pulled into schools and jobs, and when their few free hours are devoted to home and family or organized recreation, then very little time and very few people are left for hanging about. Nevertheless, this trend toward affiliating the entire population is hardly complete, not even in the United States. Where floating populations still exist, and where hanging about is standard activity, municipal ordinances can and do come into play.[7] Ordinances against loitering and blocking the streets have long been used against young black males (see, for example, Werthman and Piliavin, 1967), and in recent years they have been used against young people more generally. When the existing laws are not deemed sufficient to control newly emergent floaters, emergency measures can always be rushed through:

The anti-hippie "keep-off-the-grass" law in Carmel's [California] public parks is legal the State Court of Appeal said yesterday.

The 2-year-old law has been challenged as discriminatory and as an unconstitutional abridgement of freedom of assembly.

The Carmel City Council passed the law as an "emergency ordinance," in the summer of 1968. It prohibits climbing in trees or lounging on lawns in the parks.

The declaration of emergency left little doubt what the City Council thought it was: "[We] have observed an extraordi-

[7] It is hardly a coincidence that contemporary riots erupt among the remaining unaffiliated floaters. In the United States, these are the young and the poor. The elderly might also be considered in this category. Their reduced physical vigor, however, makes them unlikely candidates for the kind of energy-exertion required in rioting.

nary influx of undesirable and unsanitary visitors to the city, sometimes known as 'hippies,' and find that unless proper regulations are adopted immediately, the use and enjoyment of public property will be jeopardized, if not entirely eliminated."

"The public parks and beaches are, in many cases, rendered unfit for normal public use by the unregulated and uncontrolled conduct of the new transients," the declaration said. (*San Francisco Chronicle,* March 28, 1970)

This same municipality apparently felt, however, that laws, in and of themselves, were insufficient to the danger:

Carmel "welcomes" visitors with a heartwarming pamphlet that tells them what they CAN'T do. For instance, no camping, no sleeping on beaches, no sitting or lying on the grass in Devendorf Park, no panhandling, no vending without a license, no standing around rapping, no staying out after 10:30 p. m. if you're under 18. And if you were planning to hurl the pamphlet away in disgust, don't. No littering. (Herb Caen, *San Francisco Chronicle,* July 30, 1970)

Begging is another activity that in most modern cities has been declared illegal. But like hanging about, its reduction (and in some cities, complete disappearance) has probably been the consequence of extra-legal forces. The distribution of affluence made possible by industrialization, the development of a welfare state to care for the remaining indigent, and the efforts of the humanitarian, labor, and reform movements during the nineteenth and twentieth centuries were undoubtedly major factors in its demise. The fact that it has emerged again among the young tells us less, I think, about the economic conditions of industrialized nation states than it does about the joys that humans can find in "conning" one another.

These youthful beggars may merely be reviving an old preindustrial city tradition. . . .

Adults still socialize in the public space of the modern city. . . . And children will play. But both do so to a far lesser degree than did their urban ancestors. Neither activity is actually illegal, but both can be discouraged and controlled by the application of various ordinances—for example, against crowds collecting or against blocking a sidewalk or street. Again, however, other forces are at work. The modern urbanite—even the poorest—is simply far more adequately housed than was the average city dweller in times past. When he or she wants to visit with friends, the living room is as comfortable as the street or corner tavern. Many urban homes have areas specifically designed for adult and child recreation (playrooms, yards). These are made possible not only by improvements in building techniques but by the areal expansion of the city as well— the latter having made available a greater allotment of space per family. These private resources are supplemented by public ones —parks and playgrounds—another example of the modern city's propensity to relegate special activities to specialized space.[8]

Finally, some note should be made of the reduced necessity for walking in the modern city. This particular activity remains legal, but the extent to which it is approved is questionable. Like other historic necessities (for example, cooking over fire), it has,

[8] The peculiarly middle class character of urban spatial segregation is attested to by the ironic fact that those with greater access to private recreational space also are likely to have greater access to public recreational space. (The elites, of course, have little need for such facilities as public parks. Their resources enable them to build their own private "parks," and to use the entire world as a playground.) Thus, it is in the most densely packed and economically deprived sections of a modern city that we can still see the kind of public-space activity pile-up so characteristic of the preindustrial urban settlement.

in the modern world, become largely a recreational activity, indulged in by masochistic cultists. Those people who still indulge in it *for a living*, such as mail carriers, beat-policemen and night watchmen, are frequently punished with low status, poor pay and the continual threat of attack by unfriendly dogs and people. Who or what are killing walking is a complex matter. The mass-produced automobile is usually assigned the major responsibility, but it is surely being aided and abetted by the areal expansion of the city (making possible wider, straighter streets, and itself engendered by the railroad and trolley), the telegraph, the telephone, and the establishment or relatively reliable government postal systems. As an aside, it might be mentioned that one of the more fascinating characteristics of the automobile is its ability to surround its occupants in a cocoon of privacy as they move through the public space of the city. . . . It thereby enables them to avoid for long stretches of time any necessity to confront the world of strangers.

The Spatial Segregation of Persons. Given the tendency of the modern city to segregate activities, it is hardly surprising that persons should be segregated as well. Yet the segregation of the latter is even more extensive than the discussion in the preceding section has implied. For the sake of simplicity and brevity, we shall here consider person-separation only in terms of class/caste/ethnicity, age, and moral categories, although these hardly exhaust the dimensions which modern urban humans use to spatially separate themselves from one another. In later chapters, when we consider such phenomena as "colonization" and "home territories," the full complexities of this separating tendency should become more apparent.

To paraphrase the old adage, to segregate is human, to integrate, divine. Even in the preindustrial city, where many forces conspired to "mix" the populance, there were strains toward flocking together among the similarly feathered birds.[9] By the eighteenth century, neighborhood segregation by class was already apparent, for example, in London (George, 1965; Chancellor, 1907), and as the city moved outward during the nineteenth and twentieth centuries, residential class homogenization intensified.[10] In all the emerging modern cities, wherever economic status was compounded by ethnicity or wherever caste lines were drawn, different "kinds" of neighborhoods multiplied: Chinatowns and rich Jewish areas; black ghettoes with middle class and poor districts (Drake and Cayton, 1962); working class suburbs (B. Berger, 1960) and enclaves of WASP affluence; Italian "villages" (Gans, 1962) and California developments of white southern immigrants on their way up.[11]

The contributors to this *class/caste/ethnicity* residential segregation, so characteristic of the modern city, are many and varied: too much so to consider here more

[9] I do not mean to suggest here that segregation is an innate and therefore inevitable human tendency. It is surely true that among lower-status persons segregation is more likely to be imposed than preferred. Nevertheless, as recent attempts at school and neighborhood racial integration in the United States have demonstrated, the higher-status group can make life so uncomfortable for the "integrator" that being with one's own—however despised one's own may be—becomes psychologically preferable.

[10] Briggs, 1965; Dickens, 1961, described nineteenth century London's lower class areas in detail.

[11] Wilson, 1967. As a basis for the spatial segregation of neighborhoods in the United States, ethnicity (as distinct from "color") has never been very stable and continues to decline in importance (see Cressy, 1971). And it seems possible that racial differentiation may follow the same course. In their stead, age and life-style, especially as they combine with class, appear to be emerging as major bases of segregation. For an insightful commentary on this trend, see Suttles, 1972: especially 262.

than superficially. The areal expansion of the city, combined with a variety of technological innovations, made such segregation possible. . . . The desire of the emerging middle class to separate itself from the "dangerous classes" provided a motivational impetus. Developers did their bit, creating district after district of similarly valued homes, and then "protecting" those values through "covenants" and "gentlemen's agreements." Zoning, at least in the United States, has been one of the more interesting instruments of segregation. It has had a major responsibility in banning mixed land use, that is, in separating place of residence from place of work. Since work places tend necessarily to be integrated, the banning of mixed land use must be considered a separatist stroke of genius (see Schnore, 1967; Toll, 1969). Zoning has helped too, to ensure that residential areas, once developed on single-class lines, would evermore remain so.[12] And in recent years, urban renewal, despite its humanitarian guise, has operated largely to remove the black and the poor from areas impinging too closely on white middle and upper class residential and commercial territory.[13]

Commercial areas, even within the city's central business district, may be segregated as well. San Francisco, for example, a city so dense and compact that it is almost preindustrial in its spatial mix, is nevertheless very much characteristic of the modern city in its central schizophrenia:

[12] Toll, 1969. It remains to be seen how successful recent attempts in the United States to "scatter" public housing among affluent neighborhoods will be. But at least in one European city where access to housing is governmentally controlled, the segregation of social groups by neighborhood appears to be waning (Musil, 1968).

[13] Greer, 1965. For a description of one of the processes by which, under conditions of modern land development practices in the United States, large-scale specialized neighborhoods emerge, see Suttles, 1972:86–90.

The image-conscious San Franciscan nervously warns the visitor: "Stay off Market. It's no more San Francisco than Broadway is New York." A specious argument. Might as well say Post Street is no more San Francisco than Fifth Avenue is New York. Market is mucho San Francisco—our main drag, and don't linger overlong on the second word. It's a drag only if you can't face the fact that San Francisco isn't all bankers at Jack's, Dolly Fritz at Trader Vic's—and No. 263 off the Golden Gate Bridge. . . .

Market is old men spitting on the sidewalk and blowing their noses in the gutters. Women too broad of beam to wear slacks, but wearing them anyway, tucked into pointy boots. Girls with hair tossed a mile high over pouty faces filled with chewing gum. Old ladies smoking cigarettes and flipping them away expertly. Greasy-haired boys wearing pants so tight they must have been painted on, standing in silent knots, icy glance on passing girls. Young men in shiny leather jackets trying to look insolent and dangerous, which they could very well be. Slim-hipped boy-girls piloting motorcycles with frigid efficiency, returning your stare with contemptuous flick of dead eyes.

Market is rock'n'roll blaring out of little record shops, $9.95 shoes and $19.95 dresses, the smell of hot dogs, men spooning crab cocktails into faces hidden inside upturned collars, schoolgirls eating ice cream sandwiches, dirty magazines with their pages scotchtaped so you can't get a free peek, pinball games flashing their obscene lights, and bums in World War II overcoats who take your quarter without the thanks you didn't want anyway. . . . (Herb Caen, *San Francisco Chronicle*, June 14, 1964)

Perhaps it is not too outlandish to suggest that the fact that Market and Post are within minutes of one another may have something to do with municipal plans to turn the former into San Francisco's "Fifth Avenue."

Commercial segregation along class lines, of course, didn't just happen, anymore than residential segregation just happened. It too is the result of multitudinous forces, one of the more important of which, again, was zoning. In 1916, for example, zoning laws "saved" New York's Fifth Avenue:

They [the Fifth Avenue Merchants Association] wanted the garment industry to get out of Fifth Avenue, or at the very least, they wanted it literally held down. They wanted this because the things which were the essences of the garment industry—the strange tongues, the outlandish appearance and the very smell of its immigrant laborers, its relentless drive to follow the retail trade wherever it went, its great concentrations of plants and people—violated the ambience in which luxury retailing thrives. It demands insulation from gross forms of work and workers, the symbols of wealth and good living and sidewalks inviting the stroll, the pause, the purchase.
A representative of the association summed it up.

The high-class retail business for which Fifth Avenue is so well known is the most sensitive and delicate organism imaginable, depending, first, on the exclusiveness of the neighborhood; second, on its nearness to the homes of the rich and the large hotels; and, third, on its lack of congestion, especially on sidewalks, so that the customers may not be crowded or jammed in a hurly-burly crowd on their way to and from the different shops. . . . The loft buildings have already invaded the side streets with their hordes of factory employees. If an adequate move were made restricting the occupancy of the buildings so that no manufacturing could be done either on Fifth Avenue

or from Madison Avenue over to Sixth Avenue, the matter would be solved. The employees from these loft buildings cannot be controlled. They spend their time—lunch hour and before business—on the avenue, congregating in crowds that are doing more than any other thing to destroy the exclusiveness and desirability of Fifth Avenue. If the exclusiveness and desirability of Fifth Avenue are destroyed, the value of real estate on Fifth Avenue will depreciate immediately. (Toll, 1969:158–59)

Given the eloquence of the Association's plea, it is not surprising that the desired building-occupancy restrictions became law, thus protecting the inalienable right of the well-to-do to spend their money without having to rub shoulders with the "dangerous classes."

Age is another category along which the spatial segregation of persons in the modern city proceeds. Children were one of the first groups to be contained. In the United States, for example, child labor laws, compulsory schooling, and measures designed to control "juvenile delinquents" —all nineteenth and twentieth century innovations—moved children out of the work place and off the streets, at least during major portions of the day. With the development of specialized public and private play space, it was possible to keep them relatively segregated for even more hours. The separation of work and residence helped too, reducing any necessity for them to mix with working adults. Nursery schools for preschool children and colleges for postschool youth have extended the duration of their segregation from the adult world, and, at least for the college-aged, have intensified it:

Relative to age in American technological society, we may note that the coincidence between it and territory is proceeding apace and is most spectacular in the host communities of the ever-expanding multiversities. Into many of these communities in recent years, there have thronged literally tens of thousands of what we might call "youth"—human animals ranging in age from late teens to middle twenties. Because the political powers have opted for the model of a few large educational institutions, rather than many small ones, "cities of youth" are being created. (J. Lofland, 1968:127)

Age segregation, however, is not limited to children:

Indeed, there would seem to be evolving a pattern wherein an age-sex unit of early adults establishes itself in an early-adult neighborhood, its members spawn their offsping and then, at the appropriate age, move to a middle-adult territory. In this way, age-sex units are always able to be with their "own kind," territorily protected from the contamination of contact with many other age categories. . . .

Although all of this is only a tendency at present, it would seem to be a growing tendency and one which assumes additional significance in the light of the already more pronounced territorial segregation of late adults. We are all well aware that persons of sixty and over—often described with polite euphemisms such as "senior citizens"—have begun to assemble in special buildings in cities, in special neighborhoods within suburbs, and, indeed, in special areas of the nation. (J. Lofland, 1968:129)

As with all forms of spatial segregation within the modern city, many forces are at work here also. The relationship between buying power and position in the life cycle, combined with the single-value character of many housing areas, almost guarantees age segregation. If these forces are insufficient, housing developers can help the trend along. Thus, an ad for a newly developed California subdivision, outside San Jose, assures potential buyers that they will have

Nice People for Neighbors
What kind of people are these who seek out country living . . . and then add their own special flair? To begin with, by requirement, one member of each family must be at least 45 years old. This puts the general population beyond child raising and ready for new rewards in life.

By actual survey, these same people are successful, well educated, friendly, and respectful of another's privacy. Many are working professionals—teachers, engineers, lawyers. There are several sales representatives, a fireman, a carpenter, even a former locomotive engineer! Virtually all residents are the kind of people with a high respect for tradition. (*San Francisco Sunday Examiner and Chronicle,* July 26, 1970)

Perhaps, from the point of view of the developers, the delights of age segregation (including, apparently, political homogenization) will compensate for the fact that buyers are going to have to enjoy their "country living" in the midst of one of the most urbanized sections of the United States (*Newsweek,* September 14, 1970).

As is rather clearly implied in the above advertisement, segregation of persons in the modern city also involves *moral* categories. Those humans deemed "beyond the pale" are set apart from "respectable citizens." Every city, for example, has its vice section and its skid row (road)—areas where the modern world's outcasts can be contained.[14] But sometimes, in some cities, containment is thought to be insufficient and more innovative segregating tactics are called for, tactics which may even conflict with political convention, economic necessity, or aesthetic values.

In Nice, France:

Mayor Jacques Medecin is convinced that

---

[14] Containment, of course, is not intended to keep respectables out; only to keep outcastes in.

tourism can be saved on the French Riviera if the federal government will permit him to open "maisons de tolerance," better known as legal bordellos.

According to the mayor, houses of prostitution will clear the jammed streets of their most disorderly traffic "and will solve a lot of other problems, too. . . ."

If he has his way, he will house Nice's prostitutes in a vast ensemble of comfortable buildings where they may receive guests in their own studio apartments "and practice their jobs as professionals."

"They will stay off the sidewalks to the great satisfaction of shopkeepers, restauteurs and hotelmen," promised the French politician. . . . (Ferris Hartman, "French Way to Keep Girls Honest," *San Francisco Chronicle*, April 10, 1970)

In South Africa, where to be black is a "mortal sin," new segregation plans fly in the face of the demands of urban economics:

South Africa's latest plans for the country's 15 million Africans and colored is to keep them out of sight.

If the proposed new national government legislation is implemented, Africans working in white areas will be restricted to the back rooms and out of town warehouses, out of sight of the five million whites. . . .

Despite the stubborn record of the government, few businessmen really believe that the government can carry through the new plans without totally wrecking the country's economy.

African jobs prohibited under the new legislation would be shop assistants, salesmen, reception clerks, telephonists, typists, cashiers, and clerks. . . . (*San Francisco Sunday Examiner and Chronicle*, August 9, 1970)

And in the United States, even aesthetic considerations must give way before the necessities of moral separation:

The grandeur of a 40-foot-wide staircase descending to the mezzanine level of the Powell street subway station may have to be abandoned. [San Francisco's] Transit Task Force reported yesterday.

Director Jack Barron said merchants in the area . . . are increasingly afraid that such a broad stairway might be a gathering place for militants or hippies. . . [*San Francisco*, July 21, 1970)[15]

Other sorts of morally devalued categories are simply put away altogether. The "feeble-minded" and "insane," who used to roam the streets of the preindustrial city, now have their own institutions. Many of the lamed and maimed now live out their lives in hospitals and nursing homes.[16] Both groups are the recipients of nineteenth and twentieth century "reforms." So is the contemporary lawbreaker. In fact, to anticipate a bit, the transformation from appearential to spatial ordering is perhaps most clearly expressed in the fact that in the modern city, lawbreakers are not mutilated, they are segregated.

Masked Heterogeneity of Populace

There is certainly no question but that the residents of the modern city are a heterogeneous lot. Of course, there are differences *among* cities in this regard—Des Moines is undoubtedly no match for New

---

[15] In their analysis of San Francisco's world-famous tolerance for deviance—its "culture of civility"—Howard S. Becker and Irving Louis Horowitz (1970) suggest that this tolerance is largely due to a willingness among various groups to "accommodate" to the desires of each other. In essence, although they do not say so explicitly, this means spatial segregation.

[16] It seems highly unlikely that the average preindustrial urbanite was as interactionally ill-at-ease with the omnipresent "visibly handicapped" as are many of his modern counterparts. For sensitive analyses of these contemporary interactional problems, see F. Davis, 1961, and Goffman, 1963b.

York or London—but these differences appear rather minor when we compare the city to the small town or isolated settlement. In fact, given the ease of modern travel and worldwide migratory tendencies, the modern city is probably a good deal more heterogeneous than was the preindustrial. What is particularly interesting about this modern heterogeneity, however is the extent to which it tends to be masked.

As we have just seen, lawbreakers are no longer mutilated. That is, body markings no longer provide clues to the strange other's moral categories.[17] And while language (should we hear the other speak) may be of some help in identifying his or her ethnicity, home region, or class (Ellis, 1967), universal schooling, status mobility, and movies, radio, and television have done much to limit its reliability.

That leaves costuming. Surely in the dress and hair styles of the city's populace, there are reliable clues to identities. To a degree, of course, this is true. Sociologists have made much of the outward display of "status symbolism" in the anonymity of the city.[18] But what I suggest here is that they have made much out of very little. I do not suggest that city dwellers all look alike. They certainly do not, I have no brief with those who complain about the drab conformity of modern humans. To walk down the street of any modern city is to encounter the most marvelous array of get-ups and garbs. Nor am I suggesting that there are *no* structural links between costume and category. What I *am* saying is that these various costumes, in the main, provide rather unreliable clues to the "identities" of their wearers.

Many factors have contributed to this state of affairs. . . . The mass production of

clothing has blurred the overt expression of buying power. The trained eye can probably easily distinguish between a $400 original and a $30 copy, but most of us have rather illiterate eyes. The general westernization of clothing is another factor—for example, the Russian traveler in Constantinople (Istanbul) today is likely to be wearing a business suit. In addition, in their search for new ideas, fashion designers have borrowed freely from the dress styles of many countries. Thus, the New Delhi housewife may wear a sleeveless shift, while the Omaha housewife may go to a cocktail party in a sari. The spread of affluence, particularly in the West, makes it possible for large numbers of persons to choose among the abundant variety of clothing styles available. And the absence of legal support for dress regulations allows them to do so freely.

This last mentioned factor—the absence of legal support for dress regulations—is perhaps one of the most crucial factors. Given this absence, costuming becomes not a matter of law—written or unwritten—but a matter of fashion, that is, a matter of fad. *And it is the essence of fad to be copied.*

Let us consider as one example the rather widespread adoption by the American young (as well as by some of their elders) during the late 1960s of longer hair, rather "casual" dress, and—at least by the males—facial hair. To certain segments of the American public, this particular form of costuming was a clear indication that the wearer espoused a dangerous, revolutionary, and negative philosophy (usually referred to as hippie-radical, an interesting contradiction in terms) which was inimical to the interests of upstanding, respectable, and patriotic Americans. Among this same segment of the public, it was also accepted as fact that wearers of "the costume" did not bathe, were usually unemployed, plotted revolution, engaged in free love, opposed war, and, most horrible of all, used drugs other than alcohol.

---

[17] Thus Goffman is able to devote one entire section of a book on *Stigma* (1963b:chap. 2) to those "stigmas" which cannot be seen.

[18] See, for example, Form and Stone, 1964; J. Lofland and Lejeune, 1960.

Among other segments of the populace, the negative aspects of the above assessment might be absent, but the belief that "the costume" was a reliable indicator remained.

The fact of the matter is, however, that the reliability of the costume (or of any of its parts) as an identity indicator was (and continues to be) highly variable. In some conservative cities of the American Midwest or South, it might have been a fairly good one. In the more faddish climates of the east and west coasts, however, it discriminated rather poorly.

When it first emerged, during the early 1960s, the costume was probably a very good indicator. It was adopted then as an identity badge by young people, largely of middle-class origin, who were rejecting the world of their parents and were turning inward in their search for peace (hippies) or turning outward in their search for change (radicals). These young people, however, unlike the elites of old, had no access to laws or the machinery of their enforcement to keep their identity badge undefiled. They could not prevent its adoption by apolitical and aphilosophical working-class youth; they could not prevent its co-optation by the "hipper" elements of the American mainstream; and they could not prevent its mass production by manufacturers anxious to get in on the "latest thing."[19] The general result was chaos. Department stores did a marvelous business in men's wigs, catering to the desires of swinging, bearded, but short-haired conservative males to be even more swinging after working hours. Wedding pictures of the aristocratic young appearing on the "society" pages of major metropolitan newspapers were magnificent studies in incongruity. Standing amidst the symbols of wealth, power, and tradition were the bride and groom—she in her granny glasses and "Salvation Army store" dress; he in his beard, beads, and jeans. The picture was further complicated by the fact that the viewer could not be sure whether these wedding outfits were purchased in a second-hand store or at some very chic and expensive boutique. Even national entertainment figures could not be counted on to "be" what they "appeared," as the following illustrates:

Johnny Cash is no hippie, though his hair is almost long enough and his box back coat is acceptable both to his hippie audience and to his natural Oklahoma hill fans. Johnny Cash played Madison Square Garden this winter and upset his younger audience by endorsing the United States presence in Vietnam in a simplistic patriotic way. (Ralph J. Gleason, "Trains, Prisons and Some History," *San Francisco Chronicle*, March 9, 1970)

The entire situation was made even more chaotic by the fact that, simultaneously, forces were also operating in the other direction. That is, a good many persons were far less "straight" than they appeared. Dress regulations could be and were enforced in both school and work settings (although they were constantly being challenged in the courts), such that many persons who might wish to express a more "hip" identity were prevented from doing so—at least for part of the day.[20] In addition, many of the politically-oriented young—radical, liberal, and moderate—knowing that their usual appearance was offensive to the people they wished to influence, adopted what were thought to be more uncommittal styles.

[19] John Irwin (1973), in his analysis of the Southern California surfing "scene," describes an earlier instance of costume appropriation. Male high school students, who never went near the water, nevertheless decked themselves out to look like surfers—even to the extent of peroxiding their hair.

[20] See, for example, "The Taxicab Hair Dispute," San Francisco Chronicle, April 14, 1970; "The Hippie Hackies," *Newsweek*, May 4, 1970.

What I have said here regarding the hippie-radical costume might be said about any other sort of costume. There is simply very little in the modern industrialized world to prevent persons from dressing up, down or across their "appropriate" social categories. If the young wish to dress like the old, and the old like the young; if the poor wish to dress like the rich, and the rich like the poor; if the males want to "feminize" their dress, and the females "masculinize" theirs; if the lawyer wants to look like a seaman, and the seaman like a lawyer; if the Nigerian wishes to dress like an Englishman, and the American wishes to dress like a Nigerian, who is to stop them? And since there is no one to stop them, and there is a giant worldwide fashion industry to encourage them, it is hardly surprising that in the modern city, the linking of identity to costume is a very problematic activity indeed.

Identifying Strangers in the Modern City

The Dominance of Spatial Ordering

The modern urbanite, then, in contrast to his preindustrial counterpart, primarily uses location rather than appearance to identify the strange others who surround him. In the preindustrial city, space was chaotic, appearances were ordered. In the modern city, appearances are chaotic, space is ordered. In the preindustrial city, a man was what he wore. In the modern city, a man is where he stands.[21]

A homosexual male is a man in a homosexual bar and not necessarily a man in a pink ruffled shirt. A prostitute is a woman standing alone in the "Tenderloin," and not necessarily a woman in a revealing costume.[22] Elites are persons who can be

found in the stores and restaurants which cater to their incredible buying power and not necessarily the persons who wear silk. The poor are persons who live in a certain section of town and not necessarily the people who wear the most tattered clothes. A "middle American" is someone who goes to the Elk's Club, and don't let that moustache fool you. A sales clerk is someone who is to be found behind the counter, never mind that he is indistinguishable from his customers. A university professor is someone who stands facing the students in a university classroom. And the fact that he may look like his students, like a Wall Street lawyer, or like a skid row bum should not be allowed to obscure this simple truth.

The modern city dweller's penchant for linking "who" to "where" turned up again and again in my interviews with various residents of San Francisco and its surrounding suburbs. Ask them if they're ever afraid in the city, and they will tell you that it depends on where in the city they happen to be. Ask them if they ever talk to strangers and they tell you about a bar they know of where everybody talks to everybody else. Ask them about people and their responses are brief. Ask them about places and they cite chapter and verse:

Q: How do you feel when you're in a public place? Any public place.
A: That depends on the kinds, on the type of public place you're in at the time. It would vary as to the type of place you're in whether you feel comfortable or whether you don't.
Q: How about "making contact" with strangers?

---

[21] On the identity-bestowing power of space, see J. Lofland, 1969:162–72, 234–43.

[22] In San Francisco at least, mass arrests of prostitutes appear to proceed on the basis of location rather than appearance. A local resident reports being called for jury duty on the case of a young "very straight-looking" college girl who was picked up in the "Tenderloin" during a daytime "cleanup." J. Lofland, personal communication.

A: I think that the way a person presents himself, through his dress, through his walk, his mannerisms can either help or hinder making contacts with other persons. A hippie on *Montgomery Street* [San Francisco's financial district] is very unlikely to make contact because *the Montgomery Street people* in *their area* are likely to alienate him [sic] just by the way he dresses. But in another situation, the idea would be reversed. I find that for me, one of the best ways to make contact, say I'm going to a strange place, is to know something about the way the people *in that place* handle themselves, the way they dress, the way they walk, and the speech and mannerisms and everything, cause that can really help making contacts—if you have to make contacts. If you prefer to remain anonymous, the best thing to do is just the opposite, cause nobody's going to want to make contacts with you. [Emphasis added]

Note that in the above quotes, the major reference is to place and *its identity,* or, to put it more accurately, *its ambience.* The first informant does not say—as the pre-industrial city dweller might have—"That depends on how the people look who are present." Instead she says, "That depends on the kinds, on the type of public place." The second informant does not get specific about "appropriate dress, speech, and mannerisms," but she does get specific about place. She does not tell us that it would be hard for a hippie to talk to a shorthaired beardless man in a business suit. But she does tell us that the hippie would have a hard time "making contact" on Montgomery Street. . . . As is clear from the above example, the modern urbanite does, of course, use appearance to help him identify strange others. But for him, *appearance is most reliable as an indicator when it is linked with location.*

The following segment of the summary of an interview with a San Francisco woman in her late thirties, suggests just how important the spatial order of the modern city can come to be in the life of its residents:

The city to her is made up of many districts and to know where someone lives is to be able to judge him. Thus, with regard to her daughter, she can tell a lot about people her daughter meets by the school they go to, for the school they attend tells one the neighborhood they live in, and the neighborhood they live in tells one something about the kind of people they are. She notes that busing [of school children] would make such judgments impossible and she feels that this is one of the reasons she is opposed to it.

. . . When we explore the acquisition of urban meanings, we shall consider the intricate knowledge of place possessed by city dwellers in more detail. For now, it is sufficient simply to understand how crucial a part such knowledge plays when one is maneuvering in the world of strangers.

The Limited Use of Appearential Ordering

Just as the preindustrial city contained within it elements of the spatial order that would eventually dominate, so does the modern city contain within it elements of the appearential order that once dominated. Just as the preindustrial urbanite was helped along by spatial clues, so the modern urbanite is helped along by appearential clues. And when combined with location, these clues increase the probability that a "correct" identification will be made.

In the late 1950s in New York City, for example, one might have been able to make some assessment of a strange male other's class standing on the basis of such clues as the following:

I. *Upper-Middle and Upper Class:* well-groomed, clean, latest style clothes (especially suits and ties), subdued colored clothes which are neatly pressed, of good quality, not worn and are of matching colors (using as criteria the present men's fashion advertisements).

II. *Lower-Middle Class:* less well-groomed, clean, wearing suits and ties but of out-dated style, colors not so subdued, clothes showing some wear, fair to poor quality, less well pressed, articles of "clashing" colors.

III. *Working Class:* not so well-groomed, clean wash trousers, no suit coat (a waist jacket usually), no ties, "clashing colors.

IV. *Derelict:* poorly groomed, dirty, dirty wash pants, suit coat (usually out of style, worn, unpressed, dirty). (J. Lofland and Lejeune, 1960:105–6)

These little *appearential portraits* were developed by two sociologists in a study of Alcoholics Anonymous, as a means of "standarizing" observer judgments of participants' class standing. The very fact that they felt it necessary to codify in order to standardize suggests something about the less than clear-cut character of appearance as an identity indicator in the modern city. I suspect that in the preindustrial city, an intelligent and knowledgeable observer would no more have required codification of class indicators than a contemporary adult requires written instructions to distinguish between a Volkswagen and a Cadillac. In any case, portraits such as these are utilized. As we shall see later, however, the particularly skilled urbanite uses them cautiously.

Of somewhat greater reliability are the appearential clues provided by those hangovers from the preindustrial city—*uniforms*. These are not much worn in the modern city, but where they are they are of immeasurable assistance in making identifications. Most frequently they signal oc-

cupation, and since in the industrialized state, occupation is so closely tied to class, they signal the latter as well. Some of them make identification possible without any reference to location. The garb of a priest or the traditional habit of a nun are two examples. The outfits of some policemen are another example—although in a few communities, the traditional uniform is being replaced with slacks and blazer, a community relations move designed to "humanize" the force. While such a change may very well make policemen more lovable, it also makes them a good deal less identifiable—removing yet another appearential clue from the modern city's small supply of clues.[23] Many other uniforms currently in use are somewhat more tied to location. A hotel doorman, for example, is only unmistakably a hotel doorman when he is standing in front of a hotel door. A nurse (minus her cap) outside the hospital might be taken for a beautician, a waitress, a lab technician, or any one of a variety of "women in white."

As an aside, it might be noted that one of the more interesting aspects of uniforms is their capacity for signaling identity so quickly that, even in interaction, the uniformed other may be relegated to the status of nonperson, to use Goffman's term (1959:151). This is well illustrated in the

---

[23] On the controversial decision to uniform policemen in the first place, see Lane, 1967. For a general discussion of the functions of uniforms in modern society, see Joseph and Alex, 1972. While the elimination of uniforms seems a general tendency in the modern world, there is also some evidence of movement in the opposite direction. Numerous retail stores, banks, and savings and loan associations in the United States have introduced standardized "career apparel," especially for their female employees (see Beverly Stephen, "Will Uniforms Work," *San Francisco Chronicle*, January 24, 1972). Whether this trend will continue, and if it does, the extent to which these uniforms will be useful in signaling occupation, remain to be seen.

common complaint of nuns that no one ever looks at their faces, or in the ability of a uniformed workman to enter a woman's restroom without attracting any notice; or, even more explicitly, in the following account:

> A cat may not everywhere look at a king, nor does a person of position always look at a person of none. I was once a party to a practical joke, the point of which was to see whether a certain lady would recognize her own son were he to attend us, her guests, as a valet. She did not, as she never looked at his face.[24]

Finally, there are still in the modern city, as there were in the preindustrial city, what we might call *unmaskable diversities*. Skin color is perhaps the clearest example, although there are others: facial structure, age and sex (although both of these latter depend to a considerable degree on costuming), and highly visible deformities. To the degree that such physical attributes are thought to have *social* significance, they become important appearential clues. The situation of the black man or woman in the United States hardly requires elaboration here, although note might be made of the fact that until recently, skin color has operated rather like a uniform in rendering its "wearer" a nonperson. The underlying similarity between the complaint of the nun that no one ever looks at her face and the assertion of whites that "all Negroes look alike" is unmistakable.

Visible deformities as appearential

clues often appear to have a rather different effect. As a number of sociologists have pointed out, some persons in America appear to feel that a handicap renders its bearer totally incompetent.[25] As such, they feel no hesitation in approaching total strangers to offer unneeded help or to express unwanted curiosity. This willingness on the part of "normals" to intrude themselves into the affairs of the "stigmatized" (unless the latter is viewed as threatening) . . . most certainly adds to the burden of an already burdensome life as the following incident clearly demonstrates:

> A male, middle aged, is wandering about the bus depot. He is blind, or at least partially blind and has with him a mutt who apparently serves as his guide dog. The dog is wearing a special harness to aid in the signaling that must go on between them. A middle aged woman has been watching him for some time. He is now standing in front of the lunch counter, apparently preparatory to taking a seat. As he is standing there, the woman approaches, introduces herself and begins telling him about some people she knows who are blind and what was done for them and so forth. He listens politely for a few moments, then turns and begins to maneuver himself onto a lunch counter seat. The woman, noting this, desires to be helpful and she tries to assist him in getting up to the counter and on to a stool. In doing so, she bumps into the dog several times, changes positions and then gets herself, the dog and the man tangled up in the leash. During all this she keeps reaching down to pat the dog who is becoming more confused and excited all the time. Finally she leaves, the man orders coffee, finishes drinking it and leaves unaided; a far smoother departure than arrival.

---

[24] Parsons, 1914:55. Such relegation to nonperson status which the uniform makes possible would seem to be most likely to occur when the wearer is lower in the social hierarchy than the observer. As Walter Klink has noted in a personal communication, uniforms may also function to open up the possibilities for interaction between strangers, as when similarly garbed but unacquainted soldiers feel free to converse with one another.

[25] Goffman, 1963b; F. Davis, 1961:120–32.

The Tenuous Nature of Spatial Order

. . . Under the assault of human intractability, all systems of order are continually in the process of breaking down. The order of urban public space is certainly no exception. In the preindustrial city, persons were continually dressing themselves in "inappropriate" costumes. In the modern city, they are continually showing up in "inappropriate" places, doing "inappropriate" things.

We have already seen a good deal of this in the foregoing pages: prostitutes who desert their "assigned" district and solicit aboard municipal buses; young people who leave the confines of cities of youth and harass the residents of adult enclaves. This latter phenomenon, in fact, would appear to have recently become a cause célèbre among the guardians of order in many modern cities. The city of Carmel, California, as we saw, faced the "danger" squarely and passed some emergency ordinances. So did the European city of Amsterdam:

New ordinances to discourage young people from hanging around Dam Square in Amsterdam went into effect yesterday, touching off disturbances that left three persons wounded by police gunfire.

The new ordinances were intended to keep "hippies" from loitering in the square opposite the Royal Palace, and from sleeping there at night. . . . (San Francisco Chronicle, August 25, 1970)

In San Francisco, no new laws were enacted, but there was no dearth of moanings and groanings over the "terribleness" of the situation. In the spring and summer of 1970, local newspapers, carried a series of stories predicting that most horrible of consequences—a slump in the tourist business —if things were not "cleaned up." In February, for example, the Sunday paper ran an almost full-page story with the intriguing headline: "Why Vital Conventions are Deserting the City." The factors contributing to this disaster turned out to be numerous, but among them was "the hippie situation":

"I'd hate to see San Francisco lose its image of being a friendly, courteous city," he [Robert K. Sullivan, general manager of the Convention and Visitors Bureau] added. "But the kids are panhandling—and selling matter like the *Berkeley Barb* on *Union Square.*

"The conventions are not bothered by it, but the families don't want their children exposed to it."

The bureau manager said the individual tourist is getting pretty jumpy about San Francisco.

"We get more and more indications that the hippie thing is not an attraction—it is not like the flower children *in the Haight-Ashbury several years ago.*" (*San Francisco Sunday Examiner and Chronicle*, February 1, 1970, italics added)

Note that the objection is not to "hippies" per se. They were considered a tourist attraction during the late 1960s when they remained in their out-of-the-way Haight-Ashbury district. The objection is to "hippies" in Union Square, located in the middle of the city's commercial and hotel area.

In June 1970, another news headline suggested that the worst had already happened: "Tourist Slump in S.F.—'Poor Image' Blamed." Within the story—a coverage of a local Convention and Visitors Bureau annual membership brunch—a number of remedies were suggested, among them:

"Let's also clean out the reputation that San Francisco or the Bay Area has been a haven of yippies, hippies, the birthplace of disorderly demonstrations, and dope."

He [one of the meeting speakers] warned that without vigorous action a serious "economic void" would result and threaten the business of the bureau members. (*San Francisco Chronicle,* June 11, 1970)

Whether there was any connection between this warning and the events of a month later, recounted below, is, of course, difficult to say:

Union Square Drug Arrests
The Tactical Unit arrested eight persons —four of them juveniles—on narcotics charges in Union Square in an afternoon swoop yesterday.

There was no violence and none of those arrested offered any resistance.

Sergeant Edward Epting said the arrests were made as a result of continuing surveillance of the Union Square area and "because we have had a lot of complaints from citizens" . . . (*San Francisco Chronicle,* July 30, 1970)

In paying so much attention to youthful assaults on the spatial order, I do not mean to imply that they are the only persons who ever get "out of place." The movements of one group into another's neighborhood or school are also seen as troublesome by municipal authorities (even when they sponsor it). Vagrants, drifters, and "skid row bums" are another source of difficulty. As Caleb Foote has so nicely demonstrated in his article on "Vagrancy-type Law and Its Administration" (1969), eternal vigilance would appear to be the price of spatial order. Sometimes offenders merely step outside their proper districts:

In discharging defendants with out-of-the-central-city address, the magistrates made comments such as the following:

"You stay out in West Philadelphia."
"Stay up in the fifteenth ward; I'll take care of you up there."
"What are you doing in this part of town? You stay where you belong; we've got enough bums down here without you." (Foote, 1969:297)

But others have the effrontery to leave their own city:

Magistrate: Where do you live?
Defendent: Norfolk.
Magistrate: What are you doing in Philadelphia?
Defendent: Well I didn't have any work down there, so I came up here to see if I could find. . . .
Magistrate (who had been shaking his head): That story's not good enough for me. I'm going to have you investigated. You're a vagrant. Three months in the House of Correction.[26]

Eternal vigilance must be maintained not only against "vagrants and bums," but against straying young black males, as well.

Gang members report that the boundaries of neighborhoods are patrolled with great seriousness and severity. The police are seen as very hard on "suspicious looking" adolescents who have strayed from home territory.

(Do you guys stay mostly at Hunters Point or do you travel into other districts?) If we go someplace, they tell us to go on home. Because every time we go somewhere we mostly go in big groups and they don't want us. One time we was walking on Steiner Street. So a cop drove up and he say, "Hey, Hanky and Panky! Come here! And he say, "You all out of bounds, get back on the other side of Steiner Street." Steiner Street is supposed to be out of bounds. (What's on the other side of Steiner?) Nothin' but houses. (Werthman and Piliavin, 1967:77)

[26] Foote, 1969:301. On control of skid row generally, see Bittner, 1969. On the history of vagrancy laws and the various uses to which they have been put, see Chambliss, 1969.

Things don't change. Like day before yesterday. We were sitting down on the steps talking with Joe and them. So here comes the police, coming down there messing with people.

"Where do you live?" they say.
"Up on the Hill."
He say, "Where do you eat at?"
"Up on the Hill."
"Where do you sleep at?"
"Up on the Hill."
He say, "Where you get your mail at?"
I say "Up on the Hill."
He say, "Well don't you think you ought to be getting up the Hill right now!"
So we went up the Hill. (Werthman and Piliavin, 1967:98)

In Chapter Three, I suggested, rather tentatively, that the spatial order of the modern city was to some degree a creation of the middle class—anxious in the early industrial city to separate themselves, physically and socially, from the encroaching "dangerous classes." Here, I want to suggest, again quite tentatively, that the spatial order in the modern city is importantly maintained by this same group. I want to suggest, that is, that the instruments for the creation and maintenance of the segregation of persons and activities in urban public space—the underpinning of spatial order—are largely in their control. We have met these instruments over and over again in the preceding pages: zoning regulations —past and present; municipal ordinances— past and present; housing developments— past and present; laws and practices inspired by humanitarian and reform groups —past and present: and, those maintenance men par excellence, the modern police.

In a fascinating paper, "On the Demand for Order in Civil Society" (1967), Allan Silver has pointed out that the modern police organization goes back only to the middle of the nineteenth century. Prior to that time, police functions were generally handled by "ordinary, respectable citizens," or, for purposes of internal peacekeeping, by the military. With increasing concentration of large populations in small areas, neither proved very efficient. But with the creation of the police, it became possible to exercise

potentially violent supervision over the population by bureaucratic means widely diffused throughout civil society in small and discretionary operations that [were] capable of rapid concentration. (Silver, 1967:8)

We have seen repeated examples in the preceding pages of these "small and discretionary operations" at work. And were it not for the police, the effects of many of the other instruments of spatial order maintenance would be largely vitiated.[27]

Behind the police, of course, stands the middle class. It is they who control the means to keep the spatial order intact in the face of repeated assault. It is they—however unwittingly they may be of the full consequences—who perform or have performed at their direction the "dirty work" (Hughes, 1964) of sustaining predictability in a world continually threatened with unpredictability. But all urbanites, including those against whom the instruments of segregation are used, rely on this order, on this predictability, in making their way among strangers.

And a city's populace does more than simply "buy" bourgeois-produced order. Through their beliefs and understandings and through their actions, however unwitting, they reinforce and sustain it. . . .

[27] See further on the origin of modern police systems in England and the United States, Brown, 1969; Gorer, 1969; Lane, 1967, 1969; Roberts, 1969; and Tilly, 1969. On the police as surrogate norm enforcers in "aggregate" situations, see Greer, 1962:59–60.

39. Life Styles and Urban Space
ANSELM STRAUSS

The spatial complexity and the social diversity of any city are linked in exceedingly subtle ways. An examination of such connections will force confrontation of a very thorny problem: how are the various urban social words related to specified spaces, areas, and streets of a city?

Technical sociological interests in this kind of inquiry dates back to the studies of Robert Park (1925) and "the Chicago school" of urban research. Chicago's ethnic diversity was so striking, and the spatial dispersal of these populations over the face of the city was so marked, that the Chicago sociologists evolved a series of studies of ethnic (and other) worlds located in urban space. They invented a corresponding set of terms to link space and social structure.[1] The point was, as Park said, that "In the course of time every section and quarter of the city takes on something of the character and qualities of its inhabitants. Each separate part of the city is inevitably stained with the peculiar sentiments of its population."

This kind of sociological inquiry had its roots in two kinds of tradition: one was scientific—the biological study of ecological communities; the other was popular—the colorful journalistic accounts of urban social worlds. (Park himself had been a journalist before he became a professor.) Journalistic exploration of the city, as presented in full-exploration of the city, as presented in full-length book form, goes

Reprinted with permission of The Macmillan Company from Images of the American Life, by Anselm Strauss. © The Free Press, a Corporation, 1961.

[1] "Natural area" was one such concept: "Natural areas" were areas produced without planning by the natural course of laying down railroads, parks, boulevards, and by the topographical features of the city. Communities often tended to be coterminous with the boundaries of natural areas (see Park, 1925).

back at least to mid-nineteenth century, somewhat before the full tide of urban reform. Reform itself brought countless investigations of the less palatable aspects of metropolitan life, some of these rather more accurate and less luridly written than contemporary journalistic descriptions which sagacious publishers continued to offer a public hungry for images of how the other halves lived (see Browne, 1869; Campbell, Knox and Brynes, 1895; McCabe, 1868, 1881; Smith, 1868). The reader comfortably sitting at home peered into the hovels of the poor, rubbed elbows with the rich, and was fleeced by the professionally wicked. He imaginatively walked streets he would never dream of frequenting, visiting places he would otherwise shrink from visiting, and listened to the speech of vulgar and uncouth persons whose actual company would have caused him untold embarrassment.

What the sociologists later did was not so much to add accuracy, and certainly not color, to the reformer's and journalist's accounts as to study more systematically the "cultures" of particular urban communities and to relate the communities to the spatial structure of the entire metropolis. Later they became especially interested in the spatial distribution and social organization of social classes, particularly in our smaller cities.

Some of this sociological research is related to our specific interest in the spatial representations of urban populations. First, we shall observe certain aspects of several studies in order to find modes of analyzing and ordering the spatial representations of the respective urban communities. The major ordering principle to be utilized will be the city themes characteristically found in novels about urban life.

One of the persistent themes of these novels has been the search for some viable metropolitan existence by migrants with rural or small town backgrounds. Many ethnic communities formerly found in our great cities were composed of men and women drawn from the villages and farms of Europe. In some instances, emigrants from the same village clustered along a single American street, seeking somehow to reconstitute at least the non-physical aspects of village life. Among the most intriguing sociological descriptions of such an ethnic community is one by Christian Jonassen (1949). A summary description of the Norwegians of New York City will serve to illustrate a subtle rural symbolism of space.

The Norwegians who settled in New York City after 1830 came mainly from the coastal districts of Norway. That country remained unindustrialized during the last century, and even today it is among the least densely settled of Western nations. According to Jonassen, the Norwegians are "for the most part nature lovers and like green things and plenty of space about them" (Jonassen, 1949, p. 34). The original immigrants settled in such an area near the ship docks, although for occupational, as well as for "nature loving" motives. Over the decades the Norwegian colony clung to the shoreline, but gradually moved down it as deterioration set in and as invaders of lower status arrived on the scene. Jonassen believes that the continuous gradual retreat of the colony to contiguous areas was possible as long as land suiting their rural values remained available. Recently the colony has been driven into a spatial and symbolic box, its back to the ocean, for there is no further contiguous land to which to move. For this reason, Norwegians have begun to make the kind of jumps to non-contiguous areas so characteristic of other immigrant groups. Norwegians are now moving to sites that still retain some rural atmosphere (Staten Island and certain places in New Jersey and Connecticut). Among the newspaper excerpts which Jonassen quotes are two which help to illustrate his contention that the Norwegians symbolize their residential districts in rural terms (Jonassen, 1949, pp. 40–41). One man writes:

I arrived in America in 1923, eight years old. I went right to Staten Island because my father lived there and he was a shipbuilder at Elco Boats in Bayonne, New Jersey, right over the bridge. I started to work with my father and I am now foreman at the shipyard where we are now building small yachts. . . . I seldom go to New York because I don't like large cities with stone and concrete. Here are trees and open places.

Another Norwegian declares:

I like it here [Staten Island] because it reminds me of Norway. Of course, not Bergen, because we have neither Floyen nor Ulrik nor mountains on Staten Island, but it is so nice and green all over the summer. I have many friends in Bay Ridge in Brooklyn, and I like to take trips there, but to tell the truth when I get on the ferry on the way home and get the smell of Staten Island, I think it's glorious.

This representation of land, redolent with rural memories, is no doubt paralleled by the spatial representations of other rural migrants to large urban centers. Polish citizens of our cities live—quite literally—in local parishes, whether their protestant neighbors recognize this or not. In some instances the parish was settled as a village, set down near a railroad yard or a factory. Although the expanding metropolis has caught up and surrounded the parish, the invisible village still exists for at least the older of its inhabitants.

Another persistent theme found in novels about city life is that cities are conducive to personal demoralization and are characterized by the destructive impersonality of their relationships: cities are sites, in a word, that are characteristically inhabited by anomic people. In the novels, these people are ex-rural people. During the 1920's, Harvey Zorbaugh described one area of Chicago, many of whose residents subscribed to this view of the city (see Zorbaugh, 1929, pp. 69–86; Firey, 1947, pp. 290–322). The area was one of furnished rooms in houses long abandoned by their former well-to-do owners. Zorbaugh described the residents of these rooms as 52 percent single men, 10 percent women, "and 38 percent are couples, 'married,' supposedly with 'benefit of clergy.' The rooming-house area is a childless area. Yet most of its population is . . . between twenty and thirty-five." This population was tremendously mobile: a turnover took only four months. Characteristically, the rooming house was "a place of anonymous relationships. One knows no one, and is known by no one. One comes and goes as one wishes, does very much as one pleases, and as long as one disturbs no one else, no questions are asked. (Zorbaugh gives documents showing how great this anonymity can be.) The depths of loneliness experienced by some are illustrated by the experiences of a girl from William Allen White's home-town of Emporia, Kansas, who after some months in this area

> began to look at my life in Chicago. What was there in it, after all. My music was gone. I had neither family nor friends. In Emporia there would at least have been neighborhood clubs or the church. But here there were neither. Oh, for someone or something to belong to!

She belonged to no groups. People treated her "impersonally . . . not a human touch at all." Bitterly, she remarks that: "The city is like that. In all my work there had been the same lack of personal touch. In all this city of three million souls I knew no one, cared for no one, was cared for by no one." Another resident of the area reported that he was so totally alone that "there were evenings when I went out of my way to buy a paper, or an article at a drug store—just for the sake of talking a few minutes with someone." In the heart of the rooming house area there was a bridge over a lagoon, which became known as "Suicide Bridge," because so many of these people had used it as a way out of their anguish. Although not all the residents of such an urban area are lonely and demoralized, or have a corresponding perspective on city life, it seems reasonable to hypothesize that this kind of perspective would be found with much less frequency in many other urban areas. These anomic urbanites, we may suppose, have little knowledge of other sectors of the city (except downtown), and must believe that all of the city and its people are much like the city and the people that they have already encountered.

It seems unnecessary to say much about the opposite of anomie: the creative use of privacy. People who seek escape from their equally oppressive urban families have traditionally flocked to those sections of cities known as "villages," "towertowns," "near North Sides," and other bohemian and quasibohemian areas. Here are found the people who wish privileged privacy: prostitutes, homosexuals, touts, criminals, as well as artists, café society, devotées of the arts, illicit lovers—anybody and everybody who is eager to keep the small-town qualities of the metropolis at a long arm's length. (Some smaller cities, of course, do not have such a bohemian section; see Ware, 1935; Zorbaugh, 1929, pp. 87–104.) The inhabitants do not necessarily intend to live here forever; the area is used by many who plan to settle down later in more conventional areas when they will then engage in more generally socially approved pursuits: "There's at least a year in everybody's life when he wants to do just as he damn pleases. The 'village' is the only place where he can do it without sneaking off in a hole by himself" (Zorbaugh, 1939, p. 99).

Closely related to the urban perspective of privileged privacy is, of course, the view that the city is a place to be enjoyed; and many of the residents of these urban areas are there because they believe that enjoymnet and excitement are most easily obtained there. Other city dwellers may visit an area for temporary enjoyment and temporary privacy: the more or less permanent residents of the area merely want or need more of these qualities, or are perhaps wiser about how to get them.

Sociological studies of other urban communities likewise lend themselves to plausible interpretation of what may be the predominant spatial representations held by inhabitants of those communities. Walter Firey's study of Beacon Hill in Boston, for instance, demonstrates how deep an allegiance the Hill's upper class inhabitants may feel for that locale, an allegiance based upon immense respect for family inheritance and tradition, all intertwined with class pride. As one lady expressed it, "Here as nowhere else in Boston has the community spirit developed, which opens itself to the best in the new, while fostering with determination all that is fine and worth keeping in the old" (Firey, 1947, p. 121). Firey describes how close to the residences of the rich cluster the apartments and rooms of bohemian groups, a conjunction frequently found. Here they could "enjoy the 'cultural atmosphere' of Beacon Hill as well as the *demi-monde* bohemian flavor of the north slope." Beacon Hill, however, was at one time in danger of a bit too many of these exotic groups, and so in further remarks of the lady already quoted we may hear a note of querulous warning:

Beacon Hill is not and never can be temperamental, and those seeking to find or create there a second Greenwich Village will meet with obstacles in the shape of an old residence aristocracy whose ancestors have had their entries and exits through those charming old doorways for generations. . . . Those who dwell there [are] drawn together for self-defense.

The point of view of invading, but more conventional, upwardly mobile groups is given us by other sociological researches that supplement the information yielded by countless novels. The predominant meanings of the terrain for such populations are fairly self-evident: they are well illustrated by an apocryphal story about a university professor who had moved into an elite neighborhood perched atop one of the city's prominent hills. He was able to purchase a house a bit below the top. His investment was much more than financial. But the continual surge of populations to the city's outer rim is in some part an effort to find "nicer" parts of the city to live in; and a fair number of sociological researches have managed to trace the movements of various ethnic groups across the city, as their members moved upward on the social scale. Sometimes those groups that are impinged upon regard the invaders as a nuisance and sometimes as a danger, especially if the invaders are colored. We have fewer studies of how the invaders feel when they are invaded or surrounded by people whom they in turn consider dangerous, but such a volume as Clayton's and Drake's *Black Metropolis* carries hints here and there that some colored people are fully as afraid of their neighbors as are the whites.[2]

Few of the studies which I have cited are focused upon the more subtle meanings of space for the city's residents: but most studies pick up something of how people symbolize, and so perceive and use, the land upon which they are quartered. The studies tell us considerably less about the meanings and uses of near and distant ur-

[2] A colored student of mine once interviewed the residents of a city block, all Negro, and found a number of migrants from the South whose predominant outlook on the city was a mixture of rural animosity against the city and a view that life all around them was dangerous. Their street and home were a veritable island in a sea of threat.

ban areas; neither do they sketch, except for the smaller cities, a symbolic map of the entire metropolis. The only exceptions to this statement are attempts to zone the city, from the center to the periphery, roughly by social class. Such maps would depict how the many populations symbolize the city as a whole including various of its areas, and would attempt to draw together the collective representations of the more important city areas for many populations. The data and concepts necessary for making such maps do not exist. The investigation is, I suggest, worthwhile if one assumes that symbolic representations of space are associated with the use—or avoidance of use—of space.

The city, I am suggesting, can be viewed as a complex related set of symbolized areas. Any given population will be cognizant of only a small number of these areas: most areas will lie outside of effective perception; others will be conceived in such ways that they will hardly ever be visited, and will indeed be avoided. When properly mapped, any given area will be symbolized by several populations, from just a few to dozens. The sociological studies of less complex areas more satisfactorily discover the meanings of areal space than studies of areas that are used by many populations for diverse reasons. One has only to compare what is known about simple residential areas, like ethnic or suburban communities, with the Rush Street night club rows and 43rd Street theater areas of our cities.

How can we best begin to talk about urban spaces in terms of their symbolic as well as economic and ecological functions? A language for talking about the latter has been developed by the fields of urban ecology, urban geography, and urban economics, but none has been formed for the former. Consider for instance the downtown areas of our cities. Studies of the central district make clear that this district

has two centers: one defined by the focus of lines of communication, the other by the focus of lines of transportation. With the first center is associated the merchandising of credits; with the second is associated the merchandising of consumers goods and services at retail. Which of these is to be taken as the most significant center depends upon which of the two associated functions . . . characterize the economy of the central city (Johnson, 1951, p. 483).

These economic functions are manifested on certain important streets and in certain well-known buildings in the downtown area. The downtown is par excellence an area for financial and retail service—and the latter may include cultural services performed by museums and orchestras.

Yet one has only to observe closely a special city like Washington to perceive that a very considerable area of the central city is set aside for overtly ceremonial functions. A broad green belt contains the nation's ritual sites: the monuments and memorials, the Capitol, the Library of Congress and the Archives with their priceless national manuscripts on hushed display. Boston too has its historic ceremonial areas, and so does Philadelphia (the latter city has recently sought to make its monuments more visible and to give them a more dignified and attractive visual setting).

American cities as a rule do not have the elaborate ceremonial, or symbolically tinged areas downtown that many European cities possess. Cities on the Continent often evolved from medieval towns, which meant that the town's main market nestled alongside the cathedral. In time the markets grew and became the modern business district encompassing or moving from the original central market site. The church area likewise acquired, and often retained, additional functions visibly performed in additional churches, administrative buildings, and cultural institutions. In German cities, for instance, this area is often referred to as the *altstadt* (old city), since it is often coterminous with the site of earlier settlement; and it is sometimes sentimentally called the city's heart. This ceremonial area, however, does not always occupy a space separate from the central business district. In cities like Frankfurt and Hanover, the ceremonial area does exist apart; and when those areas were destroyed by the bombing during the war, the administrative and residential buildings were rebuilt in ceremonial styles, and business structures were kept off the area. But in cities like Nuremburg and Cologne, the central business district is embedded in, or superimposed upon revered ceremonial terrain. In both cities a rich symbolism is associated with the medieval street plan of the inner city. The streets themselves are considered, in some sense, sacred, and may not, quite aside from financial considerations, be tampered with. Although the area cradled within Nuremberg's famed medieval walls was terribly bombed during the war, the entire area was rebuilt thereafter with the conscious intention of recapturing the flavor of old Nuremberg; and the height and color of the buildings in the business district which lies within the walls have been carefully controlled to maintain the illusion of an old city. In Cologne, the street plan is so sacred that planners, after the war, have experienced great frustration in trying to provide for the flow of traffic because the city's street plan may not be altered. Such a city as Essen is much more like American cities, for it grew quickly during the late nineteenth century from a village to a modern industrial city; hence it did not have any great investment in treasured buildings or inviolable street plans. Its central district was rebuilt with relative freedom and with no obvious ceremonial features.

These European examples illustrate that symbolic functions (or "services," if one wishes to retain the language of economics) go on coterminously with economic and ecological functions. One can see the point dramatically illustrated by the

relaxed people who stroll up and down Fifth Avenue in New York City during any fine evening. Then this beautiful shopping street is used as a promenade of pleasure, and window shopping is part of the enjoyment. During the day, most New Yorkers who rush across or along it are too preoccupied with other affairs to use the street for viewing and promenading, but even during the busiest hours of the day one can observe people using the street and its shops exclusively for pleasure. The significance of Fifth Avenue is not merely a matter of economics or of ecology, and its symbolic meanings, we may assume, are multitudinous.

Just as the downtown area, and even single streets, are differentiated by economic function, so we may regard them as differentiated by symbolic function. This statement has implications that are not immediately apparent. A convenient way to begin seeing these implications is to examine closely a single important downtown street. It will be probably be used simultaneously by several different kinds of populations, distinguishable by dress and posture. Other kinds of people will be wholly, or to a considerable extent, missing. (These may be found on other streets; for instance, the wealthier customers and strollers will be found on upper Fifth Avenue rather than below 42nd Street.) Just as several types of economic services can be found cheek by jowl on the same street, so may there be several symbolic functions performed by the same street. A restaurant there may serve expensive food: it may also serve leisure and a sense of luxury. Close by, another type of establishment may cater to another taste, an activity not entirely reducible to economic terms. The street may attract people who seek glamour, adventure, escape from a humdrum life, and who, though they may not spend a cent, feel wholly or partly satisfied by an evening on the street. The larger the downtown area, the more obviously districted will be the various economic and symbolic functions.

A city as large as Chicago, for instance, has a separate hotel row, a separate elite shopping boulevard, a separate financial canyon; and on these streets may be seen different types of architecture, different types of clients and servicing agents, and different types of activities. During the evening some of the symbolic, if not indeed the economic, functions change on identical streets; that is, people are using different institutions, or using the same ones a little differently. The sociological question is always: "Who is found in such an area or on such a street, doing what, for what purposes, at any given hour?"

Over the years a downtown street can change wholly in economic and symbolic function, as the center of town moves or as the city center grows larger and hence more differentiated. However, in American cities, some downtown streets seem to retain a remarkable affinity for the same kind of businesses, clients, visitors, and pleasure-seekers. Streets acquire and keep reputations. They evoke images in the minds of those who know these reputations; and presumably these images help attract and repel clients and visitors. From time to time, as the downtown district becomes more differentiated, functions break off from one street and become instituted on another. Thus in Chicago, upper Michigan Avenue was opened with some fanfare during the present century, drawing away elite shops and shoppers from the more centrally located and famed State Street section. One can, if he is sufficiently imaginative, therefore, view the downtown area of any city as having different historical depths. This is easier to see in Asiatic or European cities; for instance, in Tokyo there are ancient streets, with both new and old functions, and newer streets as well. In American cities, history tends to be lost more quickly; but even here some residents are more aware of street histories than other townspeople, and derive satisfactions from knowing about the past as they walk the street; it is, one might add, not too much to claim

that they perceive the street differently from someone who does not know its past.[3] Here is an elderly Chicago lady speaking:

I am looking from the window of my office in the London Guaranty Building, on the very site of Fort Dearborn. I look from one window up the Chicago River, past the new Wacker Drive, once South Water Street, where my grandfather was a commission merchant. . . . A short distance south of the Wacker Drive, my father sat in the office of his bank and made his first loans to the merchants who were even then building their grain elevators and establishing a center for the meat industry of the world (Bowen, 1926, pp. 224–225).

Not everyone has personal and familial memories so intertwined with street histories. On the other hand, it is perhaps more characteristic of American urban memories than of European or of Asiatic that one's own personal memories are relied upon to supply temporal depth to city streets and districts. For the more obviously historic areas like the Boston Commons, personal memories are buttressed with folklore and textbook history.

To continue now with the complex symbolic functions of certain downtown streets, it is clearly observable that certain streets draw several different kinds of

[3] Donald Horton has supplied this amusing and revealing anecdote. Many years ago O. Henry wrote a story of which the scene was laid in Grove Court in Greenwich Village. Those living there then were working-class people and artists. They were succeeded by Irish men and women, who in turn were replaced by the present generation of middle-class intellectuals. One family of the later group speaks of itself as "First Settlers" because it was among the earliest of this population to settle there. Frequently devotees of O. Henry's writing seek out Grove Court, only to be disappointed that a pump which was featured in his "Last Leaf" has been removed.

populations. The term "locale" shall refer to such a street. A street like Rush Street in Chicago, for example, is a locale where in the evening one may find—on the street and in the many restaurants and bars—a variety of customers, servicing agents, and visitors. Rush Street has its own atmosphere, as many people have observed, compounded of all these people and all these institutions. It is one of the glamour streets of Chicago. There one can see, if one has an eye for them, prostitutes, pimps, homosexuals, bisexuals, upper-class men and women, university students, touts, artists, tourists, business men out for a good time with or without girl friends, young men and women dating, people of various ethnic backgrounds, policemen, cabbies—the entire catalogue is much longer. Rush Street is a locale where people from many different urban worlds, with many styles of urbanity, pass each other, buy services from each other, talk to one another, and occasionally make friends with one another. Like animals using the same bit of land, people on Rush Street can interact almost subliminally, demanding nothing of each other, making no contracts with each other, merely passing each other or sitting near each other. But the interaction can also be contractual and exploitative, as when prostitutes find clients or pickpockets find marks. But most important, perhaps, there can occur at such locales a more sociable, more lasting kind of contact between peoples drawn from different worlds. It is at places like Rush Street that the orbits of many worlds intersect, so that persons may learn something of the ways of another world. In locales, as the orbits intersect, the physical segregation of these urban worlds is at a minimum.[4]

[4] World famous streets and boulevards occasionally stimulate the writing of books about themselves. J. B. Kerfort (1911) wrote one about Broadway. Some of his feeling for the multiplicity of members of social worlds present at this locale is vividly suggested by his

Other streets in the city are inhabited and visited by persons drawn from just a few social worlds. Think, for instance, of the main street in a Polish area down whose length one can see only Polish people. The area may be visited occasionally by outsiders or patrolled by a non-Polish policeman; but for the most part, especially at night, this is a street which quite literally belongs to the residents of the parish. (If anything, the side streets are even more insular.) Let us call such a street or area, where intersect only a minimum number of social worlds, a "location." At a location, the physical segregation of the people of a social world is maximized. Here they can openly indulge in ceremonial and ritual gestures; here they may speak a foreign language without shame. For it is here that an urban world is seen in the form of relatively public activities based on relatively widely shared symbols. It is here, too, that the outsider really knows that he is an outsider: he knows that he must learn the appropriate ways of his world. This kind of area, too, is characterized by quite ex-

opening lines: "I was leaning, one afternoon, on the stone rail . . . that surrounds the fifty-second story of one of the downtown office towers, looking dreamily down into the chasm of Broadway. . . . A man alongside of me volunteered a remark. . . . 'They look like ants, don't they.' . . . From dawn to dark—and after —it . . . was lined with ascending and descending insects. What if, just once, one were to make the long journey up that crooked and curving highway, challenging every human ant one met, stopping him, rubbing antennae with him, sensing the sources he derived from the ends he aimed at, the instincts he obeyed, the facts he blinked at, the illusions he hugged—getting, in short, the essence of his errand? Suppose one covered the dozen miles in eleven days and held two hundred thousand interviews by the way. Suppose, when one reached the heights of Harlem, one set down and took stock of what one had learned?" What one had learned can only mean that the worlds of so many of these people are different from one's own.

clusive, or semi-exclusive, spaces, as anyone who has entered a Polish tavern, to be eyed by the "regulars," knows. In the streets of such an area, the stranger is quickly spotted.

Some outsiders occasionally visit such locations by design, going as tourists who are "slumming"; or they may go on flying visits for particular services, as conventioneers are said to visit Negro areas for quick trips to houses of prostitution. But a person may find himself in a more or less closed location quite without design, and respond with delight, with aversion, or with another emotion to seeing the strange world "at home." If the outsider does not see the world on its home terrain, then he can only see some of its members in action at some more public locale, as when one observes certain people downtown at a restaurant, and experiences the same kinds of reactions or gets the same impressions of them that he might get if he visited these people—whether they are poor or rich, ethnic or native citizens—at their own more local haunts.

However, some city dwellers, by virtue of their work, are frequent visitors to a number of different locations. Jazz musicians, salesmen of some kinds, policemen, and bill collectors cross many lines of normal spatial and social segregation—in a certain restricted way, at least. Their occasional roles bring them to these locations where in the course of servicing clients they may also become spectators of local acts, or on occasion participate in them.

The names "locale" and "location" are polar terms with many intervening steps between them.[5] The main street of any city's Negro area is a locale—the side streets are a location—although somewhat fewer orbits of social worlds perhaps intersect there than at the main street of the downtown area. Even at a location the

orbits of members of the predominant social world necessarily crosscut the orbits of members of some other worlds: even the most isolated elderly lady of an ethnic enclave occasionally meets an outsider, however brief and superficial the contact. Most people's orbits, of work and of play, take them beyond their immediate residential neighborhoods. Nevertheless, we need not be surprised that most people use and know only a limited number of spatial sectors of their city and know very little about the people who frequent those areas. In a large city, unquestionably most spatial segments will be only vaguely conceived, virtually geographic blurs. The places where the orbits of life take a city dweller will have special meanings to him.

The concept of "orbit" permits us to say something about space that the earlier sociologists did not make clear or obscured. The point turns about the relations of space to social worlds. The Chicago sociologists, for instance, were alternatively struck by the ecological features of urban communities and by the social color of the communities themselves. Robert Park (1936) attempted to relate these two kinds of observation by talking about "ecological order" and a "moral order," maintaining uncertainly sometimes that they were interrelated and sometimes that the ecological sustained the moral. When the human ecologists later turned away from a sharp focus upon the "moral order," certain other sociologists like Walter Firey criticized them for ignoring the probable role played by the moral or cultural side of society in ordering ecological relationships. The tenor of Firey's criticism is conveyed by an opening passage from his book (1947):

Since its emergence as a definite field of research, ecology has developed a number of distinct theories, each of which has tried to bring a conceptual order out of man's relationships with physical space. When these theories are subjected to a careful analysis their differences turn

[5] I am greatly indebted to Howard S. Becker for these distinctions which were then further explored by the two of us.

out to be, in large part, variations upon a single conception of the society-space relationship. Briefly, this conception ascribes to space a determinate and invariant influence upon the distribution of human activities. The socially relevant qualities of space are thought to reside in the very nature of space itself, and the territorial patterns assumed by social activities are regarded as wholly determined by these qualities. There is no recognition, except in occasional fleeting insights, that social values may endow space with qualities that are quite extraneous to it as a physical phenomenon. Moreover, there is no indication of what pre-conditions there may be to social activities becoming in any way linked with physical space.

Firey's answer was to contend and try to establish that cultural factors influenced ecological, or locational, processes. Human ecologists have gone their way fairly unaffected by this species of criticism, although the issue seems still to be alive.

It is not my intent to do more than comment on this issue as a background to my own discussion of spatial representations. The chief efficacy of the term "orbit" is that it directs attention to the spatial movements of members of social worlds. Some worlds are relatively bounded in space, their members moving within very narrow orbits, like the immigrant mothers already mentioned. The members of other social worlds, such as the elite world of any large metropolis, move in orbits that take in larger sections of the city as well as encompass sections of other cities—foreign as well as domestic. In any genuine sense, it can be said that the members of such a world live not only, say, in the Gold Coast area, but also elsewhere for part of the year—in a favorite resort, in a fine suburb, in Paris, or in all four places.

The important thing about any given urban world is not that it is rooted in space.

That is merely what often strikes the eye first, just as it attracted the attention of the nineteenth-century journalists and the twentieth-century sociologists. What is important about a social world is that its members are linked by some sort of shared symbolization, some effective channels of communication. Many urban worlds are diffusely organized, difficult to pin down definitely in space since their members are scattered through several, or many, areas of the city. An FM station, for instance, may draw devoted listeners to its classical programs from a half dozen areas in the city. The worlds of art or fashion or drama may find expression in particular institutions located downtown, but their members are scattered about the face of the city. These are but a few of the urban worlds to which one may belong. (As Tomatsu Shibutani (1955) has commented: "Each social world . . . is a culture area, the boundaries of which are set neither by territory nor by formal group membership but by the limits of effective communication.") The important thing, then, about a social world is its network of communication and the shared symbols which give the world some substance and which allow people to "belong" to "it." Its institutions and meeting places must be rooted somewhere, even if the orbits of the world's members do take them to many other sites in the city (just as the jazz musician moves about the city on jobs, and ends up in favorite bars for "kicks" and for job information). The experiences which the members have in those areas stem from, and in turn affect, their symbolic representations of those areas. Of an area which they never visit, they have no representations unless someone in their circle has visited it, and has passed along some representation of it. In sum: the various kinds of urban perspectives held by the residents of a city are constructed from spatial representations resulting from membership in particular social worlds.

40. *The Uses of Sidewalks: Contact*
JANE JACOBS

Reformers have long observed city people loitering on busy corners, hanging around in candy stores and bars and drinking soda pop on stoops, and have passed a judgment, the gist of which is: "This is deplorable! If these people had decent homes and a more private or bosky outdoor place, they wouldn't be on the street!"

This judgment represents a profound misunderstanding of cities. It makes no more sense than to drop in at a testimonial banquet in a hotel and conclude that if these people had wives who could cook, they would give their parties at home.

The point of both the testimonial banquet and the social life of city sidewalks is precisely that they are public. They bring together people who do not know each other in an intimate, private social fashion and in most cases do not care to know each other in that fashion.

Nobody can keep open house in a great city. Nobody wants to. And yet if interesting, useful and significant contacts among the people of cities are confined to acquaintanceships suitable for private life, the city becomes stultified. Cities are full of people with whom, from your viewpoint, or mine, or any other individual's, a certain degree of contact is useful or enjoyable; but you do not want them in your hair. And they do not want you in theirs either.

Considering city sidewalk safety, it is necessary that there should be, in the brains behind the eyes on the street, an almost unconscious assumption of general street support when the chips are down—when a citizen has to choose, for instance, whether he will take responsibility, or abdicate it, in combating barbarism or protecting strangers. There is a short word for this assump-

tion of support: trust. The trust of a city street is formed over time from many, many little public sidewalk contacts. It grows out of people stopping by at the bar for a beer, getting advice from the grocer and giving advice to the newsstand man, comparing opinions with other customers at the bakery and nodding hello to the two boys drinking pop on the stoop, eying the girls while waiting to be called for dinner, admonishing the children, hearing about a job from the hardware man and borrowing a dollar from the druggist, admiring the new babies and sympathizing over the way a coat faded. Customs vary: in some neighborhoods people compare notes on their dogs; in others they compare notes on their landlords.

Most of it is ostensibly utterly trivial but the sum is not trivial at all. The sum of such casual, public contact at a local level —most of it fortuitous, most of it associated with errands, all of it metered by the person concerned and not thrust upon him by anyone—is a feeling for the public identity of people, a web of public respect and trust, and a resource in time of personal or neighborhood need. The absence of this trust is a disaster to a city street. Its cultivation cannot be institutionalized. And above all, *it implies no private commitments.*

I have seen a striking difference between presence and absence of casual public trust on two sides of the same wide street in East Harlem, composed of residents of roughly the same incomes and same races. On the old-city side, which was full of public places and the sidewalk loitering so deplored by Utopian minders of other people's leisure, the children were being kept well in hand. On the project side of the street across the way, the children, who had a fire hydrant open beside their play area, were behaving destructively, drenching the open windows of houses with water, squirting it on adults who ignorantly walked on the project side of the street, throwing it into the windows of cars as they went by. Nobody dared to stop them. These were anonymous children, and the identities behind them were an unknown. What if you scolded or stopped them? Who would back you up over there in the blind-eyed Turf? Would you get, instead, revenge? Better to keep out of it. Impersonal city streets make anonymous people, and this is not a matter of esthetic quality nor of a mystical emotional effect in architectural scale. It is a matter of what kinds of tangible enterprises sidewalks have, and therefore of how people use the sidewalks in practical, every-day life.

The casual public sidewalk life of cities ties directly into other types of public life, of which I shall mention one as illustrative, although there is no end to their variety.

Formal types of local city organizations are frequently assumed by planners and even by some social workers to grow in direct, common-sense fashion out of announcements of meetings, the presence of meeting rooms, and the existence of problems of obvious public concern. Perhaps they grow so in suburbs and towns. They do not grow so in cities.

Formal public organizations in cities require an informal public life underlying them, mediating between them and the privacy of the people of the city. We catch a hint of what happens by contrasting, again, a city area possessing a public side-walk life with a city area lacking it, as told about in the report of a settlement-house social researcher who was studying problems relating to public schools in a section of New York City:

Mr. W——— [principal of an elementary school] was questioned on the effect of J——— Houses on the school, and the up-rooting of the community around the school. He felt that there had been many effects and of these most were negative. He mentioned that the project had torn out numerous institutions for

socializing. The present atmosphere of the project was in no way similar to the gaiety of the streets before the project was built. He noted that in general there seemed fewer people on the streets because there were fewer places for people to gather. He also contended that before the projects were built the Parents Association had been very strong, and now there were only very few active members.

Mr. W——— was wrong in one respect. There were not fewer places (or at any rate there was not less space) for people to gather in the project, if we count places deliberately planned for constructive socializing. Of course there were no bars, no candy stores, no hole-in-the-wall *bodegas,* no restaurants in the project. But the project under discussion was equipped with a model complement of meeting rooms, craft, art and game rooms, outdoor benches, malls, etc., enough to gladden the heart of even the Garden City advocates.

Why are such places dead and useless without the most determined efforts and expense to inveigle users—and then to maintain control over the users? What services do the public sidewalk and its enterprises fulfill that these planned gathering places do not? And why? How does an informal public sidewalk life bolster a more formal, organizational public life?

To understand such problems—to understand why drinking pop on the stoop differs from drinking pop in the game room, and why getting advice from the grocer or the bartender differs from getting advice from either your next-door neighbor or from an institutional lady who may be hand-in-glove with an institutional landlord—we must look into the matter of city privacy.

Privacy is precious in cities. It is indispensable. Perhaps it is precious and indispensable everywhere, but most places you cannot get it. In small settlements everyone knows your affairs. In the city everyone does not—only those you choose to tell will know much about you. This is one of the attributes of cities that is precious to most city people, whether their incomes are high or their incomes are low, whether they are white or colored, whether they are old inhabitants or new, and it is a gift of great-city life deeply cherished and jealously guarded.

Architectural and planning literature deals with privacy in terms of windows, overlooks, sight lines. The idea is that if no one from outside can peek into where you live—behold, privacy. This is simpleminded. Window privacy is the easiest commodity in the world to get. You just pull down the shades or adjust the blinds. The privacy of keeping one's personal affairs to those selected to know them, and the privacy of having reasonable control over who shall make inroads on your time and when, are rare commodities in most of this world, however, and they have nothing to do with the orientation of windows.

Anthropologist Elena Padilla, author of *Up from Puerto Rico*, describing Puerto Rican life in a poor and squalid district of New York, tells how much people know about each other—who is to be trusted and who not, who is defiant of the law and who upholds it, who is competent and well informed and who is inept and ignorant— and how these things are known from the public life of the sidewalk and its associated enterprises. These are matters of public character. But she also tells how select are those permitted to drop into the kitchen for a cup of coffee, how strong are the ties, and how limited the number of a person's genuine confidants, those who share in a person's private life and private affairs. She tells how it is not considered dignified for everyone to know one's affairs. Nor is it considered dignified to snoop on others beyond the face presented in public. It does violence to a person's privacy and rights. In this, the people she describes are essentially the same as the people of the mixed, Americanized city street on which I live, and essentially the same as the people

who live in high-income apartments or fine town houses, too.

A good city street neighborhood achieves a marvel of balance between its people's determination to have essential privacy and their simultaneous wishes for differing degrees of contact, enjoyment or help from the people around. This balance is largely made up of small, sensitively managed details, practiced and accepted so casually that they are normally taken for granted.

Perhaps I can best explain this subtle but all-important balance in terms of the stores where people leave keys for their friends, a common custom in New York. In our family, for example, when a friend wants to use our place while we are away for a week end or everyone happens to be out during the day, or a visitor for whom we do not wish to wait up is spending the night, we tell such a friend that he can pick up the key at the delicatessen across the street. Joe Cornacchia, who keeps the delicatessen, usually has a dozen or so keys at a time for handing out like this. He has a special drawer for them.

Now why do I, and many others, select Joe as a logical custodian for keys? Because we trust him, first, to be a responsible custodian, but equally important because we know that he combines a feeling of good will with a feeling of no personal responsibility about our private affairs. Joe considers it no concern of his whom we choose to permit in our places and why.

Around on the other side of our block, people leave their keys at a Spanish grocery. On the other side of Joe's block, people leave them at the candy store. Down a block they leave them at the coffee shop, and a few hundred feet around the corner from that, in a barber shop. Around one corner from two fashionable blocks of town houses and apartments in the Upper East Side, people leave their keys in a butcher shop and a bookshop; around another corner they leave them in a cleaner's and a drug store. In unfashionable East Harlem keys are left with at least one florist, in bakeries, in luncheonettes, in Spanish and Italian groceries.

The point, wherever they are left, is not the kind of ostensible service that the enterprise offers, but the kind of proprietor it has.

A service like this cannot be formalized. Identifications . . . questions . . . insurance against mishaps. The all-essential line between public service and privacy would be transgressed by institutionalization. Nobody in his right mind would leave his key in such a place. The service must be given as a favor by someone with an unshakable understanding of the difference between a person's key and a person's private life, or it cannot be given at all.

Or consider the line drawn by Mr. Jaffe at the candy store around our corner—a line so well understood by his customers and by other storekeepers too that they can spend their whole lives in its presence and never think about it consciously. One ordinary morning last winter, Mr. Jaffe, whose formal business name is Bernie, and his wife, whose formal business name is Ann, supervised the small children crossing at the corner on the way to P.S. 41, as Bernie always does because he sees the need; lent an umbrella to one customer and a dollar to another; took custody of two keys: took in some packages for people in the next building who were away; lectured two youngsters who asked for cigarettes; gave street directions; took custody of a watch to give the repair man across the street when he opened later; gave out information on the range of rents in the neighborhood to an apartment seeker; listened to a tale of domestic difficulty and offered reassurance; told some rowdies they could not come in unless they behaved and then defined (and got) good behavior; provided an incidental forum for half a dozen conversations among customers who dropped in for oddments; set aside certain newly arrived papers and magazines for regular customers who would depend on getting

them: advised a mother who came for a birthday present not to get the ship-model kit because another child going to the same birthday party was giving that, and got a back copy (this was for me) of the previous day's newspaper out of the deliverer's surplus returns when he came by.

After considering this multiplicity of extra-merchandising services I asked Bernie, "Do you ever introduce your customers to each other?"

He looked startled at the idea, even dismayed. "No," he said thoughtfully. "That would just not be advisable. Sometimes, if I know two customers who are in at the same time have an interest in common, I bring up the subject in conversation and let them carry it on from there if they want to. But oh no, I wouldn't introduce them."

When I told this to an acquaintance in a suburb, she promptly assumed that Mr. Jaffe felt that to make an introduction would be to step above his social class. Not at all. In our neighborhood, storekeepers like the Jaffes enjoy an excellent social status, that of businessmen. In income they are apt to be the peers of the general run of customers and in independence they are the superiors. Their advice, as men or women of common sense and experience, is sought and respected. They are well known as individuals, rather than unknown as class symbols. No; this is that almost unconsciously enforced, well-balanced line showing, the line between the city public world and the world of privacy.

This line can be maintained, without awkwardness to anyone, because of the great plenty of opportunities for public contact in the enterprises along the sidewalks, or on the sidewalks themselves as people move to and fro or deliberately loiter when they feel like it, and also because of the presence of many public hosts, so to speak, proprietors of meeting places like Bernie's where one is free either to hang around or dash in and out, no strings attached.

Under this system, it is possible in a city street neighborhood to know all kinds

of people without unwelcome entangle-
ments, without boredom, necessity for excuses, explanations, fears of giving offense,
embarrassments respecting impositions or
commitments, and all such paraphernalia
of obligations which can accompany less
limited relationships. It is possible to be on
excellent sidewalk terms with people who
are very different from oneself, and even,
as time passes, on familiar public terms
with them. Such relationships can, and do,
endure for many years, for decades; they
could never have formed without that line,
much less endured. They form precisely
because they are by-the-way to people's
normal public sorties.

"Togetherness" is a fittingly nauseating
name for an old ideal in planning theory.
This ideal is that if anything is shared
among people, much should be shared.
"Togetherness," apparently a spiritual resource of the new suburbs, works destructively in cities. The requirement that much
shall be shared drives city people apart.

When an area of a city lacks a sidewalk life, the people of the place must enlarge their private lives if they are to have
anything approaching equivalent contact
with their neighbors. They must settle for
some form of "togetherness," in which more
is shared with one another than in the life
of the sidewalks, or else they must settle
for lack of contact. Inevitably the outcome
is one or the other; it has to be: and either
has distressing results.

In the case of the first outcome, where
people do share much, they become exceedingly choosy as to who their neighbors are,
or with whom they associate at all. They
have to become so. A friend of mine, Penny
Kostritsky, is unwittingly and unwillingly
in this fix on a street in Baltimore. Her street
of nothing but residences, embedded in an
area of almost nothing but residences, has
been experimentally equipped with a charming sidewalk park. The sidewalk has been
widened and attractively paved, wheeled
traffic discouraged from the narrow street

roadbed, trees and flowers planted, and a
piece of play sculpture is to go in. All these
are splendid ideas so far as they go.

However, there are no stores. The
mothers from nearby blocks who bring small
children here, and come here to find some
contact with others themselves, perforce
go into the houses of acquaintances along
the street to warm up in winter, to make
telephone calls, to take their children in
emergencies to the bathroom. Their
hostesses offer them coffee, for there is no
other place to get coffee, and naturally considerable social life of this kind has risen
around the park. Much is shared.

Mrs. Kostritsky, who lives in one of the
conveniently located houses, and who has
two small children, is in the thick of this
narrow and accidental social life. "I have
lost the advantage of living in the city,"
she says, "without getting the advantages
of living in the suburbs." Still more distressing when mothers of different income
or color or educational background bring
their children to the street park, they and
their children are rudely and pointedly
ostracized. They fit awkwardly into the
suburbanlike sharing or private lives that
has grown in default of city sidewalk life.
The park lacks benches purposely; the "togetherness" people ruled them out because
they might be interpreted as an invitation
to people who cannot fit in.

"If only we had a couple of stores on
the street," Mrs. Kostritsky laments. "If only
there were a grocery store or a drug store
or a snack joint. Then the telephone calls
and the warming up and the gathering could
be done naturally in public, and then people
would act more decent to each other because everybody would have a right to be
here."

Much the same thing that happens in
this sidewalk park without a city public life
happens sometimes in middle-class projects
and colonies, such as Chatham Village in
Pittsburgh for example, a famous model of
Garden City planning.

The houses here are grouped in

colonies around shared interior lawns and play yards, and the whole development is equipped with other devices for close sharing, such as a residents' club which holds parties, dances, reunions, has ladies' activities like bridge and sewing parties, and holds dances and parties for the children. There is no public life here, in any city sense. There are differing degrees of extended private life.

Chatham Village's success as a "model" neighborhood where much is shared has required that the residents be similar to one another in their standards, interests and backgrounds. In the main they are middle-class professionals and their families.[1] It has also required that residents set themselves distinctly apart from the different people in the surrounding city; these are in the main also middle class, but lower middle class, and this is too different for the degree of chumminess that neighborliness in Chatham Village entails.

The inevitable insularity (and homogeneity) of Chatham Village has practical consequences. As one illustration, the junior high school serving the area has problems, as all schools do. Chatham Village is large enough to dominate the elementary school to which its children go, and therefore to work at helping solve this school's problems. To deal with the junior high, however, Chatham Village's people must cooperate with entirely different neighborhoods. But there is no public acquaintanceship, no foundation of casual public trust, no cross-connections with the necessary people—and no practice or ease in applying the most ordinary techniques of city public life at lowly levels. Feeling helpless, as indeed they are, some Chatham Village families move away when their children reach junior high age; others contrive to send

them to private high schools. Ironically, just such neighborhood islands as Chatham Village are encouraged in orthodox planning on the specific grounds that cities need the talents and stabilizing influence of the middle class. Presumably these qualities are to seep out by osmosis.

People who do not fit happily into such colonies eventually get out, and in time managements become sophisticated in knowing who among applicants will fit in. Along with basic similarities of standards, values and backgrounds, the arrangement seems to demand a formidable amount of forbearance and tact.

City residential planning that depends, for contact among neighbors, on personal sharing of this sort, and that cultivates it, often does work well socially, if rather narrowly, for self-selected upper-middle-class people. It solves easy problems for an easy kind of population. So far as I have been able to discover, it fails to work, however, even on its own terms, with any other kind of population.

The more common outcome in cities, where people are faced with the choice of sharing much or nothing, is nothing. In city areas that lack a natural and casual public life, it is common for residents to isolate themselves from each other to a fantastic degree. If mere contact with your neighbors threatens to entangle you in their private lives, or entangle them in yours, and if you cannot be so careful who your neighbors are as self-selected upper-middle-class people can be, the logical solution is absolutely to avoid friendliness or casual offers of help. Better to stay thoroughly distant. As a practical result, the ordinary public jobs—like keeping children in hand—for which people must take a little personal initiative, or those for which they must band together in limited common purposes, go undone. The abysses this opens up can be almost unbelievable.

For example, in one New York City project which is designed—like all orthodox residential city planning—for sharing much

[1] One representative court, for example, contains as this is written four lawyers, two doctors, two engineers, a dentist, a salesman, a banker, a railroad executive, a planning executive.

or nothing, a remarkably outgoing woman prided herself that she had become acquainted, by making a deliberate effort, with the mothers of every one of the ninety families in her building. She called on them. She buttonholed them at the door or in the hall. She struck up conversations if she sat beside them on a bench.

It so happened that her eight-year-old son, one day, got stuck in the elevator and was left there without help for more than two hours, although he screamed, cried and pounded. The next day the mother expressed her dismay to one of her ninety acquaintances. "Oh, was that *your* son?" said the other woman. "I didn't know whose boy he was. If I had realized he was *your* son I would have helped him."

This woman, who had not behaved in any such insanely calloused fashion on her old public street—to which she constantly returned, by the way, for public life—was afraid of a possible entanglement that might not be kept easily on a public plane.

Dozens of illustrations of this defense can be found wherever the choice is sharing much or nothing. A thorough and detailed report by Ellen Lurie, a social worker in East Harlem, on life in a low-income project there, has this to say:

It is . . . extremely important to recognize that for considerably complicated reasons, many adults either don't want to become involved in any friendship-relationships at all with their neighbors, or, if they do succumb to the need for some form of society, they strictly limit themselves to one or two friends, and no more. Over and over again, wives repeted their husband's warning:

"I'm not to get too friendly with anyone. My husband doesn't believe in it."

"People are too gossipy and they could get us in a lot of trouble."

"It's best to mind your own business."

One woman, Mrs. Abraham, always goes out the back door of the building because she doesn't want to interfere with the people standing around in the front. Another man, Mr. Colan . . . won't let his wife make any friends in the project, because he doesn't trust the people here. They have four children, ranging from 8 years to 14, but they are not allowed downstairs alone, because the parents are afraid someone will hurt them.[2] What happens then is that all sorts of barriers to ensure self-protection are being constructed by many families. To protect their children from a neighborhood they aren't sure of, they keep them upstairs in the apartment. To protect themselves, they make few, if any, friends. Some are afraid that friends will become angry or envious and make up a story to report to management, causing them great trouble. If the husband gets a bonus (which he decided not to report) and the wife buys new curtains, the visiting friends will see and might tell the management, who, in turn, investigates and issues a rent increase. Suspicion and fear of trouble often outweigh any need for neighborly advice and help. For these families the sense of privacy has already been extensively violated. The deepest secrets, all the family skeletons, are well known not only to management but often to other public agencies, such as the Welfare Department. To preserve any last remnants of privacy, they choose to avoid close relationships with others. This same phenomenon may be found to a much lesser degree in no-planned slum housing, for there too it is often necessary for other reasons to build up these forms of self-protection. But it is surely true that this withdrawing from the society of others is much more extensive in planned housing. Even in England, this suspicion of the neighbors and the ensuring aloofness was found in studies of planned towns. Perhaps this pattern is nothing

---

[2] This is very common in public projects in New York.

more than an elaborate group mechanism to protect and preserve inner dignity in the face of so many outside pressures to conform.

Along with nothingness, considerable "togetherness" can be found in such places, however. Mrs. Lurie reports on this type of relationship:

Often two women from two different buildings will meet in the laundry room, recognize each other; although they may never have spoken a single word to each other back on 99th Street, suddenly here they become "best friends." If one of these two already has a friend or two in her own building, the other is likely to be drawn into that circle and begins to make her friendships, not with women on her floor, but rather on her friend's floor.

These friendships do not go into an ever-widening circle. There are certain definite well-traveled paths in the project, and after a while no new people are met.

Mrs. Lurie, who works at community organization in East Harlem, with remarkable success, has looked into the history of many past attempts at project tenant organization. She has told me that "togetherness," itself, is one of the factors that make this kind of organization so difficult. "These projects are not lacking in natural leaders," she says. "They contain people with real ability, wonderful people many of them, but the typical sequence is that in the course of organization leaders have found each other, gotten all involved in each other's social lives, and have ended up talking to nobody but each other. They have not found their followers. Everything tends to degenerate into ineffective cliques, as a natural course. There is no normal public life. Just the mechanics of people learning what is going on is so difficult. It all makes the simplest social gain extra hard for these people."

Residents of unplanned city residential areas that lack neighborhood commerce and sidewalk life seem sometimes to follow the same course as residents of public projects when faced with the choice of sharing much or nothing. Thus researchers hunting the secrets of the social structure in a dull gray-area district of Detroit came to the unexpected conclusion there was no social structure.

41. The Uses of Sidewalks: Assimilating Children
JANE JACOBS

Children in cities need a variety of places in which to play and to learn. They need, among other things, opportunities for all kinds of sports and exercise and physical skills—more opportunities, more easily obtained, than they now enjoy in most cases. However, at the same time, they need an unspecialized outdoor home base from

From *Death and Life of Great American Cities*, by Jane Jacobs. © Copyright 1961 by Jane Jacobs. Reprinted by permission of Random House, Inc., and the author.

which to play, to hang around in, and to help form their notions of the world.

It is this form of unspecialized play that the sidewalks serve—and that lively city sidewalks can serve splendidly. When this home-base play is transferred to playgrounds and parks it is not only provided for unsafely, but paid personnel, equipment and space are frittered away that could be devoted instead to more ice-skating rinks, swimming pools, boat ponds and other various and specific outdoor uses. Poor, generalized play use eats up substance that could instead be used for good specialized play.

To waste the normal presence of adults on lively sidewalks and to bank instead (however idealistically) on hiring substitutes for them, is frivolous in the extreme. It is frivolous not only socially but also economically, because cities have desperate shortages of money and of personnel for more interesting uses of the outdoors than playgrounds—and of money and personnel for other aspects of children's lives. For example, city school systems today typically have between thirty and forty children in their classes—sometimes more—and these include children with all manner of problems too, from ignorance of English to bad emotional upsets. City schools need something approaching a 50 percent increase in teachers to handle severe problems and also reduce normal class sizes to a figure permitting better education. New York's city-run hospitals in 1959 had 58 percent of their professional nursing positions unfilled, and in many another city the shortage of nurses has become alarming. Libraries, and often museums, curtail their hours, and notably the hours of their children's sections. Funds are lacking for the increased numbers of settlement houses drastically needed in the new slums and new projects of cities. Even the existing settlement houses lack funds for needed expansions and changes in their programs, in short for more staff. Requirements like these should have high priority on public and philanthropic funds—not only on funds at the present dismally inadequate levels, but on funds greatly increased.

The people of cities who have other jobs and duties, and who lack, too, the training needed, cannot volunteer as teachers or registered nurses or librarians or museum guards or social workers. But at least they can, and on lively diversified sidewalks they do, supervise the incidental play of children and assimilate the children into city society. They do it *in the course of carrying on their other pursuits.*

Planners do not seem to realize how high a ratio of adults is needed to rear children at incidental play. Nor do they seem to understand that spaces and equipment do not rear children. These can be useful adjuncts, but only people rear children and assimilate them into civilized society.

It is folly to build cities in a way that wastes this normal, casual manpower for child rearing and either leaves this essential job too much undone—with terrible consequences—or makes it necessary to hire substitutes. The myth that playgrounds and grass and hired guards or supervisors are innately wholesome for children and that city streets, filled with ordinary people, are innately evil for children, boils down to a deep contempt for ordinary people.

In real life, only from the ordinary adults of the city sidewalks do children learn—if they learn it at all—the first fundamental of successful city life: People must take a modicum of public responsibility for each other even if they have no ties to each other. This is a lesson nobody learns by being told. It is learned from the experience of having *other people without ties of kinship or close friendship or formal responsibility* to you take a modicum of public responsibility for you. When Mr. Lacey, the locksmith, bawls out one of my sons for running into the street, and then later reports the transgression to my husband as he passes the locksmith shop, my son gets more than an overt lesson in safety and obedience. He also gets, indirectly, the lesson that Mr. Lacey, with whom we have no ties other than street propinquity, feels responsible for him to a degree. The boy who went unrescued in the elevator in the "togetherness"-or-nothing project learns opposite lessons from his experiences. So do the project children who squirt water into house windows and on passers-by, and go unrebuked because they are anonymous children in anonymous grounds.

The lesson that city dwellers have to take responsibility for what goes on in city streets is taught again and again to children on sidewalks which enjoy a local public life. They can absorb it astonishingly early. They show they have absorbed it by taking it for granted that they, too, are part of the management. They volunteer (before they are asked) directions to people who are lost: they tell a man he will get a ticket if he parks where he thinks he is going to park; they offer unsolicited advice to the building superintendent to use rock salt instead of a chopper to attack the ice. The presence or absence of this kind of street bossiness in city children is a fairly good tip-off to the presence or absence of responsible adult behavior toward the sidewalk and the children who use it. The children are initiating adult attitudes. This has nothing to do with income. Some of the poorest parts of cities do the best by their children in this respect. And some do the worst.

This is instruction in city living that people hired to look after children cannot teach, because the essence of this responsibility is that you do it without being hired. It is a lesson that parents, by themselves, are powerless to teach. If parents take minor public responsibility for strangers or neighbors in a society where nobody else does, this simply means that the parents are embarrassingly different and meddlesome, not that this is the proper way to behave. Such instruction must come from society itself, and in cities, if it comes, it comes almost entirely during the time children spend at incidental play on the sidewalks.

Play on lively, diversified sidewalks differs from virtually all other daily incidental play offered American children today: It is play not conducted in a matriarchy.

Most city architectural designers and planners are men. Curiously, they design and plan to exclude men as part of normal, daytime life wherever people live. In planning residential life, they aim at filling the presumed daily needs of impossibly vacuous housewives and preschool tots. They plan, in short, strictly for matriarchal societies.

The ideal of matriarchy inevitably accompanies all planning in which residences are isolated from other parts of life. It accompanies all planning for children in which their incidental play is set apart in its own preserves. Whatever adult society does accompany the daily life of children affected by such planning has to be a matriarchy. Chatham Village, that Pittsburgh model of Garden City life, is as thoroughly matriarchal in conception and in operation as the newest dormitory suburb. All housing projects are.

Placing work and commerce *near* residences, but buffering it off, in the tradition set by Garden City theory, is fully as matriarchal an arrangement as if the residences were miles away from work and from men. Men are not an abstraction. They are either around, in person, or they are not. Working places and commerce must be mingled right in with residences if men, like the men who work on or near Hudson Street, for example, are to be around city children in daily life—men who are part of normal daily life, as opposed to men who put in an occasional playground appearance while they substitute for women or imitate the occupations of women.

The opportunity (in modern life it has become a privilege) of playing and growing up in a daily world composed of both men and women is possible and usual for children who play on lively, diversified city sidewalks. I cannot understand why this arrangement should be discouraged by planning and by zoning. It ought, instead, to be abetted by examining the conditions that stimulate minglings and mixtures of work and commerce with residences, a subject taken up later in this book.

The fascination of street life for city children has long been noted by recreation experts, usually with disapproval. Back in 1928, the Regional Plan Association of New

York, in a report which remains to this day the most exhaustive American study of big-city recreation, had this to say:

> Careful checking within a radius of 1/4 mile of playgrounds under a wide range of conditions in many cities shows that about 1/7 of the child population from 5 to 15 years of age may be found on these grounds . . . The lure of the street is a stronger competitor . . . It must be a well administered playground to compete successfully with the city streets, teeming with life and adventure. The ability to make the playground activity so compellingly attractive as to draw the children from the streets and hold their interest from day to day is a rare faculty in play leadership, combining personality and technical skill of a high order.

The same report then deplores the stubborn tendency of children to "fool around" instead of playing "recognized games." (Recognized by whom?) This yearning for the Organization Child on the part of those who would incarcerate incidental play, and children's stubborn preference for fooling around on city streets, teeming with life and adventure, are both as characteristic today as they were in 1928.

"I know Greenwich Village like my hand," brags my younger son, taking me to see a "secret passage" he has discovered under a street, down one subway stair and up another, and a secret hiding place some nine inches wide between two buildings, where he secretes treasures that people have put out for the sanitation truck collections along his morning route to school and that he can thus save and retrieve on his return from school. (I had such a hiding place, for the same purpose, at his age, but mine was a crack in a cliff on my way to school instead of a crack between two buildings, and he finds stranger and richer treasures.)

Why do children so frequently find that roaming the lively city sidewalks is more interesting than back yards or play-grounds? Because the sidewalks are more interesting. It is just as sensible to ask: Why do adults find lively streets more interesting than playgrounds?

The wonderful convenience of city sidewalks is an important asset to children too. Children are at the mercy of convenience more than anyone else, except the aged. A great part of children's outdoor play, especially after they start school, and after they also find a certain number of organized activities (sports, arts, handcrafts or whatever else their interests and the local opportunities provide), occurs at incidential times and must be sandwiched in. A lot of outdoor life for children adds up from bits. It happens in a small leftover interval after lunch. It happens after school while children may be pondering what to do and wondering who will turn up. It happens while they are waiting to be called for their suppers. It happens in brief intervals between supper and homework, or homework and bed.

During such times children have, and use, all manner of ways to exercise and amuse themselves. They slop in puddles, write with chalk, jump rope, roller skate, shoot marbles, trot out their possessions, converse, trade cards, play stoop ball, walk stilts, decorate soap-box scooters, dismember old baby carriages, climb on railings, run up and down. It is not in the nature of things to make a big deal out of such activities. It is not in the nature of things to go somewhere formally to do them by plan, officially. Part of their charm is the accompanying sense of freedom to roam up and down the sidewalks, a different matter from being boxed into a preserve. If it is impossible to do such things both incidentally and conveniently, they are seldom done.

As children get older, this incidental outdoor activity—say, while waiting to be called to eat—becomes less bumptious physically and entails more loitering with others, sizing people up, flirting, talking, pushing, shoving and horseplay. Adolescents are always being criticized for this kind of loitering, but they can hardly grow up without it. The trouble comes when it is done not within society, but as a form of outlaw life.

The requisite for any of these varieties of incidental play is not pretentious equipment of any sort, but rather space at an immediately convenient and interesting place. The play gets crowded out if sidewalks are too narrow relative to the total demands put on them. It is especially crowded out if the sidewalks also lack minor irregularities in building line. An immense amount of both loitering and play goes on in shallow sidewalk niches out of the line of moving pedestrian feet.

There is no point in planning for play on sidewalks unless the sidewalks are used for a wide variety of other purposes and by a wide variety of other people too. These uses need each other, for proper surveillance, for a public life of some vitality, and for general interest. If sidewalks on a lively street are sufficiently wide, play flourishes mightily right along with other uses. If the sidewalks are skimped, rope jumping is the first play casualty. Roller skating, tricycle and bicycle riding are the next casualties. The narrower the sidewalks, the more sedentary incidental play becomes. The more frequent too become sporadic forays by children into the vehicular roadways.

Sidewalks thirty or thirty-five feet wide can accommodate virtually any demand of incidental play put upon them—along with trees to shade the activities, and sufficient space for pedestrian circulation and adult public sidewalk life and loitering. Few sidewalks of this luxurious width can be found. Sidewalk width is invariably sacrificed for vehicular width, partly because city sidewalks are conventionally considered to be purely space for pedestrian travel and access to buildings, and go unrecognized and unrespected as the uniquely vital and irreplaceable organs of city safety, public life and child rearing that they are.

Twenty-foot sidewalks, which usually preclude rope jumping but can feasibly permit roller skating and the use of other wheeled toys, can still be found, although the street wideners erode them year by year (often in the belief that shunned malls and "promenades" are a constructive substitute). The livelier and more popular a sidewalk, and the greater the number and variety of its users, the greater the total width needed for it to serve its purposes pleasantly.

But even when proper space is lacking, convenience of location and the interest of the streets are both so important to children —and good surveillance so important to their parents—that children will and do adapt to skimpy sidewalk space. This does not mean we do right in taking unscrupulous advantage of their adaptability. In fact, we wrong both them and cities.

Some city sidewalks are undoubtedly evil places for rearing children. They are evil for anybody. In such neighborhoods we need to foster the qualities and facilities that make for safety, vitality and stability in city streets This is a complex problem; its a central problem of planning for cities. In defective city neighborhoods, shooing the children into parks and playgrounds is worse than useless, either as a solution to the streets' problems or as a solution for the children.

The whole idea of doing away with city streets, insofar as that is possible, and downgrading and minimizing their social and their economic part in city life is the most mischievous and destructive idea in orthodox city planning. That it is so often done in the name of vaporous fantasies about city child care is as bitter as irony can get.

42. Some Sources of Residential Satisfaction in an Urban Slum[1]

MARC FRIED AND PEGGY GLEICHER

The gradual deterioration of older urban dwellings and the belief that such areas provide a locus for considerable social pathology have stimulated concern with altering the physical habitat of the slum. Yet the technical difficulties, the practical inadequacies, and the moral problems of such planned revisions of the human environment are also forcing themselves upon our attention most strikingly (see Gans, 1959). While a full evaluation of the advantages and disadvantages of urban renewal must await studies which derive from various disciplines, there is little likelihood that the vast sums currently available will be withheld until there is a more systematic basis for rational decisions. Thus it is of the utmost importance that we discuss all aspects of the issue as thoroughly as possible and make available even the more fragmentary findings which begin to clarify the many unsolved problems.

Since the most common foci of urban renewal are areas which have been designated as slums, it is particularly important to obtain a clearer picture of so-called slum areas and their populations. Slum areas

Reproduced by permission of the *Journal of the American Institute of Planners* (November 1961, Volume XXVII, No. 4), and the authors.

[1] This report is part of a study entitled "Relocation and Mental Health: Adaptation Under Stress," conducted by the Center for Community Studies in the Department of Psychiatry of the Massachusetts General Hospital and the Harvard Medical School. The research is supported by the National Institute of Mental Health, Grant No. 3M 9137-C3. We are grateful to Erich Lindemann, the Principal Investigator, and to Leonard Duhl of the Professional Services Branch, NIMH, for their continued help and encouragement. Edward Ryan has contributed in many ways to the final formulations of this paper, and Chester Hartman and Joan Levin have given helpful criticism and advice.

undoubtedly show much variation, both variation from one slum to another and heterogeneity within urban slum areas. However, certain consistencies from one slum area to another have begun to show up in the growing body of literature. It is quite notable that the available systematic studies of slum areas indicate a very broad working-class composition in slums, ranging from highly skilled workers to the non-working and sporadically working members of the "working" class. Moreover, even in our worst residential slums it is likely that only a minority of the inhabitants (although sometimes a fairly large and visible minority) are afflicted with one or another form of social pathology. Certainly the idea that social pathology in any form is decreased by slum clearance finds little support in the available data. The belief that poverty, delinquency, prostitution, and alcoholism magically inhere in the buildings of slums and will die with the demolition of the slum has a curious persistence but can hardly provide adequate justification for the vast enterprise of renewal planning.

In a larger social sense, beyond the political and economic issues involved, planning for urban renewal has important human objectives. Through such planning we wish to make available to a larger proportion of the population some of the advantages of modern urban facilities, ranging from better plumbing and decreased fire hazards to improved utilization of local space and better neighborhood resources. These values are all on the side of the greater good for the greatest number. Yet it is all too apparent that we know little enough about the meaning and consequences of differences in physical environment either generally or for specific groups. Urban renewal may lead, directly and indirectly, to improved housing for slum residents. But we cannot evaluate the larger effects of relocation or its appropriateness without a more basic understanding than we now have of the meaning of the slum's physical and social environment. This report is an initial essay toward understanding the issue. We shall consider some of the factors that give meaning to the residential environment of the slum dweller. Although the meaning of the environment to the resident of a slum touches only one part of the larger problem, it is critical that we understand this if we are to achieve a more effectively planned and designed urban environment.

I. The Significance of the Slum Environment

People do not like to be dispossessed from their dwellings, and every renewal project that involves relocation can anticipate considerable resistance, despite the best efforts to insure community support. It is never quite clear whether most people object mainly to being forced to do something they have not voluntarily elected to do; or whether they simply object to relocation, voluntary or involuntary. There is, of course, considerable evidence for the commitment of slum residents to their habitat. Why this should be so is less clear and quite incomprehensible in the face of all middle-class residential values. In order to evaluate the issue more closely we shall consider the problem of the meaning and functional significance of residence in a slum area. Although we are primarily concerned with a few broadly applicable generalizations, a complete analysis will take better account of the diversities in the composition of slum populations.

The fact that more than half the respondents in our sample[2] have a long-stand-

ing experience of familiarity with the area in which they lived before relocation suggests a very basic residential stability. Fifty-five percent of the sample first moved to or were born in the West End approximately 20 years ago or more. Almost one-fourth of the entire sample was born in the West End. Not only is there marked residential stability within the larger area of the West End, but the total rate of movement from one dwelling unit to another has been exceedingly low. Table 42–1 gives the distribution of movement from one dwelling unit to another within ten years prior to the interview. It is readily evident that the largest proportion of the sample has made very few moves indeed. In fact, a disproportionate share of the frequent moves is made by a small group of relatively high-status people, largely professional and semi-professional people who were living in the West End only temporarily. Regardless of which criterion we use, these data indicate that we cannot readily accept those impressions of a slum which suggest a highly transient population. An extremely large proportion shows unusual residential stability, and this is quite evenly distributed

TABLE 42–1. *Number of Moves in Previous Ten Years*

Moves	Number	Percent
Totals	473	100
None	162	34
One	146	31
Two	73	15
Three or more	86	19
No answer	6	1

between the age of 20 and 65. The present analysis is based on the pre-location data from the female respondents. Less systematic pre-relocation data on the husbands are also available, as well as systematic post-relocation data for both wives and husbands and women without husbands.

[2] These data are based on a probability sample of residents from the West End of Boston interviewed during 1958–1959. The sampling criteria included only households in which there was a female household member

among the several levels of working-class occupational groups.

The Slum Environment as Home

What are the sources of this residential stability? Undoubtedly they are many and variable, and we could not hope to extricate the precise contribution of each factor. Rents were certainly low. If we add individually expended heating costs to the rental figures reported we find that 25 percent were paying $34 a month or less, and 85 percent paying $54 a month or less. But though this undoubtedly played a role as a background factor, it can hardly account for the larger findings. Low rental costs are rarely mentioned in discussing aspects of the West End or of the apartments that were sources of satisfaction. And references to the low West End rents are infrequent in discussing the sources of difficulty which people expected in the course of moving. In giving reasons for having moved to the last apartment they occupied before relocation, only 12 percent gave any types of economic reason (including decreased transportation costs as well as low rents). Thus, regardless of the practical importance that low rents must have had for a relatively low income population, they were not among the most salient aspects of the perceived issues in living in the West End.

On the other hand, there is considerable evidence to indicate that living in the West End had particular meaning for a vast majority of West End residents. Table 42–2 shows the distribution in response to the question, "How do you feel about living in the West End?", clearly indicating how the West End was a focus for very positive sentiments.

That the majority of West Enders do not remain in or come back to the West End simply because it is practical (inexpensive, close to facilities) is further documented by the responses to the question, "Which neighborhood, this one or any other place, do you think of as your real home, that is

TABLE 42–2.   *Feelings About the West End*

Feelings	Number	Percent	
Totals	473	100	
Like very well	174	37	} 75
Like	183	38	
Mixed like-dislike	47	10	} 14
Indifferent	18	4	
Dislike	25	5	} 10
Dislike very much	23	5	
No answer	3	1	

where you feel you really belong?" It is quite striking that fully 71 percent of the people named the West End as their real home, only slightly less than the proportion who specify liking the West End or liking it very much. Although there is a strong relationship between liking the West End and viewing it as home, 14 percent of those who view the West End as home have moderately or markedly negative feelings area. On the other hand, 50 percent of those who do not regard the West End as home have moderately or markedly positive feelings about the area. Thus, liking the West End is not contingent on experiencing the area as that place in which one most belongs. However, the responses to this item give us an even more basic and global sense of the meaning the West End had for a very large proportion of its inhabitants.

These responses merely summarize a group of sentiments that pervade the interviews, and they form the essential context for understanding more discrete meanings and functions of the area. There are clearly differences in the details, but the common cores lies in a widespread feeling of belonging someplace, of being "at home" in a region that extends out from but well beyond the dwelling unit. Nor is this only because of familiarity, since a very large proportion of the more recent residents (64 precent of those who moved into the West End during 1950 or after) also showed clearly positive feelings about the area. And 39 percent of those who moved in during 1950 or after regard the West End as their real home.[3]

Types of Residential "Belonging"

Finer distinctions in the quality and substance of positive feelings about the West End reveal a number of variations. In categorizing the qualitative aspects of responses to two questions which were analyzed together ("How do you feel about living in the West End?" and "What will you miss most about the West End?"), we distinguished three broad differences of emphasis among the positive replies. The three large categories are: (1) *integral belongings:* sense of *exclusive* commitment, taking West End for granted as home, thorough familiarity and security; (2) *global commitment*: sense of profound gratification (rather than familiarity), pleasure in West End and enjoyment; and (3) *discrete satisfaction:* specific satisfying or pleasurable opportunities or atmosphere involving no special commitment to *this* place.

Only a small proportion (13 percent) express their positive feelings in terms of logically irreplaceable ties to people and places. They do so in often stark and fundamental ways: this is my home; it's all I know; everyone I know is here; I won't leave. A larger group (38 percent) are less

[3] It is possible, of course, that we have obtained an exaggerated report of positive feelings about the area because of the threat of relocation. Not only does the consistency of the replies and their internal relationships lead us to believe that this has not caused a major shift in response, but, bearing in mind the relative lack of verbal facility of many of the respondents and their frequent tendencies to give brief replies, we suspect that the interview data often lead to underestimating the strength of sentiment.

embedded and take the West End less for granted but, nonetheless, express an all-encompassing involvement with the area which few areas are likely to provide them again. Their replies point up a less global but poignant sense of loss: it's one big happy family; I'll be sad; we were happy here; it's so friendly; it's handy to everything and everyone is congenial and friendly. The largest group (40 percent) are yet further removed from a total commitment but, in spite of the focused and discrete nature of their satisfaction with the interpersonal atmosphere or the convenience of the area, remain largely positive in feeling.

Differences in Foci of Positive Feelings

Thus, there is considerable variability in the depth and type of feeling implied by liking the West End; and the West End as home had different connotations for different people. For a large group, the West End as home seems to have implied a comfortable and satisfying base for moving out into the world and back. Among this group, in fact, the largest proportion were more concerned with accessibility to other places than with the locality itself. But for more than half the people, their West End homes formed a far more central feature of their total life space.

There is a difference within this larger group between a small number for whom the West End seems to have been the place *to* which they belonged and a larger number for whom it seems rather to have been the place *in* which they belonged. But for the larger group as a whole the West End occupied a unique status, beyond any of the specific attributes one could list and point to concretely. This sense of uniqueness, of home, was not simply a function of social relationships, for the place in itself was the object of strong positive feelings. Most people (42 percent) specify both people and places or offer a global, encompassing reason for their positive feelings.

But almost an equally small proportion (13 percent and 10 percent, respectively) select out people or places as the primary objects of positive experience.

With respect to the discrete foci for positive feelings, similar conclusions can be drawn from another question: "Which places do you mostly expect to miss when you leave the West End?" In spite of the place-orientation of the question, 16 percent specify some aspect of interpersonal loss as the most prominent issue. But 40 percent expect to miss one of the places which is completely identified with the area or, minimally, carries a specific local identity. The sense of the West End as a local region, as an area with a spatial identity going beyond (although it may include) the social relationships involved, is a common perception. In response to the question: "Do you think of your home in the West End as part of a local neighborhood?"[4] 81 percent replied affirmatively. It is this sense of localism as a basic feature of lower-class life and the functional significance of local interpersonal relationships and of local places which have been stressed by a number of studies of the working class (see Hoggart, 1857; Young & Willmott, 1957) and are documented by many aspects of our data.

In summary, then, we observe that a number of factors contribute to the special importance that the West End seemed to bear for the large majority of its inhabitants.

1. Residence in the West End was highly stable, with relatively little movement from one dwelling unit to another and with minimal transience into and out of the area. Although residential stability is a fact of importance in itself, it does not wholly account for commitment to the area.

[4] This question is from the interview designed by Leo Srole and his associates for the Yorkville study in New York.

2. For the great majority of the people, the local area was a focus for strongly positive sentiments and was perceived, probably in its multiple meanings, as home. The critical significance of belonging in or to an area has been one of the most consistent findings in working class communities both in the United States and in England.

3. The importance of localism in the West End, as well as in other working-class areas, can hardly be emphasized enough. This sense of a local spatial identity includes both local social relationships and local places. Although oriented around a common conception of the area as "home," there are a number of specific factors dominating the concrete meaning of the area for different people.

We now turn to a closer consideration of two of these sets of factors: first, the interpersonal networks within which people functioned and, in the subsequent section, the general spatial organization of behavior.

II. Social Relationships in Physical Space

Social relationships and interpersonal ties are not as frequently isolated for special attention in discussing the meaning of the West End as we might have expected. Despite this relative lack of exclusive salience, there is abundant evidence that patterns of social interaction were of great importance in the West End. Certainly for a great number of people, local space, whatever its independent significance, served as a focus for social relationships in much the same way as in other working-class slum areas (for example, Gans, 1962; Mogey, 1956; Kerr, 1958). In this respect, the urban slum community also has much in common with the communities so frequently observed in folk cultures. Quite consistently, we find a strong association between positive feelings about the West End and either extensive social relationships or positive feelings about other people in the West End.[5] The availability of such interpersonal ties seems to have considerable influence on feelings about the area, but the absence of these ties does not preclude a strongly positive feeling about the West End. That is, despite the prominence of this pattern, there seem to be alternative sources of satisfaction with the area for a minority of the people.

The Place of Kinship Ties

Following some of the earlier studies of membership in formal organizations, which indicated that such organizational ties were infrequent in the working class, increasing attention has been given to the importance of kinship ties in lower-class groups (see Dotson, 1951). Despite the paucity of comparative studies, most of the investigations of working-class life have stressed the great importance of the extended-kinship group. But the extended-kinship group, consisting of relationships beyond the immediate family, does not seem to be a primary source of the closest interpersonal ties. Rather, the core of the most active kinship ties seems to be composed of nuclear relatives (parents, siblings, and children) of both

[5] These associations between feelings about the West End and interpersonal variables include interpersonal relationships outside the West End as well. Thus there is the possibility that an interrelated personality variable may be involved. We shall pursue this in subsequent studies.

spouses. Our data show that the more extensive these available kinship ties are within the local area, the greater the proportion who show strong positive feeling toward the West End. These data are given in Table 42–3 and show a quite overwhelming and consistent trend in this direction. Other relationships point to the same observation: the more frequent the contact with siblings or the more frequent the contact with parents or the greater the desire to move near relatives, the greater the proportion who like the West End very well.

The Importance of the Neighbor Relationship

Important as concrete kinship ties were, however, it is easy to overestimate their significance and the relevance of kinship contacts for positive feelings about the residential area. Studies of the lower class have often neglected the importance of other interpersonal patterns in their concentration on kinship. Not only are other social relationships of considerable significance, but they also seem to influence feelings about the area. The similar effects of both sets of relationships is evident in Table 43–4, which presents the association between feelings about the West End and the personal importance of relatives versus friends.[6]

[6] The "Preference for Relatives or Friends" item is based on four separate questions presenting a specific situation and asking if the respondent would prefer to be associated with a relative or friend in each situation.

TABLE 42–3.   *Extensiveness of Kin in West End by Feelings About West End*

| | | | Feelings About West End (percent) | | |
Extensiveness of Kin in West End	Number of Respondents	Totals	Strongly Positive	Positive	Mixed Negative
Few	193	100	29	46	25
None	150	100	37	38	25
Some	67	100	45	31	24
Many	52	100	58	27	15

TABLE 42–4. *Preference for Relatives or Friends About West End*

Preference for Relatives or Friends	Number of Respondents	Totals	Feelings About West End (percent)		
			Strongly Positive	Positive	Mixed Negative
Relatives preferred	232	100	39	39	22
Mixed preferences	81	100	35	32	33
Friends preferred	148	100	36	42	22

A greater proportion (50 percent) have a strong preference for relatives, but a large group (31 percent) indicates a strong preferential orientation to friends. More relevant to our immediate purpose, there is little difference among the three preference groups in the proportions who have strong positive feelings about the West End.

In view of the consistency in the relations between a wide variety of interpersonal variables and feelings about the West End, it seems likely that there are alternative paths to close interpersonal ties of which kinship is only one specific form.[7] In fact, the single most powerful relation between feelings about the West End and an interpersonal variable is provided by feelings about West End neighbors (Table 42–5). Although the neighbor relationship may subsume kinship ties (i.e., when the neighbors are kin), the association between feelings about neighbors and feelings about the West End is stronger than the association between feelings about the West End and any of the kinship variables. Beyond this fact, the frequent references to neighbors and the stress on *local* friendships lead us to suggest that the neighbor relationship was one of the most important

[7] We do not mean to imply that this exhausts the special importance of kinship in the larger social structure. There is also evidence to suggest that some of the basic patterns of the kinship relationship have influenced the form of interpersonal ties more generally in the urban working class (see Fried and Linemann, 1961).

ties in the West End. And, whether based on prior kinship affiliation or not, it formed one of the critical links between the individual (or family) and the larger area and community.

Localism in Close Interpersonal Ties

Since the quality of feeling about the West End is associated with so wide a diversity of interpersonal relationships, it is not surprising that the majority of people maintained their closest ties with West Enders. The distribution of relationships which were based in the West End or outside the West End are given in Table 42–6. The striking proportion whose closest ties are all or mostly from the West End is clearly evident. As we would expect on the basis of the previous results, the more exclusively a person's closest relationships are based in the West End, the greater the likelihood that he will have strong positive feelings about the West End.

A few significant factors stand out clearly from this analysis.

1. Although the kinship relationship was of considerable importance in the West End, as in other working-class communities, there were a number of alternatives sources of locally based interpersonal ties. Among these, we suggest that the neighbor relationship is of particular importance, both in its own right and in its effect on more general feelings about the area.
2. There is considerable generality to the

TABLE 42–5.   *Closeness to Neighbors by Feelings About West End*

Closeness to Neighbors	Number of Respondents	Totals	Feelings About West End (percent)		
			Strongly Positive	Positive	Mixed Negative
Very positive	78	100	63	28	9
Positive	265	100	37	42	21
Negative	117	100	20	39	41

TABLE 42–6.   *West End Dwelling of Five Closest Persons*

Five Closest Persons	Number	Percent	
Totals	473	100	
All West End	201	42	} 60
Mostly West End	85	18	
Equally West End and outside	13	3	
Mostly outside West End	70	15	} 25
All outside West End	46	10	
Unspecified	58	12	

bors; there were many interrelated friendship networks; mutual help in household activities was both possible and frequent: many of these relationships had a long and continuous history; and the various ties often became further intertwined through many activities within a common community.

The street itself, favorite recreation areas, local bars, and the settlement houses in the area all served as points of contact for overlapping social networks. Thus the most unique features of this working-class area (although common to many other working-class areas) were: (a) the interweaving and overlap of many different types of interpersonal contacts and role relationships, and (b) the organization and concrete manifestation of these relationships within a common, relatively bounded spatial region. It is these characteristics which seem to have given a special character and meaning both to the quality of interpersonal relationships and to the area within which these relationships were experienced.

We have repeatedly stressed the observation that, granting the importance of local social relationships, the meaning of "localism" in the West End included places as well as people. It is difficult to document the independent significance of either of these factors, but the importance of the physical space of the West End and the special use of the area are evident in many ways. Previously we indicated the importance of physical areas and places as sources of satisfaction in the West End. We now

observation that the greater one's interpersonal commitments in the area, in the form of close contact or strongly positive feelings, the greater the likelihood of highly positive feelings about the area as a whole. This observation holds for all the forms of interpersonal relationship studied.

What is perhaps most striking about the social patterns of the West End is the extent to which all the various forms of interpersonal ties were localized within the residential area. Local physical space seems to have provided a framework within which some of the most important social relationships were embedded. As in many a folk community (see Goodenough, 1951), there was considerable overlap in the kinds of ties which obtained: kin were often neigh-

wish to consider more systematically the way in which the physical space of the area is subjectively organized by a large proportion of the population. In understanding the importance of such subjective spatial organization in addition to the significance of local social relationships, we can more adequately appreciate the enormous and multiply derived meaning that a residential area may have for people.

III. Subjective Spatial Organization

There is only a fragmentary literature on the psychological, social, or cultural implications of spatial behavior and spatial imagery. The orientation of the behavioral sciences to the history, structure, and dynamics of social relationships has tended to obscure the potential significance of the nonhuman environment generally and, more specifically, that aspect of the nonhuman environment which we may designate as significant space. Although there have been a number of important contributions to this problem, we are far from any systematic understanding of the phenomena. We do not propose to discuss the problems or concepts, but only to start with a few very primitive considerations and to observe the working-class relationship to space in several respects. We are primarily concerned with the way in which space is organized or structured in defining the usable environment and in providing restrictions to or freedom for mobility in space.[8] In this way we may hope to see more broadly the constellation of forces which serve to invest the residential environment of the work-

[8] We shall not touch on a related problem of considerable interest, the basic modes of conceiving or experiencing space in general. We assume a close relation between general conceptions of space and ways of using spatial aspects of specific parts of the environment, but an analysis of this problem is beyond the scope of the present discussion.

ing class with such intense personal meaning.

Spatial Usage Patterns in the Middle Class

There are undoubtedly many differences among people in the way space is organized, according to personality type, physiological disposition, environmental actualities, social roles, and cultural experience. We wish to focus only on some of those differences which, at the extremes, distinguish the working class quite sharply from higher-status groups. Although we do not have comparative data, we suggest that in the urban middle class (most notably among relatively high-status professional and business groups) space is characteristically used in a high *selective* way. The boundary between the dwelling unit and the immediate environs is quite sharp and minimally permeable. It is, of course, possible to go into and out of the dwelling unit through channels which are specifically designated for this purpose. But walls are clear-cut barriers between the inside of the dwelling unit and the outer world. And even windows are seldom used for any interchange between the inner world of the dwelling unit and the outside environment (except for sunlight and air). Most of us take this so much for granted that we never question it, let alone take account of it for analytic purposes. It is the value of the "privacy of the home." The dwelling unit may extend into a zone of lawn or garden which we tend and for which we pay taxes. But, apart from this, the space outside the dwelling unit is barely "ours."

As soon as we are in the apartment hallway or on the street, we are on a wholly *public* way, a path to or from someplace rather than on a bounded space defined by a subjective sense of belonging.[9] Beyond

[9] The comment of one reader to an early draft of this paper is worth quoting, since it leads into a fascinating series of related prob-

this is a highly individualized world, with many common properties but great variability in usage and subjective meaning. Distances are very readily transgressed; friends are dispersed in many directions; preferred places are frequently quite idiosyncratic. Thus there are few physical areas which have regular (certainly not daily) widespread common usage and meaning. And contiguity between the dwelling unit and other significant spaces is relatively unimportant. It is primarily the channels and pathways between individualized significant spaces which are important, familiar, and common to many people. This orientation to the use of space is the very antithesis of that localism so widely found in the working class.

The Territorial Sense in the Working Class

Localism captures only a gross orientation toward the social use of an area of physical space and does not sufficiently emphasize its detailed organization. Certainly, most middle-class observers are overwhelmed at

lems. With respect to this passage, Chester Hartman notes: "We tend to think of this other space as anonymous and public (in the sense of belonging to everyone, i.e., no one) when it does not specifically belong to us. The lower-class person is not nearly so alienated from what he does not own." To what extent is there a relationship between a traditional expectation (even if occasionally belied by reality) that only *other* people own real property, that one is essentially part of a "propertyless class" and a willingness to treat any property as common? And does this provide a framework for the close relationship between knowing and belonging in the working class in contrast to the middle-class relationship between owning and belonging? Does the middle-class acceptance of legal property rights provide a context in which one can *only* belong if one owns? From a larger psychological view, these questions are relevant not merely to physical space and physical objects but to social relationships as well.

the degree to which the residents of any working-class district and, most particularly, the residents of slums are "at home" in the street. But it is not only the frequency of using the street and treating the street outside the house as a place, and not simply as a path, which points up the high degree of permeability of the boundary between the dwelling unit and the immediate environing area. It is also the use of all channels between dwelling unit and environment as a bridge between inside and outside: open windows, closed windows, hallways, even walls and floors serve this purpose. Frequently, even the sense of adjacent human beings carried by noises and smells provides a sense of comfort. As Edward Ryan points out:[10]

> Social life has an almost uninterrupted flow between apartment and street: children are sent into the street to play, women lean out the windows to watch and take part in street activity, women go "out on the street" to talk with friends, men and boys meet on the corners at night, and families sit on the steps and talk with their neighbors at night when the weather is warm.

It is not surprising, therefore, that there is considerable agreement between the way people feel about their apartments and the way they feel about the West End in general (Table 42–7). Without attempting to assign priority to feelings about the apartment or to feelings about the West End, it seems likely that physical barriers which are experienced as easily permeable allow for a ready generalization of positive or negative feelings in either direction.

We would like to call this way of structuring the physical space around the actual residential unit a *territorial* space, in contrast to the selective space of the middle

[10] This comment is a fragment from a report on ethnographic observations made in the area.

TABLE 42–7. *Feelings About the Apartment by Feelings About West End*

Feelings About Apartment	Number of Respondents	Totals	Feelings About West End (percent)		
			Like Very Well	Like	Mixed-dislike
Like	367	100	43	40	17
Mixed-indifferent	41	100	20	42	39
Dislike	60	100	12	30	58

class. It is territorial in the sense that physical space is largely defined in terms of relatively bounded regions to which one has freedom or restriction of access, and it does not emphasize the path function of physical space in allowing or encouraging movements to or from other places.[11] There is also evidence, some of which has been presented in an earlier section, that it is territorial in a more profound sense: that individuals feel different spatial regions belong to or do not belong to them and, correspondingly, feel that they belong to (or in) specific spatial regions or do not belong.[12]

[11] These formulations refer to modal patterns and do not apply to the total population. Twenty-six percent do select out the "accessibility" of the area, namely a path function. The class difference, however, is quite striking since 67 percent of the highest-status group give this response, but only 19 percent of the lowest-status group and between 28 percent and 31 percent of the middle- (but still low-status) groups select out various types of "accessibility."

[12] Without attempting, in this report, a "depth" psychological analysis of typical patterns of working-class behaviors, we should note the focal importance of being accepted or rejected, of belonging or being an "outsider." Preliminary evidence from the post-relocation interviews reveals this in the frequent references to being unable to obtain an apartment because "they didn't want us" or that the landlord "treated us like dirt." It also emerges in the frequently very acute sensitivity to gross social-class differences, and a sharp sense of not belonging or not fitting in with people of higher status. Clarification of this and related

Spatial Boundaries in the Local Area

In all the previous discussion, the West End has been treated as a whole. People in the area did, in fact, frequently speak of the area as a whole, as if it were an entity. However, it is clear that the area was differently bounded for different people. Considering only the gross distinction between circumscribing the neighborhood as a very small, localized space in contrast to an expansive conception of the neighborhood to include most of the area, we find that the sample is about equally split (Table 42–8). It is apparent, therefore, that the

TABLE 42–8. *Area of West End "Neighborhood"*

Neighborhood	Number	Percent
Totals	473	100
Much of West End: all of area, West End specified, most of area, large area specified	491	40
Part of West End: one or two streets or less, a small area, or less, a small area, a store	207	44
People, not area: the people around	17	4
Not codeable	58	12

problems seems essential for understanding the psychological and social consequences of social-class distinctions and has considerable implication for urban residential planning generally and urban specifically.

territorial zone may include a very small or a very large part of the entire West End, and for quite a large proportion it is the former. For these people, at least, the boundary between dwelling unit and street may be highly permeable; but this freedom of subjective access does not seem to extend very far beyond the area immediately adjacent to the dwelling unit. It is also surprising how little this subjective sense of neighborhood size is affected by the extensiveness of West End kin or of West End friends. This fact tends to support the view that there is some degree of independence between social relationships and spatial orientations in the area.[13]

Thus, we may say that for almost half the people, there is a subjective barrier surrounding the immediately local area. For this large group, the barrier seems to define the zone of greatest personal significance or comfort from the larger area of the West End. However, it is clearly not an impermeable barrier. Not only does a large proportion of the sample fail to designate this boundary, but even for those who do perceive this distinction, there is frequently a sense of familiarity with the area beyond.[14] Thus, when we use a less severe criterion of boundedness than the local "neighbor-

hood" and ask people how much of the West End they know well, we find that a very large proportion indeed indicate their familiarity with a large part or most of the area (Table 42–9). Although almost half the people consider "home ground" to include only a relatively small local region, the vast majority is easily familiar with a greater part of the West End. The local boundaries within the West End were, thus, boundaries of a semipermeable nature although differently experienced by different people.

The Inner-Outer Boundary

These distinctions in the permeability of the boundaries between dwelling unit and street and across various spaces within the larger local region are brought even more sharply into focus when we consider the boundary surrounding the West End as a whole. The large majority may have been easily familiar with most or all of the West End. But it is impressive how frequently such familiarity seems to stop at the boundaries of the West End. In comparison with the previous data, Table 42–10 demonstrates the very sharp delineation of the inner space of the West End from the outer space surrounding the West End. The former is generally well explored and essentially familiar, even though it may not be considered the area of commitment. The latter is either relatively unknown by many

---

[13] The social-class patterning is also of interest. Using the occupation of the head of household as the class criterion, there is almost no difference among the three working-class status levels in the area included as a neighborhood (the percentages who say "much or all of the area" for these three groups are, respectively, 51 percent, 46 percent, and 48 percent). But only 38 percent of the high-status group include much or all of the West End in their subjective neighborhood.

[14] Of those who include only part of the West End in their designation of their neighborhood, 68 percent indicate they know a large part or most of the West End well. Naturally, an even higher percentage (87 percent) of those who include much or all of the West End in their neighborhood are similarly familiar with a large part or all of the area.

TABLE 42–9. *Area of West End Known Well*

Area	Number	Percent	
Totals	473	100	
Just own block	27	6	} 20
A few blocks	65	14	
Large part	66	14	} 64
Most of it	237	50	
Uncodeable	78	16	

TABLE 42–10. *Familiar Areas of Boston*

Area	Number	Percent
Totals	473	*101*
West End only:		
no other area, none	141	*30*
Adjacent area:		
North End, esplanade	216	*46*
Contiguous areas:		
East Boston, Cambridge	98	*21*
Nearby areas: Revere, Malden, Brookline	12	*3*
Metropolitan Boston, beyond "nearby" areas	1	*0*
Outside Boston area	3	*1*
No answer	2	*0*

people or, if known, it is categorized in a completely different way. A relatively large proportion are familiar with the immediately adjacent areas which are directly or almost directly contiguous with the West End (and are often viewed as extensions of the West End), but only slightly more than a quarter (26 percent) report familiarity with any other parts of the Boston area. Thus there seems to be a widely experienced subjective boundary surrounding the larger local area and some of its immediate extensions which is virtually impermeable. It is difficult to believe that people literally do not move out of this zone for various activities. Yet, if they do, it apparently does not serve to diminish the psychological (and undoubtedly social) importance of the boundary.[15]

These data provide considerable evidence to support, if they do not thoroughly validate, the view that the working class commonly organizes physical space in terms

[15] We do not have data on the actual frequency of use of the various areas outside the West End. Thus we cannot deal with the problem of the sense of familiarity in relation to actual usage patterns.

of a series of boundaries. Although we do not mean to imply any sense of a series of concentric boundaries or to suggest that distance alone is the critical dimension, there seems to be a general tendency for the permeability of these boundaries to decrease with increasing distance from the dwelling unit. Significant space is thus subjectively defined as a series of contiguous regions with the dwelling unit and its immediately surrounding local area as the central region. We have referred to this way of organizing physical space as *territorial* to distinguish it from the more highly *selective* and individualized use of space which seems to characterize the middle class. And we suggest that it is the territorial conception and manner of using physical space which provides one of the bases for the kind of localism which is so widely found in working-class areas.

In conjunction with the emphasis upon local social relationships, this conception and use of local physical space gives particular force to the feeling of commitment to, and the sense of belonging in, the residential area. It is clearly not just the dwelling unit that is significant but a larger local region that partakes of these powerful feelings of involvement and identity. It is not surprising, therefore, that "home" is not merely an apartment or a house but a local area in which some of the most meaningful aspects of life are experienced.

IV. Conclusions

The aims of urban renewal and the sources of pressure for renewal are manifold: among the objectives we may include more rational and efficient use of land, the elimination of dilapidated buildings, increase in the municipal tax base, and the improvement of living conditions for slum dwellers. Although the social benefit to the slum dweller has received maximum public attention, it is always unclear how the life situation (or even the housing situation) of the working-class resident of a slum is supposed to be improved by slum clearance or even slum improvement. Public housing has not proved to be an adequate answer to this problem for many reasons. Yet public housing is the only feature of renewal programs that has even attempted to deal seriously with this issue.

In recent years, a number of reports have suggested that concern about slum conditions has been used to maneuver public opinion in order to justify use of eminent domain powers and demolition, largely for the benefit of middle- and upper-status groups. Although we cannot evaluate this political and economic issue, we do hope to understand the ways in which dislocation from a slum and relocation to new residential areas has, in fact, benefited or damaged the working-class residents involved. It is all too apparent, however, that the currently available data are inadequate for clarifying some of the most critical issues concerning the effects of residential relocation upon the subject populations.

We know very little about slums and the personal and social consequences of living in a slum. We know even less about the effects of forced dislocation from residential areas on people in general and on working-class people specifically. But rational urban planning which, under these circumstances, becomes urban *social* planning, requires considerable knowledge and understanding of people and places affected by the plans. It is incumbent upon us to know both what is wrong with the slum and with slum life and what is right about slums and living in slums. It is essentially this question, formulated as the meaning and consequences of living in a slum, that has motivated our inquiry into the sources of residential satisfaction in an urban slum. In turn, this study provides one of the bases for understanding the ways in which dislocation and relocation affect the patterns of personal and social adaptation of former residents of a slum.

In studying the reasons for satisfaction

that the majority of slum residents experience, two major components have emerged. On the one hand, the residential area is the region in which a vast and interlocking set of social networks is localized. And, on the other, the physical area has considerable meaning as an extension of home, in which various parts are delineated and structured on the basis of a sense of belonging. These two components provide the context in which the residential area may so easily be invested with considerable, multiply determined meaning. Certainly, there are variations both in the importance of various factors for different people and in the total sense which people have of the local area. But the greatest proportion of this working-class group (like other working-class slum residents who have been described) shows a fairly common experience and usage of the residential area. This common experience and usage is dominated by a conception of the local area beyond the dwelling unit as an integral part of home. This view of an area as home and the significance of local people and local places are so profoundly at variance with typical middle-class orientations that it is difficult to appreciate the intensity of meaning, the basic sense of identity involved in living in the particular area. Yet it seems to form the core of the extensive social integration that characterizes this (and other) working-class slum populations.

These observations lead us to question the extent to which, through urban renewal, we relieve a situation of stress or create further damage. If the local spatial area and an orientation toward localism provide the core of social organization and integration for a large proportion of the working class, and if, as current behavioral theories would suggest, social organization and integration are primary factors in providing a base for effective social functioning, what are the consequences of dislocating people from their local areas? Or, assuming that the potentialities of people for adaptation to crisis are great, what deeper damage occurs in the process? And, if there are deleterious effects, are these widespread or do they selectively affect certain predictable parts of the population? We emphasize the negative possibilities because these are closest to the expectations of the population involved and because, so frequently in the past, vague positive effects on slum populations have been arbitrarily assumed. But it is clear that, in lieu of or along with negative consequences, there may be considerable social benefit.

The potential social benefits also require careful, systematic evaluation, since they may manifest themselves in various and sometimes subtle ways. Through a variety of direct and intervening factors, the forced residential shift may lead to changes in orientations toward work, leading to increased satisfaction in the occupational sphere; or, changes may occur in the marital and total familial relationship to compensate for decreased kinship and friendship contacts and, in turn, lead to an alternative (and culturally more syntonic) form of interpersonal satisfaction; or, there may be either widespread or selective decreases in problems such as delinquency, mental illness, and physical malfunctioning.

A realistic understanding of the effect, beneficial and/or deleterious, of dislocation and relocation from an urban slum clearly requires further study and analysis. Our consideration of some of the factors involved in working-class residential satisfaction in the slum provides one basis for evaluating the significance of the changes that take place with a transition to a new geographic and social environment. Only the careful comparison of pre-relocation and post-relocation data can begin to answer these more fundamental questions and, in this way, provide a sound basis for planning urban social change.

43. Planning and Social Life: Friendship and Neighbor Relations in Suburban Communities[1]

HERBERT J. GANS

Studies of wartime housing projects and postwar suburban subdivisions have shown that the residents of these developments do a considerable amount of visiting with the nearest neighbors, and may select their friends from among them. Social relationships appear to be influenced and explained by *propinquity* (see Merton, 1947; Caplow & Foreman, 1950; Festinger, Schachter & Back, 1950: Festinger, 1951; Kuper, 1953; Whyte, 1953, 1957; Rosow, 1961).[2] As a

Reprinted by permission of the *Journal of the American Institute of Planners* (1961, Volume XXVIII, No. 7) and the author.

[1] I am indebted to Paul Davidoff, John W. Dyckman, Lewis Mumford, Janet and Tom Reiner, Melvin M. Webber, and William L. C. Wheaton for helpful critiques of earlier versions of this paper.

result, they are affected by the site plan and the architectural design, which determine how near people will live to each other. In fact, Festinger, Schachter and Back (1950) have suggested that:

The architect who builds a house or designs a site plan, who decides where the roads will and will not go, and who decides which directions the houses will face and how close together they will be, also is, to a large extent, deciding the pattern of social life among the people who will live in those houses.

[2] The discussion that follows draws on these studies and on my own research and observations in two suburban communities, Park Forest, Illinois, and Levittown, New Jersey.

Conversely, other studies of social life have shown that people tend to choose friends on the basis of similarities in backgrounds, such as age and socio-economic level; values, such as those with respect to privacy or child rearing; and interests, such as leisure activity preferences (see, e.g., Lazarsfeld and Merton, 1954). These findings suggest that social relationships are influenced and explained by people's *homogeneity* with respect to a variety of *characteristics,* although it is not yet known exactly what combination of characteristics must be shared for different social relationships. This explanation would imply that the planner affects social life not through the site plan but through decisions about lot size or facility standards that help to determine, directly or indirectly, whether the population of an area will be homogeneous or heterogeneous with respect to the characteristics that determine social relationships.[3]

The two explanations raise a number of issues for planning:

1. Whether or not the planner has the power to influence patterns of social life.
2. Whether or not he should exert this power.
3. Whether some patterns of social life are more desirable than others, and should, therefore, be sought as planning goals. For example, should people be encouraged to find their friends among neighbors, or throughout, or outside their residential area? Should they be politely distant or friendly with neighbors?

If propinquity is most important in

---

[3] Hereafter, when I describe a population as homogeneous or heterogeneous, I always mean with respect to the characteristics that are relevant to the particular aspect of social life under discussion, although for stylistic reasons, the qualifying phrase is usually left out.

determining friendship formation and neighbor relations, the ideal patterns—if such exist—would have to be implemented through the site plan. If homogeneity of characteristics is most important, the planner must decide whether to advocate homogeneous residential areas, if he wishes to encourages friendliness and friendship among neighbors; and heterogeneous ones, if he wishes to encourage more distant neighbor relations and spatially dispersed friendship.

Although the available research does not yet permit a final explanation of the patterns of social life, a preliminary conclusion can be suggested. This permits us to discuss the implications for planning theory and practice.

Propinquity, Homogeneity, and Friendship

The existing studies suggest that the two explanations are related, but that homogeneity of characteristics is more important than propinquity. Although propinquity initiates many social relationships and maintains less intensive ones, such as "being neighborly," it is not sufficient by itself to create intensive relationships. Friendship requires homogeneity.

Propinquity leads to visual contact between neighbors and is likely to produce face-to-face social contact. This is true only if the distance between neighbors is small enough to encourage one or the other to transform the visual contact into a social one.[4] Thus, physical distance between neigh-

---

[4] If the physical distance is negligible, as between next-door neighbors, social contact is likely to take place quickly. When neighbors are not immediately adjacent, however, one or the other must take the initiative, and this requires either some visible sign of a shared background characteristic, or interest, or the willingness to be socially aggressive. This is not as prevalent as sometimes imagined. Although the new suburbs are often thought to exhibit an

bors is important. So is the relationship of the dwellings—especially their front and rear doors—and the circulation system. For example, if doors of adjacent houses face each other or if residents must share driveways, visual contact is inevitable.

The opportunity for visual and social contact is greater at high densities than at low ones, but only if neighbors are adjacent horizontally. In apartment buildings, residents who share a common hallway will meet, but those who live on different floors are less likely to do so, because there is little occasion for visual contact (See Festinger, Schachter & Back, 1950; Wallace, 1952). Consequently, propinquity operates most efficiently in single-family and rowhouse areas, especially if these are laid out as courts, narrow loops, or cul-de-sacs.

Initial social contacts can develop into relationships of varying intensity, from polite chats about the weather to close friendship. (Negative relationships, varying from avoidance to open enmity are also possible.) Propinquity not only initiates relationships, but it also plays an important role in maintaining the less intensive ones, for the mere fact of living together encourages neighbors to make sure that the relationship between them remains positive. Propinquity cannot determine the intensity of the relationship, however; this is a function of the characteristics of the people involved. If neighbors are homogeneous and feel themselves to be compatible, there is some likelihood that the relationship will be more intensive than an exchange of greetings. If neighbors are heterogenous, the relationship is not likely to be intensive, regardless of the degree of propinquity. *Propinquity may thus be the initial cause of an intensive positive relationship, but it cannot be the final or sufficient cause.*

This is best illustrated in a newly settled subdivision. When people first move in, they do not know each other, or anything about each other, except that they have all chosen to live in this community—and can probably afford to do so.[5] As a result, they will begin to make social contacts based purely on propinquity, and because they share the characteristics of being strangers and pioneers, they will do so with almost every neighbor within physical and functional distance. As these social contacts continue, participants begin to discover each other's backgrounds, values, and interests, so that similarities and differences become apparent. Homogeneous neighbors may become friends, whereas heterogeneous ones soon reduce the amount of visiting, and eventually limit themselves to being neighborly. (This process is usually completed after about three months of social contact, especially if people have occupied their homes in spring or summer, when climate and garden chores lead to early visual contact.) The resulting pattern of social relationships cannot be explained by propinquity alone. An analysis of the characteristics of the people will show that homogeneity and heterogeneity explain the existence *and the absence* of social relationships more adequately than does the site plan or the architectural design. Needless to say, the initial social pattern is not immutable; it is changed by population turnover and by a gradual tendency to find other friends outside the immediate area (see Form, 1951).

[5] Home buyers do not, however, move into a new area without some assurance that neighbors are likely to be compatible. They derive this assurance from the house price (which bears some correlation to purchasers' income level), from the kinds of people whom they see inspecting the model homes, and from the previous class and ethnic image of the area within which the subdivision is located.

inordinate amount of intrablock visiting, I found that on the block on which I lived in Levittown, New Jersey, some of the men who lived three to five houses away from each other did not meet for over a year after initial occupancy. The wives met more quickly, of course.

If neighbors are compatible, however, they may not look elsewhere for companionship, so that propinquity—as well as the migration patterns and housing market conditions which bring homogeneous people together—plays an important role. Most of the communities studied so far have been settled by homogeneous populations. For example, Festinger, Schachter, and Back (1950) studied two student housing projects whose residents were of similar age, marital status, and economic level. Moreover, they were all sharing a common educational experience and had little time for entertaining. Under these conditions, the importance of propinquity in explaining visiting patterns and friendship is not surprising. The fact that they were impermanent residents is also relevant, although if a considerable degree of homogeneity exists among more permanent residents, similar patterns develop.

Propinquity, Homogeneity, and Neighbor Relations

Although propinquity brings neighbors into social contact, a certain degree of homogeneity is required to maintain this contact on a positive basis. If neighbors are too diverse, differences of behavior or attitude may develop which can lead to coolness or even conflict. For example, when children who are being reared by different methods come into conflict, disciplinary measures by their parents will reveal differences in ways of rewarding and punishing. If one child is punished for a digression and his playmate is not, misunderstandings and arguments can develop between the parents. Differences about house and yard maintenance, or about political issues can have similar consequences.

The need for homogeneity is probably greatest among neighbors with children of equal age and among immediately adjacent neighbors. Children, especially young ones, choose playmates on a purely propinquitous

basis. Thus, positive relations among neighbors with children of similar age are best maintained if the neighbors are comparatively homogeneous with respect to child-rearing methods. Immediately adjacent neighbors are likely to have frequent visual contact, and if there is to be social contact, they must be relatively compatible. Some people minimize social contact with immediately adjacent neighbors on principle, in order to prevent possible differences from creating disagreement. Since such neighbors live in involuntary propinquity, conflict might result in permanently impaired relationships which might force one or the other to move out.

Generally speaking, conflicts between neighbors seem to be rare. In the new suburbs, current building and marketing practices combine to bring together people of relatively similar age and income, thus creating sufficient homogeneity to enable strangers to live together peaceably. In the communities which I have studied, many people say that they have never had such friendly neighbors. Where chance assembles a group of heterogeneous neighbors, unwritten and often unrecognized pacts are developed which bring standards of house and yard maintenance into alignment and which eliminate from the conversation topics that might result in conflict.

The Meaning of Homogeneity

I have been stressing the importance of resident characteristics without defining the terms homogeneity and heterogeneity. This omission has been intentional, for little is known about what characteristics must be shared before people feel themselves to be compatible with others. We do not know for certain if they must have common backgrounds, or similar interests, or shared values—or combinations of these. Nor do we know precisely which background characteristics, behavior patterns, and interests are most and least important, or about what issues values must be shared. Also, we do not know what similarities are needed for relationships or different intensities or, for any given characteristics, how large a difference can exist before incompatibility sets in. For example, it is known that income differences can create incompatibility between neighbors, but it is not known how large these differences must become before incompatibility is felt.

Demographers may conclude that one community is more homogeneous than another with respect to such characteristics as age or income, but this information is too general and superficial to predict the pattern of social life. Social relationships are not based on census data, but on subjectively experienced definitions of homogeneity and heterogeneity which terminate in judgments of compatibility or incompatibility. These definitions and judgments have received little study.

Sociologists generally agree that behavior patterns, values, and interests—what people think and do—are more important criteria for homogeneity than background factors (see Lazarsfeld & Merton, 1954). My observations suggest that in the new suburbs, values with respect to child rearing, leisure-time interests, taste level, general cultural preferences, and temperament seem to be most important in judging compatibility or incompatibility.

Such interests and values *do* reflect differences in background characteristics, since a person's beliefs and actions are shaped in part by his age, income, occupation, and the like. These characteristics can, therefore, be used as clues to understanding the pattern of social relationships. *Life-cycle stage* (which summarizes such characteristics as age of adults, marital status, and age of children) and *class* (especially income and education) are probably the two most significant characteristics. Education is especially important, because it affects occupational choice, child-rearing patterns, leisure-time preferences, and taste level. *Race* is also an important

criterion, primarily because it is a highly visible—although not necessarily accurate—symbol of class position.[6]

Background characteristics provide crude measures that explain only in part the actual evaluations and choices made by neighbors on a block. Until these evaluations themselves are studied—and then related to background data—it is impossible to define homogeneity or heterogeneity operationally. Since considerable criticism has been leveled at the new suburbs for being overly homogeneous—at least by demographic criteria—such research is of considerable importance for the planner's evaluation of these communities and for the planning of future residential areas.

Variations in Homogeneity

The degree of population homogeneity varies from suburb to suburb. Moreover, since residents usually become neighbors by a fairly random process—for example, by signing deeds at the same time—many combinations of homogeneity and heterogeneity can be found among the blocks of a single subdivision.[7] In some blocks, neighbors are so compatible that they spend a significant amount of their free time with each other and even set up informal clubs to cement the pattern. In other blocks, circumstances bring together very diverse people, and relationships between them may be only polite, or even cool.

[6] Studies (Deutsch & Collins, 1951; Greer & Greer, 1960) suggest that where people are relatively homogeneous in class and age, race differences are no obstacle to social relationships, and race is no longer a criterion of heterogeneity. This is especially true in middle-class residential areas occupied by professional people.

[7] This is true of the larger subdivisions. Smaller ones are sometimes not settled randomly, but are occupied by groups, for example related households or members of an ethnic group moving *en masse* from another area.

Whyte's studies (1957) in Park Forest led him to attribute these variations to site planning features. He found that the small "courts" were friendly and happy; the larger ones, less friendly and sometimes unhappy. He also found that the residents of the smaller courts were so busy exchanging visits that, unlike those of the larger ones, they did not become active in the wider community. My observations in Park Forest and in Levittown, New Jersey, suggest, however, that homogeneity and heterogeneity explain these phenomena more effectively.[8] When neighbors are especially homogeneous, blocks can become friendly, regardless of their size, although the larger blocks usually divide themselves into several social groupings. Block size is significant only insofar as a small block may *feel* itself to be more cohesive because all sociability takes place within one group. In the larger blocks, the fact that there are several groups prevents such a feeling, even though each of the groups may be as friendly as the one in the smaller blocks.

Community participation patterns can be explained in a similar fashion. If the block population is heterogeneous, and residents must look elsewhere for friends, they inevitably turn to community-wide clubs, church organizations, and even civic groups in order to meet compatible people. If participation in these organizations is based solely on the need to find friends, however, it is likely to be minimal, and may even cease, once friendships are established. This type of membership differs considerably from civic or organizational participation proper. The distinction between the two types is important. Whyte recommends that site planners encourage participation by making blocks large enough to discourage excessive on-the-block social life. While this might increase the first type of participation, it cannot affect the second type. People who are inclined to be really active in community-wide organizations are a self-selected minority who will desert the social life of the block, regardless of the block's layout or of the neighbor's compatibility. They are usually attracted to community participation by pressing community problems and by interest, ambition, or the hope of personal gain. Site planning techniques cannot bring about their participation.

The Role of Propinquity

Given the importance of homogeneity in social relationships, what role remains for propinquity? Since propinquity results in visual contact, whether voluntary or involuntary, it produces social contact among neighbors, although homogeneity will determine how intensive the relationships will be and whether they will be positive or not. Propinquity also supports relationships based on homogeneity by making frequent contact convenient. Finally, among people who are comparatively homogeneous and move into an area as strangers, propinquity may determine friendship formation among neighbors.

In addition, some types of people gravitate to propinquitous relationships more than others. Age is an important factor. As already noted, children choose their playmates strictly on a propinquitous basis, though decreasingly so as they get older. This is why parents who want their young children to associate with playmates of similar status and cultural background must move to areas where such playmates are close at hand.

Among adults, the importance of pro-

[8] These comments are based on observations, however, rather than on systematic studies. Macris (1958) studied visiting patterns in Park Forest in 1957 and found considerably less intrablock visiting than did Whyte (1957). He also found that there was almost no visiting at all between tenants and homeowners, even though they were living in physical propinquity in the area he studied. This suggests the importance of neighbor homogeneity.

pinquity seems to vary with sex and class. Women generally find their female friends nearby, especially if they are mothers and are restricted in their movements. In fact, young mothers must usually be able to find compatible people—and therefore, homogeneous neighbors—within a relatively small radius. Should they fail to do so, they may become the unhappy isolated suburban housewives about whom so much has been written. My observations suggest that most women are able to find the female companionship they seek, however. In addition, the increase in two-car families and women's greater willingness to drive are gradually reducing the traditional immobility of the housewife.

The relationship between propinquity and class has received little study. Generally speaking, the "higher" the class, the greater the physical mobility for visiting and entertaining. Thus, working-class people seem to be least mobile and most likely to pick their friends on a propinquitous basis. However, since they visit primarily with relatives, they may travel considerable distances if relatives are not available nearby (Young & Willmott, 1957). Upper-middle-class people seem to go farther afield for their social life than do lower-middle-class ones, in part because they may have specialized interests which are hard to satisfy on the block.

Propinquity is also more important for some types of social activities than others. In America, and probably everywhere in the Western world, adolescents and adults socialize either in peer groups—people of similar age and sex—or in sets of couples. Peer groups are more likely to form on the basis of propinquity. For example, the members of that well-known suburban peer group, the women's "coffee klatsch," are usually recruited in the immediate vicinity. Since the participants indulge primarily in shop talk—children, husbands, and home —the fact that they are all wives and mothers provides sufficient homogeneity to

allow propinquity to function.[9] For couples, homogeneity is a more urgent requirement than propinquity, since the two people in a couple must accept both members of all other couples. The amount of compatibility that is required probably cannot be satisfied so easily among the supply of neighbors within propinquitous distance.

The role of propinquity also varies with the size of the group, and with the activities pursued. The larger the group, the less intensive are the relationships between participants, and the less homogeneity is required. If the group meets for a specific activity, such as to celebrate a major holiday or to play cards, the behavior that takes place is sufficiently specialized and habitual that the participants' other characteristics are less relevant. If the group meets for conversation, more homogeneity of values and interests is required.[10]

Limitations of These Observations

The foregoing comments are based largely on observations and studies in new suburban communities. Little is known about the role of propinquity and homogeneity in established communities, although there is no reason to expect any major differences (see Rosow, 1961, p. 131). Whatever differences exist are probably due to the reduction of much of the initial homogeneity in established communities through popula-

[9] There must, however, be general agreement about methods of housekeeping, getting along with husbands, and child rearing. Since these methods vary with education and socioeconomic level, some homogeneity of class is necessary even for the coffee klatsch.

[10] The kinds of gatherings which Whyte (1957) studied so ingeniously in Park Forest were mainly those of peer groups indulging in single-purpose activities. This may explain why he found propinquity to be so important.

tion turnover. The same process is likely to take place in new communities. Moveouts create a gap in established social groupings. Newcomers may be able to fill this gap—provided they are not too different from those they have replaced. Even so, it is hard for a newcomer to break into an established coffee klatsch or card party, and only people with a little extra social aggressiveness are likely to do so. In addition, there is the previously noted tendency of the original residents to find new friends outside the immediate area and to spend less time with neighbors. As a result of these processes, patterns of social life in new communities will eventually resemble those in established areas.

Most of my observations are at present only hypotheses that need to be tested by more systematic research. Two types of studies are especially important. The first should investigate the influence of resident characteristics by analyzing the existence of propinquitous relationships among a variety of blocks, all similar in site plan and architectural design but differing in the degree of homogeneity among neighbors. The second study should analyze the impact of site plans and housing design on propinquity, by studying subdivisions which differ in physical layout but are occupied by similar kinds of residents.

Conclusions

At the beginning of this paper, I raised three questions: whether the planner had the power to influence patterns of social life; whether he ought to use this power; and if so, whether ideal patterns existed which should be advocated as planning goals. These questions can now be answered in a preliminary fashion.

The planner has only limited influence over social relationships. Although the site planner can create propinquity, he can only determine which houses are to be adjacent.

He can thus affect visual contact and initial social contacts among their occupants, but he cannot determine the intensity or quality of the relationships. This depends on the characteristics of the people involved.

The characteristics of the residents can be affected to some small degree by subdivision regulations, lot-size provisions, facility standards, or by any other planning tools which determine the uniformity of the housing to be built and the facilities to be provided—and can therefore affect the degree of homogeneity or heterogeneity among the eventual occupants. The planner has considerably less influence, however, than the private and public agencies which combine to finance, build, and market houses. These in turn respond to housing demand—and to the fact that most buyers are willing to accept similarity in house type and want a fair degree of homogeneity in their neighbors.

Consequently, within the context of present planning powers and practices, the planner's influence on social relationships is not very great. Whether or not it should be greater can only be decided on the basis of value judgments about patterns of social life.

Needless to say, a wide variety of value judgments can be formulated. My own judgment is that no one ideal pattern of social life can be—or should be—prescribed, but that opportunity for choice should be available both with respect to neighbor relations and friendship formation.

Neighbor relations should be positive; no benefits, but many social and emotional costs, result from life in an atmosphere of mutual dislike or coolness. Beyond this point, however, the intensity of relationships should not be a subject for planning values. Whether neighbors become friends, whether they remain friendly, or whether they are only polite to each other should be left up to the people who come to live together. Each type of relationship has its pros and cons, but none is so much more desirable than another that it should be advocated by the planner.

Friendship formation is a highly personal process, and it would be wrong for anyone to presume to plan another person's friendships. Moreover, one pattern of friendship does not seem to me to be preferable to any other. Finding one's friends on the block is convenient, although propinquity may encourage so much social contact that no time is left for friends who live farther away. Also, propinquity may make life on the block difficult if the relationship should cease to be friendly. Dispersal of friendship over a larger residential area may help people to know their community a little better, but unless they are already interested in gathering and using such knowledge, this is not likely to make much difference to them, or to the community.

Prescribing the opportunity for choice requires also that no one should be forced into any social relationship not of his own choosing. For example, no site plan should so isolate blocks from one another that residents must find it too difficult to maintain social contacts outside the block. Likewise, no residential area should be so heterogeneous in its population make-up that it prevents anyone from finding friends within the area; nor should it be so homogeneous that residents socialize only on their own block.

Implications for Planning Practice

Detailed implications cannot be spelled out until considerably more data are available on the relative roles of propinquity and homogeneity. Some guides can be suggested, however.

The site planner should not deliberately try to create a specific social pattern, but he should aim to provide maximum choice. If possible, the site plan should contain a variety of house-to-house relationships, so that residents who desire a large number of visual and social contacts and those who prefer relative isolation can both be satisfied. If density requirements permit, however, the site planner should not locate dwelling units within such close physical and functional distance to each other that the occupants are constantly thrown together and forced into social contact. In areas of single-family houses, the planner should avoid narrow courts. In row-house developments, soundproof party walls are necessary. In addition, some type of separation between houses should be provided to shield front and rear doors from those of adjacent houses. Since Americans seem to dislike complete and permanent separation for neighbors, however, something less irrevocable than a solid wall is desirable.

Blocks and courts should be so laid out that they do not become prisons. At the same time, however, they should not be spread out in such a fashion that all visual and social contact between neighbors is prevented. This is a problem in areas of very low density, where lots are so large that neighbors have difficulty in meeting each other.[11]

If and when sufficient research has been done to establish the relationship between site planning and social life on a sounder empirical basis, the concept of voluntary resident placement should be explored. Thus, if the studies indicate that some locations in a site plan will inevitably result in greater social contact than others, potential occupants should be informed, so that they can take this fact into account in choosing their houses.

Since homogeneity is an important determinant of social relationships, some degree of homogeneity on the block would seem to be desirable. This would encourage

[11] Erich Lindemann (in a personal conversation) has reported that this resulted in an upper-income community which he and his associates have studied. The large lots which satisfy the status needs of their owners also create loneliness for women who have no social contacts in the larger community.

positive relationships among neighbors and would allow those who want to find friends in the immediate vicinity to do so without impairing the ability of others to seek friends on the outside. If blocks are too homogeneous, however, those people who differ from the majority are likely to be considered deviants, and may be exposed to social pressure to conform or sentenced to virtual isolation. Conversely, heterogeneous blocks would produce cool and possibly negative relations among neighbors and would eliminate the chance to make friends on the block.

The proper solution is a moderate degree of homogeneity, although at this point no one knows how to define this degree operationally or how to develop planning guides for it. Moreover, the planner lacks the power to implement such guides. *My observations suggest that, by and large, the present crop of suburban communities provides the degree of homogeneity described here. Consequently, the planner need not worry about his inability to intervene.*

My proposals in behalf of residential homogeneity are based on the value judgments defended here and apply only to one phase of residential life. Planners have long debated whether residential areas should be homogeneous or heterogeneous. Some planners, who give higher priority to other planning values, and are more concerned with other phases of residential life, have advocated balanced communities, with heterogeneous populations.

References

1. On the Nature of the Environment

Allport, F. The contemporary appraisal of an old problem. *Contemporary Psychology*, 1961, *6*, 195-196.

Ashby, W. R. *An introduction to cybernetics*. New York: Wiley, 1956.

Barker, R. G. Ecology and motivation. In M. R. Jones (Ed.), *Nebraska Symposium on Motivation*. Lincoln: University of Nebraska Press, 1960.

Barker, R. G. (Ed.), *The stream of behavior*. New York: Appleton-Century-Crofts, 1963.

Barker, R. G., & Barker, L. S. Behavior units for the comparative study of cultures. In B. Kaplan (Ed.), *Studying personality cross-culturally*. New York: Harper & Row, 1961.

Barker, R. G., & Wright, H. F. *Midwest and its children*. New York: Harper & Row, 1955.

Barker, R. G., Wright, H. F., Barker, L. S., & Schoggen, M. F. *Specimen records of American and English children*. Lawrence: University of Kansas Press, 1961.

Brunswik, E. The conceptual framework of psychology. In *International encyclopedia of unified science* (Vol. 1). Chicago: University of Chicago Press, 1955.

Brunswik, E. Scope and aspects of the cognitive problem. In H. Gruber, R. Jessor, & K. Hammond (Eds.), *Cognition: the Colorado symposium*. Cambridge: Harvard University Press, 1957.

Calhoun, J. B. A comparative study of the social behavior of two inbred strains of house mice. *Ecological Monograph*, 1956, *26*, 81-103.

Calhoun, J. B. Population density and social pathology. In L. Duhl (Ed.), *The urban condition*. New York: Basic Books, Inc., 1963.

Dickman, H. The perception of behavioral units. In R. Barker (Ed.), *The stream of behavior*. New York: Appleton-Century-Crofts, 1963.

Goffman, E. *Behavior in public places*. New York: The Free Press of Glencoe, 1963.

Gump, P. V., & Friesen, W. V. Participation of large and small school Juniors in the nonclass settings of school. In R. G. Barker & P. V. Gump, *Big school, small school*. Stanford, Calif.: Stanford University Press, 1964. (a)

Gump, P. V., & Friesen, W. V. Satisfaction derived from nonclass settings. In R. G. Barker & P. V. Gump, *Big school, small school*. Stanford, Calif.: Stanford University Press, 1964. (b)

Gump, P. V., Schoggen, P., & Redl, F. The camp milieu and its immediate effects. *Journal of Social Issues*, 1957, *13*, (1) 40-46.

Gump, P. V., Schoggen, P., & Redl, F. The behavior of the same child in different milieus. In R. Barker (Ed.), *The stream of behavior*. New York: Appleton-Century-Crofts, 1963.

Gump, P., & Sutton-Smith, B. The it role in children's games. *The group*, 1955, *17*, 3-8.

Heider, F. On Lewin's methods and theory. *Journal of Social Issues*, 1959 Supplement Series, 13.

Jordan, N. Some formal characteristics of the behavior of two disturbed boys. In R. Barker (Ed.), *The stream of behavior*. New York: Appleton-Century-Crofts, 1963.

Lawrence, D. H. The nature of a stimulus:

Some relationships between learning and perception. In S. Koch (Ed.), *Psychology: A study of a science* (Vol. 5). New York: McGraw-Hill, 1963.

Leeper, R. W. Learning and the fields of perception, motivation, and personality. In S. Koch (Ed.), *Psychology: A study of a science* (Vol. 5). New York: McGraw-Hill, 1963.

Lewin, K. Forces behind food habits and methods of change. *Bulletin of the National Research Council*, 1943, *108*, 35-65.

Lewin, K. Frontiers in group dynamics. *Human Relations*, 1947, *1*, 2-38.

Lewin, K. Defining the "field at a given time." *Field theory in social science.* New York: Harper & Row, 1951.

Maruyama, M. The second cybernetics: Derivation-amplifying mutual causal processes. *American Scientist*, 1963, *51*, 164-179.

Miller, G. A., Galanter, E., & Pribram, K. H. *Plans and the structure of behavior.* New York: Holt, Rinehart, Winston, 1960.

Murray, H. A. Preparations for the scaffold of a comprehensive system. In S. Koch (Ed.), *Psychology: A study of a science* (Vol. 3). New York: McGraw-Hill, 1959.

Ratliff, F. Some interrelations among physics, physiology, and psychology. In S. Koch (Ed.), *Psychology: A study of a science* (Vol. 4). New York: McGraw-Hill, 1962.

Raush, H. L., Dittmann, A. T., & Taylor, T. J. The interpersonal behavior of children in residential treatment. *Journal of Abnormal and Social Psychology*, 1959, *58*, 9-27. (a)

Raush, H. L., Dittmann, A. T., & Taylor, T. J. Person, setting, and change in social interaction. *Human Relations*, 1959, *12*, (4), 361-378. (b)

Schoenfeld, W. N., & Cumming, W. W. Behavior and perception. In S. Koch (Ed.), *Psychology: A study of a science* (Vol. 5). New York: McGraw-Hill, 1963.

Sells, S. B. (Ed.). *The stimulus determinants of behavior.* New York: Ronald Press, 1963.

Soskin, W., & John, Vera P. The Study of spontaneous talk. In R. Barker (Ed.), *The stream of behavior.* New York: Appleton-Century-Crofts, 1963.

Willems, E. P. Forces toward participation in behavior settings. In R. G. Barker & P. V. Gump, *Big school, small school.* Stanford, Calif.: Stanford University Press, 1964. (a)

Willems, E. P. Review of research. In R. G. Barker & P. V. Gump, *Big school, small school.* Stanford, Calif.: Stanford University Press, 1964. (b)

Zener, K., & Gaffron, Mercedes. Perceptual experiences: an analysis of its relation to the external world through internal processings. In S. Koch (Ed.), *Psychology: A study of a science* (Vol. 4). New York: McGraw-Hill, 1962.

2. Some Perspectives on the Study of Man-Environment Phenomena

Altman, I. The communication of interpersonal attitudes: An ecological approach. In Huston, T. L., *Perspectives on interpersonal attraction.* New York: Academic Press, 1973.

Altman, I., Nelson, P., & Lett, E. E. *The ecology of home environments* (Final Report, Project No. 0-0502, Grant No. OEG-8-70-0202 [508], Office of Education, Department of Health, Education and Welfare), University of Utah, 1972.

Altman, I. & Taylor, D. A. *The development of interpersonal relationships: Social penetration.* New York: Holt, Rinehart & Winston, 1973.

Barker, R. G. (Ed.), *The stream of behavior.* New York: Appleton-Century-Crofts, 1963.

Barker, R. G., *Ecological psychology.* Stanford, Calif.: Stanford University Press, 1968.

Barker, R. G., & Gump, P. *Big school, small school.* Stanford, California: Stanford University Press, 1964.

Barker, R. G., & Wright, H. F., *Midwest and its children.* New York: Harper and Row, 1955.

Bechtel, R. B. The public housing environment: A few surprises. Paper presented at Environmental Design Research Association, Los Angeles, California, 1972.

Craik, K., *New directions in psychology.* New York: Holt, Rinehart and Winston, 1970.

Galle, O. R., Gove, W. R., & McPherson, J. M. Population density and pathology. *Science,* 1972, *176,* 23-30.

Hall, E. T. *The silent language.* New York: Doubleday, 1959.

Hall, E. T. *The hidden dimension.* New York: Doubleday, 1966.

Kuethe, J. L. Social schemas. *Journal of Abnormal and Social Psychology,* 1962, *64,* 31-38. (a)

Kuethe, J. L. Social schemas and the reconstruction of social object displays from memory. *Journal of Abnormal and Social Psychology,* 1962, *65,* 71-74 (b)

Ladd, F. Black youths view their environment: Neighborhood maps. *Environment and Behavior,* 1970, *2,* 74-99.

Lett, E. E., Clark, W. & Altman, I. A propositional inventory of research on interpersonal distance (Technical Report No. 1), Naval Medical Research Institute, Bethesda, Maryland, 1969.

Lynch, K. & Rivkin, M. A walk around the block. *Landscape,* 1959, *8* (34), 24-34.

Proshansky, H. M., Ittelson, W. H., & Rivlin, L. G. *Environmental psychology.* New York: Holt, Rinehart and Winston, 1970.

Sommer, R. Small group ecology. *Psychological Bulletin,* 1967, *67,* 145-152.

Sommer, R. *Personal space: The behavioral basis of design.* Englewood Cliffs, N.J.: Prentice Hall, 1969.

Stea, D. & Downs, R. (Eds.). *Cognitive mapping: Images of spatial environments.* Chicago: Aldine Press, 1972.

Zeisel, J. Frontier paper on sociology of architecture. Unpublished manuscript, Harvard University, 1972.

3. Conceptualizations of Human Environments

Anastasi, A. Psychology, psychologists, and psychological testing. *American Psychologist,* 1967, *22,* 297-306.

Astin, A. W. *The college environment.* Washington, D.C.: American Council on Education, 1968. (a)

Astin, A. W. Undergraduate achievement and institutional "excellence." *Science,* 1968, *161,* 661-668. (b)

Astin, A. W., & Holland, J. L. The environmental assessment technique: A way to measure college environments. *Journal of Educational Psychology,* 1961, *52,* 308-316.

Bandura, A. *Principles of behavior modification.* New York: Holt, Rinehart and Winston, 1969.

Bandura, A., & Walters, R. H. *Adolescent aggression.* New York: Ronald Press, 1959.

Barker, R. *Ecological psychology.* Stanford, Calif.: Stanford University Press, 1968.

Barker, R., & Gump, P. *Big school, small school.* Stanford, Calif.: Stanford University Press, 1964.

Barry, H., Child, I., & Bacon, M. Relation of child rearing to subsistance economy. *American Anthropologist,* 1959, *61,* 51-64.

Bechtel, R. Hodometer research in architecture. *Milieu,* 1967, *2,* 1-9.

Bergin, A. Some implications of psychotherapy research for therapeutic practice. *Journal of Abnormal Psychology,* 1966, *71,* 245-246.

Berke, J., & Wilson, V. *Watch out for the weather.* New York: Viking Press, 1951.

Buehler, R., Patterson, G., & Furniss, J. The reinforcement of behavior in institutional settings. *Behavior Research and Therapy*, 1966, *4*, 157-167.

Caffrey, B. Behavior patterns and personality characteristics related to prevalence of coronary heart disease in American monks. *Journal of Chronic Diseases*, 1969, *22*, 93-103.

Calhoun, J. B. Population density and social pathology. *Scientific American*, 1962, *206*, 139-148.

Cobb, S., French, J., Kahn, R., & Mann, F. An environmental approach to mental health. *Annals of the New York Academy of Sciences*, 1963, *107*, 596-606.

Cohen, H., & Filipczak, J. *A new learning environment*. San Francisco: Jossey-Bass, 1971.

Corwin, R. G. Patterns of organizational conflict. *Administrative Science Quarterly*, 1969, *14*, 507-520.

Couch, A. The psychological determinants of interpersonal behavior. In K. Gergen & D. Marlowe (Eds.), *Personality and social behavior*. Reading, Mass.: Addison-Wesley, 1970.

Craik, K. H. Environmental psychology. In *New directions in psychology* (Vol. 4). New York: Holt, Rinehart and Winston, 1970.

Duhl, L. (Ed.). *The urban condition*. New York: Basic Books, 1963.

Endler, N., & Hunt, J. McV. S–R inventories of hostility and comparisons of the proportion of variance from persons, responses, and situations for hostility and anxiousness. *Journal of Personality and Social Psychology*, 1968, *9*, 309-315.

Galle, O. R., Gove, W. R., & McPherson, J. M. Population density and pathology: What are the relations for man? *Science*, 1972, *176*, 23-30.

Gerst, M., & Moos, R. The social ecology of university student residences. *Journal of Educational Psychology*, 1972, *63*, 513-522.

Griffitt, W. Environmental effects on interpersonal affective behavior: Ambient effective temperature and attraction. *Journal of Personality and Social Psychology*, 1970, *15*, 240-244.

Griffitt, W., & Veitch, R. Hot and crowded: Influences of population density and temperature on interpersonal affective behavior. *Journal of Personality and Social Psychology*, 1971, *17*, 92-98.

Gump, P., Schoggen, P., & Redl, F. The camp milieu and its immediate effects. *Journal of Social Issues*, 1957, *13*, 40-46.

Halpin, A., & Croft, D. *The organizational climate of schools*. Chicago: Midwest Administration Center, University of Chicago, 1963.

Holland, J. *The psychology of vocational choice*. Waltham, Mass.: Blaisdell, 1966.

Holsti, O., & North, R. The history of human conflict. In E. McNeil (Ed.), *The nature of human conflict*. Englewood Cliffs, N.J.: Prentice-Hall, 1965.

Huntington, E. *Civilization and climate*. New Haven: Yale University Press, 1915.

Insel, P., & Moos, R. The work environment inventory. Palo Alto, Calif.: Social Ecology Laboratory, Department of Psychiatry, Stanford University, 1972.

Jordan, P. A real predicament. *Science*, 1972, *175*, 977-978.

Kanfer, F., & Saslow, G. Behavioral analysis. *Archives of general psychiatry*, 1965, *12*, 529-538.

Kasmar, J. V. The development of a usable lexicon of environmental descriptors. *Environment and behavior*, 1970, *2*, 153-169.

Kates, R., & Wohlwill, J. (Eds.) Man's response to the physical environment. *Journal of Social Issues*, 1966, *22*, 1-140.

Katz, D., & Kahn, R. *The social psychology of organizations*. New York: Wiley, 1966.

Kelly, J. The coping process in varied high school environments. In M. Feldman (Ed.), *Studies in psychotherapy and behavioral change* (Vol 2). Buffalo: State University of New York Press, 1971.

Kinzel, A. F. Body-buffer zone in violent prisoners. *American Journal of Psychiatry*, 1970, *127*, 99-104.

Klerman, G., Golberg, S., & Davis, D. Relationship between the hospital milieu and the response to phenothiazines in the treatment of schizophrenics. Paper presented at the Semaine Interdisciplinaire des Neuroleptiques, Liege, Belgium, May 11-16, 1969.

Lansing, J., Marans, R., & Zehner, R. *Planned residential environments*. Ann Arbor, Mich.: Survey Research Center, Institute for Social Research, University of Michigan, 1970.

Leary, T. *Interpersonal diagnosis of personality*. New York: Ronald Press, 1957.

Leiderman, P. H., & Shapiro, D. (Eds.) *Psychobiological approaches to social behavior*. Stanford, Calif.: Stanford University Press, 1964.

Lewin, K. *Field theory in social science*. New York: Harper & Row, 1951.

Lewin, K., Lippett, R., & White, R. Patterns of aggressive behavior in experimentally created "social climates." *Journal of Social Psychology*, 1939, *10*, 271-299.

Lichtman, C., & Hunt, R. Personality and organizational theory: A review of some conceptual literature. *Psychological Bulletin*, 1971, *76*, 271-294.

Lieber, A., & Sherin, C. Homicides and the lunar cycle: Toward a theory of lunar influence on human emotional disturbance. *American Journal of Psychiatry*, 1972, *129*, 69-74.

Likert, R. *The human organization: Its management and value*. New York: McGraw-Hill, 1967.

Linton, R. *The cultural background of personality*. New York: Century, 1945.

March, J. (Ed.) *Handbook of organizations*. Chicago: Rand-McNally, 1965.

Maslow, A., & Mintz, N. Effects of esthetic surroundings: 1. Initial effects of three esthetic conditions upon perceiving "energy" and "well-being" in faces. *Journal of Psychology*, 1956, *41*, 247-254.

Mason, J. Organization of psychoendocrine mechanisms. *Psychosomatic Medicine*, 1968, *30*(Pt. 2), 565-808.

Michelson, W. Some like it hot: Social participation and environmental use as functions of the season. *American Journal of Sociology*, 1971, *76*, 1072-1083.

Milgram, S. Behavioral study of obedience. *Journal of Abnormal and Social Psychology*, 1963, *57*, 371-378.

Milgram, S. Group pressure and action against a person. *Journal of Abnormal and Social Psychology*, 1964, *69*, 137-143.

Milgram, S. The experience of living in cities. *Science*, 1970, *167*, 1461-1468.

Mills, C. *Climate makes the man*. New York: Harper & Row, 1942.

Mischel, W. *Personality and assessment*. New York: Wiley, 1968.

Moos, R. The assessment of the social climates of correctional institutions. *Journal of Research in Crime and Delinquency*, 1968, *5*, 174-188.

Moos, R. Sources of variance in responses to questionnaires and behavior. *Journal of Abnormal Psychology*, 1969, *74*, 405-412.

Moos, R. Assessment of the psychosocial environments of community-oriented psychiatric treatment programs. *Journal of Abnormal Psychology*, 1972, *79*, 9-18. (a)

Moos, R. British psychiatric ward treatment environments. *British Journal of Psychiatry*, 1972, *120*, 635-643. (b)

Moos, R. Changing the social milieus of psychiatric treatment settings. *Journal of Applied Behavioral Science*, 1973, in press (a)

Moos, R. *The Family Environment Inventory*. Palo Alto: Social Ecology Laboratory, Department of Psychiatry,

Stanford University, 1973. (b)

Moos, R. *Evaluating treatment environments: A social ecology approach.* New York: Wiley, 1974.

Moos, R., & Humphrey, B. *Group Environment Inventory: Technical report.* Palo Alto, Calif.: Social Ecology Laboratory, Department of Psychology, Stanford University, 1973.

Moos, R., & Insel, P. (Eds.) *Issues in social ecology: Human milieus.* Palo Alto, Calif.: National Press Books, 1974.

Muecher, H., & Ungeheuer, H. Meteorological influence on reaction time, flicker fusion frequency, job accidents, and use of medical treatment. *Perceptual and Motor Skills,* 1961, *12,* 163-168.

Murray, H. *Explorations in personality.* New York: Oxford University Press, 1938.

Nielsen, J. Criminality among patients with Kleinfelter's syndrome and XYY syndrome. *British Journal of Psychiatry,* 1970, *117,* 365-369.

Osmond, H. Function as a basis of psychiatric ward design. *Mental Hospitals,* 1957, *8,* 23-39.

Pace, R. *College and University Environment Scales.* (Technical manual: 2nd ed.) Princeton, N.J.: Educational Testing Service, 1969.

Peterson, R., Centra, J., Hartnett, R., & Linn, R. *Institutional functioning inventory: Preliminary technical manual.* Princeton, N.J.: Educational Testing Service, 1970.

Porter, L., & Lawler, E. Properties of organzation structure in relation to job attitudes and job behavior. *Psychological Bulletin,* 1965, *64,* 23-51.

Proshansky, H. M., Ittelson, W. H., & Rivlin, L. G. (Eds.) *Environmental psychology: Man and his physical setting.* New York: Holt, Rinehart and Winston, 1970.

Pugh, D. Modern organization theory: A psychological and sociological study. *Psychological Bulletin,* 1966, *66,* 235-251.

Purcell, K., & Brady, K. *Assessment of interpersonal behavior in natural settings.* (Final Progress Report) Denver, Colo.: Children's Asthma Research Institute and Hospital, 1964.

Raush, H., Dittman, A., & Taylor, T. Person, setting, and change in social interaction. *Human Relations,* 1959, *12,* 361-378.

Roberts, K. On looking at an elephant: An evaluation of cross-cultural research related to organizations. *Psychological Bulletin,* 1970, *74,* 327-350.

Rotter, J. *Social learning and clinical psychology.* New York: Prentice-Hall, 1954.

Russett, B., et al. *World handbook of political and social indicators.* New Haven: Yale University Press, 1964.

Schmid, C. Urban crime areas. *American Sociological Review,* 1960, *25,* 527, 542, 655-678.

Schoggen, P. Environmental forces in the everyday lives of children. In R. Barker (Ed.), *The stream of behavior.* New York: Appleton-Century-Crofts, 1963.

Sells, S. Dimensions of stimulus situations which account for behavior variance. In S. Sells (Ed.), *Stimulus determinants of behavior.* New York: Ronald Press, 1963.

Sells, S., Findikyan, N., & Duke, M. *Stress reviews: Atmosphere.* (Tech. Rep. No. 10) Fort Worth: Institute of Behavioral Research, Texas Christian University, 1966.

Sommer, R. *Personal space.* New York: Prentice-Hall, 1969.

Stern, G. *People in context: Measuring person environment congruence in education and industry.* New York: Wiley, 1970.

Swift, J. W. Effects of early group experience: The nursery school and day nursery. In M. Hoffman & I. Hoffman (Eds.), *Child development research.* Vol. 1. New York: Russell Sage Foundation, 1964.

Trickett, E., & Moos, R. The social environment of junior high and high school classrooms. *Journal of Educational Psychology*, 1973, in press.

Walberg, H. Social environment as a mediator of classroom learning. *Journal of Educational Psychology*, 1969, *60*, 443-448.

Wicker, A. Size of church membership and members support of church behavior settings. *Journal of Personality and Social Psychology*, 1969, *13*, 278-288.

Wohlwill, J. The emerging discipline of environmental psychology. *American Psychologist*, 1970, *25*, 303-312.

Wolf, R. The measurement of environments. In A. Anastasi (Ed.), *Testing problems in perspective*. Washington, D.C.: American Council on Education, 1966.

Wolfgang, M. *Patterns in criminal homicide*. Philadelphia: University of Pennsylvania Press, 1958.

Wolpe, J., & Lazarus, A. *Behavior therapy techniques*. Oxford: Pergamon Press, 1966.

4. Some Issues Facing a Theory of Environment and Behavior

Etzioni, A. *Science*, March 1973, *179*, 4077.

Hardin, G. *Exploring new ethics for survival: The voyage of the Spaceship Beagle*.

Linowitz, S. *New York Times*, April 10, 1972.

Luria, S. E. *New York Review of Books*, Feb. 7, 1974.

Medewar, P. *Smithsonian*, 1973.

5. Environmental Psychology: A Methodological Orientation

Allport, G. *Personality: A psychological interpretation*. New York: Holt, 1937.

Ittelson, W. H., Proshansky H. M., Rivlin, L. G., Winkel, G. H. *Introduction to environmental psychology*. Holt, Rinehart and Winston: New York, 1974.

Katz, D. Some final considerations about experimentation in social psychology. In C. G. M. McClintock (Ed.) *Experimental social psychology*. New York: Holt, Rinehart and Winston, 1972.

Lewin, K. *Resolving social conflicts*. New York: Harper, 1948.

6. Knowledge and Design

Colquhoun, A. *Typology and design method*. *Arena*, June 1967, 11-14.

Keene, S. C. *Introduction to metamathematics*. Amsterdam: North-Holland Publishing, 1959.

Kelly, G. *The psychology of personal constructs*. New York: Wiley, 1964.

Kuhn, T. *The structure of scientific revolutions*. Chicago: University of Chicago Press, 1962.

Lakatos, I. *History and its rational reconstructions*. (mimeo).

Lakatos, I., & Musgrave, A. (Eds.) *Criticism and the growth of knowledge*. Cambridge, England: Cambridge University Press, 1970.

Le Corbusier: *Towards a New Architecture*. London: Architectural Press, 1946. (First English edition, 1927.)

Levi-Strauss, C.: *The savage mind*. London: Weidenfeld & Nicholson, 1966.

Nagel E., & Newman, J. R.: *Gödel's proof*. London: Routledge & Kegan Paul, 1959.

Piaget, J. *Structuralism*. London: Routledge & Kegan Paul, 1971.

Popper, K. R. *The logic of scientific discovery*. London: Hutchinson, 1959.

Popper, K. R. *Conjectures and refutations*. London: Routledge & Kegan Paul, 1963.

Royal Institute of British Architects Research Committee. *Strategies for architectural research: Architectural research and teaching, 1,1*, May 1970. 3-5.

7. Undermanning Theory and Research

Baird, L. L. Big school, small school: A critical examination of the hypothesis. *Journal of Educational Psychology,* 1969, *60,* 253-260.

Barker, R. G. Ecology and motivation. *Nebraska Symposium on Motivation,* 1960, *8,* 1-50.

Barker, R. G. On the nature of the environment. *Journal of Social Issues,* 1963, *19* (4), 17-38.

Barker, R. G. Explorations in ecological psychology. *American Psychologist,* 1965, *20,* 1-14.

Barker, R. G. *Ecological psychology: Concepts and methods for studying the environment of human behavior.* Stanford: Stanford University Press, 1968.

Barker, R. G., & Barker, L. S. Structural characteristics. In R. G. Barker & P. V. Gump (Eds.), *Big school, small school: High school size and student behavior.* Stanford: Stanford University Press, 1964.

Barker, R. G., & Hall, E. R. Participation in interschool events and extracurricular activities. In R. G. Barker & P. V. Gump (Eds.), *Big school, small school: High school size and student behavior.* Stanford: Stanford University Press, 1964.

Barker, R. G., & Wright, H. F. *Midwest and its children: The psychological ecology of an American town.* New York: Row, Peterson, 1955.

Campbell, W. J. Some effects of high school consolidation. In R. G. Barker & P. V. Gump (Eds.), *Big school, small school: High school size and student behavior.* Stanford: Stanford University Press, 1964.

Desor, J. A. Toward a psychological theory of crowding. *Journal of Personality and Social Psychology,* 1972, *21,* 79-83.

Freedman, J. L., Klevansky, S., & Ehrlich, P. R. The effect of crowding on human task performance. *Journal of Applied Social Psychology,* 1971, *1,* 7-25.

Galle, O. R., Gove, W. R., & McPherson, J. M. Population density and pathology: What are the relations for man? *Science,* 1972, *176,* 4030, 23-30.

Gump, P. V., & Friesen, W. V. Participation in nonclass settings. In R. G. Barker & P. V. Gump (Eds.), *Big school, small school: High school size and student behavior.* Stanford: Stanford University Press, 1964. (a)

Gump, P. V., & Friesen, W. V. Satisfactions derived from nonclass settings. In R. G. Barker & P. V. Gump (Eds.), *Big school, small school: High school size and student behavior.* Stanford: Stanford University Press, 1964. (b)

Helson, H. *Adaptation-level theory.* New York: Harper & Row, 1964.

Petty, R. M., & Wicker, A. W. Degree of manning and degree of success of a group as determinants of members' subjective experiences and their acceptance of a new group member: A laboratory study of Barker's theory. Unpublished manuscript, Department of Psychology, University of Illinois, 1971.

Shaw, M. E. *Group dynamics: The psychology of small group behavior.* New York: McGraw-Hill, 1971.

Sommer, R. Man's proximate environment. *Journal of Social Issues,* 1966, *22* (4), 59-70.

Thibaut, J. W., & Kelley, H. H. *The social psychology of groups.* New York: Wiley, 1959.

Wicker, A. W. Undermanning, performances, and students' subjective experiences in behavior settings of large and small high schools. *Journal of Personality and Social Psychology,* 1968, *10,* 255-261.

Wicker, A. W. Cognitive complexity, school size, and participation in school behavior settings: A test of the frequency of interaction hypothesis. *Journal of Educational Psychology,* 1969, *60,* 200-203. (a)

Wicker, A. W. Size of church membership

and members' support of church behavior settings. *Journal of Personality and Social Psychology,* 1969, *13,* 278-288. (b)

Wicker, A. W. Processes which mediate behavior-environment congruence. *Behavioral Science,* 1972, *17,* 265-277.

Wicker, A. W., & Kauma, C. E. Effects of a merger of a small and a large organization on members' behaviors and experiences. Unpublished manuscript, Claremont Graduate School, 1972.

Wicker, A. W., McGrath, J. E., & Armstrong, G. E. Organization size and behavior setting capacity as determinants of member participation. *Behavioral Science,* 1972, *17,* 499-513.

Wicker, A. W., & Mehler, A. Assimilation of new members in a large and a small church. *Journal of Applied Psychology,* 1971, *55,* 151-156.

Willems, E. P. Forces toward participation in behavior settings. In A. G. Barker & P. V. Gump (Eds.), *Big school, small school: High school size and student behavior.* Stanford, Calif.: Stanford University Press, 1964.

Willems, E. P. Sense of obligation to high school activities as related to school size and marginality of student. *Child development,* 1967, *38,* 1247-1260.

Zlutnick, S., & Altman, I. Crowding and human behavior. In J. F. Wohlwill & D. H. Carson (Eds.), *Environment and the social sciences: Perspectives and applications.* Washington, D.C.: American Psychological Association, 1971.

8. Psychological Maps of Paris

Downs, R. M., & Stea, D. *Image and environment: Cognitive mapping and spatial behavior.* Chicago: Aldine, 1973.

Gould, P., & White, R. *Mental maps.* Baltimore: Penguin Books, 1974.

Hillairet, J. *Dictionnaire historique des rues de paris.* Paris: Les Editions de Minuits, 1964.

Lynch, K. *The image of the city.* Cambridge, Mass.: The M.I.T. Press, 1960.

Sondages: Revue Française de l'Opinion Publique. 1951, No. 2. 1-41. "Paris, une enquête psychosociale." Anonymous.

Suttles, G. *The social construction of communities.* Chicago: University of Chicago Press, 1972.

9. Ecological and Cultural Factors in Spatial Perceptual Development

Barker, R. G. Explorations in ecological psychology. *American Psychologist,* 1965, *20,* 1-14.

Barker, R. G. *Ecological psychology.* Stanford: Stanford University Press, 1968.

Barry, H., Child, I., & Bacon, M. Relation of child training to subsistence economy. *American Anthropologist,* 1959, *61,* 51-63.

Barry, H. Cross-cultural research with matched pairs of societies. *Journal of Social Psychology,* 1969, *79,* 25-33.

Berry, J. W. *Cultural determinants of perception.* Unpublished Ph.D. thesis, University of Edinburgh, 1966a.

Berry, J. W. Temne and Eskimo perceptual skills. *International Journal of Psychology,* 1966b, *I,* 207-29.

Berry, J. W. Independence and conformity in subsistence-level societies. *Journal of Personality and Social Psychology,* 1967, *7,* 415-18.

Berry, J. W. Ecology, perceptual development and the Muller-Lyer illusion. *British Journal of Psychology,* 1968, *59,* 205-10.

Berry, J. W. On cross-cultural comparability. *International Journal of Psychology,* 1969, *4,* 119-128. (a)

Berry, J. W. Ecology and socialization as factors in figural assimilation and the resolution of binocular rivalry. *International Journal of Psychology,* 1969, *4,* 271-80. (b)

Berry, J. W. *Ecology, cultural adaptation and psychological differentiation,* n.d.

Collins, P. Functional analyses. In: Leeds, A., & Vayda, P. (Eds.) *Man, culture and animals*. Washington: American Association for the Advancement of Science, 1965.

Cravioto, J. Nutritional deficiencies and mental performance in childhood. In: Glass, D. C. (Ed.) *Environmental influences*. New York: Russell Sage, 1968.

Dawson, J. L. M. Kwashiorkor, gynaecomastia and feminization processes. *Journal Trop. Med. Hygiene*, 1966, *69*, 175-9.

Dawson, J. L. M. Cultural and physiological influences upon spatial-perceptual processes in West Africa. Parts I and II. *International Journal of Psychology*, 1967, *2*, 115-28 and 171-85.

Ferguson, G. A. On learning and human ability. *Canadian Journal of Psychology*. 1954, *8*, 95-112.

Hammond, K. R. *The psychology of Egon Brunswik*. New York: Holt, Rinehart and Winston, 1966.

Helm, J. The ecological approach in anthropology. *American Journal of Sociology*, 1962, *67*, 630-639.

MacArthur, R. S. Sex differences in field-dependence for the Eskimo: Replication of Berry's findings. *International Journal of Psychology*, 1967, *2*, 139-140.

Meggars, B. J. Environmental limitations on the development of culture. *American Anthropologist*, 1954, *56*, 801-24.

Rappaport, R. A. *Pigs for the ancestors*. New Haven: Yale University Press, 1967.

Raven, J. C. *Coloured progressive matrices sets A, Ab, B*. London: H. K. Lewis, 1956.

Steward, J. H. *Theory of culture change*. Urbana, Ill.: University of Illinois Press, 1955.

Vayda, P. *Environment and cultural behavior*. Garden City: Natural History Press, 1969.

Vayda, P., & Rappaport, R. A. Ecology, cultural and non-cultural. In J. Clifton (Ed.), *Introduction to cultural anthropology*. Boston: Houghton Mifflin, 1968.

Whiting, J. W. M. Methods and problems in cross-cultural research. In G. Lindzey & E. Aronson (Eds.) *Handbook of social psychology*. (Vol. 1, 2nd ed.). Reading, Mass.: Addison-Wesley, 1968.

Witkin, H. A. Individual differences in ease of perception of embedded figures. *Journal of Personality*, 1950, *19*, 1-15.

Witkin, H. A., Birnbaum, J., Lomonaco, S., Lehr, S., & Herman, J. L. Cognitive patterning in congenitally totally blind children. *Child Development*, 1968, *39*, 767-84.

Wohlwill, J. F. The physical environment: A problem for a psychology of stimulation. *Journal of Social Issues*, 1966, *22*, 29-38.

Wohlwill, J. F. The emerging discipline of environmental psychology. *American Psychologist*, 1970, *25*, 303-12.

10. Structuralism, Existentialism and Environmental Perception

Beck, R. Spatial meaning, and the properties of the environment. In D. Lowenthal (Ed.) *Environmental perception and behavior*. University of Chicago Department of Geography Research Paper 109. 1967, 18-41.

Goldschmidt, W. *Comparative functionalism*. Berkeley: University of California Press, 1966.

Leach, E. *Lévi-Strauss*. New York: Viking Press, 1970.

Levi-Strauss, C. *The savage mind*. London: Weidenfeld and Nicolson, 1966.

Levi-Strauss, C. The story of Asdiwal. In E. Leach (Ed.) *The structural study of myth and totemism*. London: Tavistock, 1967.

Piaget, J. *Structuralism*. New York: Basic Books, 1970.

Sartre, J. P. *La nausée*. Paris: Gallimard

1938.

Sartre, J. P. *Being and nothingness*. New York: Washington Square Press, 1966.

Warnock, M. *Existentialism*. London: Oxford Univ. Press, 1970.

11. Environment Perception and Contemporary Perceptual Theory

Allport, G., & Pettigrew, T. Cultural influence on the perception of movement: The trapezoidal illusion among the Zulus. *Journal of Abnormal and Social Psychology*, 1957, 55, 104-113.

Bridgman, P. W. Science and common sense. *Scientific Monthly*, 1954 (July), 32-39.

Bruner, J. S. Constructive cognitions. *Contemporary Psychology*, 1970, 15 (2), 81-83.

Brunswik, E. *Perception and the representative design of psychological experiments*. Berkeley: University of California Press, 1956.

Cantril, H. (Ed.).*The morning notes of Adelbert Ames, Jr. (including a correspondence with John Dewey)*. Rahway, New Jersey: Rutgers University Press, 1960.

Chomsky, N. *Language and mind*. New York: Harcourt, 1968.

Dewey, J., & Bentley, A. F. *Knowing and the known*. Boston, Massachusetts: Beacon, 1949.

Gibson, J. J. *The perception of the visual world*. Boston, Massachusetts: Houghton, 1950.

Gibson, J. J. *The senses considered as perceptual systems*. Boston, Massachusetts: Houghton, 1966.

von Helmholtz, H. L. F. *Helmholtz's treatise on physiological optics*. Translated from the third German edition. J. P. C. Southall, (Ed.). New York: Dover, 1962.

von Helmholtz, H. L. F. The facts of perception. In R. M. Warren & R. P. Warren (Eds.), *Helmholtz on perception: Its physiology and development*. New York: Wiley, 1968.

Ittelson, W. H. *Visual space perception*. New York: Springer, 1960.

Kiss, G. Memory forgotten? *Contemporary Psychology*, 1971, 16(9), 609-610.

Neisser, U. The processes of vision. *Scientific American*, 1968, 219(3), 204-214.

Rock, I. *The nature of perceptual adaptation*. New York: Basic Books, 1966.

Segall, M. H., Campbell, D. T., & Herskovits, M. J. *Influence of culture on visual perception*. Indianapolis: Bobbs-Merrill, 1966.

Stevens, S. S. *Handbook of experimental psychology*. New York: Wiley, 1966.

Tolman, E. C., & Brunswik, E. The organism and the causal texture of the environment. *Psychological Review*, 1935, 42, 43-77.

Whitehead, A. N. *The aims of education, and other essays*. New York: Macmillan, 1957.

Wundt, W. *An introduction to psychology*. London: Allen & Unwin, 1912.

12. The Anthropology of Space

Ariès, P. *Centuries of childhood*. New York: Knopf, 1962.

Goffman, E. *The presentation of self in everyday life*. Garden City, N.Y.: Doubleday, 1959.

Hall, E. T. *The silent language*. Garden City, N.Y.: Doubleday, 1959.

Hediger, H. *Studies of the psychology and behavior of captive animals in zoos and circuses*. London: Butterworth, 1955.

Joos, M. The five clocks. *International Journal of American Linguistics*, 1962, 28, 127-133.

Osmond, H. Function as the basis of psychiatric ward design. *Mental Hospitals* (Architectural Supplement), 1957, 8, 23-29.

Mumford, L. *The city in history*. New York: Harcourt, Brace, 1961.

Sommer, R. Studies in personal space. *Sociometry*, 1959, 22, 247-260.

White, T. H. *The making of the president 1960.* New York: Atheneum, 1961.

13. Freedom of Choice and Behavior in a Physical Setting

Altman, I., & Haythorn, W. W. The ecology of isolated groups. *Behavioral Science,* 1967, *12,* 169-182.

Ardrey, R. *The territorial imperative: A personal inquiry into the animal origins of property and nations.* New York: Atheneum, 1966.

Biderman, A. D., Lovria, M. & Bacchus, J. *Historical incidents of extreme overcrowding.* Washington, D.C.: Bureau of Social Science Research, 1963.

Brehm, J. W. *A theory of psychological reactance.* New York: Academic Press, 1966.

Chermayeff, S., & Alexander, C. *Community and privacy: Toward a new architecture of humanism.* New York: Doubleday, 1963.

Doxiadis, C. A. Man and the space around him. *Saturday Review,* December 14, 1968, pp. 21-23.

Esser, A. H., Chamberlain, A. S., Chapple, E. D., & Kline, N. S. Territoriality of patients on a research ward. In J. Wortis (Ed.), *Recent advances in biological psychiatry* (Vol. 7). New York: Plenum Press, 1965.

Goodwin, J. What is a slum? *The Independent,* February 1964, p. 4.

Hall, E. T. *The hidden dimension.* New York: Doubleday, 1966.

Lewis, O. *The children of Sanchez.* New York: Vintage, 1961.

Lewis, O. *Five families.* New York: New American Library, 1965.

Leyhausen, P. The communal organization of solitary mammals. *Symposium of the Zoological Society of London,* April 1965, No. 14, 249-263.

Lorenz, K. *Aggression.* New York: Harcourt, Brace & World, 1966.

Lucas, R. C. *The recreational capacity of the Quetico-Superior Area.* U.S. Forest Service Research Paper LS-15. Lake States Forest Experiment Station, St. Paul, Minn., 1964.

Pastalan, L. A. *Privacy as an expression of human territoriality.* Unpublished paper. University of Michigan, 1968.

Rivlin, L. G., Proshansky, H. M., & Ittelson, W. H. *An experimental study of the effects of changes in psychiatric ward design on patient behavior.* Offset. City University of New York, 1968.

Schorr, A. L. *Slum and social insecurity.* U.S. Department of Health, Education, and Welfare. Social Security Administration. Research Report No. 1, U.S. Government Printing Office, 1966.

Vischer, A. L. *Barbed wire disease.* London: John Bale and Davidson, 1919.

Weingarten, M. *Life in a Kibbutz.* New York: Reconstructionist Press, 1955.

Westin, A. F. *Privacy and freedom.* New York: Atheneum, 1967.

14. The Role of Space in Animal Sociology

Calhoun, J. B. A comparative study of the social behavior of two inbred strains of house mice. *Ecological Monogaphs,* 1956a, *26,* 81-103.

Calhoun, J. B. Behavior of house mice with reference to fixed points of orientation. *Ecology,* 1956b, 37, 287-301.

Calhoun, J. B. Social welfare as a variable in population dynamics. *Symposium of Quantitative Biology,* 1958, 22, 339-356.

Calhoun, J. B. A behavioral sink. In E. Bliss (Ed.), *Roots of behavior.* New York: Paul Hoeber, 1962.

Calhoun, J. B. *The ecology and sociology of the Norway rat,* U.S. Dept. of Health, Education, and Welfare, Public Health Service, Pub. No. 1008, Washington, D.C.: U.S. Government Printing Office, 1963.

Calhoun, J. B.: The social use of space. In W. Mayer & R. Van Gelder, *Physiological mammalogy.* New York: Academic Press, 1964.

Calhoun, J. B. Ecological factors in the development of behavioral anomalies. In J. Zubin (Ed.), *Comparative psychopathology*. New York: Grune and Stratton, 1967.

Stewart, J. Q. Concerning social physics. *Scientific American*, 1948, *178*, 20-23.

Zipf, G. K. *Human behavior and the principle of least effort*. Cambridge, Mass.: Addison-Wesley, 1949.

15. Human Territoriality

Alland, A., Jr. *The human imperative*. New York: Columbia University Press, 1972.

Altman, I. Territorial behavior in humans: An analysis of the concept. In L. A. Pastalan & D. A. Carson (Eds.), *Spatial behavior of older people*. Ann Arbor: University of Michigan Press, 1970.

Altman, I., & Haythorn, W. W. The ecology of isolated groups. *Behavioral Science*, 1967, *12*, 169-182.

Altman, I., Taylor, D. A., & Wheeler, L. Ecological aspects of group behavior in social isolation. *Journal of Applied Social Psychology*, 1971, 1, 76-100.

Ardrey, R. *The territorial imperative*. New York: Atheneum, 1966.

Barker, R. *Ecological psychology*. Stanford: Stanford University Press, 1968.

Barton, R. The patient's personal territory. *Hospital and Community Psychiatry*, 1966, *17*, 336.

Becker, F. D. Study of spatial markers. *Journal of Personality and Social Psychology*, 1973, *26*, 439-445.

Becker, F. D., & Mayo, C. Delineating personal distance and territoriality. *Environment and Behavior*, 1971, *3*, 375-381.

Blood, R. O., & Livant, W. P. The use of space within the cabin group. *Journal of Social Issues*, 1957, *13*, 47-53.

Brower, S. N. The signs we learn to read. *Landscape*, 1965, *15*, 9-12.

Carpenter, C. R. Territoriality. In A. Roe & G. G. Simpson (Eds.), *Behavior and evolution*. New Haven, Conn.: Yale University Press, 1958.

Cheyne, J. A., & Efran, M. G. The effect of spatial and interpersonal variables on the invasion of group controlled territories. *Sociometry*, 1972, *35*, 477-489.

Colman, A. D. Territoriality in man: A comparison of behavior in home and hospital. *American Journal of Orthopsychiatry*, 1968, *38*, 464-468.

Davis, D. E. Territorial rank in starlings. *Animal Behavior*, 1959, 7, 214-221.

De Long, A. J. Dominance-territorial relations in a small group. *Environment and Behavior*, 1970, *2*, 170-191.

Edney, J. J. Place and space: The effects of experience with a physical locale. *Journal of Experimental Social Psychology*, 1972, *8*, 124-135. (a)

Edney, J. J. Property, possession and permanence: A field study in human territoriality. *Journal of Applied Social Psychology*, 1972, *2*, 275-282. (b)

Edney, J. J. Territoriality and control. Unpublished doctoral dissertation, Yale University, 1973.

Edney, J. J., & Jordan-Edney, N. Territorial spacing on a beach. *Sociometry*, 1974, *37*, 92-104.

Efran, M. G., & Cheyne, J. A. Shared space: The cooperative control of spatial areas by two interacting individuals. *Canadian Journal of Behavioral Science*, 1973, *5*, 201-210.

Efran, M. G., & Cheyne, J. A. Affective concomitants of the invasion of shared space: Behavioral, physiological, and verbal indicators. *Journal of Personality and Social Psychology*, 1974, *29*, 219-226.

Ehrlich, P., & Freedman, J. Population, crowding and human behavior. *New Scientist and Science Journal*, 1971, *50*, 10-14.

Eibl-Eibesfeldt, I. *Ethology: The biology of behavior*. New York: Holt, Rinehart and Winston, 1970.

Elms, A. Horoscopes and Ardrey. *Psychology Today*, 1972, *6* (5), 36.

Esser, A. H. Dominance hierarchy and clinical course of psychiatrically hospitalized boys. *Child Development,* 1968, *39,* 147-157.

Esser, A. H. Interactional hierarchy and power structure on a psychiatric ward: Ethological studies of dominance behavior in a total institution. In S. J. Hutt & C. Hutt (Eds.), *Behavior studies in psychiatry.* Oxford: Pergamon Press, 1970.

Esser, A. H. Cottage Fourteen. *Small Group Behavior,* 1973, *4,* 131-146.

Esser, A. H., Chamberlain, A. S., Chapple, E. D., & Kline, N. S. Territoriality of patients on a research ward. In J. Wortis (Ed.), *Recent advances in biological psychiatry* (Vol. 7). New York: Plenum Press, 1965.

Goffman, E. *Presentation of self in everyday life.* Garden City: Doubleday, 1959.

Goffman, E. *Relations in public.* New York: Harper and Row, 1972.

Hall, E. T. *The silent language.* Greenwich, Conn.: Fawcett, 1959.

Hall, E. T. *The hidden dimension.* New York: Doubleday, 1966.

Kaufmann, J. H. Is territoriality definable? In A. H. Esser (Ed.), *Behavior and environment: The use of space by animals and men.* New York: Plenum Press, 1971.

Klopfer, P. H. From Ardrey to altruism: A discourse on the biological basis of human behavior. *Behavioral Science,* 1968, *19,* 399-401.

Knowles, E. S. Boundaries around group interaction: The effect of group size and member status on boundary permeability, *Journal of Personality and Social Psychology,* 1973, *26,* 327-331.

Leyhausen, P. The communal organization of solitary mammals. *Symposium of the Zoological Society of London,* 1965, *14,* 249-263.

Lipman, A. Chairs as territory. *New Society,* 1967, *20,* 564-566.

Lorenz, K. *On aggression.* New York: Bantam Books, 1969.

Lyman, S. M., & Scott, M. B. Territoriality. A neglected sociological dimension. *Social Problems,* 1967, *15,* 236-249.

Morris, D. *The human zoo.* New York: McGraw-Hill, 1969.

Newman, O. *Defensible space.* New York: Macmillan, 1972.

Paluck, R. J., & Esser, A. H. Aggressive behavioral repertoire and use of space in institutionalized severely retarded and normal boys. *American Zoologist,* 1971, *11,* 51. (a)

Paluck, R. J., & Esser, A. H. Controlled experimental modification of aggressive behavior in territories of severely retarded boys. *American Journal of Mental Deficiency,* 1971, *76,* 23-39. (b)

Paluck, R. J., & Esser, A. H. Territorial behavior as an indicator of changes in clinical behavioral condition of severely retarded boys. *American Journal of Mental Deficiency,* 1971, *76,* 284-290. (c)

Parr, A. E. In search of theory. *Arts and Architecture,* 1965, *82,* 14-16.

Pastalan, L. A. Spatial privacy and differential manifestations of the territorial imperative among the elderly in various congregate living arrangements. In L. A. Pastalan & D. A. Carson (Eds.), *Spatial behavior of older people.* Ann Arbor: University of Michigan Press. (a)

Pastalan, L. A. Privacy as an expression of human territoriality. In L. A. Pastalan & D. H. Carson (Eds.), *Spatial behavior of older people.* Ann Arbor: University of Michigan Press, 1970. (b)

Proshansky, H. M., Ittelson, W. H., & Rivlin, L. G. Freedom of choice and behavior in a physical setting. In H. M. Prohansky, W. W. Ittelson, & L. G. Rivlin (Eds.), *Environmental psychology.* New York: Holt, Rinehart and Winston, 1970. (a)

Prohansky, H. M., Ittelson, W. H., & Rivlin, L. G. The influence of the physical environment on behavior: Some basic assumptions. In H. M. Prohansky, W. H. Ittelson, & L. G. Rivlin (Eds.), *Environmental psychology*. New York: Holt, Rinehart and Winston, 1970. (b)

Roos, P. D. Jurisdiction, an ecological concept. *Human Relations*, 1968, *21*, 75-84.

Stea, D. Space, territory and human movements. 1965, *15*, 13-16.

Sommer, R. Studies in personal space. *Sociometry*, 1959, *22*, 247-260.

Sommer, R. Leadership and group geography. *Sociometry*, 1961, *24*, 99-110.

Sommer, R. Man's proximate environment. *Journal of Social Issues*, 1966, *22*, 59-69. (a)

Sommer, R. The ecology of privacy. *Library Quarterly*, 1966, *36*, 234-248. (b)

Sommer, R. *Personal space: The behavioral basis of design*. Englewood Cliffs, N.J.: Prentice-Hall, 1969.

Sommer, R., & Becker, F. D. Territorial defense and the good neighbor. *Journal of Personality and Social Psychology*, 1969, *11*, 85-92.

Sundstrom, E., & Altman, I. Field study of territorial behavior and dominance. *Journal of Personality and Social Psychology*, 1974, *30*, 115-124.

Wynne-Edwards, V. C. *Animal dispersion in relation to social behavior*. New York: Hafner, 1962.

Wynne-Edwards, V. C. Self-regulating systems in population of animals. *Science*, 1965, *147*, 1543-1548.

16. Some Analytic Dimensions of Privacy

Freud, S. *The Ego and the Id*. John Strachey (Ed.) (Translated by Joan Riviere.) New York: Norton, 1962.

Laufer, R. S., & Wolfe, M. *Privacy as an age related concept*. Paper presented at the meeting of the American Psychological Association, Montreal, August 1973.

Piaget, J. *The moral judgment of the child*.

New York: Basic Books, 1966.

Tausk, V. On the origin of the "influencing machine" in schizophrenia. *Psychoanalytic Quarterly*, 1933, *2*, 519-556.

17. Stress Inducing and Reducing Qualities of Environments

Altman, I. & Lett, E. The ecology of interpersonal relationships: A classification system and conceptual model. In J. MacGrath, (Ed.), *Social and psychological factors in stress*. New York: Holt, Rinehart and Winston, 1970.

Appley, M. H., & Trumbull, R. (Eds.) *Psychological stress*. New York: Appleton-Century-Crofts, 1967.

Arnold, M. Stress and emotion. In M. H. Appley & R. Trumbull, (Eds.). *Psychological stress*. New York: Appleton-Century-Crofts, 1967.

Benson, H. Your innate asset for combating stress. *Harvard Business Review*, July 1974, 49-59.

Berkowitz, L. *Aggression*. New York: McGraw-Hill, 1962.

Berlyne, D. E. *Conflict, curiosity and arousal*. New York: McGraw-Hill, 1960.

Butler, R. A. Discrimination learning by rhesus monkeys to visual exploration motivation. *Journal of Comparative and Physiological Psychology*, 1953, *46*, 95-98.

Butler, R. A. The effect of deprivation of visual incentives on visual exploration in monkeys. *Journal of Comparative and Physiological Psychology*, 1957, *50*, 177-179.

Carlstam, G., Karlsson, C. G. & Levi, L. Stress and disease in response to noise. *Proceedings of the International Congress on Noise as a Public Health Problem*, U.S. Environmental Protection Agency, May 1973.

Carlstamm, G. & Levi, L. Urban conglomerates as psychosocial human stressors: General aspects, Swedish trends and psychological and medical implications. A contribution to the *U.N. Con-*

ference on the Human Environment, Stockholm. Royal Swedish Ministry for Foreign Affairs, 1971.

Cohen, S. I. Central nervous system functioning in altered sensory environments. In M. H. Appley & R. Trumbull (Eds.) *Psychological stress.* New York: Appleton-Century-Crofts, 1967.

Cohen, S. Environmental load and the allocation of attention. Unpublished manuscript, University of Oregon, 1975.

D'Atre, D. Psychophysiological responses to crowding. *Environment and Behavior,* 1975, 7, 237-252.

Desor, J. A. Toward a psychological theory of crowding. *Journal of Personality and Social Psychology,* 1972, 21, 79-83.

Dohrenwend, B. S. & Dohrenwend, B. P. (Ed.) *Stressful life events: Their nature and effects.* New York: John Wiley & Sons, 1974.

Epstein, Y. M. & Aiello, J. R. Effects of crowding on electrodermal activity. Paper presented at the meeting of the American Psychological Association. New Orleans, Sept., 1974.

Franck, K. A., Unseld, C. T. & Wentworth, W. R. *Urban life: The newcomer's experience.* Unpublished manuscript, Graduate School and University Center of the City University of New York, 1975.

Freedman, J. L., Levy, A. S., Buchanan, R. W. & Price, J. Crowding and human aggressiveness. *Journal of Personality and Social Psychology,* 1972, 8, 526-548.

Freidman, M. R., Rosenman, R. H., Straus, R., Wurm, M. & Kositcheck, R. The relationship of behavior pattern to the state of the coronary vasculature. *American Journal of Medicine,* 1968, 44, 555.

Froberg, J., Karlsson, C. G., Lennquist, S., Levi, L., Mathe, A. A. & Theorell, T. *Renal and adrenal function: A comparison between responses to cold and to psychosocial stressors in human subjects. A pilot study.* Reports from the Laboratory for Clinical Stress Research, Stockholm, Sweden, 1974.

Griffitt, W. & Veitch, R. Hot and crowded: Influences of population density and temperature on interpersonal affective behavior. *Journal of Personality and Social Psychology,* 1971, 17, 92-98.

Glass, D. C. & Singer, J. E. *Urban stress: Experiments on noise and social stressors.* New York: Academic Press, 1972.

Hamburg, D. Crowding, stranger contact, and aggressive behavior. In L. Levi (Ed.), *Society, stress and disease: The psychosocial environment and psychosomatic disease* (Vol. 1). London: Oxford University Press, 1971.

Holmes, T. H. & Rahe, R. H. The social readjustment rating scale. *Journal of Psychosomatic Research,* 1967, 2, 213-218.

Hunt, J. McV. *Intelligence and experience.* New York: Ronald, 1961.

Ittelson, W. H., Proshansky, H. M., Rivlin, L. G. & Winkel, G. H. *An introduction to environmental psychology.* New York: Holt, Rinehart and Winston, 1974.

Kagan, A. R. & Levi, L. Health and environment-psychosocial stimuli: A review. *Social Science and Medicine,* 1974, 8, 225-241.

Kahn, R. L. & French, J. R. P. Status and conflict: Two themes in the study of stress. In J. MacGrath (Ed.) *Social and psychological factors in stress.* New York: Holt, Rinehart and Winston, 1970.

Langer, S. *Mind: An essay on human feeling.* Johns Hopkins Press, 1967.

Levi, L. & Kagan, A. R. A synopsis of ecology and psychiatry: Some theoretical psychosomatic considerations, review of some studies and discussion of preventive aspects. *Excerpta Medica International Congress Series No. 274, Psychiatry* (Part I), 1971.

Lansing, J. B. & Marans, R. W. Evaluation of neighborhoods. *Journal of the American Institute of Planners,* 1969, 35,

195-199.

Lazarus, R. S. Cognitive and personality factors underlying threat and coping. In M. H. Appley & R. Trumbull (Eds.) *Psychological stress*. New York: Appleton-Century-Crofts, 1967.

MacGrath, J. (Ed.) *Social and psychological factors in stress*. New York: Holt, Rinehart and Winston, 1970.

Mandler, G. & Watson, D. L. Anxiety and the interruption of behavior. In C. D. Spielberger (Ed.), *Anxiety and behavior*. New York: Academic Press, 1966.

Michelson, W. *Enironmental change*. Centre for Urban and Community Studies, University of Toronto, Canada, Research Paper #60, 1973.

Milgram, S. The experience of living in cities. *Science*, 1970, *167*, 1461-1468.

Niculescue, S. The meaning of the built environment: Dwelling environments as meaning household identity. Unpublished doctoral dissertation, University of Auckland, New Zealand, 1975.

Peterson, R. *Air pollution and its behavioral effects*. Paper presented at Environmental Design and Research Association Conference. Lawrence, Kansas, April 1975.

Presscott, J. W. Invited commentary. In M. H. Appley & R. Trumbull, *Psychological stress*. New York: Appleton-Century-Crofts, 1967.

Radloff, R. & Hemreich, R. *Men under stress*. New York: Appleton-Century-Crofts, 1967.

Riesen, A. H. Excessive arousal effects of stimulation after early sensory deprivation. In P. Solomon et al. (Eds.), *Sensory deprivation*. Cambridge, Mass.: Harvard University Press, 1961.

Saegert, S. *House and home in the lives of women*. Paper presented at Environmental Design Research Association Conference, Lawrence, Kansas, April 1975.

Saegert, S., Mackintosh, E. & West, S. Two studies of crowding in urban public spaces. *Environment and Behavior*, 1975, *7*, 159-184.

Schorr, A. L. *Slums and social insecurity*. Washington, D.C.: U.S. Government Printing Office, 1966.

Selye, H. *The stress of life*. New York: McGraw-Hill, 1956.

Sokolov, E. N. *Perception and the conditioned reflex*. (Translated by S. W. Waydenfold). Oxford: Pergamon Press, 1963.

Valins, S. & Baum, A. Residential group size, social interaction and crowding. *Environment and Behavior*, 1973, *5*, 421-439.

Walter, E. V. Dreadful enclosures: Deoxifying an urban myth. Paper presented at conference: *Cognitive and Emotional Aspects of Urban Life*, Center for Research in Cognition and Affect, The City University of New York, June 1972.

Weick, K. E. The "ess" in stress: Some conceptual and methodological problems. In J. MacGrath, (Ed.), *Social and psychological factors in stress*. New York: Holt, Rinehart and Winston, 1970.

Weiss, J. M. Psychological factors in stress and disease. *Scientific American*, July 1972, pp. 104-113.

Zubeck, J. (Ed.) *Sensory deprivation: Fifteen years of research*. New York: Appleton-Century-Crofts, 1969.

18. Social Ritual and Architectural Space

Ardrey, R. *The territorial imperative*. London: Collins Fontana Library, 1969.

Argyle, M. *The psychology of interpersonal behaviour*. London: Pelican Books A853, 1967.

Blake, R., et al. Housing architecture and social interaction. *Sociometry*, 1956, *19*, (2), 133-139.

The doctor's dilemma: A report on a group practice surgery. *The Architects' Journal*, May 14, 1969, pp. 1279-1281.

Duffy, F. Role and status in the office. *Architectural Association Quarterly*, October 1969, pp. 4-13.

Goffman, E. *Behaviour in public places.* New York: Glencoe Free Press, 1963.

Goffman, E. *The presentation of self in everyday life.* London: Penguin Press, 1969.

Gullahorn, J. T. Distance and friendship as factors in the gross interaction matrix. *Sociometry,* 1952, *15,* (1–2), 123–134.

Hall, E. T. *The silent language.* New York: Doubleday, 1959.

Hall, E. T. *The hidden dimension.* London: Bodley Head, 1969.

Institution of Professional Civil Servants. *ICPS Handbook.* London, 1968, pp. 773-786.

Lipman, A. Building design and social interaction. *The Architects' Journal,* January 1968, pp. 23-30.

Lipman, A. Territoriality, a useful architectural concept? *RIBA Journal,* February 1970, pp. 68-70.

Little, K. B. Personal space. *Journal of Experimental Social Psychology,* 1965, *1,* 237-247.

Lockwood, D. *The black coated worker.* London: George Allen & Unwin, 1958.

Rapoport, A. Whose meaning in architecture? *Interbuild/Arena,* October 1967, pp. 44-46.

Rapoport, A. *House form and culture.* Englewood Cliffs, N.J.: Prentice-Hall, 1969.

School hostel at Dunoon, Scotland. *The Architects' Journal,* May 28, 1969, pp. 1441-1456.

Sommer, R. Studies in personal space. *Sociometry,* 1959, *22,* 247-260.

Sommer, R. *Personal space: The behavioral basis of design.* Englewood Cliffs, N.J.: Prentice-Hall, 1969.

Sprott, W. J. H. *Human groups.* London: Pelican Books, 1958.

van de Ryn, S., and Silverstein, M. *Dorms at Berkeley—An environmental analysis.* Center for Planning and Development Research, University of California, Berkeley, 1967.

Wilson, S. Architecture in communication with man and nature. *Architectural Science Review,* 1967, *10,* 131-135.

21. The Development of Spatial Cognition.

Amy, M. The psychologist looks at spatial concept formation: Children's concepts of space and time. In *Research needs in geographic education.* National Council on Geographic Education, Normal, Ill.: Illinois State University, 1967.

Anderson, J., & Tindal, M. *The concept of home range: New data for the study of territorial behavior.* Unpublished paper, Department of Geography, Clark University, 1970.

Appleyard, D. City designers and the pluralistic city. In L. Rodwin et al. (Eds.), *Planning urban growth, and regional development: The experience of the Guayana program of Venezuela.* Cambridge, Mass.: MIT Press, 1969a.

———. Why buildings are known. *Environment and Behavior,* 1969b, *1,* 131-156.

———. Styles and methods of structuring a city. *Environment and Behavior,* 1970, *2,* 100-118.

Arnheim, R. *Art and visual perception: A psychology of the creative eye.* Berkeley: University of California Press, 1967.

———. *Visual thinking.* Berkeley: University of California Press, 1969.

Ausubel, D. P. *The psychology of meaningful verbal learning.* New York: Gruen and Stratton, 1963.

Bachelard, G. *The poetics of space.* Boston: Beacon, 1969.

Baldwin, A. L. *Theories of child development.* New York: Wiley, 1967.

Beck, R. J. *A comparative study of spatial meaning.* Unpublished M.A. thesis, University of Chicago, 1964.

———. Spatial meaning and the properties of the environment. In D. Lowenthal (Ed.), *Environmental perception and behavior.* Department of Geography, University of Chicago, Research Paper No. 109, 1967.

Birch, H. G., & Korn, S. J. Place-earning, cognitive maps, and parsimony. *Jour-*

nal of General Psychology, 1958, *58*, 17-35.

Blaut, J. M. Space and process. *The Professional Geographer*, 1961, *13* (4), 1-7.

———. *Studies in developmental geography.* Graduate School of Geography, Clark University, Place Perception Research Report No. 1, 1969.

Blaut, J. M., McCleary, G. F., & Blaut, A. S. Environmental mapping in young children. *Environment and Behavior*, 1970, *2*, 335-349.

Blaut, J. M., & Stea, D. *Place learning.* Graduate School of Geography, Clark University, Place Perception Research Report No. 4, 1969.

Blaut, J. M., & Stea, D. Studies of geographic learning. *Annals of the Association of American Geographers*, 1971, *61*, 387-393.

Bower, G. H. Analysis of a mnemonic device. *American Scientist*, 1970, *58*, 496-510.

Brown, W. Spatial integrations in a human maze. *University of California Publications in Psychology*, 1932, 5.

Bunge, W. *The first years of the Detroit geographical expedition: A personal report.* Detroit: Detroit Geographical Expedition, Discussion Paper #1, 1969.

Buttimer, A. Social space in interdisciplinary perspective. *Geographical Review*, 1969, 59, 417-426.

Carr, S., & Lynch, K. Where learning happens. *Daedalus: Journal of the American Academy of Arts and Sciences*, 1968, 97, 1277-1291.

Cassirer, E. *An essay on man: An introduction to a philosophy of human culture.* New Haven: Yale University Press, 1944.

———. *The philosophy of symbolic forms.* (Volume 1, *Language*). New Haven: Yale University Press, 1953.

———. *The philosophy of symbolic forms.* (Volume 2, *Mythical thought*). New Haven: Yale University Press, 1955.

———. *The philosophy of symbolic forms.* (Volume 3, *The phenomenology of knowledge*). New Haven: Yale University Press, 1957.

Cobb, E. The ecology of imagination in childhood. *Daedalus*, 1959, *88*, 537-548. Reprinted in P. Shepard & D. McKinley (Eds.), *The subversive science: Essays towards an ecology of man.* Boston: Houghton-Mifflin, 1969.

Colyard, Y. (Ed.) *Field notes: The geography of the children of Detroit.* Detroit: Detroit Geographical Expedition, Discussion Paper #3, 1971.

Craik, K. M. Environmental psychology. In T. M. Newcomb (Ed.), *New directions in psychology* (Volume 4). New York: Holt, Rinehart and Winston, 1970a.

———. Environmental disposition(s) and preferences. In J. Archea & C. M. Eastman (Eds.), *EDRA Two: Proceedings of the 2nd Annual Environmental Design Research Association Conference.* Pittsburgh: Carnegie-Mellon University, 1970b.

Deese, J., & Hulse, S. H. *The psychology of learning* (3rd ed.). New York: McGraw-Hill, 1967.

DeJonge, D. Images of urban areas, their structures and psychological foundations. *Journal of the American Institute of Planners*, 1962, *28*, 266-276.

Dent, B. D. *Perceptual organization and thematic map communication.* Graduate School of Geography, Clark University, Place Perception Research Report #5, 1970.

Downs, R. M. The role of perception in modern geography. *University of Bristol, Department of Geography Seminar Paper Series A*, 1968, *11*, 1-20.

Ekman, G., Lindman, R., & William-Olsson, W. A psychophysical study of cartographic symbols. *Perceptual and Motor Skills*, 1961, *13*, 355-368.

Eliade, M. *The sacred and the profane.* New York: Harcourt, 1959.

Erikson, E. K. Toys and reasons. In *Childhood and society* (2nd ed.). New

York: Norton, 1963.

Flavell, J. H. *The developmental psychology of Jean Piaget.* Princeton: Van Nostrand, 1963.

———. Concept development. In P. H. Mussen (Ed.), *Manual of child psychology* (Vol. 1, 3rd ed.). New York: Wiley, 1970.

Flavell, J. H., & Wohlwill, J. F. Functional and formal aspects of cognitive development. In D. Elkind & J. H. Flavell (Eds.), *Studies in cognitive development: Essays in honor of Jean Piaget.* New York: Oxford University Press, 1969.

Follini, M. B. *The construction of behavioral space: A microgenetic investigation of orientation in an unfamiliar locality.* Unpublished M.A. thesis, Clark University, 1966.

Freeman, F. N. Geography: Extension of experience through imagination. In *The psychology of common branches.* Boston: Houghton-Mifflin, 1916.

Gregg, F. M. Are motor accompaniments necessary to orientational perception? *Journal of Psychology,* 1939, *8,* 63-87.

———. Overcoming geographic disorientation. *Journal of Consulting and Clinical Psychology,* 1940, *4,* 66-68.

Griffin, D. Topographical orientation. In R. Downs & D. Stea (Eds.), *Image and environment.* Chicago: Aldine, 1973.

Gulick, J. Images of an Arab city. *Journal of the American Institute of Planners,* 1963, *29,* 179-198.

Gulliver, F. P. Orientation of maps. *Journal of Geography,* 1908, *7,* 55-58.

Hall, E. T. *The hidden dimension.* New York: Doubleday, 1966.

Hallowell, A. I. Some psychological aspects of measurement among the Salteaux. *American Anthropologist,* 1942, *44,* 62-77.

———. *Culture and experience.* Philadelphia: University of Pennsylvania Press, 1955.

Harris, D. B. (Ed.) *The concept of development.* Minneapolis: University of Minnesota Press, 1957.

Hart, R. A. *Aerial geography: An experiment in elementary education.* Unpublished M.A. thesis, Clark University, 1971.

Hendel, C. W. Introduction: The philosophy of form in Kant. In E. Cassirer, *The philosophy of symbolic forms* (Vol. 1, *Language*). New Haven: Haven: Yale University Press, 1953.

Hilgard, E. R., & Bower, G. H. *Theories of learning* (3rd ed.). New York: Appleton-Century-Crofts, 1966.

Holloway, G.E.T. *An introduction to the child's conception of space.* London: Routledge and Kegan Paul, 1967a.

———. *An introduction to the child's conception of geometry.* London: Routledge and Kegan Paul, 1967b.

Howard, I. P., & Templeton, W. B. *Human spatial orientation.* New York: Wiley, 1966.

Howe, G. F. A study of children's knowledge of directions. *Journal of Geography,* 1931, *30,* 298-304.

———, The teaching of directions in space. *Journal of Geography,* 1932, *31,* 207-210.

Hudson, W. H. On the sense of direction. *Century Magazine,* 1922, *104* 693-701.

Hunt, J. M. Intrinsic motivation and its role in psychological development. *Nebraska Symposium on Motivation,* 1965, *13,* 189-282.

Inhelder, B. Operation thought and mental imagery. *Monographs, Society for Research in Child Development,* 1965, *30,* 4-18.

Kabonova-Meller, E. N. Formation of geographical representations in students of the fifth to seventh classes. *Izvestiya Akademi Pedagogicheskikh Nauk RSFSR,* No. 86, 1956. Cited in F. N. Shemyakin, Orientation in space. In B. G. Ananyev et al. (Eds.), *Psychological science in the U.S.S.R.* (Vol. 1). Washington: Office of Technical Services, 1962.

Kant, I. *Critique of pure reason* (2nd rev. ed.). New York: Macmillan, 1902.

Kaplan, B. The study of language in psychiatry: The comparative developmental approach and its applications to symbolization and language in psychopathology. In S. Arieti (Ed.), *American handbook of psychiatry* (Vol. 3). New York: Basic Books, 1966a.

————, The "latent content" of Heinz Werner's comparative developmental approach. In S. Wapner & B. Kaplan (Eds.), *Heinz Werner 1890-1964: Papers in memorium*. Worcester, Mass.: Clark University Press, 1966b.

————, Meditations on genesis. *Human Development*, 1967, *10*, 65-87.

Khopreninova, N. G. Orientation of locality by sightless persons. *Uchenyye Zapiski Chkalovskogo Gos. Pedagogicheskikh In-ta* (Chkalov State Pedagogical Institute) No. 8, 1956. Cited in F. N. Shemyakin, Orientation in space. In B. G. Ananyev et al. (Eds.), *Psychological science in the U.S.S.R.* (Vol. 1). Washington: Office of Technical Services, 1962.

Ladd, F. C. Black youths view their enviroment: Neighborhood maps. *Environment and Behavior*, 1970, *2*, 64-79.

Langer, J. *Theories of development.* New York: Holt, Rinehart and Winston, 1969.

————. Werner's comparative organismic theory. In P. H. Mussen (Ed.), *Manual of Child Psychology* (Vol. 1, 3rd ed.). New York: Wiley, 1970.

Laurendau, M., & Pinard, A. *The development of the concept of space in the child.* New York: International Universities Press, 1970.

Lee, T. Psychology and living space. In R. Downs & D. Stea (Eds.), *Image and environment*. Chicago: Aldine, 1973.

Levi-Strauss, C. History and anthropology. *Revue de Metaphysique et de Morale*, 1949, *54*, 363-391. Reprinted in *Structural anthropology*. New York: Doubleday Anchor, 1967.

Liebig, F. G. Uber unsere Orientierung im Raume bei Ausschluss der Augen. (On orientation in space without sight). *Zeitschrifet für Sinnesphysiology*, 1933, *64*, 251-282. Cited in I. P. Howard & W. B. Templeton, *Human spatial orientation.* New York: Wiley, 1966.

Lord, F. E. A study of spatial orientation in children. *Journal of Educational Research*, 1941, *34*, 481-505.

Lukashok, A. K., & Lynch, K. Some childhood memories of the city. *Journal of the American Institute of Planners*, 1956, *22*, 142-152.

Lynch, K. *The image of the city*. Cambridge, Mass.: MIT Press, 1960.

Lynch, K. Some references to orientation. In R. Downs & D. Stea (Eds.), *Image and environment*, Chicago: Aldine, 1973.

Lyublinskaya, A. A. Learning spatial relations by a child of pre-school age. *Anthology Problemy Psikhologii*, Leningrad: Izd-vo LGU Leningrad State University, 1948. Cited in F. N. Shemyakin, Orientation in space. In B. B. Ananyev et al. (Eds.), *Psychological science in the U.S.S.R.* (Vol. 1). Washington: Office of Technical Services, 1962.

Lyublinskaya, A. A. The role of speech in the development of visual perception in children. *Sb. Vaprosy Detskoy: Obshechey Psikhologii*, Moscow: Izd-vo Academiia Pedagogieheskikh Nauk RSFRS, 1956. Cited in F. N. Shemyakin, Orientation in space. In B. G. Ananyev et al. (Eds.), *Psychological science in the U.S.S.R.* (Vol. 1). Washington: Office of Technical Services, 1962.

Miller, J. W. Measuring perspective ability. *Journal of Geography*, 1967, *66*, 167-171.

Moore, G. T. *A comparative analysis of organismic-developmental theory and general systems theory.* Unpublished paper, Department of Psychology,

Clark University, 1970.

Muchow, M., & Muchow, H. *Der Lebens-raum des Grosstadtkindes. (The life space of the child in the large city)*, Hamburg: Verlag, 1939. Cited in H. Wernef, *Comparative psychology of mental development* (Rev. ed.). New York: International Universities Press, 1948.

Parr, A. E. The child in the city: Urbanity and the urban scene. *Landscape*, 1967, 16 (Spring), 1-3.

Piaget, J. How children form mathematical concepts. *Scientific American*, 1953, *189* (5), 74-79.

———. *The child's construction of reality.* New York: Basic Books, 1954a.

———. Perceptual and cognitive (or operational) structures in the development of the concept of space in the child (Summary). *Proceedings, 14th International Congress of Psychology.* Amsterdam: North Holland Publishing Co., 1954b. Also in *Acta Psychologica,* Amsterdam, 1955, *11*, 41-46.

———. Beginnings of representative imitation and further development of imitation. In *Plays, dreams and imitation in childhood.* New York: Norton, 1962.

———. *The origins of intelligence in children.* New York: Norton, 1963a.

———. *The psychology of intelligence.* Totowa, New Jersey: Littlefield, Adams, 1963b.

———. *The child's conception of the world.* Patterson, N.J.: Littlefield, Adams, 1963c.

———. *Six psychological studies.* New York: Vintage, 1968.

———. *The mechanisms of perception.* New York: Basic Books, 1969.

———. *Structuralism.* New York: Basic Books, 1970.

Piaget, J., & Inhelder, B. *The child's conception of space.* New York: Norton, 1967.

Piaget, J., & Inhelder, B. *The psychology of the child.* New York: Basic Books, 1969.

Piaget, J., Inhelder, B., & Szeminska, A. *The child's conception of geometry.* New York: Basic Books, 1960.

Pinard, A., & Laurendau, M. Le caractère topologique des premières représentations spatiales de l'enfant: Examen des hypotheses de Piaget. (The topological character of the child's first spatial representations: Examination of some of Piaget's hypotheses.) *Journal International de Psychologie*, 1966, *1*, 243-255.

Rand, G. Some Copernican views of the city. *Architectural Forum*, 1969, *132* (9), 77-81.

Rasmussen, S. E. *Experiencing architecture.* Cambridge, Mass.: MIT Press, 1959.

Ridgley, D. The teaching of directions in space and on maps. *Journal of Geography*, 1922, *21*, 66-72.

Robinson, A. R. Psychological aspects of color in cartography. *International Yearbook of Cartography*, 1967, 7, 50–61.

Romney, A. K., & D'Andrade, R. G. (Eds.), Transcultural studies in cognition. *American Anthropologist*, 1964, *66*.

Rusch, C. W. On understanding awareness. *Journal of Aesthetic Education*, 1970, 4 (4), 57-59.

Ryan, T. A., & Ryan, M. S. Geographical orientation. *American Journal of Psychology*, 1940, *53*, 204-215.

Scully, V. *The earth, the temple, and the gods.* New Haven: Yale University Press, 1962.

Shelton, F. C. A note on the world across the street. *Harvard Graduate School of Education Association Bulletin*, 1967, *12*, 47-48.

Shemyakin, F. N. On the psychology of space representations. *Uchenye Zapiski Gos. In-ta Psikhologii.* (Moscow), 1, 1940. Cited in F. N. Shemyakin. Orientation in space. In B. G. Ananyev et al. (Eds.), *Psychological science in the U.S.S.R.* (Vol. 1). Washington: Office of Technical Services, 1962.

————. Orientation in space. In B. G. Ananyev et al. (Eds.), *Psychological science in the U.S.S.R.*, (Vol. 1). Washington: Office of Technical Services, Report No. 62-11083, 1962.

Smith, W. F. Direction orientation in children. *Journal of Genetic Psychology*, 1933, *42*, 154-166.

Stea, D. The measurement of mental maps: An experimental model for studying conceptual spaces. In K. R. Cox & R. G. Golledge (Eds.), *Behavioral problems in geography: A symposium*. Evanston, Ill.: Northwestern University Press, 1969.

Stea, D., & Blaut, J. Notes toward a developmental theory of spatial learning. In R. Downs & D. Stea (Eds.), *Image and environment*. Chicago: Aldine: 1973a.

Stea, D., & Blaut, J. Some preliminary obsevations on spatial learning in school children. In R. Downs & D. Stea (Eds.), *Image and environment*. Chicago: Aldine, 1973b.

Stea, D., & Downs, R. M. From the outside looking in at the inside looking out. *Environment and Behavior*, 1970, *2*, 3-12.

Straus, E. *The primary world of senses*. Glencoe, Ill.: Free Press, 1963.

————. *Phenomenological psychology: Selected papers*. New York: Basic Books, 1966.

Sverlov, V. S. *Prostranstevennaya Orientirovka Sepykh*, *(Space orientation by the blind)*. Moscow, 1951. Cited in F. N. Shemyakin, Orientation in space. In B. G. Ananyev et al. (Eds.), *Psychological Science in the U.S.S.R.* (Vol. 1). Washington: Office of Technical Sciences, 1962.

Tolman, E. Cognitive maps in rats and men. In R. Downs & D. Stea (Eds.), *Image and environment*. Chicago: Aldine, 1973.

Toulmin, S. *Foresight and understanding: An enquiry into the aims of science*. New York: Harper Torchbooks, 1961.

Towler, J. O. The elementary school child's concept of reference systems. *Journal of Geography*, 1970, *69*, 89-93.

Towler, J. O., & Nelson, L. D. The elementary school child's concept of scale. *Journal of Geography*, 1968, *67*, 24-28.

Trowbridge, C. C. Fundamental methods or orientation and imaginary maps. *Science*, 1913, *38*, 888-897.

Tyler, S. A. (Ed.) *Cognitive anthropology*. New York: Holt, Rinehart and Winston, 1971.

Von Senden, M. *Space and sight*. London: Methuen, 1960.

Vygotsky, L. S. *Thought and language*. Cambridge, Mass.: MIT Press, 1962.

Wallace, A. F. C. *Culture and personality*. New York: Random House, 1961.

Wapner, S. Organismic-developmental theory: Some applications to cognition. In P. H. Mussen, P. Langer, & M. Covington (Eds.), *Trends and issues in developmental psychology*. New York: Holt, Rinehart and Winston, 1969.

Wapner, S., Cirillo, L., & Baker, A. H. Some aspects of the development of space perception. In J. P. Hill (Ed.), *Minnesota Symposium on Child Psychology* (Vol. 4). Minneapolis: University of Minnesota Press, 1971.

Wapner, S., & Werner, H. *Perceptual development*. Worcester, Mass.: Clark University Press, 1957.

Warren, H. C. Magnetic sense of direction. *Psychological Bulletin*, 1908, *5*, 376-377.

Werner, H. *Comparative psychology of mental development*. New York: International Universities Press, 1948.

Werner, H. The concept of development from a comparative and organismic point of view. In D. B. Harris (Ed.), *The concept of development*. Minneapolis: University of Minnesota Press, 1957.

Werner, H., & Kaplan, B. *Symbol forma-*

tion: An organismic-developmental approach to language and the expression of thought. New York: Wiley, 1963.

White, S. H. The learning theory tradition and child psychology. In P. H. Mussen (Ed.), Manual of child psychology (Vol. 1, 3rd ed.). New York: Wiley, 1970.

Williams, R. L. Map symbols: Equal-appearing intervals for printed screens. Annals of the Association of American Geographers, 1958, 48, 132-139.

Wisner, B. Protogeography: Search for the beginnings. Unpublished paper presented to the Annual Conference of the Association of American Geographers, San Francisco, 1970.

Witkin, H. A., Dyk, R. B., Faterson, H. F., Goodenough, D. R., & Karp, S. A. Psychological differentiation: Studies of development. New York: Wiley, 1962.

Wohlwill, J. F. Developmental studies of perception. Psychological Bulletin, 1960, 57, 249-288.

Wood, D. The image of San Cristobal. Monadnock (Clark Geographical Society), 1969, 43, 29-45.

Wood, D. Fleeting glimpses: Adolescent and other images of the entity called San Cristobal, las Casas, Chiapas, Mexico. Unpublished M.A. thesis, Clark University, 1971.

Wood, M. Visual perception and map design. The Cartographic Journal, 1968, 5, 54-64.

Worchel, P. Space perception and orientation in the blind. Psychological Monographs, 1951, 65, 332.

22. Children's Play and Urban Playground Environments

Barker, R. G., & Wright, H. F. One boy's day: A specimen record of behavior. New York: Harper & Row, 1963.

Bettelheim, B. Love is not enough. New York: Free Press, 1950.

Bishop, R. L., & Peterson, G. L. A synthesis of environmental design recommendations from the visual preferences of children. Northwestern University Department of Civil Engineering, 1971.

Cooper, C. Adventure playgrounds. Landscape Architecture, 1970, 61 (1), 18-29, 88-91.

Dattner, R. Design for play. New York: Van Nostrand Reinhold, 1969.

Dee, N., & Liebman, J. C. A statistical study of attendance in urban playgrounds. Journal of Leisure Research, 1970, 2, 145-159.

Friedberg, M. P., & Berkeley, E. P. Play and interplay. London: Collier Macmillan, 1970.

Ittelson, W. H., Rivlin, L. G., & Proshansky, H. M. The use of behavioral maps in environmental psychology. In H. M. Proshansky, W. H. Ittelson, & L. G. Rivlin (Eds.), Environmental psychology: Man and his physical setting. New York: Holt, Rinehart and Winston, 1970.

Nicholson, S. How not to cheat children: The theory of loose parts. Landscape Architecture, 1970, 62 (1), 30-34.

Spivak, M. The political collapse of a playground. Landscape Architecture, 1969, 59, 288-291.

Stea, D. Home range and use of space. In L. A. Pastalan & D. H. Carson (Eds.) Spatial behavior of older people. Ann Arbor: University of Michigan Press, 1970.

Wade, G. R. A study of free-play patterns of elementary school-aged children in playground equipment areas. Masters thesis. Pennsylvania State University, 1968.

Webb, E. J., Campbell, D. T., Schwartz, R. D., & Sechrest, L. Unobtrusive measures: Nonreactive research in the social sciences. Chicago: Rand McNally, 1966.

Wright, H. F. Recording and analyzing child behavior. New York: Harper & Row, 1967.

23. Black Youths View Their Environment

Appleyard, D., Lynch, K., & Myer, J. *The view from the road.* Cambridge, Mass.: MIT Press, 1964.

Carr, S., & Schissler, D. The city as a trip. *Environment and Behavior*, 1969, *1*, 7-35.

De Jonge, D. Images of urban areas. *Journal of the American Institute of Planners*, 1962, *28*, 266-276.

Gulick, J. Images of an Arab city. *Journal of the American Institute of Planners*, 1963, *29*, 179-197.

Hassan, Y. The movement system as an organization of visual form. Unpublished doctoral dissertation. MIT, 1965.

Lee, T. Psychology and living space. *Transactions of the Bartlett Society*, 1963-64, *2*, 9-36.

Lynch, K. *Image of the city.* Cambridge, Mass.: MIT Press, 1960.

Piaget, J., & Inhelder, B. *The child's conception of space.* New York: Norton, 1967.

Shelton, F. C. A note on "the world across the street." *Harvard Graduate School of Education Assn. Bulletin*, 1967, *12*, 47-48.

Southworth, M. (forthcoming) Study of children's knowledge and use of the city. Tentative title of Ph.D. dissertation, MIT.

Steinitz, C. Meaning and the congruence of urban form and activity. *Journal of the American Institute of Planners*, 1968, *94*, 233-248.

Tilly, C. Anthropology on the town. *Habitat*, 1967, *10*, 20-25.

24. Toward an Ecological Theory of Adaptation and Aging

Helson, H. *Adaptation level theory.* New York: Harper & Row, 1964.

Lawton, M. P., & Nahemow, L. Ecology and adaptation in the aging process. In C. Eisdorfer, & M. P. Lawton, (Eds.) *Psychology of the aging process*, Washington, D.C.: American Psy-

chological Association, 1973.

Lawton, M. P., & Simon, B. The ecology of social relationships in housing for the elderly. *The Gerontologist*, 1968, *8*, 108-115.

McClelland, D. C., Atkinson, J. W., Clark, R. A., & Lowell, E. L. *The Achievement motive.* New York: Appleton, 1963.

Mangum, W. Adjustment in special settings for the aged. Unpublished doctoral dissertation, University of Southern California.

Murray, H. A. *Explorations in personality.* New York: Oxford University Press, 1938.

Rosow, I. *Social integration of the aged.* New York: Free Press, 1967.

Sivadon, P. Space as experienced: Therapeutic implications. In H. M. Proshansky, W. H. Ittelson, & L. G. Rivlin (Eds.) *Environmental psychology.* New York: Holt, Rinehart and Winston, 1970.

Wohlwill, J. F. Behavioral response and adaptation to environmental stimulation. In A. Damon (Ed.) *Physiological anthropology.* New York: Oxford University Press, 1975.

25. The Comprehension of the Everyday Physical Environment

Abernathy, B. L., & Noe, S. *Urbanography. Progressive Architecture*, 1966, *47*, 184-190.

Appleyard, D. Lynch, K., & Myer, J. R. *The view from the road.* Cambridge, Mass.: MIT Press, 1964.

Barron, F. Psychology of imagination. *Scientific American*, 1958, *199*, 150-166.

Block, J. *The Q-sort method in personality assessment and psychiatric research.* Springfield, Ill.: Thomas, 1961.

Carr, S., & Kusilko, G. *Vision and memory in the view from the road: Progress report.* Cambridge, Mass.: MIT-Harvard Joint Center for Urban Studies, 1964.

Carroll, J. B. Review of: C. E. Osgood, G. Suci, & P. H. Tannenbaum, The measurement of meaning. *Language*, 1959, *35*, 58-77.

Casey, T. G. Proposed method for the description of urban form. M. Arch. thesis, College of Environmental Design, University of California, Berkeley, 1966.

Christensen, P. R., Merrifield, P. R., & Guildford, J. P. *Consequences test.* Beverly Hills, Calif.: Sheridan Supply Co., 1958.

Clyde, D. J. Self ratings. In L. Uhr & J. G. Miller (Eds.), *Drugs and behavior.* New York: Wiley, 1960.

Gordon, W. J. J. *Synectics: The development of creative capacity.* New York: Harper & Row, 1961.

Gough, H. G., & Heilbrun, A. B., Jr. *The adjective checklist manual.* Palo Alto, Calif.: Consulting Psychologists Press, 1965.

Halprin, L. Motations. *Progressive Architecture*, 1965, *46*, 126-133.

Harris, R. E. The improvisations procedure as a device for the assessment of air force officers. *I.P.A.R. Research Bulletin*, Berkeley, Calif.: Institute of Personality Assessment and Research, University of California, 1955.

Henry, W. E. *The analysis of fantasy.* New York: John Wiley, 1956..

Knapp, R. H. A study of metaphor. *Journal of Projective Techniques*, 1960, *24*, 389-395.

Lamm, J. W. Wurster Hall: A case study of people's reactions to buildings. B. Arch. thesis, College of Environmental Design, University of California, Berkeley, 1965.

Leith, E. M., & Upatnieks, J. Photography by laser. *Scientific American*, 1965, *212*, 24-35.

Michelson, W. An empirical analysis of urban environmental preferences. *Journal of the American Institute of Planners*, 1966, *32*, 355-360.

Moreno, J. L. *Who shall survive?* New York: Beacon House, 1934.

Nowlis, B. Research with the mood adjective checklist. In S. S. Tomlins & C. E. Izard (Eds.), *Affect, cognition and personality.* New York: Springer, 1965.

Osgood, C. E., Suci, G., & Tannenbaum, P. H. *The measurement of meaning.* Urbana, Ill.: University of Illinois Press, 1957.

Rose, S. W. A notation/simulation process for composers of space. Lincoln, Nebr.: University of Nebraska, n.d., mimeographed.

Saarinen, T. F. *The perception of the drought hazard on the Great Plains.* Department of Geography Research Paper No. 106. Chicago: University of Chicago, Department of Geography, 1966.

Sanford, N. Will psychologists study human problems? *American Psychologist*, 1965, *20*, 192-202.

Sarbin, T. R. Role theory. In G. Lindzey (Ed.), *Handbook of social psychology.* Reading, Mass.: Addison-Wesley, 1954.

Stea, D. Personal communication, April 1966.

Studer, R. G., & Stea, D. Directory of behavior and environmental design. Providence, R.I.: Brown University, 1965.

Thiel, P. A sequence-experience notation for architectural and urban space. *Town Planning Journal*, 1961, *32*, 33-52.

Vigier, F. C. An experimental approach to urban design. *Journal of the American Institute of Planners*, 1965, *31*, 21-30.

Weiss, R., & Boutourline, S. *Fairs, exhibits, pavilions and their audiences.* New York: IBM Corp., 1962.

Winkel, G., & Sasanoff, R. *Approaches to an objective analysis of behavior in architectural space.* University of Washington, Architecture/Development, Series No. 5, August 1966.

27. An Approach to an Objective Analysis of Behavior in Architectural Space

Alexander, C. *Notes on the synthesis of form.* Cambridge, Mass.: MIT Press, 1964.

Garner, W. R. *Uncertainty and structure as psychological concepts.* New York: Wiley, 1960.

Harman, H. Simulation as a tool for research. *Systems Development Corporation,* SP-565, September 25, 1961.

Larsen, J. W. Simulation—A tool for industrial engineers. In S. M. Selig and M. Ettelstein (Eds.), *New horizons in industrial engineering.* Baltimore, Md.: Spartan Books, 1963.

Thiel, P. *The tourist and the habitué.* Unpublished working paper, College of Architecture and Urban Planning, University of Washington, 1964.

Thomas, C., & Deemer, W., Jr. The role of operational gaming in operations research. *Operations Research,* 1957, *5,* 1-27.

Van der Ryn, S. *The ecology of student housing: A case study in environmental analysis and design.* Berkeley, Calif.: University of Californa, College of Environmental Design, 1965 (mimeo).

Weiss, R., & Boutourline, S. *Fairs, exhibits, pavilions and their audiences.* New York: IBM Corporation, 1962.

29. The Tragedy of the Commons

Bateson, G., Jackson, D. D., Haley, J., & Weakland, J. *Behavioral Science,* 1956, *1,* 251.

Comfort, A. *The anxiety makers.* London: Nelson, 1967.

Davis, K. *Science,* 1967, *158,* 730.

Fletcher, J. *Situation ethics.* Philadephia: Westminster, 1966.

Frankel, C. *The case for modern man.* New York: Harper, 1955.

Fremlin, J. H. *New Scientist,* 1964, (415), 285.

Girvetz, H. *From wealth to welfare.* Stanford, Calif.: Stanford University Press, 1950.

Goodman, P. *New York Review of Books,* May 23, 1968, *10* (8), p. 22.

Hardin, G. *Journal of Heredity,* 1959, *50,* 68.

Hardin, G. *Perspectives in Biology and Medicine,* 1963, *6,* 366.

Hardin, G. (Ed), *Population, evolution, and birth control.* San Francisco: Freeman, 1964.

Lack, D. *The natural regulation of animal numbers.* Oxford: Clarendon Press, 1954.

Lloyd, W. F. *Two lectures on the checks to population.* Oxford: Oxford University Press, 1833. Reprinted (in part) in Hardin, G. (Ed.) *Population, evolution, and birth control.* San Francisco: Freeman, 1964.

McVay, S. *Scientific American,* 1966, *216* (8), 13.

Roslansky, J. D. *Genetics and the future of man.* New York: Appleton, 1966.

Smith, A. *The wealth of nations.* New York: Modern Library, 1937.

Tax, S. (Ed.) *Evolution after Darwin* (Vol. 2). Chicago: University of Chicago Press, 1960.

U Thant. *International planned parenthood news.* February 1968, p. 3.

von Hoernor, S. *Science, 137,* 18.

von Neumann, J., & Morgenstern, O. *Theory of games and economic behavior.* Princeton, N.J.: Princeton University Press, 1947.

Whitehead, A. N. *Science and the modern world.* New York: Mentor, 1948.

Wiesner, J. B., & York, H. F. *Scientific American.* 1964, *211* (4), 27.

30. The American Scene

Alsop, S. America the ugly. *Saturday Evening Post,* June 23, 1962, pp. 8, 10.

The American outdoors, *U.S. Forest Service Miscellaneous Publication No. 1000.* Washington, D.C., 1965.

Banham, R. Urbanism: USA. *Arcitectural Review,* 1961, *130,* 303-305.

Barzun, J. *God's country and mine.* Boston: Little & Brown, 1954.

Boyd, R. *The Australian ugliness.* Melbourne: University Press, 1960.

Burnham, D. H., as quoted in C. Tunnard

and H. H. Reed, *American skyline: The growth and form of our cities and towns*. Boston, 1955.

Casson, H. Critique of our expanding "Subtopia." *New York Times Magazine*, October 27, 1957.

Chinard, G. Eighteenth century theories on America as a human habitat. *Proceedings of the American Philosophical Society*, 1947, *91*, 27-57.

Cowper, W. The task. Book I, The sofa. In *Poems*. Vol. 2. London, 1814.

Crevecoeur, M-G. S. *Journey into Northern Pennsylvania and the State of New York* (in French, 1801, translated by Clarissa Spencer Bostelmann). Ann Arbor, Mich., 1964.

Dangerfield, G. The way West: A review of Daniel Boorstin's *The Americans. New York Times Book Review*, October 31, 1965, pp. 24, 26.

Dickens, C. *American notes, and pictures from Italy* (1842 and 1846). London, New York, Toronto: Oxford University Press, 1957.

Ellis, H. F. A walk in Massachusetts. *New Yorker*, July 2, 1960, pp. 22-24.

Emerson, R. W. English traits (1856). In *The selected writings of Ralph Waldo Emerson*. New York: Modern Library, 1950.

Freneau, P., & Brackenridge, H. H. The rising glory of America, as quoted in H. N. Smith, *Virgin land*. New York: Vintage Books, 1957.

Gowans, A. *Images of American living*. Philadelphia and New York: Lippincott, 1964.

Grund, F. J. *The Americans in their moral, social, and political relations*. Vol. 2. London: Longman, 1837.

Hamburger, P. *An American notebook*. New York: Knopf, 1965.

Heimert, A. Puritanism, the wilderness, and the frontier. *New England Quarterly*, 1953, *26*, 361-382.

Hersey, J. *The marmot drive*. New York: Popular Library, 1953.

Hosmer, C. B., Jr. *Presence of the past.*

New York: Putnam, 1965.

Jackson, J. B. Notes and comments. *Landscape*, 1963-1964, *13*, 1-3.

James, H. *The American scene*. New York and London: Harper, 1907.

James, H. *The American scene*. Edited by W. H. Auden. New York, 1946.

James, W. On a certain blindness in human beings. In *Talks to teachers on psychology: And to students on some of life's ideals*. New York: The Norton Library, 1958. (Originally published, 1899.)

Jefferson, T. *Notes on the State of Virginia* (1787). Ed. by W. Peden. Chapel Hill, N.C.: University of North Carolina Press, 1955.

Jellicoe, G. A. *Studies in landscape design*. Vol. 2. London, New York, Toronto: Oxford University Press, 1966.

Jones, H. M. *O strange new world*. New York: Viking Press, 1964.

Kahn, E. J., Jr. The Hudson River. *Holiday*, 1966, *40*, 40-55, 83-89.

Kouwenhoven, J. A. What's "American" about America. In *The beer can by the highway*. Garden City, N.Y., 1961. 39-73.

Kurnberfer, F. Der Amerika-müde (1855), as quoted in D. A. Dondore, *The prairie and the making of Middle America: Four centuries of description*. Cedar Rapids, Iowa: Torch Press, 1926.

Le Corbusier, C-E. *When the cathedrals were white* (translated by Francis E. Hyslop, Jr.). New York, London, Toronto: McGraw-Hill Paperbacks, 1964.

Lévi-Strauss, C. *Tristes tropiques* (translated by John Russell). New York: Criterion Book, 1961.

Locke, J. Essay concerning the true original extent and end of civil government. In *Two treatises of government* (1690). London: Everyman, 1924.

Lowenthal, D. *George Perkins Marsh: Versatile Vermonter*. New York: Columbia University Press, 1958.

Lowenthal, D. Not every prospect pleases: What is our criterion for scenic beauty? *Landscape,* 1962-1963, *12,* 19-23.

Lowenthal, D. Is wilderness "Paradise Enow"? Images of nature in America. *Columbia University Forum,* 1964, 7, 34-40.

Lowenthal, D. The American way of history. *Columbia University Forum,* 1966, 9, 27-32.

Lowenthal, D., & Prince, H. C. English landscape tastes. *Geographical Review,* 1965, *55,* 186-222.

Marx, L. *The machine in the garden.* London: Oxford University Press, 1964.

McCoubrey, J. W. *American tradition in painting.* New York: George Braziller, 1963.

Michener, C. T. Why would anyone want to live in Tacoma? *Seattle,* 1966, *3,* 18-25, 46-47.

Miller, P. *The life of the mind in America.* New York: Harcourt, Brace & World, 1965.

Morris, J. *Coast to coast.* New York: Simon & Schuster, 1962.

Morris, L. Remaking America: The lake makers. *Holiday,* 1946, *1,* 46-48.

Nairn, I. *The American landscape.* New York: Random House, 1965.

New scene at Disneyland simulates New Orleans. *New York Times,* July 26, 1966.

Nuttall, T. A journal of travels into the Arkansas Territory during the year 1819 (Philadelphia, 1821). In R. G. Thwaites (Ed.), *Early Western travels 1748-1846.* Vol. 13. New York: AMS Press, 1905.

Only tour in Key West that will take you to the following points of interest. *New Yorker,* May 29, 1965.

Pritchett, V. S. Second steps. *New Statesman,* July 30, 1965, pp. 155-156.

Pushkarev, B. Scale and design in a new environment. In L. B. Holland (Ed.), *Who designs America?* Garden City, N.Y.: Anchor Original, 1966.

Rand, C. L. A., The ultimate city: I. Upward and outward. *New Yorker,* October 1, 1966, pp. 56-65.

Rölvaag, O. E. *Giants in the earth* (1927) (translated by Lincoln Colcord and O. E. Rölvaag). New York, Evanston, London: Perennial Library, 1965.

Sartre, J-P. New York, the colonial city. In *Literary and Philosophical Essays* (translated by Annette Michelson). New York: Philosophical Library, 1957.

Schroeder, F. E. H. Andrew Wyeth and the transcendental tradition. *American Quarterly* 1965, *17,* 559-567.

Seddon, G. Hurricane view of U. S. *London Observer,* November 18, 1962.

Shepheard, P. A. Philadelphia Enquirer. *Listener,* May 9, 1963, 787-789.

Simonds, J. O. *Landscape architecture: The shaping of man's natural environment.* New York: McGraw-Hill, 1961.

Stein, G. *The geographical history of America.* New York: Random House, 1936.

Tocqueville, A. de. *Democracy in America* (in French, 1835-1840). Vol. 2 (translated by Henry Reeve, revised by Francis Bowen, Phillips Bradley, Ed.). New York: Vintage Books, 1956-1957.

Twain, M. *Life on the Mississippi* (1875). New York and London: Harper, 1929.

Van Doren, M. *Travels of William Bartram* (1791). New York: Dover Publications, n.d.

Ward, J. W. The politics of design. In L. B. Holland (Ed.), *Who designs America?* Garden City, N.Y.: Anchor Original, 1966.

Whitehill, W. M. Promoted to glory. . . . In *With heritage so rich: A report of a special committee on historic preservation. . . .* New York, 1966.

Whyte, W. H. The politics of open space. In A. J. W. Sheffey (Ed.), *Resources, the metropolis, and the landgrant university: Proceedings of the Conference on Natural Resources,* University of Massachusetts, January-May 1963.

University of Massachusetts, College of Agriculture, Cooperative Extension Service, Publ. *410*, n.d.

Wigglesworth, M. God's controversy with New-England (1662). *Proceedings of the Massachusetts Historical Society*, 1871-1873.

Wolfe, M. R. *Towns, time, and regionalism.* Seattle: University of Washington, Dept. of Urban Planning, Urban Planning and Development Series, 1963.

Wright, T. *Islandia.* New York and Toronto: New American Library, 1958.

31. Experiencing the Environment as Hazard

Baumann, D. *The recreational use of domestic water supply reservoirs: Perception and choice.* Chicago: University of Chicago, Department of Geography Research Paper No. 121, 1969.

Baumann, D. & Kasperson, R. Public acceptance of renovated waste water: Myth and reality, *Water Resources Research, 10*, (4) August 1974, 667-674.

Burton, I. & Kates, R. The perception of natural hazards in resource management. *Natural Resources Journal, 3*, (3) January 1964, 412-441.

Burton, I., Kates, R., & White, G. *The Environment as hazard.* New York: Oxford University Press, forthcoming.

Dworkin, J. *Global trends in natural disasters, 1947-1973.* Boulder: University of Colorado, Natural Hazard Research Working Paper No. 26, 1974.

Golant, S., & Burton, I. *Avoidance-response to the risk environment.* Chicago: University of Chicago, Natural Hazard Research Working Paper No. 6, 1969.

Golant, S., & Burton, I. A semantic differential experiment in the interpretation and grouping of environmental hazards. *Geographical Analysis*, 1970, *2* (2), 120-134.

Halverson, B., & Pijawka, D. Scientific information about man-made environmental hazards. *The Monadnock*, 1974, *XLVIII*, 7-20.

Hewitt, K., & Burton, I. *The hazardousness of a place: A regional ecology of damaging events.* Toronto: University of Toronto Press, 1971.

Holmes, T. H., & Rahe, R. H. The social readjustment rating scale. *Journal of Psychosomatic Research*, 1967, *11*, 213.

Islam, M. A. *Human adjustment to cyclone hazards: A case study of Char Jabbar.* Boulder, Colorado: University of Colorado, Natural Hazard Research Working Paper No. 18, 1971.

Islam, M. A. Tropical cyclones: Coastal Bangladesh. In G. White (Ed.), *Natural hazards: Local, national, global.* New York: Oxford University Press, 1974.

Kates, R. *Hazard and choice perception in flood plain management.* Chicago: University of Chicago, Department of Geography Research Paper No. 78, 1962.

Lawless, E. *Technology and social shock— 100 cases of public concern over technology.* Washington: National Science Foundation, forthcoming.

Moon, K. *The perception of the hazardousness of a place: A comparative study of five natural hazards in London, Ontario.* Unpublished M.A. research paper, University of Toronto, 1971.

Reactor safety study: An assessment of accident risks in U.S. commercial Nuclear power plants. (14 vols.). Washington: U.S. Atomic Energy Commission, 1974.

Sewell, W. R. D. (Ed.), *Human dimensions of weather modification.* Chicago: University of Chicago, Department Research Paper No. 105, 1966.

Sewell, W. R. D., *et al., Human dimensions of the atmosphere.* Washington: National Science Foundation, 1968.

Sinclair, C. *et al., Innovation and human*

risk: The evaluation of human life and safety in relation to technical change. London: Centre for the Study of Industrial Innovation, 1972.

Slovick, P., Kunreuther, H. & White, G. Decision processes, rationality, and adjustment to natural hazards. In G. White (Ed.), *Natural hazards: Local, national, global.* New York: Oxford University Press, 1974.

Starr, C., Benefit-cost studies in sociotechnical systems. In *perspectives on benefit-risk decision making.* Washington: National Academy of Engineering, 1972.

Tversky, A., & Kahneman, D. Judgement under uncertainty: Heuristics and biases. *Science,* 1974, *185* (4157), 1124-1131.

White, G. (Ed.) *Natural hazards: Local national, global.* New York: Oxford University Press, 1974.

White, G., Bradley, D., & White, A. *Drawers of water.* Chicago: University of Chicago Press, 1972.

Wingate, I., *Penguin medical dictionary.* London: Penguin Books, 1972.

Wyler, A. R., Masuda, M., & Holmes, T. H. Seriousness of illness rating scale, *Journal of Psychosomatic Research,* 1968, *11,* 363-374.

Wyler, A. R., Masuda, M., & Holmes, T. H. The seriousness of illness rating scale: Reproductibility, *Journal of Psychosomatic Research,* 1970, *14,* 59-64.

32. Recreation as Social Action

Abraham, K. A constitutional basis of locomotor anxiety. In *Selected Papers.* London: Hogarth Press, 1927.

Burch, W. R., Jr. The play world of camping: Research into the social meaning of outdoor recreation. *American Journal of Sociology,* 1965, *70,* 604-612.

Burch, W. R., Jr. Wilderness—The life cycle and forest recreational choice. *Journal of Forestry,* 1966, *64* (9), 606-610.

Bureau of Outdoor Recreation. National Conference on Policy Issues in Outdoor Recreation in Logan, Utah (Sept. 6-8, 1966). Washington, D. C.: Bureau of Outdoor Recreation, 1967.

Burke, K. *The philosophy of literary form: Studies in symbolic action.* Baton Rouge, La.: Louisiana State University Press, 1941.

Caillois, R. *Man, play and games.* Translated by M. Barash. New York: Free Press, 1961.

Caplow, T. *The sociology of work.* Minneapolis: University of Minnesota Press, 1954.

Cesario, F. J., Sr. Operations research in outdoor recreation. *Journal of Leisure Research,* 1969, *1* (1), 33-51.

Clawson, M. *Methods of measuring demand for and value of outdoor recreation.* Reprint No. 10. Washington, D.C.: Resources for the Future, 1959.

Converse, P. E. Time budgets. In: D. L. Sills (Ed.) *International encyclopedia of the social sciences.* (Vol. 16). New York: Macmillan Company, 1968.

Davis, R. K. *The value of outdoor recreation: An economic study of the Maine woods.* Unpublished preliminary draft for Resources for the Future, Inc., Washington, D.C., 1967.

Dumazedier, J. *Toward a society of leisure.* Translated by S. E. McClure. New York: Free Press, 1967.

Durkheim, E. *The elementary forms of the religious life.* Translated by J. W. Swain. New York: Free Press, 1954.

Ferriss, A. L., et al. *National recreation survey.* Outdoor Recreation Resources Review Commission Study Report 19. Washington, D.C.: Government Printing Office, 1962.

Glock, C. Y., & Selznick, G. The wilderness vacationist. In Outdoor Recreation Resources Review Commission. Study Report 3. *Wilderness and recreation: A report on resources, values and problems.* Washington, D.C.: Government Printing Office, 1962.

Goode, W. J. Outdoor recreation and the family to the year 2000. Outdoor Recreation Resources Review Commission. Study Report 22. *Trends in American Living and Outdoor Recreation.* Washington, D.C.: Government Printing Office, 1962.

Gurin, G., & Mueller, E. *Participation in outdoor recreation, factors affecting demand among American adults.* Outdoor Recreation Resources Review Commission. Study Report 20. Ann Arbor, Michigan: University of Michigan Survey Research Center, 1962.

Hauser, P. M. Demographic and ecological changes as factors in outdoor recreation. Outdoor Recreation Resources Review Commission. Study Report 22. *Trends in American living and outdoor recreation.* Washington, D.C.: Government Printing Office, 1962.

Huizinga, J. *Homo ludens.* Boston: Beacon Press, 1955.

Kadushin, C. Power, influence and social circles: A new methodology for studying opinion makers. *American Sociological Review,* 1968, 33 (5), 685-699.

Kaplan, M. *Leisure in America: A social inquiry.* New York: Wiley, 1960.

Klausner, S. Z. The intermingling of pain and pleasure: The stress seeking personality in its social context. In S. Z. Klausner (Ed.) *Why man takes chances: Studies in stress seeking.* New York: Doubleday, 1968.

Lazarsfeld, P. F. The art of asking why. In D. Katz et al. (Eds.) *Public opinion and propaganda.* New York: Dryden Press, 1954.

Lewin, B. D. Claustrophobia. *Psychoanalytic Quarterly,* 1935, 4.

Lowenthal, L. *Literature and the image of man.* Boston: Beacon Press, 1957.

Mead, M. Outdoor recreation in the context of emerging American cultural values: Backround considerations. Outdoor Recreation Resources Review Commission. Study Report 22. *Trends in American living and outdoor recreation.* Washington, D.C.: Government Printing Office, 1962.

Merriman, L. C., Jr., & Ammons, R. B. *The wilderness user in three Montana areas.* St. Paul, Minn.: School of Forestry, University of Minnesota, 1965.

Meyersohn, R. The sociology of leisure in the United States: Introduction and bibliography, 1945-1965. *Journal of Leisure Research,* 1969, 1 (1), 53-68.

Peterle, T. J. Characteristics of some Ohio hunters. *Journal of Wildlife Management,* 1967, 31 (2), 375-389.

Reid, L. M. *Outdoor recreation: A nationwide study of user desires.* East Lansing, Mich.: Department of Resource Development, Michigan State University, 1963.

Shafer, E. L., Jr., Hamilton, J. E., Jr., & Schmidt, E. A. Natural landscape preferences: A predictive model. *Journal of Leisure Research,* 1969, 1 (1), 1-20.

Sonnenfeld, J. Equivalence and distortion of the perceptual environment. *Environment and Behavior,* 1969, 1, 83-99.

Sorokin, J., & Berger, G. A. *Time-budgets of human behavior.* Harvard Sociological Studies. (Vol. 2). Cambridge, Mass.: Harvard University Press, 1939.

Stillman, C. W. The price of open space. *Black Rock Forest Papers No. 28.* Cornwall, N.Y.: Harvard Black Rock Forest, 1966.

Stouffer, S. A., et al. *Measurement and prediction.* Princeton, N.J.: Princeton University Press, 1950.

Thomas, F. *Environmental basis of society.* New York: Century Company, 1925.

Wenger, W. D., Jr., & Gregerson, H. M. *The effect of non-response on representativeness of wilderness-trail register information.* U.S. Department of Agriculture Forest Service, 1964.

33. The House as Symbol of the Self

Bachelard, G. *The poetics of space,* Boston: Beacon Press, 1969.

Colman, A., & Colman, L. *Pregnancy: The psychological experience*, New York: Herder and Herder, 1971.

The dentist's chair as an allegory of life, *Time*, April 13, 1970, p. 70.

Eliade, M. *The sacred and the profane: The nature of religion.* New York: Harcourt, 1959.

Jacobi, J. *Complex, archetype, symbol in the psychology of C. G. Jung.* New York: Pantheon Books, 1957.

Jung, C. *Memories, dreams and reflections.* London: Collins. The Fontana Library Series, 1969.

Laumann, E., and House, J. Living room styles and social attributes: Patterning of material artifacts in an urban community. In Laumann, Siegel, and Hodges, (Eds.), *The logic of social hierarchies.* Chicago: Markham, 1972.

Malicroix, H. B., as quoted in G. Bachelard, *The poetics of space.* New York: The Orion Press, 1964.

Michelson, W. Most people don't want what architects want. *Transaction*, 1968, 5, 37-43.

Murray, W. J. C. *Copsford.* London: Allen and Unwin, 1950.

Nin, A. *The Diary of Anaïs Nin, 1931–34*, New York: Harcourt, 1966.

Lord Raglan. *The temple and the house.* London: Routledge & Kegan Paul, 1964.

Rainwater, L. Fear and house-as-haven in the lower class. *Journal of the American Institute of Planners*, 1966, 32, 23-31.

Rainwater, L. *Behind ghetto walls.* Chicago: Aldine-Atherton, 1970.

Rapoport, A. *House form and culture*, Englewood Cliffs, N.J.: Prentice-Hall. 1969.

Searles, H. F. *The nonhuman environment in normal development and in schizophenia*, New York: International Universities Press, 1960.

Spyridaki, G. *Mort lucide.* As quoted in Bachelard, *The poetics of space.* Boston: Beacon Press, 1969.

Watts, A. *The book: On the taboo against knowing who you are.* New York: Macmillan, Collier Books, 1966.

Watts, A. W. *Nature, man and woman*, New York: Random House, Vintage Books, 1970.

Werthman, C. *The social meaning of the physical environment.* Unpublished doctoral dissertation. University of California, Berkeley, 1968.

34. Architecture, Interaction, and Social Control

Architectural Forum, Slum surgery in St. Louis. April 1951, pp. 128-136.

Bell, W., & Boat, M. Urban neighborhoods and informal social relations. *American Journal of Sociology*, 1957, 62, 391-398.

Blum, A. F. Social structure, social class, and participation in primary relationships. In A. B. Shostak & W. Gomberg (Eds.) *Blue collar world.* Englewood Cliffs, N.J.: Prentice-Hall, 1964.

Bott, E. *Family and social networks.* London: Tavistock, 1957.

Demerath, N. J. St. Louis public housing study sets off community development to meet social needs. *Journal of Housing*, 1962, 19, 472-478.

Fava, S. F. Contrasts in neighboring New York City and a suburban county: In R. L. Warren (Ed.) *Perspective on the American community.* Chicago: Rand McNally, 1957.

Festinger, L., Schacter, S., & Back, K. *Social pressures in informal groups.* New York: Harper & Row, 1950.

Foote, N. N., Abu-Lughod, J., Foley, M. M., & Winnick, L. *Housing choices and housing constraints.* New York. McGraw-Hill, 1960.

Fried, M. Grieving for a lost home. In L. J. Duhl (Ed.) *The urban condition.* New York: Basic Books, 1963.

Fried, M., & Gleicher, P. Some sources of residential satisfaction in an urban slum. *Journal of the American Insti-*

tute of Planners, 1961, *27*, 305-315.

Freid, M., & Levin, J. Some social functions of the urban slum. In B. Friedman and R. Morris (Eds.) *Urban planning and social policy*. New York: Basic Books, 1968.

Gans, H. Planning and social life: Friendship and neighbor relations in suburban communities. *Journal of the American Institute of Planners*, 1961, *27* (2), 135-139.

Gans, H. *The urban villagers*. New York: Free Press, 1962.

Gans, H. Effect of the move from city to suburb. In L. J. Duhl (Ed.) *The urban condition*. New York: Basic Books, 1963.

Herberle, R. The normative element in neighborhood relations. *Pacific Sociological Review*, 1960, *3* (1), 3-11.

Marris, P. *Family and social change in an African city*. Evanston, Ill.: Northwestern Univ. Press, 1962.

Rainwater, L. Crucible of identity: The Negro lower-class family. *Daedalus*, 1966, *95* (1), 172-216. (a)

Rainwater, L. Fear and the house-as-haven in the lower class. *Journal of the American Institute of Planners*, 1966, *32*, 23-31. (b)

Rainwater, L., & Schwarts, M. J. Identity, world view, social relations, and family behavior in magazines. *Social Research, Inc.*, 1965.

Schorr, A. L. *Slums and Social Insecurity*. Washington, D.C.: Government Printing Office, 1963.

Suttles, G. D. *The social order of the slum*. Chicago: University of Chicago Press, 1968.

Wallin, P. A. Guttman scale for measuring women's neighboring. *American Journal of Sociology*, 1953, *59*, 243-246.

Whyte, W. H. *The organization man*. Garden City, N.Y.: Doubleday, 1956.

Wilner, D. M., Walkley, R. P., Pinkerton, T. C., & Tayback, H. *The housing environment and family life*. Baltimore, Md.: Johns Hopkins University Press,
1962.

Wolfe, A., Lex, B., & Yancey, W. *The Soulard area: Adaptations by urban white families to poverty*. St. Louis: Social Science Institute of Washington University, 1968.

Young, M., & Wilmott, P. *Family and kinship in East London*. Glencoe: Free Press, 1957.

35. The Early History of a Psychiatric Hospital for Children

Bayes, K. *The therapeutic effect of environment on emotionally disturbed and mentally subnormal children*. Surrey, Eng.: Gresham, 1967.

Bayes, K., & Francklin, S. (Eds.) *Designing for the handicapped*. London, Eng.: George Godwin, 1971.

Chermayeff, S., & Alexander, C. *Community and privacy: Toward a new architecture of humanism*. New York: Doubleday, 1963.

Colman, A. D. *The planned environment in psychiatric treatment*. Springfield, Ill.: Charles C Thomas, 1971.

Goldfarb, W., & Mintz, I. Schizophrenic child's reaction to time and space. *Archives of General Psychiatry*, 1961, *5*, 535-543.

Hutt, S. J., & Hutt, C. *Direct observation and measurement of behavior*. Springfield, Ill.: Charles C Thomas, 1970.

Hutt, C., & Vaizey, M. J. Differential effects of group density on social behavior. *Nature*, 1966, *209*, 1371-1372.

Ittelson, W. H., Proshansky, H. M., & Rivlin, L. G. The environmental psychology of the psychiatric ward. In H. M. Proshansky, W. H. Ittelson, & L. G. Rivlin (Eds.) *Environmental psychology: Man and his physical setting*. New York: Holt, Rinehart and Winston, 1970. (a)

Ittelson, W. H., Rivlin, L. G., Proshansky, H. M. The use of behavioral maps in environmental psychology. In H. M. Proshansky, et al. (Eds.) *Environ-*

mental psychology: Man and his physical setting. New York: Holt, Rinehart and Winston, 1970. (b)

Myrick, R., & Marx, B. S. *An exploratory study of the relationship between high school building design and student learning.* Washington, D.C.: George Washington University, 1968.

Nellist, I. *Planning buildings for handicapped children.* Springfield, Ill.: Charles C Thomas, 1970.

Piaget, J., & Inhelder, B. *The psychology of the child.* New York: Basic Books, 1969.

Rubin, T. I. *Jordi—Lisa and David.* New York: Ballantine, 1962.

Searles, H. F. *The nonhuman environment in normal development and in schizophrenia.* New York: International Universities Press, 1960.

Sorosky, A. D., Rieger, N. I., & Tanguay, P. F. Furnishing a psychiatric unit for children. *Hospital and Community Psychiatry,* Nov. 1969, 334-336.

Stanton, A. M., & Schwartz, M. S. *The mental hospital.* New York: Basic Books, 1954.

Stroh, G., & Buick, D. Perceptual development and childhood psychosis. *British Journal of Medical Psychology,* 1964, 37, 291-299.

36. The Use of Space in Open Classrooms

Brunetti, F. A. Noise, distraction and privacy in conventional and open school environments. In W. J. Mitchell (Ed.), *Environmental design: Research and practice. Proceedings of the EDRA 3/AR8 Conference.* Los Angeles: University of California Press, 1972.

Durlak, J. T., Beardsley, B. E., & Murray, J. S. Observation of user activity patterns in open and traditional plan school environments. In W. J. Mitchell (Ed.) *Environmental design: Research and practice. Proceedings of the EDRA 3/AR8 Conference.* Los Angeles: University of California Press, 1972.

Hutt, C., & Vaizey, M. J. Differential effects of group density on social behavior. *Nature,* 1966, 209, 1371-1372.

Krantz, P. J., & Risley, T. R. The organization of group care environments: Behavioral ecology in the classroom. Paper presented at the American Psychological Assn., Honolulu, 1972.

McGrew, W. C. *An ethological study of children's behavior.* New York: Academic Press, 1972.

Rohe, W., & Patterson, A. H. The effects of varied levels of resources and density on behavior in a day care center. In D. H. Carson (Ed.) *Man-environment interactions: Evaluations and applications. EDRA5 Proceedings.* Milwaukee, Wisc., 1974.

37. The Experience of Living in Cities

Abelson, P. Microcosms in a world apart. *Science,* 1969, 165, 853.

Abuza, N. The Paris-London-New York questionnaires. Unpublished paper, Social Relations 98, Harvard University, 1967.

Altman, D., Levine, M., Nadien, M., & Villena, J. Trust of the stranger in the city and the small town. Unpublished research, Graduate Center, City University of New York, 1969.

Berkowitz, W. Personal communication.

Blumenfeld, H. Criteria for judging the quality of the urban environment. In H. Schmandt & W. Bloomberg, Jr. (Eds.), *The quality of urban life.* Beverly Hills, Calif.: Sage, 1969.

Feldman, R. E. Response to compatriot and foreigner who seek assistance. *Journal of Personality and Social Psychology,* 1968, 10, 202-214.

Gaertner, S., & Bickman, L. The ethnic bystander. Unpublished research, Graduate Center, City University of New York, 1968.

Gans, H. J. *People and plans: Essays on urban problems and solutions.* New York: Basic Books, 1968.

Hall, E. T. *The hidden dimension*. New York: Doubleday, 1966.

Hall, P. *The world cities*. New York: McGraw-Hill, 1966.

Hooper, D. A pedestrian's view of New York, London and Paris. Unpublished paper, Social Relations 98, Harvard University, 1967.

Jacobs, J. *The death and life of great American cities*. New York: Random House, 1961.

Latané, B., & Darley, J. Bystander apathy. *American Scientist*, 1969, 57, 244-268.

Lynch, K. *The image of the city*. Cambridge: MIT Press & Harvard University Press, 1960.

McKenna, W., & Morgenthau, S. Urban-rural differences in social interaction: A study of helping behavior. Unpublished research, Graduate Center, City University of New York, 1969.

Meier, R. L. *A communications theory of urban growth*. Cambridge: MIT Press, 1962.

Milgram, S., & Hollander, P. Paralyzed witnesses: The murder they heard. *The Nation*, 1964, 25, 602-604.

Park, R. E. The city: Suggestions for the investigation of human behavior in the urban environment. In R. E. Park, E. W. Burgess, & R. D. McKenzie (Eds.), *The city*. Chicago: University of Chicago Press, 1967. (Originally published 1925.)

Regional Plan Association (1969). The second regional plan. *The New York Times*, June 15, 1969, 119, Section 12.

Simmel, G. The metropolis and mental life. In K. H. Wolff (Ed.), *The sociology of George Simmel*. New York: The Free Press, 1950. (Originally published: *Die Grosstadt and das Geistesleben die Grosstadt*. Dresden: v. Zahn & Jaensch, 1903.)

Strauss, A. L. (Ed.) *The American city: A sourcebook of urban imagery*. Chicago: Aldine, 1968.

Suttles, G. D. *The social order of the slum: Ethnicity and territory in the inner city*. Chicago: University of Chicago Press, 1968.

Waters, J. The relative acceptance accorded a discreditable person in rural and metropolitan areas. Unpublished research, Graduate Center, City University of New York, 1969.

Wirth, L. Urbanism as a way of life. *American Journal of Sociology*, 1938, 44, 1-24.

Zimbardo, P. G. The human choice: Individuation, reason and order as deindividuation, impulse and chaos. *Nebraska Symposium on Motivation*, 1969, 17.

38. The Modern City: Spatial Ordering

Adrian, C. R. *Governing urban America* (2nd ed.). New York: McGraw-Hill, 1961.

Anderson, N. *The hobo*. Chicago: University of Chicago Press, Phoenix Edition, 1961. (Originally published 1923.)

Becker, H. S., & Horowitz, I. L. The culture of civility. *Trans-action*, April 1970, pp. 12-19.

Berger, B. M. *Working class suburb: A study of auto workers in suburbia*. Berkeley: University of California Press, 1960.

Bittner, E. The police on skid-row: A study of peace keeping. In W. J. Chambliss (Ed.), *Crime and the legal process*. New York: McGraw-Hill, 1969.

Briggs, A. *Victorian cities*. New York: Harper & Row, 1965. (British publication, 1963.)

Brown, R. M. Historical patterns of violence in America. In H. D. Graham & T. R. Gurr, *Violence in America: Historical and comparative perspectives*, (Vol. I). A staff report to the National Commission on the Causes and Prevention of Violence. Washington, D.C.: U.S. Government Printing Office, 1969.

Chambliss, W. J. The law of vagrancy. In W. J. Chambliss (Ed.), *Crime and the legal process.* New York: McGraw-Hill, 1969.

Chancellor, E. G. *The history of the squares of London: Topographical and historical.* London: Kegan Paul, 1907.

Cressey, P. F. Population succession in Chicago: 1898-1930. In J. Short (Ed.), *The social fabric of the metropolis.* Chicago: University of Chicago Press, 1971, 109-119.

Davis, F. Deviance disavowal. *Social Problems,* Fall 1961, pp. 120-132.

Dickens, C. *Oliver Twist.* New York: New American Library, 1961. (Originally published 1838.)

Drake, St. Clair, & Cayton, H. R. *Black metropolis.* New York: Harper & Row, 1962, *1* and *2.* (Originally published 1945.)

Ellis, D. S. Speech and social status in America. *Social Forces,* 1967, pp. 431-437.

Faris, R. E. L. *Chicago sociology, 1920-1932.* San Francisco: Chandler, 1967.

Flexner, E. *Century of struggle: The woman's rights movement in the United States.* New York: Atheneum, 1970. (Originally published 1959.)

Foote, C. Vagrancy-type law and its administration. In W. J. Chambliss (Ed), *Crime and the legal process.* New York: McGraw-Hill, 1969.

Form, W. H., & Stone, G. P. Urbanism, anonymity and status symbolism. In R. L. Simpson & I. H. Simpson (Eds.), *Social organization and behavior.* New York: Wiley, 1964.

Gans, H. *The urban villagers.* New York: Free Press, 1962.

George, M. D. *London life in the eighteenth century.* New York: Capricorn Books, 1965. (Originally published 1925.)

Goffman, E. *The presentation of self in everyday life.* Garden City, New York: Doubleday, 1959.

Goffman, E. *Behavior in public places.* New York: Free Press, 1963. (a)

Goffman, E. *Stigma.* Englewood Cliffs, N.J.: Prentice-Hall, 1963. (b)

Gorer, G. Modification of national charac-

ter: The role of the police in England. In W. J. Chambliss (Ed.), *Crime and the legal process.* New York: McGraw-Hill, 1969.

Greer, S. *The emerging city.* New York: Free Press, 1962.

Greer, S. *Urban renewal and American cities.* Indianapolis: Bobbs-Merrill, 1965.

Gusslin, O. R., Hunt, R. G., & Roach, J. O. Social class and the mental health movement. *Social Problems,* Winter 1959-60, pp. 210-218.

Gusfield, J. R. *Symbolic crusade: Status politics and the American temperance movement.* Urbana: University of Illinois Press, 1963.

Hall, E. T. *The silent language.* Greenwich, Conn.: Fawcett Publications, 1959.

Hughes, E. C. Good people and dirty work. In H. S. Becker (Ed.), *The other side: Perspectives on deviance.* New York: Free Press, 1964.

Irwin, J. Surfing: The natural history of an urban scene. *Urban Life and Culture,* July 1973.

Joseph, N., & Alex, N. The uniform: A sociological perspective. *American Journal of Sociology,* January 1972, 719-730.

Lane, R. *Policing the city: Boston, 1822-1855.* Cambridge: Harvard University Press, 1967.

Lane, R. Urbanization and criminal violence in the 19th century: Massachusetts as a test case. In H. D. Graham & T. R. Gurr, *Violence in America: Historical and comparative perspectives* (Vol. 2). A staff report to the National Commission on the Causes and Prevention of Violence. Washington, D.C.: U.S. Government Printing Office, 1969.

Lofland, J. The youth ghetto: A perspective on the "cities of youth" around our large universities. *Journal of Higher Education,* March 1968, 121-143.

Lofland, J. *Deviance and identity.* With the assistance of L. H. Lofland. Englewood Cliffs, N.J.: Prentice-Hall, 1969.

Lofland, J., & LeJeune, R. Initial interaction of newcomers in Alcoholics Anonymous: A field experiment in class symbols and socialization. *Social Problems*, Fall 1960, pp. 102-111.

Musil, J. The development of Prague's ecological structure. In R. E. Pahl (Ed.), *Readings in urban sociology*. Oxford: Pergamon Press, 1968.

Parsons, E. C. *Fear and conventionality*. New York: Putnam, 1914.

Roberts, B. C. On the origins and resolution of English working-class protest. In H. D. Graham & T. R. Gurr, *Violence in America: Historical and comparative perspectives*. (Vol. 1). A staff report to the National Commission on the Causes and Prevention of Violence. Washington, D.C.: U.S. Government Printing Office, 1969.

Schlesinger, A. M. *The American as reformer*. New York: Atheneum Paperback, 1968.

Schnore, L. F. Community. In N. J. Smelser (Ed.), *Sociology: An introduction*. New York: Wiley, 1967.

Schwab, W. B. Oshogbo—An urban community? In H. Kuper (Ed.), *Urbanization and migration in West Africa*. Berkeley and Los Angeles: University of California Press, 1965.

Silver, A. On the demand for order in civil society: A review of some themes in the history of urban crime, police and riot. In D. J. Bordua (Ed.), *The police*. New York: Wiley, 1967.

Suttles, G. D. *The social construction of communities*. Chicago: University of Chicago Press, 1972.

Tilly, C. Collective violence in European perspective. In H. D. Graham and T. R. Gurr, *Violence in America: Historical and comparative perspectives* (Vol. 1). A staff report to the National Commission on the Causes and Prevention of Violence. Washington, D.C.: U.S. Government Printing Office, 1969.

Toll, S. I. *Zoned American*. New York: Grossman, 1969.

Werthman, C., & Piliavin, I. Gang members and the police. In D. J. Bordua (Ed.), *The police*. New York: Wiley, 1967.

Wilson, J. Q. A guide to Reagan country: The political culture of Southern California. *Commentary*, May 1967, pp. 37-45.

39. Life Styles and Urban Space

Bowen, L. deK. *Growing up with a city*. New York: The Macmillan Co., 1926.

Browne, J. *The great metropolis: A mirror of New York*. Hartford, Conn.: American Publishing Co., 1869.

Campbell, H., Knox, T. W., & Brynes, T. *Darkness and light, or lights and shadows of New York life*. Hartford, Conn.: Hartford Publishing Co., 1895.

Cayton, H., & Drake, S. *Black metropolis*. New York: Harcourt Brace, 1945.

Firey, W. *Land use in Central Boston*. Cambridge, Mass.: Harvard University Press, 1947.

Johnson, E. The function of the central business district in the metropolitan community. In P. Hatt & A. Riess (Eds.), *Reader in urban sociology* (1st ed.). Glencoe, Ill.: The Free Press, 1951.

Jonassen, C. Cultural variables in the ecology of an ethnic group. *American Sociological Review*, 1949, *14*, 32-41.

Kerfort, J. B. *Broadway*. Boston: Houghton Mifflin, 1911.

McCabe, J. *The secrets of the great city*. Philadelphia: Jones Bros., 1868.

McCabe, J. *New York by sunlight and gaslight*. Philadelphia: Hubbard Bros., 1881.

Park, R. *The city*. Chicago: University of Chicago Press, 1925.

Park, R. Human ecology. *American Journal of Sociology*, 1936, 42, 1-15.

Shibutani, T. Reference groups as perspectives. *American Journal of Sociology*, 1955, *60*, 566.

Smith, M. H. *Sunshine and shadow in New York*. Hartford, Conn.: J. B. Burr & Co., 1868.

Ware, C. *Greenwich Village*. Boston: Houghton Mifflin, 1935.

Zorbaugh, H. *The gold coast and the slum.* Chicago: University of Chicago Press, 1929.

42. Some Sources of Residential Satisfaction in an Urban Slum

Dotson, F. Patterns of voluntary association among urban working class families. *American Sociological Review,* 1951, *25,* 687-693.

Fried, M., & Lindemann, E. Sociocultural factors in mental health and illness. *American Journal of Orthopsychiatry,* 1961, *31,* 87-101.

Gans, H. *The urban villagers.* Glencoe, Ill.: Free Press, 1962.

Goodenough, W. *Property, kin, and community on Truk.* New Haven, Conn.: Yale University Publications in Anthropology, 1951.

Hoggart, R. *The uses of literacy.* London: Chatto & Windus, 1857.

Kerr, M. *People of Ship Street.* London: Routledge & Kegan Paul, 1958.

Mogey, J. M. *Family and neighbourhood.* London: Oxford University Press, 1956.

Young, M., & Willmott, P. *Family and kinship in East London.* Glencoe, Ill.: Free Press, 1957.

43. Planning and Social Life

Caplow, T., & Foreman, R. Neighborhood interaction in a homogeneous community. *American Sociological Review,* 1950, *15,* 357-366.

Deutsch, M., & Collins, M. *Interracial housing.* Minneapolis: University of Minnesota Press, 1951.

Festinger, L. Architecture and group membership. *Journal of Social Issues,* 1951, 7, 152-163.

Festinger, L., Schachter, S., & Back, K. *Social pressures in informal groups.* New York: Harper & Bros., 1950.

Form, W. Stratification in low and middle income housing areas. *Journal of Social Issues,* 1951, 7, 116-117.

Greer, E., & Greer, G. *Privately developed interracial housing.* Berkeley: University of California Press, 1960.

Kuper, L. Blueprint for living together. In L. Kuper (Ed.), *Living in towns.* London: Cresset Press, 1953.

Lazarsfeld, P., & Merton, R. Friendship as a social process: A substantive and methodological analysis (Part I: Substantive analysis, by R. Merton), in M. Berger, T. Abel, & C. Page (Eds.), *Freedom and control in modern society.* New York: Van Nostrand, 1954.

Macris, D. *Social relationships among residents of various house types in a planned community.* Unpublished master's thesis, University of Illinois, 1958.

Merton, R. The social psychology of housing. In W. Dennis (Ed.), *Current trends in social psychology.* Pittsburgh: University of Pittsburgh Press, 1947.

Rosow, I. The social effects of the physical environment. *Journal of the American Institute of Planners,* 1961, *27,* 127-133.

Wallace, A. *Housing and social structure.* Philadelphia: Philadelphia Housing Authority, 1952.

Whyte, W. H., Jr. How the new suburbia socializes. *Fortune,* August 1953, pp. 120-122, 186, 190.

Whyte, W. H., Jr. *The organization man.* New York: Simon and Schuster, 1957.

Young, M., & Willmott, P. *Family and kinship in East London.* London: Routledge and Kegan Paul, 1957.

Subject Index

Author Index

* Italic page numbers indicate authorship of a reading.